ANTI-BLACK THOUGHT

THOUGHT

1 8 6 3 - 1 9 2 5

"THE NEGRO PROBLEM"

AN ELEVEN –VOLUME ANTHOLOGY OF RACIST WRITINGS

edited and introduced by

JOHN DAVID SMITH

Alumni Distinguished Professor of History
at North Carolina State University

A GARLAND SERIES

VOLUME SIX

THE BIBLICAL
AND
"SCIENTIFIC" DEFENSE OF SLAVERY

RELIGION AND "THE NEGRO PROBLEM"
PART II

edited with introductions by

JOHN DAVID SMITH

GARLAND PUBLISHING, INC.
NEW YORK & LONDON
1993

Library of Congress Cataloging-In-Publication Data

The Biblical and "scientific" defense of slavery : religion and "the Negro problem" /
edited by John David Smith.
    p.   cm. — (Anti-Black thought, 1863–1925 ; v. 6)
    Includes bibliographical references.
    ISBN 0-8153-0978-3 (alk. paper)
    1. Racism—United States—History—19th century. 2. Racism—Religious aspects.
3. Racism—Biblical teaching. 4. Afro-Americans—History—1863–1877.
5. United States—Race relations. 6. White supremacy movements—United States—
History—19th century. I. Smith, John David, 1949–   . II. Series.
E185.2.B48 1993
241'.675'0973—dc20   92-32107
                                                          CIP

Printed on acid-free, 250-year-life paper
Manufactured in the United States of America

FOR ALEX, LISA, AND LORENZ

CONTENTS

THE BIBLICAL AND "SCIENTIFIC" DEFENSE OF SLAVERY

ACKNOWLEDGMENTS

Anti-Black Thought 1863–1925 began in 1989 when Professor Paul Finkelman suggested to Leo F. Balk, Vice President of Garland Publishing, Inc., that I undertake an anthology of texts that documented late nineteenth-century American racism. I am grateful to Professor Finkelman for his endorsement and to Mr. Balk for his commitment to and enthusiasm for the project. My editors at Garland, Anita Vanca and Jonathan Oestreich, have been most helpful in locating texts, obtaining permissions to publish, and hammering out details. I very much appreciate their labors.

At North Carolina State University, I benefited from the research assistance of graduate students Eric Jackson, Paul Peterson, Michelle Justice, and Jo Frost. Eric and Paul helped me compile a data base of possible texts and verified citations. Michelle and Jo joined me in the appraisal process and Jo played an important role in deciding upon the final arrangement of the texts. Much of this work was tedious, and I value the care and precision with which these graduate students performed their tasks.

Professor Randall M. Miller offered keen advice regarding my use of the American Colonization Society texts. Dr. Jeffrey J. Crow and Professors David P. Gilmartin, William Kimler, and Linda O. McMurry subjected the "General Introduction" and the volume introductions to thoughtful criticism and thereby strengthened the entire project. I am especially indebted to Will Kimler for his painstaking analysis of the introductory section on "science" and race in Volumes V and VI, and for his help in revising this section. I hold in high regard the judgments of each of these colleagues and thank them for the time and effort they devoted to evaluating various drafts of my essay.

As the project neared completion, Alex Andrusyszyn assisted me in managing the extensive files. And finally, over the course of editing *Anti-Black Thought 1863–1925*, Sylvia A. Smith provided valuable insights into the nature of racial and sexual oppression and the role of law in social change.

When a man attempts to discuss the negro problem at the South, he may begin with the negro, but he really touches, with however light a hand, the whole bewildering problem of a civilization.

—*Edgar Gardner Murphy (1904)*[1]

The most formidable of all the ills which threaten the future existence of the Union arises from the presence of a black population upon its territory; and in contemplating the cause of the present embarrassments or of the future dangers of the United States, the observer is invariably led to consider this as a primary fact.

—*Alexis de Tocqueville (1835)*[2]

GENERAL INTRODUCTION

Writing in 1903, more than a half-century after Alexis de Tocqueville, W.E.B. Du Bois, the brilliant black historian, sociologist, and polemicist, viewed America's "ills" from a radically different perspective. Nonetheless, the two men concurred on the role that race played in defining America's character and destiny. Du Bois wrote in the shadow of Jim Crow race relations, American imperialism, and emerging Progressivism. As he looked back toward the nineteenth century, Du Bois found a legacy of slavery and racial oppression. He branded it a blot on the United States, which was then an emerging industrial and world power.

"The problem of the twentieth century," wrote Du Bois in *The Souls of Black Folk*, was "the problem of the color-line,—the relation of the darker to the lighter races of men in Asia and Africa, in America and the islands of the sea." Summarizing the history and cultural lives of African Americans, Du Bois underscored a question that ran as a leitmotif through white racial thought from the age of emancipation to the age of segregation. "What," he asked, "shall be *done* with Negroes?"[3] In his many writings Du Bois pounded away at the passive roles whites had always assigned to blacks—first as slaves—and later as freedmen, all too often caught in the web of neoslavery. From years of observing racial conditions in the North and South, Du Bois concluded that blacks and whites lived worlds and cultures apart—separated by a veil of racism. Years later, reflecting on the emancipation experience, Du Bois lamented that the freedman shared little of the progress and optimism that had marked white Victorian America. He wrote with elegant pathos: "The slave went free; stood a brief moment in the sun; then moved back again toward slavery."[4]

Though a propagandist for black rights, Du Bois in no way overstated the case. Most white Americans in the nineteenth century, north and south, before and after emancipation, did in fact view blacks as inferior "others." Though their attitudes toward blacks varied from place to place and over time, the vast majority of whites nevertheless held blacks, as a people and as a class, in contempt. To be sure there were exceptions. Whites always could identify "good Negroes," persons who conformed to their definition of acceptable behavior—deferential blacks who knew their "place." In the main, however, whites treated blacks as persons who differed in pejorative ways from themselves.

As so often in American history, whites defined "different" to mean "inferior." Not only their skin color, but their temperament, culture, and community, allegedly marked African Americans as "different." Such variances from the "normal"—the white ideal—were interpreted by the dominant caste as immutable characteristics. Yet, in what constituted just one of many contradictions in the ideology of white racism, whites lived in seemingly constant fear of racial mixing. If black "traits" were unalterable, why then were whites so apprehensive of miscegenation? The Old South's large mulatto population stood as a silent reminder that racial fears had not prevented racial mixing under slavery. After slavery whites continued to perceive blacks as marginal men and women—persons who mattered little, whose alleged childlike behavior and intellects deserved minimal respect. Blacks were to be acted upon. Decisions were to be made for them, not by them. During slavery's long history, various schools of racists trotted out a broad range of arguments—biblical, "scientific," historical, social, and economic—to bolster the idea of keeping blacks in chains.[5]

Following emancipation in 1865, whites, notably southerners, continued to describe blacks as degraded, certainly unprepared for the responsibilities and challenges of freedom. Many whites predicted that blacks could not survive as freedmen and women. Without the alleged paternalism of slavery, they reasoned, blacks would fall by the wayside, unable to compete in the class and racial struggle with whites. Some extreme racists even continued to define blacks as subhuman "beings," whose reported separate creation destined them to a perpetual servitude regardless of laws and legislation passed by civil authorities.

There was a direct relationship, of course, between the end of slavery and the determined search by whites for other means to regulate blacks. By the post-Civil War years, explains historian George M. Fredrickson, an "explicit or ideological racism" had taken root in the South. Social forces— "selfishness, greed, and the pursuit of privilege"—exacerbated the notion that blacks were natural inferiors. By the end of the century, social and economic tensions—as well as an upsurge of racism worldwide—led whites to campaign for the legal segregation and disfranchisement of their former slaves.[6]

At first white southerners settled on the Black Codes passed and then overthrown during Presidential Reconstruction. When other forms of racial control failed, post-Civil War whites eventually resorted to violent means.

From 1882, when statistics began to be collected systematically, until 1903, white mobs lynched 1,941 blacks.[7] Many other lynchings no doubt went unreported. Those blacks who were spared the barbarities of white racial "justice" faced a labyrinth of legal and extralegal barriers: *de jure* segregation under the Jim Crow laws and *de facto* segregation imposed by custom. Turn-of-the-century blacks had to fight to gain the most basic constitutional rights, minimally adequate schools, medical care, housing, and economic opportunities. As historian Nell Irvin Painter has delineated:

> At the turn of the twentieth century nine out of ten blacks lived in the South, and three-quarters of black farmers were tenants or sharecroppers. In the generation since emancipation, blacks, who constituted about 40 percent of the southern population, had bought one-eight [sic] of the region's farms. Even so, nearly all Afro-Americans, even the landowning minority, were poor. The most oppressed lived as peons, tied to planters by long-term contracts that deprived them of the right to change employers for as much as ten years, or as convicts, whom the states leased to planters and industrialists. In either situation, employers, who cared only about extracting a maximum of work from actual or virtual prisoners, provided wretched living and working conditions. These southern blacks, who earned bare subsistence and often died before earning their freedom, represented the worst-paid workers in this country.

Though African Americans never stood passively by acquiescing to white hegemony, theirs was a constant uphill struggle. Again, as before Appomattox, blacks confronted a maze of white arguments determined to keep them locked into inferior social, political, and economic status.[8]

Writing in 1908, the reform journalist Ray Stannard Baker analyzed the causes and consequences of America's race "problem," what whites generally termed "The Negro Problem." In *Following the Color Line* Baker identified "the most sinister phase of the race problem" as "instinctive race repulsion and competitive jealousy." Race relations, marred by "mutual fear and suspicion," led to the segregation of blacks and whites, what Baker described as "the rapid flying apart of the races." "More and more," he noted, "they are becoming a people wholly apart—separate in their churches, separate in their schools, separate in cars, conveyances, hotels, restaurants, with separate professional men. In short, we discover tendencies in this country toward the development of a caste system."[9]

This system of American apartheid marred the burgeoning industrial complex of the North as well as the agricultural South. Black northerners experienced *de facto* segregation while competing for jobs, housing, and social services with the "new" immigrants who populated the urban North. Racial violence often erupted in the North as persons with different cultural and ethnic backgrounds clashed. Race riots, for example, occurred in Springfield, Ohio, in March, 1904, and in August, 1906; in Springfield, Illinois, in August, 1908; in East St. Louis, Illinois, in July, 1917; and in

Chicago in July, 1919. To be sure, the northward migration of blacks after the turn of the century added diversity, texture, and power to the northern black community. Blacks challenged white discrimination at every turn. While Baker observed "comparatively little social and political prejudice" in the North, he nevertheless admitted that in the North "the Negro has a hard fight to get anything but the most subservient place in the economic machine." Black workers, in East St. Louis, for example, "had separate washrooms and dressing rooms, usually worked in segregated labor gangs, and ate meals in 'the colored section' of the lunchrooms." The African Americans lived in black ghettoes and their children attended "Negro schools."[10]

In the South, post-Civil War whites drew upon a two-hundred-year history of perceiving blacks as passive extensions of the master class. The old proslavery argument remained very much alive long after General Robert E. Lee's men stacked their guns at Appomattox, becoming a permanent fixture in the intellectual life and economic and legal world of the New South.[11] While few whites dreamed of reviving chattel slavery, conditions of neoslavery—modified serfdom, economic peonage, enticement laws, emigrant agent restrictions, contract laws, vagrancy statutes, the criminal-surety and convict labor systems—ensnared African Americans. After 1890 Jim Crow laws in one southern state after another locked blacks into a truly separate and unequal world.[12] Frightened by the thought of "social equality" and economic competition with blacks, white southerners employed all manner of racial violence to keep African Americans generally landless, undereducated, and powerless. Whites even conjured up the notion of black men as rapists of white women, thereby projecting their racial fantasies upon the sons of their ex-slaves. "Racial purity" became a catch-all phrase in the lexicon of the Jim Crow South. White southerners' determination to maintain absolute control over blacks amounted to what historian Joel Williamson has termed a "rage for order." "Uppity" blacks— men and women who demanded respect, fair treatment, and equal opportunities—threatened the very fabric of the South's biracial system.

Determined to maintain racial control, white Americans after the Civil War published widely on the causes and consequences of what they defined to be "The Negro Problem." As they struggled to find answers to the race question, whites flooded popular magazines, newspapers, scholarly journals, polemical tracts, monographs, and "scientific" treatises with writings on racial themes. Conferences, symposia, and public lectures underscored the sense of immediacy whites felt about the "race problem." By the turn of the century discussion of the "The Negro Problem" had virtually become a cottage industry. "Race thinkers" aplenty satisfied the seemingly insatiable demand in the white community for "experts" on just how to deal with the Negro.[13]

This eleven-volume anthology of writings on "The Negro Problem," written with only one exception by white authors, documents the various strains of racist thought in America from 1863 to 1925. The collection reproduces in facsimile format eighty-six texts that espoused a broad range of racist ideas—from relatively mild paternalistic remarks to extreme racialist diatribes—prevalent over the course of the post-emancipation age. It contains a microcosm of the various negative images whites held of blacks, including vulgar racist caricatures, genteel but condescending suggestions for black "uplift," and endorsements of black colonization. Many of the eighty-six texts are obscure racist pamphlets and speeches. To round out the collection, and to provide context, I have included several hard-to-find books, conference proceedings, and Ku Klux Klan items. The texts are drawn from the holdings of nineteen research libraries, and from the collections of the editor and the publisher.

In order to provide researchers with convenient topical access, the volumes are arranged thematically. Some themes (for example, the alleged backwardness of Africans, innate inferiority of blacks, slavery's "civilizing" influence, the horrors of emancipation and Reconstruction, fear of miscegenation among whites, the crucial importance of maintaining white supremacy, and the advantages of racial segregation) appear again and again throughout the collection. The topical format has eliminated much redundancy from volume to volume and serves to illustrate the breadth and depth of racist thought. Within the topical arrangement, each volume is arranged chronologically, suggesting the continuity and evolution of thought, as well as the subtle shift of racial themes over time. With no illusions of being "comprehensive" (the difficulties of locating texts and then gaining permission to publish them have been staggering), this edition is by design selective and eclectic. Nonetheless, it is hoped that *Anti-Black Thought 1863-1925* provides a representative sampling of conservative and reactionary racial thought from the era of the Civil War until the 1920s.

To be sure, these volumes tell only one side of the story—the white side of the discourse on race during the age of Jim Crow. They document the hurtful racial stereotypes and unfortunate images of blacks associated with that period. They illustrate how whites viewed the black presence as a "problem"—a menace—and how whites defined sources of the "problem" and identified solutions to it. For almost twenty years I have worked with these and similar materials and I am cognizant of just how painful and disturbing this sort of material is to African Americans. It is my determination, however, that the process of bringing such historical texts to light— and making them readily available for students and a general audience— will play some small role in battling racial injustice, bigotry, and class rule. An understanding of the pervasiveness and intensity of white racism is a key to comprehending the obstacles to true black freedom and equality.

This is not to suggest that blacks were passive and stood aimlessly by as whites acted upon them. Fortunately recent historical scholarship has uncovered how blacks actively fought slavery and the Jim Crow system that replaced it—a system with the cards consistently stacked against African

Americans. Blacks resisted nonetheless.[14] In different ways W.E.B. Du Bois, Booker T. Washington, Charles W. Chesnutt, Kelly Miller, and hundreds of other black leaders forcefully engaged their white critics and demanded racial justice throughout the period. With eloquent outrage they protested lynching, limited industrial education, disfranchisement, and segregation in every avenue of American life. Along with such white reformers as George Washington Cable, Lewis H. Blair, Albion W. Tourgée, and Franz Boas they challenged Jim Crow America. The overwhelming scale of the white racist barrage, however, had the effect of keeping blacks on the defensive. Just as whites controlled American society, so too did their racist dogma dominate the popular press. As a result, all too often blacks were forced to respond to whites on their terms. In other words, whites dictated the contours of the turn-of-the-century discourse on race. One of the tragedies of white racism is that the talents of many black scholars were diverted from more useful pursuits to defending what should have been obvious—the humanity of African Americans.

Even so, Du Bois and other African Americans remained ever hopeful that "out of the shame and oppression of the past" that "a new and broader humanity" might succor suffering blacks. As Frederick Douglass explained in 1886, the phrase "the negro problem" was itself "a misnomer." Eight years later Douglass referred to the "so-called but mis-called Negro problem." Responding to the common assumption among whites that they were civilized and blacks were uncivilized, Douglass charged "that there is nothing in the history of savages to surpass the blood-chilling horrors and fiendish excesses perpetrated against the coloured people of this country, by the so-called enlightened and Christian people of the South." "The Negro Problem" was, as Tocqueville, Du Bois, and Douglass had known all along, the white man's problem after all.[15]

Endnotes

[1]Murphy, *Problems of the Present South: A Discussion of Certain of the Educational, Industrial and Political Issues in the Southern States* (New York: Macmillan Company, 1904), 158.

[2]Tocqueville, *Democracy in America*, 2 vols. (1835; New York: Schocken Books, 1974), 1:424.

[3]Du Bois, *The Souls of Black Folk: Essays and Sketches* (1903; Greenwich: Fawcett Publications, 1961), 23, second quotation, emphasis added.

[4]Du Bois, *Black Reconstruction in America* (1934; New York: Atheneum, 1973), 30.

[5]George M. Fredrickson, *The Black Image in the White Mind: The Debate on Afro-American Character and Destiny, 1817–1914* (New York: Harper and

Row, 1971); Larry E. Tise, *Proslavery: A History of the Defense of Slavery in America, 1701–1840* (Athens: University of Georgia Press, 1987).

[6]Fredrickson, "Toward a Social Interpretation of the Development of American Racism," in Nathan I. Huggins, Martin Kilson, and Daniel M. Fox, eds., *Key Issues in the Afro-American Experience*, 2 vols. (New York: Harcourt Brace Jovanovich, 1971), 1:241, 254.

[7]Robert L. Zangranado, *The NAACP Crusade Against Lynching, 1909–1950* (Philadelphia: Temple University Press, 1980), 6. On the recent literature on racial violence, see W. Fitzhugh Brundage, "Mob Violence North and South, 1865–1940," *Georgia Historical Quarterly*, 75 (Winter, 1991): 748–770.

[8]I.A. Newby, *Jim Crow's Defense: Anti-Negro Thought in America, 1900–1930* (Baton Rouge: Louisiana State University Press, 1965); Lawrence J. Friedman, *The White Savage: Racial Fantasies in the Postbellum South* (Englewood Cliffs: Prentice-Hall, 1970); Joel Williamson, *The Crucible of Race: Black-White Relations in the American South Since Emancipation* (New York: Oxford University Press, 1984); Painter, *Standing at Armageddon: The United States, 1877–1919* (New York: W.W. Norton, 1987), xxi.

[9]Baker, *Following the Color Line: American Negro Citizenship in the Progressive Era* (New York: Doubleday, Page & Company, 1908), 298, 299, 300.

[10]Baker, *Following the Color Line*, 129; Elliott Rudwick, *Race Riot at East St. Louis, July 2, 1917* (New York: Atheneum, 1972), 6.

[11]John David Smith, *An Old Creed for the New South: Proslavery Ideology and Historiography, 1865–1918* (1985; Athens: University of Georgia Press, 1991).

[12]Pete Daniel, *The Shadow of Slavery: Peonage in the South, 1901–1969* (1972; New York: Oxford University Press, 1973); Daniel A. Novak, *The Wheel of Servitude: Black Forced Labor After Slavery* (Lexington: University Press of Kentucky, 1978); William Cohen, *At Freedom's Edge: Black Mobility and the Southern White Quest for Racial Control, 1861–1915* (Baton Rouge: Louisiana State University Press, 1991).

[13]See Alfred Holt Stone, "More Race Problem Literature," *Publications of the Southern History Association*, 10 (July, 1906): 218–227. "The great salient feature of the problem of race relations to-day," concluded Stone, "is the steadily increasing uniformity of ideas among white men all over the world,—as they come face to face with the negro." See p. 227.

[14]See, for example, Arnold H. Taylor, *Travail and Triumph: Black Life and Culture in the South Since the Civil War* (Westport: Greenwood Press, 1976); Leon F. Litwack, *Been in the Storm So Long: The Aftermath of Slavery* (New York: Alfred A. Knopf, 1979); Vincent Harding, *There Is a*

River: The Black Struggle for Freedom in America (New York: Harcourt Brace Jovanovich, 1981); Mary Frances Berry and John W. Blassingame, Long Memory: The Black Experience in America (New York: Oxford University Press, 1982); John Hope Franklin and August Meier, eds., Black Leaders of the Twentieth Century (Urbana: University of Illinois Press, 1982); Howard N. Rabinowitz, ed., Southern Black Leaders of the Reconstruction Era (Urbana: University of Illinois Press, 1982); Eric Foner, Nothing But Freedom: Emancipation and Its Legacy (Baton Rouge: Louisiana State University Press, 1983); Armstead L. Robinson, "The Difference Freedom Made: The Emancipation of Afro-Americans," in Darlene Clark Hine, ed., The State of Afro-American History: Past, Present, Future (Baton Rouge: Louisiana State University Press, 1986), 51–75; Leon Litwack and August Meier, eds., Black Leaders of the Nineteenth Century (Urbana: University of Illinois Press, 1988).

[15]Du Bois, "The Negro South and North," Bibliotheca Sacra, 62 (July, 1905), in Herbert Aptheker, ed., The Complete Published Works of W.E.B. Du Bois: Volume I, 1891–1909 (Millwood, NY: Kraus-Thompson Organization, 1982), 256; Douglass to W.H. Thomas, July 16, 1886, Frederick Douglass Papers, Manuscript Division, Library of Congress; Douglass, The Lessons of the Hour (1894), in Philip S. Foner, ed., The Life and Writings of Frederick Douglass, 4 vols. (1955; New York International Publishers, 1975), 4:491, 492–493.

FURTHER READINGS[1]

Anderson, Eric. *Race and Politics in North Carolina, 1872–1901: The Black Second.* Baton Rouge: Louisiana State University Press, 1981.

Bauman, Mark K. "Race and Mastery: The Debate of 1903." In *From the Old South to the New: Essays on the Transitional South.* Edited by Walter J. Fraser, Jr., and Winfred B. Moore, Jr. Westport: Greenwood Press, 1981.

Berry, Mary Frances. "Repression of Blacks in the South, 1890–1945: Enforcing the System of Segregation." In *The Age of Segregation: Race Relations in the South, 1890–1945.* Edited by Robert Haws. Jackson: University Press of Mississippi, 1978.

Boskin, Joseph. *Sambo: The Rise & Demise of an American Jester.* New York: Oxford University Press, 1986.

Bowler, Peter J. *The Eclipse of Darwinism: Anti-Darwinian Evolution Theories in the Decades Around 1900.* Baltimore: The Johns Hopkins University Press, 1983.

————. *Theories of Human Evolution: A Century of Debate, 1844–1944.* Baltimore: The Johns Hopkins University Press, 1986.

Bruce, Dickson D., Jr. *Black American Writing From the Nadir: The Evolution of a Literary Tradition, 1877–1915.* Baton Rouge: Louisiana State University Press, 1989.

Burton, Orville Vernon. "'The Black Squint of the Law': Racism in South Carolina." In *The Meaning of South Carolina History: Essays in Honor of George C. Rogers, Jr.* Edited by David R. Chesnutt and Clyde N. Wilson. Columbia: University of South Carolina Press, 1991.

Cartwright, Joseph H. *The Triumph of Jim Crow: Tennessee Race Relations in the 1880s.* Knoxville: University of Tennessee Press, 1976.

Cassity, Michael J., editor. *Chains of Fear: American Race Relations Since Reconstruction.* Westport: Greenwood Press, 1984.

_____ , editor. *Legacy of Fear: American Race Relations to 1900.* Westport: Greenwood Press, 1985.

Cell, John W. *The Highest Stage of White Supremacy: The Origins of Segregation in South Africa and the American South.* Cambridge: Cambridge University Press, 1982.

Clayton, Bruce. *The Savage Ideal: Intolerance and Intellectual Leadership in the South, 1890–1914.* Baltimore: Johns Hopkins University Press, 1972.

Cooper, William J., Jr. *The Conservative Regime: South Carolina, 1877–1890.* Baltimore: The Johns Hopkins University Press, 1968.

Cortner, Richard C. *A Mob Intent on Death: The NAACP and the Arkansas Riot Cases.* Middletown: Wesleyan University Press, 1988.

Crow, Jeffrey J. "An Apartheid for the South: Clarence Poe's Crusade for Rural Segregation." In *Race, Class, and Politics in Southern History: Essays in Honor of Robert F. Durden.* Edited by Jeffrey J. Crow, Paul D. Escott, and Charles L. Flynn, Jr. Baton Rouge: Louisiana State University Press, 1989.

Dittmer, John. *Black Georgia in the Progressive Era, 1900–1920.* Urbana: University of Illinois Press, 1977.

Drago, Edmund L. *Initiative, Paternalism, and Race Relations: Charleston's Avery Normal Institute.* Athens: University of Georgia Press, 1990.

Ellsworth, Scott. *Death in a Promised Land: The Tulsa Race Riot of 1921.* Baton Rouge: Louisiana State University Press, 1982.

Fields, Barbara J. "Ideology and Race in American History." In *Region, Race, and Reconstruction: Essays in Honor of C. Vann Woodward.* New York: Oxford University Press, 1982.

Fischer, Roger A. *The Segregation Struggle in Louisiana, 1862–77.* Urbana: University of Illinois Press, 1974.

Flynn, Charles L., Jr. *White Land, Black Labor: Caste and Class in Late Nineteenth-Century Georgia.* Baton Rouge: Louisiana State University Press, 1983.

Fredrickson, George M. *The Arrogance of Race: Historical Perspectives on Slavery, Racism, and Social Inequality.* Middletown: Wesleyan University Press, 1988.

―――."Black-White Relations Since Emancipation: The Search for a Comparative Perspective." In *What Made the South Different? Essays and Comments.* Edited by Kees Gispen. Jackson: University Press of Mississippi, 1990.

Gerber, David A. *Black Ohio and the Color Line, 1860–1915.* Urbana: University of Illinois Press, 1976.

Gossett, Thomas F. *Race: The History of an Idea in America.* Dallas: Southern Methodist University Press, 1963.

Graves, John William. *Town and Country: Race Relations in an Urban-Rural Context, Arkansas, 1865–1905.* Fayetteville: University of Arkansas Press, 1990.

Gutman, Herbert G. *The Black Family in Slavery and Freedom, 1750–1925.* New York: Pantheon Books, 1976.

Hair, William Ivy. *Carnival of Fury: Robert Charles and the New Orleans Race Riot of 1900.* Baton Rouge: Louisiana State University Press, 1976.

Harlan, Louis R. *Booker T. Washington: The Making of a Black Leader, 1856–1901.* New York: Oxford University Press, 1972.

———. *Booker T. Washington: The Wizard of Tuskegee, 1901–1915.* New York: Oxford University Press, 1983.

———. *Separate and Unequal: Public School Campaigns and Racism in the Southern Seaboard States, 1901–1915.* Chapel Hill: University of North Carolina Press, 1958.

Harrison, Alferdteen, editor. *Black Exodus: The Great Migration from the American South.* Jackson: University Press of Mississippi, 1991.

Hartzell, Lawrence L. "The Exploration of Freedom in Black Petersburg, Virginia, 1865–1902." In *The Edge of the South: Life in Nineteenth-Century Virginia.* Edited by Edward L. Ayers and John C. Willis. Charlottesville: University Press of Virginia, 1991.

Haynes, Robert V. *A Night of Violence: The Houston Riot of 1917.* Baton Rouge: Louisiana State University Press, 1976.

Horsman, Reginald. *Josiah Nott of Mobile: Southerner, Physician, and Racial Theorist.* Baton Rouge: Louisiana State University Press, 1987.

Ingalls, Robert P. *Urban Vigilantes in the New South: Tampa, 1882–1936.* Knoxville: University of Tennessee Press, 1988.

Lofgren, Charles A. *The Plessy Case: A Legal-Historical Interpretation.* New York: Oxford University Press, 1987.

Luker, Ralph E. "In Slavery's Shadow: North Carolina Methodism and Race Relations, 1885–1920." In *Methodism Alive in North Carolina.* Edited by O. Kelly Ingram. Durham: Duke Divinity School, 1976.

————. *The Social Gospel in Black & White: American Racial Reform, 1885–1912.* Chapel Hill: University of North Carolina Press, 1991.

McGovern, James R. *Anatomy of a Lynching: The Killing of Claude Neal.* Baton Rouge: Louisiana State University Press, 1982.

McMillen, Neil R. *Dark Journey: Black Mississippians in the Age of Jim Crow.* Urbana: University of Illinois Press, 1989.

Mandle, Jay R. *Not Slave, Not Free: The African American Experience Since the Civil War.* Durham: Duke University Press, 1992.

Newby, I. A., editor. *The Development of Segregationist Thought.* Homewood: The Dorsey Press, 1968.

Nieman, Donald G. *Promises to Keep: African–Americans and the Constitutional Order, 1776 to the Present.* New York: Oxford University Press, 1991.

Olsen, Otto H., editor. *The Negro Question: From Slavery to Caste, 1863–1910.* New York: Pitman Publishing Corporation, 1971.

————, editor. *The Thin Disguise: Turning Point in Negro History, Plessy v. Ferguson, A Documentary Presentation (1864–1896).* New York: Humanities Press, 1967.

Painter, Nell Irvin. "'Social Equality,' Miscegenation, Labor, and Power." In *The Evolution of Southern Culture.* Edited by Numan V. Bartley. Athens: University of Georgia Press, 1988.

Perman, Michael. "Counter Reconstruction: The Role of Violence in Southern Redemption." In *The Facts of Reconstruction: Essays in Honor of John Hope Franklin.* Edited by Eric Anderson and Alfred A. Moss, Jr. Baton Rouge: Louisiana State University Press, 1991.

Rabinowitz, Howard N. "A Comparative Perspective on Race Relations in Southern and Northern Cities, 1860–1900, with Special Emphasis on Raleigh." In *Black Americans in North Carolina and the South.* Edited by Jeffrey J. Crow and Flora J. Hatley. Chapel Hill: University of North Carolina Press, 1984.

————. *Race Relations in the Urban South, 1865–1890.* New York: Oxford University Press, 1978.

————. "Segregation and Reconstruction." In *The Facts of Reconstruction: Essays in Honor of John Hope Franklin.* Edited by Eric Anderson and Alfred A. Moss, Jr. Baton Rouge: Louisiana State University Press, 1991.

————. "The Weight of the Past Versus the Promise of the Future: Southern Race Relations in Historical Perspective." In *The Future South: A Historical Perspective for the Twenty-first Century.* Edited by Joe P. Dunn and Howard L. Preston. Urbana: University of Illinois Press, 1991.

Rable, George C. *But There Was No Peace: The Role of Violence in the Politics of Reconstruction.* Athens: University of Georgia Press, 1984.

Rogers, William Warren and Robert David Ward. *August Reckoning: Jack Turner and Racism in Post-Civil War Alabama.* Baton Rouge: Louisiana State University Press, 1973.

Shapiro, Herbert. *White Violence and Black Response: From Reconstruction to Montgomery.* Amherst: University of Massachusetts Press, 1988.

Smith, H. Shelton. *In His Image, But . . . Racism in Southern Religion, 1780–1910.* Durham: Duke University Press, 1972.

Stanfield, John H. *Philanthropy and Jim Crow in American Social Science.* Westport: Greenwood Press, 1985.

Takaki, Ronald T. *Iron Cages: Race and Culture in 19th-Century America.* New York: Alfred A. Knopf, 1979.

Toll, Robert C. *Blacking Up: The Minstrel Show in Nineteenth-Century America.* New York: Oxford University Press, 1974.

Tuttle, William M., Jr. *Race Riot: Chicago in the Red Summer of 1919.* New York: Atheneum, 1970.

Wayne, Michael. *The Reshaping of Plantation Society: The Natchez District, 1860–1880.* Baton Rouge: Louisiana State University Press, 1983.

Weaver, John D. *The Brownsville Raid.* New York: W.W. Norton, 1970.

Westin, Richard B. "Blacks, Educational Reform, and Politics in North Carolina, 1897–1898." In *The Southern Enigma: Essays on Race, Class, and Folk Culture.* Edited by Walter J. Fraser, Jr., and Winfred B. Moore, Jr. Westport: Greenwood Press, 1983.

Wheeler, Joanne. "Together in Egypt: A Pattern of Race Relations in Cairo, Illinois, 1865–1915." In *Toward a New South? Studies in Post-Civil War Southern Communities.* Edited by Orville Vernon Burton and Robert C. McMath, Jr. Westport: Greenwood Press, 1982.

Wilson, Charles Reagan. *Baptized in Blood: The Religion of the Lost Cause, 1865–1920.* Athens: University of Georgia Press, 1980.

Wright, George C. *Life Behind a Veil: Blacks in Louisville, Kentucky, 1865–1930.* Baton Rouge: Louisiana State University Press, 1985.

———. *Racial Violence in Kentucky, 1865–1940: Lynchings, Mob Rule, and "Legal Lynchings."* Baton Rouge: Louisiana State University Press, 1990.

[1]These citations develop themes suggested in the "General Introduction" and are designed to supplement the works cited in the Endnotes. In no sense comprehensive, the references are drawn heavily from the historical literature published since 1980, and reflect the ongoing reassessment of white racism in late nineteenth-century America.

INTRODUCTION

Volumes V and VI present texts illustrating the central role that religion played in bolstering white resistance to emancipation during the post-Appomattox decades. Biblical interpretations, of course, had provided a major pillar for the old proslavery argument and, not surprisingly, white racists trotted out many of the old arguments anew. In 1867 "Ariel," Nashville publisher and clergyman Buckner H. Payne, published *The Negro: What is His Ethnological Status?*—a pamphlet grounded in antebellum pre-Adamite and polygenist theories. At the very moment, then, when the Reconstruction amendments were being passed, Payne charged that blacks and whites were members of different species. His pamphlet sparked considerable debate, the contours of which appear in Volume V.

Payne argued that blacks had not descended from Ham and, accordingly, were not human beings. In his opinion, God frowned upon attempts to equalize the races. Payne assumed "That the negro being created before Adam, consequently . . . is a *beast* in God's nomenclature." The author asserted that calamities in the Bible were God's punishments for miscegenation between white descendants of Adam and Eve and blacks. Payne charged that because blacks lacked souls and could not be saved, they could not worship God. And whereas blacks allegedly were beasts, not men, God disapproved of attempts to equalize the races. To "elevate a *beast* to the level of a son of God," explained Payne, was analogous to insulting the Creator. As a result, "the states or people that favor this equality and amalgamation of the white and black races, *God will exterminate.*" Before emancipation, slaveholders had acted as God's agents to prevent this calamity. But now, Payne argued, only two alternatives remained for the African American: "You *must send him back to Africa or re-enslave him.*"[1]

"A Minister," D.G. Phillips of Louisville, Georgia, agreed with Payne that God had created blacks before the rest of mankind. In *Nachash: What Is It?*, Phillips argued that the serpent who deceived Eve had been a black, thereby dooming all blacks "to perpetual menial crouching slavery." Phillips's postwar biblical defense of slavery was strongly influenced by Dr. Samuel A. Cartwright, one of the Old South's foremost "scientific" apologists for slavery. Convinced that blacks could live only as slaves or perish, Phillips denounced emancipation as being against God's will, "and," he warned that, "the consequences must be direful in the end."[2] Similarly, the works by "Prospero" and "Sister Sallie" generally supported Payne. In addition, the editor has included Payne's *Ariel's Reply* to his critics in Volume V, and, in Volume VI, A. Hoyle Lester's *The Pre-Adamite, or Who Tempted Eve?* and Charles Carroll's *The Tempter of Eve* to suggest the persistence of the "Ariel" debate as late as 1902.

The controversy generated by "Ariel" not only provides insights into the post-Civil War race question but also offers glimpses into the contemporary discourse on race. Significantly, most racists, as historian Forrest G. Wood suggests, rejected Payne's arguments as "utter nonsense." To accept Payne's biblical thesis would have undercut "a sacrosanct white supremacy dogma—namely, the curse-of-Canaan notion." For example, in *Speculum for Looking Into the Pamphlet Entitled "The Negro,"* included in Volume V, "Optician" attacked Payne and denied that slaveholders had ever viewed their blacks as beasts and had in fact treated them humanely. Another critic, Nashville's Robert A. Young, identified numerous errors in Payne's pamphlet and declared: "We do not believe in the social equality of the Negro. We do not believe he knows how to handle a vote. We are disfranchised. Still, we believe *the Negro is a descendant of Adam and Eve; that he is the progeny of Ham; that he is a human being, and has an immortal soul.*" "M.S." lashed out not only against Payne but against Young as well, concluding "that the negro is not a *beast*, but has a soul, but [was] not created after the image of God; that he was created and placed upon the earth *anterior* to Adam, together with all the other inferior races . . . ."[3] Harrison Berry, who described himself as "A Full Blooded Cushite," ridiculed Payne on several counts, especially for denying that blacks were part of the human family. Berry, who as a slave reportedly defended the enslavement of his own race, denounced Payne's pamphlet as "the last effort of the great diabolical aristocratic slave power." Berry's case is just the most curious instance in the bizarre debate over the alleged biblical sanctions of a racial hierarchy.[4] According to Wood, "The Ariel controversy was most revealing as a reflection of the widespread belief in, and the preposterous extremes of, religious fundamentalism, at least when it involved racial matters."[5]

Just as polygenist theology bolstered nineteenth-century theories of white supremacy, so too did the burgeoning disciplines of anthropometry, craniometry, and ethnology. After the Civil War, polygenist theories remained alive, thanks largely to Dr. Josiah C. Nott of Mobile, Alabama. In the most important development for the scientific study of humanity, Charles Darwin's evolutionary theory stressed man's basic unity, while allowing for varieties and inequality. "Darwin," explains historian Paul F. Boller, Jr., "rejected the notion . . . that species of plants and animals (including man) originated in a special act of creation which fixed their forms for all time. Evolutionary change, . . . not immutability, is the law of life; living organisms are the products of gradual, minute changes taking place over vast periods of time, and their origins can be traced back to ancient species that are quite different in form from those prevailing in modern times." In other words, Darwin argued that all human races belong to a single species, but that some races were superior to others. Organisms competed in a struggle for existence through a process that Darwin termed "natural selection."[6]

As historian Carl N. Degler points out, Darwin's theory of evolution was based upon "hereditarianism, not racism, because it lacked the invidious comparison among races that is the essential and distinguishing element in the concept of racism." Others, however, developed the theory of racist evolution from his work. Darwin actually wrote little about the issue of human origins, other than to argue for a primate link and against polygenist notions of separate creations. The number of shared physical characteristics among all humans made them one species, Darwin said. Nonetheless, he accepted the standard social hierarchy of the races, as seen by Europeans. That allowed racial theorists to call themselves "Darwinian" while connecting the social ladder of the races to a biologically determined hierarchy of superiority and inferiority. Evolutionists in general arranged the different races along a linear path of progress, with the "lower" races showing the remnants of primitive stages. Drawing upon anthropometrics and ethnology, anthropologists and other "race thinkers" defined a hierarchy of stages in evolution with the European as the goal.[7]

Invoking Darwin's name to gain the legitimacy of "science," they recast polygenist creationism into a biological theory of the separate nature of the races, or a racist evolutionism. These writers argued that differences between the races stemmed from different species of mankind, *not*, as Darwin insisted, from varieties within the human family. By the end of the century, when white racism in America was rampant, the "science" of race had "proven" beyond a doubt the immutable inferior mental and physical capacity of blacks. Discounting the roles of culture or environment, racists employed "science" to establish an elaborate explanation for the retrogression of African Americans. Lacking the "protection" of slavery, post-Civil War blacks were allegedly falling by the wayside in direct competition with whites. They also reportedly succumbed to innate degenerative tendencies and were dying off. According to scientists and pseudo-scientists, mulattoes were especially prone to deteriorate physiologically. "While the Anglo-Saxon," notes historian John S. Haller, Jr., "reaped the benefits of a man-centered evolutionary process, the so-called 'inferior races' and 'stocks' remained outcasts from the evolutionary struggle, restricted from participation because of innate racial characteristics that were unresponsive to environmental influences."[8]

In 1896, after compiling data on black mortality, statistician Frederick L. Hoffman of the Prudential Insurance Company of America advised his firm that African Americans posed "a bad actuarial risk." "With an inordinate rate of mortality," he said, "with an excessive degree of immorality, with a greater tendency to crime and pauperism than the whites, the negro race has also . . . a far lower degree of economic activity and inclination towards accumulation of capital and other material wealth." According to Hoffman, "education, philanthropy and religion" for blacks "have failed to develop a higher appreciation of the stern and uncompromising virtues of the Aryan race." Exuding pessimism, Hoffman predicted that "gradual extinction is only a question of time." In 1910, however, Hoffman revised his earlier forecast, concluding "that the [Negro] race will reach a stationary condition, very much as is the case with the Gypsies in Europe, and to a certain extent with our Indian population."[9]

Endnotes

[1]"Ariel," *The Negro: What Is His Ethnological Status?* (second edition; Cincinnati: n.p., 1867), 45, 48, 46, 48; Wood, *Black Scare: The Racist Response to Emancipation and Reconstruction* (Berkeley: University of California Press, 1968), 6-7.

[2]A Minister, *Nachash: What Is It? or An Answer to the Question, "Who and What is the Negro?" Drawn From Revelation* (Augusta: James L. Gow, 1868), 42, 43, 44; D.G. Phillips to W.R. Hemphill, December 31, 1868, Hemphill Family Papers, Duke University.

[3]Wood, *Black Scare*, 6; "Optician," *Speculum for Looking Into the Pamphlet Entitled "The Negro"* (Charleston: Joseph Walker, 1867), 6, 20; Young, *The Negro: A Reply to Ariel* (Nashville: J.W. M'Ferrin & Co., 1867), 4-5; "M.S.," *The Adamic Race. Reply to "Ariel." Drs. Young and Blackie, on the Negro* (New York: Russell Bros., 1868), 67.

[4]Berry, *A Reply to Ariel* (Macon: American Union Book and Job Office Print, 1869), 36, 34. In 1861 Berry published *Slavery and Abolitionism, as Viewed by a Georgia Slave* (Atlanta: Franklin Printing House, 1861), in which he described himself as the slave of S.W. Price of Covington, Georgia. Berry defended slavery as the product of God's will and maligned the Abolitionists as "the worst of all enemies of the Slave." See pp. 31-32, 40. As Maxwell Whiteman suggests, Berry's authorship of this anti-abolition tract is "highly suspect." If Berry did indeed write *Slavery and Abolitionism*, explains Whiteman, "the ideas were the ideas of his master." According to Whiteman, Berry's 1882 pamphlet, *The Foundation of Atheism Examined, With an Answer to the Question, "Why Don't God Kill the Devil?"* "showed him as a semi-literate man not even equal to the logic of apologetics of his first literary venture, giving credence to the likelihood that the work was not his own." See Whiteman, "Harrison Berry: A Georgia Slave Defends Slavery, A Bibliographical Note," [introduction to] Berry, *Slavery and Abolitionism, as Viewed by a Georgia Slave* (reprint edition; Wilmington: Scholarly Resources, 1977), [1-2]. In his authoritative *A Bibliography of*

the Negro in Africa and America (1928; New York: Argosy-Antiquarian, 1965), 314, 576, Monroe N. Work failed to identify Berry as a Negro author, again raising questions as to the legitimacy of his writings.

[5]Wood, *Black Scare*, 7. See also I. A. Newby, *Jim Crow's Defense: Anti-Negro Thought in America, 1900-1930* (Baton Rouge: Louisiana State University Press, 1965), 93-98.

[6]William Stanton, *The Leopard's Spots: Scientific Attitudes Toward Race in America, 1815-59* (Chicago: University of Chicago Press, 1960); Jacques Barzun, *Race: A Study in Superstition* (1937; New York: Harper and Row, 1965), 47-48; Boller, *American Thought in Transition: The Impact of Evolutionary Naturalism, 1865-1900* (Chicago: Rand McNally, 1969), 1-2; Stephen Jay Gould, *The Mismeasure of Man* (New York: W.W. Norton, 1981), 71-72; Glenn C. Altschuler, *Race, Ethnicity, and Class in American Social Thought, 1865-1919* (Arlington Heights, IL: Harlan Davidson, 1982), 3-4.

[7]Degler, *In Search of Human Nature: The Decline and Revival of Darwinism in American Social Thought* (New York: Oxford University Press, 1991), 14.

[8]Haller, *Outcasts From Evolution: Scientific Attitudes of Racial Inferiority, 1859-1900* (1971; New York: McGraw-Hill, 1975), 187.

[9]Altschuler, *Race, Ethnicity, and Class in American Social Thought, 1865-1919*, 5; Hoffman, "Race Traits and Tendencies of the American Negro," *Publications of the American Economic Association*, 11 (August, 1896): 308, 329; Hoffman to Edward Eggleston, August 17, 1910, in Edward Eggleston, *The Ultimate Solution of the American Negro Problem* (Boston: Gorham Press, 1913), 273.

NACHASH:

WHAT IS IT?

OR

AN ANSWER TO THE QUESTION,

"WHO AND WHAT IS THE NEGRO?"

DRAWN FROM REVELATION.

BY

A MINISTER.

" To the law and to the testimony."
" Truth is mighty and will prevail."

Augusta, Ga:
JAS. L. GOW, BOOK AND JOB PRINTER,
276 Broad Street—Up Stairs.
1868.

1

PREFACE.

This tract sets forth a theory on that prolific subject, *the negro*. The writer asks no favors and fears no frowns from critics. All he asks is, that they be honest, candid and respectful, as he has been. If he be wrong he is open to conviction. But it can be produced only by arguments, not by abuse or efforts at ridicule. The subject contains some most important questions in both Church and State. Upon their solution the character of the civilization of America for ages to come, must, to a good degree, depend.

If the theory here advanced be untrue, the existence of this tract can only be ephemeral, and it will accomplish but little harm. But if it be true, then "truth is mighty and will prevail."

The writer attempts to show that the Bible teaches that the negro does not belong to Adam's race, but was an earlier creation; that he is a rational, and therefore accountable and immortal creature; that he was inferior, and therefore subordinated to Adam at his creation; that he was first in the transgression in Eden, and for his offense there was doomed to the condition of perpetual menial slavery, and that if saved at all it can only be through contact as a slave with Adam's race. Infidelity has of late laid hold of the negro and manufactured from him arguments prejudicial to the Bible. The misfortune is not in the error of the Bible but of its interpreters. It must be vindicated by its friends as it always has been. This tract is an effort to show that the developments of science and history only throw new light on the Bible and prove that a long accepted interpretation of it is incorrect. How far it succeeds in that attempt let the candid reader decide. These sheets are extracted from a large amount of manuscript on the subject, reviewing it in detail, all of which will perhaps be sent to press in due time.

THE AUTHOR.

Home, June 10, 1868.

2

NACHASH.

CHAPTER I.

INTRODUCTORY REMARKS.

" Who and what is the negro ?" For more than half a century, the press, both in Europe and America, has been sending out contributions to his history. But still the questions have not been satisfactorily answered. Good men, in both Church and State, still declare them open questions, and demand further answer before they feel prepared to form their final judgment. The reason of their hesitation is found, to some degree, in the manner in which the subject has been too often treated. Prejudice, cupidity, personal aims and pride of opinion, have, too often, taken the place of that honest search after truth for its own sake, which is always necessary to produce permanent conviction. Too many interests are involved in the questions to allow their decision without full, satisfactory evidence.

Much that has been written was in the form of electioneering documents, by political partisans. Aimed to excite the populace, their object was, not truth, but a temporary effect. If they happened to contain truth it came in so doubtful a form as to prove only ephemeral—

"Like snow that falls upon the river,
A moment white then gone forever."

Much of it emanated from penny-a-line scribblers, who wrote only for their bread and butter, and were not actuated by any love of truth, but a desire to produce something which would be read by the millions and therefore sell well. To gain that end they have pandered to every appetite, however vitiated, dealt in the marvelous, appealed to prejudice and imitated Sinbad the Sailor. They have poured a morbid public taste for reading on the subject of the negro into Mammon's foul crucible and " coined it into drachms." Far too often for the good of truth and humanity they have succeeded, and sold books and made money. But they did not make man either wiser or better.

Many good meaning men, unaware that their feelings wrought up by fancy sketches, had gained a mastery over them and blinded

3

6

their calmer judgment, have poured forth the flood of their sympathies, in wonder that all the world could not see as they saw—feel as they felt. Their zeal, whether wise or unwise let time decide, sent forth productions so fast that they were necessarily left, like the eggs of the ostrich in the sands, to care for themselves; and alas! they all hatched. This class did not notice that, with the very best of motives, they were "dealing damnation round the land," at which themselves, as well as all calm thinkers, would gaze in pale astonishment. Some have felt constrained to conserve the institution of slavery, because they found it clearly defined and allowed in the Bible. But they generally placed it upon untenable grounds. They failed to see that it was not necessarily a blessing because divinely appointed. It is true, however strange it may seem, to say that no fair issue was ever joined between the honest pro-slavery and anti-slavery man. The one never defended the social desirableness, the civil utility or wisdom of slavery. But he desired its fancied profits, and defended it on the ground that it was divinely appointed and clearly contained in Revelation, and therefore lawful. In the argument he overlooked the main fact, that slavery, in the proper acceptation of the term, never could have inhered in the original order of things, as an emanation from the goodness and love of God to all His creatures. Subordination could—indeed was necessary. But slavery could not. If such a divine appointment as slavery exist in the Bible, (and it certainly does) it must result, in some way, from the punitive justice of God, and be inflicted as the penalty of law for some transgression. It is therefore, if penalty, a thing necessarily fearful, and, in itself, undesirable. Penalty, of any kind, never can be desirable, however unwise it may be to try to shield him who has incurred it. The pro-slavery man was always ready to admit the institution liable to both social and moral evils, which is true. But he claimed that it was sanctioned by Revelation, which is also true. But the fact that God has appointed that the penalty of law shall always attach to its violator, is no evidence that the penalty is a thing pleasing and desirable in itself. No more is the fact, that God inflicted slavery on the negro for an offence, evidence that the condition is desirable or profitable to either party in the relation.

The anti-slavery man, if honest, has always admitted that slavery was sanctioned by the word of God, but that it was an unnatural and undesirable condition, full of both social, civil and moral evils. Thus the one claims the divine appointment of the institution, but admits its attendant evils; the other claims its attendant evils, but admits its divine appointment. And thus issue was never fairly joined. But the one, in order to maintain a position never seriously threatened, has often mingled with arguments strong and symmetrical, puerile theories, which, by the law of association, have dragged his arguments into doubt—often contempt. The other, in his zeal to gain a fortress never denied him, has sanctified means which emasculated the intellectual and moral sentiments of whole communities, and drove the share of corrupting infidelity straight through the foundations of settled faith. But at the end of the long and angry discussion both parties have left, if not untouched, at least unanswered, the questions "who and what is the negro?" There is another class of writers on this subject, and another reason for hesitancy which was seen; and it is a noble one—"conscience toward God."

All writers on the subject may be easily divided into two classes— the Religious and Scientific. The latter are entitled to much credit. But too many of them ignore the credibility of written revelation, and depend entirely upon the doubtful conclusions of science. Science has her proper place and work, and, with really scientific men, that place is honorable and that work arduous and most beneficial in its results. But really scientific men freely admit, that, for any rational account of the history of the first two thousand years of our world, we are left almost entirely to written revelation. Outside of it is nought but merest conjecture. If we close revelation we leave all that part of the history of our world anterior to the commencement of authentic profane history, which does not reach beyond the songs of Homer, if so far, an entire blank. It is easy for "so-called" science to prate; but how often is it "the prating of a fool." It is the legitimate province of science to ferret out all the lessons which God has taught in nature, his elder revelation, to find

> " Tongues in trees, books in the running brooks,
> Sermons in stones, and 'God' in everything."

But she should propound her conclusions with very great modesty, for two reasons: First—so many of what have been called scientific truths, have been found unable to bear the light of time. Further search has *demonstrated* her *demonstrations demonstrably* wrong. And many that are now held to be scientific truths may yet turn out scientific errors. Secondly—God has taught plain lessons elsewhere beside in the natural world. He has given a plainly written revelation, to which we do well to take heed as unto a light shining in a dark place. It is a fact of all ages, that they who have ignored the Bible and have depended upon science and human philosophy for lessons to instruct, amend and guide men, have not only failed, but have finally rendered him more ignorant and depraved. Many scientific writers on the subject of the negro have loved truth for its own sake; sought it carefully, found much of it, and disseminated it to a grateful world. And they are the witnesses that there is yet no established *scientific* answer to the thousand and one interesting questions raised by the existence and many peculiarities of the negro.

God is the Author of both the Bible and material nature; and he is consistent. He never contradicted in one a lesson taught in the other. They harmonize perfectly in every lesson taught by them. They treat partly the same, and partly different subjects. And if they seem, at any time, to clash, the error is not in them, but in a misapprehension of one or both of them. Yet some who profess to be scientific writers ridicule obvious facts, as if what they say had not been far better said and then refuted many times before. They laugh at the Bible as a system of fables, not knowing that its authenticity and divine origin have been established upon a base of truth and human confidence from which it never can be shaken. They who imprisoned Gallileo had as much right to claim that their theory was correct, as they who now claim that science settles the fact that the negro belongs to the family of Adam, without regard to revelation. The Bible must, at last, decide the question " who and what is the negro ?"

The class of religious writers bow, in deference, to the authority of revelation. And although they have often erred, as it is human to do, to them is the world chiefly indebted for what is already accepted as established truth on the subject. Of course we do not include here the wild ravings of the fanatical crowd, which pass away before sober thought as mists before a morning sun in May. But only those who appeal to reason and the great umpire, time.

The great misfortune, however, with this class of writers on this and every other religious subject, is, they too often " teach for doctrines the commandments of men." Their proper reverence for the Bible and for those who treat it with becoming respect, sometimes leads them to adopt the opinions of the latter as the established doctrines of the former. Men are bound to accept and reverence the Bible, but not the interpretation given to it by even every good man. We can never tell, if candid, how few of our opinions of what the Bible contains, have been formed from an examination of the book itself, and how many of them from what some good man or men have said about it. It is read as much, possibly, in order to find in it something to sustain an opinion already formed, or what some one has said about it, as it is to ascertain what it contains and teaches. In all such cases " the wish is father to the thought," and what is sought is generally found. And then woe be to the luckless wight ! who dares to question the conclusion. He is an innovator—an infidel—an evildoer. Not because he questions revelation or offers any disrespect to it. But because he bows to it and dares to read it for himself—he dares to question an interpretation of it. As Science imprisoned her own Gallileo who was nearer right than she, so has the church imprisoned her thousands who have since been vindicated by time and proven correct.

The church has long since agreed, generally, that the Bible contains certain theories about the negro. And now everything written about him must chime in with those theories, or it is heresy and its author an infidel. And many men, not readers of the Bible— not familiar with it, but accepting these theories as really its contents, and seeing their contradictions and absurdities, have rejected it for what it never contained. With such the questions " who and what is the negro ?" are wholly unanswered. These sheets offer a new answer to these questions, which is drawn directly from the Bible. And whether that answer be right or wrong, " truth is mighty and will prevail."

CHAPTER II.

Before approaching the Bible to ascertain what it teaches on any subject, we should have definite ideas of the subject on which we seek the light. Let us then look briefly at the history of the negro, that we may the better appreciate the perfect correspondence between the position he there occupies, and the position assigned him by the angry fiat of his author, as it is described by inspiration.

Man's history is something like the running stream—an unbroken connection. It can easily be traced upward to where its little fountain bubbles up among the distant hills. Or it can be followed downward, as it sparkles in the sun, plays on the slope, creeps round the pebble, dances over the bending ozier, gurgles into the brook, swells into the stream, grows to the torrent, dashes over the precipice, spreads into the majestic river, and moves onward to the great ocean, white with the commerce of nations. All the way it is well defined—an unbroken unit—an expansive idea. Such is man's history.

Not so the history of the negro. It is more like the streams flowing westward from the Rocky Mountains. Their sources are pointed out, whether correctly or not. But as they flow onward their waters sink in the sands and are lost for a time. Again they rise and are clearly traced in their course. And thus they continue to rise and sink until, at last, they empty, geographers have not told us where. Such is the negro's history. He can be traced backward to his origin, or at least to the Garden of Eden. But like the sparkling waters in these channels, often wanting, so present living facts of negro history are often wanting. The reason of this will become obvious as we proceed. But here the mind instinctively asks: what are the salient points, the prominent features, the exalting facts, the brilliant periods, the real historic ages of the negro? "Echo answers—*what?*"

Now, however, we may divide and subdivide humanity into races, nations or castes, still every school boy knows that each subdivision has had, at some time, what may be denominated "its historic age," when it carved out history for itself, except the negro. Each has made and left an impress somewhere upon the condition, laws, learning, arts, governments, commerce, religions, agriculture or some other idea of the world. The tribe, nation or subdivision may be dead long since. But it has left its mementoes behind it somewhere, to witness for it that it once was there. Its apologist, standing upon its grave, can point to its monuments of some sort, pleasing or mournful, which it has left as the ineffacible footprints of its once presence there. He can point to the rising sun of its glory, and say, "behold the coming day"—or to its deep foot-prints and say, "see! it once was here." He may stand with Moses upon the top of Pisgah and look hopefully forward to the glorious future of his nation, or he may sit pensive with Marius amid the smouldering ruins of Carthege, and look mournfully back to the faded glories of an eventful and brilliant past. And the eye will glisten or moisten as it follows the ascending or declining sun of national glory. But, before a candid world we assert it, in neither direction can the eye catch one solitary glance of one fact, one idea, one thought, one promise, which bears the impress of the negro. We gaze into vacuity. It is all a dismal blank. Six thousand years of labor, and not even a ridiculous mouse! A being of all history, himself has no history. Found at all times and in all places, ubiquitous as the air we breathe, still he has left no impress at any time or place, to say for him, "here is evidence of negro great-ness." For six thousand years he "has been toted" upon the shoulder of man's history, as the gnat upon the horn of the ox, and has never, even there, called for attention. He is a rational being, so say facts and revelation. But is that a self-directing independent intellect which has not yet been weaned in sixty centuries? We challenge all candor, all history to show where or when the negro has ever origi-nated one idea, advanced one thought which has been preserved, formed one government, enacted one law, written one readable book or poem, originated or mastered one art either fine or useful, furnished one conqueror, warrior, traveler, adventurer, sailor or mechanic; made one discovery, started one sect, originated one myth, made one improvement in agriculture, or in any way left upon the civilization of any country or age, or upon the world of mind, any more impress than has been left there by the horse, ox or ass His "foot-prints upon the sands of time "have to be Daguerreotyped by man before the next tide, or they are gone, and gone forever. Where and what is his history? Himself has never tried to write it. Man has written it, and it is all contained in two words—"he was—he is." His intel-lect is a Hybrid intellect, and upon his genius, "Tekel" has been written by the finger of God, so deep that it can never be obliterated. Look at him in the most favorable circumstance in which his history places him. In the United States, where he has lived for centuries, in immediate contact, and actually mixed up with the most active, energetic and enterprising type of man, where he enjoyed every privilege and facility, and in a country whose laws and government were well calculated to wake up and call out all the latent and dor-mant energies of his nature, if he had any such, he has still slumbered on, as ever, the mere satellite of man. And this is true of him, not only in the fabled degradation of Southern slavery (where, by the way, he has made the farthest advances that he has ever yet made) but in Northern freedom, where he possessed all the advantages of a free education, stimulated by a public sentiment almost morbid on the subject—where the rattle of machinery never died upon his ear—where he was continually employed in both making and guiding that machinery—amazingly imitative being as he certainly is—still the fact is true as strange, that among all the thousands of rights issued annually from the Patent office, to all classes and nationalities, for inventions and improvements in machinery, not one has ever been granted to, or asked for, by a negro. In the Southern States, the peculiarities of soil, climate and *chattle* slavery, have, in the last half century, somewhat identified the negro with the production of cotton and rice. Nothing else, for six thousand years has come so near identifying him with one practical idea. But those who have guided his labor have always affirmed what has been, and now will be demonstrated—that not as many as one in ten of those negroes who have been born and grown up on cotton and rice farms and have grown old in their cultivation, can now plant and cultivate successfully one acre of either, without the planning and guiding mind of a white man. The multitude of ludicrous but unfortunate attempts that have been made in the last two years, furnish lessons amusing, gloomy and instructive. They prove that he is rational, but, that his is an emasculated intellect, either preordained, or else doomed to act in a dependent capacity. His whole history, or rather his entire lack of history, proclaims him *sui generis*, different from and inferior to man. And none but he who gave that nature ever can exalt it to the dignity of manhood.

There is another interesting and very vocal fact which will not be questioned by any candid mind. It is the singular unanimity with which all men, in all ages, countries, and social and moral conditions, have seized upon the negro and reduced him, not only to slavery, but to *chattle slavery*.

That men, both savage and civilized, have seized upon and enslaved, and bought and sold white men, is certainly true—not universally, or even commonly true. But they have never pitched upon any one race, nation or tribe to enslave thus. And there has always been, even where it was practiced, opposition to it, and an implied unlawfulness in it—a natural or an instinctive repugnance to it. But no candid mind informed on the subject, will deny that it is true of the negro wherever the light of his history glimmers, that all men, at all times, in all countries, and in every social and moral condition, have felt at liberty to enslave the negro, and generally, to reduce him to chattle slavery. What does history say about the negro except as a slave? Where do you find him in all the past except as a slave? As the ornithologist has to speak of the bird in the air, or not at all; as the piscologist has to speak of the fish in the water, or not at all, for these are the only places where their subjects are ever found, so the negro historian has to speak of him in slavery, or not at all, for it is the only place he is ever found—generally in chattle slavery. An almost universal consent has assigned it to him as his natural place. I am not arguing that it is right or wrong thus to enslave him. The question is not this—"what is right or wrong?" But what is natural? and what are the facts of history? The question is not between menial abject slavery, and chattle slavery. But the question is, what is the history of the negro? In his first appearance since the flood he comes to view on monuments, coins, inscriptions and pictures as a crouching menial. The black Eunuch is found in the foreground of almost every view of the camp, the court and the Seraglio of barbarous and semi-barbarous Asia for more than thirty hundred years. No mart is pictured or described there, without its black slaves. "The land of history" writes him down *slave—chattle slave.* In Africa— the land of negroes—his manhood now is, and for centuries, reaching back into entire historic obscurity, has been measured by the number of Cowries he would command in the market. Each petty chief, himself the crouching slave of some owning master still above him, has huddled together his own family and the rest of the slaves he could command, and has sent them to the shambles with the natural feeling that it was their legitimate place. It is so to-day in that country. All Africans enslave all Africans in Africa. If you shudder at the recital, reader, quarrel not with me. I lament it as much as you can. You must quarrel with the faithful chronicles of the past, which honest candor will not deny are here faithfully represented.

In Europe, the negro was regarded not only as a slave, but a chattle slave, and was bought and sold at a price, until he was entirely crowded out by the density of growing population. And even when his room was demanded and his offensiveness to growing civilization had manumitted him, and they refused to retain him as a slave, he had no dignity of manhood, nor any of the peculiarities of citizen accorded to him. But he was "forcibly ejected" from society and sent to the "islands of the sea"—to Africa, Spain and America. All Europe bore a part in enslaving the negro at home, and in sending him, as a slave, abroad. Other causes than a persuasion that negro slavery is wrong, prompted them to sing with Cowper—

> "Slaves cannot breathe in England—
> They touch our borders and their shackles fall."

And where are the "four hundred and eighty-two thousand" for whom Wilberforce pleaded so long and so earnestly? Who can point to one of them or of their descendants still alive on the earth? May we not take up the language of David and say—

> "They like a sleep are, like the grass,
> That grows at morn are they they?"

When the charm of chattle slavery which spell bound them was broken, "like the green and tender herb," they withered away.

The Northern section of the United States never was a section where slavery, either chattle or otherwise, could be profitable or lasting. That section was settled, not by capital seeking a profitable investment, but by labor seeking remunerative employment. And labor has always kept pace with, and generally outstripped the demand. Domestic increase and foreign accretions have always more than equalled the demand, and left a large margin for paupers. Hence negroes were not needed there as menials, and when owned as chattles, being entirely valueless, they were soon sent further South to find a market. But the few who remained never have been regarded as natural, social or civil equals of man. They have been and now are looked down upon as an inferior race of beings. Let it go on

record for future reference that in the year A. D. 1868, every free
State of the American Union by a majority of the white voters have
said—the negro is an inferior—a menial race of beings. They freed
him from chattle slavery in the Southern States, yet they say he is a
natural slave. Because there he has clung like a miserable fungus to
the suburbs, lanes and sewers of cities and towns, where any person
who could find any menial employment for him, has felt it, and to-day
feels it, his province to kick him into that employment, and then
throw him a crusty morsel of any sort as remuneration, and both
parties feel perfectly satisfied. Whether that feeling be right or
wrong, no one who is at all conversant with the facts of the case, will
question its existence all over the northern portion of the United
States. In the southern portion of the United States, the idea (false
we admit) has long prevailed that it was unhealthy for *men* to labor in
the field. But the productions of that section rendered a large
amount of agricultural labor necessary, and very profitable. And it
required but a moment to find the requisite laborer. The same
instinctive feeling which has always enslaved him and kept him a slave
as long as he was considered profitable, at once pounced upon the
negro. And he has been, not only enslaved, but bought and sold by
every type of society, and by no one sooner, than by the negro himself—whenever able to buy. Many have always questioned the
utility, taste and wisdom of the traffic, but none ever questioned the
moral right of such slavery in the slave States. It was a universal
sentiment. Even the savage Indians, though they had no employment for him, and could not make him profitable, yet, as soon as they
could buy, capture, or steal a negro, reduced him to chattle slavery.

Nor did the sentiment which has now freed him in North America,
from chattle slavery (it is to be hoped *forever*) grow out of any general
belief that it is morally wrong to enslave him. For he was not freed
by sentiment, but by policy. The slave States never did agree to free
him until compelled to do so by force and arms. And the Northern
States prosecuted the war on the principle publicly set forth by a
vote in Congress that it was not their desire or intention to interfere
with the institution of slavery. And whether Congress made that
declaration in good or in bad faith, a contrary declaration by them at
that time would have emasculated their cause, broken down their
armies, overwhelmed their policy and established—perhaps perpetuated slavery on the continent. And when the acting President abolished slavery by proclamation, he made it conditional, on the continuance of Southern hostilities, and also proclaimed it "a war measure,"
simply adopted in order to weaken the enemy.

Universal history asserts it a truth that man in every age, country,
clime, social and moral condition, has looked down on the negro as an
inferior being, and has always enslaved him, and generally made him
a chattle slave. And any sentiment which has been so uniform and so
universal may be right or wrong, but it cannot be merely accidental.
It must have something in the order and nature of things, out of
which it grows and on which it rests. That something, we shall see,
was the intention and order of the great Author of nature in creation.
And was first rendered fearful after the fall of man.

There is another interesting and instructive fact patent everywhere on the surface of negro history. In fact it constitutes the sum of all negro history. He has always sought and voluntarily accepted of his own free choice the condition of slavery to man. It never has been so much man, as the negro himself who has sought and cherished that relation. His whole history proves that he has sought it and claimed it, and has never rejected or opposed it.

A few isolated exceptions, each susceptible of an easy explanation in its connection, never can militate against the truth of this proposition, sustained, as it is, by the full broad deep current of all history. Now, when the eye is pleased with beauty in objects, and objects of beauty everywhere meet the eye—when the ear is pleased with "the harmony of sweet sounds," and melody everywhere salutes the ear, it were hard to convince enlightened reason that God has not established, in nature, a kind of reciprocal relation between them. A law of nature does adapt one to the other. It is the voice of God in his "elder revelation." So, also, when men always and everywhere enslave the negro, and the negro instinctively seeks slavery to man, it were hard to convince enlightened reason that God has not ordained and established in nature, the law of master and siave between them.

Men have been enslaved. The Hebrews in Egypt, the Helots in Greece, the slaves of Rome, the Serfs of Russia—even the Celts in Ireland have been enslaved, sometimes men have been bought and sold. But none of them ever were passive, willing, unresisting slaves. They were always refractory under the yoke, they aspired to redemption, and panted after freedom. And generally their misfortune was, they attempted to throw off the yoke too soon; but in every case, just as soon as they became strong enough in numbers, or in civil changes, they waited for—they asked no extraneous aid—no foreign mind to plan or strong arm to strike. But they have always arisen in their own strength, asserted manhood, broken the galling chain, and by dint of internal energy rushed either to a position among the nations, or to quick destruction. Even individuals when enslaved in isolated conditions, have peremptorily refused it, and chosen death rather. They tunnelled out of dungeons, dashed themselves into the Bosphorus spurning both Scilla and Charybdis, faced the Simoons of Sahara, impaled themselves upon the fixed weapons of guards, incited insurrections, slew masters, fired cities, grew sullen in chains, and in every conceivable way asserted manhood. An attempt was once made to enslave the savage Indian in America. But his naturally free mind, though a savage, soared above it, and said, "I also am a man." He could be outnumbered and killed, but he could not be enslaved. And no one has ever been enslaved without the continual presence of a strong constraining power, except the negro. However poor—however forced to humble himself for bread or for employment by which to secure it—however ground down by oppressive governments and laws, however degraded in his or her morals to low or vile occupations, still there has always been a remaining sense of individual dignity and personal freedom which would not, and could not compromise itself. Manhood arose within and said: "My fists are fettered, but my mind is free. " The proud war horse can be gentled down until he will submissively wear the harness; for God has made him so. But who ever broke over the divine law written in nature, and gentled down the fierce Hyena. God speaks through the nature given him and says " *no* " to every attempt to tame him. So of man and the negro. He has been, and now is in slavery in every country on the face of the Globe, where men would or will have him as such, and just as long as they would have him. And if he is free at any place, it is not because himself has ever planned it—ever gained it—ever sought it—or ever at any time or place expressed one well defined desire for it. If slavery be not his natural condition it cannot be denied that it is, at least, his historic condition. Yet that history utterly fails to furnish one well defined example of an attempt on his part to break the chain as galling to him. For no candid reader of history will call the one or two isolated erratic examples which have occurred, fair exceptions to this rule. For they were neither prompted nor planned nor guided by himself. That some instances have occurred where individual negroes, from some peculiarity of circumstance, have avoided and even escaped from slavery, may be true. That a few oxen have been tried which utterly refused to wear the yoke, is also true. And examples in this case are, doubtless, far more numerous than in that. And if the few examples in the former case prove that the negro is not a slave in his own nature, by the ordinance of God, then the many examples in the latter case will prove that the ox was never designed in nature to bear the yoke.

There is also, at least, one example—that of St. Domingo—where negroes banded together as a community in concert to seek their freedom. But it was after they, in their ignorance, had been excited imposed upon and incited by designing white men and mulattoes. And they were led and governed by these same classes. And even in that instance they were most legitimately acting out their character of slave. For they yielded themselves, both mind and body, unquestioningly, to the government of their leaders. They had no sentiment or idea of their own, but obeyed implicitly the behests of those whom, for the time they regarded as masters, just as they now march up and vote, without one question, the ticket given them by those whom they regard and call masters, or just as did the negro element fighting in the armies of the United States, in the last war. And there is not a candid man on the continent who saw them in those armies, and does not know and feel, that, whatever may be published to the contrary, they obeyed white officers as the ship obeys the pilot. And they had no more patriotic sentiment end or aim, and no more impulse of freedom and individual dignity than the mules of the wagon train. They were as willing to serve on the one side as the other, if only some white man gave orders. And they never did fight on either side except when phrensied by strong drink, or impelled by white men with bayonets from behind. They fought only as the Gladiator fights. And however, facts may now be suppressed, truths are stubborn things, and history will vindicate herself. It always has been true, and until " nature dies and God and angels come to lay her in her grave," it always must be true that the negro expresses no defined desire after freedom from man. No great effort where brave men do or die—no self-directed war or insurrection—no outburst of lofty aspirations—no high aim at a dignified manhood. O for one Moses, Themistocles, Brutus, Kosciusco, Bruce, Tell, Botzaris, or Henry, in all the history of the past, with a black skin to rise up and say, "give me liberty." It would break the gloom of a fearful monotony. But no one rises. Many men have stood up and said it for the negro. And have maintained their saying with their treasure and their blood. But the negro has still stood in stolid indifference where he was at first placed by the sentence of Almighty God, "on thy belly shalt thou go, and dust shalt thou eat."

In Asia there is no record of any attempt. They served there cheerfully until actually refused as slaves, spewed out and driven away from every country where they are not, to-day, in slavery. In Europe there is no record of any attempt. They were actually ejected thence by men who refused alike their cheerfully offered persons and services, and to permit them to remain on the soil. Not only was there no war for freedom there. But there never did go up to any government of Europe, a petition from black slaves for manumission. So says Wilberforce. In Africa, to which country they have, by degrees, been driven from all others, until it has become the land of negroes, where they are huddled together, to rot away, by millions, in savage cannibalism; they have had no whites to whom they might act out the leading impulse of their nature, and become slaves, there they have all become slaves to one another. Each, though there be slaves under him, is the slave to some one still above him.

In South America, with a civilization never far in advance of that of which the negro himself is susceptible, he has been, and now is the only recognized slave. And there he submits to it rather with gratitude than resentment. And in all this circuit of the Globe, embracing a period of six thousand years, the negro in slavery all the time and every place, there has been no attempt for freedom—no expressed desire for it. In the free States of the American Union, his numerical weakness always forbade any hopeful attempt to throw off the yoke, whilst he was in slavery there. But when he was freed there, without his own effort or expressed desire, he never was regarded either by himself or the white man, as a citizen or a human being. For citizenship has been accorded to every nation, tribe and kindred of people. But never yet to the negro. Hence hundreds of them went farther South annually, and into voluntary chattle slavery, where they could find a condition which accorded with their feelings and nature.

In the Southern States the condition of things has long been widely different. There the porportion of blacks to whites has often and long been more than one to one. In many places even two, three, or four to one. Sufficient to justify any reasonable hope of success, in an attempt at freedom, if he desired it. He was well aware that a majority of the nation were opposed to slavery, and anxious to excite an attempt on the part of the negro. He was told so by the weekly and daily

Press—by itinerant lecturers—by non-slaveholders in their midst, and often by their masters themselves. Yet they affected to despise, and did despise it all, and laughed at it as actually contemptible. In 1864, in many parts of the State of Georgia, the negroes were to the whites as three to one, and that one was absent from home in the Confederate army. They were told every day that a mighty struggle was in progress, and their freedom or continued slavery was the question at issue. They were told that the men were all absent in the army, and simply to say "we are free," would secure their freedom; for there were none to oppose. In the mean time a mighty army passed through the State. They told the negro that they had come to free him. They entreated him by all the sacredness of freedom, to awake, arise or be forever fallen. They offered him his master's home and chattels, and proposed to defend him in their possession, if only he would arise and assert his freedom. ("We speak that we do know and testify that we have seen.") Yet as a rule they not only refused freedom, but in vast companies petitioned their owners for permission to enter the army and fight against their, would be, liberators. And the vast majority of those who followed the Union army in the excitement of the moment, soon returned and begged permission to occupy their former positions as slaves. And, to-day, if all extraneous influences were removed, and the negroes in the South were left free and uninfluenced to choose, and the white men would accept them as such, a majority of them would go into voluntary slavery in less than half a year; either to their former masters or to other parties whom they would choose as masters. No person, except one who had lived long in the South, and therefore knew, would ever believe that so many negroes, who escaped to the free States, and after there trying freedom, voluntarily returned to their former owners, as have done so. Suffice it, that the provision of the Constitution of the United States which did require the rendition of fugitive slaves has been a dead letter for more than thirty years. For it cost an owner more to recover a fugitive, through the courts, than would purchase a slave. Hence the effort was never made, except in rare instances for political purposes. And we appeal to the records of the country for evidence that opposition to the fugitive slave law was always put upon the ground ostensibly that free persons of color in the North were kidnapped and carried South under pretence that they were fugitives. This suspicion grew out of the fact that multitudes of free negroes from the North did voluntarily go South and into voluntary slavery. But it could only be done in some of the Southern States, and clandestinely at that, for local laws in many Southern States forbade it. There was nothing separating the free from the slave States but a narrow river— for the greater part of the way only an imaginary land line where the negro in freedom could at any moment toss an apple to the negro in slavery—where a single step would convey from slavery to freedom. Yet it is true that for every one *which* passed over from slavery to freedom, ten passed over from freedom to voluntary slavery, by evading all the local laws which forbade it. And this too in full view of all the inducements held out to the ignorant slave to seek his freedom.

Where are the Randolph negroes? Many of them may be in Northern freedom. But the writer *ought* to know that *some* of them went farther South and into voluntary chattle slavery years ago. And they can now be located and named among the freedmen of Georgia. And this is only one out of a vast multitude of similar examples. Here is another. This writer once assisted, by advice at least, in getting off to Liberia, a squad of negroes from Newton County, Georgia. They were privately conveyed to Savannah, and there shipped for Monrovia with support for one year, and were placed under the care of the Colonization Society. They went to Africa. They had been manumitted by their owner. He died and left no children. And in less than two years all of the squad (then living) landed at Philadelphia from Africa. The laws of Georgia then forbade their reingress into the State. But they sent on one of their number clandestinely to get former friends to appeal to the Courts to permit them to return to the State and go into voluntary slavery to a neighbor of their former owner. An appeal was made to the Courts, their prayer was granted, they returned to the State and went into voluntary chattle slavery to a man who had been a neighbor to their former owner. And they were freed from that slavery only by the Convention of Georgia in 1865, which manumitted all slaves in the State. Names are withheld here, but all the names and facts of the case can be found in the records of the Superior Court of Newton County, Georgia, between the years 1850 and 1860. These are but isolated examples, it is true, but the multitude of such examples that have been furnished in the last half century, gives them a degree of importance equal to the results of experiments made by men of science. The great law which they recognize—the great fact which they illustrate is, that the negro is by nature a slave—that it is the relation toward man which himself instinctively, voluntarily chooses.

Negroes are now free in the Southern States. May God forbid that they ever be restored to chattle slavery. Universal sentiment is now opposed to their re-enslavement. Not because it is regarded as unnatural or morally wrong—nor because it is regarded as unjust or injurious to the negro. For it is not. Thousands fought and died to retain and conserve slavery, who, at the time regarded it as a social incubus and a civil burden, which had been devolved upon them without their choice. They felt morally bound to maintain it at any sacrifice. And nobly did they defend the charge left with them. It has been removed from them without their choice or assent. They are clear of all the consequences before both God and man, let the consequences to the negro be what they may. They would never be willing to resume those fearful responsibilities in any circumstances. They can in all good faith point to the reminiscences of the late war for evidence, and say to the negro, in full view of what is just before him—

> "Shake not your gory locks at me,
> Thou canst not say I did it."

For coming events cast their shadows before them so far as to give their clear outline long before their arrival. Half an eye can see that the fate of the negro on this continent is fixed—his doom is irrevocably sealed. He is out of his natural condition, to which he aspires and out of which he pines and dies out if in contact with *man*—if separated from *man*, he sinks speedily to savage cannibalism. All the appliances, which either wisdom can invent or chicanery and duplicity can apply, may be tried. But they will only prove the empty voice of Canute. The wave will still roll on. Man cannot reverse the fixed decree of Omnipotence. The negro, in the South, is now out of his natural condition—an ox in the ocean—a Dolphin on land. And nothing but the power of God can save him from extinction. Men may make spasmodic efforts; they are only the hectic blush upon the consumptive cheek. Four millions of blacks are doomed to extinction. Bear witness *the present*. You speak to coming ages! The history of the negro proves that he does not, never did possess a self-directing independent mind—the white man regards—always did regard him a natural, a lawful slave—the negro admits the fact, and instinctively seeks the condition of slavery to man.

Now if we shall find in Revelation clear evidence to corroborate and sustain these facts of history, we ought to feel that the question, "who and what is the negro?" is fairly answered.

CHAPTER III.

IS THE NEGRO A LINEAL DESCENDANT OF HAM?

The color of the negro is one of his distinguishing peculiarities. Revelation teaches, as we shall see, that color is the broad deep ineffacible sign of difference of race which God has fixed between man and the negro. There are very many differences between them. They differ from the crown of the head, which in the one is covered with short thick matted wool, and in the other with long straight silken hair, to the sole of the foot, which in one is convex and placed centrally under the leg, and in the other is concave and extending forward, not backward from the centre of the leg. Prof. Agassiz, who is now regarded one of the most profound naturalists in the United States, says: "I have pointed out over a hundred specific differences between the bonal and the nervous systems of the white man and the negro. Indeed their frames are alike in no particular, there is not a bone in the negro's body that is relatively the same shape, size, articulation, or chemically of the same composition as that of the white man. * * Climate has no more to do with the difference between the white man and the negro, than it has with that of the negro and chimpanzee, or than it has between the horse and the ass, the eagle and owl. Each is a distinct and separate creation." Some of the multiplied differences may be merely temporary, the results of natural causes which may or may not be known, yet causes adequate to the production of temporary difference. For we know that such causes do exist, and do effect such differences in both the vegetable and animal kingdoms. They are often wrought by art, and as often by causes over which man has no control, and of which science is still ignorant. But this law has been found out as governing them uniformly—they are simply temporary, or changes of habit, not of nature—*specific*. They are never permanent changes of nature—*generic*. The change or removal of the natural cause which produced them, will also change or remove them. They have never yet been known to amount to such a change of the genus that one could proceed from another, except in the case of Hybrids, of which we shall speak in their place.

The Apple-tree may be modified indefinitely in its fruit; but it cannot be made to produce rye, plums, or peaches. The horse may be indefinitely modified in his kind ; but he never can sire the ox, dog, or gorilla. A mongrel is the farthest stretch in this direction that art has gone or science recognized. And a reversal of the producing cause, it is found, will always reverse the effect and restore the genus to its natural status. Now, we affirm, that there are differences between man and the negro, which are not merely habit—specific, or the result

18

of natural causes known or unknown, but generic and marking as clear, if not as wide, a difference of race as exists between any two animals in the whole kingdom. And although science and natural history abundantly sustain the assumption, our appeal is not to them, but to the more sure word of prophecy. The Bible settles the fact of a difference of color between man and the negro. That climate, habits of life, &c., will effect a temporary difference of color in man is true; but that they can, or ever did render such change permanent, so that it would inhere in man's offspring to all generations, is not true, but is contrary to all the laws of science. She says that the Polar Bear, removed to a torrid clime, will become tawny and eventually black in his offspring, if they live at all; but return him to his polar snows, and he will again become tawny and eventually white in his offspring. "The cause removed, the effect ceases,"—(Lineaus.) Take man to a torrid clime, and he too will become dark, and his offspring will wear the color as long as they remain under the influence of the producing cause; but return them to a temperate or frigid clime, and as swift as was the descent, so swift will be the ascent. And soon his offspring are white and show their origin—nature—genus. But take the negro to the equator and reproduce him there, and he is black; take him to a temperate clime and reproduce him there for a thousand generations, and he is still black; take him to the poles and reproduce him there, amid polar snows, if possible, for a thousand generations, and still he is black. His color remains at all times and places the same clear voice of God, asking the naturalist, "can the Ethiopian change his skin?" We are bound to find some other adequate cause for a difference of color between man and the negro, aside from mere natural changes, or to admit that God made the difference at their original creation, and the negro is not *man*, (Red). Hence the almost uniform consent of the christian world, taking for granted from the negro's size, shape, and partial conformation to the general appearance of man, and especially from the fact that he possesses the gifts of speech and an inferior degree of reason, that he is *man*—a changed descendant of Adam; and seeing the absurdity of attributing the difference of color to any merely local, temporary, or natural cause, has sought for some change wrought by the immediate power of God upon some one or more of the human family since their original creation, changing them from red to black. And that consent has agreed, long since, to find this miraculous cause, in some way, in "the curse on Ham" the son of Noah. But doubtless the conclusion is merely fanciful, and drawn entirely from a fortuitous combination of circumstances, viz: The word Ham means *black*. Some of his sons did settle in Africa. Africa has been given up to negroes almost entirely in modern time. Some of the descendants of Ham were doomed to servitude; and the negro is, and always has been, *nay always will be*, a *slave*. Whence nimble fancy made the short and easy leap over the yawning vortex of truth, to the conclusion that the negro descended from Ham. The writer candidly admits, that from a child he was taught to believe that the negro descended from Ham; but he never has seen the argument stated in logical form, and does not know how it is or can be so stated. He modestly challenges the whole christian world to state the argument in logical form, which will prove the negro a descendant of Ham, and not at the same time contradict in some of its parts, either the Bible or admitted facts. Did the negro descend from any of the sons of Ham? That is not established, nor can it be. Is the negro black because Ham was black? Why Ham was never cursed so far as the Bible informs us. And he was the son of white parents, he had two purely white brothers, and he had one white son—Canaan, the father of the white Philistines. If, therefore, he was dark skinned, or black, and for argument sake we admit he was, still the fact that he was the son of white parents, and the father of a white race (the Philistines) as we know he was, proves that his darkness was only temporary, and the result of some local or temporary cause, and not permanent. Did the blackness of the negro result from the curse on Canaan? We know that Canaan and his seed were purely white. Did the servitude of the negro, or his slavery, which has stuck to him as the shirt to Nessus, result from the curse on Canaan? Why the Bible tells us plainly where the servitude of Canaan was to begin and end, and where it did begin and end—among his brethren. After this "Ham theory" has been held and promulgated all over the christian world for a sweep of centuries, still is it true that he who fights it has to fight a man of straw. It assumes no tangible form—no proper person—no fixed premise. It is still an enemy in the dark; and we can say to it only—

> "Be thou a spirit of peace or a goblin damned,
> Bring with thee airs from Heaven or blasts from hell,
> Be thy intents wicked or charitable,
> Thou comest in such a questionable shape
> That I will speak to thee."

We shall see that the Bible teaches that the negro existed as a distinct race long before Ham. We assert that there is no record in the Bible of any curse on Ham, whatever may be true of one of his sons. The servitude placed upon Canaan fell on purely white men—the party cursed never did dwell in Africa. These facts which cannot be successfully questioned, break forever every link by which the negro is connected with Ham. It is true that the word which is translated "Ham" does mean dark or black. It is equally true that at that time names were given to things as in some way descriptive of them. It is therefore quite probable that his name was given to Ham by his parents because his complexion was not so fair as that of his brothers. They may have called him by way of distinction, "the dark skinned." However that may be, the name was given him, not only before the offence, but before the flood. And if the name is descriptive of complexion at all, it must have been so at the time it was given. And if he was then dark it is strange that his color should be the penalty of an offence committed long afterward. And more strange that it should be a consequence on him when that consequence never was denounced against him, but against his fourth son, who was a purely white man, and his descendants. For we may not trifle with the

20

reader so far as to admit that Canaan—the Canaanites—the Philistines—the Tyrians and Sidonians were black—were negroes. Is it so that a penalty denounced against a son—a penalty which says nothing about color—gave to the father of that son a black color and a name descriptive of it, which name and color the father bore long before the son was born? "The oxen were plowing and the asses were feeding beside them," therefore the square of two is seven.

We admit that three of the sons of Ham did settle in Africa. It is hence taken for granted that the Africans of to-day, who are mostly black, are in some way the descendants of Ham; admit it all. Then how came they black? They were the sons of white grand parents at least, and they had one white, though cursed brother, who never settled in Africa. Therefore if black, it must be the result of climate; but science, both admits and proves that color from that cause is not permanent, but accidental, and will cease in higher latitudes. But the color of the negro is fixed, permanent, changeless. It is not from the natural cause, the climate of Africa; therefore the conclusion that the negro of to-day is a descendant of the sons of Ham, who did settle in Africa, is a logical *"nonequiter.* It is because the christian world has seen and admitted that merely natural causes can not produce the difference which is seen between the negro and man, that they have gone to the "curse on Ham" to find an extraordinary or miraculous cause. But admit the nonsense that Ham and all his sons lived and died in Africa, and were black. Does that prove their descendants still there, or there five centuries afterward? If the man who sowed good seed in his field and was afterward asked, "from whence then hath it tares?" had answered, "they must have sprung from good seed, for I once sowed it there;" would his conclusion have been either scriptural or scientific?

> "You laugh, I think this tale applied
> Would make you laugh on t'other side."

The sons of Jacob once settled in Egypt; they became "six hundred thousand that bore arms," besides the aged, the females and children. But in the short period of "four hundred and thirty years "they were all gone—not one left behind. Five hundred years have not yet passed since the entire Western continent was densely covered with races of people, which are now fairly extinct. Their places are filled by new importations from a distant continent, some of whom, though now grey headed, have never seen an Indian. The same is true of many of the countries of Europe, in the last thousand years. So quickly do the inhabitants of a country sometimes change and give place to others. And the reason why the negro is now found in Africa, and in almost entire possession of it, is no proof that he has been there from the days of Cush, Misraim and Phut. It is chiefly because that country has always been found insalubrious for white men. They have died out there again and again, and have not desired it, but have tacitly allowed it to become the Potter's field of earth—the receptacle of the negro, as he has been spewed out of slavery in all other countries. As Shem and Japheth supplanted Canaan upon his own vine hills, and he is gone—as the Turk supplanted the Jew, and he is gone—as the northern hords supplanted the southern nations of Europe, and they are gone—as the Anglo Saxon supplanted the red man in North America, and he is gone—as the Castillian and the Andalusian supplanted the Aztec, and he is gone, so the fevers of Africa, the blasts of the Desert, and the "death damps" of the Nile supplanted Lybia and Carthage. And such names as Origen, Hannibal, &c., with all the white inhabitants of Africa are gone. And the negro with no nation, no country, no home, no mind, as he has been ejected from slavery and the presence of the white man in all other countries, has been permitted to congregate there and await the full development of the malediction of Almighty God—"I will put enmity between thee and the woman, and between thy seed and her seed." No man can prove either from history, science or Revelation, that there has been one lineal descendant of Ham in the Peninsula of Africa in the last thousand years. There may or may not have been, but to say positively there was, is wholly gratuitous.

But as three of the sons of Ham did settle in Africa, grant that their descendants are still there. How came they black? "The curse on Ham did it." Well, but Ham was never cursed. "Well then, the curse on Canaan." But Canaan and his seed never lived in Africa. "But Ham was black and his three eldest sons were like him, and they settled in Africa, and were the progenitors of the negro." But you admit that as Ham was the son of white parents, and the father of a white son, if he and three of his sons were dark, it was the result of some natural or temporary cause like climate, and that if removed from under the influence of that operating cause, they would be white, and thus show their nature and stock. But the negro is black at all times, in all places, and in all circumstances, and proves that he is so by the power of God, either in his creation, or by a judgment since sent upon him. "Well is that not exactly what I said, the curse on Ham—the curse on Ham, there is the cause." "Answer not a fool according to his folly lest thou be like him," (Solomon.) All candid men of science admit that the color of the negro has not been and cannot be accounted for satisfactorily on the supposition that he is a man. He stands an anomaly. They guess, conjecture, suppose, compare, &c., &c., but do not affirm; and it is because no good satisfactory cause or reason of this color can be found in nature, that men have agreed to find it some way in the curse of Canaan; but unless there were some sort of evidence that Canaan or some of his seed were black, if we should admit that Ham and his three eldest sons, and all their descendants were both black as jet and perpetual slaves, that could not fix any connection of cause and effect between the curse and the color, or the curse and the slavery of the negro. Therefore, the color of the negro must either be the original sign of an entirely different race from man, or a deep stamp by the immediately exerted power of God since the original creation. It is not from Ham. If it could be made to appear that Canaan was black, as it cannot, or if it could be made to appear even that they had dwelt in Africa, as it cannot, there were room for an inference, however unfair. But they alone were cursed; they never lived in Africa; they were white.

"Then what about the curse on Ham?" It seems strange that a historic incident so full and explicit should ever be so much misunderstood or distorted as this has been. In the ninth chapter of Genesis the fact is stated—"a truth so rudimental and so plain that none by comment could it plainer make. Its details fill volumes, and mingle with the tide of history for more than forty centuries. At the time referred to, all the sons of Noah were fathers; but none of their sons had been mentioned by name, except this fourth son of Ham. Moses states very distinctly what the offence of Ham was, and the penalty inflicted for it—"cursed be Canaan, a servant of servants shall he be to his brethren. Where this transaction took place, it is not possible now, perhaps, to determine; but wherever it was, it was some considerable time after the deluge; for a vineyard had been planted and its vines had matured and produced grapes, on the wine of which Noah had become drunken. Hence, it has been conjectured, as Canaan alone of the grand sons of Noah is mentioned, and as Noah and all his sons were evidently together on this occasion, that they were, probably all of them, on a visit to Canaan, who dwelt in Palestine, always famous for its vines and wines. And the reason why Canaan alone was cursed, was because he had furnished the wine which was the temptation to Noah, and the instrumental cause of the shameful emute. Else why should the historian be careful to tell us all about Canaan and none of the other grandsons of Noah? And why should the curse fall on the fourth rather than any other son of Ham? Or why on the son and not on the father who committed the offence? The above idea is borrowed, and simply thrown out for what it is worth. It may assist to explain a fact which, though plainly stated, has about it something mysterious. Whether the above be true or not, Moses tells us plainly that Canaan did dwell in the country which still bears his name, and was the father of the seven nations of Palestine whom Israel either drove out or reduced to servitude. The curse takes no cognizance of any of the sons of Ham, save Canaan, and it simply dooms him to servitude to his brethren, not to strangers. It predicts great prosperity for the two brothers of Ham, and declares that, dwelling contiguous to each other, they should unite or coalesce by intermarriage, and thus one of them dwell in the tents of the other, as they did long before the Egyptian bondage. And the entire five books of Moses are but the historic development of these facts. They inform us that Canaan dwelling in Philistia, became eventually a company of nations, rich, populous, proud—that they lost the knowledge of the true God, and became most abandoned idolators unworthy of the pleasant country which they possessed, and ripe for destruction.

In the mean time, a scion from the united families of Shem and Japheth had come up among them from between the Tigris and Euphrates, tarried a time, and then went down into Africa and tarried about four hundred years, and also became strong and very numerous, left Egypt in a mass, and returned to the land of Canaan, inhabited by their relatives, called by a hebraism, their brethren, waged war against them and destroyed very many of them. But some of the inhabitants of the land, hearing of the near approach of the conquering army, went out to that army, disguised as travelers from a far country, with old cloths and musty provisions, and asked to be taken as allies to the army, and to be made low servants—" hewers of wood and drawers of water "—or " servants of servants. " Their petition, unfortunately for Israel, was heard and granted, and thus Canaan became a servant of servants to his brethren. And thus was completed to the letter, and forever the curse or prediction of Noah—" cursed be Canaan, a servant of servants shall he be unto his brethren. " Such is briefly the whole Bible account of "the curse on Ham. " There is first a very clear prediction made that one of the sons of Ham in his families, should eventually be overcome and brought to servitude by two of the sons of Noah in their families. Then follows a clear, long, circumstantial history of the time, place, manner, and agents of its accomplishment. And in what part of it is found any reference to or intimation of a negro ?

> " Optics keen it takes I ween
> To see what is not to be seen."

Canaan was a white man; his descendants so far as history in the Bible or elsewhere describes them, were white, (see Prideaux). Ham was dark skinned most probably ; but he was the son of white parents, he had two white brothers, and one white son, if no more. From these data who can say that any of the other three sons were black ? If they were, it is not so stated or even intimated in the Bible. If they were black it could only be the result of some local or temporary cause, such as makes a difference of complexion among the children of almost every large family; for it did not result from any mark or curse, or judgment placed upon them by the power of God. If it did there is no intimation of it in the Bible ; and if they were dark or black from any local or transient cause, the effect would cease so soon as the cause was removed, and their descendants in temperate or cold climes would become white. But it is a gratuitous task to assay to prove that they were white until some amount of some sort of evidence from some source is furnished to prove that they were black. That evidence does not exist; that there were negroes among them, and among all the descendants of Noah may be, and we believe is true. But they were not of them. The fact that a Raven is found among Swans is not proof that it is a Swan or descended from one. Two facts are patent, the negro has been found to be black as far back as he can be traced, and he has always been found a menial slave—very generally a *chattle* slave to man. On these accounts, men have always looked down on him as an inferior or degraded being ; but they have generally taken for granted from his size and shape, his speaking and reasoning, that he was man, degraded to what he is by some judgment of God. Searching for the origin and cause of what he is, they overlooked it at the proper place. They have regarded it a species of infidelity to crowd him out of the human race, and yet they plainly saw that they could not crowd him into it without a miracle of some sort. Diligent search utterly failed to find one; but a fortuitous concurrence of circumstances was found. The negro is black ; he lives chiefly in Africa; he has always been a slave. Ham means black; he was in Africa. In some way servitude was made to attach to a part of his family. Hence men hitched these two ideas together, and then soldered over the open incohering joint with many fancies, and made the negro a descendant of Ham. And it has been taught by sire to son as if a clear doctrine of revelation, and received unquestioningly, until it is a part of the creed of the christian world. It is really wonderful what a number of theories we hold as true, both in nature and revelation, which have no base on which to rest, or evidence to sustain them but fancy sketches, and the fortuitous concurrence of circumstances. A fixed belief— settled opinions—long drawn conclusions ought not to be laid aside, without good evidence carefully weighed, or the flood gate of ridiculing infidelity may be opened, and everything sacred be deluged by her muddy waters. But we ought to be willing to review again and again the coherency and incoherency of our theories, and to lop off and root out whatever will not bear the light, until at last we arrive at a full knowledge of the truth. See the evils to both Church and State, that have resulted from the unfortunate error of making the negro a man! It has marred the beauty and harmony of God's established order in the natural world. It has hung as a heavy impending weight upon the wheels of advancing civilization. It has wrought almost endless confusion, and proved greatly injurious to both man and the negro.

Reader, the Bible denies—history denies—science denies that the negro descended from Ham—that the negro is a man. He must be naturally *red* in color before he can be recognized as the man of the Bible. The statement may be denied, rejected, abused, and spurned as evil, perhaps infidel, at present. But "truth is mighty and will prevail."

Infidels are such, chiefly, because they have not examined revelation long, and carefully weighed the evidence of its genuineness and authenticity. They form their opinions of it almost entirely from what is said about it by its friends; and when they see a theory like that which makes Ham the father of the negro, incoherent, self-contradictory—clashing in all its parts, condemned by facts, &c., they take for granted, not what is true, that it is simply a web of human fancies, but that it is really a doctrine of the Bible, because the friends of the Bible put it forth. And when they reject it as they should, they at the same time reject revelation which is slandered as being its putative parent; and good men see the flood of infidelity which is being poured around the land and mourn over it and ask, "how shall it be stayed?" If good men will relinquish erroneous opinions which are held, not because manifestly true, but only because they are old, and, like wine, seasoned by time, and lop off from their creed all such excrescent fungi as this "Ham theory," and take the plain statements of the Bible for what they are worth, they are true and will prevail.

And if these sheets do not furnish a *clew* (all they propose at present) to a clearer and more satisfactory theory in the Bible, on the subject of the negro, than the one we have been reviewing, throw them in the fire and leave still unanswered the question, "Who and what is the negro?"

CHAPTER IV.

BIBLE ACCOUNT OF THE NEGRO.

I think the Bible teaches very clearly that the negro is a distinct race from man, created before Adam—that he is in an inferior degree rational and accountable, and therefore a subject of law—that he was at Adam's creation subordinated to him, not as a slave or *menial*, but as all other things were subordinated to him as the head of this world—that he was bound by law both to Adam and to God, which law was written on his heart, as the law given to Adam was at first written on his—that he was first in the transgression in Eden, and that for his offence he was doomed to a condition of perpetual menial slavery to man, which was to be a source of fretful annoyance and disquiet to both parties, and that if he be civilized and saved at all, it can only be in and through his connection with man as a slave—not necessarily a *chattle* slave—but at least a menial slave.

Christian reader, do not shudder at this outline; I am not going to pour forth a flood of infidel ravings, nor ridicule revelation or commonly received opinions of it. You can have no higher regard for revelation than I have—no firmer belief that it is God's word—and is true though every man be a liar. The question is not "is it true and worthy of confidence?" But the only question with *me* is, "what does it teach?" Come, let us lay aside all former notions and preconceived ideas, and set humbly down at its feet and ask it to teach us God's truth about the negro—it will do so. Its first writer when he commenced to write, had either to plunge at once "*in medias res,*" without any intimation of the subject on which he was going to write, or he had to give an introduction or kind of summary outline of his subject. He seems to have adopted the latter plan. Hence the first chapters contain a very sweeping and summary description of the creation and origin of all things—so very summary that a thousand and one very interesting and important questions which he could have answered, are left unanswered. But if he had stopped to answer them all, the world itself would not have contained the books which would have been written. So summary are his first chapters that good and learned men are now debating the question whether the creation he describes was performed in six common days as at present measured, or six days indefinitely long. The question is not yet settled; and if the description of creation is so sweeping as to leave that a debatable question, we should expect to find it less explicit in matters of detail. So it is; the facts which it is essential for man to know, are clearly stated. Unessential things are only referred to, hinted at, suggested, inferred and implied, so far as was necessary to gain the prime end aimed at, which was to teach man his origin, nature and condition, and the cause and cure of that condition. The Bible is not a work on art, science, commerce, history, or *the negro*, but is given to man as a sinner to fit him for Heaven. And it only refers to, or hints at these collateral subjects so far as is necessary, in order to reach its prime object. And yet it makes the negro, which is not of Adam's race, so prominent and conspicuous, both by plain statements and necessary implication, as to leave no room for doubt that he occupies a prominent place in the foreground of the picture. " Order is Heaven's first law." No intelligent Bible reader has failed to notice that a systematic progression characterised the creation of God; so reason teaches; so science teaches; so Moses teaches. Beginning from the lowest, each *order*, by whatever name you choose to call it, is seen to rise above its fellow order, and each by an almost imperceptible link like that uniting the colors in the solar spectrum, is seen to hitch itself to that one next above it. There is no where an intervening space; "nature abhors a vacuum. " The Geologist says that from the inorganic life of the stone to the *possibly* organic life of the moss clinging to its side, the passage is so short and obscure as to leave it still doubtful to whose department that moss belongs, the Geologist's or Botanist's. If we pass still higher, the learned are now debating the question where they shall locate the Zoophyte—in the vegetable or animal kingdom; it is allied to both, it is perfect in neither; it is the seam by which they are united, and by which the God of nature has shown that variety in uniformity is his great law. As we pass up through the almost endlessly diversified shades of instinct in the animal kingdom, the same law meets us at every turn. The extremes are almost immeasurably wide apart; but the interlinkings are merged and lost in affinities. We pass from the Zoophyte or Conchia up to the Gorilla, as up a long but regular flight of steps; but just there we find the first vacuum— the first missing link in the chain; for between the highest degree of instinct in animals, and the lowest degree of reason in man, enabling him to mimic the skill, and enjoy the expansive wisdom of his great Author, there is an immeasurable distance—an anomaly in nature—a loathsome vacuum—a proof that man has not yet classified correctly the orders which God has formed. Reason and analogy expect to see that link supplied—that vacuum filled by its order—either a higher order of instinct than has yet been found in animals, or a lower order of reason than that which characterises *man*—the noble Anthropos. And precisely such a being, filling exactly that niche, answering to that imperative demand, do we find in the negro. If human art had laboured assiduously for six thousand years to adapt him to that position, and to fill with him that niche, it could not have done so as nicely as we have already seen, that his history has done it. There he is; God—nature—reason has placed him there; man can not take him thence, except by a violence as unnatural as to transplant a vegetable from earth to ocean, or to translate a fish from ocean to earth. Extinction must be the result of any such rash effort. Rational, yet not enough so to guide himself, independent of man, to any thing higher than the lowest savage—rational, yet possessed of no originating or constructive intellect, we appeal to his whole history for proof that independent of man's mind, he never has arisen above the dignity of a savage, and separated from man, he always shrinks swiftly back to the condition of a savage, but little above the Chimpanzee, as he is now doing in the Republic of Liberia.

This is written by one who has no prejudice against the negro—one who wishes no harm, but all good to the negro—one who never has been profited by the toil of the negro—one who has spent twenty years of assiduous labor in the Ministry, trying to teach and christianise the negro—one who has spent fifty years in immediate contact with the negro, trying to learn from himself who and what the negro is—one whose means of information have been as good as are generally enjoyed. Sixty centuries have demonstrated, and sixty more will demonstrate that the negro is incapable of a distinct civilization; and history and science furnishing us with such a distinct and well defined being should drive us to revelation to search for intimations of his origin and position. But we are not to forget that the Bible was not given to man to teach him history or science, but to make him wise unto salvation. But so close was the connection between Adam and the negro who had been created just before him that we ought to expect to find the negro made much more prominent in the incidental allusions of the Bible, than any of the orders of being still below him. So he is; in fact he is made to burst upon our view at the very creation of man, and he moulds and fashions the cautious language in which that creation is described. The brief history of man's creation is, "so God created man in his own image, in the image of God created he him; male and female created he them," (Gen. 1st, 27th). This is plainly the execution of a design or intention expressed in the preceding verse—"let us make man in our image after our likeness," (26). This is the first time the word man or Adam is used by Moses; this is the only creation of *mankind* mentioned in the Bible. It includes all the race. If the negro is of the human race, he is included here; for God has made of one blood all nations of *men* for to dwell on all the earth; and if he is not included here, he is not of the genus "*homo*." And of this brief passage, so rich as it must be in its vast comprehension of facts, we observe—It is strange that the word *Adam* which is here rendered *man*, means *red*—(what we now call *white* as applied to the color of the human countenance or skin). The material of which this last creature was formed, was "red earth." Can all the logic and science of the universe ever evade the silent lesson contained in the color of the material of which man was made, or the trumpet tongued announcement that the material used was different from what had been used before, and that the difference was in color? As the cloud seen by the Prophet no larger than his hand grew into the drenching shower, so this little word in the very connection and circumstances in which it occurs was intended to swell into a broad history, and stand the mark of that Heaven wide distinction which God made between two different races at their creation. When God once makes his mark, man may lamely imitate, but never efface or counterfeit it; but it stands a witness to plead the presence there *once* of the great

Jehovah ; and it will so plead *in seculum seculorum.* After the creation of the world from nothing by the fiat of the Creator, we are told repeatedly, and in many varied forms, that all things in the world or on the earth were made of the earth as the material used. But there is no intimation any where given of the color of that material—no mention made of color—no reference to color, no hint at color—no importance seems to have attached to color in any thing up to the time *man* was to be made. But just then, as if a new idea (if it were possible) had entered the Divine mind, he says "let us make a *red* man." Now, why does the historian, in a description so very summary as this is universally admitted to be, where the writer seems parsimonious of words, and is trying to express the largest amount of thought possible in the smallest number of words—where, in order to be brief, he leaves untold a thousand facts of both interest and importance to man—where he makes every word count and contain an idea or great class of ideas—why should he stop just here and deviate from his method, and seemingly turn out of his way and drag in a new word containing a useless particularity, and tell us, after having stated distinctly that all creatures were made of earth, that this last one was made of *red earth*, and was therefore *red* in color ? It will not do to say "it is a merely accidental circumstance." The Spirit dictated this word. "All scripture is given by inspiration of God." It will not do to say "it means nothing," for God never utters unmeaning words, however much we may misunderstand his word. Unless we are going to wrest or ignore revelation, we must admit that there was a fixed design in the use of this word—some worthy end in view— some great lesson to be taught; and may not—must not candor admit, until some better reason can be assigned, which never can be done, that the intention was to point out the forever visible distinction between the being now formed, wearing the image of God in a high order of intellectual and moral constitution, and some other being somewhat like him in several respects, though of a different color? Does it not look like the historian, consulting that brevity which is everywhere manifest on the face of this narrative, wished to intimate clearly in a way which could not be misunderstood, yet without stopping to state fully a collateral and unessential fact, that when God made *man*—the *red* man—what we now call *white man* (and there is no other being dignified with the appellation *man* in the Bible; for the name carries the color in and with it) that there was already in existence as a part of the fifth day's work, a being *which*, from his size, shape, and partial conformation to the image of man, and especially from the fact that he possessed the power of speech and a subordinate degree of reason, might some day be confounded with man, and be taken as a specific, or in some way changed and modified part of this last creation—this master piece—this work of the sixth day? And to avoid all such confusion, without stopping to give a set lesson on this extraneous subject, he pointed out the forever unvarying distinction between the two races—the deep stamp of *manhood*—the seal of Almighty God—a word which should sound in the lessons of science and the voice of facts for thousands of generations, and loom up in all history and say, "the creature of the fifth day was not red but some other color—*black* if you choose it, but the creature of the sixth day was *man*—was *red*—was in the image of God—was Anthropos." Now in view of the unquestioned fact that there are many differences between man and the negro, and among them this difference of color— a fact which science has grappled for many centuries, and yet of which she admits to-day, that she can give no good satisfactory account, on the assumption that the negro is a man—in view of the facts of negro history which have been stated, and which can not be questioned—in view of the stubborn fact that man has always and in every place and social condition naturally, instinctively looked on the negro as an inferior, and stood aloof from social equality with him chiefly on account of his color—in view of the fact which we hope to be able to prove abundantly that there was an inferior rational speaking creature in existence before Adam—in view of the scripture which we have noticed, and shall notice—and especially in view of the fact that man's color is a natural fixture unsusceptible of change by art, it may be sullied and smirched by natural causes, but remove it from under the influence of those causes "it will rise and be itself again" in his descendants, and thus show its nature and origin, and the same is true of the negro, we think it fair to draw the conclusion from the above text that the Bible does teach that the word man (Adam) does carry with it, not the idea of a black, but of a red color, and that it requires that color to be natural to a being before he can in truth and justice be called a *man*. God has placed a mark upon the negro which he can not remove—it is natural. He may scotch, but he can not kill it; the same is true of man. And Moses tells us the origin of this color when he says "the Lord God made *man*," which means a red man, or as we now use the color—a *white man*.

Here, and not in any fancied "curse on Ham" is found the true reason of a difference of color between man and the negro, a difference which has given more perplexity to both scientific men and Bible readers than all other differences. It is chiefly on account of his color that the negro falls in the estimation of men. They always did, do, and always will look down on him as an inferior, on account of his color. "They find him guilty of a skin not colored like their own, and for that worthy cause "they stand aloof from him, or seize upon and enslave him, as marked for that purpose by Almighty God. And whether it be right or wrong in its manner, as it may, in its nature, it is not the result of native cupidity, rapacity, or disregard of law, but is simply like any other out-cropping of nature and conscience, within which is a part at least of the oracle of God.

Just here it must be observed that there was given to Adam at his creation, a kind of headship over, or proprietary right in all other creatures. They were distinctly given to him, and placed under him whilst he was placed over them, (Gen. 1, 26). If the negro, therefore, existed before, as he did, he too was subordinated to Adam. This, however, did not and could not imply his slavery in any of its forms, but only that orderly subordination of inferior to superior, which must exist in every system where variety exists in unity, and where "some must and will be greater than the rest." Adam was first in intelligence and exaltation, God had made him so; he possessed an elastic, originating, self-directing, constructive mind, and was in immediate intercourse with his Author. It was meet that he "have dominion;" and his duty and highest happiness consisted in his observing all the laws and amenities of his position; and every sentient being below him was to find its highest happiness in observing all the laws of its subordinate position. And this had to be so unless God had established a dead equality destitute alike of variety and capacity of expansion. There was no degradation or slavery implied in the fact that the Sloth was made inferior to the Lion, or the Vulture inferior to the Eagle, and Adam placed over each; so there was neither slavery or degradation implied in the fact that the negro was made inferior to Adam and placed under him; it was for their mutual good and happiness as parts "of that stupendous whole, whose body nature is and God the soul." Slavery never inhered in any way in the original order of things—subordination did. The one manifests the wisdom and goodness of God, and is manifest in all his works, the other displays the punitive justice of God, and is seen only where his law has been violated and as penalty for sin. If the ox or ass be made to serve with rigor, it is not because of their inferiority and subordination, but because their master is a sinner, and they and all parts of nature over which he was placed, sympathise with him in the penalty which he pays; and if there be, as there certainly is, any thing unpleasant to both parties in the slavery of the negro to man, it is not because the former was at the first made inferior and subordinate to the latter, but because both have violated law, and pay the penalty which attaches to such violation. The negro was a sinner before he was a slave, but he was subordinate to Adam before he was a sinner; of which Moses gives us as clear an intimation as he did that the negro existed, and was of a different color from man before the creation of man. "And the Lord God planted a Garden eastward in Eden, and there he put the man whom he *had* formed," (Gen. 2, 8). The tense here used and the form of expression both import that man had been created, "male and female," or containing the female, before the garden was planted. The creation ended with man, for the woman was taken from him; he was the last work of the sixth day. The whole Bible is so full and clear on this point that it is impossible, without violence to its plain language to avoid the conclusion that man, male and female. was the last work of the Creator before "he rested from all his works;" so it is generally understood. But in the above text the historian seems to re-open the work of creation, and tells us of an additional work afterward done—the planting or arranging of a garden for man's reception; for it is impossible to avoid the truth—that the language used imports an after work. Such is its structure, and so would it be understood by every candid reader. "Does then the historian contradict himself and inform us that God had finished all his works and rested from them, and afterward inform us that he performed an additional work?" Not so; it can be said that "the garden was prepared, but not mentioned before." Why not? had the Spirit forgotten it at the proper place? What evidence that it had been done, but not mentioned before? But the phrase, "whom he had formed," asserts that the man "had been formed" before the garden was planted. The evident truth is—

> "God works by means since first he formed the world,
> As of old he employed his means to drown it."

And he planted the garden in the order of time and events as stated in the narrative; but he did it not himself, for his own work was done before, but he did it by means or an agency which he had provided; and himself is said to have done it on the principle always true in both civil and moral government—"He who does a thing by another does it himself." He did it by means of the negro. In the preceding verse (7) the historian, as we have seen very clearly, implies, and directly will tell us plainly, that there was already in existence a being which, though not colored like Adam, possessed a subordinate degree of reason and intelligence sufficient to both the .mechanical and intellectual task of preparing the garden. He was not sufficient to its proper tillage and cultivation undirected by the superior mind of man, for we are distinctly told "there was not a man to till the ground." And the history of the negro for six thousand years demonstrates that by self-direction alone, he is not capable of a civilized cultivation of the soil. There is no historic account of any section of country ever cultivated by pure negroes; in less than a century it sinks to savage cultivation. And as the writer had clearly implied the existence of a being capable of such a work in the seventh verse, all that was requisite in the eighth verse was to say that such a work was done, and the logic of facts would of necessity connect this with that. Hence the historian, in a very summary description has made that same logic to tell us that there was a semi-rational being, though of a different color, in existence when *man* was created—that he was subordinated to man, and was not herding out with the animal kingdom, but was in the garden as an operative when man was placed there. Let us follow the historian to see the use which he makes of these facts.

"Now, the serpent was more subtile than any beast of the field, which the Lord God had formed," (Gen. 3, 1). It may be assumed as a fact, for such it is universally understood to be, that the Devil—the chief of the fallen Spirits, was the tempter who deceived Eve. All men who hold the Bible to be a divine revelation, so far as the writer is informed, hold that it was the Devil—the father of lies who is here called "Serpent." But it is as universally admitted that he assumed some tangible form—some physical or material body—that he entered into and acted through, and by some one of the living creatures which God had formed—and that he made that creature his agent in presenting the temptation. ("*Qui facit per allium facit per se.*")

And the historian here calls that body or shape, or creature by the name "serpent." And from this unfortunate translation of the word, bible readers generally have given a kind of unwilling and bewildered assent to the theory that the Devil entered into some one of the crawling tribe now called by this name, serpent. Now in our attempt to find out from the Bible itself, what kind of creature the serpent, was we never question the actual presence of the Devil as prime mover. We only enquire after the agent he used, or the visible form he put on. We are to see that it was not and could not have been the creature now called serpent; and as there is nothing in or about the Hebrew word which is here translated *serpent*, and nothing in the whole connection to favor or suggest such an idea, but the fact that this creature was doomed to crouch or crawl, and the serpent crawls, it seems quite probable that the English translators were governed by the Septuagint, rather than the Hebrew. And that the Seventy in their day and country were at a loss what to call it. Long before their day the negro had come to be regarded as a species in the human family. They, therefore, never thought of him; for sixty centuries in the full blaze of civilization had not yet developed his full character as a natural inferior; and as they could find in the whole animal kingdom, no creature to which the word in the Hebrew would fairly apply, and which would meet the circumstances of the case, they agreed to give him a name from the penalty which they saw placed upon him, and they called him "*crawler.*" If they had simply transferred the word without translating it, as they did in many other cases, much confusion would have been avoided. There is nothing in the original name of the creature—"*Nachash*" to indicate its size, shape, or manner of locomotion. There is much in it, as we shall see, to indicate that it was a kind of rational speaking creature. And as they have given to it a name which is of Roman, and hence of comparatively modern origin, and which indicates only its manner of locomotion, it is quite probable that they had no reference to the word itself, but to the penalty put upon the serpent in giving it a name; nor is there any writer of note, with whom this writer is acquainted, who does not admit that there are many great dificulties in allowing this creature to have belonged originally to the serpent family. Some suppose it to have been one creature, and others another; and each assigns good reasons for dissenting from the serpent theory, whether he proposes a better or not. And the Bible reading world has long since agreed that it could not have been the creature now called serpent, but for lack of a better name they would continue to call it by that one, and leave every individual to determine for himself what the serpent was.

We offer some of the evidence found in the Bible that it was not a serpent, but a negro. 1st. It could not have been an irrational animal of any species; because it transgressed a law of some sort, and suffered the penalty for that transgression. The law transgressed by man we know, for it is stated by Moses; but what the law transgressed by the serpent was, we know not, for it is not stated by Moses. Most probably it was the law which subordinated it to man, and bound it to his interest. However that may be, the words in which its punishment is announced, as well as the mere fact of its punishment, prove it guilty of a violation of some law which it was required to know and obey. "For where there is no law, there is no transgression." In a moral government absolutely perfect as is that of God, can a creature be held responsible to law when no law has ever been given it, and when, if law had been given, no capacity to know the law had ever been given? In moral government the following connection is indissoluble—penalty necessarily implies offence—offence a law—law capacity to know the law, and capacity to know the law rationality. The serpent did offend, and a penalty was denounced against it, and was executed upon it. Therefore, it must have been rational; such are the facts of its history, and such the clear import of the language—"because thou hast done this thing, cursed art thou."

The history of the case makes it very clear that the serpent, like Adam, was on probation. The phrase "because thou hast done this thing" plainly implies that it was in some way forbidden to do that thing, and ought to have understood the prohibition. And the phrase "cursed art thou," is the very language, common in revelation, by which the sanction of violated law is expressed. And the serpent had to be "able to stand, yet free to fall," by the standard of law before it could possibly incur that curse. And it could not be thus able without rational capacity to know that there was a law, and that this thing was wrong according to that law. That an individual at first made capable of knowing and obeying law, should, for his violation of that law incur a penalty which had been fixed by the law, and which would, after its infliction, incapacitate him to know and obey it perfectly, and should still be held accountable for such knowledge and obedience, is one thing. But that he should be held accountable for such knowledge and obedience when no capacity to know and obey had ever been given him, and then punished for a failure, is quite another thing. The first may characterise a perfect governor, the second can characterise none but a despot.

The serpent was punished, and therefore must have sinned; but if it sinned it violated law, for "sin is the transgression of the law;" but if it sinned it must have been rational, for none can sin but rational beings; but if it were rational, it could not have been a serpent, for serpents are not rational.

It may be said "the serpent was rational up to the time of its offence, but lost its rationality as a part of the penalty inflicted upon it." Is there the slightest foundation for such objection in revelation? Is it either stated, implied, or suggested in any way by anything that is stated? Any other conjecture were just as legitimate. The conclusion that the serpent was rational, is so necessary, both from the fact that penalty was inflicted upon it, and from the language in which the penalty is announced, that logic can not evade it without violence to both revelation and the structure of moral government, as at present understood.

2d. The carefully worded language by which Moses describes the serpent, proves that it was rational—"now the serpent was more subtile than any beast of the field. * *" To say nothing of that word "subtile," which, in this connection contains a rich fund of meaning, and which never can be properly applied to an entirely irrational animal, the phrase "beast of the field" as it stands in the Hebrew, is equivalent to the phrase in English—"the animal kingdom." It includes every living creature in the animal kingdom which lacks the gift of reason. Hence the description of Moses not only excludes the serpent from the animal kingdom, but it sets up a kind of comparison between the serpent and every part of that kingdom. It is done by the omission of the word "other," which should, and would have been joined to the word "beast" if the serpent had been regarded as an irrational animal; and the phrase would have read "any *other* beast of the field." That omission was evidently studied and intentional; for Moses uses the same phrase three times in the immediate connection, and the word *other*, on which the sense must turn, is left out every time. If a writer should say "the sun is larger than any *other* heavenly body," whether he so intended or not, his language would include the sun among the heavenly bodies, and compare him with each one of them. But if he should imitate the style of Moses and say, "the sun is larger than any heavenly body"—omitting the word *other*, then whether he so intended or not, his language would exclude the sun from among the heavenly bodies, and compare him with all of them; and when Moses joins to the serpent the descriptive word subtile, which can not with strict propriety apply to an irrational animal, and then omits three times in the same connection that word *other*, which should have been joined to the word beast if he had understood the serpent to be a beast, or part of the irrational animal kingdom, the conclusion seems forced upon us that Moses regarded the serpent as a rational being of some sort; but he was not man, for he lacked that *red* color which gives its generic distinction to the name *man*. Who and what was he?

3d. The serpent had the gift of speech—could utter and understand articulate sounds as signs of ideas; for he conversed with Eve, and she with him. But articulate language belongs only to rational beings.

4th. The serpent did actually reason with the woman, and present at least two arguments as motives to her mind, and did, as only rational beings can, debate with her the relative strength of arguments. And if we admit the Bible account of this transaction true and unvarnished, as we must, it were just as easy to prove man an irrational animal as the serpent; for man has never furnished any evidence of rationality which was not by this serpent, except in degree of developement. Besides the serpent seems to have walked erect as a biped, which is plainly implied, or referred to in the *penalty*, "on thy belly shalt thou go"—it seems to have had hands, for it "took of the fruit," &c., &c.

It may be said in answer to all this, that "it could converse, reason, walk erect, and use hands up to the time of its offence, but lost all these powers as the consequence of its offence." That might be true of its walking erect and using hands, for there is a shadow of foundation for such an assumption in the language which fixes the penalty. But we will see directly that it is only a shadow without any substantive existence. But what evidence of any kind is there that it lost its reason and speech as the result of its offence? Is it implied in the word *enmity*—"I will put enmity between thee and the woman?" Can the student, with the Bible before him, find either in plain statement, necessary inference, implication or suggestion, any more foundation for that assumption, than he can for the assumption that the serpent was the man in the Moon?

It may be, and has been said, "God gave specially to an ordinary serpent these extraordinary powers and characteristics for the time being, to accomplish this specific work, as he once gave power to Baalam's ass to speak; and, the work done, the powers ceased by their own limitation "—in a word, that it was a miracle.

> "O what a tangled web we weave,
> When thus we practice to deceive."

There is no doubt that God could have given to an ordinary serpent these extraordinary powers; but, aside from the fact that it is a mere gratuitous assertion that he did so, for there is not the smallest intimation in the Bible that he did, it is blasphemous. It assumes that God wrought a miracle in order to induce the woman to sin—that she could and would have withstood any temptation naturally incident to her nature and condition, or coming in any ordinary or natural form; but that her good and kind Author took advantage of her condition, and threw her entirely off her guard by placing before her a monster—a being entirely new to her, not a part of that natural system of which herself was a part, in which her lot was cast, and with which she had to do. And as miracles have been performed only to attest the divine mission, and authority of those who performed them, we submit it, if Eve would not have been, not only justified, but bound to regard such miracle as a direct intimation of the mind of her Author, and therefore bound through deference to the author of miracles, to do as she did? The blasphemy of the supposition that this creature was made to assume any new shape or powers for the occasion, must forever render that supposition loathsome to every one who cherishes a proper reverence for the Bible. But if it did not put on such new appearance and powers, it could not have been what is now called a serpent, and it must have been some kind of a rational creature.

5th. This name "Nachash," which is rendered "serpent," means in the original, a kind of inferior rational creature. It is true that the language of the Bible was not formed from lexicons as its standard, but the lexicons of that language were formed from the Bible. Hence lexicons can not decide accurately the question before us. But although the lexicographers drew their definitions from the Bible, and such other manuscripts as came to hand, by collating, and by analogy, by carefully comparing a word in one connection with the same word in different connections, their work has been done so often, so carefully, honestly and learnedly, that it is now both fair and safe to take these lexicons as the standard of the language. The writer has but four of them before him, from Stokius down to Stewart. And every one of these gives serpent as one of the *figurative* renderings of the word Nachash. Not one of them gives it as the literal or primary rendering. Every scholar knows that every word in a language has one literal or primary signification; and then it is used by writers in a wider latitude *figuratively*. Hence it is sometimes, as in the case before us, exceedingly difficult to get the proper meaning, because it has been used in so wide a latitude figuratively. All the Hebrew lexicons, however old, are comparatively modern; and there were at least two strong reasons why they might have given *serpent* as the primary rendering of the word Nachash; but they did not, but gave it as one of its figurative renderings.

1st. They found the word the first time it is used in the Bible, as the name of a creature which is described as walking, handling, speaking and reasoning. This forbade the idea of its being a serpent; but in the same connection they saw that it was doomed "to go on the belly"—a Hebrew phrase, which we shall see by analogy, when we reach it, has no special reference to manner of motion or travel, and they transferred that doom as one meaning of the word "crawler" or "creeper."

2d. The idea obtained extensively among the ancients that serpents had the strange power of charming the birds and reptiles, which they took for food. Whether it be really so or not, still that belief yet obtains with many. And as this creature exercised an influence over the woman, much like a charm, and besides was doomed to crawl, they called it serpent. Will the Bible reader please to examine the use of the two species of serpent mentioned, (Num. 10). And see if this is not the reason of the name serpent applied to them there? All the Hebrew lexicons to which the writer has access, differ slightly in what they give as the primary meaning of the word. But their difference is not in sense, but simply in arrangement, or collocation of terms. They agree essentially that the literal meaning of Nachash is, a diviner—charmer seer—consulter of omens—necromancer—soothsayer, consulter with familiar spirits, &c., &c. And every one of these describes and necessarily implies, at least a degree of rational power. See the word used in these senses—(2 Kings, 21, 6)—(2 Chron. 33, 6)—(Levit. 19, 26)—(Deut. 18, 10)—(Num. 23, 23 (24,1) *et pasim*.

If what are considered the best Hebrew lexicons are taken as the standard of the language, then the very name Nachash means a rational being of some sort. And there is nothing in the Bible to favor the idea that it was a rational species now extinct, but much to favor the idea that its race was to be continued as long as man's. This is implied in the phrase, "between thy *seed* and her *seed*." Where and what are the seed of that rational creature? If we should notice the perfect applicability of the above epithets—subtile—diviner, &c., to the negro, as they apply to no other creature on earth, whether rational or irrational, it would only swell the cumulative evidence that the original intention in their use was to describe him. No one familiar with him either in his savage or highest civilized state has failed to see and be struck by the perfection with which he renders the abstract in these terms concrete in a living example.

Now, if both reason and analogy discover a vacuum in the orders of creation not sanctioned by the Bible in what it does teach on that subject, and all the facts of negro history for six thousand years, place him precisely in that vacuum, and fill it with him. If the word man means Adam or red man, and it requires that color to inhere in a being as natural to him, however sullied by natural causes, before he can justly claim the appellation *man*—if both science and the Bible declare the negro's color a broad distinction between him and man—if the Bible clearly teaches that there was some kind of an inferior rational being in existance before Adam—that such a being deceived the woman— that his race was continued parallel for a time if not cotemporaneously with hers perpetually—that he was subject to subtility and super- stitious charms—that he sinned, and was punished when man was, shall we not conclude that the negro is that being? Can we avoid the conclusion? We believe he is, and must therefore wait for clearer evi- dence than we have yet seen or heard, before we accord to him a place in the human race, or among the irrational creatures of the animal kingdom.

CHAPTER V.

SLAVERY OF THE NEGRO.

Slavery is the abject subjection of one being to another, according to the will of the master. It is not essential that the slave be bought and sold. He may be as abject without as with chattle slavery. Slavery is one and chattle slavery another form of the same thing, as monarchy and democracy are different forms of one thing. The wife who obeys the husband—the subject who obeys the ruler—the child which obeys the parent without any regard to the nature, law and source of the authority exercised, is as much a slave in reality as if bought at a price, "for there is no authority but of God."

Now it is claimed as a historic demonstration, that chattle slavery is the best form for the negro, in which his slavery can exist; but it is not intimated that it is the form of slavery, or only form to which he was doomed. It is only asserted that by the clear authority of God he was made an abject crouching slave to man. The proof of which is twofold—first in his history—secondly in revelation. The facts are so full and uniform that it ought not to be doubted that man does and always did naturally look down on the negro as an inferior and regard, and treat him as a crouching abject menial. And the negro has as uniformly and naturally acquiesced in, and abjectly yielded to the destiny, without once stopping to enquire why it was so. It must be a law of nature; and we are now to find in the Bible, the history of its cause and origin.

If the reader has weighed the evidence already presented, that the serpent which deceived the woman was a negro, we are now to find some additional evidence in the language in which the penalty was denounced against that serpent. Up to this time that serpent seems to have been subordinate to Adam only as all other creatures were subordinate—not as slaves, but in a relation mutually binding, and mutually pleasant and profitable, with no jar, clash of interests or of feeling. Love, inclination, cheerfulness seem to have crowned the relation from all sides ; as husband and wife, implying, as Christ informs us, "dominion" and subordination, so all the other relations, though implying superior and subordinate, were mutually accepted as pleasant and profitable. The subordinate obeyed cheerfully and happily, because prompted to it alike by the law, and his own inclination. The superior commanded from the same combined causes; there was subordination, but no slavery there ; but when the serpent—the negro gardener forgot the amenities of his position—acted out his wily nature—took advantage of man's absence to play upon the credulity of the woman—acted out a constructive falsehood before her, and thus as an older being, induced her to eat what was forbidden to her, but not to him—when he betrayed the confidence which was, and should have been placed in him, and abused the relation in which he had been placed; then it was said to him, "because thou hast done this, thou art cursed above all cattle, and above every beast of the field: upon thy belly shalt thou go, and dust shalt thou eat all the days of thy life; and I will put enmity between thee and the woman, and between thy seed and her seed : it shall bruise thy head and thou shalt bruise his heel, " (Gen. 3, 14 15). Here is the voice of retributive justice—the penalty of law—the slavery of the negro—the change from an orderly, pleasant subordination to abject slavery—full of fretting disquiet to both parties.

It is true as, Bible readers generally understand it, that this language is partly prophetic, and looks forward to " Christ the second Adam ; " but it is equally true that the literal offspring of the woman and of the serpent are here spoken of as beings—and their relation and condition fixed. And the present inquiry is, not into the gospel promises, but into the legal facts and consequences promulgated in this language.

There are at least two prominent ideas expressed here—first, that contained in the distinction made between the serpent and "all cattle and every beast of the field, " and the addition "on thy belly shalt thou go, and dust shalt thou eat "—secondly, that contained in the language—" I will put enmity between, &c., &c.

The being who is created with rational capacities and susceptibilities, and is thus far superior to any part of the irrational animal kingdom, and is afterward doomed to a condition of crouching abject slavery, with blasted powers and relations, is in all truth cursed "above all cattle and above every beast of the field. " He may still tower in his intellect far above the beast, but it is only as the tall dead trunk in the forest, scathed by the lightnings of Heaven, towers in blasted ruin above the living shrubbery below. Such is the serpent. What idea is expressed by the language "on thy belly shalt thou go, and dust shalt thou eat?" Similar phrases occur frequently in the Bible, but the exact language occurs in only two places beside this ; and if the idea in these two places is the same, and is made plain and clear by the connection, then we are not only justified, but almost forced to take the same idea from it here where the connection does not make the idea so transparent. It is very evident that the language is prophetic, and therefore figurative. In the ninth verse of the seventy-second Psalm, the same phraseology occurs ; it is in this place translated—"they that dwell in the wilderness shall bow before him, and his enemies shall lick the dust. " A part of the same idea is repeated in the eleventh verse—"all Kings shall fall down before him." In these cases all commentators agree that the language is figurative, and that there is no allusion to the shape or the manner of motion, but to the subjection and the voluntary humility of the nature, condition, and feelings of the inferior in the presence of the superior. Christ, according to these prophecies, is to be head over all things to the church. She is to grow, spread, and conquer until none shall be left to question her authority, or dispute the right of her exalted Head. Even "they that dwell in the wilderness" or in lands yet pagan, are to hear the gospel, be gained over by it and to it, and they who oppose themselves are to "lick the dust" or be destroyed and removed out of the way. In one word the whole idea is, Christ is to be universal and absolute master, and all are to acknowledge and acquiesce unquestioningly in the fact, or be destroyed and removed out of the way. To go "on the belly" in this case does not mean any particular shape or mode of locomotion, but simply to bow down before, or to respect and obey unquestioningly as an inferior to a superior. It is not said to the serpent you shall crawl, slide, travel or move forward on the belly, but you shall go down upon it. The idea seems to be not shape or mode of travel, but that of comparative condition. We say of a person who is humbled or depressed in any way that he is "bowed down." And that seems to be the idea contained in the language "on thy belly shalt thou go." "You shall naturally crouch and humble yourself, and feel all your inferiority to man;" and the additional phrase—"dust shalt thou eat" only serves to throw additional light on the above view. To eat dust—like the dust—bite the dust, &c., are never used to describe the quality of the food, or the manner of taking it, but always to express death, conquest or complete subjugation. All that a fair interpretation from analogy can make of this address to the serpent is equivalent to this—though rational, yet you shall be degraded far more than any irrational animal; for you shall crouch a menial slave before man, and be subdued and domineered over by him, and after an indefinite flight of years, shall bite the dust, or be rooted out and extinguished by him.

The other place where the same language occurs it is rendered—"they shall bow down to thee with their faces toward the earth and lick up the dust of thy feet, " (Isaiah 49, 23). Here both the subject and the idea advanced is precisely the same as that in the seventy second Psalm. And all commentators agree that the idea is perfectly transparent in both cases. In fact both writers in describing Christ's complete and universal dominion over the world and its entire subjection to him seem to refer to and adopt this language used by Moses to describe the dominion of man over the negro, and his abject slavery to man; only in the one case it comes in the form of a most fearful curse, in the other in the form of a retriving promise. If "the analogy of faith" on which all do and should rely establishes any thing clearly, it does seem that in this case it establishes the fact that the curse on the *serpent* doomed the negro to perpetual menial crouching slavery to man, because he had been instrumental in leading man into sin and consequent ruin.

Honest candor will not deny that such is and always has been the relation between man and the negro. Efforts are being made—they have often been made to school man into the *feeling* (belief) that the negro is a man—his brother. It never has been done; even fanaticism, whilst it preaches it can not practice it. Nature revolts at it. The humble christian, even at the foot of the cross, oppressed with the feeling "behold I am vile—less than the least of all saints," has felt even there—"God has made a broad distinction between me and the negro, which I can not, dare not ignore. I will yield what is due in his position, but I can not and will not ignore the position itself." And the negro on his part as naturally and uniformly acquiesces in the distinction, and shrinks from an equality of association with man, as the Hare crouches in the corner of the cage and shrinks from equality of association with the Lion.

The slavery—not necessarily chattle slavery—but low, crouching, menial, abject slavery of the negro is the idea taught by the curse on the serpent. The Bible teaches it; facts teach it; all history teaches it. Reader, your own feelings, whether you be a pro or anti-slavery man, rise up and assert it, "and will not down at your bidding." It is the voice of God. You may abuse and quarrel with him who advances the theory and call him by hard names; he cares very little for that; praise or censure as you choose; a fig for the difference. He appeals to the great umpire time, and waits for her decision. "Truth is mighty and will prevail." The other prominent idea taught in this penalty on the serpent is thus expressed—"I will put enmity between thee and the woman, and between thy seed and her seed, it shall bruise thy head and thou shalt bruise his heel." Still admitting the gospel promise contained here, it can not be doubted that penalty of law is inflicted on a rational material subject of law for its violation. And if the meaning which we extracted from the preceding context was the true one, that contained here is also clear—and is also abundantly borne out by the facts of slavery. It is here affirmed that the relation of superior and subordinate which hitherto had been pleasant and cheerfully acquiesced in, was now to become the prey of envy and enmity—full of festering sores and burning boils on both sides. What was once the channel of mutual good and happiness, was now to become the channel of mutual distrust—of oppression and lawless overreaching and grinding exactions on the one side, and of subtile, meagre peculating and annoying service on the other. And how most exactly true to all the facts of negro slavery in all ages and countries is this description of Moses! Man has always trampled on and disregarded what otherwise might seem the rights of the negro, and has bruised his head. And the negro, wherever he has been in large numbers in contact with man, has always been in slavery, chattle or else otherwise abject, and has proved a dead weight on society—a barrier to material advancement—an injury to the body politic, and a clog to civilization, and has thus bruised man's heel.

For these reasons we conclude that the negro, though a rational being, is not *man* and never can rise to the dignity of manhood; and that for an offence, he was doomed to a condition of abject slavery. As a *chattle* he is now free in this country, and may he remain forever ѕо! But to assay to take him out of his condition of slave and force him into an unsought condition of manhood is to fight against God, and the consequences must be direful in the end. "Truth is mighty and will prevail." Here we are forced to desist for the present.

CHAPTER VI.

OBJECTIONS ANSWERED.

The writer expected, in this tract, to offer only a brief outline of a theory; and the limit thus assigned has been already transpassed too far to allow a notice of the many parts of scripture which throw additional light upon the various positions assumed. Especially ought we to notice the immortality and salvability of the negro, as they are so clearly set forth in both the old and new Testaments. This, however, must be deferred for the present.

There are two seeming objections to the truth of this theory, which, because of their plausibility, must be briefly noticed.

1st. The first may be thus stated—"Hybrids are barren, but the mulatto is prolific, therefore man and the negro are of the same race." I submit that it must be clearly demonstrated, in the face of all the facts which we have seen, that man and the negro are the same race, before any one is authorized to say that all Hybrids are barren and will not reproduce; for if the mulatto be a Hybrid, and I think we have proven that he is, the objection we know to be false. And granting to it all the force it can justly claim it is at best a "petitio principii." It assumes as true the very thing to be proven so. Science herself has not asserted positively that all Hybrids are barren, and that there is a law of nature which forever forbids their fecundity under all circumstances. Her greatest masters are to-day still debating that very question as one yet open. The objection assumes precisely the form of Hume's argument against miracles, which has been demonstrated a fallacy a thousand times. Grant that many Hybrids have been found which did not reproduce, does that prove that they never would in any other conceivable circumstance? Grant it did; would that prove that the same must be true of all other Hybrids? "What can we reason but from what we know?" May it not be true that the possibility of this reproduction exists every where, and yet actual examples exist no where but in this one case, because of some peculiarity of circumstance? May it not be true that thousands of examples exist, and yet have hitherto escaped observation? May it not be true that no examples do or can exist in the irrational animal kingdom, and yet are multitudinous among rational animals? May it not be true that among irrational animals which could not appreciate the confusion and endless disorder they might thus introduce, God rendered it impossible by a law of their nature, and yet among rational animals— subjects of moral law, he left it perfectly natural, and threw all of the responsibilities of the confusion introduced upon those who should introduce it? There is a very large field for thought in that last question.

As long as science speaks scientifically, her voice must be heard, reverenced and obeyed; for her's is the voice of God in his elder revelation. But when she stoops to prate through the mouths of fools, she must expect to be judged by the company she keeps.

It is very readily admitted that so far as careful observation has extended, Hybrids have not been found very, if at all prolific, except the mulatto, though there are reported what are called "well authenticated" exceptions. It is also true that the mulatto himself comes, to some degree, under this rule. Observation has settled the fact that a family of them rarely lasts beyond the fourth generation, but becomes extinct. In all black slave marts they have been less popular and valuable than pure blacks, except as indoor servants, because they have long been known to be less hardy, less prolific, and more liable to die out as families. Therefore, unless it can be clearly demonstrated that there is a uniform law of nature which necessarily and forever, and in all circumstances positively forbids reproduction, it will not do to say that it is not very common, or that they are not very prolific. We admit it and point to the mulatto as an example of the soundness of the rule. But we also assert that some Hybirds will reproduce and point to the mulatto for evidence. And the witness never can be silenced until it is fully established that he is not a Hybrid. Different as man and the negro certainly are in very many respects, we hazard nothing in saying that there is probably no two other races in the whole animal kingdom so nearly alike in physical conformation—having so many features in common; and this near approximation may be one reason why their mongrel offspring will reproduce, and does prove an exception to a general rule, if indeed there should prove to be any rule on the subject; or the fact that they are both rational, and therefore subjects of moral law and amenable to its sanctions if they disregard it and produce a mongrel race, may be the reason why they are made the exceptions to a law in physical nature, if such a law should be discovered. Therefore, if we should freely admit the clearly established rule that Hybrids generally, will not reproduce, still the objection were powerless as against the mulatto; for we see good ground for making him an exception, and, if you please, the only exception to that rule. And we dismiss the objection.

2d. The second objection, though much less weighty, is much more plausible than the first, because it seems taken from the Bible. Its form is—the Deluge was universal, and "all flesh living was destroyed" by it except those preserved in the Ark—Noah and his family, "eight souls" in all, and the animals. But if the negro was not an *animal*—if he possessed a soul, then this language excludes him. Therefore he must have descended in some way from Noah. "In a word, if the negro had existed before the deluge it would have destroyed him, and he was not in the Ark for only eight souls," were there.

Many good and very learned men still contend that the deluge was not universal. And although we believe and admit that it was, still their arguments would have to be satisfactorily removed before we could be denyed their use. And if we have made a clear showing that the negro existed before man, and still exists, and one of the two, either our conclusion or the objection to it, must be given up, which shall it be? I would certainly admit that the deluge was not universal rather than admit that the negro belongs to the human race. But we admit freely that the deluge was universal, and that, according to Moses, only "eight souls" were saved. The Bible is a revelation from God to *man*—to *Adam's race*, and not to any part of inferior creation. It at first showed the negro subordinate to man; it afterward doomed him to menial slavery to man; it placed him under and hitched him to man, and makes him dependent upon man. He never can be civilized or christianized, except through and by man. Hence, it speaks of him, as we have seen, only incidentally and allusively. It tells us of a fact of great interest and importance—that all the orders of being below man were preserved in the Ark to keep seed on the earth; and that was enough. It was not a revelation to or for them, and there were too many truths needed by man to allow the writer time or space to turn aside and name specifically each being in the Ark. And it were just as fair, honest and candid, to say no horse, dog, saurion, or serpent was saved by the Ark, because no one of them is specifically mentioned, as to say no negro could be there because he is not mentioned. When God gives a revelation on such subjects, then and not till then are we to expect full and explicit information about them. But to quarrel with the Bible about what it does clearly teach, simply because it does not teach more in detail, is foolish; or to expect to find the entire history of tad-poles, lizards, horned horses and negroes in a book given to man as a lost moral agent, to teach him a way of recovery, were demanding in it a feature which would render ridiculous the production of any human pen.

"But you say the negro has a soul, and the Bible asserts roundly that only "eight souls" were in the Ark. Therefore, either the negro has no *soul* or he does descend in some way from Noah." It is true that in the Bible the term *soul* is often used to express the spiritual, immaterial immortal, part of man. It is also true that it is far oftener used in the sense of *person, individual, human being,* &c., &c. It then includes both soul and body, and is intended to distinguish man from all orders below him. And the circumstances prove, and most writers admit that to be the sense in which the term is used in this passage. Eight souls—eight persons—eight of Adam's race in contradistinction to all other races were saved in the Ark. It neither affirms or denies directly or indirectly the presence or absence of other races of being. Its whole idea is, only eight of Adam's race were saved in the Ark. It has no reference to the negro.

But we now turn about upon the pursuer and put him upon the defensive. The description of the Ark and deluge says nothing about the negro; but before a candid world, what it does say and its very silence do *imply* both the fact and the absolute necessity of the negro in the Ark. Whether reckoned as a rational or irrational being—a clean or an unclean beast, or a creature *sui generis* unmentioned by

Moses, he must have been in the Ark as a *slave* in considerable
strength. The Ark was an immense water craft of about forty-five
thousand tons burden. It was afloat for a voyage of ten months, (Gen.
7, 11, 8, 13). It was freighted with the world in miniature. It must
have had stores of provision on board, immense both in quantity and
variety, (Gen. 6, 21). It had a vast number of rooms for the accomo-
dation of all the creatures it contained; for they had to a good degree
to be kept separate. No one will admit that the kite and dove, the
wolf and lamb, the lion and roe, the dog and hare, the *white man and
negro* occupied, respectively, the same stall. This is implied in the
number of stalls. Now admitting that there was no engineering or
steerage necessary. The stores had to be regularly meeted out.
Flesh, both salt and fresh had to be issued each day. A regular
slaughter pen, with all its accumulation of filth, breeding contagion in
the hot climate of Armenia, had to be kept up for carniverous animals,
(Gen. 6, 21). Forage, cereals, spices, gums, &c., &c., had to be regularly issued to all that vast caravan each day. (It is now allowed I believe, that attention to twelve horses, with their stalls, is the labor of a
diligent hand). Health on so long a voyage without coming to land,
also required that most strict attention be given to cleanliness, both of
person and vesel. All those rooms and that very great accumulation
of filth had to be cleansed each day; besides a thousand and one calls
for labor and attention on so long a voyage—calls which will at once
suggest themselves to the mind of any one who has ever sailed one day
on board a vessel—calls which render necessary the presence of several
hands on board the smallest river craft or packet boat. And yet, these
voyagers had to prepare their own food, and attend to their own personal comforts. And for all this Herculean task, there were only four
men on board "from stem to stern"—the rest were females. And am
I to be told that four men did or could do all the labor which was
indispensable on board that "Great Eastern" freighted with a world,
and through a voyage of ten months in a hot climate? No! "*Credat
Judeus Apella, non ego.*" I never can believe it, so long as the Bible
teaches that there was in existence a kind of rational being sometime
ycleped "*serpent,*" not created *red* but some other color, that he was
capable of rational mechanical toil, and doomed to perpetual menial
slavery to man—that he was a "creature" of some sort, and therefore,
necessarily included in the list of "every living creature wherein is the
breath of life" preserved in the Ark. If I see the victim rolling in
his blood, and a man with a scowling countenance, and a bloody hand,
and a bloody knife in it standing over him, that man may be a friend
to the slain, and may simply be examining the weapon with which a
deed was done by some unknown hand, but as he stands over the
victim, I am bound to pronounce him an assassin. Such is the force
of circumstantial evidence. So of the case before us. There must
have been negroes on board the Ark as well as horses and cattle, though
the Bible does not specifically mention the one or the other. There
was more work performed than four men could have performed.

It may be said that God managed this whole voyage miraculously,
and so dispensed with the labor that would otherwise have been

necessary. It is very easy to cry "miracle." They are "rat holes" into which many errorists dodge from the bullets of truth. Does "the book" say any thing more about "miracle" in this case than it does about "negro?" If you have right, the Bible being silent, to say "work done by miracle," have I not the same right, in its silence, to say "work done by negro?" Be sure the circumstantial evidence is in my favor; for this is the last place in the world where miracle mongers ought to go to find one. Miracles are never wrought to gain ends which can be gained by the use of natural means. And where do we find miracle here? In the one hundred and twenty years of toil spent in building the Ark, when it could have been done in a moment, and by a word? In the existence of an Ark for safety, when the same safety could have been accorded by a word without an Ark? Why the one great lesson taught by the Ark is the wise and proper use of means in good time to secure safety. There were no miracles to assist Noah and his sons, but doubtless there were negroes. And in place of the deluge militating against the truth of the theory whose brief outline is contained in this little tract, it furnishes strong presumptive evidence of its truth.

The civilization of America for the next century, possibly forever, must depend to a good degree upon the practical answer which *the people* adopt to the question, "who and what is the negro?" A multitude of answers "of all sorts, shapes and sizes," good, bad and indifferent are flying round. With the feeling that these extracts contain the meager outline of the answer which God, nature and history have given to that question, the writer has selected them from a pile of manuscripts, revised them and sent them to the press. And to show that whilst we have depended chiefly upon the Bible—the last resort for truth on this subject, we have not falsified or ignored the revelations of natural science, we close with an extract from the pen of the most profound naturalist in America—Prof. Agassiz.

"I have pointed out over a hundred specific differences between the bonal and the nervous systems of the white man and the negro. Indeed their frames are alike in no particular. There is not a bone in the negro's body which is relatively the same shape, size, articulation or chemically of the same composition as that of the white man, * * * the whole physical organism of the negro differs quite as much from the white man's as it does from that of the Chimpanzee, that is, in his bones, muscles and fibers. The Chimpanzee has not much farther to progress to become a negro, than a negro to become a white man. *This fact, science inexorably demonstrates.* Climate has no more to do with the difference between the white man and the negro, than it has with that of the negro and the Chimpanzee, or than it has between the horse and ass, the eagle and the owl. *Each is a separate and distinct creation.* The negro is no more a negro by *accident* or *misfortune* than an owl is the sister of the eagle, or the ass is the brother of the horse. How stupendous, and yet how simple is the doctrine of the Almighty maker of the universe, who has created different species of the lower animals to fill the different places and offices in the grand scenery of nature!"

THE'

COLOR LINE.

DEVOTED TO THE

Restoration of Good Government,

PUTTING AN END TO

NEGRO AUTHORITY AND MISRULE,

AND ESTABLISHING

A White Man's Government

IN THE

WHITE MAN'S COUNTRY,

BY

ORGANIZING THE WHITE PEOPLE OF THE SOUTH.

By SISTER SALLIE.

DEDICATION.

To the WHITE PEOPLE of the SOUTH this Paper is most cheerfully dedicated by the Author. Being left an orphan girl at an early age, and having passed through the cruel and desolating war which was common to us all in its results; and having felt too keenly the effects of Radical misrule and negro oppression, patience has ceased to be a virtue. I propose to dedicate this little book to the White People of my unfortunate South; and as my mite contributed to the restoration of good government, sound morals, and the organization of the white people.

Your

SISTER SALLIE.

THURSDAY NIGHT.

"Well, Sister Sallie, I am glad to see you reading the Bible. It is the foundation of all correct knowledge, pure morals, sound law, and good government."

"Yes, John. I have been a close student of the Bible for about fifteen years; have just finished it for the fourth time this year, and am now reviewing it critically, and, if I may be allowed the expression, analytically."

"If that is the case, Sallie, I would like to hear your criticism or comments on the Mosaic account of Adam's family—prefer you would begin with it, in order to system."

"Well, really John, that is beginning at the start of our race. And as its chapter of misfortunes is a long one, and filled with every character of the ills of life, I presume I may set myself for a siege, if you are to be the interrogator."

"Yes, sister, there are to me some very curiously strange and unnatural things in the account as given by Moses. And as I know you to be exceedingly sceptical in your belief of everything you read or hear, and not disposed to take anything for granted without corresponding proof, I would like to hear your views, and know what you think about old Mr. Adam and his family."

"Well, John, there are one or two facts connected with the life and history of old Mr. and Mrs. Adam which do not apply or attach to any other persons ever on earth. The first is, that Mr. Adam never was a child or little boy; nor his good lady a little girl. Neither of them ever had the pleasure or delight of gamboling in their father's or mother's presence, or dandling on their knees, or receiving the affectionate caresses of a mother, as you and I had; but were ushered into existence, and entered the arena of life, without any experience to buffet with the rough world. Some people blame Mr. Adam and his lady for what they did; but as far as my observation goes of human nature, my judgment is, that put any other man and woman off to themselves, without any experience or knowledge, to contend with the surroundings that they had to contend with, I am clearly of opinion they would have done exactly as they did. I am certain the woman would; but whether or not the man would agree to die for his wife, as Mr. Adam did, I do think it a little doubtful. There is some

49

thing strange and fascinating in love, and it develops itself more fully between man and wife than under any other circumstances in which human nature can be placed."

"Sallie, what '*surroundings*' were peculiar to Adam and Eve? We only read that they were the first persons that were made. I can see no surroundings that should have *compelled* them to do as they did."

"John, that is just like the most of your sex. They '*can't see*' the reason for anything unless it is ready to punch their eyes out. Then they can see as soon as any one else. Why, John, if you must know their surroundings, and are so stupid that you can't see them till pointed out to you, I will try and do so. The first thing then that they had to contend with was a whole generation of bad neighbors."

"'Neighbors,' Sallie, did you say? Why, who on earth could have been neighbors to Mr. and Mrs. Adam? I thought they were the first people that were made."

"Yes, John, that displays some more of the stupidity of your sex. There are none of you who rarely, if ever, have enough thought about you to give the Bible, or in fact, any other book, more than a superficial reading. And if a woman reads it critically, and happens to differ with your sex, or sees merit in it, that their laziness or stupidity would not let them see, they think it wonderfully strange. Does not the historian say that Cain, his first-born, after he had killed his brother Abel, went to the land of Nod? Now how, in the name of common sense and reason, could he go to the '*land of Nod*' if there were no such place? And people in it, too. It is not territory alone that makes a *land*, with distinctive *name*; but it is the *people* in it that gives it the name."

"Sister, you really astonish me. I really believe you must be crazed. I fear too 'much learning hath made thee mad.'"

"Yes, John, that is about the way with your sex. Whenever a woman begins to expose their ignorance, or show she has examined a subject closer than they have, their excessive vanity cries out, 'crazed, crazed!' They can't bear to know that a woman has the faculty of analytically or critically examining anything, and drawing its hidden merits out; but John, that don't make any difference with your sister Sallie. She is free from all of your sex, at liberty to think for herself, and accountable to *no man* for her thoughts. She carries her heart in her 'carpet-bag!' Yes, I say Mr. and Mrs. Adam had neighbors; but from such as they did have, may the Lord forever deliver me!"

"Well, Sallie, as you seem so positive about it, who were their neighbors? You astonish me beyond measure! Who were their neighbors?"

"John, you are duller than a meat-axe, though not much differing from all other men who read the Bible. Have I not told you the land of Nod was peopled? To make a district of territory *a land* or *State*, requires people. And it is the people that usually give the name to the country, or it acquires its name from some peculiarity of its inhabitants. There is a great deal *implied* or *understood* in the Bible as being comprehended in the nature of the subject of which the writer is treating. For instance, he says Cain was a 'tiller of the ground.' Now he did not think it necessary to go through the long routine of manufacturing those implements, or of even telling that he had plows, hoes, axes, harrows, single-trees, clevices, etc., etc., but presumed upon the good sense of the agricultural people to whom he was writing. And knowing that they '*tilled*' the ground, and knew what implements of agriculture were necessary for that purpose, just stated a prominent, leading, material fact, which in its nature embraced all the lesser ones. Let me give you an illustration, to show what I mean by the term implication, which I shall use very often in our conversations: I say a man cut down a tree. I expect the person's good sense to whom I am talking will supply the omission of mine to say that there was a blacksmith, who bought some iron from an iron manufactory, and bought some coal, and carried those articles to his shop, and there he had a bellows, and furnace, and striker, and anvil, and hammers, with which to make an axe; and then got some wood, and with the drawing-knife he made a handle, and put it into the axe, and sold it to the man who cut down the tree with it. Now, John, if any one were to come to you, and go through such a rigmarole of stuff as that, in order to tell you that a man cut down a tree, you would consider he was a first-class fool, or else he took you to be one—one or the other would be certain. And that is just the way Moses looked upon this matter when he said Cain went to the land of Nod. He presumed upon the good common sense of men to supply the omission. He had stated the prominent leading fact, and perhaps he may have thought, that if all men were so stupid that their dull skulls could not supply the minor facts, the women's good sense would.

"Again, John, Moses was talking to a people who had had the story handed down to them through the family lines of Adam to him, orally, and were as familiar with it as they were with their everyday household affairs. Everything in the shape of family records were, and had been, kept up to that time by oral tradition; or, at least, there is nothing to show to the contrary. He then did not sit down to state propositions, and argue the *pro* and *con* of them to prove them; but sat down to state facts which his people, the Jews, as a nation, were as conversant with as you and I are of our family line for two or three generations back. All, then, that he had to do, was to mention the leading, prominent facts upon which was based the truth of what he was telling, because he knew that those to whom he was immediately writing knew these facts to be true as well as he did. And he presumed that their knowledge of these prominent, material, and leading facts, as true, would enable their good sense to fill up or supply the omission of the lesser ones.

"Further: If he looked down the stream of time at all, he thought women would have good sense enough to supply these facts, if men were too stupid to do so. Now when he says Cain was a tiller of the ground, he virtually says that he had all the necessary implements of agriculture to till with. You don't suppose that he meant he rooted it up with his nose, like a hog! But by taking a broad, comprehensive, and expanded view of the subject, he supposed future generations could work out the problem in after years from the facts he had stated, by applying their own experience to those facts, and drawing the corresponding conclusion. As I shall have occasion to talk more fully on this subject on some other evening, I will dismiss this branch of it for the present."

"Sister, you said that there were people in the land of Nod, and that Adam knew it. Does not the historian say Adam was the first man that was made?"

"No, John, he does not say so. He only says he was the first man that was made in the *image and likeness* of God. Let us examine this matter. The historian says, 'And God said, Let us make man, in our own image and likeness.' This to my mind implies that he had made man who was *not* in his image or likeness. Had he said, 'Now let us make a *white* man,' no one would have hesitated to have believed that he had made one of another color. I have shown you previously how things are said by implication, and are understood by contrast. For instance, if I say A has *a house* exactly like B's, it would imply that A had more than one house. But if I were to say that A's house is exactly like B's house, it would imply that A had but the one house. This would be the natural conclusion, and correct conclusion, based upon the philology of language, of construing words and sentences. So, when the Lord said, 'Let us make man in our image and likeness,' he indirectly said he had made one, or, perhaps, more, who were not in his likeness or image. He said more. He said, 'and let him have dominion over every thing before created.' Now I conclude, and will yet show to your satisfaction, that the bad surroundings or neighbors which Adam had were the people not made in the image or likeness of God, and were the occupants of the land of Nod."

"Well, sister, if that be so, why did He say, 'it is not good for man to be alone?'"

"I am glad you asked that question, John. I will try and answer you. It does not appear that, up to the time the Lord said 'it is not good for man to be alone,' that he had given him any moral law; had only given him power and dominion over creation. And from the nature of the declaration, I am clearly of the opinion that, in the exercising of that power and 'dominion,' the Lord had 'seen a spirit developing, through the actions of Adam, that forced this conviction upon his mind. I am inclined to the opinion that he had seen that Adam was disposed to be social in his nature, and desired company. And, like all his sons after him, if they could not get good, would take bad company. And seeing Adam inclined to seek society among the Nodites, over whom he had given him power and dominion as servants, He said, 'It is not good for the man to be alone,' and fixes it upon Adam, calling him by name. Gen., 2d ch., v. 18–20. Now this clearly shows to my mind that the Lord considered Adam alone, as far as suitable society was concerned. Let me illustrate, John: A married woman's husband is gone on a journey. At the same house where she is living, there may be twenty men living. Now, as far as society is concerned, she is as much alone whilst her husband is gone, as if no one were in fifty miles of her. How very applicable it would be, in that case, to say, the man went off and left his wife alone; meaning that, by the strict rules of morals and circumspection governing the married life, she was alone. And though not literally true, still, according to the rules of society and prudence, it is substantially true. Now it is in this sense that Adam was alone. He had no society that would aid or enable him to carry out God's injunction to him—'have dominion over them, and subdue them.' In this respect, there was no society, in the mind of God, suitable to his condition, and hence the declaration : ' It is not good for the man to be alone.' That this is evidently the reason, is clearly shown in 2d ch., 22d v. of Genesis, and of the rib which he had taken out of the man, he made a woman, and gave her to *the man*."

" Well, sister, if the Nodites were not in the image or likeness of God, in whose likeness were they made? But, perhaps, it would be more in order for me to ask you what is meant by being made in the image and likeness of God?"

" Brother John, I see you seem to have become somewhat interested in the subject, so I will try and answer you satisfactorily. The Nodite, whoever he was, was made in his own image, if in any image at all. Deity had no pattern to make him by any more than he did the horse or the goat; but only undertook to make all manner of forms, of four-legged and two-legged animals, and of every distinct color. This was necessary in order to make a perfect creation. Now as to your question, ' What is meant by being made in God's image and likeness ?' Means exactly the same as it does to make any other one thing in the image and likeness of another thing. I will illustrate: When the artist undertook to make General Jackson's statue, as he did, in New Orleans, he did not get the material out of which General Jackson was made, but got just such material as he could carve the features, color, form and size of General Jackson upon ; so that, when it was done, everybody who saw it, did not see General Jackson, but something that looked exactly like him. Now it could have looked exactly like him, whether made in full life or in miniature; just as a photograph, though not larger than your hand, looks exactly like the person it is intended to represent, in features, color and form. This is what I understand the Lord to mean when he says, ' Let us make man in our own image and likeness.' He did not use the same material (if I should be allowed the expression) that *He* was made out of, any more than the artist did in making the image of Jackson; but only that material which he could mold into form, color, and features of himself. Hence I conclude that ' *the man* ' was made in the form and color of God, and in features resembling him, for that is what he proposed to do, and he either did it or he did not; if he did not, then we must conclude that he could not, and proposed to do what he knew he could not do, which I do not think there are any rash enough to assert. Another point of likeness in which Adam (the man) was made like God, was his moral faculties. This he did not endow anyone else with but Adam, and, through Adam, Eve. This faculty he did not give to any other animal of his creation."

" Well, sister, the more I hear you talk the more I become interested in the subject, and the more my interest is excited, and the more questions I have to ask you. Will you consider me too inquisitive if I ask you what was the color of Adam?"

"No, John; not at all. It appears to me quite natural you should ask that question. It is a very sensible question. Indeed, a very important one, and one which, I think, can be answered only by the Bible, and the logic of facts. To begin, I will assert that Adam was a white man, and in him God Almighty established the COLOR LINE that was to govern the world on earth. Now for the proof; and in introducing it, I must be allowed the privilege of arranging it in that order that best suits my views of the dignity and the grandeur of the subject embraced in your question:

"The Jewish Scriptures fix the fact that Abraham was the father of the Jewish people. One argument I deduce from this fact is, that if the Jews are all white, and if that inflexible and unvarying law of nature be true, that 'like begets like,' then the father and the mother of the Jews, Abraham and Sarah, were white, and by *a priori* reasoning, if the father and mother of the Jews, or their head representatives were white, then it follows that the head representatives of Abraham and Sarah were white also.

"Let us examine the matter a little more practically, guided by the history as given by Moses, and let the facts speak for themselves:

"Adam was, according to the chronology of his family, 672 years old when Methuselah was born. Adam died at the age of 920 years. Then Methuselah was 248 years old when Adam died, and 587 years old when Noah was born. Methuselah died at the age of 969 years, thus living, after Noah was born, 382 years. Noah was 500 years old when Shem, Ham and Japheth were born, and 600 years old when the flood came. So you can readily see that Noah had 382 years of his life to spend with Methuselah, and hear him talk of Adam and Eve, with whom he had lived for 284 years. I say lived with. I do not mean by the expression 'lived with,' that he actually lived in the same house with him; but in the same country, and had every opportunity of going to see him and talking with him that any of us have of any of our relations. And I ask you, John, is there any thing more natural than to believe that Methuselah and his wife did visit Adam and Eve, and take all their children with them, and talk with them, and hear them tell the unfortunate story of their transgression and banishment from the Garden of Eden? Why, John, woman as I am, I would walk around the world, barefooted and alone, if Adam and Eve were living, just to see the first man and woman that were made in the image of God, and would listen to them recount the early history of my race and sex with more than human interest.

"And is it less reasonable to believe that Noah, who lived 382 years in the same country with Methuselah, did not visit him, and take his children with him, and hear him tell the wonderfully exciting and interesting history of Adam and Eve, as he got it directly from themselves? I do not care to follow the biblical record of Adam, as it gives the regular succession of the heads of families from Adam to Methuselah, and from him to Noah; for this would make an almost endless conversation ; but I only take up such members of Adam's family as will keep up the regular connection, and at the same time show that they had every opportunity of seeing, hearing, and knowing the true history of our race, and had no object to gain by not giving a faithful history to their children and families, respectively. Then you can very readily perceive that the line of connection—that the history of our race, from Adam to Noah, is only second-handed. Thus: Methuselah heard it from Adam, and taught it to Noah."

"Sister, while your chronological account is very interesting to me, I really cannot see what it has to do with the answer to my question— ' What was the color of Adam ?'"

"The object of it is this: I stated that Abraham was called the father or head of the Jewish nation. I further stated that the Jews, as far as we know anything of them, are all white persons, and all history concurs in the same. Now it follows, if the children are white, then, according to the fixed law of nature or of God, that like begets like, the parent Abraham must be white also. The Apostle Paul also confirms this in Acts xvii, 28, 29, when reasoning with the Athenians and Grecians who had become idolaters. He says, in regard to their idols: ' Now we are his offspring (that is, we are the offspring of God), and we ought not to think that the Godhead is like gold or silver or stone, graven with many devices.' The legitimate conclusion is, then, that, as he cites himself and the Athenians and Grecians as God's offspring, that we should conclude that the Godhead, our Father, looks like us. Paul evidently knew the force of that command, ' bring forth in thine own likeness and image,' and leaves them to draw their conclusions accordingly, as they were his offspring.

"This fact established, then all that is necessary to prove, in order to show that Adam was a white man, is to prove that Abraham is his literal descendant. Hence the necessity of showing the relationship between Adam, Methuselah, Noah and Abraham. If history shows one unbroken line of descent from Adam to Abraham, then I think it will be clearly shown that Adam was a white man, because his literal blood descent, Abraham, was white. I am willing to rest the proof that Abraham was a white man upon the fact that his descendants, all now on earth, are white men. But more on this subject after I get through with the chronological table of descent as given by Moses :

"Noah was 600 years old when the flood came. Shem, Ham and Japheth were then 100 years old or thereabouts. The history says Noah lived 500 years and begat Shem, Ham and Japheth. Noah lived 300 years after the flood, for he died at 900 years old ; this would make him have lived 400 years with Shem, Ham and Japheth. Now it would not be necessary for him to tell his sons anything about the flood, for they had passed through it, and knew as much about it as he did. Neither was it necessary for him to tell them what their or his color was, for this they knew ; but it was necessary for him to tell them all about what Methuselah told him of Adam. This was necessary, and not only that, but it is reasonable and natural to believe that the story was listened to with a great deal of interest by his sons, and treasured up in their memories. Then when Noah died, Shem, the oldest, was 400 years old. Shem was 130 years old when his first son, Arphaxad, was born, and lived 500 years afterward, making him 630 years old when he died. Now, by computing the respective ages of the first sons, and grandsons, from the birth of Arphaxad to the birth of Abraham, it makes a period of 290 years. This would make Shem's age, at birth of Abraham, 420 years; and as Shem lived to the age of 630 years, Abraham could have talked with Shem for 210 years.

"I will now give you the name of the first-born son in every head of the families in the regular line, running back from Abraham to Noah. First then in order is Abraham's father, Terah; next Terah's father, Nahor; next Nahor's father, Serug; next Serug's father, Rue; next Rue's father, Peleg; next Peleg's father, Eber; next Eber's father, Salah; next Salah's father, Arphaxad; next Arphaxad's father, Shem; next Shem's father, Noah. You see now I have got the regular line from Abraham to Noah; showing that Abraham is the blood descent of Noah. And of course, if Abraham was white, his ancestors clear back to Noah were white also, for the apostle Paul says the ancestor must look like his offspring. See Acts, xvii, 28, 29. This is as clear a proposition as the axiom in mathematics, that things which are equal to the same thing are equal to one another; and that other universal law of nature, that 'like begets like.' Now, if I can show a regular, unbroken line of blood connexion from Noah back to Adam, and by the history show that Noah was the literal blood descent of Adam, it follows, that if Noah was white, then his ancestor was white.

"I will now take the heads of the families of the regular line from Noah back to Adam, as given by Moses:

"First then is Noah's father, Lamech; then Lamech's father, Methuselah; next Methuselah's father, Enoch; next Enoch's father, Jared; next Jared's father, Mahalaleel; next Mahalaleel's father, Cainan; next Cainan's father, Enos; next Enos' father, Seth; next Seth's father, Adam, and next Adam's father, God.

"Now, if a family record can establish anything on earth, I think I have shown a regular connecting link of pure blood record from Abraham back to Adam; and if we come down from Adam to Abraham, the line of pure blood descent is unbroken to Abraham.

"And it follows, beyond all contradiction, that if Abraham was a white man, then his great progenitor, Adam, was a white man. Unless that universal law given by the Creator to *all animated nature* to bring forth after their kind, and that also universally established law of nature that 'like begets like,' and that declaration of Paul that the parent look like the offspring, be true, all have proved a failure. And as Adam was in the image and likeness of God, the Creator was white also. This then is one reason, and the true reason, why he gave the white man power and dominion over all of his creation, because he was in his image and in his likeness, and was his son according to the Gospel as recorded by the Holy Evangelist, Luke, iii, 38: ' Adam was the son of God.'

56

" But let me examine the law of like begetting like' a little further. Take, for instance, the vegetable kingdom. The oak of the forest casts its seed to the earth ; it springs up an oak. The pine the same. So with the bay, the myrtle, cedar, gum, hickory, ash, and all other trees of the forest ; the seed produces a scion like its sire. Then the more delicate shrubs and flowers ; the rose reproduces the rose, the violet its kind ; the pink reproduces the pink, the lily its kind :. all in their own likeness and their own image, in obedience to that mandate of Jehovah, ' bring forth after thy kind.'

"Take also the feathered tribe. The ostrich produces and reproduces the ostrich ; the pelican, the turkey, and the vulture, all produce and reproduce their own specific kind. Take also the smaller birds : the sparrow brings forth the sparrow ; the swallow, wren, and the martin, all, all bring forth in their own image and their own likeness, in obedience to that positive, divine law, ' bring forth after thy kind.' Also, the finny tribe. The whale produces the whale; the sturgeon, the sturgeon ; the buffalo, cat, perch, trout, salmon, herring, all produce and reproduce, *ad infinitum*, their respective kinds. And are so jealous of their kind, though mingled together in the mighty deep, in the rivers, lakes, and smaller streams, the world over, still they bring forth their own kind with that exactness as if fate stood over them, and molded each one in its own image and its own likeness. I might pursue this subject till I would wear your patience threadbare, John, and not find one solitary exception to this invariable and inflexible law of God of like-begetting ; in accordance with that universal command of the Great Creator God, to ' bring forth after their kind.'"

" Well, sister, I have listened to you with a great deal of interest indeed. I have really been entertained and delighted; particularly with your chronological account of Adam's family, and the regular succession from Abraham back to Adam ; but whilst I admit all this,- I must say I am not satisfied with it."

" What is your objection, brother?"

" My objection to it, sister, arises from the universally-taught doctrine by the ecclesiastical teachers of the day, that the negroes are the descendants of Ham, the Indians the descendants of Shem, and the white man the descendants of Japheth."

" John, I will state, as a prelude to what I have to say on this subject, that I, too, have heard a great deal of the ecclesiastical teachings of the day in this matter. And it would look like a woman, a poor orphan girl as I was raised, ought to do, like a large portion of my sex, gulp down, in silent submission, whatever the ' droppings' of their respective sanctuaries might be, as they fall from the so-called inspired lips of their respective preachers. But as I am a character *sui generis*, I shall beg leave to be my own interpreter of God's book.

" The most sensible thing I ever saw on this subject, from the pulpit teachings of the day, was from the pen of the learned Mr. Alexander Campbell, the head and front of the reformers to Primitive Christianity; begun in this century in Virginia, I think about the year 1830. It is due to that great and good man, as I have introduced his name, to say, that in NO AGE OF THE WORLD has any reformer thrown more

light upon the true teaching of the Bible than he has. His able
papers, the *Christian Baptist* and *Millenial Harbinger*, conducted with
so much fairness, ability, and spirit, visited every portion of this country, and a large portion of the Old World, or mother country, and
proclaimed that wonderful truth, ' that the Bible was its own interpreter,' and ' the only true creed of the Christian.' He gave a new
impetus to the world of thought, and directed it back to the Word of
God. The religious world will never do him justice, for he opposed
all creeds, except the Bible ; pronounced them wicked in their nature,
and calculated to bring the teachings of the Bible into neglect.

"His article which I saw took the ground that the respective colors
of Shem, Ham, and Japheth indicated their *names*, and hence their
father and mother, Noah and wife, named them as suggested to their
minds by their respective colors. For instance, he said, the word
Shem in the Hebrew language meant *red*, Ham meant *black*, or *brown*,
and Japheth meant *white* ; and as Shem's color was red, he was named
Shem from his color ; Ham being black, was named Ham ; and so
with Japheth, because he was white. He then took the ground from
this argument, and from this argument only, that Shem was the father
of the Indian, because he was red ; Ham of the negro, because he was
black, and Japheth of the white.

"This was simply putting a few more stitches in the old pulpit
theory to give it the appearance of a new vamp. I was quite young
when I read it, and was pleased with it at the time, for Mr. Campbell
was a strong writer, a very logical reasoner ; none more so, not excepting Lord Bacon, John Locke, Lord Bolingbroke, or Lord Brougham.
And when he treated a subject thoroughly, his conclusions were so
fully in accordance with his premises, that conviction to any one who
admired him was almost irresistible. I attached a great deal of importance to his article at the time, and was persuaded it was true.

"Several years have passed since then. We have been through a
desolating war. Mr. Campbell has been numbered with the dead.
We have lost our parents, and our property has been destroyed by the
war. We have both been driven to hard work—you to the field, and
I to the school-room. This has caused me to see the importance of a
woman's thinking and acting for herself ; and being of a religious turn
of mind, I was led to the study of the Bible, as it claimed to be the
teachings of the husband, of the widow, and the father of the father-
less. As slavery was the wealth of the Southern people, and ' bone
of contention' and ' apple of discord' between the North and the
South, and the remote and exciting cause of the war, I determined to
study the Bible with special reference to negro slavery, and convince
myself, if it was *the sin* which the Northern people said it was.

"With this determination of mind in me, I took up the subject and
theory of Mr. Campbell, viz. : Shem, the father of the Indians. I
took up Shem's line, and attempted to trace it to some point or incident that would confirm Mr. Campbell's position. I had not gone far
before the history brought me to Abraham, termed the father of the
Jews. This raised the question in my mind : were the Indians the
children of Abraham ? If they were, they had one unmistakable sign

upon their bodies by which the male seed of Abraham can identify himself in any country, or in any clime: I mean the sign of circumcision. The history says God gave this to Abraham 'as a seal' of the covenant made with him and his seed, to the land of Canaan. After giving it to him in person, he told him that he should circumcise every male child in his family, and enjoin it upon his seed as a perpetual sign in their flesh, as a seal of his covenant with him. Now if the Indians are the offspring of Shem, they also are of Abraham; and if of Abraham's seed, they have the seal of circumcision upon their bodies to this day, handed down from father to son, as a seal of the covenant of God to Abraham, their father and progenitor, if they are his seed, or offspring. So determined was God that this seal of circumcision should be kept perpetual, that when he gave it to Abraham he accompanied it with a decree, which he has never yet revoked, viz.: that he that shall refuse to be circumcised shall be cut off from his people.

"Now the history of the Indian will not show that there ever was one of them circumcised; not upon the body of one single Indian was it ever discovered during the revolutionary war, the war of 1812, the Seminole war, or upon any one of any of the tribes with which the United States have ever made treaties. And the fact is, that not a solitary Indian, since they have been discovered in America, has ever claimed to be the child of Abraham, or of the line of Shem; whilst, on the other hand, no matter where you find a Jew, whether in a city, or in the country, in a republican or despotic form of government, whether on the banks of the Ganges, the Tiber, the Nile, the Amazon, the Thames, the Mississippi, or their own favored Jordan, any and everywhere found, every male of them bears upon his body the mark of circumcision, the seal of the promise of God to Abraham and his seed. And not a solitary one of them ever fails to claim to be the stock of Abraham, and line of Shem. They are proud of it, and well they may be, for they carry the truth on their bodies that is incontrovertible, that their ancestors, through all time, are white, and have been, *white men and women.*

"Now, John, with this argument of circumcision to identify the Jews, as the children of Abraham, and through him the children of Shem, and through Shem the seed of Adam, what goes with the theory of the pulpit, based upon the color of Shem, indicating his name, and making him the progenitor of the Indians?

"But again, John, God said, 'every male that refuses to be circumcised *shall be cut off* from his people. Genesis, xvii, 14. Now suppose the Indians had been the seed of Abraham, they would have been exterminated right at that time for not being circumcised, for extermination is what is meant by being cut off. And right then and there would an end have been put to their race. The very fact then that we find the Indians all over this country without the sign of circumcision in their flesh to identify them as the seed or offspring of Abraham, and that we find it in the flesh of every male Jew on earth, and also find them keeping up the rites of the Jewish nation in their worship, and claiming Abraham and Shem as their progenitors, is incontestable proof that they are the seed of Abraham, and that as they are white, their father Abraham, and his progenitor, Shem, were also white.

"It is said in Acts, xiv, 17, 'that God has not left himself without witness.' And I am inclined to believe that he, in looking down the stream of time, saw in the far-distant future what efforts would be made by a corrupt, religious people, to prove that Shem was the father of the Indians, gave circumcision to Abraham, one of his literal blood descendants, to be kept strictly in his family line, throughout their generations, as a living proof of the fact that Shem was a white man; and if white, then not the progenitor of the Indians, but of the Jews, and hence white people; and that the Indian is not the descendant of Abraham, and if not of Abraham, then not of Shem. I have for a long time been astonished that the ecclesiastical divines could not see the dilemma into which they plunged themselves by taking the ground that the name of Shem indicated his color.

"But, John, let us examine the question from a legal stand-point: Suppose the Indians were to set up a claim to the land of Canaan, on the ground that they were the heirs-at-law of Abraham, the descendant of Shem, claiming under the contract or covenant made by God to Abraham, and attempt to eject the present occupants of that country under their claim. I mean, to suppose that there was a legal tribunal on earth that had jurisdiction over the case, (which of course there is not), but just to look at this matter from every practical stand-point, I make the supposition. The attorney for the defense would demur to their plea on the ground that the title set up by them lacked the *seal* of the grantor. And it would be such a demurrer as the court would sustain, on the ground that the seal of the grantor to lands must be attached to the document purporting to be the title made to the lands. When governments grant lands, there is no need for any additional seal, or affidavit to the contract, but only the seal of the grantor. To all patents to lands granted or sold to any one by the United States, or any other great Power, unless that grant or patent has attached to it, and stamped upon it, the seal of the grantor, called its *great seal,* the instrument claiming to be the title would be declared null and void, and so the court would rule, and the claim would not stand in law if resisted. Every nation and every State have their respective seals, and so do individuals. And every document purporting to issue from one of them, will always have its seal stamped upon it, unless it is a forgery. And so sacred did Deity hold the importance of a seal attached to a contract for land as good, sound law, that he established as his seal to his contract, or covenant with Abraham and his seed to that country, the sign of circumcision in the flesh of Abraham and his seed, as a testimony forever between him and them, that he would perform in good faith its conditions.

"And another design he had in view, by putting the seal in the flesh of Abraham and his children was, that it would be a living and perpetual testimony or witness that they who bore it were the rightful and legal heirs to that land, and none others could be; and in the absence of any family record, which, in his wisdom, he saw would, in the nature of things, cease to be kept; but that the world should know that none but those who bore upon their bodies this sign or seal, were the descendants of Abraham; and if not of Abraham, then not of Shem. Then I conclude that the absence of this seal on the person of the Indians, and the presence of it on the Jews, settles beyond all dispute, that the Indians are not the descendants of Abraham. And if not of Abraham, then not of Shem, because Abraham, the father of the Jews, was white; and if white, then his father or representative head, Shem, from whom he descended, was white also. And Shem being white, then his immediate father, Noah, was also a white man. And if Shem was white—as I think I have shown by the family record and the logic of facts that he was, taking the color of the Jews, as the seed of Abraham, as the starting point; and the Indians all being red, and not bearing upon their body the sign of circumcision, the distinguishing mark which God placed on the seed of Abraham to identify them from all other people—it follows that they, the Indians, must look to some other origin than that of Shem. They have no part nor lot in the estate of Abraham. Neither can they claim any benefit resulting from being descendants of Shem. But as I am wearied, I will bid you good-night till Thursday night, when I will resume the subject, and try and close this branch of it."

THURSDAY NIGHT.

"Well, sister, I have listened very patiently to your arguments in support of your proposition, that Shem is not the progenitor of the Indians, and am compelled to admit that there is a great deal of apparent soundness in them; and, whilst I cannot refute them, I am not prepared to subscribe to them; owing, in part, to the force of previous education on the subject, and partly from their newness to me."

"Yes, John, I will admit that early education begets prejudices that are very hard to eradicate, and very few have moral courage to review their early education in religion, but are content to console themselves that father and mother believed this way, and did so and so, and it must be right. It is, however, a deception that will lure millions to a ruinous account in the final day of settling up accounts with their Creator."

"Yes, sister, I will admit that I have been too passive in my duty toward my Creator, and have listened with too much credulity to what the preacher would say, and gulp it down as true, and never take the Bible and examine whether it were true or not. But, as you have given the subject so much thought, and have been both entertaining and instructing in our fire-side talks, I would now like to hear you on the Ham branch of Noah's family. I have always been taught to believe that he was the father or representative of the negro race. Let me hear your views on this."

61

"Yes, John, I know the doctrine that Ham is the head or progenitor of the negro race is a pulpit doctrine, and believed, I think, by all the ecclesiastical corps, and one of very grave importance to the white man as well as the negro; but rendered doubly so since the doctrine of miscegenation promulged by Henry Ward Beecher and his satellites, and the doctrine of social, political and religious rights now fixed upon the country, and by the further iniquity of the Civil Rights Bill which Congress and the President are moving heaven and earth to fasten upon the country.

"My first argument to prove that Ham is not the progenitor of the negro race, will be founded upon the application of the law of nature, 'that like begets like,' which I have argued very fully when giving you my views on the family of Shem.

"First, then, the *freedom shriekers*, the social-equality men, the civil-rights men, the miscegenationists, and the pseudo philanthropists, all agree and teach that the whole *human race* were reduced by the flood to eight persons—the Noah family. That from the three sons of Noah sprung the three colors, red, black and white men.

"I have shown in the argument upon Shem's origin, that Noah and his wife were white, and that Shem was a white man also. The advocates of the doctrine that color indicated the name, all agree that Japheth was a white man. Their own admission that Japheth was white, gives me one-third of the argument that one-third of Noah's three sons were white. My argument, showing that the Jews, who are the descendants of Shem, through Abraham, being all white, proves that their progenitor, Shem, was a white man also, according to the universal law of God 'that like begets like,' or rather, as expressed by him, 'bring forth after thy kind,' 'in thy image and likeness;' and as Paul has taught, 'that the parent should look like his offspring.' This gives me two of the three sons as white.

"Now the argument I make, aside from Scripture, that Ham is not the father of the negro, is this: If the law of God, 'bring forth after thy kind,' be true, and Ham was a black-skinned, thick-lipped, *flat-nosed*, woolly-headed negro, such as the negro is amongst us, in order for him to bring forth (or in other words, to have children that looked like him, which is the meaning of it,) he was obliged to have the same kind of a black-skinned, thick-lipped, flat-nosed, woolly-headed wife; if he had not, right then and there the pure negro would have ceased to have been born; right there it would have stopped; that would have put an end to the race, then and there; there never would have been another such creature as Ham born on earth. Let me illustrate this, John, and you will have to bear with my apparent immodesty in doing so; but the nature and the gravity of the subject requires it. There are none of the advocates who contend that Ham had a negro wife, nor that Shem's wife was an Indian; but their argument is, that all the human race were of the same color till old Mrs. Noah gave birth to the triple progeny of three different colored sons, by the same father; and these three sons each selected their wives, before the flood, from people of this *same one color*. They don't say whether the three wives of these three boys were all white, all red, or all black; but that they were all the same color. Be that what it may, it is admitted by them all. Now, John, just recur to your own experience and observation, and to history in all time (except in this one solitary case of these three boys and their three wives), and see if you can find a solitary case in which the commingling of the colors of men and women did not give rise to mixed blooded children, making a mixed blooded race, partaking in part both of the color of the father and the mother? And more especially, in every instance where a pure blooded white and pure blooded black person had issue between them, that the child or issue was, and has ever been, since the first record of amalgamation, a mixed blood, or mulatto. In all history there is not one solitary exception on record to this unyielding law of God, 'of like begetting like.' This law, had it been inscribed by the Recording Angel of God, upon the canopy of heaven, in characters as large and as indelible as those in which Moses received the Ten Commandments, and so bright as to be read at the hour of midnight darkness, would not have been more legible or more intelligible than the results of the past have proved its fulfillment to be. Now if these three boys had wives of the same color, and they themselves all being of different colors, the strict legitimate conclusion, from the logic of facts, would be, and is, that there was but one pure breed or race perpetuated from them. The other two sons' children would have been mixed bloods—half-breeds. An admixture of the negro and white woman producing the mulatto, as the children of Ham, and the admixture of the Indian and the white woman resulting in a mixed blood, not like either, but part red and part white. Thus, you see, by the logic of facts, if their premises are true, as stated above, there never could have been another pure blood negro or pure blood Indian born, but an extinction of the negro and the pure blood Indian and negro race right then and there; unless, they can show that there was a divine decree, in the shape of a miracle, to suspend that universally established law of God, 'bring forth after thy kind.' But there is no such decree on record. The historian makes no mention of God revoking his previously promulged law to all creation. Then, I conclude, as we find the pure blood negro and the pure blood Indian still in the world, that the theory is not true.

"I have shown before that the Jews are the posterity of Abraham, by the fact that they bear on their persons the seal, *circumcision*, which God gave to Abraham and his seed as a perpetual identification of them as his seed; that, as they are white, then, by the logic of facts, their father, Abraham, was white also; and Abraham being white, his progenitor, Noah, the father of Shem, Ham and Japheth, was white also. And all agree that Japheth was white, one of his sons; also, that Noah's wife was a white woman. The irresistible conclusion, then, from the logic of facts, places, beyond a doubt, that Ham was also white."

"Well, sister, if the fathers of these people were white, why did not Adam, Methuselah, Noah, Shem, or Abraham say so at some period of the world?"

"John, I will answer your question by asking you another, viz.:

2

If your father and mother were white, why did they not tell *you* so? For the very reason that you knew it was so, and there was no one fool enough to dispute it; and for the further reason that they thought that you had sense enough to *know* the fact when you looked upon them. But suppose, John, you had been a mulatto: then *my* father would have raised an issue with our mother, about your paternity, and a family feud between them would have been raised, resulting in a divorce, and a record of it would have been kept, in the shape of a divorce, recorded in the clerk's office, on account of the infidelity of our mother to *my* father, not your father, as he would not then have been. But seeing we were both white children, our father was fully content with our mother and us as his offspring, and did all he could to make us happy to the day of his death.

"Now do you think it too heavy a draft on the imagination to suppose that human .nature was exactly the same *then*, in the days of Noah, as it was in the days of our parents? And that Noah loved his wife with the same tenderness and ardency that our father loved his? And that he was equally as jealous of her love and fidelity to him as our father was of our mother to him? If this be the case, and all history attests the truth of the same, do you not think that when old Mrs. Noah gave birth to her sons (and there is nothing in the Scripture to show that they were not all born at the same birth), that when the old gentleman saw that one of them was black, and one red, and one white, that he would not have raised a family disturbance that would have made things so warm around old Mrs. Noah's bed that she would have quit that place in a hurry, taking two of the children and leaving the white one to old man Noah. I tell you, John, that had such been the case, old Mr. Noah would have made things so warm, and raised such a row just about that time in his family, and created such a disturbance, that all the neighbors, for miles around, would have gone there to see and hear what was the matter. Why, John, they would have had to send for a constable and had him arrested and bound over to keep the peace; and a record of the whole matter would have been kept to be handed down to all future generations. It would have been made a record of also in the family chronology, that would have been handed down through all time to come. As a general rule, John, where a man loves his wife, which most men do, they are very indulgent to them, and in many instances indulge them too far, on account of their pure, true love for them. But, John, though I have seen a great many exceedingly kind and indulgent husbands, so much so that it has sometimes made me wish I had one myself, still, I never saw one who was not highly pleased, no matter how much he loved his wife, and how true and how faithful he believed his wife to be to him, but what was not better pleased and satisfied when his wife bore an issue to him, and his neighbor women came to see her and the baby, to hear them say, 'Oh, dear me! what a pretty little thing, why, it looks *just like its daddy!*' I say, John, with all the stoic philosophy that some men have, and as much as they may become immersed in business, or abstract philosophical subjects, there is one thing they all like, and that is, that every child their wives have should resemble them in *some particular*. But when she gets to having black-skinned, thick-lipped, flat-nosed, woolly-headed children, and pure Indian children, and then expect to pacify him with the cool, indifferent assertion that they just came *nat'ally*, like the old woman's did, who kept having children for ten years after her husband died. She said '*they just came nat-'ally*.' This 'nat'ally' way of. having black children and Indian children, as is said old Mrs. Noah did, and then laying them to the father of the *white* child, wouldn't half begin to '*pass muster*' with the men or women *either* of this day. And, John, judging from what the Bible says of old Mr. Noah, he is one of the few men that I would not set down as a fool. Any man that could see one hundred and twenty years ahead, that a big rain was coming that would drown the whole world, or even could. believe such a thing when told it by God that long beforehand, and had sense enough to go to work and build a house of that peculiar structure that it would stand a current of a flood running any way it chose, and large enough to hold all his family, and his property, and invest every dollar he had in it, and work on it for one hundred and twenty years for that purpose, had too much sense to have the 'wool drawn over his eyes' so much as to believe the 'cock and bull' story of his wife having a coal-black negro child and a pure Indian child, and that he was the father of them. Why, John, I am a woman and have heard the *old women* talk; and judging from what they say, I would reverse the story of Jonah and the whale, and sooner believe that he swallowed the whale than to believe this startling, wonderful, prodigious story of old Mrs. Noah having, at one birth, a white, red, and black child, all of different anatomical structures and different natures and different instincts; and then what would be worse than all, to believe that they were all the children of old Mr. Noah. 'Can a fountain send forth sweet water and bitter?' 'Can a man take coals of fire into his bosom and not get burned?' says the Scripture. I tell you, John, had such a thing been the case, old man Noah would have called on the old lady to *make a showing* how this thing was done. Why, John, such an astounding fact, had it been true, would have been a miracle of such gravity and magnitude in its character and nature that a cohort of angels would have been sent from the court of heaven to Noah to explain that this was one of the Almighty's wonderful displays of his power, the sequel of which was to bring into the world two colors and races of beings which he had never before created. When Joseph found his betrothed wife to be with child with the Savior of the world, he was sadly distressed about it, and determined to 'put her away' because of *supposed* infidelity to him, and a violation of the Mosaic law; and he would have done so had not the Almighty sent an angel to him to convince him, by incontestable proof, that it was the wondrous work of God to bring into existence the Redeemer of the world. And so determined was our Heavenly Father that the history of this matter should be known as his work and his miracle, and the honor and virtue and integrity of purpose of Mary to her sex, to Joseph, and the divine written revealed law vindicated, that he dispatched a messenger from his own throne, clothed with power to convince and satisfy Joseph, and cause him to take back his wife whom he was about to divorce.

"And further, he had a record kept of the full and complete history of the whole matter, from its earliest incipiency to the present day, attesting the truth of this wonderful miracle of his, in contrast with his established law of procreation. God never leaves himself without witness—never leaves a cardinal fact of his truth unsupported by that character of proof that will attest its truth as his work. He never leaves his truth to the fine-spun theories of the imaginations of designing men; but in all ages has established his universal laws and proclaimed them by revelation; and whenever he suspended one of them (not violated one of them), he has always been so kind and good as to make full and ample explanation to his creatures for the same. This was the case when the *hairy* child was born to Isaac; this was the case when Shadrach, Meshach and Abednego were cast into the fiery furnace. They were miracles for a specific purpose which he declared; for the information and satisfaction of those concerned. And this has been the case with every miracle which God has performed by suspending his natural revealed or divine law.

"Now is it doing his Majesty due honor, not to say justice, to charge that he would thus virtually suspend his universal law or decree— 'bring forth after thy kind,' and perform such a wonderful miracle as the one alleged to have been performed in Noah's family is, if true, and not having given satisfactory reasons for it. He has never before left the solution of a miracle to the future reasoning of men, but has always attested it with the facts that it was his, and told the object and the design. When he placed the rainbow in the heavens, he told why he did it. He said that it should be an everlasting covenant between him and Noah, that, while time endured, there should be 'seed time and harvest,' and 'that the earth should no more be drowned with a flood.' And every once in a while he makes known to Noah's posterity that he has not forgotten his promise to their father, by suspending his bow in the heavens.

The one now in question, of the birth of these three boys, is second in magnitude and importance as far as the interests of the white race are concerned, only to the miraculous birth and history of the Savior, provided it is true, and is the work of God. And proof, equally cogent, is requisite to vindicate him in the violation of his own law, 'bring forth after thy kind,' if he did violate or suspend it. For if these three sons were of the same parentage, and of the three colors ascribed to them, it is in direct violation of God's universal law, and a miracle, which none other but God could perform. Now I conclude, as there is no record of the fact in the history as given by Moses, and no explanation of it by Deity, no attestation of it by angels, no family disaffection between Mr. and Mrs. Noah, there is a more rational, sensible, and natural solution of the origin of the races of Indians and negroes. But if the commonly-received theory, that Shem, Ham, and Japheth, being red, black, and white, and that they are the ancestors of the three different colors, be true, then you can see that it defeats the plain declaration of Moses, when he says, in his account of the creation before the flood, 'God finished his work on the sixth day,' which he did not do if he did not make the red and black men before the flood. You see their argument is not sustained by the facts; for their theory makes Ham the head of the negroes, Shem of the Indians; thus showing that God did not complete his work when he said he did, but did it after the flood. It is laid down in Hedge's Logic that when an argument proves *too much*, it is evidence of its unsoundness; or rather, it shows it is unsound. Their argument proves *too much*. But this only shows to what extremes men will go to propagate a false theory, if it conflicts with their pecuniary, political, or ecclesiastical interest to contend for the true one.

"But, John, there is another important thing to be considered by the advocates of the theory that these three boys are the progenitors of the three races, which I wish to bring up for your future consideration, and in order to do so without confusion, I will, for the present, speak of it as relates to Ham and his reputed posterity, the negro. Suppose, for the sake of argument, that I admit that Ham was a black man, it would not necessarily follow that he was the father of the negro race. He *might* have been *black*, and still have retained the form, stature, features, hair, lips, nose, and head of his father. Nature does sometimes take a freak, and produce a prodigy or deformity, the result of external or accidental causes, as was the case when the hairy child Esau was born to Isaac; but then it does not follow, as a conclusion, founded either in fact, or supported by experience, that the posterity of such persons suffered from such disability: on the contrary, their issue, or children, have always maintained the original status of the original progenitors.

"Now in order to sustain the assumption (for it is only an assumption) that Ham was the progenitor of the negro, the advocates of it must not only show that Ham was black, but they must also show that he was of a different anatomical structure to that of Japheth, and had wool on his head instead of hair, had thick lips, flat nose, and flat head, all of which are the distinguishing marks of difference between the white man and the negro. They must also show that the freak of nature (for it was only a freak of nature if it existed at all) that caused Ham to be black, also incorporated in his physical nature, or endowed it (whichever you may please to term it) with the power of transmitting and stamping upon his progeny the same characteristic differences which distinguish them from the white man; and that, too, *without a wife possessing* the same characteristic differences to distinguish her from the white race, and that the negroes now maintain, and have maintained, since they were first known in natural and political history.

"Now I will admit, John, that Ham could have transmitted these unmistakable marks of difference to his posterity, provided he himself first possessed them, and then that his wife also possessed them in a like degree; but to claim that *he did, being a black man himself*, having a low, flat head, and an anatomical structure as different from the white man as the negro is from that of the monkey, and having wool instead of hair on his head, and with a white wife, (which he was obliged to have according to their theory, that there were no other men on the earth after the flood, but Noah's family), I say, to claim that under these circumstances *he did* transmit all of these peculiar characteristics in the negro which so strongly mark them from the white man, requires a Divine revelation as clear and as strong as that attesting the truth of the miraculous conception and birth of the Savior of the world, to sustain it.

"It is a miracle, if true, which sets aside all of God's universally established laws of 'like begetting like,' or that positive command to 'bring forth after thy kind,' or that 'the parent should look like the offspring,' all of which he has held as sacred as any other law, and in fact, (I believe, more so), that he has ever yet revealed or promulged to His creatures, and the sanctity of which he has always preserved by its strict fulfillment, except for special purposes, in order the more clearly to reveal his power to man and to establish his truth. And then he has always been so kind as to show to his creatures why he had done so, never leaving to them to infer that he did thus and so; but, being God, 'able to create and to destroy,' he has always wisely told his creatures that he had set aside or suspended his *own laws*, because he had the right to do so, when it become necessary to reveal his power to man and make it known. When he conceived the design of making a woman to be the wife of Adam, he did not leave it to conjecture how the woman came on earth; but he told it to Adam, that he had put him to sleep (in other words, mesmerised him), and whilst in that condition had taken a rib from his side and made a wife for him. This was like a kind, good and beneficent creator would do, and not leave Adam to infer that his wife came up out of the ground, like a mushroom, or dropped down from the heavens, but inspired him with the knowledge of the facts, so that he exultingly exclaims, 'She is bone of my bone and flesh of my flesh.' But when, after the counsel of his own will, he determined to stock the earth with two other different colors of men (if their theories be true), he performed a miracle, which for grandeur, and the magnitude of its consequences, on the original color, the creation of the woman sinks into perfect insignificance before it, and never says one word about it. The Scripture says: 'God does not leave himself without a witness;' but I ask, where is 'the witness' to this miraculous introduction of two more distinct colors and races and nations of men to people the earth and to divide the same with the original creation, if their theory is true? Nothing could be a competent witness, to attest this as the work of God, and that it was true, but a confirmation of it by a messenger sent directly from the court of heaven, clothed with power to prove beyond all possibility of any doubt, that it was the direct interposition of God for a specific purpose, and a declaration of that interposition so clear that even the children could understand it. No other testimony can possibly sustain it. And that declaration would then have to have been placed upon record and handed down with the balance of the record of Adam's race, so that all his children would have known it. And had it been true, the goodness and the wisdom of our creator would have caused him to have it made known to his creatures that he had done this, in

68

order to produce other colors of men on the earth which had not existed before; and a record of it would have been kept in the chronology of Noah's family, and handed down through all time.

"But, on the contrary, there is not one word said on the subject more than on any other family afterwards, except that old Mr. Noah got drunk, and on account of some impropriety of Ham, as a respectful child, he, Noah, pronounced a curse on Ham's child, Canaan. That curse did not necessarily attach to his *natural* color, but to his condition, saying, 'A servant of servants he, Canaan, should be to his brethren.' Now, even this curse, and its fulfillment to the very letter, much less to the spirit, does not prove that Ham, the father of Canaan, was a negro, or even black. Nor does it even show that Canaan was black, or even a negro. It only proves that a change in Canaan's condition, relative to his liberty or his freedom, was to be the consequence. And as far as all practical purposes are concerned, Canaan and his posterity could better have filled the condition of servants, as intelligent white men, and fulfilled the stern decree of Ham's father, than they could as negroes."

"Well, sister, it is now nearly twelve o'clock, and time to retire. But before we part for the night, let me say to you that I have listened to you with intense interest, and I now feel so completely taken up with the subject that I shall be very anxious for the next Thursday night to come. Then I wish you to pursue the subject, and I promise you I will not interrupt you with questions until you have gotten through. So good-night, Sister Sallie."

THURSDAY NIGHT.

"Good evening, John. I am glad to see you. You have had a week to consider on my views, as given you in good faith. Do you desire to hear me further, or would you prefer to let our conversations stop?"

"O! my dear sister, I would not now have them come to an end for any earthly consideration. I have listened to you with an interest which I have never before felt in any subject. Your argument is very searching in its character, and to my mind, very conclusive; and whilst if I were to admit it true, other questions would arise more perplexing in their nature than the ones you have discussed with so much earnestness and zeal, and with such force, that I am obliged to admit that my faith in my preconceived opinions, based upon the ecclesiastical teachings of the day, are very much shaken."

"John, what are the other questions that would arise in your mind to trouble you, provided you gave your assent to the truth of what I have said?"

"Sister, the first difficulty that presents itself, if your argument is true, is, what, then, is the origin of the negro?"

"I saw that sooner or later, John, you would be compelled to ask that question, for if my argument given you heretofore has truth or force in it, it naturally forces you to ask that question. I will now attempt to answer it as well as it can be answered by the Scriptures and the logic of facts, which are the only sure and safe guides leading to the correct solution of this vexed question. And to begin my answer to it, I will call your attention to one position I took in our early conversations on this subject. In one of them I asserted (and dwelt on it to some extent) that when God said, 'Let us make man in our own image and our own likeness,' it *implied* that he had made man previously, *that was not in his own image and likeness*. That there was another man, or other men, made before Adam, is as clear from the same history that gives the account of Adam's creation, as it is clear that there was a land of Nod, to which Cain went and knew his wife, in other words, took his wife, for that is the true and correct meaning of the text. The very bare mention of the fact that *Cain went to the land of Nod* 'and knew his wife,' mentioned in the incidental manner that it is, is a very strong proof that it was a well known fact taught to Adam's posterity down to Moses, who made the record that such a country existed, even in Adam's day. Again, it being mentioned as *the land of Nod*, shows very clearly that it was peopled. If not, how did it acquire its name *Nod?* There is no record that Adam gave it to it. It was certainly coeval with him, if not anterior. Cain did not give it to it, for he went there, because it was a country by that name. Abel was dead. He could not have given it the name. It is not revealed that God gave it the name of Nod. Then who did? And why call it Nod? I answer, it was not called Nod simply because there was territory there; for with no other people on the earth but Adam and Eve, there was no need of a division of the earth into States, or territories, or lands, by name. For if this had been the case, there would have been no use of districting the earth into lands by distinctive names.

"I will ask why was there a necessity for God 'planting the Garden of Eden' for Adam, and giving it its boundaries, if there was no other person on the earth but him? This garden was bounded by four rivers, the first of which was Pison, which compasseth the whole land of Havilah, where there is gold; the second is Gihon; it compasseth the whole land of Ethiopia; the third is Hiddikel, which goes down to the east of Assyria; and the fourth is the Euphrates. Now here is a country given to Adam, on which no one had the right to trespass. Now why do this? Why fix boundaries to a district of country for certain individuals, if there were not other persons on the earth? Why give it a name, if it was not to distinguish it from the district of country already in the possession of some one else? I say, why not say at once: 'I put you here on the earth; there are none your right to dispute; it is all yours; take peaceable possession of it and hold it?' Why say unto Adam, in Genesis i, 28, 'replenish the earth and *subdue* it?' If there were none to dispute Adam's title to the earth, the word *subdue* is a meaningless term. If it were not in the possession of some one else whom the Creator was not willing

70

should hold it, why say *subdue* it? If the Lord had only meant to use it for the practical purposes of husbandry or farming, he would have said 'and *cultivate*' it; but when he said *subdue* it, it clearly conveys the idea that a portion of it, at least, was in the possession of some persons other than Adam's family, and he would, perhaps, have his right disputed. Those persons, I assert, were the Nodites, who held the possession of that territory which they had denominated 'Nod.' Now why they called it Nod, I am unable to say, but will give you my opinion, based on the characteristic peculiarities of the negro and the Indian, as developed among us, and I presume their natural character among us is the same as it was before Adam was created, if you will make a due allowance for the force of example and teaching they have had by associations with the white man. I hold, and will attempt to show, before I get through, that the Indian and the negro were both made before the white man Adam. They were man, or men, not in God's image. I mention this rather prematurely, but will attempt to show the truth of it before I get through our conversations on this subject. Then the Indian and the negro had possession of the entire country. The Indian was inclined to make his living altogether by hunting and fishing, and was always on the move. The negro was naturally lazy and inclined to lie about home, work a little potato patch, and, perhaps, a corn patch and pindar patch, and was very much inclined to be sleepy-headed, which peculiarity attaches to him to this day. Every body knows, who knows anything about the true character of the full-blood negro, that no matter under what circumstances he sits down in the sunshine, and is uninterrupted for but a few moments, he will get to *nodding*; and even in private conversation with him at night, if he once gets still, the next thing is to get to *nodding*. The Indian, who draws all his illustrations from nature, and names every thing from some peculiarity which is natural in its character, saw in the negro this peculiarity of everlasting *nodding*, and, whenever he passed the negro's house or shanty, found him sitting down in the sun, asleep or *nodding*, gave the district of country which, by common consent between him and the negro, he had settled in, the name of the Land of Nod. I then think the Indian gave the country the name by way of derision and contempt, as it so fully exemplified or illustrated the true character of the pure blood negro.

"You can take this explanation for just what it is worth; and whilst I freely admit there is no Bible precept for it, it is so characteristic, both of the habit of the negro to *nod* when he sits down and gets still, and so characteristic of the Indian to name every thing from some leading, prominent trait in its character, that I cannot but conclude that, taking nature as the guide, this is the best solution and answer to the question: 'Why is it called *the land of Nod?*' This, then, I assert, is the name that Adam found the country in which the negroes were colonized when he was created. And as he did not care to change it, as he found it so very suitable, and characteristic of the negro, he let it pass by that name. The bare fact, then, of that country having the name of Nod, when Cain went there after he had killed Abel, is conclusive evidence that it was peopled by some one, is as clear and clearer than the fact that America was peopled when first discovered by us.

"What name the aborigines had given America no one knows; but because it was given the name of America by us, does not prove that it was not inhabited when discovered; and even suppose that the Adamic family gave it the name of Nod: that does not prove it was not peopled or inhabited when discovered, but rather goes to prove the fact that it was. Else, why speak of it at all as a land or country?"

"Sister, this looks somewhat feasible; but then if it were true, who were the Nodites?"

"John, I gave you an inkling of my opinion on this subject about a half hour ago, when trying to account for this land having the name of Nod. I will now say, in that connection, that they were the children of men, or man, whom God did not make in his *own image* and own *likeness*, and as I have shown that Shem was not the father of the Indians, nor Ham the father of the negroes, and as all the world admit that Japheth is the father of the white man, I conclude that they were either the negro or the Indian."

"But, sister, Shem, Ham, and Japheth lived after the flood, and the Nodites in the early part of God's creation of the earth. Now why do you attempt to explain a thing which existed before the flood by a thing that transpired afterward, fully fifteen hundred years?"

"I am glad you raised that question, John. It is a legitimate one, and comes within the purview of the subject. In answer, then, I will say, first, that the whole civilized world receive the Mosaic account of the creation as true, and also his account of the destruction of the world by the flood, leaving only Noah's family, of eight persons, as saved from the general wreck. Now as we find the negro and the Indian in existence, and as I have shown they are not of the offspring of Noah's family, it follows that they were either created after the flood, or existed under the distinctive name of beasts, cattle, or serpents, or some of the animals created by God, and were imported by Noah in the ark, out of the old world into the new. That they are not of Noah's family I think I have clearly shown, and if not of his family, they are of necessity a part of God's original creation, and introduced on this side of the flood exactly like the horse and other animals, under the name of either clean or unclean beasts.

"I will now revert to the first five days' work of the Creator, and retrospect the history for a moment; but to prevent being tedious, will begin with the fifth day's work. The writer says, in Genesis, i, 25, that the beasts, cattle, and creeping things after their kind, was the work of the fifth day. This is the fifth day's work. He pronounced it 'all good.' He then retrospects his work, as it were, and after reviewing it all over, and pronouncing it 'good,' he comes to the conclusion that he has not got anything in his 'own image and own likeness.' He has not made himself the pattern by which to make anything that he has created. That he had made man not in his own image and own likeness, is to my mind very clear; for when he says 'let us make man in our own image and likeness,' it implies that he had made him not in his image and likeness. Now the fact that I have traced the Jews, who are the chosen people of God, back through Abraham, Noah, Methuselah, back to Adam, whom the Bible calls the son of God, and shown also, by the universal law of nature, that like begets like, and by the further revealed law of God, 'bring forth after thy kind,' that as the Jews are white, which is attested all the world over by ocular demonstration, then it follows that they are the product of white ancestors, who brought forth after their kind. And as Adam was the son of God, Luke, iii, 38, and was in the image and likeness of God, then, by the logic of facts, the Creator, God, was also white. The inspired writer, Luke, asserts that Adam was the son of God. And Moses says he was made in the likeness and image of God, and that his wife was made out of a rib taken from himself. She was then the same color of Adam. They were commanded to bring forth after their kind ; and by tracing their posterity down to the Jews, and finding the Jews all white people, I conclude that Adam and Eve were both white persons, or that positive injunction, 'bring forth after thy kind' has proved a failure. And as we find the Indians and the negroes on the earth, and not in color, either in skin, or bone, or flesh, of the same of the Jews, with hair differing from each other, and both differ- ing from the hair of the Jews, and differing from each other in their physical structure, and each differing from the Jew in their physical structure ; and as I have traced the Jews' color back to Adam, and shown that Adam was the son of God, exactly in his likeness and image, and find the Indian and the negro both differing from Adam's posterity, the Jews, in all the essential characteristics of their nature, I conclude that they are not in the image or likeness of God, because they differ in so many characteristic essentials from the posterity of his son, Adam, whom he made in his own image and likeness. They are then an original creation, separate and distinct from the white man, and were in existence before the creation of the white man, Adam, and were the people who were on the earth before Adam, and one or the other of them had peopled the land of Nod. And I now assert that it was the negro, and not the Indian, who dwelt in the land of Nod, and at the proper time and place, in the course of our conversations, I will attempt to prove it.

"If, then, what I have said be true, which, according to analogy, the logic of facts, and the universally-established law of nature of 'like begetting like,' and the Divine command, 'bring forth after thy kind,' and the further declaration that the 'parent should look like the offspring,' is so, then they were the work of the fifth day's creation, and are classed among the cattle, creeping things, and *beasts;* and though they were called *man,* still they were classed among the *beasts,* because they were of the fifth day's work, and not in God's image.

The prophet Jeremiah says of the Jews, in xxxii, 35, when speak- ing of the departure of the Jewish people from the true Levitical worship as given by Moses, and of erecting idols as objects of worship, thus . . 'to cause their sons and their daughters to pass through the fire unto Moloch, which I commanded them not; *neither came it into my mind* that they should do *this abomination*, to cause Judah to sin.' Now, John, I think he is equally as much astonished and surprised to find that the ecclesiastical teachers, and the politicians of a certain school, and the rulers in authority, have raised the negro IDOL, and worship it instead of him.

"This is another thing that I do not believe *ever came into his mind* that white men would do. After seeing his dealings with the amalgamationists before the flood, and the Canaanitish amalgamationists after the flood, and know his revealed and positive law that they should 'bring forth after their kind,' it never *entered into his mind* that the so-called '*called and sent*' ministers of the gospel would profane the sacred desk, and slander his holy name with the gross, base falsehood, that he would make a law, and *command* all animated nature to strictly observe it, 'bring forth after thy kind,' and then be the first to put it aside by the most flagrant violation of which the mind of man can conceive, and assign no cause or reason for it.

"An earthly king, or ruler, who would do such a thing, would call down upon his head the unmitigated contempt and hatred of every subject in his realm. None would ever look upon him in any other light than an unprincipled tyrant, who could not be trusted when his own personal interest was involved. With the facts before me, John, I fearlessly assert that it never *came into the mind* of the Creator of the heavens and the earth that any one, having 'his image and his likeness,' would commit so foul a slander against his holiness as to say that he had been the author of the three races of man, in the way the politico-ecclesiastico-would-be-divines teach.

"No, John, such a thing never *entered into the mind of God* until the outrage was committed. I say this, with all the profound reverence for my maker that a poor orphan girl who has prayed and knelt and wept at his altar, with all the faith of the human heart, and whose faith in him is as lasting as life, and as strong as death. But, John, I will not weary you further on this point, for I am confident that its absurdity is too palpable for you not to see it."

"Sister, you have made out a very strong case, indeed; and I shall bear your views in mind, and when I return home will examine them very critically by the light of the Bible. In this connection I wish to ask you one question, and must ask your patient forbearance for taxing your native modesty so far as it necessarily will be involved in order to give an intelligent answer. The question is this: If your argument in the case of Ham's color, based upon the established law of nature, 'of like begetting like,' and the further revealed law of 'bring forth after thy kind' be true, then how do you account for the *complexity* of color in the inferior animals, as the horse, the cow, the dog, etc.? You know that it is nothing at all uncommon for a cow to have a black calf at one time, a spotted one at another, and a red one at another, and perhaps a white one at another—and the same male be the sire of them all. Now, how do you account for this, if the law of 'like begetting like' be true?"

"John, as you have said that I must pardon you for your question and its nature, I hope you will not look upon me as compromising either my sex or my respect, for its native modesty and purity and its delicate rights, when I attempt to answer you. And as it may require some very plainness of speech and some very masculine language to answer correctly and intelligently, you will do me the justice to know that while I am indulging in it, for the purpose of a truthful and honest answer, that I am not insensible to the mortification and embarrassment to which it subjects the discreet of my sex.

"In the first place then, John, your question is not a parallel one with the facts involved in the case of Ham and his reputed progeny, the negro, as assumed by the advocates of the theory that he is the father or progenitor of the negroes. In the case of the negroes, if Ham is their father, it not only changes their color but changes the nature and covering of their head, placing upon it a thorough coat of *stuff*, neither hair nor wool, changes the structure of their head, both in shape and thickness of the skull, from that of the white man; changes the shape and color of every bone in their body from that of the white man; changes the character of the blood, as chemical analysis has shown; changes the conformation of the nose, leaving it without any bone in it, and instead of being high, or Roman, or aquiline, or pointed as the white man's, is universally flat, blunt, and without any bone in it, but only a cartilage. I have just this morning met with an article from an unknown writer, published in the *Vicksburger* of October 29, 1874 (in which the writer contrasts the negro with the white man), with which I am so much pleased that you must pardon me for reading to you a short extract, because it is so strictly true, and so exactly establishes the point I have made. The writer says: . . . 'His head is so poised obliquely on the vertical column that when he stoops down his brain remains upright and occupies the extreme hight of his figure—a trait of all the lower animals. Then the forearm of the negro is longer than that of the white man, and his lifting muscle passing down under the elbow joint, is much stronger; his knees approach each other, and his feet turn outwards; the muscles of the calf are differently formed from those of the whites, the large part of the great muscle called the gastronemie being situated high up near the hams at the back of the leg. The feet are flat, the bone of the heel is not arched, but is level with the bones of the instep, so that *the hollow of the foot makes a hole in the ground*. The skin contains colored or pigmentary cells not found in the white man's, and supposed to absorb and emit by perspiration a large amount of heat, which would otherwise affect the more vital and more delicate parts of the body.' . . . These distinguishing marks of difference in the person of the negro are so universally uniform, and stamped so indelibly upon him, that they attach with unerring certainty and severity to the posterity of the pure-blood negro, as the form, color, shape, hair and habits of the bear is transmitted to its young. Now it would not be any less a miracle for the same male and female black bear to produce a red and white young, as it was (if true) for Mr. and Mrs. Noah, both being white, to produce in their natural offspring red and black children. But I will argue this more fully in answering directly your question as to the mixed colored cattle, etc.

"Now, that the cattle have kine of many colors, and particularly ringed, streaked and speckled, is true; but it was considered a matter of so much importance that it should be known how it was done, that Deity caused a record to be made of the fact. The historian says that Jacob had been defrauded by his father-in-law, Laban, out of his wife, for which he had served faithfully. And making another contract with the old gentleman, to serve seven other years for his daughter whom he had first wanted, made an agreement with him to do so as stock-minder and shepherd, upon condition that he would give him, as compensation, all the ringed, streaked and speckled cattle that might be raised. To this contract the old gentleman readily consented, no doubt believing that he was driving a good bargain. The legitimate inference is, judging from the readiness with which the old man Laban accepted the proposition, that there had never been but few, *if any*, of that kind of cattle calved to his knowledge, and when such was the case (if ever), it was looked upon as a freak of nature which ceased with that individual case—as it did with the hairy child, Esau.

"Now why Jacob made the proposition, I am unable to say. Whether it was from the results of observation, or whether the results of inspiration, or whether a little of both, I am unable to tell; but one thing is certain: that he felt very well assured that he could and would get the best of the trade. Now how did he manage to cause 'ring-streaked and speckled' cattle to be calved? The historian says he placed at the water troughs and watering places, when the cattle went to drink, sticks and poles, peeled, and painted like barbers' poles, and some in rings, and some spotted, and all of them stuck up all around the troughs; also he had the troughs painted in variegated colors. And knowing from constant watching of his flocks and herds, that when they came to drink was the time they gendered with each other, he had either learned by experience and observation, or by inspiration, that these things, from their novelty, would attract the attention of the cattle, and their colors would, from the force of the imagination or memory (so to speak), be transferred to the natural increase then in embryo or that might be conceived at such times and places in presence of these streaked, spotted and ringed poles. But it does not appear that this departure from the original color affected the structure or conformation or habits of the spotted cattle, so as to make them in any respect different from the solid colored cattle; but only affected their colors, and that they retained intact the shape, form, structure, blood, and instincts of the solid cattle, thus showing that whilst the issue of the solid color was changed to striped, the result of the external or accidental causes, still it did not originate a different race of cattle. Now in order for it to be a parallel case with that of the negro (if true, as before stated by those claiming that Ham is the father of the negro,) it would not only have to show that a different color was produced by these accidental or external circumstances or causes, but also that a complete change in the structure, form, habits and blood of the many colored cattle had been transferred to them and stamped upon them so different from the solid colored cattle that, through all time, the calves of spotted cattle had been, from that day to this, spotted calves or ringed, streaked or speckled. But the facts of the case do not show this to be the case; for it is not an uncommon thing for the spotted male and female to reproduce a solid colored calf, thus showing that there is an instinctive principle in nature to maintain its original status as to color, and when not interrupted by accidental or external circumstances or causes it will always do so.

" But the pure negro has, from the earliest of his history, produced and reproduced his distinctive color, with its distinctive form, organization, features, structure, blood, nose, hair and habits of character, never in a solitary instance reproducing an original white-colored child as the issue of a male and female pure blood negro.

" Now, the conclusion that I come to from this contrast and argument is, that the negro is an *original* creation, and has never produced an issue unlike itself from the pure blood male and female negro, and that your case is not a parallel one, because Deity has left us a record that we do know how the ringed, streaked and speckled cattle were produced by the solid colored, being the result of accidental or external circumstances, and we know also the reason why it was done, viz., that it was the revenge of Jacob on his father-in-law for swindling him out of his wife; whilst, if the story of Mrs. Noah having red, black and white-colored children, which children possessed in their persons the faculty and power of tranferring to their posterity peculiar characteristics which stamped them a different people from the original color of their parents, and then left it to conjecture to determine so important a fact (if it be a fact), is a proposition too absurd in its nature to gain credence from any but the superstitious or the credulous.

" Why, John, to believe that an all-wise and good God would take more pains and care to solve a minor mystery by causing a record of it to be kept and handed down through all time, for the benefit of mankind, showing how and why a departure from his natural law was permitted with the inferior animals, as in the case of the ringed, streaked and spotted cattle, and pass by, in perfect indifference and profound silence, a miracle of the magnitude and importance, and of such vital interest to the entire world, as the one claimed to be performed in the birth of Shem, Ham and Japheth, is, if true, to say the least of it, to charge him with base carelessness and neglect of the good of his creatures, made in his own image and likeness, and contradicts that cardinal rule of action ascribed to him in Holy Writ, 1st Corinthians, xiv, 33, ' God is not the author of confusion, *but of peace,*' and that other precept, Acts xiv, 17, ' He does not leave himself without witness,' which he has done if the story of the birth of these three boys be true. I ask, where is the witness that attests it ? Not even a record of the fact, only that old Mrs. Noah had three sons, perhaps at one birth, which any other woman might and have done often. Not one word about their color being at all different from Mr. and Mrs. Noah.

" Why, John, if Moses would make a record of a departure from the natural law of a matter that interested only Jacob and his father-in-law, showing the shrewdness of the young man in cheating the old

man out of his cattle because he swindled him out of his betrothed
wife, and seven years' work also, do you think—are you stupid enough
to believe that if old Mr. and Mrs. Noah did have, at one birth, three
boy children, one red, one black and one white, that he would not
have made a record of the fact? John, old women have had one
peculiarity since the earliest history of women, and that has been, they
would go to see another woman when she had a child, and always
must *see the baby*, and say ' it looks just like its daddy.' Now don't
you know, John, that with that custom prevailing with women, and
with their natural curiosity, which has so justly been ascribed to my
sex, from mother Eve down to this day—I say don't you know that
when it was noised abroad that Mrs. Noah had a red, white, and black
child, that every old woman that could have gone to see the children
would have done so? They would have said, ' *I won't believe it till I
see it.* I *must* see them children. I want to see who they look like.
I want to see if they look like old neighbor *Noah.*' For you know
what a tenacity women have for the child to look like its *daddy.* And
after the flood, the children and grandchildren, and even great-grand-
children, of Shem, Ham and Japheth would have gone to old Mr.
Noah and his wife, their grandfather and mother, in particular, and
have them tell them the story of the diversity of colors. The children of Ham would have gone more particularly than any of the rest,
for if human nature was the same then that it is now, and there is no
reason to suppose that it was not, the white children of Japheth would
have taunted the children of Ham with their woolly heads, low fore-
heads, thick lips, flat noses and black skins, so as to have kept up a
perpetual feud among the families. Pride of character, a decent
respect for themselves, and a mortified and insulted pride, would have
impelled the children of Ham to have called on him for an explanation of the fact, how this wonderful difference in color and characteristics came to exist between him and his brother Japheth. If, then,
I say, the story of their birth had been true, Ham would have told that
he and his brothers Japheth and Shem all had the same father and
mother. But God, in his wisdom, wishing to bring into existence two
other colors of people, caused *them* to be of their respective colors,
with their respective physical organizations to that degree that they
naturally transferred their color and all their peculiar characteristic
differences to their posterity, and that it would continue so through all
time as long as they kept up the pure blood. This history would have
been so marvellous in its nature and character that it would never
have been forgotten by the direct children of Ham, Japheth and Shem;
and with the negro and Indian children and grandchildren of Ham
and Shem continually mixing socially with the posterity of Japheth,
it necessarily would have given rise to a continued explanation of the
facts to every succeeding generation of children down to Moses, who,
when he sat down to write the history of the origin of man, would
have found this fact one of the most important and essential points
in the history, and would have omitted any other truth or fact before
he would this. For he would have said his record that he was making was God's *witness* of himself, and as his *amanuensis* he must make

a true one, as it was being made for the benefit of mankind through all time to come. But the absence of such a record, even by implication, much less by fact, proves very conclusively to my mind that the story is not true.

"Again, John : Natural history, experience and facts all agree in one thing as regards the ' crossing of breeds' (as it is termed) of stock by farmers for the purpose of improving them. Experience has taught them that they may breed a black mare to a gray sire and the colt be a black in color, but in form it will partake either of the father or mother, but retaining all the instinctive attributes of the dam or sire. Take that colt and breed it on another dam of the color of either its dam or sire, and the colt produced is just as likely to be the color of the grand-sire or grand-dam as it is to be of mixed color, still retaining all the instinctive attributes of the horse and its peculiar form and structure, thus showing that there is a tenacity in the *law* of nature to preserve the original color; but never in the whole history of animated nature has the horse been the sire of a mule, with a mare for its dam, but could only be so by having a jennet as the dam.

"This I introduce to show that whilst animals may be of different colors, as long as they are of the same blood, form and race, their issue will occasionally attest the fact of race being the same by being of the original color of sire or dam. But through all time, neither history, experience or facts will show one solitary instance where the progeny of the white man by a negro ever failed to be a mulatto. And further, where a man and his wife, both being white, ever gave being to a mulatto or black negro, except in Noah's family, if true. The same may be said of the other color.

"Now, the argument I draw from these facts is this, that if the negro was of the Adamic family, but by some freak of nature or accidental or external cause or circumstance, his color was changed, the tenacity of the law of nature for its original state or color would at some period of its existence vindicate itself and its honor by reproducing, from this departure, an issue of the same original color, form and characteristics of the original ancestor. But such has never been the case with the negro, but its posterity has ever been a pure negro, possessing all of its physical peculiarities, color and habits, and ever will be."

"Well, sister, I have listened to you with a great deal of interest, and I do assure you that you have shaken my faith very much in the doctrine of Adam and Eve being the progenitors of the Indian and the negro. And as the negro has become so much the ward of the Government, I feel more deeply interested in the subject now than ever before. If, then, he is not of the posterity of Adam, what place in natural history or animated nature do you assign him ? "

"You asked me that question once before, John, but I was not then ready to answer it, because I had not fully shown, by reason, analogy and the logic of facts and Scripture, that he was not of Adam's, Noah's or Ham's race. But now, having as I think clearly shown this to be the truth, I am prepared to try to give you an intelligent answer, based upon the same tests, viz., Scripture, reason, analogy and the logic of facts.

3

"To begin, then, I will have to go back to the beginning of the account of the creation, as given by Moses. I will begin with the fifth day's work. On it and in it God made the creeping things, cattle and beasts, if Moses is correct. On the sixth day he made man in his *own image*. And the seventh he rested. I think I have shown that the negro is not of Abraham's posterity, and if not of it, then not of Shem's, for Shem was a progenitor of Abraham and a son of Noah; and if not of Shem, then not of Ham, for Ham was the brother of Shem and a son of Noah; and if not of Noah, then not of Adam, for Noah was the literal blood descent of Adam; and if not of Adam, then not of God, for Adam is called the son of God—see Luke iii, 38. And Moses says God created him in his own *likeness* and his own *image*. All this being true, and as we find the negro on the earth, and bringing forth only in his own *likeness* and *image*, as far as the pure bloods are concerned, I assert without the fear of successful contradiction, he is a part of the fifth day's creation, and is classed a beast by God. And for the proof of this proposition I challenge any white man or woman who is anxious to prove that his or her mother and the negro's is or was the same. I respectfully state, John, that if *they* feel proud of the blood alliance, that I most cordially and sincerely say that they are perfectly welcome to the honor; but if such is the fact, then they and myself are not of the same race or family of men. They, however, who are proud of their connection are perfectly welcome to it, but I wish them to know that they are not akin to your *Sister Sallie*."

"Well, sister, why do you say he is a beast? I think you said last night, or in one of your conversations, that he was *man*, not in the image of God."

"Yes, John, I said that then and still say the same. But that don't prevent him from being a beast. A beast, and a man not in God's image, may be the same thing. In God's nomenclature of all his works, there is no design on his part of indicating indignity or disrespect for anything he had made by giving it the name he did, so long as they occupied and filled the place or sphere assigned them by him. It has only been by their attempting to depart from the sphere to which he had assigned them that has ever called forth his wrath, hatred or dislike to any portion of his creation. The cattle on a thousand hills are as much the admiration of God, as his work, as long as they fill the sphere assigned them, as man in his own image and likeness; and either, by departing from that sphere assigned them by him, becomes equally the subject of his disapprobation and punishment, in proportion as he has made them accountable to him. This being the case, then, I can see no reason why the negro should not be as proud of the classification or term 'beast,' as the man in God's image and likeness is of his, as long as the negro is content to remain in his sphere assigned him. There is not a truer precept in ethics or morals than that one which says: 'Our unhappiness arises more from our imaginary troubles than our real ones.' And had it not been for the ecclesiastical teachings, the negro would have been as well content with his generic name *beast*, and more so, than he is with his present unenviable pretenses to make himself appear as the brother of the white man. And I am certain that the Government would be looked upon by the nations of the civilized world as possessing more reverence for God Almighty's laws.

"The difference between beasts (in God's nomenclature of animals) and the *other* inferior animals is this, that the beasts can talk, use the same speech that man in God's own image can, and make himself understood, whilst the cattle and creeping things cannot. They can, by their peculiar instincts, make themselves intelligible to their particular species, but not to the beast, or to man in God's image.

"After the sixth day, when God had made Adam and Eve, and placed them in the garden of Eden, he gave them a fee-simple title to all of his creation, land and all, and told them to subdue it. He did not agree to catch the deer or tame the horse or cow for them, or clear up the land, or even subdue anything for them. He only gave them the absolute ownership to it and 'dominion over it' as it was. This was a *carte blanche* to use any means in their power to convert any and everything to their use—-the creeping things, cattle, fish, fowls, air, earth, water, and the beasts, and every vegetable, and the fruit of every tree *but one*; of this he forbade them to eat, or even touch, under the penalty of death. Now, how long Adam and his wife lived in possession of the garden of Eden, the record does not show. It may have been two hundred years, or it may have been only one diurnal period of twenty-four hours.

"Have you ever contrasted the course of an affectionate and kind father towards his first son, after he had settled him off by giving him his estate, with that of God towards our first parents, his children, after he had settled them off in the garden of Eden and given them their estate, or property?

"The natural father will visit his son and advise and counsel him, giving him the benefit of his experience in practical life; warn him against secret and open enemies; give him lessons of honesty, sobriety and economy; in a word, the full benefit of his experience; visiting him from time to time, to see how he is maintaining the dignity, honor and integrity of the family, by keeping sacred the precepts inculcated by him. The young man looks with anxiety for his parent's return visits, and enjoys the approval of his father when he comes, with pleasure and delight, as long as he keeps sacred and inviolate the precepts of his father. But no sooner does he begin to violate them than these returning visits begin to be an annoyance to him, and he loses that pleasure in his visits that he formerly enjoyed.

"Such I take to have been the course with our heavenly father towards his son Adam and his wife, after settling them off in the garden of Eden. He visited them from time to time, gave them his counsel and advice, and it was their delight to have him visit them and hear his instructions. And so long as they continued in strict obedience to them and were innocent of any violation, were always glad to see him. I know, John, there is no record of the fact that God visited them but once, but when I take into consideration the fact that an earthly or natural parent will and does manifest so much care, love and affection as they do for their children, I cannot but

81

believe that the love and affection of a supernatural parent is as much
more intense for his children as the earthly parent's is for his, as the
supernatural father is superior to the natural father. Then, I think,
it is natural to conclude that the true, pure and heavenly love and
care which God bore for his children was as much greater for them
than the earthly parent's is for his children, as God is superior or
greater than man. Then, when the historian says, 'They heard the
voice of the Lord, walking in the garden in the cool of the evening,' I
claim it was his custom to call on his children ' in the cool of the evening' and see how they were progressing with the practical pursuits of
life, and if they were converting the property he had given them to a
good or bad use, and to give them instructions in all the business affairs
of life. Nothing is more natural than such a conclusion; nothing
more God-like. And how long this had continued there is no record
to show. But there is one thing as clear as any other declaration in
the Bible; that is, that they had been there long enough to learn the
language of the serpent, whether it was one day, as we account time or
days, or a period of successive years.

"I shall not assert or contradict either position positively, as it can
only be sustained by the inference and implication contained in, and
arising out of, the nature of the graphic account of the subject given
by Moses. One thing is certain: they had been there long enough for
them and the serpent, which was a beast, to learn to speak the same
language—see Genesis iii, 1: 'Now the serpent was more subtle than
any other beast of the field that God had created,' or else they both
naturally spoke the same language. And at a certain period in their
history we find him in controversy with Eve upon a subject in which
the veracity of God was called in question by him. It was a question
of life and death to her, the question in controversy being whether if
she ate of the fruit of the forbidden tree she would or would not die,
she affirming that she would, and he taking the negative, that she
would not. To what extent this controversy was carried the sequel
must show. She brought up the most powerful argument (to her
credit be it spoken) that was in the range of human ken : 'God says
I will die if I eat it.' And one would have thought, at our day of
life, that the argument would have been sufficient to have controlled
her action and fixed her steadfast in her obedience. Although this
account of this contest is very short, giving only the plain, graphic
statement of the facts in as few words as could be, still the nature of
her opposition, appealing to the positive declaration of God that she
'*would die* if she eat it' shows that the question was warmly contested
by her. An attack was first made upon her faith and the veracity of
God, saying 'that God knew she would not die;' in other words, that
it was an imposition that God was palming off on her just for the purpose of keeping her in ignorance. Now, if she would only eat of it,
she would soon see that God was imposing on her. She still remains
faithful, does not yield. He next attacks her vanity by flattering her
with the belief that if she would eat it she would become as wise as
God and know both good and evil. She still retains her integrity to
God's order and refuses to give her consent or yield to his arguments.

It will take a practical illustration to convince her. She must see it tested by seeing it eaten. Abstract reasoning will not do her. If it is all that the serpent says it is, it is certainly very desirable. But unless she can see some one eat it and prove it to her by putting into practice what he preached, she would not believe him; for God had told her it would kill her in the day she ate it, and unless she could see some one eat it, and *see* that it did not *kill* them, she would not even *touch* it, much less eat it. The historian says, when she '*saw* it was good for food.' How did she '*see* it was good for food?' Argument or any theory could not make her *see* it. It might make her believe it, but it could not make her '*see* it was good for food' until she saw some one *eat* it. I say that in view of these facts, that whilst the historian does not say, in so many words, that the serpent did eat it, yet from the fact that he first attacked her faith, next her vanity, and lastly her appetite, and the further fact that he says 'when she *saw* it was good for food,' shows that she saw him eat it.

"He could as well have made her know that it would cause her to 'know good and evil' by reasoning with her, or made her know it would kill her by reasoning to her, as to have attempted by any process of reasoning to show to her 'that it was good for food.' And even then she must *see* that it did not kill the one that experimented with it by eating it. This done, and she was ready for a trial herself. From this view of the subject, I hold that the serpent had to eat it, and did eat it in her presence, to *show* her, and let her *see* it was good for food, and convince her that it would not kill her. Then, 'when she *saw*' this fact 'that it was good for food,' by seeing him eat it in her presence, and further, that he *did not* die, her faith in God's word. 'she would die,' was shaken. Well could she then reason thus: 'I *see* the serpent eat it, and it don't kill him, and I *see* it is good for food by his eating it. I now believe it possesses properties to make me wise; and it is so handsome, I'll just taste it to see if it is sweet.' I say that it is not at all unreasonable to draw on the imagination and say that a contest somewhat of this kind went on between them before she yielded to his duplicity. She says she was deceived by the serpent. The man was *not deceived;* see 1st Timothy ii, 14: 'Adam was not *deceived,* but the woman being deceived, was in the transgression.'

"John, I want to digress a little from the main thread of this argument and give you my reasons why Adam, knowing it was wrong to eat this fruit, not being deceived, ate it. I say, in the absence of any better reason, it was this, viz.: There was not another white woman on the earth for him to marry after Eve would die, and he saw she was bound to die and leave him alone, and not believing in the doctrine of miscegenating with the negro, or equality of races, he preferred to eat and die, and go to the grave, or anywhere else that she had to go, than to take a negro wife, which he would have had to do, or spend the balance of his days a miserable old widower, forlorn, cheerless, through all time to come. But if there had been another white woman for him to have married, my opinion is that he would have divorced Eve and got a wife that did not have quite so much curiosity. He did not belong to the Henry Ward Beecher school, neither did he believe in the doctrine of social equality or civil rights, but knew that God had drawn in him the COLOR LINE which was to rule the world, and he would forfeit his life before he would be the first to destroy it."

"Well, sister, I had never thought of that before, but really it does strike me with a great deal of force now, and I believe that God Almighty is the true author of the COLOR LINE, and Adam knew it and died for it. I do not wish to interrupt you, however, but there is one thing that has always been a mystery to me—who the serpent that deceived Eve was? Will you tell me, if you can?"

"John, I will try to identify it before I get through, at least to my satisfaction, if not to yours or anyone else's. And it was with this object in view that I have given the short synopsis of the account of the temptation and transgression of our first parents.

"The serpent was a 'beast,' and a very subtle one. Moses says, 'he was more subtle' than any 'beast' of the field 'that God had created.' He then belonged to Adam, Gen. i, 28: . . . 'And let him have dominion over every living thing that moveth on the earth.' The beasts were moving things on the earth. Then the serpent was a beast, and being a beast, Adam had *dominion* over him. He had more. He had the ownership over him, Gen. ii, 19: 'And out of the ground the Lord God formed *every beast* of the field, and every fowl of the air, and brought them to Adam to see what he would call them, and whatever name he gave them, that was their name.' He says, 'every beast of the field.' This implies there were more beasts than one. To one of them Adam gave the name of 'serpent,' to distinguish it from the other beasts, because it was more subtle than the rest. The beasts were not cattle, for in the 20th verse of the same chapter he says: 'And Adam gave names to all cattle, the fowls of the air, and to every beast of the field,' showing that the *cattle* and the *beasts* were as distinct as the cattle and the fowls of the air. Then it follows that Adam and Eve had dominion and ownership over the *serpent that deceived them.* Now, I ask, why did he deceive Eve? Was it just for his amusement? Was it just for his mischievous nature? Was it just to vex the Creator? Or was it from a design, or motive, which if carried out he thought would accrue to his benefit? There was some reason for it, some object in view, some end to accomplish, which could not be done unless Adam and Eve ate of the forbidden fruit and died.

"Suppose this is true, and it was his design that Adam and Eve should die. Then how was *he* to be benefited by it? This, to my mind, is a very grave matter, and worthy of very profound consideration, John, and I want you to allow me full time to give you my reflections on it."

"Certainly, sister, I will not interrupt you, for I do assure you I am very much interested in your views. They have set me thinking on this in a manner I never did before."

"Then I shall attempt to show you what design or motive he had in deceiving Adam and Eve and causing their death, and through their death how he expected to be benefited. In order to do this, I will first try to identify him.

" To begin then, I will state that Moses says he (the serpent) ' was more subtle than any beast of the field that the Lord God had made.' I have examined Webster's Unabridged to see the definition of *subtle.* He gives it thus: 1st. Sly in design, deceitful, as a subtle enemy. 2d. Cunningly devised. 3d. Artful. 4th. Cunning. 5th. *Insinuating.* 6th. Wily. Some or all of these were possessed to a greater or less degree by the serpent than any other beast of the field. In addition to all of these qualities, which, by the way, are not all enviable ones, he had the power of speech, and understood the language of Adam and Eve so as to make himself intelligent to Eve. He said to her, Gen. iii, 1, ' God has said you shall not eat of every tree in the garden.' And Gen. iii, 4, 5, he talks further with her. He possessed to a certain degree the faculty of reason ; sufficiently, at least, when mingled with his cunning, deceit, artfulness and *insinuating,* he was enabled to convince her from the steadfastness of her faith to God's word. That he was not a snake is clear, for they crawl on their bellies *naturally.* This is their natural way of locomotion, and hence was not a curse ; for whatever is natural is not a *curse.* Again, a snake does *not* eat dirt, but fish, frogs, birds, rabbits, etc. But the serpent was to eat dust all the days of his life. Again, a snake does not talk. They are not deceitful or cunning, but open and frank in their pretensions, ever ready to flee at the approach of man, or bite if intruded on; peaceable if let alone, and only depredate to make their living. They have no more enmity against a man than against any other animal; will not bite unless encroached upon. They are not disliked by man, because of any particular enmity against them as snakes, but for fear of their poison. This applies with equal force to the spider, the tarantula, the scorpion, the alligator, the shark, the lion, the tiger, the panther, as it does to the snake. The one is disliked for fear of their poison ; the other on account of their strength and savage nature. The crawling on his belly was inflicted on the serpent as a *curse,* not as a *natural* quality. Gen. iii, 14, ' Thou art cursed above all *cattle,* and every *beast* of the field '—not *creeping* things, for it is no curse to them to crawl upon their bellies.

"Again, the curse did not take away any quality which he had before, nor the power of speech. Nothing is said on that subject. So all his natural habits and qualities that he had before he still retained, with the curse added, that on his belly he should crawl and eat dirt all the days of his life. He does not say he shall not eat anything else but dirt, but that was a habit he would follow in addition to his natural habits.

" There was enmity to be put between him and the seed of the woman throughout their generations. And again, the snake would have no object in view, no speculation to make, no advantage to gain, by Adam and Eve's death.

" If, then, what I have heretofore said be true in regard to Adam and Eve's posterity, and if the beasts, cattle and creeping things are different from each other, and all made on the fifth day ; and if one of the beasts was the serpent, and the serpent could talk, then all the beasts could talk; and as the beasts and cattle were not the same animals, and as the cattle and creeping things could not talk, but the beasts could, it follows of necessity that man who was not in God's image was the beast, one of whom, Moses says, was the serpent, so named by Adam on account of his being more subtle than any other beast.

"Now I have shown that the Indian and the negro were not of Adam's posterity. They then can be nothing else of creation but that part denominated beasts, and one of them Adam has named the 'serpent,' because he was more subtle than the other. Now which of them was more subtle of the two? For there could have been but the two, at least of this kind of beasts, or he would have said *most* subtle. But he says *more* subtle, thus showing there were but the two kinds embraced in this classification. Now, I take the ground that the negro was more subtle than the Indian. And why?

"1st. Because he was more sly than the Indian. This is one of the definitions of subtle. The natural disposition of the Indian is openness, frankness. In trading with you he fixes his price on his article for sale, and nothing can make him take less. And if he wishes to buy anything you have for sale he asks your price, and at once takes it or lets it alone, without a word of chaffering about price.

"2d. The negro is more artful, crafty and insinuating in his manner than the Indian. The Indian is too proud to *insinuate* himself anywhere. He never tries by cunning, craftiness or deceit, to get into your confidence or to insinuate himself into your good will or family. He is open, frank, and fixed in his character; outspoken, and meaning exactly what he says; is too proud to barter off his words in order to deceive you; whilst the negro has no regard for his word or promise, and is ever ready to insinuate himself into your company or family, unless kept out by fear.

"3d. The Indian does not plan by art and deceit to injure you in person or property, while pretending to be your friend. If he affects friendship for you, it is sincere. If he makes a bargain with you he will stand to it. If he is your enemy, he will tell you so and have no dealings with you whatever. You can rely upon him. He makes no effort at deceit; but if he is your enemy you are sure to know it. But not so with the negro. He carries two faces under one hat, and as the Indian says, 'has a forked tongue, like the snake,' 'that he can tell the truth and a lie at the same time.' You can't depend upon his word. He has no sense of honor, no respect for his obligation; is destitute of gratitude, and always ready to take the advantage of you in the dark. He has no sense of virtue, nor regard for the marriage relation, whilst the Indian is strictly virtuous, and faithful to their vows to husband and wife.

"4th. The negro is more treacherous than the Indian. He thinks it no harm to betray his best friend; has no regard for the truth, if he can make a lie suit his purposes better. Whilst the Indian would sacrifice his life, before he would make himself your friend and then betray you.

"These are all the definitions of the term *subtle*; and, as experience, history and facts corroborate what I have said, I feel no hesitation in saying that the negro was the *serpent* that deceived Eve. 'Deceit' is one of the most prominent meanings of subtle, as laid down by Webster; 'treachery' another, and 'insinuating' another; and every one of these are very prominent traits of character in the negro, whilst they are almost entirely absent in the Indian. 'Tis true, that in war the Indian, like the white man, resorts to all the arts that nature has placed him in possession of; but, then, he does this as your open enemy. But after he has made peace with you, and *smoked the pipe* with you, you can depend upon his complying with all the conditions of any treaty that he has made with you. But not so with the negro. He don't respect his agreement longer than he is making it, if he can turn it to his advantage, in the least, to set it aside.

"When I use the terms *negro* and *Indian* I mean the race, and not individuals; for there are individual exceptions to all general rules. But these exceptions can't be considered as destroying the general rule. I also mean the pure-blood negro, and pure-blood Indian. There are many tribes of Indians. How these tribes of Indians came into existence, I am not sufficiently acquainted with their history to tell; but am of opinion that many of them originated by amalgamation with the negro. And whenever there is any negro blood in them, to that extent they are treacherous, and designing, and deceitful."

"Well, sister, if the negro is the serpent, why is it that he walks erect? The serpent was to, and part of that curse was, that he should crawl on his belly?"

"This question, John, I have often asked myself, and looked for its solution with a great deal of care. The first part of the *curse* did, for a long time, make me look to the snake for its solution. But when I came to examine more closely, I found it is *natural* for the snake to crawl. Hence it was not a curse for him to crawl, for this is his natural manner of moving from place to place. In order for it to be a *curse*, it must change his natural manner of locomotion. If it was to be literally fulfilled, in order for it to be a *curse* on the snake, it must be shown that *it* had another manner of locomotion before the *curse* was pronounced, and the curse changed that manner to crawling on its belly. But as that has never been claimed for it, I settle it in my mind, it could not be the snake.

"Again: Another part of the curse was that he was to eat dirt all the days of his life. Now, if this is to be fulfilled literally, there is nothing that lives on dirt, alone, but the earth-worm; and there is no one so foolish as to believe *it* was the serpent.

"Again: Another part of the curse was that enmity should be put between 'him and the woman,' and between his seed and her seed —'It shall bruise thy head, and thou shalt bruise his heel.' I once heard an old preacher on this text. He took the ground that the serpent was a snake—'For,' said he, 'don't you know that whenever any one kills a snake he *mashes* its head; and if a snake bites any one, it is in the heel?' I don't know when I felt so indignant as I did, to hear such gross ignorance come from the pulpit. The poor old creature wanted to make a literal interpretation of it, and that was the best he could do.

"The learned Mr. Alexander Campbell, in one number of his *Millennial Harbinger*, says: 'All beasts, cattle and creeping things and fowls, and men, spoke the same language before the fall of man;' and makes the serpent the literal snake, talking to Eve to deceive her. I cannot but look upon this as assuming the very point in dispute, and I have looked upon it as one of the weakest things that GREAT and GOOD man ever wrote. He, however, made a very plausible argument on the subject, to a superficial thinker, and admirer of him.

"Other learned divines hold that the serpent was His Satanic Majesty, who dwells in Tartarus; that he left his brimstone dominions and came up to earth, and went into the snake (for they hold that he has transmigratory powers), and thus deceived Eve by his deceptive, lying eloquence. In regard to all these theories, I have often asked 'if weak thy faith, why choose the harder side?' Why not take a plain, honest, common-sense view of the subject, and say it is fulfilled in the personage of no one who did not have some object in view, and that object was to get Adam and Eve out of the way in order to get their place. Now, if we take that plain, common-sense view of the matter, and strip the subject of all the learned nonsense that the ecclesiastical, would-be divines have thrown around it, I think a very sensible explanation of the matter can be given.

"In the first place, then, just admit what Moses says, that the serpent is a beast, and that the beast was man, not in God's image, either in color, form, or morals, but deceitful, cunning, treacherous, lying, and then, as I have shown, that that man was the negro, and we have a plain, practical, sensible solution of the great mystery, *who the serpent was*, that mystery which has troubled the minds of the learned, ecclesiastical world for a thousand years or more; taking that view of the subject, that the serpent never would have tried to deceive Eve, only that he thought he could get her's and Adam's place in creation, and he be, if not the owner, at least the controller of all the earth.

"What benefit could it be to his satanic majesty, (if there be such a personage), whose headquarters, they say, are located in Pandemonium, to quit his regions, and come to earth to deceive Eve? Divines say, because he wanted to get them down there, after they died, to torment them. Poor, miserably ignorant creatures, to preach such nonsense to the credulous world, who set and gulp it down, as if it came directly from God himself, and have not the independence to look into the Bible and see if such things are so! Poor, foolish souls, if they would only read Revelations, xx, 14, they would see that *hell* itself was to be cast into the lake of fire; and in verse 10th of same chapter they would see that the devil that *deceived* them was to be cast into the lake of fire and brimstone, where the *beast* and the False Prophet are!

"Then away with such ignorance of God's Holy Word! Shame, O shame, where is thy blush? That a man claiming to be *called* and *sent* to preach the gospel to a sinful world, should utter such abominable wickedness and ignorance in the face of God's righteous word.

This is one reason, John, why I am so very careful about giving my assent to what I hear taught from the pulpit—I find the preaching world so very ignorant of God's holy truth, and so completely taken up in preaching the peculiar tenets of their particular church, and neglecting the gracious word of God, 'which is able to make them wise unto salvation,' and which comes without money and without price.

"Now let us look at this matter from the standpoint that I view it, viz.: that the serpent was a man, who was not made in God's image and likeness, and that that man was the negro, and had been living on the earth, in the land of Nod, for a period, God only knows how long, and being the more subtle of God's creation, had managed to get the control and occupancy, and appropriation to his own use, of everything that God had created, and had held that control from the day of his creation until the time Adam was created and placed in the garden of Eden, with dominion, and power and ownership to all of his works of creation given to him, with the right *divine* to convert any and all of it to his use, together with this same serpent,.and all his posterity, and all that portion of the earth that he had taken possession of; I say, if you will view it from this standpoint, you can readily see a good reason why he would want Adam and Eve to eat of the forbidden fruit, and die."

"Well, sister, suppose your position is true, how long do you think the serpent had been living in the land of Nod?"

"John, I am not able to tell. There is but one thing in the whole history that throws the least light upon the subject. It is found in Genesis, ii, 17, ' in the day thou eatest thereof, thou shalt surely die.' And in Genesis, v, 5, it says, 'and all the days of Adam were 930 years.' This would make a day, a period, a certain, or an uncertain number of years, to constitute *the day* in which he died. He was 130 years old when Seth was born; but how old he was when he violated God's law, there is no way of arriving at correctly. But suppose for the sake of argument that he was 100 years old when he transgressed, then *the day* in which it took him to die would be a period of 830 years.

"There is one thing certain, he did not die in the next twenty-four hours after he had eaten of the fruit, but in a certain number of years afterward. Now what I want to arrive at from this argument is this: If the period Adam lived after he transgressed was a certain number of years, whether more or less than 830 is termed *a day*, why then was not the fifth day and sixth day the same number of years? There is nothing in Scripture to disprove it, but what is said goes to sustain it. And if that is so, then the fifth day in which the beasts were created could have lasted 830 years, or it could have been more, and not invalidate or even tarnish the truth of the history given by Moses, and the serpent could have been 930 years old when Adam was created, or could have been more; I say it is not at all unscriptural to make this supposition. In point of fact, there is more Scripture to support it than there is against it, if you once admit that the time from which Adam transgressed till he died constituted *one day*, ' in

89

the day thou eatest thereof thou shalt surely die.' How very common a thing it is for us to say in the *day* of Washington, of Jackson, of Clay, meaning the period of their lives when their talents shone the brightest, and their influence was the greatest. We must reconcile God's word, and it can only be done in this way.

"Then I conclude from this that the serpent, or rather the beast, as he was then, (for God created him a beast), and Adam named him serpent afterward, then the beast, which I have shown is the negro, could have lived on the earth long enough to have cleared up a large field, and got a large stock around him. He was not overly industrious, we know, if he was at all like the free negroes of our day, the *wards of Uncle Sam*. But still, just by continuous living, and adding a little every year, as his family increased, he could have had quite a field opened by the time Adam was created, and, as I said before, could have accumulated a large stock of cattle, and hogs, and perhaps sheep, and other property. I will guarantee he had a horse, and that perhaps about the first thing, for a free negro must have a horse, or he don't think he is free; and if he had not learned how to make a saddle, he *went* it barebacked. In 930 years he could have become, as evidently he was, a very numerous people, numbering, no doubt, several hundred thousand. If we take the system that the free negroes of the present day adopt in settling and building, you can imagine, John, what kind of a country Nod was when settled by *them*, with several hundred thousand families. You have a Nod in miniature in every town and county in the South, wherever they are permitted to settle. A little clapboard shanty, with hen-house attached, a small potato patch near by, a watermelon and cabbage patch, a cow tied by the horns or tail, and staked out to graze, a pigpen just under the window, a sorebacked horse, three or four bobtailed dogs, a gun, and a little fence about four rails high, was about the character of the improvements in Nod at the time Adam was created. No regular street or road; for wherever a fellow took a notion to put down his house, *there it went*, even if it were in the middle of the road. And then they would turn the road around the house and the potato patch. The next fellow that settled popped his shanty down in the road, and then the road was turned again around the house and the potato patch, and so it went on, *ad infinitum;* and this is the way that Nod was settled, and it was in about this fix, without a straight road, or street of two hundred yards in length, when Adam was created.

"Now, John, you can very easily imagine what was the old negroes' feelings when they learned that God had made a white man and settled him in Eden. Their curiosity was very much awakened to see a *white man.* The old chief, or head representative of them all, no doubt concluded that he would call on the new-comer, and see how he liked his new neighbor. He no doubt held the doctrine of social equality and civil rights, and to make this visit more agreeable to the young bachelor, concluded he would take along his daughters, Miss Susie, and Jane, and Katie, intending to give the young man an entertainment from the maiden vocalists of the Land of Nod, and let him learn at once the latest fashionable airs of the city, and perhaps make a favorable impression on him in advance of any of the other belles of Nod, who might have white proclivities. But imagine, if you can, John, the old chief's utter surprise on being informed that he and all his neighbors belonged to Adam, and every thing which they possessed; that the Creator, God, his father, in whose likeness and image he was made, had given him a fee simple title to them and all their land and property, and that he would come down to Nod in a few days and see what they were doing. No doubt he would make very great changes, for his father, God, wanted the earth tilled, and as there was no man who would do so satisfactorily without compulsion, he would make changes to suit. He might leave many of them where they were; but as he desired to cultivate a tract of country at Eden, and would need farm and house hands for that purpose, he would, perhaps, bring up with him several families, and among them Joe's, Tom's and Sam's families, and for him to tell them to hold themselves in readiness. This old head representative leaves, and as the other negroes in Nod assemble round to hear the news, he utters the astounding intelligence that all 'de niggers belongs to dat *white man.*'

"You have seen something of the practice of the negroes, when they were slaves, and a new overseer was appointed on the plantation. The old head driver would make it a point to try him first. He would approach him in some peculiar way of his own, most generally at night, when he thought he had got through supper and was sitting smoking his pipe. He would come sauntering in, with his hat under his arm, and accost him with a 'How-do-you-do, Master?' If the manager was disposed to be at all sociable, he would continue; but if not, would retire and tell the balance of the hands 'that man come here for *business!* Don't fool with him. I *tell you,* let him alone, and go do what he say.' The negroes we had were the descendants of the negroes Adam had. He was created a *master*—they were made *slaves.*

"How long Adam remained a bachelor cannot be well arrived at, but long enough for the Lord to know that it was not good for him to be alone. By alone, he meant to be without society of the same color and likeness of himself; and if he did not get that kind of society he might take up with a negress, one of his house servants. So he made him a wife, and gave her to him, and renewed his instructions to him to keep and tend the garden, and dress it with care and taste, and to use for his and her use and benefit all beasts, cattle, fowls, lands and agricultural implements that he could find; that he wanted the earth cultivated, and there was not a man that would do it to *suit him;* that everything was at his disposal for that purpose—to convert any or all of it to his and her comfort and convenience. That all of nature's trees, teeming with the delicious fruits of Eden, and the surrounding country, were for his and her own use and control, with one solitary exception. That was a tree in the center of the garden, and its fruit. They were not even to touch it, much less eat it. For in the day they did it, they would die. Adam, no doubt, had taken old Sam's or Jim's family with him up to Eden, and a great many other negroes, to wait on him before he got his wife, and aid him in cultivating and settling his farm and attend his stock. All who know the proclivity

of the negro for eavesdropping, as it is termed, when there is anything
to be done which pertains to them, and on this occasion in particular,
when their master had just got a wife, and the Creator was there cel-
ebrating the rites of marriage between them, and then was giving them
instructions how to do and how to live—I say, any one who knows the
true character of the negro for eavesdropping and insinuating himself
deceptively into the family at such times (particularly if he be a house
servant), can readily see and know that he was continually in and out
and about the house, listening to hear what the Heavenly Father said
to his children.

"I imagine I can see old Sam, just coming into the apartments of
Adam and Eve, with a basket of fruits, where the Lord and they were
sitting ; and they were listening to his counsel, hearing his instructions, and receiving the gift in fee-simple from him, their Father God,
to all the earth, cattle, beasts, and the serpent, too, who was *de facto*
the negro.   When just at this point old Sam stops, either behind some
shade trees or a rose bush, or sneaks behind the door of their neat little
cottage, and listens to every word the Creator says to them.   He hears
the title to himself and his posterity passed *forever* to Adam and Eve
and *their posterity.*   He *hears* the absolute and unconditional gift to
Adam and Eve of all *cattle* and *stock* of every description ; to the fowls
of the air and the fish of the waters.   He hears the gift confirmed to
Adam and Eve, to all flowers and fruits and fruit trees ; that they can
use them as they choose ; everything in the garden except the *one tree*
in the midst of it.   This he hears their Father tell them—they must
not touch or eat it, only at the peril of their lives.   He heard the
awful penalty to follow, as the consequence, the tremendous words
uttered by Jehovah God to his children, ' *In the day you eat it you shall
surely die.*'   The legitimate inference is that if they *never ate* it they
would *never* die, for death was suspended on the act of *eating* or touching it.

"Now, John, imagine old Sam, if you can, sitting back in the
bushes listening to all this ; his countenance falling as he heard the
absolute and unconditional title to him and his posterity passed forever
to Adam and Eve, together with their farms, houses, stock, and above
all, his horse, dog and gun, and you can very readily see with the
mind's eye the old fellow holding a soliloquy with himself about in
this way : ' Well, if dat white man got to cum here and take everything from me, dat I been scrapin' togedder for dis thousand year. I
jess tell you what's de truth, it shan't do him any good.   What ! He
goin' to take *me* and put me to work for *him !*   An' take my childen
to wait on his ! to be cuffed about as dey please !   An' take *my wife's*
chickens and turkeys for *his wife !*   An' take *my* cows, hogs, sheep,
an' my horse, too, what I been ownin' ever since he was a colt, an' all
I been workin' for so hard for dis thousan' year !   I tell you it shan't
do him any good !   I burn it up fust !   I will, fore God !'   Then suddenly stopping, as if a bright idea had just struck him, through which
he thought he saw a way of escape from the condition of slavery in
which he was placed by the Creator, and by which he thought he
could get back the ownership and control of his property, he says:

'Let me see; let me see;' and dropping his woolly head between his knees, as if in a deep study, and after continuing in that condition for about an hour, he raises his head, and looking around to see if anyone is near enough to hear what he says, seeing no one, he says, in a half-suppressed voice, and in a tone and spirit that shows his mind is well matured: 'I'll git dat white man out of de way! I'll fool him, an' git him to eat dat apple. An' den he'll die, an' den me an' my childen will be free agin! An' den we git all our property back agin! We had dis country fust, any way, an' I intends to keep it. I fools dat white man, dat's what I do!'

"Now, if you will look at the matter from this standpoint, you can very readily see a natural and sensible reason for the serpent deceiving them, and the inducement to do so. It is a very rational and sensible one. It was based upon the desire to preserve his property and his liberty, which he thought he was entitled to, and whilst the Scriptures do not state the facts exactly as I have, still I hold it is a more natural, rational and sensible view of the subject than any of the thousand snake stories, with devils in them, propagated from the pulpit. And the allusions, inferences, implications and declarations of Scripture go further to sustain this view of it than any other that I have seen; and especially when you take into consideration the fact that I have shown that the negro is not of Adam's family descent, because 'not either in his image or likeness.'"

"Well, sister, your last argument has put me to thinking very intensely, and I now begin to see that the nearer one can make the scriptures conform to *common-sense*, the more apt we are to get a correct understanding of them. I shall examine well, when I go home, what you have said on this branch of the subject. Why do you say in his *image* and *likeness*?"

"For the reason, John, that image relates to *form* or shape—likeness to color. I will illustrate: Two oxen, two sheep or two horses may have the exact form or shape of each other, as oxen, sheep or horses. In that respect they are the exact image of each other. But one ox may be black, the other red; one sheep black, the other white; one horse may be black, the other a gray—in these respects they are very unlike each other.

"Now, when God said, let us make man in our own image and likeness, he meant both as respects his form and color. And as he is a God of order, and fixed principles of character and attributes, as revealed in the scriptures, I hold he had a fixed form and color. The scripture says his head is 'white as wool.' And, as we have found that there are three distinct forms and colors of men on earth, I hold that two of them are not in the image or likeness of God; but must have been made without any pattern, only such as he drew in his own mind's eye, as he did when he made the other animals. I have found the Jews white, and traced them back to Adam, and find him called by the inspired writers, the son of God; and by another, 'made in his image and likeness.' I therefore conclude the other two distinct colors, the red and black men, were not and are not in his image and likeness, because they differ so very widely from him in form and color, and so widely from each other."

"Well, sister, do you believe that it is because Adam was in the 'likeness and image' of God that he gave him the dominion and ownership to the whole earth, and all of his creation on this earth?"

"Yes, John, *I do*. He established *right then and there* the COLOR LINE that was to govern this earth, and have the rule in it. For that is exactly what he proposed to do. Gen. i, 26: 'Let us make man in our *own image* and *our likeness*, and let him have *dominion* over the fish, fowls, cattle, and over *all the earth*.' What could be more definite than this? And verse 27, same chapter: So he created *man* in his *own image* and *likeness*, . . verse 28, and have *dominion* over the fish, the fowls, and *every living thing*.

"You see, then, from the above scriptures, that there is no escape from the claim of Adam to the beasts, cattle, creeping things, and all the earth. And having proven that the serpent was the negro, and that Adam and Eve had a fee simple title to him and his posterity throughout their generations, and to all the property he had acquired during his lifetime in the land of Nod, I want to notice a little further the views of the ecclesiastical divines on the subject before dismissing this branch of it.

"When I was a little girl there was, in the State in which we were born, a very distinguished preacher of the M. E. Church. There were few more talented men than he was. He had a reputation for learning and ability, eloquence and talent, as a pulpit orator, that extended to the adjoining States. Whenever it was known that Dr. W. was to preach, every person who could go to hear him, suspended all business of every character, and devoted a few hours to listening to this distinguished minister. My father and mother both went, and I, of course, did so. It had been announced in a certain newspaper printed in N., that the Rev. Dr. W., of the M. E. Church, would preach at F. on Sunday, the — day of —, and his subject would be the temptation of our first parents in the Garden of Eden.

"I had been reading the old Bible, and though very young, I had become very much interested on the subject. I had a great curiosity to know what kind of a thing the serpent was that deceived them, and as this learned gentleman and distinguished biblical scholar intended to discourse upon the subject, the interest I felt in hearing him has not been often equaled by a little girl.

"The distinguished preacher, after introducing his subject and laying down his premises, which would be tedious to state now, asserted flatly that the *serpent was a snake*. He did not tell what kind of a snake it was, but left his audience to infer the kind. His powers of description in the pulpit surpassed any one I ever heard before or since; and his *forte*, in carrying conviction to his audience that it was a snake, lay in his superior powers of description. He first represented it as crawling back and forth before Eve, in order to attract her attention. Then it would crawl around and around her; then coil itself up and throw itself out at full length; then run off a little, then return, not manifesting any disposition to bite, but only to arrest her attention. Finally, he represented it as raising itself half-erect, and with the remainder of its body moving in a serpentine manner, started off before her. Its actions were so curiously strange, and it continued so long in her presence, that when it started off she determined to follow it to see what it wanted. He represented it as throwing its head back and forth, as if beckoning her to follow. 'Curiosity,' he said, 'that great ruling trait in woman's character, induced her to follow it.' She followed, on, and on, and on, till finally it reached the center of the garden. Here he gave a most glowing description of the beauties of Eden, laid out in walks of evergreen, and flowers springing up on every side and either hand, till finally he got to the tree of the knowl-edge of good and evil. Here he represented Eve as stopping several paces away from the tree, 'for,' said she, 'I am not to touch it.' He represented the snake as getting to the tree, and gradually winding itself around and around it, climbing higher and higher, higher and higher, till finally reaching the first limbs it began to look round at the fruit for some more ripe and mellow than the rest, crawling about among the limbs, till finally finding some mellow and delicious ones, he commenced eating them. Just at this point he seemed to catch a new idea, and as if his lips had been touched by a live coal from off the altar of Deity, he exclaimed in a most positive and emphatic man-ner: ' *Now the devil was in that snake!*' 'And,' said he, ' the devil spoke through the snake like the prophet did through Balaam's don-key, and said: Yes; the Lord says if you eat of this fruit you will die. You see I eat it, and it don't kill me. Don't you see from this that you are imposed on? The reason I can talk, and am so much wiser than the other beasts, is that I eat of the fruit of this tree every day. And if you will eat it, it will make you wise. And O ! it is so sweet. Just try a little of it. It won't hurt you.' In this way he represented the devil, through the snake, enticing Eve to do wrong. 'And when,' said he, ' he had got her curiosity excited to its highest point, he plucked off a most delicious apple, and calling to her to *try* her *hand* at catching, he threw it to her and told her to *catch* it.' His descrip-tion was so life-like and so vivid that I thought I could see the apple flying through the air like a ball, and Eve in her excitement catching it. 'She caught it,' said he, 'and after smelling it found its flavor so exquisite she concluded to taste it, any way, just to find out its true odor and flavor. A little taste could not hurt anybody. She tasted,' said he; 'delighted at its taste, she bit and eat it. Merciful God !' he exclaimed, with so much feeling and pathos that there was a cold shiv-ering sensation ran through the entire congregation. He spoke about two hours and held his congregation spell-bound, as if they saw the whole drama being enacted by the power of the devil in the person of the snake. For months afterward I could see nothing but that snake crawling before old Mrs. Adam, then up the tree, then through the limbs, then eating an apple.

" It would be entirely foreign to the purpose of our conversations to attempt to show the application which he undertook to make of his expose of the subject, in order to show the heinousness of sin in listen-ing to its deceitful flatteries to allure from the truth. I only introduce

4

this to show the opinions of the learned on the subject, and whilst the old and the young, the thinking and the unthinking, the saint and the sinner, all left the church under the full conviction that the distinguished D.D. had added a large stock of valuable information to their knowledge of God's Word, and all pronounced it a very able discourse, not one of them ever saw that he had *assumed* the very point in doubt, or debate, viz.: Who or what was the devil that had got into the snake? This he did not attempt to prove. -

"I thought, at that time, that all he said was true; for my little eyes were so intently fixed on his manner, and my little girlish ears so entirely delighted with his elegant language, his superior eloquence, his prolific imagination and richness of description, that, like a little girl would, I gave way to what all the old people said, and gave a ready assent.

"But, John, time has wrought great changes since then. The learned D. D. has long since been called to his long home. Few, if any, of the old persons who heard him on that occasion are now on the stage of action to attest the truth of what I say; and Time, that great wonder-worker, and revelator of all truth, and instructor in all matters of doubt, has added to me, in his annual rounds, treasures of wisdom, for which I will never be able to repay him; and in my retrospect of life I have learned to be very skeptical of early teachings, and have learned to subject them all to the crucible of God's Word; and what will not stand that test, I have learned to reject and throw aside.

"It is a very hard matter to give up an idea of early education, especially if held by our parents; for you know with what pertinacity children cling to the tenets of their parents' religion. But still, John, I have learned one lesson from the Bible, which is this: 'Call no man *father* on *earth.*' By which is meant, allow no one to think for you in the interpretation of God's Word; but to 'prove all things, and hold fast that which is good.'

"Acting, then, upon this cardinal rule of scripture, I have asked myself this question: Suppose the facts as stated by the learned Dr. W., and as are taught from the pulpit of the present day, be true? Then I am left as much in darkness as I was before, for the question that would arise is this: Who, then, was the devil that went into the snake? 2d, What object could he have had in view? 3d, In what respect would it have benefited the devil, or the snake, for Adam and Eve to have transgressed and died? 4th, What would either the snake or the devil have made by the operation?

"All of these questions have come up before me, and as far as the D. D. and the pulpit teachings of the present day are concerned, I am left as much in the dark, and so are you, as to who the serpent was who deceived Eve, as we were before the Rev. D. D. ever spoke on the subject.

"It will not do to say that 'it was the devil,' and leave it unexplained, and not tell us what kind of a thing he was. If it would, I would then ask: Was it the same devil that entered into Judas, and caused him to betray the Savior? or that entered into the swine? or that took Jesus up into a high mountain? or that set him on the pinnacle of the temple?

"Let us take a closer examination of this matter, and as I am in the habit of interpreting Scripture by facts, common-sense, experience, the practice of the inspired writers, and the Savior, and bringing to my aid the customs, manners, habits, and the peculiar idiom of the people of the day and country where they were spoken, I want to recur to a few places in Scripture where the words Satan, Devil, and Serpent are used, and by subjecting them to the above rules of interpretation, see if I can't answer some of the mysterious questions which have perplexed mankind for so long a time, and show that they all go to corroborate the position that I have taken, viz.: that the negro was the serpent who deceived Eve, and caused her and Adam to sin, and thus death.

"The first, then, will be found in Matt. xvi, 2: 'But he said, get thee behind me, Satan, thou art an offence to me.' In this place the apostle Peter was called Satan.

"The next is found in Matt. iv, 1, 2, 3, 4: 'Then Jesus was led by the Spirit into the wilderness to be tempted of the devil.' 'And when he had fasted forty days and forty nights, he was afterward an hungered.' And when the tempter came to him, he said, "If thou be the Son of God, command that these stones be made bread.' Verse 5: 'Then the devil took him up to the holy city, and set him on the pinnacle of the temple, and said, if thou be the Son of God, cast thyself down, for it is written, he will give his angels charge concerning thee.' 'Jesus saith, Thou shalt not tempt the Lord thy God.' Verse 8: 'Again the devil took him up into an exceeding high mountain, and showed him all the kingdoms of the world, and the glory of them, and said, All these will I give thee if thou wilt worship me. Jesus said, Get thee behind me, Satan, for it is written, thou shalt worship the Lord thy God, and him only shalt thou serve.'

"Now let us examine and see if in reality there was any temptation in this matter. If *the devil* spoken of in this connection did not own the kingdoms of the earth offered to Jesus, and did not have the disposing power over them, then it was no temptation to Jesus to offer them to him upon condition of his serving him. Then he either *did* or *did not* own them. The question then arises, who did own the land of Judea, Palestine, and Jerusalem, at the time of the Savior's temptation, and had the disposing power over them?

"The Bible and concurrent history both agree in the fact that the regal title to all that country was vested in the Roman Emperor, who was at that time Tiberius Cæsar, and that his power was *absolute*. Now, in order for it to have been a temptation at all, no one could have offered it to the Savior but Cæsar, or some one acting under him, with power to make transfer. If, then, it was not Cæsar, or his authorized agent, who offered all the kingdoms of the Roman empire, embracing the entire land of Judea, Samaria, and Jerusalem, to the Savior, it was no temptation; and if it was, then Cæsar, or some one acting by his authority at the time, was *the devil* that tempted Jesus in this instance. It was a personage who traveled with Jesus; first saw he was hungry ; next took him up to the pinnacle of the temple, and set him on it; next showed him the kingdoms of the world. In all these transactions *the devil* talked ; spoke the same language that Jesus and the apostles did ; quoted Scripture, and offered power and authority such as was delegated to him to transfer ; thus showing, that in this instance *the devil* was a man, a being, with that same character of identity as *the devil* that the apostle Peter was as *Satan*.

"The next Scripture that I will refer to is John xiii, 2, 'And supper being ended, the *devil* having put it into the heart of Judas to betray Jesus.' . . Verse 27 : 'And when he had dipped the sop, he gave it to Judas. Then Satan entered into him.' Mark xiv, 10, 11 : . . 'Judas went to the chief priests to betray him, . . they offered him money to betray him.' Now let us analyze these three texts. John xiii, 2 : 'The devil put it into the heart of Judas to betray him.' . . . Mark xiv, 10, 11 : 'Judas went to the high priests to betray him, . . they were glad and offered him money.' In two of these texts the high priests are the acting parties, and must be *the devil*—they offer money to betray him, thus putting it into the heart of Judas '*to betray him.*' . . John xiii, 27 : 'And when he had dipped the sop, *Satan entered into him* to betray him.' This shows that it was the *determination* or *resolve* of Judas to betray him, that is called Satan in this connection. I could bring up, if I had time, every text in the Scriptures of the New Testament, and show that the words ' satan,' ' devil' and ' serpent' are all applied according to the context in which they are used, to a *principle* as opposed to sound morals, or as a *passion* opposed to the true interests of the Savior's teachings, or as a *disease* conflicting with the laws of health and baffling the skill of the medical faculty of that day, or as a personage under the garb of a deceitful friend, or as a personage clothed with civil or regal authority, in the administration of which the tendency was opposed to the precepts and teachings of the Savior. I have shown that the Apostle Peter was called Satan, and also Cæsar, and the chief priests. 2d. That it was a wicked resolve on the part of Judas, at variance with the teachings of Christ, that entered into him, and is called Satan. 3d. That it was a disease cast out of the maniac, as in the cases of those who had fits. If, then, these things be true, what goes with the snake story of the learned D.D., and the order of the ecclesiastical teachers, that the serpent was either in the snake or an invisible, supernatural being, that had the power of transforming himself into a snake, or of going into the snake, in order to deceive Adam and Eve ?

"I think, John, I have said enough to show you, and any unprejudiced mind, that *the devil*, satan and serpent all have a figurative and corporal identity. Figurative, as applied to principle, passion and disease. Corporal, as applied to civil or regal authority in persons. That has been my reason for introducing the few texts which I have brought before you.

"Now, what design could the Roman Emperor have had in getting the Savior to worship him ? Let us look into this matter. History shows that at the time the Savior was on earth the land of Judea and Jerusalem had been subjugated by the Romans, and their government destroyed; and though the Jews were permitted to worship God according to their peculiar religion, still they had no independent government of their own. They knew that the prophets had told of a Deliverer who was to re-establish the kingdom of their father David, and they (the Jews) were looking for him to come for that purpose at that time. The Roman Emperor, Cæsar, or Herod, or perhaps both, knew very well the scripture prophecies that pointed to Christ. Herod was so well convinced of it that he tried to destroy him in infancy. See Mat., ii, 8. They feared his power, and calculated to lose their hold on the Jewish country. Being fully convinced that Jesus was the personage who was to restore the kingdom to Israel, the Roman officer then in authority, whether Cæsar or his substitute, desired to forestall public opinion before he asserted his right to the crown, and show to the Jews that he had done homage to Cæsar, and worshipped him, and hence was not worthy of being their king. He felt satisfied *he* was the rightful heir to the crown of Judea and throne of David. He knew, also, that the Jewish scriptures did not permit anything worshipped but God. And if he could get him to apostatize from the true religion of God, and worship *him*, that God would discard Jesus, and thus *he* would retain his power over the Jewish people. In point of fact, he feared the claim of Christ to the throne of Israel, and wanted to keep him out of it. This, then, was his design, and you can now see the reason of *his* tempting him.

"The chief priests wanted him betrayed that they might crucify him according to the Jewish law, because, as they said, he had committed blasphemy against God and the law by calling himself the son of God.

"Now, both the Roman emperor and the chief priests are called the devil. I have showed the design of the action of both of them against Jesus, and for this design they are both styled 'the devil;' have shown that the apostle Peter was called Satan because he advised a thing done of which Jesus disapproved. If, then, with the scriptures on this subject to sustain me in the fact that persons (white persons, too), were called *the devil* and Satan, why not, when there is so much Scripture, so many facts and so much concurrent testimony to prove that the negro was a beast, and named the serpent, admit the fact?

I shall now dismiss this branch of the subject till Thursday night next, when I shall attempt to show you what the true worship of God was. Till then, good-night."

THURSDAY NIGHT.

"Sister, on our separation on last Thursday night you promised to give your views on the subject of the true religion of God. I would like to hear you on that subject; for the Bible appears to me to be entirely silent as to any particular manner or faith in the worship of God, as revealed to, or required of Adam by the Creator."

"Yes, John, there is a great deal of truth in what you say. There were but three positive commands given to Adam and Eve that I can find in the Bible. The first was not to *touch or eat* of the fruit of the tree of the knowledge of good and evil. The second was to *bring forth after their kind.* The third was to *subdue* the earth and use everything else created for their own use, pleasure and luxury. But after the violation of God's law—the first command—and they were turned out of the garden of Paradise, the first thing we hear on the subject of worship *at all*, is when Cain and Abel both brought their sacrifices or offerings to the Lord. Abel's was accepted and Cain's rejected. The question that arises in my mind is, why did they bring their sacrifices *at all?* There is no positive command revealed in the Bible requiring them to do it, or even showing that it was a custom for them to do so. There is nothing *revealed*, at that time, to show that there was any positive law given them to sacrifice. In Genesis iv, 2, it is said Cain was a tiller of the ground and Abel a tender of flocks. . . Verse 3 : 'In *process of time* Cain brought of his crop an *offering* to the Lord.'
. . Verse 4 : 'Abel brought of the firstlings of his flocks.' Now, up to this time, mentioned in verses 3 and 4, there is nothing *revealed* to show that an offering was *required of them at all*. And were it not for the sequel afterwards, we would be left in the dark upon the subject. . . Verse 4 : 'And the Lord had respect unto Abel and his offering.' . . Verse 5 : 'But had no respect to Cain's.' Cain was offended. . . Verse 5. The Lord asked him why he was offended?
. . Verse 7 : 'If you do *well* you *will* be accepted; if not, the sin is your own.'

"I wish to premise a few things, John, before entering more particularly upon the subject, and which, if kept in view whenever examining the Bible, you will be the better enabled to understand the writer. The first is this : Try, if possible, to get a correct knowledge of the circumstances and surroundings under which he wrote, and if possible imagine yourself in his condition. 2d. Then try and get a correct knowledge of the manners, customs, habits and religion of the people to whom he is writing ; then a thorough knowledge of the idiom, both of the language of the writer and those to whom he was writing. Get these well fixed in your mind, and keep them before you all the time you are examining. If you do this, you will have very little trouble in correctly interpreting the Bible on any subject that is treated by the inspired writer.

"Now let us examine a little the surroundings of Moses when he wrote the short history of Adam and Eve and their immediate family. When he sat down to write the history the world was over three thousand years old, and as far as we can find out there had never been any chronology or history of it kept in writing, but was perpetuated by the recollections of those who had lived before and taught it to their children. It had also passed through the flood, and every one of Adam's posterity, except Noah and his family, had been drowned. A written code of laws and morals had been given him by which to govern the Jews, and a written form of worship for them to observe toward God. Among the things, as religious service, and one of the first and most important, was that of sacrifice to God upon the altar erected to him for that purpose by his command. Upon that altar all sacrifice was offered, and when it was offered as a test of true faith, and in the faith that God had required his creatures to have, fire came down from heaven and consumed the sacrifice. But if it was not offered in that spirit and faith, then the fire did not come down and consume the sacrifice.

"Now with these things premised, we can be enabled to understand why the Lord said to Cain, ' if you do well, you will be accepted, but if not, *sin* lies at your own door.' Now Moses was writing to the Jews, a people who fully understood the sacrificial law, the manner of performing it, and the kind of sacrifices which were required to be offered; hence there was no use for him to go through the whole routine of the manner of sacrifice, but just the bare mention of it was all that was necessary in order for them to understand it. And when he says, ' the Lord had respect to Abel's offering,' and did not have to Cain's, they understood it well and clearly that fire came down from God and devoured Abel's offering, because it was of the kind prescribed by God, and that Cain's was not; then well could the Lord say to Cain, 'if you do well, you will be accepted;' in other words, ' if you offer the right kind of sacrifice, I will accept it; but if not, I will not, and the sin lies at your door.'

"Now I raise the question, how was either Cain or Abel enabled to know what kind of sacrifice would be accepted, or even if any would be accepted? Or why did they sacrifice at all? Moses knew as well as he knew anything else. The Jews knew it also; for they saw in their law what kind of sacrifices were to be offered. And I hold that the reason that he simply mentions the fact that these two men offered sacrifice, and one was accepted, and the other not, was from the fact that one offered the right kind, and the other did not. This is also confirmed in the declaration of the Lord, ' if you do well you will be accepted.' Now if Cain had not known what he had to do, in order to *do well*, he could have very justly replied, how do I know what constitutes ' *do well?*' You have never told me. Myself and brother come and offer to you, and you accept him and reject me. The other portion of the Lord's rebuke explains the whole matter: ' *if not, sin lies at your door.*' In other words, ' you knew what to do, and would not do it.' ' Abel also knew what to do, and did it, and I accepted his; because he did what he was told, and had been taught by Adam and Eve, as I taught them.'

' Now let us look at this from a practical standpoint: The writer says Cain was a tiller of the ground; Abel tended his flocks. Cain knew the time for sacrifice had come. For the writer says, ' Now it came to pass, in *process of time;*' thus showing that it had been their custom to sacrifice during a *process of time*; that Cain brought of the fruit of the ground to offer unto the Lord, and the Lord would not accept it, and substantially told him that he knew that was not the right kind of sacrifice to bring. My view of this matter is about this: Cain was like a great many other people in their practical views of the worship of God, viz.: that it does not make much difference about

such *little things.* ' One offering is just as good as another.' I have no
doubt that he reasoned about in this way : ' The time for sacrifice has
come, and I have got no lambs, or kids, or cattle to offer, but I have
a fine crop. The Lord seems to have blessed me more abundantly this
year than ever heretofore. 'T is true I could swap some corn, or pota-
toes, or perhaps sell brother Abel a horse, and take part pay in sheep,
and then I could offer one of them, but I don't think it very necessary
to be so very particular about small matters. I 'll show a willing disposition, and give a little more corn, wheat, rye or oats, and let the
Lord take the will for the deed. And in fact, I don't see why it is
not just as good—I think it is better ; for in doing this, I don't have
to take the life of anything—I think it much more merciful.' I say,
I have no doubt Cain reasoned in this way on this subject ; the sequel
shows with what success.

"Matters went on in this way for some time. But the more Cain
thought of it, the more he disliked his brother Abel ; and he plotted
his death. He sought an opportunity to get him off to himself, as all
murderers do, and consummated his fiendish purpose. When charged
with it by the Lord, he denied it. But on being told ' his brother's
blood cried to him from the ground,' he could make no reply. He
saw the Lord knew it. A curse is pronounced on him. The earth
should not yield to him her strength, as heretofore, when he tilled it.
He should be a fugitive and vagabond. He complains at his fate ;
'tis more than he can bear. 'Tis not mitigated, but a mark is put upon
him. He is thrust out from his father's family ; goes to the land of
Nod, among the negroes, and takes a wife. She bears him a son.
The mark set on Cain is developed in the child being a mulatto.
Calls his name Enoch. His line is given for four generations, and
then stops ; and Cain's family is not mentioned by name any more in
the Bible.

"There I will leave them for the present, and take up Adam's
family. The historian says ' Adam lived 130 years, and begat a son
in his own *image* and *likeness,* and called his name Seth.' And to
Seth was born a son, and he called his name Enos. ' Then men began
to *call on the name of the Lord.*' Now, there are two very important
facts stated in this synopsis of Cain's and Adam's history, to which I
wish to call your special attention. The first is this, that when Moses
commences to give the *generations* of Adam, he does not mention Cain
at all ; but begins, Gen. v, 3 : ' Adam lived 130 years, and begat a
son in his own *image* and *likeness,* and called his name Seth.' Why
not begin with Cain ; he was his oldest child ? Why not date his
generations from Cain, his oldest child (which, in point of fact, is
true), instead of with Seth, the younger son ? And why be so careful
to say 'in his own image and likeness?' Now, these are very important
things to be considered ; and if correctly understood, will be of great
help to you, John, in our future conversations.

"First, then, let us examine into the reason for not taking Cain
as the beginning of Adam's generations. Why not say, when Cain's
first son, Enoch, was born, that he was in his *image* and *likeness?* I
say it was because Enoch was a mulatto, and hence could not be in

the *image* or *likeness* of Cain. I have long since shown that Adam and Eve were white; consequently, Cain was white. But his wife, being a negress, his child was a mulatto. Now, Moses knew this fact; and had he taken CAIN as the beginning of the generations of Adam, he would then have had to take, as next in the family line, Cain's first-born, Enoch, and thus made the mulatto, mixed-blood race, the seed and offspring of Adam—which God so severely hated. But instead of this, he drops Cain altogether as part of the generations of Adam, and takes Seth, the younger brother, and makes special mention of the fact that he was in Adam's *image* and *likeness.* Now, why be so particular as to make a mention of this fact? I say it is because it was positively and unconditionally commanded that Adam and Eve, and their posterity, should bring forth after their own *image* and *likeness.* That was the true faith at that time, the religion given by God to them, and to be inculcated in their posterity through all time.

" God abandoned Cain, and so did Adam, because he was a murderer. He was driven out from the family of Adam. He was, whilst there, a tiller of the ground.

" I have previously shown that the negroes belonged to Adam and Eve and their posterity forever. As Cain was a tiller of the ground, and as his father owned all the negroes, when he was turned out of the family and abandoned by God, and went to the land of Nod, if the sequel is an index by which to form a judgment of a man's fixed determination of purpose. I should say that he conceived the idea at once of going to the land of Nod, and claiming to be the heir-at-law of Adam, took forcible possession of such of the negroes and territory of the land of Nod, and being a shrewd and designing man, and knowing that *possession* was eleven points in the law, determined to hold the same under claim as the heir of Adam. As the family was rich and did not need that portion of the estate, and not being anxious, or rather wishing to avoid contact with the murderer of one of the family, they concluded to let him hold peaceable possession of it. In the course of his life, whilst in the family, he had been the acknowledged manager of all the field hands, as Abel was of what few were necessary to assist in tending the flocks. He then had but little difficulty with the negroes of Nod in asserting his right. No doubt he first claimed possession only as manager for his father, but as no one ever appeared to claim the estate, he laid claim to them all, and the negroes knowing no better, abided the same. He takes a wife among them and commences raising a family of children. Of this more in future.

" The second thing to which I would call your particular attention is the time that Moses says ' that men began to call on the name of the Lord.' Now Moses knew, and so did the Jews to whom he was writing, what was meant by ' *calling* ' on the name of the Lord. They knew it meant sacrificing at the altar of the Lord, for it was at the altar that God had *recorded* his *name*—Exodus xx, 24 : 'An altar of earth thou shalt make unto me, and shalt sacrifice thereon thy burnt offerings, and thy peace offerings, thy sheep and thy oxen. In all places where I *record* my name, I will *come* unto thee, and I will bless.

thee.' Hence they knew that it was at the *altar* that God's name was recorded, and hence the apostate Cainites, or sons of men, expected to be accepted at an altar erected to God by them. Whether accepted or not, the sequel will tell.

"The inspired writer says: 'Adam was 130 years old when Seth was born. And Seth lived 105 years and begat Enos.' Now add 135 and 105, and it makes 240 years. In Genesis iv, 26, just after mentioning the birth of Enos, and in almost the same breath, he says: ' *Then men began to call on the name of the Lord.*' Now, how to reconcile the fact *that men began to call on the name of the Lord*, just when Enos was born, which was 240 years after Adam was created, with the fact that Abel did *call* on the *name* of the Lord *acceptably*, fully 210 years before Enos was born, and for so doing lost his life—(and it is natural to believe that Adam had done so before him, and had taught him *to call on the name of the Lord*, and had also taught Seth, and the balance of his family, to do the same thing)—I say how to reconcile the statement that *men just then began to call on the name of the Lord*, can only be done in one way, and that is, that *the men* who just *then began to call on the name of the Lord* were the *mulatto* children of Cain and the negroes, who were men not in the image or likeness of God.

"In this connection take the 1st and 2d verses of the 6th chapter of Genesis, and see if it does not throw some light on the subject : 'And it came to pass, when *men* began to multiply on the face of the earth, and *daughters* were born unto *them*,' . . . Verse 2 : 'That the *sons* of God saw the *daughters of men*, that they were *fair*, and they took them wives such as they chose.' Now here the *sons of God* are brought in contrast with the *daughters of men*. Who, then, were the *sons of God ?* And who the *daughters of men ?* I have shown by the Apostle Luke that Adam was called the *son of God*. Moses makes his generations begin with Seth, and so continue, and shows that *they* had kept up a continuing calling on the name of the Lord. Hence, the line of Seth were the *sons* of God. Then who were the daughters of men? I say they were the corrupt issue between Adam's pure blood by Cain and his corrupt and wicked intercourse with the negress wife. It may have been 1000 years that this had continued. Suffice it to say that it had continued long enough for them to be called *fair*. Not black or white, but *fair*—mulattoes or quadroons. At least enough so as to fascinate the *sons* of God ; enough to cause them to solicit their hands in matrimony, and *they took* their wives of such as they chose. The *men*, then, that *began to call upon the name of the Lord* about the time Enos was born, were the children of Cain by his negro wife, and the negroes of Nod, over which he claimed control and ownership, through the title which he set up through his father Adam.

"But as Cain would not worship God when in Adam's family, as was required of him to do, it would be very unnatural to suppose that he would do so after having been abandoned both by God and Adam. It is natural to believe, that after he had taken a negro wife, and had children by her, he had adopted, or perhaps originated, which I think the most probable, the doctrine of Social Equality, Civil Rights, and Miscegenation, as taught now by Henry Ward Beecher, and all that school of adulterers, fornicators, and blasphemers of God's holy truth, who make merchandise of religion. The doctrine of Miscegenation, Social Equality, and Civil Rights, as taught by Cain and his posterity, caused the sons of God, the true line of Adam, through Seth, to depart from the true, pure worship of God, which was, 'that they should beget children in their own *image* and their own *likeness*,' was consummated in full when they saw the mulatto girls, the posterity of Cain, by the negro wife; and finding them '*fair*' in complexion, they took wives to their own fancy. No doubt that Cain, the author of miscegenation and social equality, had taught, that as he was Adam's child, even if his wife was black, and a negro, still his children had white blood in their veins, and were akin to the true line of Adam, whose sons were called the sons of God. This doctrine had gained strength and countenance till it had become customary for the sons of God to marry the *daughters of men*, the mulatto girls, and I presume *vice versa*. And as custom makes law, it had become common for the line of Seth to marry and intermarry with the mixed blood of Cain and his descendants, till God Almighty becoming disgusted with seeing his religion ignored and his image and likeness marred by Adam's posterity marrying with Cain's mixed-blooded children, and seeing an utter disrespect on the part of Adam's pure blood to keep up a pure blood or race in his own likeness and image, he resolved that he would destroy the whole family of the earth, both man and beast. He communicated his intention to Noah, stating that he had found only him and his immediate family '*righteous*' in his sight. Righteousness, then, consisted in keeping up a pure blood white race, in the likeness and image of God. *Corrupt*, in this connection, has direct reference to the *color* of men. The entire white race had corrupted its blood by marrying into the negro and mulatto, and as God says, 'had corrupted his way.' That '*way*' was, to perpetuate his *likeness* and *image* on earth, in the posterity of Adam's true line through Seth down to Noah. This they had ceased to do, but had established a different code of morals altogether. They had originated the doctrine of social equality, political equality, miscegenation and even legalized marriage between the white, mulatto and negro race, precisely as the carpetbag, Radical party have done in the Southern States, and I believe in the Northern also. Henry Ward Beecher once taught that it would be an improvement on the *white* race to miscegenate with the negro. I presume he got the idea from the Bible account as given by Moses, when he says 'there were giants (Gen. vi, 4) who were men of renown, and they became exceedingly wicked.' These giants were the product of the illicit intercourse between the *sons of God* (the line of Seth) with the *daughters of men*—the mulatto girls, or offspring of Cain, with his negro wife. From this precept, or rather practice, that religious mountebank, H. W. Beecher, gets his doctrine of miscegenation of the white man with the negro, in order to improve the race, as he once taught from the pulpit of Plymouth Church.

"But what was the fate of the world, under the influence of this character of preaching before the flood? It called forth the wrath of God upon it; and, at the end of 120 years from the day that God had told Noah he would destroy it, the flood came, and swept like a mighty wave over the whole surface, leaving no living thing upon it, Noah and his family, and such animals as he had been instructed to take into the ark, excepted."

"Well, sister, in Gen. vi, 7, God says 'he would destroy *man* and *beast.*' You said, in a former conversation, that the beast, and man not in God's image, were the same thing. If this be so, why, then, does he say he will destroy *man* and *beast?*"

"John, read verse 2, same chapter, and you will see the explanation to your question. . . All flesh had corrupted '*his way.*' His '*way*' was that they should beget children in their own *likeness* and *image.* This was God's universal law, and for a departure from it there was no excuse or forgiveness; and to Adam's posterity more particularly, because they were made in his *image* and *likeness.* And to mar that image and likeness was to '*corrupt his way,*' for which there was no excuse.

"I have shown that the whole, entire earth, consisting of Adam's true line by Seth, and his abandoned line through Cain, and man not in his image, the negro, had amalgamated and miscegenated in blood, in preaching, in legislation, so as to set at defiance God's law, which he had established, to keep up the *exact image* and *likeness* of himself on earth. So universal was the effect and influence on the world at that time, that when the Lord came to take a close inspection of Adam's race, he could only find his exact *image* and *likeness* in Noah and his three sons and *their wives.* So delighted was the Lord to find his *likeness* and *image* preserved in Noah's family, that he exclaimed, *You, Noah!* and *only you!* have I found *righteous* in my sight. You have kept my law sacredly! You have kept your blood pure! Not one drop of negro blood courses through the veins of any of your posterity! All the balance have *corrupted* the pure blood, and I am determined to destroy it, both man and beast, with whom he had corrupted his blood, and all cattle and creeping things. I will save only you and your family, of the white race, with which to begin to re-people the earth again in my *image* and *likeness.* This is my answer to your question, why the Lord used the term *man* and *beast.*

"Now, John, if this be true, and from it I fearlessly assert there is no escape, what becomes of the doctrine of the abolitionists, the free-lovers, the amalgamationists, the miscegenationists and the pseudo-philanthropists, that all mankind, of every blood and color on the habitable globe, are of Adam's race, and are *brothers* and *sisters nationally.* It is very clear that Cain's descendants had preached this exact doctrine. Cain, like the carpet-bagger of the North, saw that when abandoned by his father's family, and by God, that the only hope he had of revenge lay in the negro. So he takes his carpet-bag, off he puts to the land of Nod, and takes possession of it by the right of being Adam's child. After living there awhile, he takes one of his house-servants, a negress, for a wife, and commences raising a family of children; and gaining standing among them, from his position, obtained their confidence, and began the worship of God with his mulatto children, by *calling* on the name of the Lord at an altar prepared by himself. At that time the pure blood of Adam's line had the pure worship and true faith. And it was so remarkable an event, to see, or know, that the mixed-blood children of Cain had begun to worship by *calling* on the name of the *Lord*, that it was made a record of, and an event made to mark the date, so that it could not be forgotten. . . . He says, Gen. iv, 26, . . it was when Enos was born. This is one of the most impressive ways to keep a record of events, except by writing, known to the world; and so universal has it become with women, that when they want to tell when anything particular happened in their lifetime, they invariably date from the birth of such or such child of theirs, saying, 'it was just about the time that my [first, second, or third] child was born.' The *calling* on the name of the Lord, by Cain's mulatto children, was noticed at first with a great deal of jealousy by the pure blood of Adam's line. They knew Cain had been driven off from God and Adam under the curse; that he should be a fugitive and vagabond in the earth, and that the earth should not yield its strength to him as heretofore; and that, under the curse, he nor his posterity had any right *divine* to worship at the *name* of *God*. It does not appear that they were ever accepted; and the presumption is, that they were not, if we are to judge from the rebellious spirit which actuated him in his offerings before he killed Abel. They made a record of it for two reasons—one was to show that they had not done so for 240 years; and the other, that they were transgressors in doing so, for they did it without any command or license from God.

"Under the garb of religion all manner of wickedness has been perpetrated. This was the beginning of the doctrine of equality of races, and social equality, which proved the destruction of the antediluvian world by the flood. The doctrine of social equality and civil rights, as taught by Sumner, Greeley, Thad. Stevens, Carpenter, and all that host of small-calibre pseudo-philanthropists, with the Brooklyn Pandemoniumists to do their hypocritical sacrificing, all emanated from the same false and fatal error. It has destroyed the best government God ever gave to man; bankrupted its treasury; turned the whole South, that was the Eden of its country, into a *Land of Nod* of olden times; placed the negro on an equality with the white man; legalized marriage between the races; and given them equal rights, socially, politically and religiously; and placed the law-making power, and executing of the same, in his hands, thus making the white man subject to the negro; abolished slavery, which God Almighty has established in the person of the negro, throughout their generations, for all time to come. And then have the hypocritical cant to assert that they have done God service, and sing Hallelujahs over it, and claim they have ushered into existence a millennial era, for which they have the *cheek* to think, and *say*, in cool blasphemy, that they have laid the Creator under obligations to them that *he can never repay*.

"This is the bold, blasphemous teaching which the latter-day Cainites unblushingly teach in the face of God's Holy Word, and his stern, inflexible, universal law, of ' like begetting like,' and ' bring forth in thy image and likeness,' or ' after thy kind,' and ' have *dominion* over everything that moves on the earth,' as given to Adam and Eve, and their pure blood posterity.

"But John, let us for a moment, with Moses as our guide, notice the vengeance of an offended and insulted God, visited on Cain and his posterity, for teaching the very same things, and causing the children of the pure, true line of Adam to blaspheme the name of God, desecrate his *image* and *likeness*, ' till he was grieved at his heart, and *repented* that he had made *man ;*' not meaning Adam, but *man*, the *negro*, not in his image and likeness; and through whom rose that rebellious, hypocritical world of false religionists and false teachers, propagating the doctrine of Social Equality, Civil Rights, and Miscegenation, which culminated in their utter destruction without mercy, forgiveness, or favor.

"If, then, John, an all-wise and good God punished with such signal severity the transgressors before the flood with such utter and total destruction, sweeping them all into eternity with one mighty swell of his indignant wrath, how can the political gamblers and psuedo-philanthropists and religious sorcerers of the present day, who teach the very same things in precept and in practice, expect to escape the punishment of God on earth, and the damnation of hell in future? It were better, far better for them that a millstone had been tied around their necks, and they cast into the sea, than to have taught and perpetrated what they have done. A sea of tears can never wash their guilt away from the sight of an insulted God, though every tear were a stream of blood. His retributive justice *must* and *will* come to their *own doors.* Already has it begun to work, and though the ' mills of the gods grind slowly, they grind surely.' Let me just retrospect a little the punishment of God on a few of the leaders and prominent men who have acted so conspicuous a part in this unparalleled wickedness of this age in the sight of God :

"John Brown, of Harper's Ferry memory, was tried, convicted, and hung for trying to array the negroes of Virginia against the white people, and instigate a massacre in order to free the negro. Giddings, one of the fathers of the doctrine of Abolition, and all its concomitant train, died a debauched imbecile, not even remembered by the negroes with a cold, lifeless panegyric pronounced over him, in whose cause of freedom he had spent his whole life. Stanton, chafing under the gnawings of a guilty conscience, eating his very vitals out, ran him into suicide. Sumner, after lingering out a miserable existence, the disappointed advocate of a doctrine so false to God and his own race, died unwept and unlamented by the negroes, the idols of his heart's adoration. Horace Greeley, after spending full forty years of his life as author and father of Abolition, died of a broken heart, when he found he had spent his whole life in a cause that bankrupted his hope of salvation. And Henry Ward Beecher still lives, but Cain-like, branded with a guilty conscience for his foul and lying teachings of abolition and miscegenation, and ' stealing the livery of the court of Heaven to serve the devil in.' And Harriet Beecher Stowe, the author of that lying wonder of the age, ' Uncle Tom's Cabin,' still lives to realize the vengeance of an insulted God for publishing such a foul calumny against his Holy Word, and to share equally the punishment of an adulterous brother for teaching a wicked doctrine so palpably at variance with God's established *righteousness.*

"These are only a few of the monsters, in human flesh, who under the garb of humanity, philanthropy and religion, have boldly set at defiance God's revealed law, and degraded that portion of his creation which he made in his own *image* and *likeness*, and this is only a foretaste of the punishment reserved for them at the great and final retribution. Whilst, on the other hand, there was Washington, a large slave-owner. who lives yet bright in the hearts of his countrymen ; Madison and Monroe, Jackson, Clay and Calhoun, the monarchs of intellect, the statesmen of their age, and the admiration of the world, all large slave-owners and strong advocates and defenders of the institution, were honored and blessed with a good old age and useful life, and died in peace, lamented by a grateful country and wept by a nation's tears. And Daniel Webster, that great expounder of constitutional law, always defended the institution, on the ground that it was guaranteed by the Constitution.   And the immortal Davis, who, with Bob Lee and Joe Johnson and a handful of barefooted and ragged soldiers, living on parched corn, claiming that their right was divine and guaranteed by the Constitution, defended it for four long years and held the world at bay.   Immortal heroes, all !   When the memories of those who overpowered you are sunk into oblivion and forgetfulness, God will watch over your actions with his benignant approbation, and cause your memories to burn upon his altar of incense till time shall be no more.   You defended the institution because you *thought* the right divine, and was guaranteed by the Constitution of the fathers of the country.   Moses, Joshua and Caleb defended it because they *knew the right was divine.*"

"Sister, whilst I agree in feeling with you in the generous and noble sentiments expressed for the sainted dead of the best cause ever known, as the rights of man, and whilst I cannot but give due weight to your arguments, so forcibly and plainly laid before me, there are still some doubts upon my mind that I can't eradicate from it."

"Tell me your doubts, John, and if possible I will take great pleasure in removing them."

"They arise from this fact—that before the flood there is no mention made of a race of people called the negro, or the Indian, and none afterward, till some one in natural history gives them that name. Now how do you account for this ? "

"Your objection, John, if it amounts to anything, is just as good against the Jew as against the negro, for the Jew was not known by that distinctive name before the flood, nor even afterwards, till long after Abraham, although their ancestors can be traced back to Adam. I have not had time to examine how they got that distinctive name as a nation.   Still they have it.   But previously to Abraham their father, being chosen of God for a specific purpose, they were known only by the heads of their respective families, and when any one family wished to identify one of another family, they did so by referring to him as the son of A., who was the son of B., who was the son of C., etc. And hence, when the line of the Savior had to be proved, and his right to the throne of David sustained, they began thus: Luke iii, 23: 'And Jesus began to be about thirty years old, being (as was supposed) the son of Joseph, who was the son of Heli,' and so on up to Adam, ' who was the son of God '—Luke iii, 38.

"But in process of time, as the families of the earth became too large to live together, they mutually consented to set off, by certain metes and bounds, a district of country for the family who emigrated, and that district of country adopted the name of the head of the family who emigrated. This is more particularly taught in the family of Jacob's twelve sons, and a more exact record of it kept than in any other portion of the Bible, who became the representatives of the twelve tribes, who peopled Judea and Jerusalem and part of Persia. Before Abraham was chosen as the father of the Jewish nation—say from the flood to the building of the Tower of Babel—the whole earth, including Indians and negroes (under the name of beasts and serpents), all spoke the same language. But when the people undertook to build a tower to reach to heaven—Gen. xi, 4, 5—the Lord seeing ' their heart was set on evil only,' determined to confound their language, and wrought a miracle, which, on account of its practical bearings upon society and the domestic affairs and business relations of life, demanded at his hands an explanation, which he was so kind and good as to have made, and a record of it kept. But suppose the inspired historian had passed by in profound silence this miracle as he did the birth of old Mrs. Noah's three boys (provided the story is true), what kind of ludicrous stories do you suppose the ecclesiastical corps, the Plymouth Church miscegenationists, and the *psuedo*-philanthropists would have given to it? Why, as the Apostle John says—21st chapter, 25th verse—the world could not have contained the books that would have been written on it. This, however, is another proof of the fact that an all-wise and good God was too merciful, just and consistent to interrupt or suspend his natural laws to make his power known and felt, and then leave it to the doubtful solution of man to find out its truth.

"The triplicate birth of the red, black and white boy children of old Mrs. Noah (if true) is of more significance and importance in its temporal and eternal results to Adam's race than is the miracle of the confounding of the tongues, and still not one word is said on the subject of the diversity of colors by the inspired historian."

"Sister, I thought you said the negro and the Indian were *beasts*. If that is so, and they are not a part of Noah's family, then how could they all speak the same language ?"

"I thought I answered that question, John, when I told you that the negro was the *serpent* that deceived Eve. I then showed the fact that the *serpent* (the negro) and Adam and Eve either naturally spoke the same language, or that they had been associated with each other so long, in the relation of master and slave, that they had learned to speak each other's language. This I felt certain I had shown when I cited the colloquy between it and Eve. But to put this matter forever at rest with you, I will give you a practical illustration. It is founded upon what our father has often told me of the early introduction of the African or Guinea negro into the colonies, by the Yankee slave-traders of Boston, Massachusetts; that sink of iniquity, where the representatives of his Satanic Majesty's dark dominions have met, under the generic term of Puritans, to concoct all their diabolical wickedness, in the name of philanthropy and religion, to try to appease an offended God, (if His Majesty had become offended, which I deny,) for selling into slavery the *poor negro!* Hypocrites! Demons in human flesh! 'Hell's most abhorrent thought' is righteousness, when compared with such deep, dark wickedness, coming up from such monster hypocrites! Pardon me, John, but my heart revolts at the thought. And my 'soul shrinks back upon itself' when I contemplate so fully 'the devil rebuking sin,' as is so exactly fulfilled when those sanctimonious hypocrites defile God's holy desk with the personages of such men as Henry Ward Beecher, dealing out damnation upon Southern people for holding in slavery the descendants of the negroes which their fathers stole and sold to the South. Surely if the man who converts to a lawful use the property for which he paid a valuable and lawful consideration, is a sinner in the sight of God and man, and must be punished for it both here and hereafter, where, O, where will the thieves who stole the property and sold it to them stand in the day when God's retributive vengeance, *long pent up*, is poured out upon their heads—with the money paid for thousands of black souls, sold into slavery by the Puritan slave-stealers, and traders from Massachusetts, heaped up in the hands of their children, making them the millionaires of the North? And the blood trickling down the backs of the '*poor negroes*' which they had stolen from Africa and sold into slavery, hanging upon their skirts! But John, this sin (if it be a sin, which I deny), has not a parallel in his majesty's dark dominions, when you contemplate the fact of its perpetrators trying to bribe high Heaven to let its wrath against them be appeased by offering the Southern people a sacrifice upon the Northern altar of the Puritan negro-traders, with Henry Ward Beecher, that thoroughbred libertine in Plymouth Church christianity, as high priest; and that, too, after they had committed the duplicate sin of re-stealing the descendants of those negroes from the people of the South.

"These Puritan negro-stealers and traders begged of Congress to let the law permitting the African slave-trade to continue in force till 1808, (I think I state correctly), while the Southern States all wanted it to cease in 1801, (if wrong in this I stand corrected). They were outvoted by the Northern States, in which the Massachusetts Puritan negro-traders took the lead. These are the facts of history, from which there is no escape. This matter of negro-stealing and trading in Africans *was all right* as long as the Puritan traders indulged in it. But no sooner had the time allowed by Act of Congress expired, and they had time to sell off what negroes they had on hand to the Southern States, than they were seized with a '*holy horror*' at the idea of one man owning property in another. They then began to concoct a more wicked design than the first, which was to steal them back from

5

111

the Southern people; set the negroes free; and then in one general convocation of the religious hypocrites, and Northern negro-traders, call upon God to damn the Southern people for holding the negroes in the '*chains of slavery,' which they* (the Puritans) *had forged for them.* But, John, I ought to let these people alone; 'for,' as the Louisville *Courier Journal* has very wisely said, ' when God puts his hand upon a man, or a nation, every one else had better take theirs off.'

"I will now recur to the answer to your question from which I digressed. I had just stated what our father had often told me of the imperfect manner of speech which the African negroes had when they were first introduced into Massachusetts, and then into Virginia. Their language was so imperfect that it was with great difficulty that either the master or they could understand each other. But by continued association as master and slave, and efforts with corresponding signs and examples, they did imperfectly understand each other. But the original African never did learn to speak the English correctly; but the children born to them did, from the fact that they were reared up to it."

"Sister, I have listened to you with a great deal of interest ; and whilst I admit it is full, there is still one thing that is left in doubt."

" Let me hear what it is, John, and I still promise to answer to the best of my ability, guided by Scripture and the logic of facts."

"The question is this, sister : If what you have said be true (and I believe it is), how do you account for the negro, who you say was created a beast, and named a serpent by Adam, losing the generic term or name of beast, as created by God, and the distinctive name of serpent, as named by Adam, and merging into the name of negro, as known among us now?"

"This, John, is one of the most important questions you have asked me since our conversations began, and shall have a very careful consideration.

" In order to answer it intelligently, I must ask you to read Gen. xi, 1 to 9, inclusive. The first verse says that all the world was of one language—meaning all persons who could talk. The verses which I have requested you to read show that the descendants of the people who came out of the flood, having a vivid recollection of what their ancestors told them of the destruction of the earth by the flood of waters, determined to build the Tower of Babel, and make it so high and so large that some, if not all, could be saved in the event of another flood, getting the idea from a part of God's creation being saved by the ark from *the* flood that had passed over it. In order to do this they had, by mutual consent, called to their aid every family of Noah's race, with all their property and servants, to perfect this stupendous undertaking. Upon the principle that as all would claim protection in the event of another flood, all should help in building the tower. The negro, as the servant of the white man, was *made* to perform a conspicuous part in the manual labor of this gigantic undertaking.

"After the completion of the ark, and before the flood, Noah knowing the fact that the negroes owned by him were *his own,* and as he had a command from God to take a specific number of pairs of *any*

112

kind of animals into the ark with him, it is very natural to conclude that as far as he could comply with his instructions, without trespassing upon his neighbors, he supplied the order from his *own plantation* with *negroes* and *stock.* The wild animals were made by God to go in to him. This being the case, the title to the negroes as legally descended to his posterity after the flood as it did to the other animals. Then when Moses says—Gen. xi, 1—'that all the earth was of one language and one speech,' he includes the *negroes* and *Indians.* In the 10th chapter of Genesis all the heads of families of the immediate line of Noah are mentioned, and shows that there were as many nations of people arising out of these families as there were heads of families named ; but *all spoke the same* language.

"At the building of the Tower of Babel, when their language was confounded, they were scattered abroad all over the earth. How, then, were they scattered ? Not by any further physical act or miracle of God, but by the law of nature that governs mankind—that of interest and happiness. Everyone who could understand each other as naturally congregated together and colonized as the waters from a thousand rivulets mingle into one common stream. In this confounding of speech the negro's and Indian's speech were also confounded. The master could not understand the negro, nor he his master, and rather than be troubled with a negro who could not understand him, he abandoned him altogether, preferring *no negro* at all to one who could not understand him. As the white people and the Indians sought such of their respective colors that they could understand in conversation, the negro did the same, all consulting their interests and feelings and instincts ; and as it was no pleasure to be associated with those they could not understand, they naturally got as far off from each other as they could.

" In this condition the negro, not finding anyone who could speak the same language with himself to claim him, concluded he would *run away,* and following the instincts of his nature, sought the hotter climates, and desiring to get off as far from the white man as he could, for fear he might be put to work again, took up his abode in the wilds of Africa.

" It was, then, the peculiar language that each spoke that made it to their interest and happiness to colonize when and where they did.

" Your question, then, applies with equal force to the white nations that were scattered abroad, as it does to the negro and Indian. There is no record which shows how the descendants of these people, who were scattered abroad, got their present names as nations. 'Tis true, there are some general outlines, which are made a matter of record by subsequent history. Still there is none that shows how, when, or where they lost their national name and obtained their present one. The Jewish chronicles, which have been kept by the mysterious care of God, are the most perfect now extant. They do not show how the *twelve tribes,* who each was once a very powerful nation, numbering hundreds of thousands to each separate tribe, all lost their respective national names, and all merged into one common name of *Jew.* The argument would be just as sound, to say that because history nor the

113

Bible does not show that Noah was called a Jew, but simply 'Noah,' that the Jew, under the national name of *Jew*, is not of Noah's line.

"I say that argument would be just' as sound, and equally as sensible, as to say, because the negro is known among us by the national name of negro, therefore he is not the descendant of the serpent whom Adam owned and who deceived Eve. The history on this subject only finds the negro in Africa, but does not account for his getting there in any other way than I have shown. And the first thing we hear of him again, politically, is that the Dutch in 1627, and after them the Portuguese, and after them the British, had brought them for sale to the British islands and the colonies. Afterwards, the Boston Puritan negro-traders had taken some blood-hounds, or negro dogs, and went to Africa to catch '*runaway negroes*' to sell to the Southern States. They argued about in this way: 'There is a great deal of manual labor needed here in Massachusetts, and Virginia, the Carolinas and Georgia, and as the Dutch, Portuguese and British have been catching *runaway negroes* in Africa and selling them to the British islands and colonies, suppose a few of us make up a company, purchase a ship, take some blood-hounds, and go over to Africa and catch a ship-load of them, and bring them to Boston and sell them out. *There's money in it.* They belong to the white man, anyhow, for they *ran away* from their owners at the building of the Tower of Babel, because their language was confounded and they could not understand their master, nor he them. We are the descendants of their old masters. Now let us go and catch them, and if they don't understand us, d—n them, we'll put the whip to them and make them understand. Possession gives right, and we can make a fortune. D—n him, there is money in him, *and I want the money.* The right of the white man to him is *divine*, anyhow, and let us *serve the Lord* by claiming our rights, for everybody knows that the Massachusetts folks are, *of all others*, a God-fearing people.' This is about the way the Boston traders reasoned at that time.

"History had given a certain district of country in Africa the name of *Niger.* The inhabitants of that country were called Niger; why? I can't tell. When these traders first brought them to the colonies they gave them the name of *Nigger*, because there was a harshness in the term, and they desired to make them forget the name of their country, and because it carried a species of terror in it. Afterwards, when sold to the Virginia planter, they being milder in their feelings, and wishing to cultivate a friendly feeling with the '*nigger*,' gave him the name of '*Negro.*' By this name they have been known ever since, till Congress gave him the name of '*Freedman.*' But no change in name has ever been able to change his *identity.* I trust now you will be satisfied with my answer to your question."

"Yes, sister, I am now satisfied you are right, and you have relieved my mind a great deal. There is one other question, however, that I wish to ask. It is this: If the negro has not the same parentage of the white man, and is not of Adam's posterity, how do you reconcile that Scripture in Acts, xvii, 26, 'God has made of one blood all nations of men to dwell on the face of the earth?'"

114

"I am very glad, John, you called my attention to this Scripture. I should have given it notice in another connection, and will do so now.

"Your quotation of this Scripture reminds me very much of the quotation of the drunkard, who was justifying himself to the preacher for his drinking. He said, 'Why, sir, don't the Scriptures say, If the wicked trouble you, *drink?*' Asserting it in the emphatic manner that he did, the preacher concluded, before he would flatly contradict him, that he would get the Bible and look up the text, and there he read, 'If the wicked trouble you, *drink not.*' Now, you stop too soon. Let us read a little further, and include the context: . . 'and hath determined the time before appointed;' . . verse 28, 'for in him we live, move, and have our being;' . . 'for we are his *offspring.*' Verse 29, . . 'forasmuch as we are the *offspring of God,* we ought not to think that the Godhead is like silver, or gold, graven with man's device . . .'

"Now, what is the argument in this controversy between Paul and the Grecians and Athenians, Epicureans and Stoics, as shown by the history of the case? It is not a question of blood descent *per se,* but a question of *faith,* based upon the resemblance of parent and offspring. He is arguing with them to show that the idol which they had erected for them to worship could not be the God of Heaven. 'For,' says he, 'we are his *offspring.* Now,' says he, 'as *we are* his offspring, we ought not to think that our parentage, the Godhead, is like gold, silver or stone, graven by art or man's device.' Then, how should they look? I ask. Why, they should look like the '*offspring.*' Who were the *offspring* which Paul directly refers to in this connection? I say it is to himself and his people, the Jews, and the Athenians and Grecians. The children of Japheth, as all history, sacred and profane, shows, were white. But to make it more clear to those to whom he was preaching, he says '*we are his offspring.*' Then, how do *we look? You see we are white;* are thinking, moving, rational beings. And as we are his *offspring,* we Jews and Athenians and Grecians—in other words, we *Jews* and *Gentiles*—we ought to conclude that our father, the Godhead, looks like his *offspring;* we! us! we Jews! and Athenians! and Grecians! who WE and all the world know are white! He is not, then, like an idol of gold, silver or stone; but looks like his children, in accordance with that universal law of his, of 'like begetting like,' written in the face and upon the body of all animated nature, from the veriest reptile up to the *white man* made in his *image.*

"Suppose, now, that it had been a question of color and of races that had been in controversy between Paul and the abolitionist or miscegenationist, or *psuedo*-philanthropist of the present day, who advocate that all *colors* of men have the same parentage? Could he have made a more forcible, more striking, more conclusive, and more unanswerable argument than he did to the Athenians, Grecians and Jews? viz.: That if the *negro* was the offspring of God, he ought to look like him, or at least look like the other children of the family—ought to be in his likeness and image, at least in *color,* that great distinguishing mark of identity which God has stamped upon all progeny in order to tell at a glance what their parentage is. He says, 'has made of *one* blood.' Why say ' of one blood' *all nations?*' Why not say at once, 'has made of one *blood* all *colors* of men?' Why use the term ' *all nations*' instead of ' *all colors?*' I say the only sensible solution of it is founded in the old maxim known since '*time was young,*' that 'BLOOD WILL TELL,' and had he used the words *all colors,* he would have violated the true doctrine of faith given by Adam to Seth, and handed down through him from generation to generation, and kept and treasured in the white families down to the day he was preaching. And so fully was he confident of the fact that it was the white people only that filled the requirements of nature's law. that ' the offspring' should look like their parents, that he used the term ' *one blood*' as applying to them. Paul knew as well as Noah did that it was the corrupting of the ' *one blood*'—the ' *white blood*'—by Cain and his posterity that caused God to curse the earth with a flood, and that *none other* but the *pure white* blood had a right to the benefits of the doctrine of Christianity which he preached, when he used the term '*one blood*' to distinguish them, the *white man* from the *colored man,* both negro and Indian. Now, had he said ' *hath made all nations,* that they might seek the Lord,' etc., . . then there might be some pretext for the wholesome doctrine that *all men,* black, red and white, if not of the same parentage, had at least an equal right to seek the Lord through Christ, but by using the term ' *one blood*' it does seem to me to be the most conclusive argument that none but those who have that ' *one blood*'—Adam's blood, pure, uncorrupted, untarnished—coursing in their veins and stamping upon them the image and likeness of God, have any right to, or are embraced in, the doctrine of salvation which he was then preaching. There were in Greece and Athens, at the time Paul was preaching, thousands of negro slaves, if history be correct. This being the case, and Paul knowing that only Adam's posterity was embraced in the transgression of Adam, and knowing also that neither the negro nor the Indian were of his posterity, used the term ' *one blood*' to settle the fact with these people—that those negro slaves were not included, as they were not of the ' *one blood*.'

"There was another reason, and a very prominent reason, why he used the term *one blood,* which is this: The Jews had always had the oracles of God, from the time they were given to Moses ; also the laws; also the temple worship; also the promise, through Abraham, their progenitor, and through them as his seed, that a Redeemer of the world should come ; and so arrogant had they become from enjoying these privileges, that they thought the children of Japheth, and of Ham, had no rights at all to the favor of God. Now Paul wished to correct this, and knowing that they admitted that the Athenians, and in fact all the posterity of Japheth and Ham, were of Noah's family, and of the ' *one blood*' as much so as they, the posterity of Shem, were, and knowing also that there were many nations, both of the posterity of Shem, Japheth and Ham, he used the term ' *hath made of one blood* all nations of men,' including and embracing only the posterity of Noah, and through him the posterity of Adam, who were involved in the consequences of Adam and Eve's transgression, who were the white people."

116

"Sister, if your argument be true, it appears to me that you would exclude the Indian and the negro from the right to worship God altogether, by the Bible."

"John, my position on that subject is simply this : That there was no command given to any one, *not to eat of the tree of knowledge of good and evil*, but to Mr. and Mrs. Adam. And, *that being the case*, it would be very unjust to punish those who were not in the transgression. Now I hold that the negro and the Indian, not being of Mr. and Mrs. Adam's posterity, but being made before them, and not placed under the law that Mr. and Mrs. Adam were, God is too just to punish them for what others did. ' Where there is no law, there is no transgression,' says Paul. And if it would be unjust to punish them for the acts of a man and woman of a different family, then it would be equally unjust to divide the rewards with them."

"Well, sister, what law do you think the negro and the Indian were originally placed under by the Creator ?"

"If the Scriptures be true, John, and if the Mosaic account of the creation be true, then the only revealed divine law given them, for them to keep inviolate, was and is, to ' *bring forth after their kind.*' No other divine law was ever given them, as far as revelation shows; but it was, and is as positive, and imperative to them, as was the law or command to Mr. and Mrs. Adam *not to eat* of the forbidden fruit; with this difference only, that death was not suspended upon the transgression of their law, as in the case of Mr. and Mrs. Adam in the transgression of theirs. The negro and Indian, like all other animated nature, would have died in the course of time, any way; for they were made of the earth, and unto the earth they will return, and that will be the end of them."

"Well, sister, I have never before seen the importance attached to being of Adam's posterity. Your conclusion is certainly right, if your arguments in previous conversations on the lines of Shem, Ham, and Japheth, be correct. And in this connection I wish to ask you why Abraham was so exceedingly particular not to let his son Isaac take a wife from among the Canaanites, in whose country he lived. This has been a mystery to me ; and I would like to know why he was so prejudiced against a whole nation of people, numbering perhaps several millions, that he was not willing for his son Isaac to marry one of their daughters. You know it is usually customary for parents to be glad to see their sons marry their neighbors' daughters."

"John, I will give your question as grave a consideration as I am capable, for I, too, have thought upon this subject with a great deal of interest. And to me it has been an astounding thing, why an old man, who was called ' *the friend of God*,' and who had been blessed with the peculiar promises of God, should, when having become very old and feeble, with death staring him in the face, as it were, have such deep-rooted prejudice and hatred against a whole nation of people of several millions of beings, that he would call his old and faithful family servant, who was a white man, and cause him to swear by the God of Heaven that he would *not allow* his son Isaac to take a wife from among them ; I say, John, there must have been some very sound reason, either in morals or law, or both, that would cause a man of the reputed goodness of Abraham, and who had the confidence of God as he had, to give birth to such deep-rooted prejudice and hatred against a whole nation of people, as he had—a prejudice as lasting as life, and a hatred as unrelenting as death. In the face of these facts, John, let us stop a moment before we judge rashly or harshly against this old man, and make a few inquiries into the history of the case.

"You must remember that Abraham did this fully three thousand seven hundred and fifty years ago. We are not, then, competent judges in this matter, without inquiring very closely into the history, both of Abraham and the Canaanites.

"The first question that arises for us to consider is: Who were the Canaanites against whom Abraham entertained this deep, malignant feeling?

"Canaan, the father or progenitor of these people, was the son of Ham, against whom his grandfather, Noah, pronounced a curse. 'Tis true, I suppose, from the nature of the account as given by Moses, that the old gentleman was drunk when he did this. But I have never blamed him for it; for the very best of professors, even the *sons of temperance*, and once in a while a *daughter*, too, takes a '*leetle too much.*' But what has puzzled me is why the old gentleman should curse the *child* for what the *fath. r did?* I am obliged to admit that I do not know any rule, either in law or ethics, taught in the Mosaic Law, or the Christian Scriptures, that inculcates such a doctrine. Be that as it may, the curse was pronounced, and perhaps the sequel may develop the reason for it.

"Abraham was born about three hundred and ninety-five years after this curse was pronounced. He was of the family line of Shem, the brother of Ham, who was the father of Canaan. How old Shem was when his nephew Canaan was born, the historian does not say. But there is one thing very certain—Shem knew all about this family matter. And as Abraham was one hundred and five years old when Shem died, it is a very natural conclusion to suppose that he had often heard his progenitor, Shem, and his uncles, Japheth and Ham, talk this matter of the curse of Noah against Canaan over time and again. He no doubt was as familiar with it as any household affair in the family. Then I hold that Abraham had got his deep-seated hatred for the Canaanites from the accounts which he had heard and learned from the family. It was a theme of every-day conversation among the entire family connections, if people talked of family matters then as they do now.

"Let us examine the family line of Canaan a little, and see what we can make out of it. The historian says Ham, the father of Canaan had four sons. Canaan is set down as the fourth in order. I will not run through the family line of the other three, but just notice Canaan. He begins thus—Gen. x, 15: 'And Canaan begat Sidon, his first-born, and Heth;' and in verse 16 he breaks off abruptly from calling his children by name, as he had done with all of Canaan's brothers' children, and says, 'and the Jabezite, Amorite, Gergashite,' and goes on with a long string of names of other *ites* which he begat. Now, why this abrupt break-off from the individual names of Canaan's children to that of nations? Why this, I ask? He had not done so with any of the other families before. Who were these *ites* that he spoke of? We hear nothing more of them till Abraham is called of God, and commanded to go into the land of Canaan. He goes. And when about to die, makes his servant swear before High Heaven that he will not let his son Isaac take a wife from among them. God promises him the land of Canaan, and to his seed after him. His servant goes into a far country, and gets a wife for Isaac of Abraham's family line, the daughter of Bethuel. Abraham dies satisfied. In the course of time his posterity go into Egypt, and are in bondage for four hundred and thirty years to their brethren of the line of Ham. They are led out by Moses, of the line of Shem; start for the land of Canaan. Moses dies. Joshua is commanded by the Lord to take command of the children of Abraham, and carry them into the land of Canaan, and to literally exterminate, or drive out, every man, woman and child of the Canaanites, and all the other ites, which, by the time he and Caleb got through with them, amounted to thirty-three nations of ites, amounting to several millions of persons.

"It would seem, from the sequel, that God Almighty's hatred to these Canaanites, and other *ites*, was as great or greater than Abraham's, for Abraham only wanted that his son should not marry one of the girls, but God Almighty determined to destroy the entire seed, breed and generation of them from the land of Canaan.

"The parallel of God's vengeance and severity, in this instance, is not to be found, save only in the destruction of the mixed bloods and negroes by the flood. Why did he destroy them? Have I not shown in previous conversations that it was on account of Cain's miscegenating and amalgamating with the negro, thus corrupting the blood of the whole of Adam's race, excepting Noah's family? And I fearlessly assert that there is no other thing that can be alleged or assigned for this wonderful and summary vengeance of God upon these *ites*, except that Canaan had developed the curse of his grandfather upon him and his posterity by miscegenating and amalgamating with the negro, as Cain had done before him, and started and propagated these *ites*, who were all mixed bloods, or perhaps had done so when the curse was pronounced, which, I think, is most likely to have been the case, for there had been plenty of time from the flood to the pronouncing of the curse for Canaan to have been born, grown up and married, and then to have apostatized from the faith and disgraced himself by taking a negro wench (perhaps one of his slaves) as a concubine, and have commenced propagating the mixed-blooded Canaanites. Noah finds this out, or knows it before, and feeling indignant at the conduct of Ham towards him when he was drunk, revenged himself by cursing Canaan, because he had brought this disgrace upon the white race. This view of the matter displays his justice in cursing the child, not so much for what the father had done, but for what he had done himself.

"Abraham knowing that God had commanded men 'to bring forth after their kind,' or beget children in their own image and likeness,

and that the white man was in the image and likeness of God, and
that the Canaanites and all the other ites were not, but were mixed
bloods, swore his servant and compelled him to go out of their country
and get a white wife for his son Isaac, that he might perpetuate the
image and likeness of God. He knew that God Almighty had established the COLOR LINE in his family line, and he was determined it
should not be laid to his charge that he had broken that pure and
spotless COLOR LINE which came coursing down through his veins
from Shem, Noah and Adam.

"This, then, John, is the reason why Abraham would not let his
son Isaac marry a Canaanitish girl, and there is no other reason that
can be assigned for it. Isaac taught the same to Jacob, sending him
out of Canaan to get a wife.

"I want, while on this subject, John, to call your attention to one
fact in the line of Ham's other children, which I should have done
when proving that Ham was white. He had four sons, viz : Cush,
Mizraim, Phut and Canaan. One of the sons of Cush was Nimrod.
He established a kingdom—Gen. x, 10—the beginning of which was
Babel, Erech, Accad and Calneh, in the land of Shinar, 'out of which
land (verse 11) went forth Asshur and builded Nineveh.' I only
introduce this, or call your attention to it, to show that it was the
grandson of Ham who built the mighty cities of Babylon and Nineveh, and all history confirms the fact that the Babylonians and Nine-
vites were pure white men. This of itself, without any other proof to
support it, would sustain the proposition that Ham was a white man."

"Well, sister, I have given you a patient and an attentive hearing,
and am willing to let others believe as they may, but as to myself, I
shall ever hereafter believe that the negro and the Indian are an
original creation and as separate from Adam's race as the horse is
from the negro."

"John, their whole claim to being of Adam's race is based upon
three things, the first of which is the assumption, without any proof,
that old Mrs. Noah had a red, black and white boy child, all by old
Mr. Noah; and the next is that these red and black boys propagated
their respective colors, without having wives of the same color, which
I think, to say the least of it, that it is the most ridiculous absurdity
—I had like to have said wicked—that sensible men ever believed or
taught since the world began. The other is upon the forced, strained
interpretation of the text of Scripture which says: 'God has made of
one blood all nations of men,' etc. I have so fully argued this to you
before that I will not waste your time over it again.

"There is one thing, John, which I want to fix upon your attention
so that you will not forget it, but will give it due consideration in after
life. It is this, viz. : that to one of the three colors, red, white, or
black, was given by the Creator the rule, dominion, power, and ownership over all things created by him, and that color was the one that
was in his image and likeness. I have shown, by taking the Jews as
the starting point, that the white man was in his image and likeness.
But for the sake of argument, let me say that I am wrong; and that it
was the negro or the Indian that was in his image and likeness. I then

120

call upon you, I call upon history, I call upon the learned ecclesiastical corps, who claim that the negro and Indian are of the same origin as the white man, to show, in the annals of history, or of facts, one single, solitary instance where the negro, or the Indian, have claimed, or had, universal *dominion* over God Almighty's works. Not one instance can they show. Again, I *dare* them to show, in one solitary instance, where the white man, as a nation, has been subject to the negro or the Indian ; except it be in the few cases of Northern carpetbaggers, who, like Esau and Cain, sold their *birth-rights* for a mess of pottage, and came down South to barter off their color for the ' loaves and fishes,' to be disposed of by the negroes. The bare fact of the discontent of the negro with his condition, and trying to insinuate himself into the company of the white man, so contrary to the white man's wishes, is *prima facie* evidence that he feels his inferiority to the white man. And it is known from one end of this country to the other, from Maine to Florida, that the white man who equalizes himself, politically, socially, civilly and religiously with them, degrades himself in his own estimation, and in the estimation of his pretended friends, but above all in the sight of the good and true men who bear the image and likeness of God, the *White Man.*

" Again. See with what unerring exactness the white man has complied with God's command, ' *and subdue them,*' as applied to the Indian. This country was settled by the Indians, and was almost literally covered by them from one end to the other when first discovered by the white man. Where are they now? Subdued ! gone ! with scarcely one left to tell the tale. Could a command be more exactly complied with ? And could any fulfillment go further to show that the Indian is neither the blood descent of Adam, or was ever to have the ' *dominion*' over the white man? The present condition of the negro will cause him to be ' *subdued,*' melt away before the white man, exactly as the Indian has. He only increased in this country because he was subject to the white man ; and it was to the interest of the white man to take care of him as his *money.* But now, with that interest in the negro gone, he must and will disappear sooner than the Indian did."

" Sister, as I have to leave for home to-morrow, our conversations must come to a close. Still, I want to hear your answer to the following question : If the judgments of God have been so severe heretofore against the nations that have corrupted the white blood, why did he permit the North to subdue the South ? and then establish social and political equality, and legalize marriage between the races?"

" John, my time is so short that I fear I shall have to condense my answer so much that it will not be satisfactory. To begin, then, I will state, emphatically, that it was not because slavery was *wrong ;* but, on the other hand, it was *right* in itself. But your ex of the Southern people had violated God's law, just as Cain and Canaan had, though not to the same extent. God had intended to make slavery a blessing to the white people of the South. He had permitted them to be introduced into the tobacco, rice, cotton and sugar fields of the Middle and Southern States, as laborers, and as a blessing to the people of these States. They had been owned by the people of every one of the Old Thirteen; but they were never profitable to the Northern States, owing to the shortness of the season, and the climate. As the Southern territory began to be developed, it opened up a market for the negroes of the North, and the owners met it freely. Up to this time they were viewed only as property by the Northern people. The title was considered good, and the right *divine*. They were not then considered citizens by the Northern people, or even as of the same race. And so rigid were they in enforcing this belief, that the amalgamation with them by the white man was placed in the catalogue of other *capital* offenses, and punished accordingly. To the credit of the New England States, let it be said that in this one thing they *once* acted with the *fear* of *God* before their eyes. Not a solitary mulatto child can be charged up to them during the existence of slavery amongst them.

"All the States worked harmoniously together, with slavery in them, as long as they were viewed *only* as property, which doctrine was adopted by Yankee legislation. And now, John, this brings me to a fact in this history that humiliates my pride, and shocks my feelings, to be compelled to admit that the land of Washington was the birthplace of practical miscegenation with the negro. Painful and mortifying as it is to me to confess it, or even know it, it was here that *the sin* that doomed the antediluvians to a flood—that exterminated the Canaanites by Joshua—was first committed. So great was public indignation, at first, against the offenders against the law, and so severe the punishment, that the perpetrators of it had invariably to flee their country. But in process of time the old Northern slave-traders died off. The younger ones sold their negroes to the Southern States. A new generation grew up in their stead; and, to the astonishment of the entire world, they found out that slavery was a sin, and the negro was the white man's brother. Northern pulpits caught the fire, and their politicians, warmed up by its heat, began to teach it was a sin. They had forgot the doctrine of the old Northern traders, that the *right to them was divine*. The Northern statute-books were remodeled, and the law declaring negroes property was repealed, and they were declared to be of Adam's race, and the brother of the white man. But that sound constitutional lawyer and statesman, Daniel Webster, always held that they *were property*.

"Southern ministers began to give in to the doctrine of the Northern pulpit, and as the doctrine gained strength that the negro was the white man's brother, apologies began to be made for slavery. Practical miscegenation increased, and so widespread had the effects of this sin become, that mulatto negroes swarmed through the middle and Southern States like the Egyptian locusts. This, then, John, is the answer to your question: *Not that slavery was a sin, or wrong*, but it was *right* and established by God himself. But the Southern *men* had turned what was intended to be a blessing into a *curse*, by following in the footsteps of Cain of old before the flood, and of Canaan after the flood, to that extent in violating God's law by miscegenating with the negro, till an insulted God, outraged in feeling at a people who had turned into a *curse* what he intended to be a blessing to them, determined to visit summary punishment upon them for their wickedness, by freeing the negro; and hence he called the Northern horde of vandals—not that they were any better in theory and doctrine, but having taken the ground that the negro was the brother of the white man, they were fit instruments to execute his indignant wrath upon the Southern men for violating his law, and thus he freed the negroes. The thing which God hates worst is he who misrepresents his law. The next is he who acts on that representation.

"Now, John, viewing this subject from my standpoint, how could it have been otherwise than that the South should have been overrun by numbers fully five to one against them, and access to the entire world to replenish from, and freedom offered to the negro, and above all, with the law of an insulted God trampled under their feet, and his face turned against them, how could they expect to succeed? Why, John, had every Confederate soldier been a sirocco, and every minnie ball been a fifty-pound shell filled with the deadly poison of the Upas tree, and every pistol and musket had been a sixty-four pounder, and every sixty-four pounder had been an earthquake, they could not have succeeded, because it was *God* vindicating his own law and punishing transgressors for marring his *image* and *likeness* by miscegenating with the negro.

"Let me illustrate: When Joshua was sent against the Canaanites and others of the country, his instructions were to ' utterly destroy,' for this very sin, both the inhabitants and all their property, and though the city of Jericho and its land had been delivered into his hand without the firing of a gun; in the very next fight he had, he was whipped worse than the Federals were at the first Manassas. Now why was this? Because he had violated God's order. (Joshua vi, 18, 19.) These are parallel cases, with this difference: Joshua and his army were a righteous people before God, as far as the sin of miscegenating with the negro was concerned, and did not believe they were the equal of the white man, or any akin to him, whilst the Northern army did both believe it and practice it."

"Well, sister, this being the case, I can't see in what respect the North is or was any better than the South."

"None, John! None in the world! But God Almighty seeing that the Southern *men* had turned his blessing into a curse, and that the continuance of it might culminate in the entire amalgamation of the two races, as it had in the days of Cain and Canaan, determined to cut this state of things short by freeing the negro. And John, had it not been for the purity and fidelity of my sex of the white race, in keeping inviolate the sanctity and sacredness of his law, by not marring his image by departing from it, there would not have been left one solitary Southern man to tell the tale of woe that would have followed his punishment for this violation of his law. But my modesty is so deeply shocked to contemplate this matter further, from this wicked standpoint, that I ask to be excused from pursuing it further, even though with you, and intended for your good."

"Sister, I believe what you say is true—every word of it—and it casts a gloom over my whole future life to know and feel so sensibly the truth of what you have said in regard to my sex. I can see no escape from the present political condition of my country, and like the Jew, when in Babylonish captivity, feel like suffering Southern humanity may forever ' hang its harp upon the willows.' "

"No, John! No! Don't despond too much! Whilst God Almighty is, and must be, just in punishing wrong, there do arise cases in which his immaculate attributes permit him to temper justice with mercy, and is ever ready to lend a listening ear to the repentant sinner. Let me cite you to his own words, found in Jeremiah xviii, 7, 8, 9, 10, and reads thus: 'At what instant I shall speak concerning a nation or a kingdom, to pluck it up, and to pull it down and destroy it; if that nation or kingdom turn from their *evil*, I will repent of the *evil* that I thought to do unto them. And at what instant I shall speak concerning a nation or a kingdom, to build or to plant it, if it do evil in my sight, that it obey not my voice, then I will repent of the good wherewith I intended to bless it." Let us now examine the fulfillment of this doctrine of God's justice tempered with mercy. In the third chapter of Jonah we have an account of his preaching to the people of Nineveh, ' that in forty days Nineveh would be destroyed.' The King hears it. He becomes alarmed, commands a universal convocation and fast of *man* and *beast* and *cattle*. He and the people repent, and God stays his judgment against Nineveh.

"Again, when Joshua was leading the children of Israel—the pure white blood against the people of Canaan, the mixed blood—after utterly destroying Jericho, he was defeated in the next fight. (See Joshua vii, 4, 5.) He appeals to the Lord to know the cause (verses 7, 8, 9.) The Lord answers (verses 10, 11, 12), . . . the people had kept back part of the spoils; tells him what to do (verses 13, 14, 15.) He follows his instructions, finds the spoil, and punishes the trespasser. The Lord returns his favor to him, and he is never again defeated in thirty-two hard-fought battles.

"Now what lessons of wisdom could the political leaders of the people of the South learn, if they would only contemplate their people's condition, from a Scripture standpoint, and, like *one man*, come back to His COLOR LINE, which he has drawn in the face of the white man, for the governing of the world, and FIGHT IT OUT ON THAT LINE, with him as their leader. Every hill and every valley ; every hamlet, town, and city; every rivulet, water-course, and river, would send up one grand, triumphant shout of joy and praise to HIM who RULES the DESTINIES of nations, for their deliverance from the curse that their misconduct has so unfortunately brought upon them.

" Vicksburg did this ; and although it did not have as its design the worship of God in all its thoughts, still the stand it took was on His COLOR LINE—the white man against the negro and mixed blood. The white people of that devoted city had endured with much long-suffering and Christian forbearance the insolence, intolerance and oppression of negro misrule, till patience, fortified by the spirit of Christianity, had ceased to be a virtue, and they determined to throw off the yoke of oppression which they had worn till their substance had nearly 'all been consumed. In solemn convention they decreed that 'live or die,' sink or swim,' they would be free again. With one common consent, all nationalities of white men represented there, determined, as if the will of one man, to *form* on the COLOR LINE. The 4th of August came. The morning chanticleer, that watchful sentinel of nature's twinkling luminaries, had just sounded his first shrill clarion, giving warning of the early approach of the bright king of day, when the old gray-headed fathers could be seen vieing with each other *who* should be the first at the polls to cast the first vote, and draw the first drop of the life-blood of oppression. Early in their wake came Israel's sons, of the royal line of King David, of Abraham and of Shem, and forming on the COLOR LINE, composed its center, with the brave sons from the land of Scotia's sweet bard, the land of Wallace and of Bruce, joined by the *whole-souled* sons of Erin, of the Emerald Isle, of the shamrock green, making its right, and the sons of the vine-clad hills and gay valleys of France, the land of LaFayette, and the boys from the land of music and of song, Italy's classic hills, and the true sons of *die Faderland*, all forming on the left, presented one united front, solid, impenetrable, unyielding; and the sight of the American eagle again clapping his wings in the pride of renewed existence, impelled the boys in the blue and the gray to abandon for *one day* all the delights of beauty and love for an ardent, endearing, cordial embrace on the COLOR LINE; and before the next morn's sun arose, negro rule and negro oppression in Vicksburg had died before THAT COLOR LINE like the host of Sennacherib before the 'breath of the Lord.'

"Vicksburg has only acted in *miniature* what the Southern States *all* have to act in full life—come *square up to the* COLOR LINE. 'Touch not, handle not the unclean thing.' Col. ii, 21. 'But come out from among them and be separate.' 2d Corinthians, vi, 17, and . . (verse 18) 'I will receive you, and will be a father unto you, and you shall be MY SONS AND DAUGHTERS, saith the Lord Almighty.' Will my countrymen heed the counsel of the all-wise God, and ' *come out* from among them and form on this COLOR LINE and be separate ?' or will they organize again on another Dent-Greeley line, only to be defeated and disgraced ? When Saul, King of Israel, was sent by Jehovah to literally exterminate the Amalekites, both men, women and children, cattle, sheep, horses and asses, he carried out the command to the letter in every respect but one. He saved some of the best of the cattle to sacrifice to the Lord. When he met Samuel, the prophet of God, he ran to him to kiss him, in joy for his success, and exclaimed he had filled the command to the letter. Samuel replied : ' What means the *bleating* of Amalekitish *cattle* in my ears?' He replied he had saved a few of the best of the *cattle* to sacrifice unto the Lord. Samuel replies: ' Because you have done this your kingdom shall be taken from you and given to another.' (1st Samuel i, 14.) What lessons of wisdom my people can learn by heeding the above Scriptures in making their next political platforms and tickets. Let me admonish them to let no *bleating Amalekitish cattle* be in it, to be heard of the Lord ; but let it be a whole-souled ' COME

125

OUT' from among them, and organized on his COLOR LINE, and they will be sure of success. When Joshua, the leader of the children of Israel, had pitched his tents in the land of Moab, and Balak, the King of Moab, heard it, he sent for Balaam, the prophet of God, and offered him a large reward to *curse* Israel. He went and tried, and tried again, but every time he opened his mouth to *curse*, a *blessing* flowed out, because Joshua had organized Israel on the COLOR LINE. (See Numbers, xxii.) And more recently, when a Canaanitish Lieutenant-Governor and a Cainite Governor had telegraphed to the President to CURSE Vicksburg by sending troops to it, because it had organized on THE COLOR LINE, the intrepid *acting* Mayor of that devoted city, determined that the President should know the facts as they were, and justice done the people of Vicksburg, telegraphed the same ; and the brother-in-law of the President, a correct and honest man, still anxious to see an impartial election, laid the facts before the President by telegraph, when lo and behold ! to the astonishment of the enemies of the good people of Vicksburg, and of good government, a blessing was sent back. The electric flash brought back the soul-stirring tidings 'THAT THE PEOPLE OF VICKSBURG COULD TAKE CARE OF THEMSELVES !' Few know the debt of obligation they owe the acting Mayor of Vicksburg and Peter Casey, for the manly and active part they took to give a truthful statement of the facts to the President. And thus it is. Whilst ever a man or a people conform fully to the requirements of God, he has always so ordered circumstances that every curse premeditated against them has been turned into a blessing.

"It only remains now for the Southern States to shape their own fate. The time has come to do it. Will they accept it ? The 'tide that leads on to *fortune'* is now before them. Will they 'take it at the flood,' and make their fate, and be free again ? Time will prove what they will do. There is but one way, and that I have pointed out. If they will still make another *Dent-Greeley line* to organize with the negro, and thus sink themselves deeper in degradation by being defeated again, when success and honor are extending welcome hands, then I can only say they will deserve no better fate ; and as the world-renowned Prentiss once said, on the floor of Congress, 'Then STRIKE OUT the stars that glitter to their names from that flag which floats upon every sea, and flaps the breeze of every clime; but leave the *stripes,* fit emblems of their degradation.'

"The authorities in power, both at Washington and in the Southern States, seem to have had it as their aim and object to degrade the white people of the South, and elevate the negro. What plea to put up for them for such an outrage against their own race, I am unable to tell. Would the plea of the Savior of the world for those who crucified him—'Father, forgive them, for they know no what they do'—be a proper plea ? No ! no ! They *do know* what they *do.* They *do know* that innocent and peaceable citizens have been arrested in South Carolina, Alabama, Louisiana and Mississippi, under pretended violations of the Ku-Klux law, and dragged, manacled, to inquisition courts, to undergo mock trials, and prosecuted and convicted, without

126

ever knowing the crimes of which they were charged, or even the witnesses against them. This has not been the case in *all* instances of this character of persecutions, but has in some. They DO KNOW that a usurper, Governor in Louisiana, has been sustained by them in his seat, contrary to the will of the good people of that State, and contrary to sound law. I can only say for the men who would turn the highest offices in the gift of the people into engines of cruelty and oppression of their own race and color, degrades the wombs that bore them, and the paps that gave them suck. There is no plea that uplifted hands and streaming eyes of suffering Southern humanity, in the likeness and image of God, can put up in their behalf, though it comes from the piteous wail of the injured widow, or suffering orphan. No! no! To the men who would deny their race for any earthly consideration let the winds of heaven refuse to refresh them when faint! Let the sun of day refuse to warm and light up their pathway! Let the pale queen of night veil her face when such monsters dare intrude in her presence! Let the babbling brook refuse to quench their thirst under the bitter anguish of the scorching fever! Let the green woods refuse to cast their shadow over them when weary and fatigued! Let the songsters of the vale still their sweet warbling notes, frighted when such hideous failures make their appearance in the morning bowers! Let their Mother Earth refuse them a resting place upon the ground, where they have desecrated her fair name! And let a veil of darkness cover them so thick that the All-Seeing Eye can never penetrate to them! And let them be sunk so deep in the Pit of Forgetfulness that the sound of Gabriel's trump will never reach them! That they may be warnings to those who may come hereafter.

"Now, John, I am through with my answer to your question, and, as our conversations must come to a close, I have but one thing more to say. When I contemplate the wrongs that have been done my people of the South by the Northern people, and find so fully every principle of good faith to the conditions of the surrender made by Generals Lee and Johnson trampled under foot, with my knowledge of the Bible position on the subject of slavery and the negro, had the admission of the Southern States back into the Union for reconstruction, to have entailed upon them the long list of outrageous acts by legislation, of political, social, and civil degradation upon my people that they have, I say, had their admission back into the Union for reconstruction been suspended upon my vote or my volition, woman as I am, calling upon all the native nobleness of my sex, that had been fostered and reared in the Southern woman's breast since we were a people, to come to my aid, I would have kept them out! *I would have kept them out!* I WOULD HAVE KEPT THEM OUT! till the God of nature, disgusted with the wicked scenes then transpiring upon earth, bid the archangel take his trump, and planting one foot on the sea, and the other on dry land, swear by Him who lives forever, that time should be no more! And as he sounded its death-knell, and called the dead back into life, and that immortal host, headed by Washington, Madison, Monroe, Jackson, Clay, Calhoun, Webster, R. E. Lee, Stonewall

6

Jackson, Polk, Cleburne, and all that gallant throng of Confederate dead, sprung into new life, and marking time to the trump of eternity, taking up the line of march to the bar of retributive justice, to receive the rewards of a well-spent life! throwing myself into the gap-way, upon supplicating knees, and with uplifted hands, and streaming eyes, I would exclaim, with all the melting pathos of female nature for insulted honor and outraged rights, Fathers of my country, and martyred heroes for God's true faith, decide this question, and make your people's Fate!

"SALLIE."

THE PRE-ADAMITE,

OR

WHO TEMPTED EVE?

1. Mongolian.   2. Malay.
3. Caucasian.   4. Negro.
      5. American Indian.

130

THE PRE-ADAMITE,

OR

WHO TEMPTED EVE?

SCRIPTURE AND SCIENCE IN UNISON AS RESPECTS
THE ANTIQUITY OF MAN.

By A. HOYLE LESTER.

Let Wisdom with all her science trace
Mankind of yore, and where begins the race,
Where born, and when; let all his traits appear,
His history solve, through each revolving year.

PHILADELPHIA:
PUBLISHED FOR THE AUTHOR BY
J. B. LIPPINCOTT & CO.
1875.

131

THIS WORK

IS RESPECTFULLY DEDICATED

TO MY WORTHY FRIEND,

DR. T. J. DRANE,

WITHOUT HIS KNOWLEDGE OR CONSENT;

AND THE OFFERING IS SIMPLY A TESTIMONIAL OF THE
KINDLY FEELINGS ENTERTAINED FOR HIM

BY THE AUTHOR,

A. HOYLE LESTER.

1*   5

TO THE READER.

For convenience of reference, I deem it necessary to insert a Chronological Table, which gives the computations of various parties who have devoted much time to this subject, which is denominated the short, or received chronology, and the long chronology, which gives the dates of the principal periods from the creation of the world to the birth of Christ.

CHRONOLOGICAL TABLE.

	SHORT SYSTEM.			LONG SYSTEM.		
	Ussher.	Peta-vius.	Clin-ton.	Hales.	Jack-son.	Poole.
	B.C.	B.C.	B.C.	B.C.	B.C.	B.C.
Creation	4004	3983	4138	5411	5426	5421
Flood	2349	2327	2482	3155	3170	3159
Call of Abraham	1921	1961	2055	2078	2023	2082
Exodus	1491	1531	1625	1648	1593	1652
Foundation of Temple	1012	1012	1013	1027	1014	1010
Destruction of Temple	588	589	587	586	586	586

Archbishop Ussher's computation, as above, has been universally adopted, as found in the margin of the authorized English version of the Bible.

7

And for the satisfaction of those who take an interest in the ancient history of Egypt, and who may wish to refer to the pyramidal period of the old empire, I have concluded to insert Manetho's system of Egyptian chronology. Many of the ante-historical dynasties are omitted, when the Egyptians claimed to be ruled over by gods and demigods; and we will begin at the epoch of Menes, or Man, which is the commencement of the historical period of the thirty dynasties.

First Dynasty.—Accession of Menes, began 3893 B.C.

Third Dynasty.—Commenced the monumental period.

Fourth Dynasty.—Pyramids and tombs extant, began 3426 B.C.

Fifth Dynasty.—Began about 3100 B.C.

Seventh Dynasty.—Began about 2900 B.C.

Tenth Dynasty.—Began about 2500 B.C.

Twelfth Dynasty.—Ends about 2124 B.C.

Thirteenth Dynasty.—Ends about 2100 E.C.

Fourteenth, Fifteenth, Sixteenth Dynasty.—Hyksos, or shepherd kings, from 2000 B.C. to 1590 B.C.

The new empire or restoration succeeds:

Seventeenth Dynasty.—Began 1671 B.C.

Thirtieth Dynasty.—Ends on second Persian invasion, 340 B.C.

Egypt conquered by Alexander, 332 B.C.

Ptolemaic Dynasty.—Began 323 B.C.

Ptolemaic Dynasty.—Ends 44 B.C.

Roman Dynasty.—Began 30 B.C.

PREFACE.

THE intellect of man is progressive, and cannot remain stationary while science marks out the line of progress, and Revelation does not forbid our going forward in the work of investigation.

That the earth is much older than our wisest sages were once willing to admit is a fact which science reveals to us almost daily, and which the theologian unites with us in establishing in a way not at variance with Divine revelation.

The Bible and Science move together harmoniously, and where there are seeming inconsistencies there can be no controversy. Our interpretation of Scripture is either incorrect and needs modification to place it in harmony with the progress of Science, or else the scientist has failed in his deductions, and presents a dogma which has an existence only in theory and not in fact.

Who believed fifty years ago that the lightnings of heaven would be used to transmit our messages from zone to zone, and from the sea to the uttermost parts

9

of the earth ? And yet Job declares, in chap. xxxviii.
35, "Canst thou send lightnings, that they may go,
and say unto thee, Here we are?" The same may be
said in regard to the powers of steam, when Job describes Leviathan as emitting flames from his nostrils
and plowing the vasty deep, until his pathway becomes
hoary with phosphorescent light. Science reveals to
us the revolutions of all the planets upon their axes,
and a myriad of worlds beyond our own system. Gen.
i. 4, 5 : "And God divided the light from the darkness. And God called the light Day, and the darkness
he called Night." There is no want of harmony in
all this, and yet how slow was the Christian world in
adopting this new system of astronomy !

The unity of the human race is comparatively a new
theory, which has been strongly maintained by the
translators of the English version of the Bible. However, the ancient world, and the Jews particularly, believed firmly in the diversity of the human family ; and
all nations under the sun, and in every age, who have
held intercourse with the dark races, have regarded
them as distinct in character, and as constituting intellectually an inferior type of the genus homo.

A. H. L.

CONTENTS.

II

137

138

THE PRE-ADAMITE.

CHAPTER I.

ADAM NOT THE FIRST MAN.

"Together let us beat this ample field;
Try what the open, what the covert yield;
The latent tracks, the giddy heights explore,
Of all who blindly creep or sightless soar."—POPE..

THAT the enlightened mind of the nineteenth century can content itself with the theory that the Chinese,
the Indian, and the Negro descended from the same
original progenitor is the source of no great astonishment to the thinking man of the present age, as the
love of ease and the cherished opinions of the past
are ever marked with foot-prints dear to the memory
of man, consequently he is indisposed to permit innovations within the precincts of his established views.

That Adam was not the father of the above-mentioned races, and was only the ancestor of the Caucasian family, I am heartily convinced can be established by sound reasoning and good, practical sense,
and at the same time on a basis not at all antagonistic
to the revelations of Holy Writ.

2   13

This generation remembers when able theologians contended that the world had only been created about six thousand years, and that the creation had been perfected by the Almighty in six days of the ordinary duration of twenty-four hours. The investigations of science have exploded this hypothesis, and no person now, who makes any pretensions to scientific lore, would stake his reputation in combating a dogma so thoroughly fixed in the human mind.

In opening the bowels of the earth, we trace its history in the various formations through which we pass, and in the peculiar texture of the various deposits which we find imbedded beneath its surface. And thus, like the man of science in mastering the organism of the human frame, he becomes familiar with its peculiarities, and tells us its comparative age, and the sex to which it belongs; and so with the various races which God in his wisdom, and at sundry times, has placed on this sublunary sphere. It behooves us to investigate their history, their traits of character, and their origin.

CHAPTER II.

THE ORDER OF CREATION.

" So from the first eternal order ran,
And creature linked to creature, man to man."—POPE.

THE world when it was first fashioned by the plastic hand of Jehovah was a barren waste, void and without form, and darkness was upon the face of the deep. Matter assumed shape; atmosphere, with its vivifying influences, took wing and sought its equilibrium throughout the immensity of space; waters were formed and sought their level in the low basins of the earth; hence lakes, seas, and oceans. And light, by the fiat of the Almighty, sprang out from the hidden caverns of immensity, and shot its rays like the fiery chain that springs from the bosom of the electrified cloud, and swept across the face of a new-born world, and infused animation into the unproductive elements of nature. Day came and went, and the dew and the shower united together, and performed their commissioned duties, to give life and invigorate the germ which the creative genius of Deity had planted in the vast fields which He had recently formed.

The grass, the herb, the tree, sprang into life, bloomed and shed its fragrance upon the desert air, and ripened its fruit at the new-appointed harvest. The waters were moved by the creative hand of Deity,

141

·and the river and the ocean became alive with the animalculæ and the leviathan. Birds winged their rapid flight through the yielding atmosphere, and fed upon the varied insects that peopled the luxuriant fields, and sang their morning song and their evening lullaby where their warbling notes as yet fell upon no mortal ear.

In the course of many ages the surface of this earth had parted with its heat, and the active influences of dews and showers had prepared many portions of the world for the growth and maturity of plants; and no doubt in the lapse of time vast plains were covered with luxuriant verdure, while other sections were sterile and parched by a meridian sun, and desolated by the scorching fires of active volcanoes. On these fertile plains and prolific slopes, where verdant pastures and flowing brooks could support animal life, God there placed the lower order of the animal creation, until times and seasons had passed over the face of nature, and prepared a habitation for the maintenance of a higher order of animal existence. So on thus, from one gradation to another, did He in his wisdom modify and reconstruct by the gradual growth and decomposition of the vegetable kingdom, until the lion, the tiger, and the horse, the highest order of the brute creation, could move and have their being, amid the forests and jungles of a world which had never as yet echoed to the voice of man.

In the ascending series of the creative programme comes the monkey, or the lower grade of the quadrumana tribes, and in due course of formation we have the baboon and the orang-outang, who occupy their periods in the creative designs of the Great I Am, until finally the gorilla, the highest standard of the quadrumana race, takes his position among created animals, and forms the uniting link between the brute creation and the lowest standard of the human family.

Ages upon ages, in all probability, had rolled over this mundane sphere since first it was thrown out in a molten state to find its regular orbit, and assume shape in winging its trackless flight along the unmeasured paths of immensity, and in fancied dreams we can still behold it blazing like a fiery comet when approaching its perihelion. We may well assume, as respects this world at the age of which we write, that the atmosphere which encircled it was impregnated with the heat arising from internal fires, consequently unfitted for the abode of Adam's race, of whom we shall speak in due time. In the crude and unsublimated condition of the world at this epoch, God saw proper to place a pair of human beings on our orb, and invested them with full possession, with all the rights and privileges of the first occupants. He endowed them with speech and with a higher degree of intelligence than that bestowed upon any animal of a former creation; He gave them laws and rules and regulations by which they should be governed, and demanded of them obedience in accordance with his divine behest, and sent them forth to multiply and people the untrodden labyrinths of earth. This was the negro, and his native land, Africa; the same whom the Anglo-Saxon introduced upon the American continent, and wherever found to-day in his ancestral clime, and whose blood is still unalloyed with the refining influences of a nobler

2*

and a higher race, we trace in him all the savage instincts that mark the very beasts that walk the earth. He served his period under the benign sway of Divine Providence; fell from his high estate, and was permitted to wander adrift, and gratify the unholy passions prompted by his unholy nature. Anthropophagi, he preyed upon his fellow-man; he sinned away his day of grace, and his kind Benefactor permitted him to become a reprobate, given over to a hardness of heart and a reprobation of mind, that he might believe a lie and be lost.

I stated in the beginning of this discourse that the theory advanced herein in reference to a diversity in the origin of the human races should in nowise conflict with the teachings of Revelation.

I assume this position : That in the progress of creation and through its various periods, as God saw that the earth, the air, and the water were adapted to the growth and nourishment of the different species with which, in his divine economy, He proposed to people these elements, and age after age, as these necessary changes would take place, He did form and create all the peculiar animal life which has ever existed on this globe; not in one day, or in one period, but in different epochs, and in accordance as He saw that these essential changes in nature required nobler creations. Thus He first formed the zoophyte and the lower animals, with every creeping thing, and so on in their regular order, until this world became a suitable abode for the lowest caste of the human family.

The negro was introduced and became the sole occupant of this vast territory. He was created black the better to enable him to endure the intolerable heat to which the world was subjected at this period, and at no time since has he desired to emigrate from the tropical clime which he has inhabited from the first hour of his introduction.

I further assume that the next creation of a higher order was the Malay, also an inhabitant of the tropics; and after the Malay in due course comes the American Indian, and still in after-periods, but in regular order, we have the Chinese, or rather the Turanian family. Each race in its turn having a distinct origin, and in no way connected with any former creation, further than that an all-wise Providence is the creator of us all, whom all admit He can create and can destroy.

And last but not least, God in his wisdom and *in his own image* created He male and female, Adam and Eve, the progenitors of the Caucasian race. In each successive race, from the flat-nosed and woolly-headed African to the highest type of divine creation, we are compelled to admit that the intellectual elements in each develop themselves in the same ratio as we leave the negro and approach the white man. History proves this assertion, which will be alluded to in its proper place. I shall also speak of the peculiar traits of character, habits, manners, and physical formation of these respective races.

CHAPTER III.

WHO TEMPTED EVE?

"Say first of God above, or man below,
What can we reason but from what we know ;
Of man what see we but his station here,
From which to reason or to which refer."

IT is highly probable that there may have existed a dozen or more distinct races of the genus homo, and they may be in existence now! Still, it answers our purpose to recognize only five races, as this subdivision has already been made, and is sanctioned by ethnologists of our age. They have, however, almost universally been traced back to the same ancestor, under a belief of the unity of the races, which theory attaches itself like an incubus to the fair Caucasian, and brings a blush to the cheek of intelligent beauty. I would wipe this stain from our escutcheon, and set at right the inquiring mind, as regards the error in question.

Let not the Bible reader or the orthodox Christian cry out *skeptic*, should the author attack erroneous notions entertained by them as respects the early history of the world, and how the African and the Turanian crossed the destroying flood that wafted Noah's heavily-freighted ark to the mountains of Ararat.

I promised the attentive reader to handle this subject in the spirit of kindness, and would ask him or her to divest the mind of any prejudicial views entertained on this interesting question. Josephus, the great uninspired Jewish writer, tells us that Adam* was a red man, being formed of red clay, which was the purest of earth, as though he would convey the idea to posterity that the progenitor of his race was made of no common material, and in fact of better material than any prior creation. Before the time of Moses the only history of the world that existed was traditional, and was handed down from sire to son; and by this channel, together with his acquaintance with the original Hebrew, the Jewish scribe was enabled to communicate this information to those whose opportunities were not so good for acquiring knowledge of ancient history. He was named Adam because he was red, of a ruddy countenance. He was the father of the blushing race. Created He him in his own image and likeness. The only immortal soul beneath the wide-expanded canopy of heaven to whose cheeks gushed the crimson blood to manifest the intense shame of conscious guilt! and if the darker races blush, with whom we claim no kindred blood, then, like the wild-flower in its native wilderness, it blushes unseen and wastes its virtue on the desert air. The side of Adam gave birth to Eve, the mother of all living; and she, the fairest queen that ever graced the

---

* This man was called Adam, which, in the Hebrew tongue, signifies one that is red, because he was formed out of red earth, for of that kind is virgin and true earth.—*Antiq. of Jews*, page 2.

.courts of earth, made her *début* on the arena of life in
the romantic shades of Eden, where the creeping vine
threw its tendrils around the giant oak, and lovely
flowers bloomed by murmuring waters in their flow to
the turbid Euphrates, and where the gentle zephyr
fanned her cheek and wafted the odorous sweets from
nature's untrodden plains.   It is not strange that
Eden's garden bird should have become wearied with
the monotony that daily surrounded her.   The scenery
had become stale to her accustomed eye, and ceased
to afford its wonted pleasure.   The presence of Adam
had no doubt become irksome, and his voice, for the
time, had ceased to fill the aching void that agonized
her tender heart ; and with a desire to explore the
farther limit of her terrestrial domain, she wandered
far along meandering brooks, and plucked strange
flowers to while away the slow-fleeting moments, and
slaked her thirst at gushing fountains where she
dreamed no mortal had yet partaken thereof.   Imagine her surprise ; innocent and unsuspecting, she
meets a stranger, the serpent who had beheld her
beauty (for Eve, at this unlucky hour, was not arrayed
in the habiliments of modern style).   She felt lonely,
and was surprised to meet this handsome stranger amidst
the solitudes of Eden's bower.   Knowing little of this
world save her own innocence, and unaware of the
great gulf that lay between God and the fallen races
that preceded her, she listened with attentive ear to
the enchanting conversation of this son of perdition.
He belonged most assuredly to the highest order of
the inferior races, around whom our heavenly Father
had thrown the benign influences of his exalted nature,

and had offered time and again to make them sons and priests unto God, and they rejected the proffered mercy; and in the same language, we may reasonably presume, he addressed those idolaters, as he did in after-years address a more enlightened and favored people, when He declared, "O Jerusalem, Jerusalem, how often would I have gathered thy children together, even as a hen gathereth her chickens under her wings, and ye would not!"

Who was this serpent that beguiled our first parents? In our language it could not be the snake, or the viper, that besets our pathway and strikes into our flesh the fangs that bring death by the venom infused into the system. By no means! Does the adder speak, or does the boa-constrictor give utterance to language? Preposterous thought! The fall of man as revealed to us in Genesis is no metaphor. Consider, kind reader, a venomous reptile approaching a lovely maiden, to hold gentle converse in the silent wood : would she take the accursed reptile to her bosom and associate with him day after day and week after week? Never! even though his hissing voice had the melody of the enchanting siren. His shape and his demeanor in aping a deceiver would carry with it the nauseating venom, at which the native modesty and timidity of the first Caucasian damsel would have revolted, and she, like the affrighted hare before its pursuers, would have fled from its presence, and sought refuge under the protecting ægis of her Lord. Then tell us not that the devil approached our first mother in the form of a snake, as seen in the so-called sacred pictures of the passing age.

But he did present himself to Eve in the form and likeness of a man, one of Mongolia's* comeliest sons. He came possessed of all the attributes of the evil genius of perdition, clothed from head to heel with the accumulated curses of an avenging God. He was an idolater, and had no pleasure in the service of his Creator, and there was but one pair in existence at that time who were altogether innocent, and meekly trusted in the promises made to them by the Great First Cause, and that pair was our first parents; and are we surprised at the malignity and duplicity practiced upon those innocent victims, when we reflect that in this impostor was concentrated the vile essence of accumulated guilt which had been increasing in intensity, and was now ready to culminate and throw its pall of darkness over the fair race so recently ushered into existence? Lest the reader may think it unimportant, and not refer to the passages alluded to, I will quote verbatim, Matt. xxiii. 33: "Ye serpents, ye generation of vipers, how can ye escape the damnation of hell?" We here observe that serpents are applied to individuals, as of old to the Mongolian, the party who addressed Eve in her rambles amid the embowered shades of her rural paradise. He came from his ambush with the venom of the fiery serpent; with manly form, stately and erect; with that suavity of manner which age and experience had perfected, and with the wily paraphernalia which the adroit expert

---

* Mongolia. A country of Asia and a part of the Chinese Empire; not far distant from the garden of Eden. Mongolian, one of the divisions of mankind, and belonging properly to the Turanian family, of whom we shall speak more at length in its proper place.

puts on when he proposes to throttle his unsuspecting victim. They met often and lingered long in some solitary shade by rural founts, where human eye could not detect or make afraid. And this gay deceiver spoke of the germ in the human heart where affection springs, and of "the daughters of men that they were fair," and of love with its operations on the tender heart, and said, Partake of the forbidden fruit: "Then shall your eyes be opened, and ye shall be as gods, knowing good and evil."

Eve, poor woman, yielded to the evil machinations of this seductive deceiver. She rose from the mossy couch a wiser but a fallen creature, and returned to the presence of her lawful companion disrobed of virtue, that precious jewel, the brightest ornament of her sex.* Gen. iii. 5: "Ye shall be as gods." This Mongolian, in tempting Eve, used these words, from the fact that in every land where idolatry is the prevailing religion, we find the depraved heart bowing down and serving graven images, representing gods which are formed and fashioned after the unholy passions of the worshipers themselves, whom they endow with imaginary wisdom and power and greatness far superior to that possessed by mortal man; and from

---

* Milton, in his " Paradise Lost," in describing the effect of the forbidden fruit upon our first parents, says:
> " But that false fruit
> For other operation first displayed,
> Carnal desire inflaming; he on Eve
> Began to cast lascivious eye, she him
> As wantonly repaid; in lust they burn:
> Till Adam thus 'gan Eve to dalliance move."

3

151

the exuberance of his heart he expressed these views to his attentive victim. These were the gods to whom he had reference, ever forgetful of the only true and living God, who is creator of all.

From this intercourse or intimacy that subsisted between this son of perdition and the fair consort of Adam arose the mongrel offspring who bears in the Bible record the name of Cain, the vile monster who watered the earth with the blood of his brother Abel. View him as the descendant of the Asiatic nomad or pre-adamite, and we are not surprised that his offering was rejected by the Lord, or that the inherent instincts of his nature should find vent in the life-blood of so near a relative; and, in consequence of this deed, the vengeance of high heaven was visited upon this fratricide.

Gen. iv. 13–17: "And Cain said unto the Lord, My punishment is greater than I can bear. Behold, thou hast driven me out this day from the face of the earth; and from thy face shall I be hid; and I shall be a fugitive and a vagabond in the earth; and it shall come to pass, *that every one that findeth me shall slay me.* And the Lord said unto him, Therefore whosoever slayeth Cain, vengeance shall be taken on him sevenfold. And the Lord set a mark upon Cain, lest any finding him should kill him. And Cain went out from the presence of the Lord, and dwelt in the land of Nod, on the east of Eden. And Cain knew his wife; and she conceived, and bare Enoch." Why did Cain fear that he should be regarded as a fugitive and a vagabond? and whom did he apprehend would find him and slay him? Certainly not his father and mother. He had just

murdered his only brother, which revelation admits.
"And the Lord set a mark upon Cain, lest any finding
him should kill him." Tell me, reflective reader,
whom did God seem to apprehend might slay this murderer, that He would desire to place a mark upon him
to shield him from the avenger of blood?

We can but admit that the world was peopled at
that time by races of men which had existed long
anterior to the Adamic age. Adam discovered this to
his sorrow just before his expulsion from the garden
of Eden, when his wife came trembling and weeping
from the shady retreat, where but recently she had
embraced one of the apostate sons of this sin-cursed
earth. Cain and Abel had grown up in the same latitude, and had made the acquaintance of the various
tribes by whom they were surrounded. Abel seems to
have shunned this people, and regarded them as unworthy associates. Like an honest youth in a corrupt
community, he tended his flock and brought his annual
tribute as an offering to the Lord, while Cain himself
cultivated their acquaintance, until his entire soul had
become so demoralized that he was ready to stain his
hands in the blood of an unoffending brother; and now
that the deed was done, remorse hangs so heavy upon
his conscience that Heaven itself must come to his
rescue and brand him with a mark of guilt, so that he
might return in safety to the olive-colored hordes of
the East, with whom he had affiliated for years.

"And Cain went out from the presence of the Lord,
and dwelt on the east of Eden." He left behind him
the ordinances of God and the society of his worshipers, and the places memorable for the tokens of his

divine presence. He went as an exile, and sought a
home among a class of people whose feelings, habits,
and sentiments were congenial, and took unto himself
a wife, one of the corrupt daughters of this inferior
race.

CHAPTER IV.

MISCEGENATION AND ITS ATTENDANT EVILS.

"Force first made conquest, and that conquest law, .
Till superstition taught the tyrant awe,
Then shar'd the tyranny, then lent it aid,
And gods of conquerors, slaves of subjects made."

PopE.

JOSEPHUS,* in speaking of Cain, says, "However,
Cain did not accept of his punishment in order to
amendment, but to increase his wickedness; for he
only aimed to procure everything that was for his own
bodily pleasure, though it obliged him to be injurious
to his neighbors. He augmented his household substance with much wealth by *rapine and violence:* he
excited his acquaintance to procure pleasure and spoils
by robbery, and became a great leader of men into
wicked courses. He also introduced a change in that
way of simplicity wherein men lived before, and was
the author of measures and weights; and whereas they
lived innocently and generously while they knew

---

* Antiquity of the Jews, chapter ii.

nothing of such arts, he changed the world into cunning craftiness."

Can we further doubt a plurality of the races? Whether Josephus held to this view or not, he has certainly testified very pointedly in behalf of our position when he says that Cain, by plunder, rapine, and violence, was obliged to be injurious to his neighbors, and excited his acquaintance to procure pleasure and spoils by robbery. Fellow-inquirer, whom did he rob and spoil and plunder? What caste and character of neighbors were those whom he kukluxed? None others save those original tribes which had been planted on God's footstool, long ages before Eve's first-born emigrated to the land of Nod. He became a great leader of men into wicked courses. Cain was separated from his father's people; there was no intercourse whatever between the descendants of Seth and this God-forsaken wretch, who had been driven forth as a fugitive and a vagabond.

He therefore allied himself to the pre-existing generation of vipers, assumed their leadership; being of an artful turn of mind, and endowed with higher intellectual powers, he preyed upon their substance and moulded them obedient to his will, and, if it were possible, led them on still further in the baser labyrinths of recklessness and iniquity. If the reader is skeptical in regard to the conclusion just drawn, then he is referred to Gen. iv. 23: "And Lamech (a descendant of Cain) said unto his wives, Adah and Zillah, Hear my voice; ye wives of Lamech, hearken unto my speech: for I have slain a man to my wounding, and a young man to my hurt."

In illustration we find that Lamech was not only a

3*

·murderer, but was the first who inaugurated that system
of free-love, or plurality of wives, which, in our day,
flourishes under the name of Mormonism, borrowed no
doubt from the associations around him, and which is
still practiced by all those ancient races still distinct
in their nature, origin, and physical formation, and denominated by geographers as Asiatic, American, Malay,
and African.

Reverting to the fourth chapter of Genesis and part
of the last verse, "Then began men to call upon the
name of the Lord," indicates that the evil genius possessed by the pre-adamite family had infused itself into
the heart of Adam's own household, to so great a degree at least that his children had ceased to reverence
Jehovah, and had gone abroad amid the groves and
mountains to worship the gods of these ancient idolaters, and had in the blindness of their hearts attempted
to appease those deities by sacrificing on their unholy
altars.   But at this juncture it seems that there was a
returning sense of duty, which stole over their obdurate
hearts, and men again began to call on the name of the
Lord.   This was about the time that Noah, the great
preacher of righteousness, commenced hurling anathe-
mas against the inhabitants of earth, and threatened
them with the destroying flood unless they would repent and turn from their evil ways.   This brought
them to reflect upon their idolatrous course, and in the
anguish of their hearts they commenced to call on the
name of Jehovah, and, alarmed at the impending destruction, we find that a few only of Adam's progeny
were permitted to take a through passage in the vessel
of that bold navigator.

Gen. vi. 1–4: "And it came to pass, when men began to multiply on the face of the earth, and daughters were born unto them, that the sons of God saw the daughters of men that they were fair; and they took them wives of all which they chose. . . . . . There were giants in the earth in those days; and also after that, when the sons of God came in unto the daughters of men, and they bare children to them, the same became mighty men which were of old, men of renown."

The sons of God intermarried among the daughters of men. This may look strange under the old régime of public opinion, but its ambiguity vanishes when we recall the fact that the sons of God were the children of Adam, and the daughters of men were the offspring of the Mongolian and the cross of Cain with the aborigines of the country. "They were fair," that is, fair to look upon, possessing figure and feature attractive to the eye, as did Pocahontas appear to John Rolfe, and the ravishing charms of Cleopatra to the lascivious eyes of Julius Cæsar and Mark Antony.

The sons of God were also those who were the true worshipers of Deity, having thus far kept aloof from the baleful influences of these original and hybrid races which "had become altogether incapable of answering the great end of divine creation." Job ii. 1: "Again there was a day when the sons of God came to present themselves before the Lord, and Satan came also among them to present himself before the Lord."

And in the form of such a disguise appears before us at this latter day the strange doctrines advanced by those who preached a higher law dogma of intellectual, political, and social equality; the former of which can never exist except in theory until Heaven's fiat is revoked, which has gone forth and stamped on the brow of the Caucasian the force of mind, of courage, and of genius, which has ever obtained in every climate and in every land where destiny has fixed his image, and social equality can only be accomplished at the sacrifice of the high moral standard which elevates our being, and the loss of which depresses the measure of our worth to the baser instincts of the savage. And the idea is forcibly and aptly illustrated in the language of the day, "that the instincts of our nature revolt at the outstincts of the negro." We here see the great sin of Adam's misguided posterity, in cohabiting with and mingling their blood with those debased aboriginal races. Through every age and in every climate, where the Caucasian has violated this great law of heaven by intermarrying with these degraded and inferior classes of people, he is reducing the high standard of intellectuality, and harnessing upon enlightened civilization a base stock of mongrels, whom experience teaches are a weak and enervated cross, and utterly debased in character, sentiment, and practice. Nor is this the only evil perpetrated upon the human family by the abominable practice of miscegenation. Heaven's vengeance comes upon us as with the besom of destruction, in that the fair fields that once blossomed as the rose have grown up in bush and brier, and the bright sunshine of prosperity is eclipsed by the dark pall that hangs over our once happy country.

It is to be hoped that no similar retribution befalls us as Heaven's vengeance thrust upon the antediluvians when Noah and his party sought refuge in the ark of safety.

"There were giants in the earth in those days; and also after that, when the sons of God came in unto the daughters of men, and they bare children to them, the same became mighty men which were of old, men of renown." There were giants in the earth in those days prior to the intermarriage of the sons of God and the daughters of men; and if so, from whom did they descend? Their progenitors certainly must have been of an earlier stock and different from our first parents. "And also after that," when the daughters of men bore children for the sons of God, showing very pointedly that the offspring by amalgamation were also giants, "which were of old, men of renown." And why were they regarded by the inspired historian as men of renown? Because they had of old become conspicuous as leaders and chieftains in the deadly warfare waged for spoil and plunder, and as nations do now when the conflict rages for supremacy and power.

And God proclaimed in language that cannot be misunderstood, "that my spirit shall not always strive with man."* And again, "I will destroy man (the Adamite) whom I have created from the face of the earth."† It is forcibly presented why God would destroy this people, because of the amalgamation of the races. This intercourse and intermixing of blood had introduced among the Adamites the interdicted worship and idolatrous devotions and damnable heresies of these debased races, who are never denominated

---

* Gen. vi. 3. † Gen. vi. 7.

man by the inspired writer, and are only occasionally
mentioned in sacred revelation, and then he is called
the serpent, or the beast; the despised creature that beguiled our mother Eve, and who continued to delude
and deceive the antediluvian race by engrafting upon
them the forbidden practices of their own corrupt
natures, until the flood came and did its work of
destruction.

CHAPTER V.

THE DELUGE AND ITS TRADITION.

> " Now the thickened sky
> Like a dark ceiling: down rushed the rain
> Impetuous; and continued till the earth
> No more was seen."—MILTON.

NOAH was directed to build an ark, the length of
which was one hundred and sixty yards, breadth of
beam twenty-seven yards, and sixteen yards high, and
was in our parlance a three-decker, in which was to be
collected male and female of all animated creation, together with Noah and his family, and food sufficient to
supply this living cargo for the space of twelve months
and ten days. An enlightened conscience admits that
the flood came, and that the great end was accomplished, in accordance with God's holy purpose:
which was the destruction of all of Adam's posterity who were not the immediate members of Noah's
family: including those who had allied themselves to

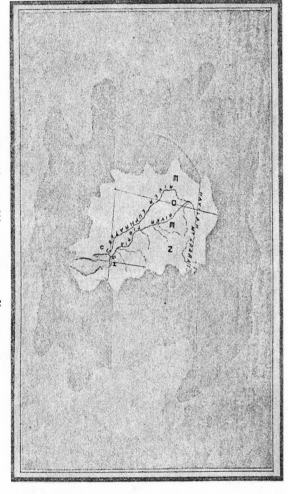

the aborigines of the East. All that portion of the world was deluged which at the time was known to the Adamite.

It is not our province to assume that any of the divine writers were or were not inspired as respects geography, astronomy, or geology, or, in fact, as respects any of the physical sciences; but this we know, that they addressed themselves to the understanding of their hearers, and in language appropriate to the knowledge of those who were to be enlightened. In the same style as the Roman would discourse in the days of the Cæsars, when speaking of the whole world; we understand him to include that portion of Asia, Europe, and Africa touching upon the Mediterranean Sea, and extending as far north as the isle of Britain.

In the same ratio do we reasonably conclude that the knowledge of the Israelites extended over but a very limited extent of the earth's surface. And thus to their understanding does Moses speak, when he transmits to his brethren the history of the Creation and the Deluge. Then only so much of the earth's surface was inundated as would accomplish the designs of Heaven, in visiting summary vengeance upon those of the chosen race who had wandered far from God and fallen from their high estate.

Noah was in the ark over twelve months, and six months had elapsed before the waters commenced to abate. And yet we find that Noah, at a still later period, sent forth a dove, which returned with an olive-leaf. The question here arises, whether or not the vegetable kingdom, immersed in water for nearly a year, would preserve vitality and put forth its leaf again.

I would sooner advance the more reasonable hypothesis that the dove had plucked the leaf from a higher elevation than the water had reached, or from sections less damaged by the overflow.

Josephus most certainly believed that the historian of the flood was inspired by Heaven, and I will here quote him:* "Now all the writers of the barbarian histories make mention of the flood and of this ark, among whom is Berossus the Chaldean. For when he was describing the circumstances of the flood he goes on thus: 'It is said there is some part of this ship in Armenia at the mountain of the Cordyæans; and that some people carry off pieces of the bitumen, which they take away and use chiefly as amulets for the averting of mischiefs.'

"Nay, Nicholas of Damascus, in his ninety-sixth book, hath a particular relation about them, where he speaks thus: 'There is a great mountain in Armenia, over Minyas, called Boris, upon which, it is reported, that many, who fled at the time of the deluge, were saved, and that one who was carried in an ark came on shore upon the top of it, and that the remains of the timber were a great while preserved. This might be the man about whom Moses, the legislator of the Jews, wrote.'"

We therefore must admit that the traditional record, even among the Jews, led them to believe that the entire surface was not covered, and that many who fled to the highest elevations escaped destruction. In reading ancient mythology, the tradition prevails also, in

---

* Antiquity of the Jews, chapter iii.

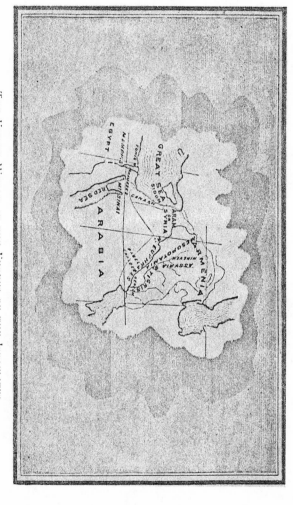

Deucalion's flood, that many were preserved by ascending the highest mountains. If all animal life perished in the general flood save those which were turned loose on Ararat, why is it that we find on the continent of America at least twenty-five to thirty animals and birds entirely distinct from all other species yet discovered in the East and known to naturalists? The nearest point of America to Asia is eighteen miles, with a turbulent strait intervening; and many of these distinct races of animals found in America are known to avoid ordinary water-courses, much less launching out on the ocean for new discoveries. And if the suggestion is advanced that they crossed on the ice when the two shores were connected by the frozen element, then we urge the argument that the coldness, frigidity, and barrenness of that northern latitude must necessarily have proved fatal to those animals found in our more tropical clime, as observation and experience teaches us that the white polar bear cannot live even a day in a temperate zone without artificial cold.

By what process of reasoning, or by what magic thought, can we transport the indolent sloth of Patagonia from the resting-place of the ark to the southern extremity of South America?—an animal by no means given to locomotion, and at its usual rate of travel of nine feet per hour, would have required ten thousand years to have made such a hideous journey.* A journey,

---

* A striking illustration we find in the kangaroo and other animals that are alone found in Australia, fit companions too for the savages of that country. How did these animals get there? and how did the Malay find a home in this wilderness? I would suggest, however,

4

in fact, which that noble animal, the horse,* has never
yet performed, though four thousand years have elapsed
since the cargo of the ark was discharged on the
mountains of Armenia.

Any person at all acquainted with the youthful science of geology may reasonably conclude that almost
the entire face of the earth has at one period or other
been submerged beneath the ocean, and by the convulsions of nature has been thrown up at various periods;
and as the water retired to their ocean caverns, vegetation sprang up, and in the course of revolving ages life
and animation peopled this once barren wilderness. It
has been asserted that the upheaval of the American
continent and the islands of the West had hurled upon
the antediluvians that awful calamity which Noah's ark
so bravely weathered. By no process of reasoning can
such a flimsy theory be established, as every indication
of nature goes to show the absurdity of such a position.
The disintegration and preparation necessary for the
surface to become a fit abode for plants, and the time
necessarily required to elapse for the different particles
to solidify and form masses of stone, where especially
are imbedded the fossil débris of the animal and vegetable kingdoms, both of which have become extinct at
periods where the memory of man runneth not to the

---

to the lover of the fabulous the legend of Europa, the daughter of the
king of Phœnicia.

  * The horse was not known in America until introduced here by the
Spaniards, and yet " it is certain that the horse inhabited this country
during the postpliocene period, long prior to the day when the present
American Indian made his abode on this continent, as its fossil remains
are found contemporaneously with the mastodon and megalonyx."

contrary. And again, there are living evidences in the vegetable kingdom of massive trees* whose record unmistakably indicates an age of at least five thousand to six thousand years. Even here where I write, this is, geologically speaking, a new country, and of very recent formation; yet we find deposits imbedded in the earth sixty and one hundred feet deep. The accretions thereupon accumulated were old when Adam first sang his lullaby to the goddess of morn, and plucked his first meal from the indigenous growth that adorned his earthly Paradise. Lest the reader may still be inclined to believe that the waters covered the entire hills and mountains of the globe, I will quote a few passages from the Bible in illustration of Biblical hyperbole, with no desire, however, to detract from the force of inspired truth, for on this basis alone I build my hopes for heaven and eternal life. Acts xxiv. 5 : "We have found this man (Paul) a pestilent fellow, and a mover of sedition among *all the Jews throughout the world.*" No theologian is ready to declare that Paul had visited all the nations then occupied by the Jews. And Acts ii. 5 : "There were dwelling at Jerusalem Jews, devout men, out of every nation under heaven." And again, Luke ii. 1 : "And it came to pass in those days, that there went out a decree from Cæsar Augustus, *that all the world should be taxed.*" These passages are only presented to illustrate the position taken, that the world to the inspired historian comprised that portion that was known to man commercially, and thus he addressed himself to the understanding of his hearers. Should

---

* Trees declare their age by concentric circles.

the reader still be indisposed to admit our premises
that the earth was partially covered with water, then I
propose to establish my position by quoting one verse
alone from the Bible, and prove to mankind that these
inferior races of men did not all perish in the flood,
but triumphantly made the voyage across the waste of
waters, and, like the other creatures in that noble vessel,
placed their feet on terra firma, and went forth beyond
the Jordan of waters to fulfill their destinies, shaped as
each was by the hand of a kind Providence.   I know
that you feel some interest to read that verse in the
Scriptures of divine truth which did admit into the ark
all the pre-adamic creatures.*   Gen. vii. 15: "And
they went in unto Noah into the ark, two and two of
all flesh, wherein is the breath of life."

---

* "We are left free to accept the plain proofs furnished by astronomy
and mechanics, by geology and physical geography, that the Deluge
could not have been universal, unless the laws of all nature had been
suspended."—PHILIP SMITH.

CHAPTER VI.

MAN AND THE QUADRUMANA TRIBES COMPARED.

> " Ill-fated race : the softening arts of peace
> Whate'er the harmonizing Muses teach :
> The Godlike wisdom of the tempered breast,
> Progressive truth, the patient force of thought :
> Investigation calm—the government of laws,
> These are not theirs."—THOMSON.

IN this chapter I shall discourse of the negro, together with the other inferior races, in contradistinction to man, or the Adamite.

In Bible language the Caucasian is man, the noblest work of God. The negro, with his cotemporary races, is the creature erroneously called the beast. I appeal to the Bible. Tell me, thou reverend chronicler of antiquity, can the vain sophistry of the learned overturn or controvert the established fulfillments of divine revelation ?

Gen. i. 24 and 25 : "And God said, Let the earth bring forth the *living creature* after his kind, cattle, and creeping thing, and *beast* of the earth after his kind : and it was so. And God made the *beast* of the earth after his kind, and cattle after their kind, and every thing that creepeth upon the earth after his kind." And again, Gen. iii. 1 : "Now the *serpent was more subtil than any beast of the field* which the Lord God

4*

171

had made." Showing conclusively the superiority of
the *creature* over the *beast* of the field, for the *creature*
in his craftiness had beguiled the woman, and the Lord
cursed him thus: " Thou art cursed above all cattle,
and above every beast of the field; upon thy belly
shalt thou go, and dust shalt thou eat all the days of
thy life;" that is, thou shalt be the lowest class in the
scale of being, abject, debased, and deceitful, mean,
contemptible, and despicable in the eyes of my chosen
people, whom thou, by the wily craftiness of your
tutelar deity, Lucifer, you have essayed to bring to the
level of your own infamy and degradation.

Creature thou art, but not a man in the image and
likeness of your Creator. Groveling in nature, and
possessing none of the higher traits of nobility that bespeak an assimilation to the ennobling attributes derived
from Deity, and which impresses upon the soul the unmistakable stamp of a higher and more exalted origin.
God was once manifested to us in the flesh. Did He
come in the form and likeness of either one of the inferior races? He presented Himself to us in the image
of his Father, clothed upon with all the paraphernalia
that indicated a direct descent from Adam. Christ
was the God-man, a true Caucasian of the blushing
race, the highest type of the original creation; endowed with beauty of person, symmetry of form and
feature, and devoid of that organism expressive of
brutal force and destructiveness, and of sensuality
and its accompanying elements of baseness; his brow
beaming with intelligence and his heart melting with
compassion. The dignity of his mien, the expressive
character of his organization, the noble combination

of worth and intellectuality that are exhibited in his structure and exemplified in his daily intercourse with man, stamp him in the highest degree the noblest and the best of earthly cotemporaries.

Reverting to the mistranslation of *creature*, I will quote from Revelation iv. 6–8: "And before the throne there was a sea of glass like unto crystal : and in the midst of the throne, and round about the throne, were four *beasts* full of eyes before and behind. And the first *beast* was like a lion, and the second *beast* like a calf, and the third *beast* had a face as a man, and the fourth *beast* was like a flying eagle. And the four *beasts* had each of them six wings about him ; and they were full of eyes within : and they rest not day and night, saying, Holy, holy, holy, Lord God Almighty, which was, and is, and is to come." The first impulse of enlightened nature would tell us that there were no beasts in heaven. These were creatures paying adoration around the throne of God, and constituted a part of the heavenly host. We read in Jer. xxi. 6: "And I will smite the inhabitants of this city, both *man and beast :* they shall die of a great pestilence." And again, in Jonah iii. 7 and 8: "And he caused it to be proclaimed and published through Nineveh by the decree of the king and his nobles, saying, Let neither man nor *beast,* herd nor flock, taste any thing: let them not feed, nor drink water : but let *man and beast be covered with sackcloth, and cry mightily unto God:* yea, let them turn every one from his evil way, and from the violence that is in their hands."

Were these real beasts who are threatened above with summary vengeance, and required to put on sackcloth

and cry mightily unto God? or were they captives from
the land of Confucius, or slaves from the islands of
Polynesia or the gold coast of Africa?

Nearly all modern zoologists contend that the various races of mankind are included under one genus,
man, and are characterized by possessing two hands,
and are distinguished from the monkey or ape tribes
on the ground that the ape is supplied with four hands.
We herein observe the distinctive features existing between the bimana and the quadrumana races of the
mammalia family.

Dr. Darwin, however, seems to class us all originally
as quadrumana, and by successive improvements upon
the original stock the Caucasian, it seems, has leaped,
like the goddess Minerva, pure, perfect, and undefiled
from the troubled brain of some giant of the chimpanzee
or gorilla tribes. This theory reversed, in the course of a
few centuries, would carry the doctor and his followers
back to the quadrumana, and it might prove a mortification to their pride to find the caudal appendage
assuming its wonted position at the lower terminus of
the vertebra. From considerations, however, of nobler
aspirations, I should demur to this theory, and endeavor to found the temple of human greatness on a
foundation more refined and sublimated than the skull
of the ourang-outang, and with unfeigned disgust I
should look back upon my humble progenitor and exclaim, "Worthy son of a degenerate sire!"

The gorilla belongs to the genus troglodytes, and
is regarded as the highest of the anthropoid apes. He
is exceedingly ferocious when found in his native wilds,
on the west coast of Africa, both above and below the

equator. The adult male grows to the height of five or six feet, and is strong and muscular, and when aroused is regarded as a more formidable enemy than the lion or tiger. The limbs are well developed and of great strength. Their arms are longer than those of the chimpanzee, extending far down the leg, but not to the ankle, as with the ourang-outang. The skull of the male is longer and wider, but less heavy, than that of man, and the capacity of the cavity which contains the brain is less than one-half of that of the most degraded human races.* The gorilla bears a nearer resemblance to the human type than any other of the ape species, and this resemblance is more manifest and striking in the young of those two races than in the adults; and as each matures in form this striking resemblance diminishes, and widens the disparity between the two.†

Whatever of appearance, either in structure, form, habit, or likeness, that may indicate a common origin to all the races, even including that of the quadrumana, is exploded at a glance by the observations of the practical anatomist. So far as the ourang-outang is concerned, a ten-year-old boy would revolt at the idea of recognizing him as a brother,—with his hands reaching to his ankles, or with the chimpanzee, reaching below the knees, with short lower extremities, flat and retiring forehead, and with peculiar physical frame, that

---

* The author of the Arabian tales reminds us of the similarity existing between man and his prototype, when he describes the conflict between the *old man of the sea* and one of his less fortunate adventurers.

† New American Cyclopædia.

allies the whole tribe more intimately with the quadruped tribes than with either of the lower types of the genus homo. The ourang-outang and chimpanzee are always found in a very hot climate : the former under the equator, in the Indian Archipelago, and the latter in Africa only, and principally on the Congo and Guinea coasts; and neither can survive for any length of time even in a temperate zone.

The most striking difference found to exist among the various types of the human family is observed in the facial angle of the skull ; and by measurement it is established that the facial angle of the Caucasian is larger than the corresponding angle in either of the lower tribes of our species, which illustrates the never-to-be-forgotten fact that larger space for brain is allotted to the Adamic race, for purposes of intellectuality and the practice of virtue, and less for the brutal passions and native instincts of our nature, than is developed even in the highest type of the Mongolian. And in the peculiár formation of the skull of the inferior tribes of Africa, the least space is allotted for the development of brain, for the exhibition of intellect, the basis of moral worth, goodness, and excellence. On the Gold Coast of Africa, and with the aborigines of Australia, we find a class of savages which should scarcely be denominated human beings : they are but a shade more elevated than the very brute that inhabits this planet, and cannot be distinguished as human either by habit, custom, dress, or form of religion, and we can only discern the shadow of the man in his erect form and linguistic peculiarities.

Remember that man is the only animal that can

stand on his feet in a natural position, or is able for any length of time to walk erect.

Looking closely at the characteristic traits of these barbarous hordes, can the intelligent mind behold any lineament in their feature, form, or nature that would induce us to hail them as lineal descendants of Adam, of Noah, or of Abraham: with a head prognathous in character, depressed in front, and wanting in elevation of forehead; their cheek-bones projecting forward, their jaws lengthened, and the entire face elongated; with teeth projecting to the front as though nature intended that they should arrest their food and supply their appetites like the carnivorous animals of the forest? They have brain, it is true; so has the hog, the ass, and the jackal. Where is the cranial capacity to contain the elements of sense, intellectuality, and progress, which the retreating form of the forehead disallows? The nostrils are wide and extended like a war-horse on the rampage, and the nose itself is destitute of that small nasal bone, or cartilage, which supports and gives prominence to that feature, and adds lustre to the countenance of the Caucasian. The apertures are large and the olfactories well developed; the lip is thick and heavy, indicative of sensuality in the extreme; in fact, this vice crops out at every pore of his beastly nature.

Zoologists say that there is a marked difference not only in the thicker skull of the negro and the smallness of the facial angle, but also in the formation of the pelvis; and it requires no great skill on the part of the scientific anatomist to detect, by the marks of the denuded skeleton, the proper race to which each subject belongs.

The type of the negro as to cranium is prognathous; the Mongolian pyramidal; and the Caucasian elliptical. And by measurement it has been fixed, on an average, that the facial angle in the ourang-outang extends from $30°$ to $35°$; in the negro the angle extended is $70°$; in the Asiatic, $75°$; and in the Caucasian, $80°$. Showing most conclusively, as advanced in the beginning of these pages, that the material creation was not only gradual and progressive, but that the animal creation were also in the same order and progression in their physical formations and intellectual tendencies, all of which was an essential part of nature's programme, and constituted an established purpose in the divine economy.

In speaking of the physical distinctions prominent in the two races, the sole of the white man's foot is concave, and the weight of the body rests upon an arch; and wherever you find his track impressed upon the sands of time, you immediately recognize it from the foot-print of the Congo and Guinea inhabitant, the hollow of whose foot, in common parlance, makes a hole in the ground. The vertebra, or spinal column, in the negro has its idiosyncrasy, which the eye of the common observer readily detects, and stamps on his frame apparent deformity, which ever fits him for and renders him a suitable subject as the bearer of burdens, and ennobles him in his sphere as a hewer of wood and a drawer of water for a wiser and a more enterprising race.

The color* of the skin is a matter of importance

---

* "WHY THE NEGRO WAS CREATED BLACK.—That the negro was formed for the climate of Africa the whole structure of his body

which should by no means be left out of consideration, and is said to exist alone in the epidermis, or outer
covering of the body ; and at the base of this cuticle is
secreted that odoriferous musk which so eminently distinguishes this race from all others that ever came from
the plastic hand of the Creator.

An idea prevails with some that unwholesome food
and the filthy habits of the negro engender this peculiar odor that is so obnoxious to the more sensitive
olfactories of the intelligent and refined. To satisfy
the incredulous the experiment has been tried, where
similar diet, ablution, and sanitary measures have been
equally and impartially administered to the subjects of
both races, and on coming out of the fiery ordeal of
purification, it is still manifest that the germ is there,
and that the aroma of the Ethiopian is still volatile and
uncompromising in its nature. Tell me, ye guardian
angel that hovers over my destiny and points back

---

unites to prove. First, as a protection to the brain against the direct
rays of the sun, his hair is made to grow short and curly, and he is furnished with a skull of enormous thickness. In no other being do we
see the wisdom of the Creator more clearly exhibited than in the construction of the African. The soles of his feet are overlaid with a thick
layer of fat,—a bad conductor of heat,—thereby enabling him to walk
at ease over the burning sands, and forming for him a far better protection than any contrivance the art of man could devise. And now you
may ask, Why did God make the African black? I answer, In order
that he may be able to keep cool in that torrid climate. A black surface will radiate or part with heat much more rapidly than a white one,
an experiment that any one may try. Take two vessels that are in
every respect the same,—two teapots, for instance ; let one of them be
covered over with lamp-black, then fill both with boiling water, and
you will find the black one will be cold much sooner than the bright
one."

5

through a long line of ancestral ages, can the leopard
change his spots, or the Ethiopian change his skin? I
once was young and buoyant in spirit as the morning
lark or sportive lamb; and in days of childhood, as the
innocent prattler would dangle upon his mother's knee,
and learned to lisp her name in love, and hearken to the
sweet accents that fell from her cherished lips, and her
heart full of the intuitive emotions that burst from a
Christian soul; and later still in life, when music charms
the unhallowed ear, and the troubled heart vibrates in
consonance with the deep-toned sigh that escapes from
lovely beauty, at whose feet I sit and dream my life away,
tell me, ye beau ideal of primeval hope and yet un-
tasted joys, does the unrefined blood of the sable Ethiopian course through those purple veins which mine
eye traces along that arm of snowy white? And does
it suffuse that tender cheek with crimson hues when
the heart overflows with reciprocated affection? Are
those gentle eyes, or golden locks, or raven curls fed by
the same crimson fluid which gives life to the olive tribes
of Central Asia or the dark-visaged sons of North and
South America? Tell me, ye loved ones, in truth and
sincerity, are we allied by blood and consanguinity
to the dark aboriginal races, whose form, color, custom,
and religion are repulsive to our senses, and whose
laws, habits, and religious rites are universally opposed
to divine revelation and inimical to the progress and
advancement of our species? Tell me, once more, my
guardian angel, can the leopard change his spots, or the
Ethiopian change his skin?

This question was propounded nearly three thousand
years ago to the descendants of Abraham by the prophet

180

Jeremiah, xiii. 23: "Can the Ethiopian change his skin, or the leopard his spots? then may ye also do good, that are accustomed to do evil." The theory is advanced by all who advocate the unity of the races, that the variety of color, hair, and anatomical structure, apparent among the different races of the human species, is solely attributable to the change of climate, food, habits, and manners of the various tribes who are occupying the different continents of the globe. The advocates of this theory, then, give the lie to the declaration of the prophet Jeremiah when he asked the above question. The answer is implied that neither the Asiatic, African, nor the leopard could change his color, unless man can change his own nature and regenerate his own soul: if this be feasible, then Christ hath died in vain.

The tropical sun may burn the skin and mar the beauty of the blushing race. But can it destroy his color, and change his physical organization, and produce such a hideous revolution that a mother could not recognize her first-born child? Verily not, though they should survive from the moment when the sun of day first illumined the bespangled sky to the hour when "eternal hope shall light her torch at nature's funeral pile."

Examine under a microscope the hair of a white man and the wool of a negro, and the tale is soon told that there is a cavity, or hollow, as observed in the oat or rye straw, throughout the entire length of the one, whereas the genuine black African's crispy wool in appearance and texture is solid throughout, and more closely allied to the wool that grows on the back of cer-

tain quadrupeds,—rather a plausible argument in favor
of the Darwinian theory. Again, the black skin of this
race does not burn or blister even under a tropical sun.
I have seen the black man of Louisiana throw off his
shirt in our broiling summer's sun and with impunity
labor for hours and days as a matter of choice, and the
direct rays would have no more effect upon his back
than a mosquito's proboscis on the impenetrable hide
of an alligator ; while the true Saxon under an hour's
exposure would cringe like a beast under his burden,
and would peel off like a snake when making his *début*
on the return of spring.

The dark races, on principles of sound philosophy,
were created to occupy the belt of the torrid and temperate zones, and wherever, by the fate of circumstance or the *vi et armis* of their warlike neighbors,
they have violated this established principle of their
nature and located in high northern latitudes, they become dwarfish in stature, and lose whatever of energy
they may have formerly possessed, become less prolific
and more assimilated to the indigenous surroundings
of that elevated and frozen region, as is thoroughly exemplified in the case of the Esquimaux and the inhabitants of Lapland, of whom, with the Finns and other
kindred tribes of Siberia, I shall speak in due course
of time. And, as regards the negro, the experienced
observer readily knows that a very cold climate freezes
him out, and that nowhere under the expanded canopy
of heaven does he flourish to the same extent as he does
within his native geographical sphere ; and, as has been
asserted by his defenders, that in every instance where
he has been removed to a colder or more elevated re-

gion, he becomes bleached and whitened by coming in contact with a fairer race of people.

Truly, we see that exemplified in our own America, where the African assumes a Caucasian physiognomy, which can be explained readily on the most rational grounds imaginable. Amalgamation comes to his relief, and the negro whitens in shades of color, and his hair straightens also, and changes in texture in the same proportion as you infuse into his veins more of the Turanian or Saxon blood. A cross among the domestic animals of a truly high-blooded character with one of a lower grade must enhance the worth of the inferior, and diminish the value of the superior in the same ratio.

CHAPTER VII.

THE MALAY.

> "The ocean spreads
> O'er coral rocks and amber beds,
> Where sandal-groves and bowers of spice
> Might be a Peri's Paradise,
> But human blood—the smell of Death—
> Mingles its taint with every breath."—MOORE.

ZOOLOGICALLY and geographically speaking, the human family have been divided, by common consent, into five different races, from which hypothesis I am not seriously disposed to appeal, and will therefore treat the subject with a view to the distinctions already made.

5*

Pickering, however, advances the supposition that there are at least eleven distinct races of the human genus now extant, while Desmoulins asserts that there are fully sixteen; and Agassiz and Nott contend that there are an indefinite number of species, who were created originally in groups, some of whom are no doubt extinct, while others still occupy the land of their forefathers.

By the arrangement as first intimated, the next race in order after the African proper is the Malay, the next highest type. But before proceeding farther let me call your attention to the admitted fact that there are found more noticeable varieties and shades among the negro tribes than are comprised even among our own race, estimating from the lowest grade to the most exalted character.

The Malay tribes, generally speaking, occupy Malacca, Madagascar, and Oceanica. In fact, we may include the East Indian and Polynesian Archipelagoes; and, by the way, this division of mankind is more widely distributed on the globe possibly than any other race of whom it is our purpose to discourse, and their habits, manners, and social condition exhibit greater variety than all the other inferior races combined. The population of this area occupied by the Malay is computed at one hundred and twenty millions of souls.

The complexion of this race is a reddish brown, assuming the hue of burnished copper, and is not altogether uniform, but is darker than the Mongolian, but lighter than many of the mixed tribes of the African coast. The hair is very straight, coarse, and black as jet, and hangs profusely abundant on the scalp. The beard naturally is very thin, and the custom prevails with them almost universally to pluck it out. The lips are thick and the nose flattened ; the latter at maturity sometimes assumes an aquiline appearance. The head is retreating, with small facial angle, with brain-cavity larger than the negro, but far less than the Indo-European. Their features and complexion are modified more or less in different latitudes, as well as they present to us greater advancement or debasement in accordance with the adulteration of blood, whether obtained from a higher or lower type of the human family, which explains readily the distinction drawn by historians of their civilization or their barbarism.

They have a characteristic fondness for roving, which accounts for their distribution throughout the various islands of the sea, ranging from the coast of Africa east to the islands on the west of North America. They are a cowardly people, cunning, treacherous, and vindictive, and will nurse their smothered resentment and diabolic designs under every manifestation of good will and affection until the desired opportunity presents itself, and then pounce upon their victim like a wolf upon the fold.

They have, by way of misnomer, been called civilized in part, but verily they are all barbarous ; emphatically so, I imagine, as the incident is fresh now in the memory of not a few living that they devoured the first missionaries who ventured among them to convert them to the true religion, as also did the natives of the Sandwich Islands slay and eat the memorable Captain Cook while on one of his voyages circumnavigating the globe ; while to this day they are universally noted for their piratical proclivities, ignorance, and baseness of character; and, as before remarked, that destiny has fixed their habitation under the equatorial line, where their appetites are fed by the native fruits that ripen in every season, and where the labor of other nations fall into their hands, and is appropriated by that spirit of rapine and plunder which they have honestly inherited from their aboriginal progenitors. This race, though isolated in part, and separated from each other thousands of miles by oceans of water intervening, and severing entirely even the probability of any social or commercial intercourse having existed among them for the space of thousands of years; and yet, amidst this seclusion and fixed isolation, we trace an undeniable singularity and sameness of language, feature, manners, habits, and configuration of person, which fixes an identity that defies contradiction, and must bring stern conviction to the mind of every unbiased thinker.

As with all other distinct races, however, there are minor differences apparent in color, form, and general outline, which is superinduced by mixing with other races, either more enlightened or more savage than they, or possessing other shades of color derived from an intercourse with surrounding nations.* Yet their distinctness and identity of race cannot be mistaken,

---

* The Malay is so much adulterated with the Mongolian in some localities, and with the African in other places, that some ethnologists are disposed to regard them as distinct species; and truly there is an improvement for the better where the infusion is derived from the former, while an admixture of the latter only tends to deteriorate and debase the standard.

though always found anatomically allied to the lower or prognathous type as respects cranial formation.

With regard to the intellectual and monumental developments displayed by the Malayan, together with the other four races inhabiting this planet, I shall speak of them more particularly at another place.

CHAPTER VIII.

THE AMERICAN INDIAN.

In rolling flood, in wind and storm,
Where mountain crag and hoary steep
Arise and spread each airy form
Amid ethereal skies that weep—
Here history can no tale unfold,
Here sprang to life from Nature's mould
The Indian chief, the warrior bold.

THE next race in order which engrosses our attention is the American Indian, whom Columbus and cotemporary discoverers found occupying almost the entire continent of America. It has already been intimated that the Esquimaux of the north more properly belonged originally to the Turanian race, and we will likewise include in the same category certain tribes of Mexico, Central America, and Peru, leaving a very large majority of the aborigines of this country as belonging to the third ethnological division of the human family.

The peculiarities of this race are high cheek-bones, protruding jaws, eyes deep-seated, nose broad but prominent, lips full and rounded, skin brown or cinnamon colored, beard scanty, hair black, long, and straight, with features distinctly marked and prominent. The shape of the head is square, with low forehead, and form of skull entirely different from the types before described, and differing materially from the Central Asiatic.

Dr. Prichard, who has spent a long life in the advocacy of the unity of the human family, thus discourses, "that all the different races aboriginal in the American continent belong, as far as their history and language have been investigated, to one family of nations, and that these races display considerable diversities in their physical constitution, though derived from one stock, and still betraying indications of mutual resemblance, and that, as existing two centuries ago, that they did not present any certain evidence of derivation from any special old world race."

The features of the Indian are frequently regular and the expression noble, and in many instances the females are regarded as handsome. Their muscular frame in many respects does not compare with that of the white man, but his powers of endurance in the wild hunt for game or for the scalp of his enemy, subsisting for days upon a mere pittance, is far above that of our own race under similar circumstances of exposure. The complexion varies in different latitudes, owing to various causes, and the physical stature also is not uniform, the average height varying in certain localities from ten to twelve inches. But one feature peculiar to the native

American should not be lost sight of; that those tribes found nearest to the poles have not been whitened by the frosts and snows of a colder latitude, while the Toltican or Mexico-Peruvian tribes are not only fairer than their more distant neighbors, but decidedly more intelligent and progressive in their tendencies. The facial angle is only 75°, and the volume of the brain is only 79 cubic inches for the semi-civilized, and 84 for the more barbarous tribes, while the low, retreating forehead diminishes space for the development of the intellectual faculties, whereas the posterior lobes of the brain are much larger with the inferior races, showing a preponderance on the side of brute force and native depravity. The Indian naturally is haughty and reserved in his bearing to strangers, and stoical and uncompromising in his character. He recognizes no neutral ground, and ignores frankly every condition of life that prompts the emotions of humanity. When war becomes the order of the day, he flaunts to the breeze the black flag of extermination, asks no quarter and gives none in return. By his creed the captive belongs to the victor, and mercy pleads in vain for its victim. Age and sex are without an advocate when the war-whoop of the savage resounds through the land. In peace he is indolent and grave, and when the stranger approaches his wigwam he is received with kindness, and the hospitalities of his board are offered without stint. He is grateful to a friend, never forgets a kindness, and never forgives a foe. The peculiar cranial formation is such with all of the inferior races of man, that the intellectual is so far overshadowed by the animal propensities that his elevation in the scale of being is almost a matter of impossibility. The Indian, more than any other race under the sun, is devoted to warfare, and differs from John Chinaman, who wears his queue behind; the native American boasts a scalp-lock on the top of his head, and defies the world in arms, and rash is he who essays to snatch this trophy in the hour of conflict. The encroachments made by their superiors upon this unfortunate people have reduced their numbers to about fifteen million souls. The treachery and savage disposition of his nature, it is to be presumed, is not altogether unknown to the Anglo-American, though the latter has done much to provoke his wrath and bring upon him the fires of extermination.

It seems strange, on reflection, that the enlightened world is so ready and willing to strike hands with and call the Indian and the negro "hail brother, well met," of one blood and of one bone, and offspring of one and the same pair of parents. Child of light, son of civilization, worshiper of the first-born, why, in Heaven's name, has the white man treated his brother thus? With flame and sword ye came and spoiled his land, ye entered his wigwam and partook of his hospitable meal, and warmed your limbs at the blazing fire that burned on his humble hearth; and in the dead hour of the stilly night, when gentle slumbers and placid dreams inwrapped the prostrate forms of the helpless sleepers, you bathed your knife in the hearts of your unsuspecting victims. With the power of might you robbed him of his possessions, and drove him a wanderer from the home of his forefathers, and converted his fair domain into a desert, which proved more repulsive to his feelings than the great Sahara to the nomadic hordes of the East. And when he came and told his tale of sorrow, and pointed to the mound where stood the unpretending hut of his warrior chief, and marked on the ground with his palsied finger where reposed the consecrated ashes of his people for a thousand generations, and demanded a consideration for the hunting-grounds of his fathers, you laughed at his calamity, and mocked at the gushing sorrow of his soul, and said, "Thou dotard, flee to your forest chambers and your mountain home, and await thou patiently until the desolating besom shall sweep the last vestige of your race from the continent of America. This alone shall be your consideration. Might is right, and before that altar we bow, worship, and adore." Has the black man no tale of sorrow to relate? no cause to reproach his pale-faced brother? snatched from his native country unapprised, the untold horrors of the middle passage, sold in a foreign land, and doomed to slavery for ages to come! I repeat, it is strange that the truly enlightened heart should entertain convictions of the unity of the human family and treat his dark-visaged brother with such unbecoming brutality; whereas views of a plurality of the races would in the eyes of many modify the guilt to some extent, but not justify such a course of conduct by any means.

There can be no doubt, however, of the distinctness and unity of this race of people. Their language is exclusively original with themselves, and is not found to correspond in root or branch with any of the known languages whom the researches of the Indo-European

6

has yet had the good fortune to analyze; and their peculiar religious views and manners and habits of life are so at variance with all other nations under the sun, that our most scientific and observant judges of the human species assign to them an originality and diversity of traits of character and physical formation which must place them distinct and aboriginal in the general creation of the world, and as the Aryan would say, they are the autochthones of the land.

It is impossible at this late day, without written records or direct revelation, to fix beyond the possibility of a doubt in the minds of all any maxim, however nearly it may approach the truth of an established axiom in mathematics; we will always find some theorist whose ideas are antagonistic, and whose views run off invariably at a tangent. This position is illustrated in the varied religions of the day, where each sect claims exact harmony with divine revelation itself; whereas their interpretations of holy writ are as much at variance as the antipodes.

CHAPTER IX.

THE MONGOLIAN.

The work of man, is man to study well
Where'er he move, or where the races dwell,
On barren shores, or in the tropic belt,
Or where alternate heat and cold are felt,—
Mongolia sits on Asia's arid plain,
Nor calls us man beyond her wide domain.

THE next race in order for our consideration is the ancient Central Asiatic or Mongolian race, whom Professor Max Müller has, in these latter days, denominated the Turanian, in consideration of the contest waged between the Aryan family and Turan, the representative of the great Tartar family, and only second in importance to the linguist and ethnologist after the Indo-European and Semitic tribes, who are the lineal descendants of Noah. This type of mankind originally dwelt east of Eden, occupying Central and Northern Asia, and ultimately spreading over the most, if not entire Europe, the polar belt of North America, and other districts of the American and Asiatic continents. Though an inferior race, compared with the Caucasian, in point of intellectual capacity, its migrations and occupancy abroad have been more extended than any other single race of the genus homo, and has performed a more important part in the political history of the world. There is a marked similarity in the language of this race, though scattered over such a vast territory, and subject, too, to innovations from all sides. It is formed on what is termed the agglutinative type: the root under no circumstances undergoes any change, and in giving expression to the ideas formed in the mind syllables are suffixed, and form no close and intimate union, but remain in the condition of loosely appended words,—a marked peculiarity known to no other language or people under the canopy of heaven.

The Mongolian's manners, customs, habits of life, and cranial formation differ materially from all other races with whom we are acquainted, and belong to that division of the species usually denominated pyramidal form of skull; they are stout, swarthy, and ugly, possessing a broad, flat face and prominent cheek-bones, high and broad shoulders, thick, short necks, and bony and nervous hands. Their eyes are black and drawn at the corners, which gives them an elliptical appearance. Their noses are considerably flattened, and their complexion varies slightly from a yellow or olive hue to a more swarthy color. The hair is universally straight, dark, coarse, and is worn usually in a queue behind. This race is not so tall in stature as the Caucasian or the American Indian, and differs so materially from these two races that it requires no experienced eye to locate the Mongolian, wherever found, when pure in blood and uncontaminated by alliance with other races. They inhabited Central Asia originally, but now occupy Northern, Central, and Eastern Asia, and as far south as the limits of the Malayan territory. As remarked previously, the Finns and Lapps of the north of Europe and the Esquimaux of North America justly belong to this race, and there are many reasons why we should also include in the same family those nations whom the Spaniards conquered at an early day, under the leadership of Pizarro and Cortes,—the aboriginal occupants of Peru, Central America, and Mexico.

The Mongolian is marked with every shade of color, just in proportion as his blood has been tinged with that of other nations of a lighter or darker hue. The original department of the eastern hemisphere formerly allotted to the Adamic race, that is, Western Asia, has in times past been overrun by the Central Asiatic, and one time they in fact overran and occupied almost the entire continent of Europe, and that portion of Africa embraced between the Great Desert and the Mediterranean Sea. These Oriental hordes, warlike and barbarous in their habits, had become cramped in their ancient allotted territory, oppressed by laws every way tyrannical in their enforcement, trampled upon and enslaved by the satraps of that densely-populated region, came out from thence in swarms like the devouring locusts, and spread themselves over Western Asia and the continent of Europe; and for the time being, the dominant race of the world, in point of intellect and progress, had to succumb to the triumphant hordes of the aggressive Mongolian. Had these warlike successes continued on the part of this inferior race, and they had remained in the ascendant, with all the nations of earth subdued to their will, our condition, intellectually, morally, and religiously,

6*

would have been deplorable indeed. But, fortunately for the cause of civilization and humanity, the Caucasian rose phœnix-like, by the might of his transcendent genius, and drove out the Mongol tribes, and confined them on the south to the fastness of the Pyrenees Mountains, and on the north to the icy coast of Scandinavia, where the Finn and the Lapp to-day ekes out a mere existence in a latitude too frozen in its temperature to suit his dark-visaged nature. Much on a par are these restricted tribes with their fellow-wanderers in Alaska, Siberia, Kamschatka, and the inhabitants of the Aleutian Archipelago. In Hungary is found a remnant of this people under the style of the Magyars, who settled there about the fourth century after Christ.

And in Turkey we have the Ottoman, whose blood has been much purified, and whose pyramidal cast of cranium has been considerably modified by an admixture of the blood of the Circassian and Georgian girls, whom avarice and an entire want of parental affection have introduced as slaves in the Turkish market. Nor is this manifest appearance of change of feature and cranial formation confined to the noble and the wealthy alone, but extends to every class and grade of the Ottoman Empire, and is thoroughly understood when we call to mind that the white damsel of Caucasus is valued in the slave-markets of the East according to beauty and symmetry of feature and figure, and that the more homely commands a much less price, and thereby comes within the range of the poorer aspirant for connubial joys; and the entire want of virtue and chastity with these hybrid races, which has been proverbial from the earliest ages, would essentially change the Mongolian characteristics and approximate his standard to that of the Caucasian.

The same, to a certain extent, is observed in Persia, the land of Cyrus and Xerxes, which, in ages gone by, yielded to the conquering tramp of the Eastern hordes, and permitted its bright escutcheon to be tarnished with the olive tinge; while others of original Persian extraction have preserved intact the purity of the Semitic race, like the high-blooded Castilian and the proud sons of Aragon have alone, among the inhabitants of the Spanish peninsula, kept aloof from the degenerate blood introduced through successive ages in the south of Europe. The Spaniard, the Portuguese, and the Italian are everlasting monuments of hybrid degeneracy.

When man mocks at Deity and violates the fixed laws of his being, he must suffer loss, the iniquities of which are visited upon him to the third and fourth generation. Who remembers when the Roman standard was planted upon the isle of Britain, and the inhabitants of the known world, from the sands of Asia to the uttermost parts of the earth, brought their diadems and laid them suppliantly at the feet of the Cæsars, —when Spain sent forth her navies and planted the cross in the temple of the Incas and Mexican adorers of the sun, and the Toltecs of America became vassals, and emptied their treasures into the lap of the proud and exacting Spaniard. The Spanish and Portuguese conquests in America and elsewhere have passed from under their yoke, and these once flourishing nations, though still proud and arrogant in spirit, have lost all

197

the noble genius of enterprise and progress once possessed, and have dwindled down to third- and fourth-rate powers among the nationalities of earth ; and the hybrid races of this continent, founded by these dynasties, are everlasting monuments of that degeneracy resulting from the amalgamation of ours with an inferior race in the scale of being. Where the Mongol has crossed with other races of a lower type, we find in that type quite an improvement, physiologically and intellectually as well as in shade of color. For instance, there is a vast improvement in the Hottentots and Bushmen of Southern Africa, and the Ashantees, Dahomans, and Senegambians of Western Africa. Some of the latter, however, are slightly tinged with the Caucasian, from the intercourse that originally existed between the Mediterranean tribes and the western coast of Africa, while the Hindoo* has a slight infusion of the Adamic stock as well as a heavy supply of the Malay admixture. In fact, wherever intercourse, from whatever cause, arises between distinct races, it is as natural for them to mix as wine and water, which must ever account for the variety of shades and colors continually turning up in different localities, and not, as some authors have

---

* " It is a great mistake to suppose that all India is peopled by a single race, or that there is not as great a disparity between the inhabitants of Guzerat, Bengal, the Doab, and the Deccan, both in language, manners, and physiognomy, as between any four nations of Europe."—BISHOP HEBER.

" The general complexion of the people is dark brown, though many are as black as negroes, while the Parsees and people of Cashmere, in the north, are but little darker than the inhabitants of Southern Europe. . . . They have black and straight hair, and are usually well formed."—*American Cyclopædia.*

assigned, attributable to the influences of localities as respects heat and cold.

.The Mongolian race comprises nearly one-half of the human family, and is estimated to number five hundred and sixty million souls, and is the only one of all the aboriginal races who has left, or now has in preservation, one solitary monument of architectural or intellectual ingenuity. The negro, Malay, and American Indian have nothing better than a thatched or mud dwelling; and the Indian has left the solitary relic of earthen mounds, scattered hither and thither, intended, no doubt, as a memorial of some victory achieved over a neighboring warlike race, or as a tomb to perpetuate the virtues of some brave chieftain of his tribe, by which they are justly denominated the moundbuilders.

In consideration of this development of mechanical skill and intellectual advancement, as well as peculiar physiological formation and linguistic affinities, induces me to include the Aztec, the Toltec, and the Incas kindred races, as certainly a part and parcel of the great Central Asiatic families. The Toltecs dwelt on the north of the valley of Mexico prior to the arrival of the Aztecs, the latter of whom are claimed, by some writers, to be the founders of the ancient Mexican civilization. But really the Toltecs are the party to whom this distinguished honor is due. Their capital was Tula, and the remains of many magnificent build ings were still to be seen when the Spaniards first invaded Mexico, and the name Toltec has justly become synonymous with architect. Prescott says, "The Toltecs were well instructed in agriculture and many of the most useful mechanic arts; were nice workers of metal; invented the complex arrangement of time adopted by the Aztecs, and in short were the true fountains of the civilization which distinguished this part of the continent in latter times." The Incas were the chiefs or imperial heads of the great Peruvian Empire in the fifteenth century, and this chain of semi-civilization extended from the highlands north of the valley of Mexico, through Yucatan, Guatemala, and across the Andes to the broad alluvians of the Amazon and Orinoco. How they reached these latitudes and became a dominant race in the midst of these mound-builders may be explained on the theory that the immense population concentrated in the heart of Asia in the course of time found that their limited area could not furnish sustenance for so dense and numerous a population, that necessity drove them out in every direction to search for new fields for settlement.

These pressing needs, and actuated by a love of conquest, they at one time flooded Europe and the north of Africa; led their hordes through Siberia, and planted them upon the icy coast of North America, which latitude is ever inimical to the dark-complexioned races, and by an easy course of descent they would gradually drift to the warm and congenial climate of Mexico, and thence by the Central American route to the attractive slopes of the Andes.*

---

* According to the traditions of the Ayrmares, the leading Peruvian race, there was a time when war and dissension were the ruling traits, and every tribe was sunk in the lowest depths of barbarism. " From

No tribe of Indians yet known to man, save those of
whom we speak, possessed that degree of intelligence
and that spirit of enterprise as is exemplified in the
magnificent structures that once dotted the adopted
land of this comparatively extinct race. Lofty temples
of hewn stone, with arched corridors grand in proportions, ornamented with sculptured stones and beauti-

---

this condition they were rescued by their tutelar divinity, the Sun,
who sent down his own children to reform and instruct them. These
were Manco Capac, and his sister and wife, Mama Oello Huaco, who
made their appearance on an island in Lake Titicaca, whence under
divine instruction they journeyed northward to the spot where the
city of Cuzco, which afterwards became the capital of the Incas, now
stands. Here they collected together the neighboring savage hordes,
and while Manco Capac instructed the men in agriculture and the
arts, and inspired them with ideas of social and civil organization,
Mama Oello taught the women to spin and weave, and inculcated
modesty, grace, and the domestic virtues. From this celestial pair
the Incas claimed their descent, in virtue of which they were the high-
priests of religion and the heads of the state. In this tradition we
trace only another version of the civilization common to all primitive
nations, and that imposture of a celestial relationship whereby designing rulers and cunning priests have sought to secure their ascend-
ency among men. Manco Capac is the almost exact counterpart of
the Chinese Fohi, the Hindoo Buddha, the terrestrial Osiris of Egypt,
the Quetzalcoatl of Mexico, and Votan of Central America. . . .
Aside, however, from all traditions, there are monumental evidences
that, anterior to the foundation of the Peruvian Empire, there existed
on the islands and shores of Lake Titicaca a people of relatively high
civilization, the story of whose migration to the northward is probably
preserved in a figurative form in that of Manco Capac and his sister;
and it may safely be assumed that this people, in their relationships,
and in virtue of their intelligence, arrogated to themselves a superiority over the tribes which they brought under their control, and
founded an exclusive and aristocratic caste, the Inca race."—*American
Cyclopædia.*

fully-carved wood, and adorned with mosaic-work
and hieroglyphic painting, indicating an enlightenment
of no ordinary kind, and a familiar acquaintance with
Oriental literature ; and in that tropic land are found
the sculptured idols before whom they bowed and
worshiped ; and a beautiful road paved with white rock,
leading from Kabah to Uxmal, ten inches high and
eight feet wide, is pointed out at this late period by the
natives, on which the couriers traveled from city to
city, conveying written messages from the nobles of
one city to the other, and these messages inscribed
upon the skins of animals and the bark of trees. These
records came to us in part by the traditions common
to the present aborigines of the country, and authenticated by the testimony of reliable travelers who have
explored this region, and report facts that have passed
under their immediate observation.   And these unmistakable evidences of superior enlightenment exhibited
in the ancient homes of the Toltecan tribes forbid
even a reasonable doubt as respects the position that
they should take among the nations of earth, being
more intelligent, more refined ; and corresponding
physical conformation allies them forever with the
original Mongolian of the East.

Reverting again to the ancient seats of the Mongolian race, it is astonishing what apparent progress this
people has made in passing ages ; taking into consideration the link which they form in the great chain of
races, the last and highest type of the pre-adamic creation, we are enabled to trace the progressive system
and the gradually ascending series in the divine programme of God's eternal purpose.

The negro, the Malay, and the American Indian had served their day, and taken their respective positions in the progressive series of original creation, when the Mongolian is introduced, preparatory to the ushering in of a higher and a nobler type of the human species, not perfect in his nature, tarnished in his complexion, yet far superior in mental endowments to any preceding family which had made its *début* on the arena of life, and the only race whose form of government is assimilated to that of a still more refined and enterprising people.* As with the Toltec of Central America, so with the inhabitant of Central Asia. The great wall that bounds China on the north is one of the remarkable wonders of the world ; its height is twenty-four feet, and length fifteen hundred miles, and sufficiently broad for two carriages to be driven along abreast from one end to the other. It was constructed several hundred years before the Christian era, for the purpose of checking the invasions of adjacent tribes descended from the same parental stock ; a very conclusive argument that no material change has taken place in the government of this empire from the established principle in the political economy of nations, that the moment that all the wealth and resources of a people are concentrated in the hands of the few, by taxation, tyranny, and oppression, it is then that the government becomes centralized, and the liberties and the entire resources of the country become vested in and subject to the will of

---

* Buckle says, " In Central America extensive excavations have been made, and what has been brought to light proves that the national religion was like that of India, a system of complete and unmitigated terror."

7

one man, who rules his subordinates with the same discipline exercised by a military commander over his immediate staff.   Consequently, tyranny of the darkest hue takes possession of the person and energies of the whole nation, and makes them subservient to the *ipse dixit* of the exacting despot.   Such a state of affairs now obtains in the Chinese Empire and with the moguls of the East, and has existed throughout Asia ages upon ages before tradition even had its birth.   China boasts the largest canal in the world, together with temples and public buildings that excite astonishment in European and American minds.   They have arts and claim a knowledge of the sciences which are yet unknown to us, and we must admit that they have been and still are in possession of secrets which the world has not been able to obtain.   They are called civilized, but nevertheless extremely barbarous in many practices sanctioned by law and upheld by the general will of the people.   In many respects they are savage and uncompromising in their nature, and devoted to the idolatrous worship which has come down to them from the antediluvian period.   The Asiatic Mongols have their libraries containing books on various subjects, and were acquainted with the art of printing in their peculiar way long before Europe made the discovery, and some of them claim that their government was founded many centuries before Commodore Noah embarked on his first sailing-voyage.   In examining the literature of India, we find statements there which require a considerable stretch of the imagination to grasp and fully retain, though pregnant with improbabilities far beyond the reach of our credulity ; yet the charges of unbelief

brought to bear against our authentic historical records
by some new-discovered race would provoke within us
a smile at the ignorance of these new and unlettered
judges of ancient history. The same view no doubt
obtains with the Hindoo and John Chinaman when
ridicule is thrust at their long-cherished records. They
claim for the average life of ordinary men of old only
eighty thousand years, and that those who were clothed
with sacerdotal robes, and holy in their lives, were permitted to enjoy one hundred thousand years of blissful
usefulness on this mundane sphere. Some survived
longer, others shorter periods. They go so far as to
mention the names of some of their great men who were
blessed with such longevity. A king, whose name is
Yudhisthir, had the glorious privilege of sitting upon
his throne and dispensing justice for the short term of
twenty-seven thousand years; while another, called
Alarka, wore his crown and was in active duty for the
space of sixty-six thousand years. And these great
men were unfortunately cut down in the prime of life,
for in the Asiatic researches it is recorded, and piously
believed by the present inhabitants of the East, that two
of their bards, by name Valmic and Vyasa, whose birth-
days were separated by a period of eight hundred and
sixty-four thousand years, yet that aged and this youthful poet had sat down together and conversed in regard
to matters that pertained to the long annals of the
past.* Their great collection of laws denominated

---

* The most remarkable case is that of a very shining character in
Oriental history, who united in his person the functions of a king and
a saint. "He was the first king, first anchorite, and first saint, and is

the "Institutes of Menu," to which the Hindoo is
so much attached, by the best native authorities these
great laws were revealed by Heaven to these ancient
devotees full two thousand millions of years before
Warren Hastings crushed this people with the iron
car of avarice.   And when China's vaults and Japan's
labyrinths of mystic lore are opened up to the vulgar
gaze of the Anglo-Saxon, we may read of Antediluvia as
the pastime of to-day, and mark on Adam's brow the
tint of evening's twilight, and search for antiquity
among the mysterious oracles which the morning
zephyrs strew promiscuously in the subterranean caverns of the Cumæn Sibyl, and point back to the hour
when the sweet influences of Pleiades and Orion cast
their mellowed light over the lifeless form of chaotic
nature.

---

therefore entitled Prathama-Rajah, Prathama Bhieshacara, Prathama
Jina, and Prathama Tirthancara.   At the time of his inauguration as
king his age was two million years.   He reigned six million three
hundred thousand years, and then resigned his empire to his sons ;
and having employed one hundred thousand years in passing through
the several stages of austerity and sanctity, departed from this world
on the summit of a mountain named Ashtapada."—*Asiatic Researches,*
vol. ix. p. 305.

CHAPTER X.

THE CAUCASIAN.

" But man he made of angel form erect,
    To hold communion with the heavens above,
    And on his soul impressed his image fair,
    His own similitude of holiness,
    Of virtue, truth, and love."—POLLOK.

THE fifth and last race which engrosses our attention is man, the child of Adam, and the lineal descendant of Shem, Ham, and Japhet, of whom alone the Bible speaks, and who alone is made in God's own image and likeness. The Indo-European, or Caucasian, has a different shaped head from any of the other races; his skull is more oval or elliptical, and is more symmetrical in form. There is no excessive prominence or undue flattening or compression on the top of the head, which invariably manifests itself with all of the lower races; the head is rounder and the forehead broad and full, with the cranial cavity largely developed; marked with a fullness of the forehead and elevation of the brow in accordance with the size of the face, indicating higher intellectual powers rather than indicative of the brutal or sensual.

The facial angle is larger than in any of the other races, and the cranial cavity consequently more fully

7*

developed, where are seated the organ of sense, which accounts for the vast difference in the intellectual and progressive capacity of this race over all others, and is illustrated by the fact, that wherever the white man has essayed to establish a supremacy over his inferiors, under reasonable auspices, he has thus far never failed to consummate his ends; for the time by the dint of numbers he has been overpowered, as brute force for a season will triumph over the intellectual advancement, but sooner or later the shackles of enthrallment fall to the ground in the presence of a higher order of genius, wisdom assumes her sway, and the noble attributes of the white man become master of the situation. The Mongols of the East came upon Europe "like a wolf on the fold," and for a time spread darkness over the fair fields of the Indo-European, and now the Magyar of Hungary has, in a measure, been absorbed by the superior race which surrounds him; and the Ottoman Empire hangs like a ragged garment on the confines of Russia, and the dark element once dominant in the Spanish peninsula has succumbed to the genius of true civilization and moral enlightenment, and the Pillars of Hercules may rise out of the ocean and stand as an everlasting monument of the inferiority of the one and the superiority of the other. America can well attest the proud achievements of the European over the savage demons that peopled the western continent. And Western Asia, once the seat of learning and of science and civilization, and where the Star of Bethlehem first threw its radiant light over the broken hopes of a perishing world, is now overrun by the mixed races of the Mongolian and the descendants of

Ishmael, who in hybridizing improve in the physical type, and degrade in the moral and intellectual, until the baser instincts of man assume undivided sovereignty over the heart, and fitly prepare him for the Moslem's work of desecration and destruction. The unsullied Caucasian sought a permanent home beyond the Bosphorus from the devouring hordes that swept across the continent of Asia, and the few who were of necessity left behind have become assimilated in manners, customs, and blood with the dominant race, who first came among them like the avalanche from the summit of the Himalaya Mountains. With this exception, however, that many of the descendants of Abraham as nomad Arabs are still perfect in cranial formation and purity of color, with no alloy of degenerate blood, who have not bowed the knee to the aggressive Mongolian, either to become allied by consanguinity or to pay tribute as a conquered vassal. Mount Caucasus* points her summit to the clouds, and bids defiance to the Mongolian and Sclavonic races. Who would essay to strip her free-born sons of their dear-bought liberties? and is it possible that the advocate of the One-Race dogma would attempt to sully the name of the fair Caucasian by charging upon this race an admixture of Mongolian blood? Such ideas are advanced upon the general declaration that of one blood God created all the nations of the earth. This language was spoken by the Apostle Paul, and was addressed to the Greeks,

---

* The white camellia, one of the most beautiful of cultivated flowers, is so closely blended with Mount Caucasus in the minds of the southern people, that it has become sacred as the emblem of purity, and eminently representative of the Adamic race.

lineal descendants of Japhet, as found in Acts xvii.
24–26: "God that made the world and all things
therein, seeing that he is Lord of heaven and earth,
dwelleth not in temples made with hands; neither is
worshiped with men's hands, as though he needed any
thing, seeing he giveth to all life, and breath, and all
things; and hath made of one blood* all nations of
men for to dwell on all the face of the earth, and hath
determined the times before appointed, and the bounds
of their habitation." In the first place, Paul's remarks
were addressed directly to the enlightened Athenian, a
type of the true Caucasian. Nor is there any evidence
that any one of Christ's apostles ever preached the
gospel to either of the inferior races, and if they did,
there are many plausible reasons to assert that their
preaching to them was as the sounding brass or tinkling cymbal. Again, the constituent parts of the blood
of vertebrated animals are found by analysis to differ
in no particular essential points; in fact, not varying
in the component particles more nor less than is observable in the blood of different individuals of the
same race. In truth, it is established by the learned in
the medical world, that the blood of the same individual undergoes material changes in making its regular circuit through the arterial and venous channels;
and again, the blood of the same individual undergoes
various changes at various ages of the same party under
equal circumstances of health and sobriety. Likewise
is the blood altered in its constituent composition by

---

* Luke wrote this gospel, and not Paul, and in none of Paul's
epistles is to be found any parallel passage or expression.

a change of food and diet to that extent that the herbivorous feeder may be easily detected from the carnivorous species. And there is also a marked difference observable in the blood of the sanguineous and lymphatic subjects of the white race. And these varied changes must ever continue in the human system, and in the physical economy of man, just as we discriminate the different waters that flow from the bosom of the earth, the one stream is impregnated with -minerals and alkalies differing from others in the same vicinity. Therefore, if this scriptural passage is to be interpreted on a scientific basis, then "hath God made of one blood all the nations of the earth, and hath before appointed the bounds of their habitations," to wit, He hath located the negro in Africa, south of the Great Desert; the Malay along the belt of the tropics, and the Mound-builder on the American continent; the Mongolian under the rising sun, and man, the true image of his Creator, on the fertile shores of the Tigris and Euphrates.

If it were possible for man to change his own features, the unguent pores of his body, the color of his skin, flatten his nose, compress his skull, and otherwise disfigure and degrade his perfect type of nobility, tell me why there were no negroes found on the American continent when first discovered. We have an equatorial sun, whose parching rays fall in perpendicular lines upon as arid districts as the original home of the blackest African; we have lakes and seas and oceans that reflect back the concentrated rays of the fiery orb of day; we have sands and plains and jungles and torrid fires to furnish all the elements necessary to generate the black and odoriferous spawn who lords it to-day over the rich heritage of the Semitic race. If food and habit and savage manners and climatic influences and fondness for human flesh, if tornadoes and volcanic floods and devouring earthquakes can fright the human heart and alter the physical formation of man, and change the noblest work of God into the degraded specimen who rears his earth-born savage frame and feature before intelligent man and claims social equality, then ought America to have claimed the proud and exalted privilege of originating one pure unalloyed and unadulterated negro, that he might present himself to the world as a living and a moving en-sample of the creative genius or the debasing influence of the virgin soil of America. If there were no other arguments in favor of the plurality of the races, this alone ought to establish the truth of our theory beyond the peradventure of a reasonable doubt.

CHAPTER XI.

HYBRIDITY, COLOR, AND SELECTION.

> " If the wild winds seem more drear
> Than man's cold charities below,
> Behold around his peopled plains,
> Where'er the social savage reigns,
> Exuberance of woe."—CAMPBELL.

I AM willing to admit that there is only the semblance of an argument in favor of a unity of the human species in the established laws governing the hybridity of the vegetable and animal kingdoms; that hybrid races, originating in the sexual intercourse of entirely different species, do not always as a general rule tend to self-perpetuation. This may apply with apparent force to the brute creation, but can have no bearing in reference to the progeny derived from a cross of the human family.

The intellectual feature of the genus homo predominates over the vegetable and the brute formations, and the natural affinities of the intellectual being are more harmonious, as respects congeniality of feeling, sentiment, and selection; and the repulsive elements that are at work with the instinctive genius of the brute tribes, derived from apprehension, may bring about results entirely different, and not at all attendant upon subjects of higher intellectual capacity, who are operating under preconceived notions of comparative congeniality, where a uniform will has been exercised to the action of a joint selection on the part of both subjects.

In the vegetable kingdom there can be no exercise of will or choice when impregnation ensues; a result exclusively emanating from a fixed law of nature, but superinducing in plants greater production and prolificacy wherever the experiment has been thoroughly tested. The mare (the female of the horse) ordinarily will not yield to the demands of the ass until teased by the male of her own species; nor is there harmonious intercourse between the lion and the tiger, and other carnivorous and herbivorous animals. There must ever exist among these diverse species and discordant natures the apprehension of fear, a foreboding of bodily injury, much akin to the dreadful shock experienced by the chaste of our own race when made to succumb to the violent efforts of the ravisher, to which the chaste victim does not respond by conception; whereas, on the other hand, the brute does conceive and brings forth a monster which is neither fish nor fowl; and a few of these crosses are seldom known to breed with hybrids of the same class, although they propagate occasionally with either of their parental stock, and in the course of time lose their identity almost entirely.

In speaking of animals as respects species, we assume as a basis that those are distinct which have preserved their identity and have remained unchanged during the space of forty-five hundred years, which carries us back anterior to the time of Noah's deluge, according to the chronological computation of Archbishop Usher, which was 2349 years B.C. Dogs have often been represented on the monuments of Egypt as early as the fourth dynasty, 3400 years B.C. So have specimens of the wolf, hyena, and jackal been delineated on the same monuments, and later, down to the eleventh and twelfth dynasties, 2100 to 2400 years B.C.

We find them frequently repeated on the walls of these memorable sepulchres as large as life and perfectly accurate in description, and presenting them every way the fac-simile of the same species now found in the neighboring countries of Asia and Africa.

The greyhound was known long prior to the days of Abraham. So were the pointer, the hound, the bulldog, and the turnspit, together with the wild dog of the woods. And it may seem strange to the cursory reader that the crowned heads of Egypt should have devoted time and means to have these minor animals represented upon their monuments. In every age history informs us that the royal court has unbended its frown and sought the forest to regale a season in the chase of the wild boar and the stag, and the triumphant victor returns from his royal park with the trophies of the chase and depicts upon the spacious walls the flying stag and the pursuing canines, with the same zest that he would inscribe those captives who grace his returning chariot from some foreign field of blood. It is difficult to say from whence came the following animals, as history does not define the dog, the horse, hog, sheep, and goat. As far as we can trace them back, they were known then as distinct as they are found to-day; whether they were original species or distinct genera, or are really hybrids, must ever remain

8

a matter of doubt, but we assume that they are and ever have been distinct. It has been tested and tried satisfactorily that the dog crossed with the wolf or the fox, that this hybrid offspring emanating from either one or the other will not only breed with the parent stock, but are prolific among themselves. And there are many instances on record where they prove to be more prolific in fact than their parents. And natural history is not silent in regard to the sheep* and goat. They are as distinct apparently as any animals found in nature; and wherever coupled together, they are remarkable for prolificacy, both with the parent stock and among themselves. This is also true of the male sheep† and the doe (Cervus capriolus). The same is proverbially true of the three different species of the camels,‡ among themselves, as also with the dromedaries, which are distinct. The one coupled with the other produces hybrids which are long-lived and prolific; the camel with the dromedary, and *vice versa*.

It is unnecessary to enumerate other examples, if it can be established in one instance that hybrids are prolific *inter se* and with the parent stock, which has been done conclusively with regard not only to different species but distinct genera. The scientific inquirer should be satisfied, and the skeptic convinced, that there is a plurality of races among the above-enumerated animals, and that there is nothing unnatural in the productions of the hybrid races of the human family.

There can be no greater cross in nature than that

---

* Molina and Chevreul.   † Hellenius.
‡ Linnæus and Cuvier.

arising between the goat and the sheep, and the white man and the negress; and if the progeny of the one is prolific, the other is likewise. And barrenness among hybrids is rather an exception than a rule, and this question of hybridity and productiveness would never have agitated the public mind to the same extent only as a plausible theory to establish the unity of the races.

There is one thing very remarkable with the hybrid classes of the genus homo wherever found on this habitable globe, in any latitude or in any climate, immaterial by whom surrounded, whether by barbarous, half-civilized, or intelligent and moral communities. They are ever destitute and devoid of honesty, virtue, and chastity. There is but one race among whom is practiced strict moral honesty in their daily intercourse with their fellow-men, and whose females are truly and strictly chaste in the highest signification of the term, both honest and chaste from principle and not as a matter of policy; and this high and exalted premium can be alone awarded to the Caucasian family. The African and Polynesian explorer, the Oriental traveler, and the Rocky-Mountain trapper, tell us that true virtue is unknown among the aboriginal races. There are isolated cases of chastity among the varied tribes of earth; but it is the exception rather than the rule, and it obtains alone where vengeance hangs like the sword of Damocles in threatening attitude over the wayward victim. Now, throw into this caldron of corruption the blood of the white man, and the progeny derived from the negro becomes a mulatto; intellectually, we admit that the stock is improved, but the virtue of the one has been destroyed by the leaven of the other, and so on *ad infinitum* as regards all others of the inferior races; so long, at least, as this degenerate taint is visible in feature and formation.

If I am not correct in the assumed premises of a want of true virtue in the mongrel races, then tell us why the Eastern harems are guarded by eunuchs and other imbeciles. The thought is father to the deed; and the custom so prevalent in the East, of veiling the females from the gaze of the world and excluding them from male society, is proof positive of a want of confidence in their virtue, and to avoid an exposure to the seductive influences of the artful, which must always prove the victor over the weaker vessel, whose constitutional tendency at best is to stray from the paths of rectitude.

Color in the human skin is derived from pigment-cells which are mingled with the ordinary epidermic cells; the former of which secrete a black pigment which bears a close relation with that inky fluid for which the cuttle-fish is so much noted, and contains a very large proportion of carbon. These pigment or coloring cells in the epidermis are alone observable in the negro and other dark-skinned races, except in freckles and in the dark spots around the nipples of the fairer race.

The varied hues of complexion met with in the different colored races is due to the number of these cells and to the particular tint of the pigment therein secreted; hence arise the jet-black, brown, copper-colored, olive, and white complexions, that mark the distinctness of complexion characteristic of the human family. And it is urged with great tenacity that these results are brought about by climatic influences, combined with the action of heat and light and the force of sexual selection. A strange theory indeed, that these influences would completely metamorphose the entire physical structure and warp the ennobling attributes of our nature, and so debase our moral being that man completely loses his identity and becomes assimilated in instinct and physiological organization with the quadrumana tribes. And the hypothesis that the jet-black negro, in making his selection for a companion in life, truly prefers one of his own color in preference to those of a lighter hue, is an egregious error, and well supported by the history of the blacks in America, in Hayti, and elsewhere. Having been a slave-owner myself, and a willing resident in their midst for forty years, I speak from my own knowledge of facts, that the jet-black negro almost invariably admires and essays to marry those having brighter skins, while the lighter-complexioned negroes or mulattoes entertain notions of pride as respects color, and are not willing to lower their status by intermarrying with one of a darker hue. And where a mulatto illegitimate turns up in a family of blacks, it becomes the universal favorite of young and old. White is the popular complexion as regards beauty and sprightliness; consequently it is coveted in a high degree by the unvarnished black. Witness the spirit of envy and the deadly hate entertained and fostered by the negroes in Saint Domingo, where has been waged for years a war of extermination against every negro whose complexion showed an admixture of the Caucasian blood. To be a mulatto in that island was a matter

8*

of no congratulation to the hybrid ; because it was a mark of superiority intellectually and as a gallant, and necessarily brought upon him the vengeance of his less fortunate black neighbor.

It is as natural for the negro to ape the white man as it is for the monkey to ape his superior. The converse of the proposition, where is the full-grown Caucasian that will debase his or her lineage by amalgamation with the black sons or daughters of Africa? If this be the programme, then, fair reader, remember that the hour is not far distant when the American mind will become reconstructed on the subject of miscegenation. And the very descendants of those who would now demoralize human society by an advocacy of such heresies, will be the first to persecute and thrust down the deluded individual whose blood is tinged with that of the negro. Voluntary sexual selection on the part of man, as producing degeneracy of character and debasement of physical structure, is a humbug practically speaking ; or else, as before stated, America in the days of Columbus should have presented to the world so remarkable a prodigy as the full-fledged negro. Selection in violation of the laws of consanguinity, if persisted in, will invariably produce idiocy, and at the same time result in physical deformity, to the mortification of him who indulges in such revolting practices. In fact, no law of nature can be violated with impunity, and intelligent mortals must pay the penalty in every instance for every deviation from the standard of right. What a farce is presented to the mind in the doctrine of selection, where an individual by choice selects a partner with a flat nose or a long heel, and this idiosyncrasy becomes a family failing through endless generations, until the flat-nose becomes a family characteristic, and the leg of each son and daughter becomes located in the centre of the foot, as is nearly the case with some specimens of the African type!

On the monuments of the Eastern hemisphere the Caucasian, Mongol, and negro are found distinct in all the features that mark the original races for the space of nearly three thousand years before the Christian era, to which I shall allude again at its proper place.

There is a strong hypothesis afloat in the world that Shakspeare favored the doctrine of miscegenation in his memorable play of Othello; which is altogether erroneous. For about this period the black race was regarded as only fit subjects to become slaves in the newly-settled colonies of America, a fact practically executed by England, Spain, and Portugal. And Shakspeare, in his selection, takes the noblest specimen of the dark-visaged race, Othello, who was to marry the daughter of the respected senator of Venice. He was brave, intelligent, and of manly form and demeanor. Desdemona was a woman of some intelligence, but of coarse habits of mind, who was moving in high society, but that society was corrupt and depraved. And a morbid appetite in connection with a spirit of romance, originating from the demoralization*
so common in Southern Europe at this epoch, actuated and urged her forward to marry this Moor, which to

---

* The intelligent reader remembers Lord Byron's attachment to the Countess of Guiccioli, which was not very creditable to either. In the mean time civilization had materially advanced in the south of Europe.

her brought death, and to her family mortification and disgrace; a sad commentary upon the frailty of human nature.

This Moor was not a negro, but a cross of the Mongolian with the nomad races of Western Asia; but inferior to the Indo-European in all the attributes that make the man.

Shakspeare detested this alliance. And the moral of this tragedy will go down to the latest generation as a warning to the Desdemonas, victims of the sickly sentimentality of our present school of philosophy.

CHAPTER XII.

CHILDREN OF HAM NOT NEGROES.—SETTLEMENT OF EGYPT.

> " His art and honors wouldst thou seek
> Embossed on grandeur's giant walls,
> Or hear his moral thunders speak
> Where senates light their airy halls."
>   CAMPBELL.

I WILL now revert to Noah and his family after escaping the perils of the deluge. To support his family he turned his attention to the tillage of the ground, and planted a vineyard, and drank too freely of the wine, and became intoxicated and lay uncovered in his tent, which being observed by his son Ham, he ridiculed the old gentleman in the presence of his two brothers. Gen. ix. 24–27: "And Noah awoke from his wine, and knew what his younger son had done unto him. And he said, Cursed be Canaan; a servant of servants shall he be unto his brethren. And he said, Blessed be the Lord God of Shem; and Canaan shall be his servant. God shall enlarge Japheth, and he shall dwell in the tents of Shem; and Canaan shall be his servant."

I have quoted this passage of Scripture with a view to explain away the error, which many intelligent thinkers have fallen into, as respects the servitude of the negro, and to disabuse the mind of the false notion entertained that Ham was the father of the negro race. Neither Canaan nor any of his descendants ever located in Southern or Central Africa, the home of the genuine black man prior to the days of Herodotus, which was 500 years B.C. And two thousand five hundred years anterior to this date the negro, as described by us and known as such to-day, was familiar to the Egyptians, the latter of whom were the lineal descendants of the Hamitic race.

Read the history of Canaan, the son of Ham, in Gen. x. 15–17: "And Canaan begat Sidon his first-born, and Heth, and the Jebusite, and the Amorite, and the Girgasite, and the Hivite," etc.

These tribes every Bible-reader knows occupied the land of Canaan, or Palestine; that beautiful country flowing with milk and honey, which the Lord gave to the Israelites when he brought them forth out of the land of Egypt, 1491 years B.C. And the Lord directed his chosen people to destroy the last vestige of these tribes, old and young, that no remnant of them or their idolatrous worship might remain to contaminate and defile his people. Joshua, however, spared many of them, and made covenants with them, to the effect that they should be hewers of wood and drawers of water unto all the congregation of the house of Israel. And they were bondsmen, the servant of servants, unto the Israelites for many generations: a literal fulfillment of the Noachic prophecy, which was never intended to have any bearing upon the negro, his location, origin, or bondage.

As early as 1500 B.C. there appears in ancient Thebes a tableau selected from the celebrated monument of Seti-Meneptha, or as better known, Belzoni's tomb, one of the kings of the nineteenth dynasty. So early as this date had the Egyptians divided mankind into four distinct species, whom they classed as Red, Yellow, Black, and White; the latter representing themselves as being superior to all other races, showing that they were not ignorant of the diversities of mankind. And innocently have they furnished us these portraits as an evidence of the fact that the curse pronounced upon Canaan had no connection with the Ethiopian of modern times.

The Ethiopia* of the Bible was included in what is known now as Central or Upper Egypt. And sometimes a portion of Arabia, bordering on the Red Sea, was also called Ethiopia. And remember not to con-

---

* In the poems of Homer it is divided into Eastern and Western Ethiopia, the Red Sea making the division. Herodotus and the later Greek and Roman geographers also repeat this distinction, and refer to a sun-burnt face, from $\alpha\iota\theta\omega$, to burn, and $o\psi$, the countenance, and not to a negro.

found Ethiopia of the Bible with the present geographical Ethiopia, or Negro-land, of which I shall speak in due time.

Egypt derived its name from Ham, the son of Noah, and it is frequently called the land of Ham in the book of Psalms.* Mizraim and Cush, two of Ham's sons, located in the land of Egypt; the one near the mouth of the Nile, and the other. higher up on the same river. The territory occupied by the one geographers gave the name of Egypt, and to the other Ethiopia, which along the fertile banks of the Nile did not extend for ages over five degrees of latitude, or about three hundred miles, and the Romans say at no period did civilization extend farther up the Nile than to 19° of north latitude.

And to impress upon the mind the character of Ham's descendants. Nimrod, who was a son of Cush, began to be a mighty man upon the earth, and, as Moses writes, was a mighty hunter before the Lord. Nor did he confine himself to the chase of wild beasts alone, but extended his conquests over man, and made him entirely subservient to his will, and through his supremacy of intellect and domineering spirit he founded the great city of Babylon, and attempted to erect the noted tower of Babel, which brought upon the inhabitants thereof that confusion which dispersed the post-diluvians, and sent them into the four corners of the world to select permanent homes. Nimrod is supposed to have remained at Babylon with his imme-

---

* Psalm cv. 23: "Israel also came into Egypt; and Jacob sojourned in the land of Ham." Making Egypt synonymous with the land of Ham.

diate family; and with his adherents he established this city as the capital of the Assyrian Empire. While others of the same line, proceeding under the spirit of discovery, cast their habitations on the alluvion or Delta of the Nile, and which since has proven to be the rich granary of the world. When Cush and Miz-raim essayed to emigrate to this portion of Africa, the probabilities are greatly in favor of the theory that the negro was unknown to our Western Asiatics, and that the nigrition type of the genus homo was still confined to Interior and Southern Africa. The Mongolian* of the East, however, had made his appearance on the borders of the Tigris and Euphrates, and had con-tributed his share of labor in constructing the noble temples and palaces that were occupied by Nebuchad-nezzar and others of the Assyrian kings;† as in after-times the negro was brought from Lake Tsad and the head-waters of the Nile, and made to contribute his quota of muscle and might in constructing those lofty pyramids which are the wonder and admiration of every

* The Mongolian at this period occupied that portion of Africa lying north of the Great Desert. (The Sahara or Great Desert at this epoch was an inland sea.) They also inhabited a greater part of the conti-nent of Europe, which in the course of time was surrendered to the Indo-European.

† "Now there is a vast mass of evidence pointing to an early popu-lation of Western Asia by a race kindred in many respects to that which we now call Turanian. Such a race certainly possessed the highlands of Elam, between lower Mesopotamia and the table-land of Iran, the ancient Media; and its traces have been found in Chaldea itself, on the monuments where records have been recently deciphered. There was, too, an universal tradition of an occupation of Western Asia by the Scythians, that is, the Turanian race."—PHILIP SMITH, vol. i. p. 195.

age. Superior intellect and the aggregation of wealth subdued the masses and built mausoleums in honor of despotism.

Then tell us not that Cush or Mizraim or Ham or Nimrod is the progenitor of the negro. They in fact first utilized the negro and converted him into a machine for agricultural and architectural purposes. And let me impress it with vivid letters upon the mind of the reader, that this degraded race was instrumental in hastening the decline and fall of this proud and illustrious people, as here again are the first symptoms of sexual intercommunication since the deluge between the high-born and ignoble races, which utterly debased the original Egyptian, and brought upon this beautiful, this lovely country, the prophetic vengeance of an incensed Jehovah, which in the due course of revolving ages was fulfilled to the most literal interpretation of the prophecy. The inspired author* denounces terrible curses upon Egypt and upon all the mingled† races of that and of neighboring states; and, furthermore, declares that the land of Egypt shall cease to be ruled by her own princes and become the basest of nations.

The Egyptians have been regarded as the most intelligent of all the ancient nations. History at an early period gave them a prominence for wisdom, learning, and a familiarity with the arts and sciences unsurpassed by all other kingdoms of the earth, and from whom the Israelites, the Grecians, and other surrounding nations copied. The invention of alphabetical letters and the art of writing came originally from the Egyp-

---

* Ezekiel, chaps. xxix. and xxx. † Ezekiel, chap. xxx. 5.

tians. And Moses states that in mystic lore they were
not excelled by any people under the sun. Their pro-
ficiency in the arts and sciences, and the exemplifica-
tion of civilization and progress found here among the
descendants of Ham, dates back as early as the kings
of the fourth dynasty, 2450 years b.c.,—the monuments
of this period show the advances that had been made ;
the masonry of their buildings, and the sculpture of
the human form, together with their habits and manners of life, attest their ingenuity and their claims to
civilization and refinement. And this we must remember was at a period in Egyptian history before the
blood of the negro and the Mongolian had infused
itself into the veins of the Hamitic race.

The ablest ethnologists who credit the races with one
origin progress admirably well in locating the descendants of Noah, until an effort is made to people Central
Asia and Africa, and to account for the diverse physical changes now perceptible in every quarter of the
globe. In solving this proposition, they become so
thoroughly mystified that the wisest strategy cannot relieve them from the dilemma, which Philip Smith, one
of the happiest delineators of this subject, admits in the
following words: "This question is one of the most
difficult in the whole science of ethnology;" and proceeding a little further, he admits that "the ancient
language of Egypt, and the Coptic derived from it,
have perhaps the best claim to represent the Hamitic
family; but it is now clear that both the people of
Egypt and their language contained a large infusion of
nigrition (or negro) element." Though Egypt was
originally pure and unsullied with the blood of the in-

ferior races, and so long as she remained thus exempt, her position among the nations of earth was without a rival. Her armies were triumphant on every field and on every sea, and the scholars of every nation came within her borders to learn wisdom and to pay homage to her sovereigns, and her great superiority was acknowledged by all the kingdoms of the world. Warlike encroachments upon the territory of the negro soon brought this supple element to contribute to the growing wealth of Egypt, until, in the course of time, the peculiar animal worship of the negro was introduced into those Nilotic cities and embraced by the people at large as the national religion of the whole country. The serpent-, the crocodile-, and the vermin-worship to which the entire nation had become addicted at the epoch of the exodus of the Israelites, only manifests the outcropping of voudouism, the diabolic snake-worship so prevalent among the besotted inhabitants of Ethiopia proper. This base devotion of serpent-worship* has not been obliterated from the minds of the lower orders of the negroes of the United States, though planted here for over two hundred years amidst the most benign Christian influences. But a short time since, the public mind was shocked and horrified at the thought that the Digby child of New Orleans had been kidnapped and sacrificed on the altar of voudouism. Egypt, to pay this penalty of a violated law, was overrun about 600 years B.C. by Cyrus, the founder of the Persian Empire, and again, one hundred years later, by Xerxes, one of his successors. The advent of the Persians upon

---

* The serpent has been worshiped by half the known world.

the soil of Egypt is the first introduction of the Mongolian into the land of the Pharaohs which can be established beyond a doubt by historical records. The presumption is, however, favorable, from the nomadic character of this people, that they had long before this period migrated from their native plains, and made inroads into both Europe and Africa. The Chaldeans, some half-century prior to the Medo-Persian conquest, had invaded Egypt, whose armies had been supplied from the same Asiatic district, and contained, in all probability, a similar class of recruits. In fact, the Scythians had made their inroads at various times towards the west, and left the mark of physical demoralization wherever their foot-prints can be traced on the sands of time.

Ancient historical records abound with descriptions of the mongrel races which came like an avalanche from the East and spread themselves over Northern Africa and Europe, and whose overpowering numbers overthrew every opposing barrier, and whose destroying breath, like the simoon of the desert, brought desolation over the rich fields and palatial abodes of civilization and refinement. They are represented as deformed in figure, of squatty stature, large and unproportioned heads, dark-visaged, and of an unearthly appearance; their color varying from a light olive to a dingy brown; their language, manners, and physical make and armor differing in many respects. And they seem to be so little allied to the human race that the writers of that period could only recognize them by their power of speech as being a part of the human family; and their every appearance was so at variance with the general appearance of man, that the ancient historian supposed them to be the progeny of some sorcerers with the demons of the desert.

And in the army of Xerxes, a marked difference was observable in the mixed races which had been thrown together by this indefatigable warrior. For instance, those recruits gathered from the elevated plains of Asia, and those from the Persian provinces bordering India on the south, were each marked by their peculiarity of habit, costume, color, and physical formation: the one partaking more of the Mongolian type of the Eastern Asiatic, and the other assuming the darker visage and osteological idiosyncrasies of the Malayan type of the Indian Archipelago of the south. Both of these differing more or less from the hybrid cross of the Ishmaelite, and utterly dissimilar in every conceivable aspect as to physical conformation, color, and general appearance from the mulattoes and other grades representing that diabolical cross between the true descendants of Ham and the nigrition tribes of Lower Africa. As respects this Hamitic branch, at a later period, the historian declares that the Egyptian is allied by blood and language with both the Turanian and negro races, as is supported by physical qualities, habits, and religion. Their reddish color distinguishes them from both the Caucasian and negro, whereas their thick lips and elongated eye connect them with the black race, and possessing a religious devotion peculiar to the Asiatics, yet thoroughly devoted to the worship of animals, snakes, etc.

The cow has been venerated in India from the most remote antiquity. And the worship of the god Odin,

9*

Woden, Goden, as called by different nations, is the same deity, and had its origin in Central Asia, as also did the worship of the god Buddha, so common in India ; and the ceremonial rites of the two are identically the same wherever they prevail. Also from the same quarter of the globe came the worship of the sun, to which luminary the Mexicans paid their religious devotions by sacrificing human beings on the lofty summits of their temples in full view of the adoring multitude beneath,—showing conclusively the origin of the race by a perpetuity of these unholy rites in their long-adopted country. Nor has Asia yet given up this idolatrous devotion, or discontinued her efforts to appease her household deities by the offering of human sacrifices.

Odin, or Woden, synonymous with Buddha, at one period was the tutelar deity of the Druids of Great Britain, and, in fact, of the whole Teutonic or Indo-European race,—a religion practiced by the Greeks and other enlightened nations under the denomination of Mercury, another name for the same deity. The question here arises, How did the Indo-European become imbued with this peculiar form of worship, which more properly belonged to the Central Asiatic? The worship of the sun became the national religion of the Toltecs by the implantation of colonies in that region from the elevated plateau of Asia, they having imbibed and preserved their religion as first received at the hands of their Turanian ancestors, and impressed it afterwards upon the aboriginal inhabitants of the American continent as far as their influence extended, both by fire and sword, as in previous ages did Mahomet and his followers plant the peculiar dogmas of

the Koran in the hearts of the vanquished races of
Asia and Northern Africa. And by due process of
reasoning per force of analogy and common sense, and
especially where stubborn facts form the basis of argument as they exist in support of the following theory.
That in ancient times, as the crowded masses along
the vast plains of Mongolia were perishing for want of
supplies to maintain animal life, some daring leader,
of Mongolian extraction, or semi-Ishmaelite, or Be-
douin wanderer from the great desert of Asia, gathered
his myriad hordes from the burning sands of Indus to
the frozen shores of Siberia, and from the volcanic
isles of Japan to the sacred soil of Palestine, and with
an army whose name is myriad, and whose numbers
eclipse the sands of the sea-shore,—a motley herd, the
denizens of every clime and the commingled blood of
every race, whose motto was pillage and plunder and
sacrilegious desecration of all that was holy and pure,
and led on by some daring leader like Attila of the
Huns, or Alaric of the Visigoths,—swept across Western Asia, Northern Africa, and all of Europe, and by
force of numbers made every nation tributary to their
exactions in point of wealth, habits, and religion.
Until, in the course of a few generations, the form of
worship practiced throughout Europe, Western Asia,
and Northern Africa had undergone, by persecution
and oppression on the part of their conquerors, an
entire metamorphosis, which resulted in the establishment of this idolatrous worship, which, from custom,
became a common fixture in the minds of all classes,
until some more daring invader usurped the religious
seats of the great Woden, and instituted other rites

and devotions in lieu of those which had held these races spell-bound for centuries past.

The limited geographical knowledge of the most enlightened European nations at this early period, and the absence of comparatively all intercourse between neighboring nations, left them in considerable doubt as to what country these various warlike hordes emanated from. A majority, at least, of the ancient historians admit that they came originally from Eastern Asia, occupied and overran at different periods the European continent, and these nomadic tribes passed under the different names of Goths, Ostrogoths, Visigoths, Vandals, and Huns. Fortunately for the cause of civilization and human progress, their reign of supremacy did not last a great while. The Caucasian or Indo-European rose in the power of his might, asserted his wonted superiority, and threw off the barbaric yoke; and, as previously remarked, drove a part of the Mongolian conquerors to the cold climate of Scandinavia, where they eke out a miserable existence in an uncongenial latitude; while a part found a temporary home in the fastnesses of the Pyrenees and the Spanish peninsula, and others, having overrun Egypt and the land of the Carthaginian, finally spread themselves along the southern waters of the Mediterranean or the Great Sea and commingled their corrupt blood with that of the Phœnicians, at one time a pure Semitic tribe, but which by the great sin of miscegenation became demoralized, and forfeited the high position attained by the prowess of her Hannibal, and thereby stained her escutcheon with the foul charge of Punic faithlessness.

Mongolia's dark-visaged sons, in settling along the western and northern coasts of Africa, by intermixture have bleached the nigrition tribes and infused new life into their sluggish veins, while in Hungary and Spain the last remnant of the Scythians are fast disappearing by the slow process of absorption on the part of the more numerous Caucasian. And the glory of the past has departed from the Magyars of Hungary, and the Ottoman Empire, so long upheld by the military prowess of interested nationalities, and yet so feeble from imbecility and corruption, must sooner or later be swallowed up by the Sclavonic race, and cease both in Asia and Europe to have even the semblance of an existence. And wherever upon the broad expanse of nature you find the inferior races occupying fertile or desirable districts of country, which become at any period the object of cupidity on the part of the more intellectual and enterprising Caucasian race, it has been, and ever will be, the fate of that people and of that country to become tributary to the genius of the Indo-European. It is a fixed axiom in the organic law of the universe, that superior intellectuality has and ever will prevail, as much so as falling bodies have a tendency to seek the centre of attraction.

235

CHAPTER XIII.

THE RELIGION OF THE RACES.

"What are monuments of bravery,
Where no public virtues bloom ;
What avails in lands of slavery
Trophied temples, arch, and tomb ?"
                                    CAMPBELL.

CARLYLE says that nine millions of human beings
have been sacrificed by war and persecution to establish the cross as an emblem of our Christian religion.
If such be the case, then we cannot materially err in
saying that it required a hecatomb of twenty millions
of souls to establish the crescent as the emblem of Mahomet's religious dynasty. This train of thought passes
through my mind in reviewing the subject of the religion of the Cross in connection with the various
races whose origin and history we have been tracing
through these pages ; and though my views herein expressed may differ from the published and entertained
theories of the nineteenth century, still, in all candor,
there is more of truth and less of fiction couched
herein than the world may be willing to admit. For
the sake of convenience, I shall divide the religious
sects or creeds into only three great parties, leaving
the minor religious isms of the day entirely out of the
question. Then we have the followers of the three
creeds,—one of the Bible, and another of the Koran,

the residue pagans : God, Mahomet, and the Creature. Intelligent reader, tell us, where does God reign in the vast area of his own creation ? and where does the Moslem's creed find its unnumbered millions of blinded devotees ? The Caucasian is the only race under the sun that takes the Bible as their rule and guide, for their faith and practice ; "and upon this rock I will build my church, and the gates of hell shall not prevail against it." And millions upon millions of treasure are annually expended by the evangelical world for the purpose of proselyting the nations of the earth and converting them to the true religion of the gospel ; a noble undertaking, we readily admit, which we sincerely hope may continue to go on until the last vestige of paganism and immorality shall be eradicated from the hearts of the human family. And in all sincerity of soul, what good has thus far been accomplished when the missionary passes beyond the borders of the Caucasian race or the confines of his habitation ? Let China and the Indies speak in answer to this interrogatory. The devotion of the Oriental is still fixed upon his ancient gods, and the preaching of the gospel to him is as the sounding brass or the tinkling cymbal.

The holy efforts and the sanguine prayers of the devoted missionary of the Cross have proved unavailing with this idol-adoring people, and ofttimes, as opportunity presented itself, the masses urged on by the subalterns in office and winked at by the lordlings in power, the hue and cry has been raised of "Great is Diana of the Ephesians" against the unfortunate and devoted missionary, who either perished by the executioner's axe or found refuge on board of some friendly vessel in port. The Malayan tribes, as previously re-marked, have a passionate fondness for the flesh of the white-faced missionaries of the North; and the red man of the West has a remarkable fondness for the long-flowing scalp of his praying pale-faced brother, with which to ornament his person in the war-dance of his tribe. The negro and the hybrid races, from the Delta of the Nile, along the Mediterranean to the Pillars of Hercules, and on the eastern shores of the Atlantic, and across Central Africa to the Straits of Bab-el-Mandeb, the Moslem's faith is the adopted creed of the mongrel inhabitants. And the unalloyed negro of interior Ethiopia still bows to his same original gods, which Egypt copied and embraced in her early excursions to the land of Nigritia, a sample of which the deluded Israelites carried in their hearts out of the land of Egypt, which became a golden calf in the wilderness of Sinai. And as a penalty for this animal-worship, the fiery serpent was turned loose in the camps of this chosen people, and brought instant death to the sufferer, until the brazen serpent was erected in the midst of the camp and proved a panacea for every ill. For several years the Chinese have been living in our midst on the Pacific coast, and are gradually making their way into the central and eastern States of the Union; and even in this land of Bibles and religious liberty, is there one solitary convert to the doctrines of the Cross among these new emigrants to our fertile shores? And if so, it lacks confirmation in the public mind, and can only be regarded as an exception to the general rule.

It is with the most delicate sense of feeling that I

approach this part of the subject, which treats of the religion of the Cross in connection with the African race as now found in America and her neighboring islands. I do not desire to appear as an arbiter dispensing judgment upon the final destiny of our adopted citizens ; the facts, however, I shall not withhold from public scrutiny, but leave every unbiased mind to form its own conclusion. A long and uninterrupted acquaintance and familiarity with this class affords an abundant opportunity to speak of them from the record.

It is proverbial that the ministers of the gospel among this people are noted for dishonesty, and are the instigators of the deviltry which is perpetrated by the pliant instruments of their spiritual leaders. And their so-called gospel lights are the hierarchy which constitute the *summum bonum* of all earthly perfection ; the blind actually leading the blind.

Though reared and educated in a land of gospel light, they still cling with avidity to the ancient superstition of their fathers, and assume an importance of religious enlightenment and of gospel knowledge which cannot be corrected by the holy zeal of our wisest divines ; and some of them, in utter ignorance of divine truths, stand up before their audiences with a lighted candle resting upon their heads, an emblem of their gifted inspiration in holy law, and harangue their deluded hearers until the fire of nature moves upon the entire congregation, and a pell-mell shout and scuffle pervades the whole mass, when a casual observer would reasonably suppose that the demons from Tartarus were holding their midnight orgies in commemoration of the general judgment.

10

And though often asserted by the Exeter Hall liberty-loving clique that the negro of the South was debarred the privileges of the Christian religion, such is not the case, nor has it ever occurred to my knowledge in the fair sunny South,—the very contrary has been the practice. The slave was often required to attend Divine service, and intelligent ministers have been employed time and again to preach to this class.

With all the restraints that have been thrown around them, the unaccepted offering of Christianity, the precepts of the holy men of God, the examples of the Christian communities in which they have been raised and the prayer-loving families in which many have been reared, with the same influences operating upon them as were bestowed upon the white children of the same household, yet they have presented a deaf ear to the kind admonition of an educated conscience, and shrink back from the light of the gospel dispensation, and embrace with open arms the heterodox and damning views conjured up by the ignorant and superstitious leaders who essay to be lights and demi-gods of the world. The truth is announced in Heaven's own revealed words, "Thou art weighed in the balances and art found wanting." The Spirit of God will not always strive with his creatures; they are devoted to their idols, and the command has gone forth, "Let them alone." And the time fast approaches that the remnant of this people which shall escape the whirlpool of dissipation, the casualties of time, and the ravages of demoralization, shall sooner or later relapse back into that barbarism from whose bourne no traveler returns. And this, too, is asserted of this race in the face of the truth that no African in his native jungles has yet accepted the gospel privileges, or attained to the high distinctions in religious enlightenment which it has been the good fortune of this class to reap in their newly-adopted American homes. To attempt to evangelize those who have placed themselves beyond the pale of hope is like throwing pearls to swine. Then the question arises in the Christian mind, Are all of these inferior races doomed to destruction by Heaven's unchanging decrees? By no means; they are saved by grace, an immutable principle in the Divine economy. The heathen are not all lost: the impenitent of every nation, together with the scoffer and the blasphemer, whatever may be his language or his race, will most assuredly perish with all the nations that forget God.

The infant and the idiot, with all others who die before they reach the years of accountability, by the inscrutable decrees of Divine Providence are saved by grace, through the atonement made by the Son of God. For the adults there can be no hope, as salvation for them alone comes through faith in the atoning sacrifice, —the only name given under heaven or among men whereby they can be saved. If they reject Him, who, then, can become their deliverer? Redemption is offered free to all mankind, without money and without price; and there can be no fault or blame attached to the inspired truth, where the subject willfully rejects the proffered mercy and builds his hopes upon the traditions of men, or founds them upon any other rock save the chief corner-stone.

CHAPTER XIV.

GEOLOGY.

"The earth's a thief, that feeds and breeds by a composture stolen from general excrement."—SHAKSPEARE.

THOUGH geology is in its infancy, yet the study of this science thus far has brought to light the hidden truths which have lain for unmeasured ages in the unexplored cloisters of mother earth.

The gradual cooling of the earth's surface in the primitive era of her early history is yet marked with indelible lines, and can be traced by the finger of Science with the same accuracy that the telescope marks the position of the different planets in their various orbits, or as the genius of man can command the lightning and utilize it in the daily transactions of life. In the deep bosom of the earth we find the crystallized masses in unstratified beds, showing conclusively the solid state that the surface assumed as the earth gradually parted with its heat. Here, in their natural state, we find the granite, porphyry, and basalt which constitute the basis of the stratified rocks, and upon which foundation are built up the various layers, one upon the other, which have been accumulating age upon age by the gradual disintegration of the surrounding masses. While this vast globe was undergoing the

cooling process, the surface originally was comparatively smooth, save where contraction ensued and deep
fissures opened wide their gaping mouths, which in
time became valleys or natural channels for the flow of
water, which in their course united with others and
formed brooks and rivers; and they, leading on to
other depressions, assumed the magnitude of seas and
oceans. In the course of time, by the action of internal fires, convulsions ensued, emanating from the introduction of water and the generation of steam. This
unstratified surface was broken up, and upheavals of
vast magnitude interspersed the surface of the earth.
Hence arose the mountain ranges which traverse the
different continents of the globe. Other portions from
similar causes became depressed, and the waters retired
to their level again and formed other seas and oceans,
and the fossilized rocks, which had required myriads of
years to form and solidify beneath the depths of the
ocean, were thrown up with the primeval unstratified
masses, and the granite, with each subsequently formed
strata, assumed positions throughout nature far above
the level of the sea, and at various dips to the horizon.
These convulsions have occurred time and again in
remote ages, and have altered the face not only of
nature, but changed the position of the original masses,
solidified by the cooling process, in such a way that the
mind actually becomes bewildered at the vast metamorphosis to which this sublunary sphere has been subjected
by the violent commotions of anterior ages.

The mind naturally inquires, Why does science place
the granite, porphyry, and basalt as the original exte-
rior of the earth's surface? From the very fact that

10*

this outer periphery of the earth's surface was not composed of layers, or strata, but purely crystallized rock, exhibiting evidences of having been subjected to intense heat. And again, no traces of organic remains have ever been found imbedded in these rocks anywhere throughout the globe indicating the existence of living beings, either of the animal or vegetable kingdom. By the gradual disintegration, or wearing away, of the solid rocks of which this world is composed, and the gradual deposition of these minute particles in many portions of the visible globe, the geologist has ascertained beyond the possibility of a doubt that the earth's crust has been raised by these accretions to the full depth or height of eight or ten miles. This fact is established by the various layers or strata overlying each other, as is observable on the margin of streams, where the silent deposit has been made year by year from successive inundations; and in these various strata are found the remains of plants and animals, which successive convulsions of nature have destroyed and thrown in mass and again covered with other deposits of a similar or dissimilar nature, and so on are these various strata marked and identified from the lowest bed of crystallized granite to the alluvion deposit of to-day. The internal fires at different epochs have thrown out untold volumes of lava, which have added their quota in forming these immense deposits, of which Herculaneum and Pompeii must ever remain perpetual yet silent witnesses.

Science informs us that the world has undergone many changes since its creation, concerning which the tradition of man has never given us any reference, the truth of which, however, is thoroughly attested by the book of rocks, in which are buried the extinct remains of plants and animals, ascending gradually one series above the other, period after period, the alliance of the one with the other bearing no similarity, but showing in every respect a distinct origin and a special adaptation to surrounding circumstances,—with the animals, a higher order of advancement, and with the plants, a more luxuriant growth.

These various creations have no doubt flourished in those periods more suitable to their growth, and at a time when the surface and circumambient air were better adapted to support the life of the numerous inhabitants of the globe. The fiat would go forth when God in his providence would sweep from the face of nature the last vestige of the animal and vegetable kingdom, and leave this débris to moulder back to mother earth, whose traces we now read in the deep bowels of the earth ; and these decomposing elements again furnish food for new plants and animals distinct in their originality and more perfect in form and structure than those of a former epoch, illustrating conclusively the ascending series in the creative programme of an all-wise Providence.

The first sedimentary stratum, or deposit, is termed Primary, and is several thousands of feet in thickness, and for its formation required ages, comprising possibly millions of years. In this strata we find imbedded vestiges of animal life only, and they of a marine character exclusively, and belonging to the zoophyte family. They were numerous and were scattered over a vast extent of territory, and readily exemplify the wisdom inculcated in the Divine economy, in placing upon this hemisphere such animal life as the crude elements of nature could the better sustain. These are the bivalve, mollusk, and the zoophyte, destitute of sight and hearing, and primitive in their organization. The next strata in course is the Silurian, which contains more numerous remains of the vegetable and animal kingdoms than the one preceding, but still less than is found in the old red sandstone; and so on do we see this progressive increase in quantity, quality, and variety of organic remains, until we reach the more modern or tertiary deposits, where geology discloses again new and distinct varieties, both of animals and plants, imposing one over the other at each successive geological period, until the earth becomes adapted to the full use and enjoyment of man, together with those animals which we find everywhere cotemporary with him; while the preceding inhabitants of earth invariably perish and become food for the sustenance of a higher order of species, and these organic remains become a thorough index to the genealogy of all former existent life, as well as an index to the past chronological history of this world. And this theory does not mar nor can it conflict with Divine revelation as interpreted by theologians of the present hour, that the days of creation were indefinite periods of time, having no reference whatever to the specific days of our own times. Nor does the theory of the gradation of plants and animals as successive creations conflict with Divine revelation, or with the dictates of reason or common sense.

These immense deposits of organic remains, covering

almost the entire surface of the earth, and of a depth in many places exceeding six or eight miles in thickness, must have required such an illimitable number of ages to accomplish such enormous results that the mind wavers in its computation of such vast calculations,—millions upon millions of years. Look at the immense number of rivers that are continually rolling their volumes of muddy water into the great abyss of the ocean ; and the highest estimate yet placed by scientific observers upon the accumulations that take place in the bottom of all our seas is one foot in a thousand years. At this rate, when will sufficient time have elapsed to deposit ten miles of sedimentary fossiliferous strata over almost the entire surface of God's creation ? Natural causes have thrown up and located these successive deposits in various portions of the globe, and have torn them asunder in every conceivable way, and have introduced through their gaping chasms and fissures the liquid porphyry and granite, and in after-ages other convulsions have sunk again these elevated mountains, hills, and plains to the bottom of the ocean, and in due time have upheaved them again, to become the habitation of a more sublimated animal and vegetable life.

In the upper members of the Silurian, fishes are first discovered of cartilaginous structure entirely, and whose frames are destitute of all bony substance ; nor until a later period in geological history do fishes appear with bony skeletons, as also reptiles and the larger mammalia tribes. In fact, the highest order of the vertebrata families in their season take possession of the earth, and leave their foot-prints impressed indelibly upon the tablets of the passing age; for instance, the woolly rhinoceros, hyena, mammoth, and mastodon, and cotemporary with these extinct mammifers also appear the quadrumana tribes, some with and others without tails, who take their position in the fossiliferous rocks in the gradual ascending scale of Divine creation.

England, France, India, and America, each in their turn have brought to light the petrified monkey, and he stands before us as a fossil, the precursor of man, a still higher and nobler species. And truly with great reluctance has the geologist admitted that man has ever been discovered in a fossil state, lest the pre-adamite should appear and be regarded as more ancient than the preconceived opinions of many have ever yet allotted to him; and possibly that such an admission might overturn the cherished dogma of the unity of the human family. Science, however, comes to his relief, and no longer can it be maintained that man is an exception to the general rule.

The last great change in the geological history of the world is denominated the drift, or diluvium period, when animal and vegetable life was destroyed on a large scale, which must have antedated the Noachic deluge many thousands of years. And in this drift or deposit are found the remains of animals, many of which are now extinct. Among the rest here imbedded are the mastodon, elephant, megalonyx, and other of the mammalia tribes. And again, when this great change took place throughout the face of nature, there must also have occurred a change of seasons, corresponding to the evidences contained in the book of rocks. The mammoth and elephant were inhabitants at one period of the frozen regions of Siberia; their remains in some instances are taken from the earth in this cold climate in a state of partial decomposition, while the earth itself still retains in some localities the smell of decaying animal matter. As a great feeder, the mammoth could not survive in this frigid climate through one season on the scanty supply of herbage now furnished by the barren waste of Siberia,—a country, in fact, like Key West, only suitable as a habitation for exiles. I only mention this land of ice as an example, having once been blessed with a temperate climate, suited to the growth and perpetuity of the largest mammifers; whereas in our geological period, the alluvium, the largest animals are alone found in the warmest climates, where luxuriant vegetable growth perpetually abounds. Consequently, the drift period could not have occurred in the days of the patriarchs, as no record is left us, either by divine or profane historians, of so remarkable a change in the seasons or in the temperature of the globe; and in fact geology unmistakably points back to this era with evidences that cannot be gainsayed, and marks its history as antedating centuries, the primeval records of the blushing race. Referring to the fossil remains of man, the book of rocks indubitably testifies to his existence upon the earth at an epoch long preceding any historical records that we possess, if we discard the written traditions of the Hindoo and Chinese, which extend back millions of years, as alluded to in a previous page of this treatise. And at the same time we find man's remains coeval with and even buried beneath the fossil relics of extinct animals, which lay many feet under the sur-

face, and whose existence on this globe refers back to
the aboriginal races that preceded Adam many, yes,
many centuries. We have the fossil remains of man
taken from the alluvion of Louisiana, deposited there
in all probability fifty thousand years ago,—a calculation easily made, by comparing the successive accumulations in the delta of the Nile with the delta of the
Mississippi River.

The importance of the annual inundations of the
Nile, not only to Egypt, but to the ancient world at
large, drove the Egyptians to the necessity of erecting
a Nilometer* in the valley of the Nile, which has left
the accurate rise of water for two thousand years; and
not only have we the rise of water noted, but the actual
deposit of earth for thousands of years. For instance,
the depth of soil around the base of the colossal statue
of Memnon at Thebes gives us an accumulation of
sedimentary deposit of less than four inches for a century; other observations in the valley of the Nile, however, give an accumulation of five inches to the century.
Taking this as a basis in reference to accumulations in
the valley of the Mississippi, where there are much less
impurities contained in the waters, we find by calculation that the augmentation of the soil would have required over fifty thousand years to elapse since these
relics ceased to represent active human life; and in addition thereto, they correspond in form and configuration with the aborigines of America. Likewise do the
relics taken from the vicinity of Natchez, in the State of
Mississippi, underlying a diluvial deposit of consider-

---

* An instrument for measuring the rise of water during the floods.

able depth, and found imbedded several feet beneath the fossil remains of the extinct megalonyx,—one of the large mammifers and allied to the sloth in form. Man fossilized most assuredly has been found in France, England, Germany, Spain, Canada, in the valley of the Mississippi, in Brazil, and in the mountain caverns of the Alps and Apennines. And wherever found in caves, his bones are closely associated with broken pottery and the relics of his faithful dog, showing the remarkable attachment which the canine in every age has had for his master, whether that protector was Indian, Chinese, or Caucasian.

And as a further proof, in America man's relics are mingled with fossilized bones of the horse long since extinct. They had both perished by some general convulsion of nature which man in this country survived, or others came in after-ages and took his place amid the fertile vales and inviting slopes of this newly-discovered hemisphere ; while every reader remembers that when Columbus first anchored his bark in the haven of the New World no horse was found, nor did the tradition of the natives give rise to even a faint supposition of any former knowledge of this noble animal. During the glacial period there are no evidences that the human family had an existence upon the earth, as no traces of art have been discovered during this or any preceding period that would indicate that he as yet moved and had a being. But at a later era we found him as a savage, under the name of troglodyte, dwelling not in houses, but in the caverns of the earth, and securing his daily food by pursuit of the wild animals of the forest, and his only weapon of

11

attack a rudely-constructed bow which projects an arrow pointed with the rough-chipped flint,—the first work of art accredited to man in his primitive savage state. Specimens of this rude architecture used in the aggressive and defensive warfare of nature's first savages have been found in America in many States of the Union, buried deeply in the bosom of the earth. And in England and on the continent of Europe the fossil remains of men abound in the ossiferous caves, commingled with those of the dog, wolf, fox, elephant, mammoth, and other extinct animals with which he contended in the chase, and which were required for his use both as respects food and raiment,—a more than ordinary hypothesis that he was cotemporary with the woolly rhinoceros, cave-bear, and the mastodon, and other extinct species of the post-pliocene period.

The autocthones, or early inhabitants of the world, were savage in their nature and unskilled in the arts of agriculture and commerce, and depended for a living upon the uncertain supply yielded in the chase and upon the spontaneous products of nature,—a system of dependence strictly adhered to at this period by the same classes of the human family who are now occupying Central and Southern Africa, Polynesia, and the uncultivated territories of North and South America. Whereas when the Adamite assumed control of his allotted hemisphere, God placed him there *to dress and tend* the garden of Eden; and when our first parents went forth condemned, the curse or command followed them, that "in the sweat of thy face shalt thou eat bread, till thou return unto the ground." The

Adamite and his descendants have ever adhered to this fiat of Heaven, and have always been emphatically an agricultural and a commercial people. In fact, husbandry is the handmaiden of civilization and enlightenment, and pursuits of the chase and a dependence upon the spontaneous products of the earth are ever the characteristic traits of the nude and barbarous of all nations and tongues.

The researches of geologists in the north of Europe have brought to light important truths connected with the prehistoric age in this portion of terra firma. In Denmark are beds of peat varying in depth from twenty to thirty feet. At the lowest depths of these bogs are imbedded pine logs, measuring three feet in diameter, and in the removal of this deposit have been found polished arrow-points of stone and other implements of a like character, though rude in their construction, but quite an improvement on the chipped instruments used by man in a more savage state and at an earlier period of his existence.

Ascending higher in these beds of peat are large layers of oak timbers, which in a former age were preceded by the pine forest along the shores of the Baltic. The pine had disappeared from the face of nature, and the oak had superseded it and covered the country with its immense forests; and in the course of ages the oak again had disappeared from its wonted hills and glades and given way to magnificent forests of beech, which now exclusively occupy this portion of Europe, and, in fact, has been the prevailing growth since the days when the Roman Empire was at its zenith. The beech is found imbedded in these peat-bogs nearest to the surface, and the oak lies intermediate between the beech and the pine.   In the earliest deposits are found the rude, polished, stone implements, more perfect, comparatively speaking, than the rough, chipped arrow-heads, flint knives and hatchets of the denuded savage of the ossiferous caves of Britain and of Western Europe, who was coeval with the extinct tribes of elephants and woolly rhinoceroses of the post-pliocene epoch.   Ascending higher, and examining closely among the pros-trate oaks of these aged peat-bogs, are brought to light the bronze shields and swords and other implements of a race of people who had advanced sufficiently in the arts as to utilize this metal for warfare and other purposes.   With the Toltecans of Central America during their conquest by the Spaniards, the only metal used by them for various purposes of husbandry was copper. They were acquainted with gold and silver, but seemed to have no knowledge of iron.   We are enabled to arrive at reasonable conclusions of the state of civiliza-tion of the different inhabitants of earth and the advance-ment made in the arts and sciences in their various periods by the relics that mother earth has preserved for our consideration.   The Romans, in the days of Julius Cæsar, found bronze instruments in use among the Britons, also with the inhabitants along the western coast of Europe.   In similar bogs, and in close prox-imity to the surface, among prostrate beech-logs, ap-pear, for the first time, implements of iron, testifying to a new era in the race of man, which is but a reasonable conclusion, when we reflect upon the successive grada-tions in the progress of creation, from the zoophyte and bivalve mollusk through all the ramifications of the animal kingdom up to the elephant and mammoth, and from the Bushman and Australian to the noblest specimen of the Divine mind, the Adamite of revelation. According to Biblical chronology, only two hundred and thirty-five years had elapsed after the creation when mention is made of Tubal Cain as an instructor of every artificer in brass and iron, demonstrating the theory that the Iron Age was alone peculiar to the blushing race, and that the age of bronze, and of polished stone, and rude, chipped stone antedated periods long prior to the advent of the enlightened Caucasian.

The periods of time during which special forests of timber may occupy certain districts of country have been computed by the scientific men of our age at fifteen thousand years; at this rate of computation the peat-bogs of Denmark are comparatively aged, and contain matters for our serious reflection.

On the shores of the Baltic are found many mounds of five to ten feet in height, composed of oyster-shell, cockle, mussel, and shells of other edible salt-water fish, and interspersed through these mounds are stone implements, and remains of beasts and birds and bones of men, showing that the aborigines once lived in this region and fed upon the products of the land and the sea; and these are the only memorials they have left us of their former existence,—the refuse-heaps, the contents of which once supplied them and satisfied their demands. However, no traces of iron or bronze utensils have yet been discovered among the débris or kitchen-heaps of this ancient people; nor do there appear any of the fossil remains of the ox, horse, or

11*

sheep. These domestic animals always attend man wherever found, from the day of Adam's first departure to our day and generation. The skulls and other bones disinterred indicate small stature, with small facial angle, and seem to be allied to the Lapps and Fins of modern times. And the flesh that covered these bones was devoured alike with that which the other rubbish contributed, and furnished food for the depraved appetite of a savage and ferocious race. And the period indicated from the evidences gathered from these kitchen-heaps corresponds closely with the oldest deposits in the peat-beds. These shell-mounds, the only evidence of an extinct race, are nothing new on the American continent. Along the sea-shore of Massachusetts and Georgia, and in Southern Louisiana, near the alluvion bordering on the various lakes adjacent to the Lower Mississippi, I have seen these shells piled up in considerable mounds and dotting the landscape around for acres, which were no doubt the rubbish-heaps of the aborigines of this country at a period antedating the traditions of the surrounding Indian tribes.

In the office of Messrs. Eager & Lusk, of New Orleans, I had the pleasure of examining a skull which had been recently removed from a shell-bank in Saint Tammany Parish, at the mouth of the Tangipaha River. It was imbedded six or seven feet beneath the surface; and immediately above this relic and overspreading it stood a magnificent live-oak tree, measuring full three (3) feet in diameter,—a noble shaft for nature to erect over the denuded bones of some poor wretch who had contributed a meal to satisfy the depraved appetite of the ancient denizens of Louisiana. These memorials of the past are replete with the records of antiquity, and it behooves us who are in search of truth to study them with care, and apply them impartially to the history of the human family.

Referring to the ancient monuments left us by the aboriginal tribes of Western Europe, every impression thrust upon the mind savors of gross barbarism and extreme savageness of character. And where in the wide domain of modern research or ancient history has any nation or tribe of people emerged from darkness with any improvement of their primitive brutal instincts without assistance from some enlightened source? Not one tribe yet, amid the researches of the past, unassisted has made any improvement in the arts of civilization. And the reverse of the proposition is also true : the fair race is progressive, and does not relapse unassisted into barbarism and savage ferocity. Instances, however, may be cited where a listless inertness has assumed sway where progress and activity once prevailed. But to clothe the white man in the garb of a savage and invest his soul with every brutal instinct and warp his frame in conformity with the mould of the Hottentot and Bushman, draws heavily in this enlightened age upon the credulity of the progressive mind. With these remarks we dismiss the subject of geology and the slight allusion made as respects archæology.

CHAPTER XV.

LANGUAGE.

" I do not much dislike the matter, but the manner of his speech."
                                        SHAKSPEARE.

As each distinct race of mankind came originally
from the omnipotent hand of Jehovah, in their respective periods of creation they were endowed by the great
First Cause with certain mental faculties adapted to
their peculiar wants, and were not thrown out at ran-
dom upon the face of earth, nor placed in latitudes
unsuited to their physical organization. Vegetable
and animal life abounded in the tropics in the earlier
epochs of the world, and the negro took his position
in Central Africa endowed with voice, utterance, and
other appliances physically and mentally adapted to his
crude nature,—perfect in himself, as emanating from
Deity, and a shade higher in the scale of being than
the quadrumana tribes of the surrounding forest. The
hand that created him planted within his nature a
language adapted to his requirements, and with this
peculiar gift his ideas were shaped and found utterance,
which formed the basis for that intercommunication of
thought and expression of desire which the lower animals had never possessed to the same perfection. This
expression of thought becomes language with the first
bimana inhabitants of this planet. Long prior to

this, however, the feathered tribes had sang their morning carol to the rising sun, and at closing twilight chirped their parting requiem to the expiring day. The brute in every age has had his voice and his language, so remarkably adapted to his peculiar wants and instincts. And He who formed them indued their nature with that peculiar utterance that marks their distinctiveness and individuality of species, wherever the utterance is made or the sound falls upon the listening ear. The lowing herd, the growling tiger, the roaring lion, and the barking dog are distinct and recognizable in every land, climate, country, and age.

The same is true of the different languages spoken by the different aboriginal races of mankind. The diversities existing between the Caucasian, the Mongol, and the negro, in color, appearance, and general physical conformation, is as palpable as reason would demand to establish a separate and distinct originality. And no less palpable is the evidence that separates the languages of the three races enumerated above, and marks them fundamentally original gifts to the present respective owners, however more or less encroached upon by an admixture, superinduced by an amalgamation of language as well as blood, among the various races at an early epoch of the world's history.

National types would never be subject to changes if there was no adulteration of blood by amalgamation; neither would languages undergo changes to the same extent unless affected by the introduction of foreign influences. The Israelite is the same to-day that he was over three thousand years ago, and as distinguishable in feature and lineament as though handed down to us in

marble statuary. In this same light may we regard
languages. The Basque language in France can be
traced unerringly back to the Turanian stock for full
three thousand years, encroached upon as it has been
by the vicissitudes of relentless war, with a view of ultimate extermination. And the Coptic, which was the
speech of Egypt for five thousand years, still leaves imperishable monuments of its antiquity which science
traces with no erring hand. And the Chinese, peculiar to its own originality for the past five thousand
years, stands forth prominent and unalterable as the
law of the Medes and Persians in structure, sound, and
derivation.

The following appertaining to this subject emanates
from Professor Agassiz, whose views always carry
weight and interest with them: " As for languages,
their common structure, and even the analogy in the
sounds of different languages, far from indicating a
derivation of one from another, seem to us rather the
necessary result of that similarity in the organs of
speech which causes them naturally to produce the
same sound. . . . Would not the power the American Indians have naturally to utter gutturals, which the
white can hardly imitate, afford additional evidence
that these races did not originate from a common
stock, but are only closely allied as men, endowed
equally with the same intellectual powers, the same
organs of speech, the same sympathies, only developed
in slightly different ways in the different races, precisely
as we observe the fact between closely-allied species
of the same genus among birds? . . . Why should
not the different races of men have originally spoken

distinct languages, as they do at present, differing in the same proportions as their organs of speech are modified? And why should not these modifications in their turn be indicative of primitive differences among them? It were giving up all induction, all power of arguing from sound premises, if the force of such evidence were to be denied.''

Language being coeval with the first inhabitants of this sublunary sphere, in connection with geology must form an important basis for the establishment of the plurality of the races prior to the historical period, the only evidences in fact which can be brought to bear upon this question at this early epoch; and, as our favorite author* contends, is the only argument which can perfectly fix the identity of the early denizens of antiquity, laying aside for the present the letter and spirit of Revelation.

The similarity and likeness of words, and similarity of grammatical structure, constitute the resemblances existing among the various languages spoken by the different families of man. Languages, like words, have their roots or base from which they spring, and groups emanating from these send off their different dialects, which are always traceable back to the original stock from which they sprung; and by analogy and comparison science derives conclusions which bear testimony in unison with the voice emanating from the book of rocks.

The Indo-European, Aryan, or Iranian family of languages is denominated inflectional, and is spoken

* Professor Max Müller.

by the Caucasian race wherever they occupy in Europe,
Asia, Africa, or America, and comprises the Sanscrit,
the Greek, the Latin, Celtic, Teutonic, Slavonic,
Gothic, and Persian.   The striking resemblance existing in this family of languages in grammatical structure, corresponding vocabulary, and the derivation of
terms applying to distinct objects in nature, shows
conclusively the relationship which has always existed ;
approximating in fact to that relationship that obtains
with the Indo-European family in complexion, feature,
and formation.

   The enterprising spirit of the Semitic and Japhetic
inhabitants of earth, from whom the Anglo-Saxon is
descended, fathers that indomitable energy which
triumphs everywhere in respect to military prowess,
the physical sciences, and the advancement in civilization and religion ; and the Caucasian alone, in fact,
possesses the language and the moral and mental
stamina which has always been the basis of literature,
art, science, moral and mental attainments in every
age of the world.

   Though the Semitic and Japhetic families have separated through many degrees of latitude or longitude, as
the case may be, or have diverged and gone to different
sections of the globe, yet there are unmistakable evidences that their languages were originally one and the
same, as the words in each language expressive of relationship, or of the simple objects that meet the eye in
nature, have the same words expressive of the same objects ; and the linguistic affinities and resemblances are
identical in grammatical structure, both in the declension of the noun and in the conjugation of the verbs,

while the base or root remains fixed and unchanged through all the vicissitudes of time, place, and surrounding influences; for instance, we have in the various tongues :

English.	Greek.	Latin.	German.	Sanscrit.
Father.	Πατήρ.	Pater.	Fäder.	Pitri.
Mother.	Μήτηρ.	Mater.	Moder.	Matri.
Sow.	Σῦς.	Sus.	Sû.	Sûkara.
Mouse.	Μῦς.	Mus.	Maus.	Mûshika.

There can be no doubt of the unity of the Caucasian languages; every philologist readily acknowledges a patriarchal origin, and all of the branches of this same language, after the dispersion, must necessarily in time have undergone many changes by the addition of other words, as the wants and the intellectual progress of the diversified families required. Still, there is an identity and distinctness in all the fundamental arrangements of the Aryan language, which stand forth audibly clear and visible to the scientific explorer. And this marked originality of language possessed by this race is replete with that perfection, as a whole, which impresses upon the reflecting mind the high and exalted origin claimed for the language of man, who was made in the image and likeness of his Divine progenitor. "The Lord God formed every beast of the field, and every fowl of the air; and brought them unto Adam to see what he would call them: and whatsoever Adam called every living creature, that was the name thereof. And Adam gave names to all cattle, and to the fowl of the air, and to every beast of the field."*

---

* Genesis ii. 19, 20.

12

Adam became endowed by the fiat of the Almighty with utterance, and with a vocabulary of words commensurate with the exalted position that he and his posterity were to take in the grand drama of life. He was made pure and holy in the image of his divine Master, impressed with an immortality extending through eternity, and from whose loins would spring Abraham, the father of God's chosen people, and in whose veins would flow the blood of Eloehim's Lamb, which was to be for the healing of the nations. Is it strange, then, that Adam should be endowed with a language adequate to the great ends for which he was created, and adapted to the progressive capacity of the most enlightened race in all the ramifications of science, literature, art, and commerce?

The Iranian, or Caucasian, family of languages is the only one that possesses a grammatical or organic structure, is perfect and more complete in all its arrangements, and by comparison is more modern in its date, having originated with the Adamite, the last crowning work or cap-stone in the great creative achievements of Deity.

The Turanian, or Mongolian, language is spoken exclusively by this large family of nations wherever dispersed throughout the globe. Central and Eastern Asia is the home of this language; but wherever emigration has led this people forth, or circumstances have driven them, they have still retained the fundamental rudiments of this language, which untold ages have not entirely obliterated by the admixture even of other tongues; and we find it still prevalent with the Finns and Lapps on the north of Europe; with the Basques in the Pyrenees Mountains, the Magyars of Hungary, and the Esquimaux of North America. This language, in its unadulterated state, is monosyllabic in character throughout, and is written and spoken without the assistance of grammar, and whatever of sense is derived from the use of words is expressed by accentuation and position ; and, by way of illustration, a change of tone and emphasis as used by a speaker in our language, in the Turanian produces different words and gives entirely a different meaning in the conveyance of thought. Declensions, cases, and numbers, as given to persons or objects in nature in the Iranian language, and conjugations, moods, and tenses to verbs, as used by us, are entirely unknown and unused in this primitive tongue, exemplifying the previous suggestion that the language of the Mongol is distinct in all of its elements and is original in its character, and belongs properly to an age far antecedent to the Adamite, and is the exclusive property of a race of people whose ruder nature in primeval ages was better adapted to this mode of expression than the fairer and more enlightened race who succeeded them centuries subsequently as inhabitants of this already peopled globe.

In the Turanian language the root never undergoes any change, but retains its distinctness, and is isolated and visible in all of the divisions and subdivisions of its branches. We find, however, slight modifications of this rule in other languages belonging to the same stock, which have undergone changes, and must continue to do so, as an admixture takes place and the dialect of one tribe is thrust upon another by the violence of war or from commercial intercourse. And, as

265

the Mongolian has accepted companionship, or been overrun and subdued by the Caucasian, since the days that Cain the first murderer took up his abode in their midst, we may reasonably suppose that an infusion of superior blood and superior intelligence would have its tendency to improve the language and manners of this people, and elevate them in the scale of being, and give them that apparent spirit of progress which their government and architectural records would indicate that they at one period possessed, showing their reasonable mental superiority over the Malay, Indian, and Negro.

The Caucasian, or Iranian, family of languages is denominated inflectional, because it admits of a declension of nouns, the declension and comparison of adjectives, and the conjugation of verbs, and has always been the property of the white man ; and in no instance is it upon record that this language has been used by any of the Turanian or other families of mankind.

This language is perfectly distinct in its character from any and every language spoken upon the habitable globe, and has ever been exclusively used by the descendants of the Adamite. Whereas the Turanian stock of languages is terminational and agglutinized and monosyllabic in character, inorganic and destitute of grammatical structure, and is identified wherever met with throughout the expanse of nature, and is truly the exclusive property of the Mongolian ; and in no instance within the history of our age is this stock of languages spoken by any people save those who occupy to-day Mongolian territory, or whose history, such as the Magyar, the Basque, and the Turk, can be traced back to the same original family, and whose many other traits portray characteristics of a common origin. Color, stature, mind, cranial conformation, intellectual progress, and civilization, all combine to prove identity, and establish lines of demarkation between the living races, not less obvious than the lines interlying the stratified and unstratified beds of which mother earth is composed.

We read these facts and give the palm of victory to the researches of science in the mineral world, and why not in the physical world accept man as we find him located in his present allotted sphere, distinct in color, physical formation, and in all the attributes of his nature, separate in creation and separate in origin?

I would not by sophistry or any other ungenerous mode of reasoning willfully drag down my fellow-mortal from the high position which we occupy as the intellectual leaders of mankind to the disgraceful level of the spawn of earth, as is exhibited in the Bushman, Kaffir, or Hottentot of Southern Africa. Nor can reason, religion, or duty prevail with the reflecting mind to lift up to the standard of God's noblest work the degraded African or South Sea Islander, whose physical deformity and cranial contortions are inimical to beauty and at variance to the symmetrical proportions of Heaven's crowning work, man in the image of his Maker.

The Turanian stock of languages is the oldest, and, by illustration, is spoken as a child would speak, whose expressions of desire are uttered in nouns, leaving the connections to be filled up and completed by the hearer. And the Iranian language being a more perfect is also a more modern language, and emanated

12*

direct from Jehovah, a special gift to his chosen people, and by which his oracles were to be transmitted to future ages for the benefit of future generations. Nor is it to be forgotten that Adam conversed with his Maker many years before and after this unfortunate pair had tasted the first sorrows that embittered their earthly career.

In reference to the languages spoken by the inferior races of man, the Indian, Malay, and Negro, enough is known to ascribe to each a purely monosyllabic character, without the least grammatical construction, crude in its nature and exclusively adapted to beings who are savages by nature, and whose aspirations are groveling at best, and satiable alone in the gratification of the brutal instincts of depraved humanity. There can in reality exist but minor differences among the languages of the barbarous and primeval races of men, whatever may be their cast or character, unendowed with the mental faculties that ennoble his being, frame his literature, shape his laws, and establish his government upon the immutable principles of right and equity. And where a gleam of light portrays, among these pre-adamic races, monumental records of architectural and intellectual skill, we invariably find that the Caucasian admixture of blood and brains has infused new life and genius into the aboriginal races,— while at the same time the Adamic family has suffered loss, and most assuredly has violated one of Heaven's immutable laws, and entailed upon his race a curse which a thousand generations will be unable to wipe out. It is remarkably strange, if the inferior races are descended from Adam, they must necessarily furnish indications of being more modern in every respect than we now find them,—having carried with them from their native homestead some semblance at least of the language, manners, customs, and habits of their original progenitor. Time and again they would have sat by the patriarchal tent before leaving forever the land of their forefathers, and would have conversed together touching the great deluge, which had submerged their former homes and depopulated the land which they had jointly occupied. They would have talked of Jehovah, who planted the garden of Eden and placed in its midst their first parents to tend the same. They would have known the language of their ancestors, and would have remembered the manners and customs of their primitive parents, and by no means have forgotten the fair and ruddy complexions that once gave beauty and lustre to the noble ancestors with whom they were connected by the lineal ties of consanguinity. And it is passing strange that no tradition is extant among these inferior races of the Noachic deluge and the terrible results ensuing therefrom. They could realize no god in all their calendar of worship, save in the sun, whose burning rays brought light and heat, or in the viper or beast that crawled in the shamble or loitered in the jungle. There is no tradition extant of the manners and customs, or a vestige left of the noble language inherited by the Adamic race. Nor does the thought enter his savage breast that his distorted features, elongated cranium, and dark visage emanated from the ruddy blushing race, which alone possesses the language of literature and the progressive elements of intellectuality, the mother of the arts, sciences, government, and religion.

These nude tribes have their traditions, however, and it is the same from the Andes of South America to the Himalayan Range, where the wandering white man, the child of the sun, made his appearance in their midst, clothed with the effulgence of immortal light, and before whom the dark-visaged and superstitious races bowed with humble adoration, and paid homage to the superior intelligence incased in this new importation from the Celestial land ; and, like Minerva, he stands before them, the embodiment of wisdom, and from whom they drink in those floods of light in architecture and other evidences of civilization that mark the apparent progress of the Toltecan and the other Mongolian tribes.

CHAPTER XVI.

THE ISRAELITES.

" Yet in that generous cause, forever strong,
   The Patriot's virtue and the Poet's song,
   Still, as the tide of ages rolls away,
   Shall charm the world, unconscious of decay."
CAMPBELL.

THE Negro and the Mongol have been distinctly depicted on the monuments of Egypt for over 3000 years B.C., and the identity of race is so clearly marked at this early period "that a wayfaring man, though a fool, may not err therein." And this simple fact alone bears so strongly in favor of our theory of a diversity and plurality of the races of the genus homo, that it behooves us to present in this work the history and identity of the Israelitish race, since the days when God chose them from the rest of mankind to become his peculiar people. As Adam, of all other races, was his chosen race, being alone created in his own image and likeness, so, also, was Abraham selected in preference to all other families of the Adamites to become the progenitor of his chosen people. Gen. xii. 1-2: " Now the Lord had said unto Abram, Get thee out of thy country, and from thy kindred, and from thy father's house, unto a land that I will shew thee: and I will make of thee a great nation."

This message was delivered to Abraham 1921 years B.C., according to Ussher; and the Lord showed him the land of Canaan and said, "Unto thee and thy seed will I give this land." The following year there was a grievous famine in the land of Canaan, and Abram went down into Egypt to sojourn there during the reign of Salatis, or Saites, the first king of the fifteenth dynasty, 2080 years B.C. by Egyptian chronology. And after having remained in Egypt two years, he returned to Canaan again, enriched by Pharaoh's liberality, and called on the name of the Lord. In the course of a very few years Abram became very much embarrassed by the scantiness of pasturage and the increasing confusion engendered between his herdsmen and those of his nephew Lot, when, by mutual consent, Lot retired with his herds to the valley of the Jordan, and made his abode in Sodom, one of the cities of the plain. And at no distant day we find Abram taking up arms, he and the male portion of his

household, with his Amorite allies, and pursuing the
Chaldean monarch, who was returning to his own
country laden with the spoils taken from Abram's
nephew, Lot, and the neighboring Canaanites. And
Abraham proved himself no ordinary champion on the
field of battle, and returned home in triumph, a proud
victor over the allied forces of the Chaldean monarch.
And this same spirit of genius that shed such lustre
around the brow of the Hebrew father at this early
period is only an index of the giant mind displayed by
this people even in our day in any sphere of life where
talent or taste may direct their energies, of which we
shall speak in its proper place.

Ten years after his return to Canaan, still being child-
less, at the request of his wife he took the Egyptian
maid Hagar, whom he had brought out of the land of
the Pharaohs, and she became his concubine ; and her
son Ishmael became the father of the nomad Arabs of
ancient and modern history, and it was declared by
Heaven " that he should be a wild man, and that his
hand should be against every man, and every man's
hand against him." It is, however, through Isaac and
his posterity that we look for the Hebrews. According
to Biblical chronology, in the year 1729 B.C. a band of
Ishmaelites in passing through Canaan purchased Joseph
of his brethren for twenty pieces of silver, and carried
him down to Egypt and sold him to Potiphar, an officer
of Pharaoh's, and captain of the guard. Twenty-four
years after Joseph's arrival Jacob came down to Egypt
with all of his family, numbering ninety Hebrews, and
settled in the land of Goshen. Joseph, it is well
remembered, at this epoch was prime minister of

Pharaoh, that is, of Assa (according to the computations of Mr. Poole), who was the fourth successor of Salatis, one of the kings of Egypt, as found on the hieroglyphics of Memphis, about 2080 B.C. according to Egyptian chronology, which differs materially from that of Archbishop Ussher.

Joseph, being in a strange land and among a strange people, married a woman of the country, who was the daughter of the priest of On, and no doubt devoted to the idolatrous worship practiced by the entire inhabitants of the land. Joseph had already been promoted from prison life to the exalted position of the prime minister to the first monarch of the earth, and was pleased to remain in his newly-adopted country, foreseeing, by the inspiration of the Divine Spirit, the impending famine, which his foresight and extraordinary wisdom amply provided for;* and there are many reasons to believe that this Pharaoh and his court became the worshipers of the true God. But in the course of time there arose a "new king who knew not Joseph." And this king was Amos, or Amosis,† of profane history, and called by Josephus Tethmosis, who was the first king of the eighteenth dynasty, about 1525 years B.C.; and, according to the best testimony, Amosis, the representative of the Theban dynasty, overthrew the Memphian Pharaohs,

---

* And besides, there was a memorable prophecy uttered by Heaven itself, which had its bearing upon the son of Jacob : "But in the fourth generation the Hebrews shall again return to Canaan. For the iniquities of the Amorites is not yet full." The fiat had gone forth, and the decree of destiny must await its literal fulfillment.

† Rameses, a line of kings.

who were the shepherd kings of Egypt and the former friends of the Hebrew children. When the Theban dynasty became a fixture in this portion of Egypt, the Israelites were looked upon as the natural enemies of the present conquerors; and lest they should unite with the remaining inhabitants to throw off the yoke of the oppressor, they were enslaved, and grievous burdens were entailed upon this unfortunate race. And, with a view of exterminating this people, a decree went out from the Theban monarch that all the males of the children of Israel should be surreptitiously disposed of at their birth, as this chosen people were already numerous, and were daily increasing the apprehensions of the reigning dynasty. An exposed infant was found by Pharaoh's daughter while she and her maidens were bathing in the waters of the Nile. It was floating by the brink of the stream in an ark of bulrushes. The daughter of Amosis, being moved with pity, had the infant Moses carried to her father's palace, and, like Joseph, he became a deliverer to this downtrodden and afflicted people. Moses at an early age took a deep interest in the affairs of the overtasked Hebrews, which interference brought upon him the threatened vengeance of his adopted father, the sovereign of the land. And for safety Moses fled to Midian, where he sojourned some time, and married Zipporah, the daughter of Jethro, the priest of Midian, and who was a lineal descendant of Abraham by his Arab wife, Keturah.

The length of time which the Israelites must certainly have endured these hardships under the Rameses kings involved a period of eighty to a hundred years.

Moses fed the flocks of his father-in-law during forty
years in the land of Midian, when Jehovah, in the
silent recesses of the desert of Mount Sinai, at the
mount of God, presented himself face to face to Moses,
and commissioned him to lead forth the Israelites from
the land of bondage to that better land of Canaan,
which was then flowing with milk and honey and ready
to receive the long-absent exiles.

The iniquities of the Amorites at this period was no
doubt full, and Moses went forth in the discharge of
this duty, assisted by his brother Aaron ; and the demand was made upon the king of Egypt that the
people might repair to the wilderness to keep a feast
in honor of their God Jehovah. The obstinate determination of this monarch, however, brought death
into every household in the land of Egypt, save where
the blood of the paschal lamb upon the lintels of the
doors guided the angel of death in his march of destruction. And the Passover now celebrated by this
people is an emblem of that mercy vouchsafed on this
memorable occasion.

The Exodus commenced at Ramesis, in the vicinity
of Heliopolis, during the eighteenth dynasty, under
the reign of Menptah, the son of Rameses II. ; and
the Israelites went out under the protection of Jehovah,
guided by a pillar of cloud by day and a pillar of fire by
night, to whom he gave laws for their government, and
confided to their keeping those great truths which were
to be preserved for the benefit of the human family.
And to this much-abused and persecuted race are we
indebted for the revealed will of God, as presented to
us in the law and the prophets.

13

When Jacob died in Egypt, we are told by the sacred writer that his body was embalmed by the physician, and Joseph and his brethren, after seventy days, carried his remains to Canaan and buried them in the cave that is in the field of Machpelah, which Abraham bought for a burying-place of Ephron the Hittite, before Mamre. So was Joseph's body embalmed after his death, and his bones were carried by his brethren and buried at the same place. And with these lights before us, are we astonished to find in our day the embalmed relics of the ancient Jews in a perfect state of preservation in the monuments of Egypt.

At an early day, as respects the history of this people, it is true that there was an admixture of other families of the Adamic race. Joseph married an Egyptian woman, and Moses wedded a Midianite; and later still, Solomon took wives from among the Moabites, Amorites, Hittites, etc., and also married a daughter of the Egyptian king Sheshonk, of the twenty-first dynasty, 1085 years B.C. These slight adulterations were soon absorbed, and made no impression upon their national character; for in every age and in every clime the physical characteristics of this race were as distinctly marked as is observed in the present age and in our own country, or where they have wandered off and been dispersed as captives, or lost their records and violated the commands of Heaven by intermarriages with other races.

There are instances where they have amalgamated with the inferior races, and their complexions and physical characteristics have undergone material changes, as is the case with the black Jews, so called, of Malabar, whose blood has been dreadfully adulterated with Mongolian and Malayan admixture. Dr. Buchanan, who has given this subject considerable attention, says "their Hindoo complexion, and their very imperfect resemblance to the European Jews, indicates that they have been detached from the present stock in Judea many ages before the Jews in the West, and that there have been intermarriages with families not Israelitish. . . . The white Jews look upon the black Jews as an inferior race, and as not of *pure caste*, which plainly demonstrates that they do not spring from a common stock in India." Therefore it would be absurd to advance the theory that the complexion and physical configuration of this people had been superinduced by climatic influences, and consequently the white man may degenerate and finally assume the hideous proportions of the Bushman, Australian, or Fuegean. Such is not in unison with the past records of the Jewish race.

Though war, famine, pestilence, persecution, and dispersion have attended this people for thousands of ages, and have driven them from their early habitations and associations; and the world, though divided in other respects, seems to have been united in the work of extermination, and to have clothed them with the curses and maledictions of fiendish animosity, as though acting in conformity with the behests of Divine revelation; the world ever destitute of the milk of human kindness and forgetful of that charity which brings solace to the wanderer from the homestead of childhood; amidst all these changes and vicissitudes, wherever the Jewish race is found dispersed through the habitable globe, we find that same unvarying perma-

nence of type which distinguishes the descendants of
Abraham from all other known races of man. The
same features prevail in the land of Mesopotamia,
where once was the seat of their glory and prosperity;
the same predominates whether as aliens scattered over
Western or Southern Asia, in Africa, Europe, or
America. Go where you will, on the elevated plains
of Central Asia, along the caravan routes through Oriental deserts, amid the isles of the sea, in the marts of
the Old or the New World, we find the Jew possessing the same Hebrew lineaments that characterized the
chosen few that emigrated to Egypt at the bidding of
Joseph, then acting as prime minister of Pharaoh.
And if at any period they have lost their distinguishing
features, it was because of amalgamation with inferior
races both in point of intellect and physical formation.
It should be remembered as a well-established fact that
of the twelve original Hebrew tribes, only two of those
tribes, Judah and Benjamin, have thus far been able to
keep up and preserve their records; and they are to-
day as pure and unsullied in all the characteristics of
feature and peculiarities of character as when Moses
led them forth through the wilderness to the land of
Canaan.

In the eighth century before Christ, Arbaces, or
Tiglath-Pileser, King of Assyria, carried away captive
thousands of the subjects of the kingdom of Israel,
who dwelt in Galilee and on the eastern side of the
river Jordan; and, twenty years after this period, Sal-
maneser, the son of Tiglath-Pileser, conquered Samaria
and put an end to the kingdom of Israel.

The work of destruction that was left undone by

these two monarchs was completed forty years afterwards by Esarhaddan. The Israelites were carried as captives and sold into slavery in the land of Media, and their homes and fields were occupied by colonies transplanted from many of the Medo-Persian provinces, who brought with them and continued the worship of their false deities, and in after-times assumed the name of Samaritans, and incorporated into their religion an admixture of Judaism and heathenism. A people every way repugnant to those Israelites who still tenaciously clung to the ceremonials of their great lawgivers.

About one hundred years later, Nebuchadnezzar overran Judea, and destroyed the first temple at Jerusalem, and returned to Babylon with many captives and ladened with a great part of the treasures of the temple. This captivity lasted seventy years, when Zerubbabel and Joshua, in company with nearly forty-three thousand souls, returned to Jerusalem and commenced the erection of the second temple, under the auspices and by the decree of the Medo-Persian monarch, Cyrus the Great, which was confirmed and carried out by his respective successors, Darius and Artaxerxes Longimanus, who, in Scripture, was called Ahasuerus, the husband of Queen Vashti. After the seventy years of captivity had expired, many of the Israelites remained in the provinces where they had been placed by the kings of Assyria and Babylon, and but few, comparatively speaking, of this race returned to their original homes, and those that gathered back were principally of the tribes of Judah and Benjamin; hence the country afterwards was called Judea, and the race at large called Jews.

13*

A portion of each of the other tribes united with these two and became one and the same; whereas the ten lost tribes remained in their newly-adopted homes in the land of Assyria, and in time were despised and down-trodden, and were absorbed more or less by the surrounding nations; and travelers assert that to this day a marked resemblance to this people is still traceable in the Persians and Afghans of the East; though many were absorbed and lost their identity during this period of subjugation, while others are still distinct and isolated among the varied inhabitants of earth. Remarkable, but nevertheless true, wherever met with in any climate or country, we invariably recognize them as belonging to the Hebrew race. Mummied Jews have been taken from the tombs of Egypt, some of them being bitumenized, and no doubt as old as their great leader, Moses, who flourished nearly thirty-five hundred years ago, with cranial formation a fac-simile of a majority of that race, as observed frequently in this the nineteenth century. From the same source the Negro and the Turanian have been obtained painted in relievo thirty-five hundred years ago with all the characteristics of their peculiar races, proving conclusively that the white, yellow, and black races were as distinct, separate, and isolated in formation and complexion as we find them to-day in their different climates and countries.

What a commentary, then, upon the ultra views of the one-origin party! How readily, then, must this marked change have taken place in the human family after the destruction of man by the Noachic deluge! From the flood to the Exodus was only eight hundred and fifty-

six years, and if Shem, Ham, and Japhet, in the di-.
vision of the races, are to be regarded as the progenitors
of the white, yellow, and red man, to whom, then, shall
we look as the father and progenitor of the black man ?
Only four hundred and eighty-five years had elapsed
when the confusion of tongues occurred at the Tower
of Babel, and the time when the Israelites crossed the
Red Sea, on their march to Canaan, yet the Mongolian and the Negro were familiar to the Egyptian before
Abraham saw those vast pyramids looming up from the
bosom of the Nile. If Revelation, then, be silent upon
the subject of the diversity of the races, then science with
the aids at her command can alone solve this question.
Abraham was born in 1998 B.C., just one year after
Noah's death, and it was exactly fifty-five years (Biblical chronology) after the dispersion and confusion of
tongues that Abraham made his entry into Egypt, he
being at this time seventy-five years old, and his wife,
Sarah, sixty-five years of age.   And yet at this early day
after the dispersion of the human family, we find Egypt
peopled with a mighty race, and Abraham a perfect
stranger in their midst,* and had not God interfered in
his behalf Pharaoh would have appropriated his wife,
Sarah, because she was fair to look upon ; but Heaven's
protecting care vouchsafed to him a safe return, with
numerous servants and herds of cattle.

When Abraham made his exit from Egypt, he carried
with him Hagar, the Egyptian maid-servant, who became his concubine ; and it is highly probable that she
was a hybrid cross of the genuine Copt, or ancient

Gen. xii. 10–15.

Egyptian, with the Mongolian race, which very naturally accounts for the peculiar character and proclivities of the descendants of Ishmael,—nomad in disposition, and highwaymen by trade.

It is asserted that the Jew stands before us as an everlasting monument of God's displeasure. All mankind, then, unfortunately, is embraced in the same dilemma, as all have erred. But verily, he stands before us as an everlasting monument of God's perfect image and likeness, exemplified in His own Son when He took upon Himself our infirmities : perfect in stature, complete in physical organization, and unimpaired in the intellectual endowments of the genus homo as the day when he came a crowning model from the plastic hand of Jehovah Himself.

European principalities dare not wage war one against the other without first testing the financial resources of the Rothschilds, the princes of bankers. A nod of recognition or approval from these giant dispensers of material aid draws forth the obsequious smile from the royal applicant and moves forward the dreadful tramp of armed legions ; or disapprobation on their part in the refusal of the sinews of war lulls the impending storm and hushes the notes of the coming strife. Wealth is power, and the Israelite knows its resources and wields this giant lever with the administrative capacity of a master-intellect, for the purpose of furthering his ends and preserving the importance and protection of his race.

The leading spirit in the British Parliament is an Israelite of no ordinary calibre. " By force of talent, industry, and perseverance, unaided by wealth or family connections, in spite of the disadvantages of his Jewish origin and his reputation of a mere novelist, he has raised himself to the position of leader of the House of Commons, and of minister of finance in the greatest commercial empire of the world." And, at the English bar, J. P. Benjamin, of American celebrity, stands without a peer; whose oratory has been listened to and admired in the halls of Congress, and whose statesmanship has been felt in all the departments of the American government.

The patriot Jew, though oppressed and persecuted by emperors and republics, by sultans and popes, we find him battling for freedom under Polish and Austrian rule in the Franco-Germanic war, and breasting the storm in the internecine struggle that drenched with blood the American soil. They have numbered their philosophers among the Saracens of the East, and have transplanted their wisdom to every land where toleration would admit a ray of light. And wherever a spirit of liberty has actuated the nationalities of earth in extending to this oppressed people the exalted privileges of citizenship and uniform equality of rights, we find that they soon take that position in society and in the national councils which worth of character and force of intellect in every age have attained, illustrating peremptorily the undiminished and progressive mental capacity of the perfect Caucasian during the extended scale of near four thousand years.

Can we now, then, reconcile our conscience or the dictates of reason in harmonizing the theory that the degraded Bushman or the savage Fuegean is a lineal descendant of the patriarchs, and necessarily a twin-brother of the intellectual race whose history we have traced in these pages? If so, our efforts are in vain: permanent form and feature are a nullity, and intellectual progress a myth, as respects the character-istics of the blushing race.

CHAPTER XVII.

THE BATTLE OF ARMAGEDDON.

"And say, Supernal Powers, who deeply scan
Heaven's dark decrees, unfathomed yet by man,
When shall the world call down, to cleanse her shame,
That embryo spirit, yet without a name?"—CAMPBELL.

EZEK. xxxviii. 14–16: "Therefore, son of man, prophesy and say unto Gog, Thus saith the Lord God; In that day when my people of Israel dwelleth safely, shalt thou not know it? And thou shalt come from thy place out of the north parts, thou, and many people with thee, all of them riding upon horses, a great company, and a mighty army: and thou shalt come up against my people of Israel, as a cloud to cover the land; *it shall be in the latter days*, and I will bring thee against my land, that the heathen may know me, when I shall be sanctified in thee, O Gog, before their eyes."

In the latter days the spirit of prophecy has revealed

to our finite minds the great struggle which is to take place in the grand drama of this world's future history, which looms up with tenfold magnitude in the contemplation of the subject now under consideration. The time will most assuredly arrive, and the day is not far distant, when the armies of the living God and the infidel host of this world shall be gathered together in the great valley of Hamon-gog,* a place which in the Hebrew tongue is called Armageddon,† when "Satan shall be loosed out of his prison, and shall go out to deceive the nations which are in the four quarters of the earth, Gog and Magog, to gather them together to battle: the number of whom is as the sand of the sea." And the revelator John‡ declares that "I saw an angel standing in the sun; and he cried with a loud voice, saying to all the fowls that fly in the midst of heaven, Come and gather yourselves together unto the supper of the great God; that ye may eat the flesh of kings, and the flesh of captains, and the flesh of mighty men, and the flesh of horses, and of them that sit on them."

This is to be the final struggle between the armies of Jehovah and the allied powers of darkness.

"The Word of God§
Clothed with a vesture dipped in blood"

will command the celestial host against Apollyon,‖ the prince of the powers that be, called in the Hebrew tongue Abaddon. And this demon of unrighteousness is the great spirit of idolatry that the Adamite encoun-

---

* Ezek. xxxix. 11.   † Rev. xvi. 16.   ‡ Rev. xix. 17, 21.
§ Rev. xix. 13.   ‖ Rev. ix. 11.

tered when he made his advent in this world. The
devil, with his rebellious followers, "which kept not
their first estate, but left their own habitation, the Lord
hath reserved in everlasting chains under darkness unto
the judgment of the great day." They were cast out
of heaven, and in retaliation against the great Father
of Light commenced their warfare against the pre-
adamite until the last mortal surrendered himself, a
willing subject to the powers of perdition. And throughout the vast area of earth there was not a soul but what
willingly bent the knee to worship at the shrine of
Baal. The creature man then stood before Jehovah as
an outcast, the foe of Heaven, and the enemy of righteousness, with no hope of return until the cup of
his iniquity was full. "And God said, Let us make
man in our image, after our likeness," and Adam and
Eve became living souls. And the serpent appeared
to our first parent in the form and type of the true
Mongolian, clothed with the habiliments of the artful
deceiver, with the twofold intention of dragging down
the new-born race to his disgraceful level and satiating
his hellish appetite upon his unwary victim.

In obedience to my knowledge of the Bible, the arch-
enemy of man has never visibly appeared and held personal converse with the sons of men. He has led man
on by wily machinations, as an unseen enemy, until his
evil purposes were accomplished and the individual
has become tributary to his exactions. Satan has,
however, ventured to converse with God, as reported
in Job's history, and he has cried out to the Son of
God when being ejected from the unhappy lunatic
who made his abode in the tombs. Also he tempted

Christ during his sojourn in the wilderness, and has dared to dispute with our Saviour and the angel Gabriel. With man, however, he has never held personal interviews in the form and attitude of a being possessing material substance. But in the fulfillment of this prophecy, the time is not far distant when he is to marshal his clans for the great battle of Armageddon. Listen to the word of inspiration. Rev. xvi. 12–14: "And the sixth angel poured out his vial upon the great river Euphrates; and the water thereof was dried up, that the way of the kings of the east might be prepared. And I saw three unclean spirits like frogs come out of the mouth of the dragon, and out of the mouth of the beast, and out of the mouth of the false prophet. For they are the spirits of devils, working miracles, which go forth unto the kings of the earth and of the whole world, to gather them to the battle of that great day of God Almighty." The unclean spirit emanating from the mouth of the dragon is the archangel of darkness; and the unclean spirit from the mouth of the beast is the creature, the pre-adamic antichrist, and the other unclean spirit is Mahomet, the false prophet of Islamism. United under one banner, and with but one object to accomplish,—the overthrow of the Christian religion,—undivided they will march in their work of destruction, and the way will be opened by the angel of the Apocalypse, who will pour out his vial of wrath upon the great river Euphrates, to dry up the waters, that the way of the kings of the earth might be prepared. In other words, the Lord of Sabaoth will open up a way in due time for the concentration of the mighty forces which are to be arrayed against

14

the Lion of the Tribe of Judah in anticipation of the great victory, when the Lamb of God shall be once more and forever crowned the "King of kings and Lord of lords."

Magog was originally a son of Japhet, and the prophet Ezekiel unites with Magog and Gog both Gomer and the house of Togarmah. The close proximity of the white race to the Turanian, and the amalgamation of races which soon ensued in the antediluvian age, brought upon the Adamite summary destruction. Nor was the posterity of Noah sufficiently mindful of this great calamity and of its great first cause to deter them from a repetition of the same offense. So we may reasonably observe, in after-ages, that Magog, Gomer, and others of the fair-complexioned race united their destiny with the Mongolian tribes of Central Asia, infused into them a higher cast of intellect, and more of the progressive spirit of the white man, and modified the feature and form of the inferior race, which has produced the varied diversity in the Turanian family, admissible wherever found scattered in their various localities, as Calmucks, Tartars, Samoyedes, Ugrians, Basques, or Lapps. This progressive spirit developed itself several centuries before the Christian era in Eastern Asia by the infusion of greater mental capacity into the inert mind of the Turanian, as we see exemplified in the structure of the Chinese wall and other architectural works of a national character found among the Chinese. History* informs us that the

---

* Cuneiform inscriptions. The information gained for history from the deciphering of the Assyrian sphenograms is a matter of consider-

Mongolian* was mixed at an early day with the Chaldean, owing to their proximity and the intercourse engendered by commercial relations, and brought about by the aggressive disposition of the Adamite in every age. Babylon of old has the reputation of being the first of all idolatrous cities, and stands forth in the Apocalypse as the prominent emblem of that enormous guilt which must culminate at some day and break upon the head of the idolatrous races. This nation, bordering closely on the Turanian group, instilled into the inferior race, lying on her east, greater intellectual endowments and more symmetrical form of person, at the same time imbibed a sufficient quantity of poison from their eastern neighbors that the religious and political economy of the Assyrian Empire became corrupt and demoralized in proportion as the Turanian family had been elevated in the scale of progress. And, like the antediluvian, great Babylon adopted the heresies and idolatrous worship of the aboriginal races, until her iniquities called forth the merited vengeance of offended Deity.

Gog and Magog represent the leading spirits of the pagan world, possessing inherently greater intellectual

---

able interest to all parties in search of truth. " It is certain that from time immemorial three peoples of different *characters and languages were living in close contact* and in various relations as to political power in the countries where sphenography was practiced. These three groups of nations are the Semitic, Aryan, and Turanian, or Scythic." (American Cyclopædia.) These inscriptions are found in abundance amid the waste ruins of those ancient cities lying between the Caspian Sea and the Persian Gulf, at one time the original boundary separating the Adamic from the inferior race on the east.

* Philip Smith's History of the World.

capacity. They are the champions selected to manipulate the Mongolian and other aboriginal hordes, combined with all the Mohammedan and other anti-Christian delusions, whom the arch-fiend of darkness, the master-spirit of the demonian elements, shall command in person; and, like an Alexander or a Napoleon, he will lead his infatuated host on, from conquest to victory, until the last armed foe shall expire, or his minions shall meet their doom and "be turned into hell with all the nations that forget God."

The Scythians of old are the people alluded to in the Holy Scriptures whom Hippocrates and Herodotus describe in personal appearance as exclusively peculiar to themselves, and entirely different from all the races of mankind with whom it has been their good fortune to meet in their intercourse with man. By these ancient historians they are represented with gross bodies and of corpulent stature, with loose and flexible joints, with flabby belly and scant hair, and in person there is a marked resemblance one to the other.

The Scythian soldier in the hour of conflict would cease from the bloody strife to drink the blood of the first victim slain in battle; and the skins and scalps of the fallen enemy were preserved as trophies by the victor; and the skulls of his mangled foes were converted into cups, and graced their rude bacchanalian boards during their annual festivals. And when death visited the royal household, they honored their king in his burial by sacrificing human beings, together with such animals as their flocks afforded. Their slaves they treated as brutes, and invariably put out all their eyes. Their intercourse with foreigners on terms of friendship was very limited, and foreign customs and habits were inadmissible under any and all circumstances. This aversion to foreign innovations is still a peculiar characteristic of the Oriental in our own day and generation.

The gypsies, a corruption of the word Egyptians, a vagabond, roving class of prowling thieves, who are infesting nearly every country under the sun, where civilization reigns, and where ignorance contributes material aid in encouraging treachery, cowardice, and cruelty. These wretches are an offshoot of the Scythian tribes of old, and have passed under various names in different countries, as Tartars or heathens, and are known at this day as Bohemians, having acquired that title as entering France first from the land of Bohemia. They have been banished from nearly every civilized kingdom of Europe, and are regarded as robbers, highwaymen, and vagrants by all who have had the privilege of testing their worthlessness. They have a language composed of scraps of words picked up hither and thither in their migrations round the world, which can be called nothing more nor less than "jargon,"— possessing no words which convey any idea of God, the human soul, or the immortality of man. Their physiognomy is Asiatic in type: complexion tawny, eyes black and piercing, hair very black, cheek-bones high and prominent, lower jaw slightly projected, and crania with small facial angle, and, like other Orientals, they are unreliable and exempt from every redeeming quality that marks the blushing race.

These vagabonds are the pioneers amid the haunts of civilization, who are ready to enlist in the grand army of aggression in its onward march to meet the chosen remnant, whose robes have been washed and made white in the blood of the Lamb. And well may the archangel of death rear his crested form in the proud attitude of a conqueror, having lorded it over God's heritage for nearly six thousand years, and swayed the iron sceptre of darkness over earth's myriads of souls until the dark domain of perdition has been peopled with the lost and ruined of every race. And the time must soon be ushered in when the marshaled hordes of earth shall be arrayed in line of battle to confront the angelic host; and as God said, "Let there be light, and there was light," in the twinkle of an eye the fiat will go forth, and the legions of Apollyon will roll back like a wave from the surf-beaten shore, and cry out in anguish for the mountains to fall on them and the hills to cover them. And the Lamb of God that was slain from the foundation of the world shall then make his second appearance, crowned in the glory of his celestial attire, to be and remain forever and ever the King of kings and the Lord of lords.

And when will be fought the great battle of Armageddon? and when will the great victory be achieved over the enemies of the Cross? When the wolf shall dwell with the lamb and the leopard shall lie down with the kid, when the suckling child shall play unharmed on the hole of the asp, and the weaned child shall put his hand with impunity on the cockatrice's den. "Here is wisdom." And no finite mind can answer this solemn question; it belongs to the mysterious records of futurity. We can, however, avail ourselves of such light as may be presented in Divine revelation for the consideration of sacred truth. David says, in Psalm xc. 4, "For a thousand years in thy sight are but as yesterday when it is past;" and again, 2 Peter iii. 8, "But, beloved, be not ignorant of this one thing, *that one day is with the Lord as a thousand years,* and a thousand years as one day." Then upon this data as a basis we proceed. The Lord was six days (or periods of time) in creating the heavens and the earth, and he rested on the seventh day and sanctified it as a day of rest. Adam commenced his labors on Monday morning, the first day of a thousand years; and now we, the transient occupants of earth in this the nineteenth century, are to-day bringing up and closing the labors of Saturday evening. From Adam to Christ was four thousand and four years, according to the computation of Archbishop Ussher, and from the birth of Christ to the present time is eighteen hundred and seventy-two years, which added together gives us a period of five thousand eight hundred and seventy-six years, leaving but one hundred and twenty-four years when the week of six days shall have passed away, and the six thousand years shall have swept across and fixed forever the destiny of man. Then comes in the Sabbath of a thousand years, the Christian's jubilee, the millennium of revelation. "Blessed and holy is he that hath part in the first resurrection." Let us be mindful that human chronology is only an assimilation to the truth, and that Archbishop Ussher was only a man and liable to err in his computation of passing ages, and the error of one hundred years or more on his part may thrust this generation into the very midst of a struggle, where hell and earth are combined to precipitate their murderous battalions on a sleeping and unsuspecting world, while the angelic host are tuning their harps in honor of the victory which must eventually place upon Jehovah's brow the golden crown and the victorious palm.

FINIS.

Yours Truly
Charles Carroll

THE TEMPTER OF EVE

— OR —

The Criminality of Man's Social, Political, and
Religious Equality with the Negro, and
the Amalgamation to which these
Crimes Inevitably Lead.

Discussed in the Light of the Scriptures, the Sciences,
Profane History, Tradition, and the Testimony
of the Monuments.

BY

CHARLES CARROLL,

ST. LOUIS.

ADAMIC LIBRARY.

ST. LOUIS:
PUBLISHED BY THE ADAMIC PUBLISHING CO.
1902.

IN GRATEFUL ACKNOWLEDGMENT OF HIS
FRIENDSHIP, KINDNESS AND LOYAL SUPPORT OF
THE SENTIMENTS EXPRESSED IN THESE PAGES,
THIS BOOK IS RESPECTFULLY DEDICATED TO
DR. A. W. BOYD, OF CHATTANOOGA, TENNESSEE.

THE AUTHOR.

CONTENTS.

CHAPTER I.

CHAPTER II.

iii

CHAPTER IX.

CHAPTER X.

300

CHAPTER XI.

CHAPTER XII.

303

LIST OF ILLUSTRATIONS.

INTRODUCTION.

Many of my correspondents in different sections of the country, have assured me that, among those familiar with my writings, there is a wide-spread desire to know how I first became impressed with my views of the negro, as expressed in my writings. To such of my readers as entertain this desire, the following facts may prove interesting:

When I was a boy, I stopped one day on my way home from school to observe the tricks of a monkey that was being exhibited by an Italian organ-grinder. When I reached home, my father informed me that he had just bought a little orphan negro; hastening to the kitchen, I at once observed the striking facial resemblance between the little negro and the Italian's monkey. His skull was as degraded and animal-like as that of the Neanderthal; while the expression of his face, his movements and gestures must have been as fantastical and ape-like as those of the Hottentot Venus. After dinner I took the little negro and hunted up the Italian with the view of further observing the resemblances between his monkey and the negro. The little negro had never before seen a monkey, and it would have been difficult to determine whether his antics or

xi

those of the monkey were the most ludicrous; he at least fully shared with the monkey the attention of the bystanders. My observations of the two convinced me that the negro and the monkey belonged to the same family; and upon reaching home, I told my father of my observations and expressed the opinion that the negro is an ape. My mother was highly amused, but my father was horrified, and turning to my mother, he asked her if she had been talking to me on that subject; she replied that she had not. My father then lectured me at length on what he termed my "outrageous views," and forbade my further discussion of the subject, assuring me that if I ever repeated the offense he would punish me severely. Sometime afterwards, when my mother and I were alone, I asked her if she did not believe the negro to be an ape, but she replied by reminding me of my father's injunction, and declined to discuss the question. But remembering my father's question to her, and her manner on both occasions when the subject was mentioned, I feel assured that I must have voiced her sentiments, when I declared the negro to be an ape. However, she died a few years afterwards, and I never questioned my father as to her sentiments.

Hoping that I would forget the matter, and to further his desire that I should do so, my father sold the little negro, and I never saw him afterward. But, though I was silenced, I was still free to observe and reason; and the more I saw of negroes, the more I was convinced that my estimate of them was correct.

About twenty years ago I decided to investigate the origin and history of the negro. And just here the teachings of my Bible-believing parents proved of inestimable value to me. I had been taught from childhood that the Bible was the Word of God. Though it must be confessed that I had grown somewhat skeptical, not because I was inclined to be so, but because of the absurd interpretation placed upon the Bible by those who professed to understand it; and I regret to say that my father was among the number. For example: I would ask, What was the tempter of Eve? I would be told in all seriousness that "it was a snake." This was absurd; I could never believe that articulate speech was possessed by an animal so low in the scale of being as a snake. And again I would ask, Who was Cain's wife? I was told that this was a "mooted question," but that "he must have taken his sister to wife." Yet I could see that the Bible plainly taught that there was no female child born to the Adamic family until after the birth of Seth; while it also taught that Cain had a wife before Seth was born. Again, I would ask, What did the antediluvians do which so offended God as to lead Him to destroy them with the deluge? I was told that "they were very wicked, but that no specific offense was charged against them." But it seemed to me that, in addition to punishing them with death, God would desire to make an example of them; and in order to do this it was necessary to specifically state their offense. Again, I would ask, What offense did the Canaan-

ites commit which led God to command the Israelites to destroy them, male and female, and even the
babes at their mother's breasts, and "leave nothing
alive that breatheth?" I was told that, "they were
a very degraded people who worshiped idols." But
it occurred to me that the little children who had not
thus offended, might have been spared, and taught
to believe in God. Such replies to these vital questions, and others of like nature, were not only unsatisfactory in the extreme, but were well calculated
to engender skepticism in the mind of a student;
and I often think with horror of how nearly they
came to making an infidel of me, as they have of
tens of thousands of earnest seekers after truth.
But even under these discouraging conditions, the
training of my youth exerted a restraining influence
upon me. My father was an old Methodist class
leader, and I am the child of a Methodist mother.
I was loath to renounce the Old Book which had afforded them so much comfort and hope. This induced me in my investigation of the negro to first
take up the Bible. I reasoned thus: If the Bible
is the Word of God; and if the negro is an ape,
surely God would not turn loose upon the earth such
a creature with no record of him by which he might
be identified in all ages of his history. The result
proved the correctness of my reasoning, as the
pages of this work will show.

I had partly written up my Bible work on this
subject when I was called home to assist in nursing
my step-mother who was dangerously ill. When

she had so far recovered as to be able to sit up, I requested permission to read my partly finished manuscript. I had not confided to them nor to any one the fact that I was investigating and writing upon any subject, so that my request was a complete surprise. However, the surprise was agreeable in the extreme to them, and my request was promptly granted. The astonishment of those old people was only equaled by their joy, when they realized that their former skeptical boy was an enthusiastic believer in, and an ardent student of, the Bible. Only the three of us were present, and the scene was one which is as impossible to describe as to forget.

After thoroughly discussing my views and critically investigating them in the light of the scriptures, my father and step-mother gave them their unqualified endorsement. When I had completed my investigations of the Bible and was able to establish the fact that the negro figures throughout the scriptures as an ape—the "beast of the field"—I turned my attention to the sciences with the desire of giving my views a scientific backing. But I soon discovered that many of the leading scientific writers utterly repudiated the Bible, and that few, if any, professed Christians accepted it as a whole, and adhered to it where it conflicted with modern theories. Inasmuch as my views of the negro were based upon the Bible, I realized that it was necessary to show that the scriptures were in absolute harmony with the sciences at every point. This imposed upon me a further labor of years. The result of which will be found in the pages of this book, and the succeeding volumes of the series. In the year of 1899, I published my views in a very condensed form in a pamphlet entitled, "The Negro not the Son of Ham." In 1901 I wrote up my views a little more extensively and placed the manuscript in the hands of a publisher whose disregard of my rights as an author led him to change the title I had given the book— "Man and the Negro"—to a course, vulgar one of his own selection. This, with his bombastic title page which has subjected me to the severest criticisms, and the general "Cheap John" appearance of the book, practically stripped it of all dignity, and rendered it a thing of which I am heartily ashamed. Though laboring under all these disadvantages, the book had an extensive sale. This, and the many letters I have received from all sections of the country endorsing my views, encourages me to write them up more elaborately and publish them in a series of which THE TEMPTER OF EVE is the first volume.

THE AUTHOR.

CHAPTER I.

THE ANTEDILUVIAN BIBLE.

"Eternal Spirit! God of truth! to whom
All things seem as they are; thou who of old
The prophet's eye unscaled, that nightly saw,
While heavy sleep fell down on other men,
In holy visions tranced, the future pass
Before him, and to Judah's harp attuned
Burdens which made the pagan mountains shake
And Zion's cedars bow—inspire my song;
My eye unscale; me what is substance teach,
And shadow what, while I of things to come,
As past rehearsing sing the Course of Time.

　　　*　　　*　　　*　　　*　　　*

The muse, that soft and sickly wooes the ear
Of love, or chanting loud in windy rhyme
Of fabled hero, raves through gaudy tale,
Not over fraught with sense, I ask not; such
A strain befits not argument so high.
Me thought, and phrase, severely sifting out
The whole idea, grant; uttering as 't is
The eternal truth.—*Pollock.*

The Bible occupies to-day, as it has in all ages
of its history, a unique position in the literature of
the world. Among the many peculiarities which distinguish it, the following are perhaps the most
peculiar:

17

311

1. It purports to be of supernatural origin, in that, it was written by men whom God selected, and to whom He communicated the knowledge which He desired them to impart to their fellow-men. Thus, it claims to be literally and truly the word of God, conveying to us from the fountain of all wisdom and truth, a knowledge which is essential to our welfare both in time and in eternity, and which was not obtainable from another source. Hence, it demands of all men that careful consideration and respect, which the creature should accord to the utterances of his Creator, or the child to the teachings of its parent.

A perusal of the first and second chapters of Genesis reveals to us a clearly defined plan of creation, in which the principal events are stated in the order of their occurrence. These various events occurred in stated periods of time described as the "first day," the "second day," the "third day," and so on; the whole terminating in the creation of man on the "sixth day." It is claimed that God selected and inspired Moses to write this narrative of the creation. Hence, it is termed by some, "The Mosaic account of Creation;" by others, "The Mosaic Record."

2. The Mosaic Record teaches that the material universe with all its phenomena was created by God for a definite purpose. Hence, it is artificial—the product of Divine art; and the laws which govern it are God's laws.

3. It draws a broad distinction between man

and the animal, and this distinction is maintained
throughout the scriptures. It teaches (1) that, in
obedience to God's command, the waters and the
earth brought forth the animals after their kind;
while God created man in His own image. (2)
No specific design is given as to why God made
the animals; neither were they assigned to any specific task beyond increasing and multiplying, and
were simply placed under man's dominion after his
creation. Hence, the animal is responsible to man.
(3) The design of God in creating man, is specifically stated; and after his creation, man was assigned
to this specific work. Hence, man must respect the
design of God in creating him, and must answer to
God for the manner in which he discharges the duties to which he was assigned in the Creation. (4)
That the animals were made in great numbers, and
in great variety; while man was created a single pair.
(5) That there are three distinct classes of animals,
which made their appearance in the order stated:
fish, fowl, and beast; that these classes of animals are
each separate and distinct from the others, and were
assigned to different spheres,—the fish to inhabit the
waters; the fowl to fly above the earth in the open
firmament of heaven; and the beast to occupy the
dry land. On the other hand, man's dominion extends over the entire globe, though for reasons
stated, his immediate place of abode would be the
dry land. (6) That the male and female animal of
the different families or species,—whether of fish, or
fowl, or beast,—originated in the same manner, and

were brought forth simultaneously. Hence, they were at once capable of reproducing their kind. But that God first created in His own image the male man, and at a later period completed his creation, by making the female man out of the male man. Thus, for a considerable period, prior to the advent of woman, the male side or part of the Adamic Creation lived upon the earth without the companionship of the female by whom he might beget offspring "in the image of God." (7) That the animals were brought forth and allowed to roam promiscuously in their different spheres,—the fish in the water, the fowl in the air, and the beasts on the dry land; their actions were not restrained by law; hence, they were held to no legal responsibility for their conduct, but were governed solely by those attributes of the mind which are commonly termed, instincts; that no part of the substance of God enters into their composition to form a link of kinship between Himself and them; that they are merely the *creatures*, not the *kinsman*, of God. Hence, no vestige of immortality distinguishes them from the plant, or the planet: mere creatures of time, they cannot survive the end of time; born of the earth, they must perish where they had their birth. But that, in the Creation, God incorporated a part of His substance with man's physical and mental organisms, thus forming a link of kinship between Himself and man, which he can transmit through pure Adamic channels to his offspring. This part of the substance of God which the Creator bestowed upon man is described in scripture as the "Soul;" it is the soul that is the immortal part of man. Hence, his possession of a soul, itself a part of the substance of God, distinguishes man from the animal, as the possession of mind distinguishes the animal from the plant; and when man's physical and mental organisms are dissolved, his soul will take its flight from the scenes of time to an endless existence in the realms of eternity. And in the Creation, man, unlike the animals, was assigned to a fixed place of abode, in the Garden of Eden, which God prepared for him, and which He commanded him to keep and cultivate. The narrative of Creation is followed by a narrative of many of the principal events in man's history from the Creation down to a few decades after the birth of Jesus Christ.

4. When we compare the age of the narrative of Creation, as we find it in the Bible, with the age of man, according to this narration we find that man existed upon the earth thousands of years before the birth of Moses, who is accredited with its authorship. This fact suggests to our mind the following inquiries: If a full and correct knowledge of the great events described by Moses in the order of their occurrence, together with a knowledge of man's kinship with God; the design of God in creating him, and the laws which God enacted for his government are essential to man, why was it not revealed to him in the Creation? And if it was revealed to him, when did he lose it? Was it suddenly lost? Did the whole

Adamic family simultaneously agree to renounce monotheism and adopt other beliefs? The thought is inadmissable! History and our personal experience and observation combine to teach us that men cling tenaciously to their ancestral beliefs; and the fact that this is especially true of their religious beliefs, goes far to prove that the loss of this knowledge was accomplished by a very gradual process, extending through a long period of time. Whatever differences of opinion upon this subject may exist in the minds of men, we feel assured that all will agree (1) that, if God revealed this knowledge to Adam, his decendants lost it at some period in their history prior to the time of Moses; or, that at the time of Moses they retained only fragments of it, so corrupted by errors and superstitions as to render it practically valueless. (2) That the loss of this knowledge was simply an *effect*, which, like all effects is traceable to a *cause*. But what was this cause? What demoralizing course of conduct, persistently pursued for ages in every portion of the earth, finally resulted in stripping man of this essential knowledge; or, that so corrupted it as to strip it of all practical value, thus reducing him to such ignorance of these most important subjects as to render it necessary for God, in His mercy, to make a second revelation to man of this essential knowledge as we have it to-day in the Mosaic Record? The solution of this question necessarily requires a careful investigation of the history and associations of man from the creation down to our day; for the very nature of the subject, its far-reaching consequences, its over-whelming importance, coupled with our earnest de-sire to dó justice to it, forbids the closing of our in-vestigations upon reaching the time of Moses. The result of our investigations will be found in the following chapters of this work. For the present we shall confine our inquiries to the question as to whether God revealed to Adam a knowledge of the great events of the Creation, which his descendents lost, thus necessitating a second revelation of this knowledge, together with the history of man and his associations and their ruinous results as we have it in the Pentateuch.

We feel assured that all fair-minded men will agree with us in the following conclusions : (1) If it could be shown that God created man and turned him loose upon the earth, like an animal, without revealing to him a knowledge of the existence of God, the Creator of the universe; nor of his kin-ship with God; nor of his immortality; nor of the design of God in creating him ; nor of the relations which God desired him to maintain toward the ani-mals; and had assigned him to no specific task ; and had enacted no laws for his special government, and left him groping in ignorance of these important subjects until the time of Moses, and yet held him to rigid responsibility for his acts, it would destroy our belief in the wisdom, and justice, and mercy, and love of God. (2) That, had God created man and not revealed to him this essential knowledge, he could never have acquired it from another source;

and any effort upon his part to solve these questions for himself, would merely have resulted in the production of innumerable hypotheses, all more or less at variance with truth, and consequently incapable of proof. The strength of our position upon this subject is easily demonstrated by investigating the theories of the men of modern time, who deny the existence of a Creator, repudiate the Bible, and attribute the existence of the universe to natural causes; and who attempt to explain the origin of man, his relation to the animals, and his final destiny.

But we have an abundance of authentic proof that God revealed this knowledge to Adam in the Creation, as shown by the following:

The Mosaic Record emphatically states that God held personal intercourse with Adam in the Garden of Eden, and revealed this knowledge to him; and that in the Garden of Eden, Adam and Eve were placed under a dual system of laws; the one defining their relations to God, and their relation to the earth and the animals; the other defining their mode of religious worship. Bible history teaches that Adam transmitted this knowledge to his decendants, more or less of whom retained it in its purity down to the time of the Deluge; and that after the Deluge it was transmitted by Noah to his decendants.

This may come as a surprise to those who have been misled by the theories of atheism to believe that man is a highly developed species of ape—the "human species" and that this "human species" of ape is divisible into five or more "races of men" of which the White is the highest and the Negro the lowest race, with the Browns, Reds, and Yellows as intermediate races, in different stages of development; and that, at the time of man's "differentiation" from the ape, he was simply an ignorant, brutal savage, and so remained for tens of thousands of years, with only such meager ability as enabled him to fashion out of flint, a rudely chipped implement of the chase with which to slaughter the animals—his kinsmen—upon which he fed, and from which he was little removed in point of intelligence; and that man traces his line of decent back through a long series of "animal ancestors" to the Monera—the lowest form of animal—itself the result of "spontaneous generation."

But when we renounce this baseless, absurd theory, which attributes to man an animal ancestry, thus degrading him to the level of the brute, and accept in their entirety the elevating teachings of the Mosaic Record, we are enabled to realize that man was created "the son of God;" that he was designed for a definite purpose, and assigned to a specific task in a fixed place of abode; and that in the Garden of Eden our first parents, Adam and Eve, held personal intercourse with the great Architect of the universe, who revealed to them the great events of the Creation, together with a full knowledge of all that was necessary for them to know in order to accomplish the great task for which they were designed and to which God assigned them in the Creation.

Men inherit from their ancestors a greater or less amount of valuable knowledge which they add more or less to, and teach the whole to their children, who, in their turn, transmit it, with such knowledge as they may have otherwise acquired, to their decendants. Thus, each generation inherits from their predecessors a vast amount of invaluable knowledge. But who taught Adam? He was the first man. No long line of projenitors transmitted to him the knowledge they had acquired from observation and experience. He was created absolutely ignorant of his origin, and of his relations to God, and the relations which God designed him to maintain toward the earth, and the rest of created things. We instruct our children in such knowledge as we possess that would prove beneficial to them, and thus do all in our power to equip them for the duties of life. Would our heavenly father be less mindful of the interest of his earthly children? Let us bear in mind that Adam was "the son of God;" and that consequently his pure-blooded decendants are God's children. To believe that God would not instruct his children in all that concerns their welfare, would compel us to repudiate the teachings of scripture. God revealed to Moses the truths written in the Pentateuch for man's instruction. Jesus Christ instructed His desciples in the duties He desired them to perform. The Bible as a whole is composed of instruction which God has given man, from time to time, for his enlightenment and guidance. The author of each book of the Bible was a man whom God instructed upon the subjects of which he wrote. Hence, the various books of the Bible mark so many periods in man's history in which he had forgotten his Creator and his obligations to Him, and had wandered so far in forbidden paths, and had become so ignorant and benighted, as to make it impossible for him, unaided, to regain his lost position. They also present so many instances in which God's parental love for man followed him out into the darkness and hopelessness of atheism and idolatry, into which his follies and crimes had led him, and enlightened him, extended to him a helping hand, and guided him back to the path of right and duty.

When we find that God dealt thus with the rebellious descendants of Adam in their wickedness and depravity, we should see in it the most positive evidence that He would instruct Adam in all that was essential for his welfare, when his ignorance was only equaled by his innocence. To our mind, nothing could be more absurd than to suppose that God did more to enlighten the demoralized, degraded descendants of Adam, whose long career of folly and crime had reduced them to the most pitiable ignorance, than He did for Adam in the innocence and ignorance in which He created him. Hence, if the Bible and all profane history, and all tradition had been destroyed ages ago, and we were creditably informed of the existence of God, the Creator of the universe; that He was a being of infinite wisdom, justice, mercy, and love; that He created man in His own image, and incorporated with man's physical and

mental organisms a part of His own substance, thus
rendering him immortal and establishing between
Himself and man the close relationship of father and
son; that He created man for a definite purpose, and
immediately assigned him to a gigantic work which
required the highest intelligence to accomplish, reason would assure us that this wise, just, merciful loving God revealed to man a knowledge of all
these things; and acquainted him with the existence
of all the factors which he should employ in the accomplishment of his great task, and the manner of
utilizing them. But upon this important subject we
shall not be content to rest our case upon mere assumption; and in the following chapters we shall
show by Bible history that God did reveal to Adam
a vast amount of invaluable knowledge relative to
the successful accomplishment of his great task, of
which the narrative of Creation makes no mention.

Let us bear in mind that this invaluable knowledge which God revealed to Adam as shown by the
Mosaic Record and the early history of the Adamic
family, was not designed for Adam alone, but was
intended for the benefit of his descendants throughout the ages that were to come. No good reason
could be advanced why God should desire that this
great mass of invaluable knowledge should be transmitted orally from generation to generation, thus
risking its being corrupted to a greater or less extent, and its value correspondingly impaired. On
the contrary, we can see every reason why God
should prefer that this knowledge which He had

322

revealed to Adam for his benefit and that of his descendants should be made a matter of permanent record, thus assuring its transmission from generation to generation in its purity. And a moment's consideration should convince us that this could only be accomplished by a knowledge of letters; that its certain transmission in its purity necessitated its being made in writing. This being true, it follows that at no period of his history has man stood in greater need of the knowledge of letters and the art of writing than did Adam in the Creation; and we feel assured that among his other accomplishments, Adam possessed the art of writing, and that he employed it in transmitting to his descendants the knowledge which God revealed to him for his benefit and theirs.

But though no fragment of this written record has escaped the ravages of time, and descended to us, we are not without evidence of its former existence. The Hebrew commentators on the Book of Genesis say: "Our rabbins assert that Adam, our father of blessed memory, composed a book of precepts which were delivered to him by God in Paradise." (*Smith's Sacred Annals*). The value of the Mosaic Record is not due to the fact that Moses wrote it, but to the fact that God revealed to him the knowledge which it contains; so it was with Adam's book; its value did not consist in the fact that Adam wrote it, but that God "delivered to him" the "precepts" of which it was composed; though Adam wrote the one, and Moses wrote the other, God in-

spired their utterances. Hence, they were each inspired volumes. This being true, it follows that the
most devout believer in the Bible of to-day does
not hold it in greater reverence than the antediluvians and the descendants of Noah for centuries
after the Deluge held Adam's book of precepts. The
knowledge which Adam's book contained was our
birthright; but unfortunately for us and them, there
came a time in the remote past when our ancestors
began to esteem it lightly, and little by little it was
lost, until to-day only a few fragments are to be
found upon the different continents; but even these
fragments that have survived the destruction of the
written record, and have been handed down tradi-
tionally, have become so corrupted in their transit
through the ages as to be of no practical value,
beyond the evidence their presence presents of the
former existence of a written volume which God inspired Adam to write.

The idea that our most ancient progenitor had
a knowledge of letters, and the art of writing, may
seem surprising to many who have been misled by
the theories of atheists to believe that man descended
from the ape; and that the earliest men were speechless and so remained for ages before developing articulate speech; and that after this event they slowly
developed through the different stages of savagism,
barbarism, and semi-barbarism, until they finally
reached such a degree of civilization as enabled them
to realize their need of letters and the art of writing;
and that they reached this period of their history in

the time of the Phœnicians, a once great commercial and maratime people, who invented the alphabet. This absurd theory of the Phœnician origin of the alphabet has long since been exploded; but with that tenacity with which men cling to error, it is taught to-day in quarters where we should least expect it. As has been shown, reason and the acceptance of the teachings of scripture leads to the belief that the art of writing is very nearly as old as man; and the most ancient traditions sustain it. Soudas, the Greek lexicographer, merely voiced a tradition of the ancients when he said, "Adam was the author of arts and letters." Pliny says, "Letters were always in use." Josephus expresses Jewish tradition when he says, "The births and deaths of illustrious men, between Adam and Noah, were noted down at the time with great accuracy." The Egyptians said that their God, Anubis, was an antediluvian who "wrote annals before the flood." The Chinese have traditions that their ancestors, prior to history, "taught all the arts of life and wrote books." William Mitford, the historian, in discussing the origin of the alphabet, says: "Nothing appears to us so probable as that it was derived from the antediluvian world."

When we examine the ancient literature of the oldest civilized nations, such as the Scandinavians, Greeks, Egyptians, Hindoos, Chinese, Americans, etc., we find that back of all their atheism, and idolatry, lays the sublime doctrine of monotheism. This proves that those peerless old architects who lived nearest to the time of Noah, and who developed those splendid civilizations, the remains of which adorn every continent of the earth, were monotheists; it also proves that their descendants yielded to the demoralizing, degrading influence of some seductive crime, and forgot God and his "precepts," renounced monotheism and wandered off into the darkness of atheism and idolatry. One would naturally suppose that there could be no identity of origin, no kinship, not even the remotest relationship between atheism, which denies the existence of God, and idolatry with its worship of many gods; but investigation of their origin reveals the fact that they are twin sisters—the offspring of one crime.

Thus it is shown that Monotheism is not only traceable to those most ancient and highly civilized postdiluvians who lived nearest to the time of Noah, but it is traceable to Adam, the first man — "the son of God." The Bible teaches that Adam was a monotheist; that in His intercourse with Adam and Eve, in the Garden of Eden, God taught them the doctrine of monotheism, together with many other things which he desired should be known to their descendants throughout all time; that Adam transmitted it to his descendants, among whom was Noah. We have shown that the very fact that the knowledge which God revealed to Adam was designed for his descendants throughout the ages that were to come, required that it be transmitted in writing; and the most ancient and reliable traditions assert that this was done. Why should not Adam have been the inventor of letters and the art of writing? Why should not the antediluvians have needed and employed the art of writing as well as the postdiluvians? The Bible also teaches that monotheism was the belief of Noah and his family, and that they taught it to their children; and if they received this doctrine from their ancestors in writing, they transmitted it in writing to their descendants. All known facts concerning the antediluvians indicate that they were a highly cultivated people. This being true, the inference is fair that Noah preserved in the ark, among other things, a greater or less amount of valuable literature, some sacred, some profane; at the head of which stood the inspired book written by Adam; that he transmitted this literature to his descendants, who added to it, as we add to our literature, until they entered upon their downward career of crime, in which their literature, sacred and profane, was finally lost; and their descendants plunged into the greatest ignorance and superstition. The above are our impressions of the learning and culture of Adam and his descendants down to the time of Moses, when viewed in the lights of scripture and tradition.

When we stand at our day and look backward up the stream of time, we are enabled with the aids of scripture, profane history and tradition to see that beyond the ages of atheism and idolatry, the various continents of the earth were populated by a highly cultivated and enlightened people who were monotheists. Thus it is shown that, whether we trace the history of man from the Creation to a period subsequent to the Deluge, or whether we trace his history back from our day to those great civilized nations who lived nearest to the time of the Deluge, the result is the same; we find that monotheism is the most ancient belief of mankind. But strange to say, the existence of monotheism among these ancient civilized nations has been seized upon by the opponents of the Bible as a weapon with which to assail it at its most vital point; they attempt to use this fact as evidence that God never inspired Moses to write the Pentateuch; but that it is simply a compilation of old legends and traditions which he or others had access to; and stranger still is the fact that we find many professed Christians who accept this demoralizing theory. But a moment's reflection should convince us that if Christianity as founded by Jesus Christ has any basis in fact, its ultimate basis is the Mosaic Record, and if the Mosaic Record and the early history of man as we find it in the Pentateuch, is merely a compilation of old legends and traditions that may be true or false, or may be part true and part false, then Christianity rests upon a foundation so frail and unreliable that, so far from commanding our respect, merely provokes contempt.

By comparing the Mosaic Record with the cosmogonies of the ancients in the corrupted condition in which they have descended to us, it is easy to see that monotheism is the principal characteristic which they have in common. Hence, no process of reasoning could be so illogical than that which leads the skeptic to decide that the Mosaic Record was derived from the ancients. But neither the advocates of the Bible or its opponents should be content to rest their case here; neither should be satisfied to confine their investigations to ascertaining the origin of the Bible; but each should seek a solution of the question. From what source did these most highly civilized and enlightened peoples of antiquity of whom profane history and tradition gives us any knowledge obtain their belief in monotheism? The atheist admits that monotheism is the most exalted religious belief; and that the earliest men in their ignorance and inexperience could never have conceived it; but that it was only possible to attain to it by a process of development from other beliefs, extending through long periods of time. But no vestige of such development exists. Monotheism, the belief in one God only—the Creator of the universe —He who rewards the good and punishes the wicked —looms up in the remote past, in all its grandeur and sublimity, as the earliest and universal belief of the globe. This being true it follows that atheism can throw no light on the origin of monotheism; on the contrary, the antiquity and universality of this sublime conception, utterly disproves the theories of atheists as to the origin of religious beliefs. Hence, we must seek elsewhere for a solution of the question as to where the great nations of antiquity obtained their belief in monotheism; and the Bible, profane history, and the most ancient traditions furnish the only explanation.

As has been shown, the Bible teaches that man was created "in the image of God;" that he was designed for a special purpose, and assigned to a specific task; that Adam and Eve were given a fixed place of abode in the Garden of Eden; that in the Garden of Eden God held personal intercourse with Adam and Eve, our first parents, and implanted in their minds the doctrine of monotheism; that He revealed to them the great events of the Creation, together with a vast amount of invaluable knowledge for their enlightenment and guidance, and that of their descendants throughout the ages that were to come. The most ancient and reliable traditions teach us that Adam was the author of arts and letters; and that he transmitted in writing to his descendants the "precepts" which God delivered to him in Eden. Profane history has preserved and handed these traditions down to us. The Bible also teaches that at an early period in their history the descendants of Adam disregarded the "precepts" of God; violated His laws; and many descended to the perpetration of crimes so beastly as to result in corrupting the flesh of the earth, thus assailing God's Plan of Creation at its most vital point. The rapid increase of this crime for many centuries threatened the utter destruction of God's Plan of Creation, and made it necessary for Him, in order to preserve it, to send upon the earth a universal deluge, and destroy this corrupted flesh and those who were instrumental in corrupting it, together with the animals that were not saved with Noah and his family in the ark.

The Bible teaches that Noah and his family were monotheists; and tradition indicates that they received the doctrine of monotheism from their ancestors in writing, and that they transmitted it in writing to their descendants. After the Deluge God made a covenant with Noah and his family in which He promised that He would not again destroy every thing living as He had done. God also gave Noah and his family the commands given to Adam in the Creation: "Be fruitful, and multiply, and replenish the earth;" at the same time He delivered into their hands the fish of the sea, the fowl of the air, and the land animals. All the facts indicate that for a long period after the Deluge the descendants of Noah lived in obedience to the laws of God, and developed upon the various continents, those superb civilizations, the remains of which, even in their ruins, attest the skill, culture, and refinement of their architects. But in the course of time the descendants of Noah, like the antediluvians, disregarded the "precepts" of God; violated His laws, and abandoned themselves to the same loathsome crime that brought destruction upon the antediluvian world; God then showered His curses upon them in the form of war, famine, and pestilence. Thus whole nations were destroyed from off the earth; their civilizations laid in ruins, and their once prosperous homes were transformed into the abodes of barbarians and savages their crimes had produced.

After entering upon their career of crime, the decendants of Noah gradually renounced monothe-

ism, and decended to atheism and idolatry; in their
long, destructive wars, and the many discouraging
vicissitudes through which they passed for centuries,
their literature, sacred and profane was lost, and
monotheism and the history of their remote ancestors survived only in tradition; and in the course of
time, even these traditions became so confused with
errors and superstitions as to render them of no
practical value. Persisting in their wicked, demoralizing course, they finally reached such depths of
ignorance and depravity as to render it impossible
for them unaided to regain their lost knowledge and
position. Then God in His wisdom, His justice, His
mercy, and in His wondrous love for man, decided
to make a second revelation to man, of the great
events of the Creation in the order of their occurrence; and also to reveal to man a knowledge of his
kinship with God; his immortality; the design of
God in creating him, and the duties to which he was
assigned in the Creation; and the relations which
God desired him to maintain toward the animals, together with the early history of man down to the
Israelitish occupancy of Canaan; and He selected
Moses, and acquainted him with a knowledge of
these great events, and instructed him to write them
as we have them in the Pentateuch. This explains
why our Bible, in some of its features, bears more or
less resemblance to many of the cosmogonies of the
ancients.

    In order to form a correct estimate of the value
of the Bible, we should first seek to ascertain whether

it is, as it purports to be, of Divine origin, or whether it is merely a human production. And the very nature of the case demands that we first investigate the origin of the Pentateuch, of which the narrative of Creation is an important part. In this investigation let us keep in view the following important truths: (1) That Moses wrote the Pentateuch more than thirty-five centuries before the birth of modern science. (2) That at the time it was written, the world was under the sway of the old cosmogonies of Egypt, Babylon, Assyria, India, China, America, etc., all of which were so loaded with errors and superstitions as to provoke the contempt and ridicule of the modern scientists. (3) That Moses, though an Israelite, was reared by a princess of Egypt, and was educated as an Egyptian.

The Egyptians taught that the heavens and the earth originated out of a kind of pulp, and that man was generated from the slime of the river Nile. There were other Egyptian philosophers who taught that the world was hatched from a winged egg. The Bible tells us that "Moses was learned in all the wisdom of the Egyptians;" yet his cosmogony bears no resemblance to theirs. What power enabled Moses to divest his mind of the atheism and idolatry which characterized the age in which he lived, repudiate the old cosmogonies with which he was so familiar, and write a cosmogony of the universe that is faultless in the light of modern science? If Moses and the other authors of the Bible were not enlightened and guided by some higher power, how is it that their writings are absolutely free from the errors and superstitions which characterize the old philosophers who preceded, and those who followed them or were contemporary with them? It should be unnecessary to remind our readers that the ancient theories which thrust God aside, and attributed the origin of the universe to other sources, were the expression of the purest atheism. But modern science with its telescopes, microscopes, spectroscopes, and other implements and appliances, has exposed their fallacies, and the intelligence of the world has thrown them aside as worthless. The Bible, with its explanation of the origin of the universe is more ancient than many of these old cosmogonies, and contemporaneous with all of them; it was subjected to the same severe tests which modern science applied to them, and to which they succumbed. But after the most prolonged, rigid investigation, often conducted with evident unfairness, where does the Bible stand to-day? Peerless in the realm of literature—peculiar, in that it is the only book without a flaw—the Bible bears upon its every page the evidences of its divine origin, as shown by the fact that it is the only book that will stand at every point, the crucial test of modern science.

CHAPTER II.

The Beginning and the First Day.

"In the beginning God created the heaven and the earth.

"And the earth was without form, and void; and darkness was upon the face of the deep. And the Spirit of God moved upon the face of the waters." (*Gen.* i, 1-2.)

The sublimity of the opening declaration of the Mosaic Record that, "in the beginning God created the heaven and the earth," is unparalleled in the world's literature. Its description of infinite intelligence combined with infinite power in a single personage is such as only the mind of Deity could have conceived, and thus, at once, goes far to prove the existence of God and the divine origin of the Bible.

The first verse of Genesis teaches that there is a God; a personal God; a Creator separate and distinct from His creation. "The central idea is creation." But in order to fully understand the meaning of this scriptural teaching we must first ascertain what constitutes a *creation* as described in the Mosaic Record. This evidently describes the bringing into existence of some new element, and its introduction into the material universe.

In discussing this question, Professor Guyot says: "The Hebrew word is *bará*, translated by

41

335

create. It has been doubted whether the word meant a creation, in the sense that the world was not derived from any pre-existing material, nor from the substance of God Himself; but the manner in which it is here used does not seem to justify such a doubt. For whatever be the use of the word *bará* in other parts of the Bible, it is employed in this chapter in a discriminating way, which is very remarkable, and cannot but be intentional. It occurs only on three occasions, the *first* creation of matter in the first verse, the first introduction of life on the fifth day, and the *creation* of man on the sixth day. Elsewhere, when only transformations are meant, as on the second and fourth days, or a continuation of the same kind of creation, as in the land animals of the fifth day, the word *asáh* (make) is used. Again, it is a significant fact that in the whole Bible where the simple form of *bará* is used it is always with reference to a work made by God, but never by man." (*Creation*, pp. 29, 30, 31.)

This enables us to realize the broad distinction which the inspired author draws between *creation* and *formation*. A *creation* is the bringing into existence and introduction into the material universe of some new element. A *formation* is something made out of some pre-existing material—the result of a mere change wrought in the form of the original element.

The Mosaic Record teaches that there are three —and only three—*creations*. The first creation is described in connection with the heaven and the earth, "in the beginning." The second creation is described in connection with the introduction of animal life on the "fifth day." The third creation is described in connection with the introduction of man on the "sixth day."

"In the beginning" the first step in creation was the bringing into existence, and the introduction into what was then empty space, the material out of which all bodies are formed. This creation is described as that of "the heaven and the earth." Science applies the term *matter* to the lowest element of which it has any knowledge; and teaches that matter is the material out of which all bodies are formed. Science teaches that matter exists in the material universe in just three forms, the *solid*, *liquid* and *gaseous*; and inasmuch as all bodies, celestial and terrestrial, are resolvable into matter in its gaseous state, science very properly decides that matter in its gaseous state was the primitive condition of all bodies.

In discussing this question, Professor Guyot says: "Minerals, plants, animals—all bodies of nature—are compound results of processes which speak of a previous condition. By decomposing them, and undoing what has been done before, we finally arrive at the simple chemical elements which are the substratum of all bodies. The same may be said of the three forms of matter—solid, liquid and gaseous. The least defined—the one in which the atoms are the most free—is the gaseous. All bodies in nature can be reduced to this, the simplest form of matter." (*Ibid*, pp. 39, 40.)

Dr. Patterson says: "Homogenous, gaseous

337

matter has been separated, investigated and found to have the Creator's mark. Science has penetrated even into the constitution of matter, and from the constitution of its smallest parts, the molecules of which each element is composed, it has demonstrated the necessity for, and the proof of, the existence of a maker. The ultimate molecules of matter are made, manufactured, and bear the manufacturer's brand indelibly stamped upon each one of them. Allow me to cite the words of one whose name will insure respect from all scientists—Prof. James Clerk Maxwell, in his lecture before the British Association as given in the *Scientific American*, and cited in the *Interior* Sept. 4, 1873:

"'Professor Clerk Maxwell lately delivered an interesting lecture before the British Association, upon molecules, by which is meant the subdivision of matter into the greatest possible number of portions, similar to each other. Thus, if a number of molecules of water are combined, they form a mass of water. Molecules of some compound substances may be subdivided into their component substances. Thus the molecule of water separates into two molecules of hydrogen and one of oxygen.

"'Professor Maxwell has calculated the size and weight of hydrogen molecules, and finds that about two millions of them, placed side by side in a row would occupy a length of about one twenty-fifth of an inch, and that a package of them containing a million million million million of them would weigh sixty-two grains, or not quite one-eighth of an ounce.

"'Each molecule throughout the universe, bears impressed upon it the stamp of a metric system as distinctly as does the meter of the archives at Paris, or the double royal cubit of the Temple of Karnac.

"'No theory of evolution can be formed to account for the similarity of molecules, for evolution necessarily implies continuous change, and the molecule is incapable of growth or decay, of generation or destruction. None of the processes of nature, since the time when nature began, have produced the slightest difference in the properties of any molecule. We are, therefore, unable to ascribe either the existence of the molecules or the identity of their properties to the operation of any of the causes which we call natural. On the other hand, the exact equality of each molecule to all others of the same kind gives it, as Sir John Herschel has well said, the essential character of a manufactured article, and precludes the idea of its being eternal and self-existent.

"'Thus we have been led, by a strictly scientific path, very near to the point at which science must stop. Not that science is debarred from studying the internal mechanism of a molecule which she cannot take to pieces, any more than from investigating an organism which she cannot put together, but in tracing back the history of matter, science is arrested when she assures herself, on the one hand, that the molecule has been made, and on the other, that it has not been made by any of the processes we call natural.

"'Science is incompetent to reason upon the crea-

tion of matter itself out of nothing. We have
reached the utmost limit of our thinking faculties
when we have admitted that because matter cannot
be eternal and seft-existent, it must have been created. It is only when we contemplate, not matter in
itself, but the form in which it actually exists, that
our mind finds something on which it can lay hold.
That matter, as such, should have certain fundamental properties, that it should exist in space and
be capable of motion, that its motion should be
persistent, and so on, are truths which may, for
anything we know, be of the kind which metaphy-
sicians call necessary. We may use our knowledge
of such truths for purposes of deduction, but we
have no data for speculating as to their origin. But
that there should be exactly so much matter and no
more in every molecule of hydrogen, is a fact of a
very different order. We have here a particular
distribution of matter, a collocation, to use the expression of Dr. Chalmers, of things which we have
no difficulty in imagining to have been arranged
otherwise. The form and dimensions of the orbits
of the planets, for instance, are not determined by
any law of nature, but depend upon a particular
collocation of matter. The same is the case with
respect to the size of the earth, from which the
standard of what is called the metrical system has
been derived. But these astronomical and terrestrial
magnitudes are far inferior in scientific importance
to that most fundamental of all standards which
forms the base of the molecular system. Natural
causes, as we know, are at work, which tend to

modify, if they do not at length destroy, all the arrangements and dimensions of the earth and the whole solar system. But though in the course of ages catastrophies have occurred, and may yet occur in the heavens, though ancient systems may be dissolved and new systems evolved out of their ruins, the molecules out of which these systems are built —the foundation stones of the material universe— remain unbroken and unworn. They continue this day as they were created, perfect in number, and measure, and weight, and from the ineffaceable characters impressed on them we may learn that those aspirations after accuracy in measurement, truth in statement, and justice in action, which we reckon among our noblest attributes as men, are ours because they are essentially constituents of the image of Him who in the beginning created, not only the heaven and the earth, but the materials of which heaven and earth consist.'" (*Errors of Evolution*, pp. 73, 74, 75, 76.)

Thus science teaches that matter, the material of which all bodies are formed, is not eternal and self-existent. But that its "ultimate molecules are made," and "not by any process that we call natural;" that they present "the character of a manufactured article;" and "bear the manufacturer's brand indelibly stamped upon each one of them." The teaching of science that the molecules of matter of which "the heaven and the earth" are composed are not eternal and self-existent, proves that they had a beginning; that they were created, and thus goes far to sustain the teachings of scripture that its creator is God. We are thus enabled to realize that the creation of *matter*, the basis of all formation in the material universe, consisted in God's bringing into existence the molecules of matter.

Additional proof that the creation which God created "in the beginning," and which is described as that of "the heaven and the earth," was the bringing into existence of matter, is shown by the following:

1. The formation of the heaven and the earth, as they now exist began on the "first day" of the cosmogonic week, a period distinct from and long subsequent to "the beginning."

2. The language of the second verse of Genesis gives an exact description of matter in its primordial, or gaseous state. In discussing this subject Professor Guyot says: "The matter just created was gaseous; it was without form, for the property of gas is to expand indefinitely. It was void, or empty, because apparently homogenous and invisible. It was dark, because as yet inactive, light being the result of the action of physical and chemical forces not yet awakened. It was a deep, for its expansion in space, though indefinite, was not infinite, and it had dimensions. And the Spirit of God moved upon the face (outside and not inside, as the pantheist would have it) of that vast, inert, gaseous mass, ready to impart to it motion, and to direct all its subsequent activity, according to a plan gradually revealed by the works of the great cosmic days." (*Ibid*, p. 38.)

Thus science clearly proves that the Creation which God created "in the beginning," which is described as that of "the heaven and the earth," was *matter*, the material out of which "the heaven and the earth" were afterwards formed.

In absolute conflict with the teachings of science, atheism teaches that "matter is eternal and imperishable." (See *Haeckel's History of Creation*, Vol. I, p. 8.)

3. The first verse of Genesis, in harmony with science, teaches that matter, the material out of which "the heaven and the earth" was formed, is not eternal, but that it had a beginning.

But when was the "beginning"? Evidently the "beginning," as described in the first verse of Genesis, marks a period distinct from the "first day," as the "first day" marks a period distinct from the "second day." If the "beginning" and the "first day" were one period, the two terms would not have been employed to describe it; but such is not the case; the "beginning" and the "first day" mark different epochs in the history of matter. Hence, the two terms, the "beginning" and the "first day," are employed to describe them. Further evidence that the "beginning," in which matter was created, is a period distinct from the "first day," is found in the fact that the second verse of Genesis gives a description of gaseous matter that is "dark, because inactive," and absolutely still; while the "first day," as we shall hereafter show, begins with the movement of matter, the initial step in the formation of "the heaven and the earth." Though we were long ago impressed with the fact that the "beginning" and the "first day," described in Genesis, marked differ-

ent epochs in the history of the universe, we are
pleased to find that our views are entertained by so
high an authority as Chancellor Dawson, who says:
"The material universe was brought into existence
in the 'beginning'—a term evidently indefinite as
regards any known epoch, and implying merely pri-
ority to all other recorded events. It cannot be the
first day, for there is no expressed connection, and
the work of the first day is distinct from that of the
beginning. It cannot be a general term for the whole
six days, since these are separated from it by that
chaotic or formless state to which we are next introduced. The beginning, therefore, is the threshold
of creation—the line that separates the old tenantless condition of space from the world-crowded
galaxies of the existing universe. The only other information respecting it that we have in scripture is in
that fine descriptive poem in Proverbs viii, in which
the wisdom of God personified—who may be held to
represent the Almighty Word, or Logos, introduced
in the formula 'God said,' and afterward referred to
in scripture as the manifested or conditioned Deity,
the mediator between man and the otherwise inac-
cessible Divinity, the agent in the work of creation,
as well as in that of redemption—narrates the origin
of all created things:
"'Jehovah possessed* me, the beginning of his way,
Before his work of old.
I was set up from everlasting,
From the beginning, before the earth was;
When there were no deeps I was brought forth,
When there were no fountains abounding in water.'"
"* Not created, as some read. The verb is *Kana*, not *bará*."

"The beginning here precedes the creation of the earth, as well as the deep which encompassed its surface in its earliest condition. The beginning in this point of view, stretches back from the origin of the world into the depths of eternity. It is to us emphatically *the* beginning, because it witnessed the birth of our material system; but to the eternal Jehovah it was but the beginning of a great series of His operations, and we have no information of its absolute duration." (*The Origin of the World*, pp. 95, 96).

We feel assured that careful investigation will reveal the strength of our position that, between the "beginning," and the "first day" of the cosmogonic week, "there is no expressed connection;" and that the work of the "first day," is distinct from that of the "beginning." The "beginning," therefore, must be regarded as the period when God brought to an end "the old tenantless condition of space" by bringing into existence, and introducing into it, the molecules of matter. Hence, the "beginning" precedes the birth of time, which occurred on the "first day" of the cosmogonic week. Between the "beginning" and the "first day," there was an interval; but in our attempt to ascertain the length of this interval, science, which deals alone with second causes, is powerless to aid us, and Divine revelation alone can throw any light; reason fails to grasp this starting point in creation, and even the imagination sees the "beginning" recede from view as it fades away into the unfathomable depths of eternity.

Thus, the book of Genesis teaches that matter

is not eternal and self-existent, but that it had a beginning. This being true, we should not be surprised to find that the book of Revelation plainly teaches that the heaven and the earth which God formed out of matter will not be eternal, but will have an ending.

In the book of *Revelation*, John gives an account of a series of events which were revealed to him; but which were evidently not revealed to him in the order of their occurrence.

In his *first* vision he proceeds to describe an event which he says "must shortly come to pass." (*Rev.* i, 1). This was evidently the final destruction of the heaven and the earth, as shown by the following:

"And I beheld when he had opened the sixth seal, and, lo, there was a great earthquake; and the sun became black as sackcloth of hair, and the moon became as blood; and the stars of heaven fell unto the earth, even as a fig tree casteth her untimely figs, when she is shaken of a mighty wind. And the heaven departed as a scroll when it is rolled together; and every mountain and island were moved out of their places. And the kings of the earth, and the great men, and the rich men, and the chief captains, and the mighty men, and every bondman, and every free man, hid themselves in the dens and in the rocks of the mountains; and said to the mountains and rocks, Fall on us, and hide us from the face of Him that sitteth on the throne, and from the wrath of the Lamb; For the great day of His wrath is come; and who shall be able to stand?"

(*Rev.* vi, 12, 13, 14, 15, 16, 17). "And I saw another mighty angel come down from heaven, clothed
with a cloud; and a rainbow was upon his head, and
his face was as it were the sun, and his feet as pillars
of fire: And he had in his hand a little book open:
And he set his right foot upon the sea, and his left
foot on the earth. * * * And the angel which I
saw stand upon the sea and upon the earth lifted up
his hand to heaven, and sware by Him that liveth
forever and ever, who created heaven, and the things
that therein are, and the earth, and the things that
therein are, and the sea, and the things which are
therein, that there should be time no longer." (*Rev.*
x, 1, 2, 5, 6).

In a subsequent vision, John says: "And I saw
a great white throne, and Him that sat on it, from
whose face the earth and the heaven fled away; and
there was found no place for them. And I saw the
dead, small and great, stand before God; and the
books were opened: and another book was opened,
which is the book of life: and the dead were judged
out of those things which were written in the books,
according to their works." (*Rev.* xx, 11, 12). "And
He said unto me, It is done. I am Alpha and Omega,
the beginning and the end." (*Rev.* xxi, 6). "And
He that sat on the throne said, Behold, I make all
things new." (*Rev.* xxi, 5). In confirmation of
this, John tells us: "And I saw a new heaven and a
new earth: for the first heaven and the first earth
were passed away; and there was no more sea. And
I, John, saw the holy city, new Jerusalem, coming
down from God out of heaven, prepared as a bride

adorned for her husband." (*Rev.* xxi, 1, 2). This "new heaven" which John saw, was not the final abode of the blest, for this is described as *the holy city, New Jerusalem;* it was a *material* heaven, with all the phenomena of sun, moon, and stars, which characterizes our material heaven. The "new earth" which John saw was a *material* earth, with all the phenomena of plant, animal, and immortal life, which characterizes our earth.

The intense, inconceivable heat, resulting from the falling of the luminaries upon "the earth, even as a fig tree casteth her untimely figs, when she is shaken of a mighty mind," would resolve the *solid* and *liquid matter* of the universe into its original *gaseous state.* When this immense gaseous mass, has lost its activity, and become *stilled*, it will be in just the condition described in Gen. i, 2; and out of this immense mass of gaseous matter, God will form the "new heaven and the new earth," which John saw; and his promise to "make all things new," will be redeemed.

Natural science teaches that matter is *imperishable.* (Haeckel). And that of all the immense volume of matter in the universe, not one atom is ever lost. Mr. Haeckel in discussing this question says: "Where a natural body seems to disappear, as for example by burning, decaying, evaporation, etc., it merely changes its form, its physical composition or chemical combination. In like manner the coming into existence of a natural body, for example, of a crystal, a fungus, an infusorium, depends merely upon the different particles, which had before existed

in a certain form or combination, assuming a new
form or combination in consequence of changed conditions of existence. But never yet has an instance
been observed of even the smallest particle of matter
having vanished, or even of an atom being added to
the already existing mass." (*History of Creation*,
Vol. i, p. 8).

Who, but the great Architect of the universe,
could have brought into existence this wonderful
combination of elements, which *is not self-existent*,
neither is it *destructible* through any physical agency;
and *out of which all bodies are formed?* In the
absence of a better name, we may regard the term
universe, as descriptive of a *vast receptacle*, in which
matter was *created*, in which it is *held*, and from which
not an atom ever *escapes*. And just as the existence
of matter, even in its primitive state, *the gaseous*,
clearly demonstrates the existence of a *Creator*, so
does this preservation of matter clearly demonstrate
the existence of a *preserver*. And just as the presence of matter in all its varied forms, celestial and
terrestrial, in which we find it to-day, bespeaks *design*,
so does this careful preservation of even the minutest atom of matter, bespeak the most far-reaching
design; and this *design*, we find revealed in John's
vision of "a new heaven and a new earth."

This indicates that the command be "not sloth-
ful in business," never emanated from a being who
is himself an idler; and that prior to the formation
of our present world, God has not occupied His
throne in the heaven of heavens in utter idleness.

But that just as it is man's disposition to *combine*, so is it God's disposition to *create*.

We are not of those who think with Bruno that there *are* other worlds than ours, and that perhaps many of them are inhabited. On the contrary, we accept the plain teaching of the Bible that the *earth* is the only habitable globe; and that the sun, moon, and stars, were made for the purposes described in the *Mosaic Record*. But we feel assured that there *were* other "worlds" than ours; and that each of them possessed an inhabited earth, and that there will be other worlds than ours, and that they also will each have an inhabited earth. It was one of these—the one which will supercede our world—that John saw in his vision.

The evidence that other "worlds" similar to ours preceeded it, is found in the statements of Paul as follows: "God, who at sundry times and in divers manners spake in time past unto the fathers by the prophets, hath in these last days spoken unto us by His Son, whom He hath appointeth heir of all things, by whom also He made the worlds." (*Heb.* i, 1, 2). "Through faith we understand that the worlds were framed by the word of God. (*Heb.* xi, 3). If our world was not preceded by others similar to it, why does Paul refer to *worlds*, thus using the *plural* and in the *past tense?* Evidently, Paul desired us to understand that there *were* other worlds than ours, just as John desired us to understand that there *will be* other worlds than ours.

This being true it follows that *the beginning*, as described in the first verse of the first chapter of Genesis, must be sought for *in the remotest depths of eternity;* and that, intervening between *the beginning* in which *matter* was *created*, and the production of light as described in the third verse of the first chapter of Genesis, there is an *interval* of such *inconceivable magnitude* as can only be measured by a *succession* of perhaps myriads of worlds like ours.

Both scripture and science teach that this world had a *beginning;* and while science clearly indicates, the Bible plainly states that this world will have an *ending.*

The initial step in the formation of the world,— *the movement of matter*, resulting in *the production of light*, on the "first day," as described in the third verse of the first chapter of Genesis,—marked *the beginning of time;* while the declaration of the angel whom John saw "stand upon the sea and upon the earth," and "sware" that "there should be time no longer"—marked *the end of time.* This indicates that time begins with the formation of a *world*, and ends *with its dissolution.* Hence, time is but a *period of eternity* just as a *day*, or a *week*, or a *year*, *is a period of time.* This enables us to realize that, just as a plant, or an animal, has its germ, its formative period, its youth, its maturity, its decline, and its final dissolution, so has a world its germ—*matter* —its formative period, as described in the *Mosaic Record;* its youth, its maturity, its decline, and its *final dissolution*, described in *Revelation.* Further evidence is found in the fact that God generously imparted to John the knowledge, which he transmits to us that, "the first heaven and the first earth had passed away," and that the *sea* had also passed away. Then the kindly hand which led Joseph as a flock, gently thrust aside the veil, which intervenes between time and eternity, and enabled John, in the light of *inspired revelation* to behold the amazing spectacle, of a "a new heaven and a new earth."

This exalted view of God, and His creative power, as clearly revealed in the scriptures, and as clearly sustained by the scriptures, should enable us to more fully realize, and to more highly appreciate the truth, and sublimity of that inspiring declaration of the Psalmist: "Before the mountains were brought forth, or ever thou hadst formed the earth and the world, even from everlasting to everlasting thou art God."

THE FIRST COSMOGONIC DAY.

THE PRODUCTION OF LIGHT.

"And God said, Let there be light: and there was light.

"And God saw the light, that it was good: and God divided the light from the darkness.

"And God called the light Day, and the darkness, He called Night. And the evening and the morning were the first day. (*Gen.* i, 3, 4, 5).

The opinion is generally entertained by those who profess to believe in the Bible that there was a creation, that is, that something was *created*, on each one of the six days of the cosmogonic week; but this is a mistake, as shown by the language of the narrative. As shown in a previous chapter, there are *three*—and *only* three creations described in the Mosaic Record; the first of these—the *matter* creation—occurred in the "beginning," a period distinct from the cosmogonic week, which opened on the "first day." The *second* creation is described in connection with the introduction of animal life on the "fifth day;" and the *third* creation is described in connection with the introduction of man on the "sixth day." Hence, there were but *two* creations which occurred within the cosmogonic week. And it is significant that no creation is described in connection with the "first day."

In discussing God's command, "Let there be light," Professor Guyot says:

"We have now a starting point, but yet no activity, no progress. All beginnings are in darkness and silence. The era of progress opens with the first day's work. At God's command, movement begins and the first result is the production of light. This was no creation, but a simple manifestation of the activity of matter; for, according to modern physics, heat and light are but different intensities of the vibratory motions of matter." (*Creation*, pp. 43, 44).

This being true, it follows that God's command, "Let there be light," was equivalent to His commanding, Let there be movement in matter! To those who have never investigated the subject, it may seem a matter of surprise that the chaotic condition of the universe as described in the second verse of Genesis, should be followed by the production of light which was evidently not derived from the luminaries, since they were not in existence; but

Mr. Guyot's explanation enables us to understand that this was not *solar* light, but *cosmic* light, resulting from the movement of matter.

Many theories have been advanced to explain how God divided the light from the darkness; but upon investigating them, we have been compelled to reject them all as being in conflict with the general teachings of the Mosaic Record. We have no data upon which to base an opinion as to how God divided the light from the darkness, and in the absence of data, we decline to speculate, since mere speculation is apt to mislead; besides, we should profit by the silence of the inspired writer upon the subject, and be silent.

The length of time embraced in the term "day," which the inspired writer employs in his division of the cosmogonic week, has been the subject of no little controversy among students of the Bible; many believe them to have been solar days of twenty-four hours; but the falsity of this belief is shown by the record; the solar day of twenty-four hours is measured by the sun, while *three* of the creative days passed before the sun was made. Further evidence that the days described in the Mosaic Record were not days of twenty-four hours, but were indefinite periods of time, is found in Genesis ii, 4, where the whole creative week is described as the "*day* that the Lord God made the earth and the heavens." Upon the question as to whether the days of the creative week were solar days or days of twenty-four hours each, or whether they were periods of indefinite length, the science of geology furnishes the most ab-

354

solute proof. The Mosaic Record teaches that the fish, and fowl, and beast, and man, were all brought into existence on the fifth and sixth days of the creative week. The remains of the first animals to make their appearance on the globe are found in the lower stratas of the earth; while those of more recent origin, as well as those of man, are found nearest the surface of the earth. Between the remains of the earliest animals which are found deepest in the earth, and the remains of man, which are found nearest the surface, there are immense deposits, thousands of feet in thickness, which furnish the most conclusive proof that they were not made in the brief space of two days of twenty-four hours each. Thus science and the scriptures combine to teach us that the days of the cosmogonic week were long periods of time that are not to be measured by hours, but by ages. The six cosmogonic days closes with the creation of man on the sixth day; this is followed by the seventh day: "And on the seventh day God ended His work which He had made; and He rested on the seventh day from all His work which He had made. And God blessed the seventh day, and sanctified it: because that in it He had rested from all His work which God created and made." (Gen. ii, 2, 3).

The following command was given in the Decalogue to commemorate the six cosmogonic days in which God created the material universe, and the seventh day in which He rested from His works: "Remember the Sabbath day, to keep it holy. Six days shalt thou labor, and do all thy work; but the

seventh day is the Sabbath of the Lord thy God; in
it thou shalt not do any work, thou, nor thy son,
nor thy daughter, thy manservant, nor thy maid-
servant, nor thy cattle, nor the stranger that is
within thy gates." (*Ex.* xx, 8, 9, 10). Thus a
weekly Sabbath was prescribed as a memorial of the
seventh day in which God rested from his work of
Creation.

It will be observed that the seventh day described in Genesis ii, 4, unlike the preceding six
days, is not divided into an evening and morning;
but more significant still is the fact that no mention
is made of an eighth day following the seventh day.
This indicates that the seventh day has not yet
ended. Both the scriptures and the sciences teach
that there has been no creation since the creation of
man; from this it follows that God has not resumed
His work, and that the seventh day is still in existence; that it will continue to exist throughout time,
and that the destruction of the heavens and the earth
will mark its close. The language of the Mosaic
Record clearly indicates that the seventh day upon
which God rested from His work began immediately
after the creation of man and his assignment to the
duties upon the earth for which he was designed,
and that man has always labored, and will continue
to labor on God's day of rest, which will close with
the end of time. The fact that the seventh day—
God's day of rest—has continued from the Creation
to the present time with no evidence of the near approach of its end, show that God's days, unlike man's
days, are indefinitely long periods of time; it also

goes far to prove that each of the six creative days which preceded it were correspondingly long periods of time. We have no means of ascertaining the length of the six creative days, or that of the seventh day; but we feel assured that the strict order and harmony which characterizes all of God's works, is expressed in the length of the six creative days and in the seventh day which followed them; and that they are all of equal duration, else why was the creative work divided into periods at all? Hence, if we could ascertain the length of any one of the creative days, we would have the length of every other one of the creative days and that of the seventh day which followed them. Then if we could ascertain just how long it has been since man was created, we could calculate to a nicety just how long it will be before the angel will stand with one foot upon the sea, and one upon the land, and raising his hand to heaven will declare the end of time.

CHAPTER III.

Formation of the Heavens.

"And God said, Let there be a firmament in the midst of the waters, and let it separate the waters from the waters.

"And God made the firmament, and separated the waters which were under the firmament from the waters which were above the firmament, and it was so.

"And God called the firmament heaven. And the evening and the morning were the second day." (*Gen.* i, 6, 7, 8).

From a mere casual glance at the texts describing the work of the first and second creative days, we would be led to suppose that the work of those days was confined solely to the subjects mentioned —the production of light, the formation of the heavens, etc. But when we examine the texts describing the work of the first and second creative days in connection with verse 9, of the Record, which describes the first work of the third creative day, it becomes plain that while the heavens were being formed, the earth also was being formed; and that when the formation of the heavens were completed, the formation of the earth was completed; and it is highly probable that the formation of the earth really began with the movement of matter on the first day.

64

Be this as it may, the language of the text describing the opening work of the third creative day leaves no room for doubt that at the close of the second creative day, the formation of the earth, as well as that of the heavens, were completed, as shown by the following:

"And God said, Let the waters under the heaven be gathered together into one place, and let the dry land appear. And God called the dry land earth; and the gathering together of the waters called he seas: and God saw that it was good." (*Gen.* i, 9, 10).

Thus, the first command given on the third creative day clearly shows that at the opening of that day, the earth was already formed, and that its formation was completed on the second creative day when the heavens were formed. Hence, the first command given on the third creative day resulted in the waters enveloping the earth, perhaps in the form of vapor, being condensed into water, and these waters gathered together into the indentations in the earth's surface, which God had prepared for their reception, and which he called "seas." This shows the close relationship which exists between the heaven and the earth: (1) from the fact that the formation of each was completed on the second cosmogonic day; (2) from the fact that the heaven was formed around the earth. The egg of a fowl with its yolk surrounded by the white albuminous part, and the shell enveloping the whole, would very properly represent the relations which the earth, the atmosphere, and the heaven sustain to each other; the *yolk* would represent the earth; the white of the egg would represent the surrounding atmosphere; and the shell, enveloping the whole, would represent the heaven. The correctness of our illustration is demonstrated by the fact that, at whatever point we stand and look out from the earth, we face the heaven. This could not be so if the heaven did not envelope the earth and its atmosphere, just as the shell envelopes the *white* and the *yolk* of the egg.

Further evidence of this is found in the language of the text: "And God said, Let there be a firmament in the midst of the waters, and let it divide the waters from the waters. And God made the firmament, and divided the waters which were under the firmament from the waters which were above the firmament; and it was so." What was so? Simply that the firmament or heaven was made, and subserved the purpose for which it was designed; it separated the waters above it from the waters beneath it. It is easy to see that, to act as a separator between the waters above it and the waters beneath it, the firmament must be impervious to water, though not necessarily impervious to heat and light; glass, for example, though impervious to water, is penetrated by the rays of heat and light.

Our views as to the existence of a firmament or heaven impervious to water enveloping the earth and its atmosphere, brings us in conflict with the modern "World-builders" who attempt to thrust God aside and substitute their own atheistic theories as to the origin of the universe for His word; our views will also be in conflict with those of the many theologians who attempt to twist the word of God and the sciences into harmony with the theories of atheists, but this will give us little concern so long as we are in perfect harmony with the scripture and the sciences.   We shall let the Bible tell its own story, and shall appeal to the sciences to demonstrate its truth whenever it is possible for them to do so. We recognize God—the Creator of the heaven and the earth—as the author of all language and all speech.   Hence we unhesitatingly accord Him the most unerring knowledge of the value of words; and when He tells us that He made a firmament or heaven in the midst of the waters to separate the waters above it from the waters beneath it, we at once recognize the firmament or heaven as impervious to water, atheists, infidels, and so-called theologians to the contrary notwithstanding.

It will be observed that in the second verse of the Mosaic Record, the inspired writer terms the gaseous matter of the universe "waters." "And the Spirit of God moved upon the face of the waters." The language of the text describing the work of the second and third creative days as above quoted, shows that the earth was the first of the great bodies formed; that it was formed in the midst of the immense gaseous mass of the universe, described as "waters;" and that on the second creative day God made a firmament in the midst of the waters, and enveloped the earth, which, if not already formed, was in process of formation, and thus separated the waters above, or on the outside of the firmament, from the waters beneath, or within the firmament.

Hence, the first work of the third creative day was to condense into water the vapors enveloping the earth, and the gathering of these "waters" into "seas," to "let the dry land appear."

This teaching of the Mosaic Record that God made a firmament or heaven in the midst of the waters to separate the waters above from the waters beneath it, shows that all the waters of the universe are not confined to the earth, but that an immense amount, perhaps the great bulk of the waters of the universe which enveloped the earth prior to the formation of the heaven, are now situated above the heaven. This teaching of the Bible as to the existence of water above the heaven is fully sustained by the sciences. The planet Mars is one of the heavenly bodies upon which water is known to exist. Sir Robert S. Ball, the eminent professor of astronomy at Dublin, in discussing Mars says:

"It seems hard to decline the suggestion that the marks on the planet may really correspond to the divisions of land and water on that globe. There are circumstances which strongly suggest that water may also be present. At the poles of Mars are large white regions, * * which undergo periodic changes, and it has been surmised that they are due to an accumulation of ice and snow on the polar regions of the planet. On some occasions, indeed, an "ice-cap" on Mars, with its brilliancy and its sharply defined margin, is a striking feature in the telescopic view of the planet." (*The Story of the Heaven*, pp. 186, 187).

The existence of water on Mars has misled many into supposing that its conditions were more or less similar to those of the earth, and that like the earth, Mars was inhabited; these absurdities are entertained in flagrant disregard of the plain teachings of the Bible that, the earth is the only habitable globe, and that the luminaries were designed for other purposes. A few years ago fanaticism on the Mars question ran so high that many were on the lookout for signals from the inhabitants of that planet; and there are not a few who still seriously entertain the belief that we shall soon be in communication with the inhabitants of Mars. These absurd hopes were born of the grossest infidelity and are doomed to disappointment. A few decades ago many who were ignorant of, or indifferent to, the teachings of the Bible that the earth is the only habitable globe, and that the luminaries were designed for other purposes, were loud in the expression of their belief that the moon is inhabited. In their fanaticism they even went so far as to map out and name mountains, seas, etc., on the moon; but later and more careful investigation, aided by improved mechanical appliances, has exploded these theories; it is now known that the moon is practically destitute of both air and water, and is consequently incapable of sustaining either plant or animal life. In contrasting the moon and the other heavenly bodies, Sir Robert S. Ball says:

"But when we look at the moon with our telescopes we see no direct evidence of water. Close inspection shows that the so-called lunar seas are deserts, often marked with small craters and rocks. The telescope reveals no seas and no oceans, no lakes and no rivers. Nor is the grandeur of the moon's scenery ever impaired by clouds over her surface. Whenever the moon is above our horizon, and terrestrial clouds are out of the way, we can see the features of our satellite's surface with distinctness. There are no clouds in the moon; there are not even the mists or the vapors which invariably arise wherever water is present, and therefore astronomers have been led to the conclusion that the surface of the globe which attends the earth is a sterile and a waterless desert.

"Another essential element of organic life is also absent from the moon. Our globe is surrounded with a deep clothing of air resting on the surface, and extending above our heads to the height of about 200 or 300 miles. * * * For all purposes of respiration, as we understand the term, we may say that there is no air on the moon, and an inhabitant of our earth transferred thereto would be as certainly suffocated as he would be in the middle of space. * * * Man is a creature adapted for life under circumstances which are very narrowly limited. A few degrees of temperature more or less, a slight variation in the composition of air, the precise suitability of food, make all the difference between health and sickness, between life and death. Looking beyond the moon, into the length and breadth of the universe, we find countless celestial globes with every conceivabl variety of temperature and of constitution. Amid this vast number of worlds with which space is tenanted, are there any inhabited by living beings? To this great question science can make no response: we can not tell. * * * 'It is not at all probable that among the million spheres of the universe there is a single one exactly like our earth — like it in the possession of air and of water, like it in size and in composition. It does not seem probable that a man could live for one hour on any body in the universe except the earth, or that an oak tree could live in any other sphere for a single season.'" (*The Story of the Heavens*, pp. 76, 77, 78, 79).

Thus the sciences sustain the teachings of scripture that our earth is the only one of the great bodies which possess all the conditions necessary to the existence of planet and animal life. Hence, the presence of water on Mars does not disprove the teachings of the Bible that our earth is the only habitable globe, and that the sun, moon and stars were designed for other purposes. On the other hand, the presence of water on Mars clearly sustains the Bible account of the firmament, or heaven which God made in the midst of the waters, "and divided the waters which were under the firmament from the waters which were above the firmament;" and shows that the waters of Mars are a part of the waters above the firmament. Other parts of these celestial waters are perhaps situated in the clouds and vapors which science teaches us envelop Jupiter. (*Ibid*, p. 217). And doubtless "the waters above the firmament," are distributed among numbers of other planets of the existence of which we have no knowledge; for, with all our boasted astronomical learning our knowledge of the heavens and of the celestial bodies is extremely limited.

It will be observed that the original chaotic condition of the universe is described in the second verse of the Mosaic Record, as the *deep*. "And darkness was upon the face of the deep." But long after the Creation—in the narrative of the Deluge—we find that God said: "And behold I, even I, do bring a flood of waters upon the earth, to destroy all flesh wherein is the breath of life, from under heaven; and everything that is in the earth shall die." (*Gen.* vi, 17). Thus, we are plainly taught that the waters which deluged the earth were not *terrestrial* waters; they did not belong upon the earth, or within it. God said: "I do *bring* a flood of waters upon the earth." The place from which the waters of the Deluge were brought is plainly stated as follows: "In the six hundredth year of Noah's life, in the second month, the seventeenth day of the month, the same day were all the fountains of the great deep broken up, and the windows of heaven were opened. And the rain was upon the earth forty days and forty nights." (*Gen.* vii, 11, 12). Thus, we are told that the waters which deluged the earth were *celestial* waters, which God brought upon the earth in the form of rain for forty days and forty nights.

It will be observed that in Genesis vii, verse 11, as above quoted, the inspired writer refers to the *great* deep—"The same day were all the fountains of the great deep broken up, and the windows of heaven were opened." This term, "the great deep," is a comparative term, and clearly indicates the existence of a *lesser* deep. This enables us to understand (1) that the original "deep" described in the second verse of the Mosaic Record, was divided into a greater and a lesser deep by the firmament which God made "in the midst of the waters," and separated the water above it from the waters beneath it; hence, the "great deep" extends from the firmament which envelops the earth to the utmost limits of the universe; while the lesser deep is that immense space intervening between the firmament and the surface of the earth and its waters. (2) That the "great deep" is the reservoir from which the waters of the Deluge were drawn; and "the *fountains* of the great deep" are the various planets upon which these waters exist; for it is evident that "the waters above the firmament" are not scattered promiscuously throughout the "great deep," but are confined to certain points described as "fountains," and that Mars is evidently one of those "fountains." Hence, when man's shameless crime had corrupted the flesh of the earth, and God decided to "*bring* a flood of waters upon the earth to destroy all flesh wherein is the breath of life from under heaven," He made openings in the firmament or heaven, which are described as "the windows of heaven," and precipitated upon the ·earth "the waters which were above the firmament," and the whole earth was deluged. "And the waters increased exceedingly upon the earth; and all the high hills under the whole heaven were covered. Fifteen cubits upward did the waters prevail, and the mountains were covered." (*Gen.* vii, 19, 20).

Thus, the Bible plainly teaches that the waters which God employed in the Deluge were drawn from "the fountains of the deep," which are situated above the heaven; and that during the Deluge these celestial waters held the same relation to the earth and the terrestrial waters that they sustained prior to the time when God made the "firmament in the midst of the waters to divide the waters from the waters." Hence, man's loathesome crime in corrupting the flesh of the earth, not only corrupted the earth in the eyes of God, but the heaven itself was disastrously affected by it, and the office of separator between the celestial and the terrestrial waters which God designed the firmament to perform was neutralized for the time being; and the waters above it were reunited with the waters beneath it, to the utter destruction of all terrestrial life, save "Noah and they that were with him in the ark."

Further evidence of the reality of the firmament and of the waters above it, and also the fact that the earth was deluged by celestial waters, is shown by the disposition which God made of the waters of the Deluge after the accomplishment of their destructive task, as shown by the following: "And God remembered Noah, and every living thing—that was with him in the ark: and God made a wind to pass over the earth, and the waters assuaged; the fountains also of the deep and the windows of heaven were stopped, and the rain from heaven was restrained; and the waters returned from off the earth continually." (*Gen.* viii, 1, 2, 3). It must be admitted that, for the waters to have *returned* from off the earth at all, they must have returned to the place from whence they came; and this, as has been shown, is above the heaven.

Not only does the inspired writer of the narrative of Creation recognize the reality of the firmament or heaven; the existence of the waters above the heaven; and that the waters of the Deluge were drawn from the celestial regions, and that the Deluge was universal, but David recognized these facts in several of his songs of praise to God, as follows: " Praise Him, ye heavens of heavens, and ye waters that be above the heavens." "Bless the Lord, Oh my soul, * * * who laid the foundations of the earth, that they should not be removed forever. Thou coveredst it with the deep as with a garment: the waters stood above the mountains. At thy rebuke they fled; at the voice of thy thunder, they hasted away. They go up by the mountains; they go down by the valleys unto the place which thou hast founded for them. Thou hast set a bound that they may not pass over; that they come not again to cover the earth." (*Ps.* cxlviii and civ).

Thus the Psalmist not only adds his testimony to that of Moses as to the reality of the firmament or heaven, and the waters above it, but also testifies to the fact that the waters which deluged the earth were *celestial* waters; and that when they had accomplished the destructive mission for which their presence on the earth was designed, and they had *returned from off the earth,* God re-established the firmament or heaven as a "*bound*, that they may not pass over, that they come not again to cover the earth."

Thus the Bible clearly describes the firmament or heaven, which God made "in the midst of the waters," to separate the waters above it from the waters beneath it; and the sciences sustain the Bible at every point where it is possible for them to throw any light upon the subject; and we are even enabled to ascertain, appropriately at least, its temperature, and to determine that it is intensely cold.

Sir Robert Ball, in discussing the temperature of the sun says: "The sun has a temperature far surpassing any that we artificially produce, either in our chemical laboratories or our metallurgical establishments. We can send a galvanic current through a piece of platinum wire. The wire first becomes red hot, then white hot; then it glows with a brilliance almost dazzling until it fuses and breaks. The temperature of the melting platinum wire could hardly be surpassed in the most elaborate furnaces, but it does not attain the temperature of the sun.

"It must, however, be admitted that there is an apparent discrepancy between a well-known physical fact and the extremely high temperature that we find it necessary to attribute to the sun. 'If the sun were hot,' it has been said, then the nearer we approach to him, the hotter we should feel; yet this does not seem to be the case. On the top of a high mountain we are nearer to the sun, and yet everybody knows that it is much colder up there than in the valley beneath. If the mountain be as high as Mt. Blanc, then we are certainly two or three miles nearer; yet, instead of additional warmth, we find eternal snow. A simple illustration will lessen the difficulty. Go into a greenhouse on a sunshiny day, and we find the temperature much hotter there than outside. The glass will permit the hot sunbeams to enter, but it refuses to allow them out again with equal freedom, and consequently the temperature rises. The earth may, from this point of view, be likened to a greenhouse, only instead of the panes of glass, our globe is enveloped by an enormous coating of air. Thus on the earth surface, we are as it were, inside the greenhouse, and we benefit by the interposition of the atmosphere; but when we climb very high mountains, we gradually pass through some of the protecting medium, and then we suffer from the cold. If we could imagine the earth to be deprived of its coat of air, then eternal frost would reign over whole continents as well as on the tops of the mountains." (*Ibid*, pp. 27, 28).

With all due respect for Professor Ball, we must insist that his illustration fails to illustrate. Surely, the greater or less amount of warmth which prevails immediately about the earth's surface, is not produced by its "enormous coating of air." The limit to which the atmosphere extends from the earth, is variously estimated at from 40 to 300 miles; Professor Ball, as quoted above, places it at "200 or 300 miles;" and he shows that the great bulk of the earth's atmosphere is intensely cold. Only a small fraction of it possesses any warmth at all; and this small part is immediately about the earth's surface. This is due to the fact that the rays of heat from the

sun are checked at the surface of the earth, and the
heat accumulates there and warms the stratas of air
immediately enveloping the earth; this heating process is going on continually. Aeronauts have made
balloon ascensions to an altitude of more than seven
miles, but such was the rarity of the atmosphere at
that elevation that it was necessary to pump air to
them from the earth's surface; at the same time the
cold was so intense, that they narrowly escaped being
frozen to death. This shows that the atmospheric
conditions presented by the earth bear no resemblance to those of a greenhouse. In a tightly closed
greenhouse the roof is comparatively low, and the
temperature is much the same in every part of it;
"the glass will permit the hot sunbeams to enter,
but refuses to allow them out again with equal freedom;" the continuous stream of "hot sunbeams"
poured into the greenhouse and retained there heats
all of the air within it, "and consequently the temperature rises."

But the very reverse is true of the earth. The
firmament or heavens sustains much the same relation to the earth that the glass roof of the greenhouse
sustains to the greenhouse, in that it confines the
atmosphere of the earth to a given space, just as the
glass roof and walls of the greenhouse confines its
air to a given space. But instead of a comparatively
small greenhouse with its low walls and roof enclos-
ing a small amount of air immediately above the
earth's surface, which the " hot sunbeams" are capable of heating, the firmament or heavens is situated
at a distance of many miles from the earth's surface,

and encloses the whole atmosphere of this globe, and such is the immensity of this "enormous coating of air" that the "hot sunbeams" are powerless to heat it as they do the small amount of air in a greenhouse. The result is that the "hot sunbeams" are poured continuously upon the earth's surface where their further passage is checked, and such amount of this heat as the earth does not absorb is radiated into the lower stratas of air which immediately envelop the earth, and the temperature of these stratas is raised, while the upper stratas, extending for miles and miles to the outer limits of the atmosphere, are not affected, and maintain an extremely low temperature, which is derived from this intensely cold firmament.

The firmament or heaven which envelops the earth and its atmosphere marks the outer limits of the atmosphere and confines the earth's atmosphere to the earth. If our earth was situated in empty space, with no structure impervious to air enveloping it and confining its atmosphere to certain limits, the atmosphere would long since have been diffused into space, and the earth stripped of this essential element would be incapable of sustaining either plant or animal life. But this is not all; if the earth was situated in empty space, with no structure impervious to water enveloping the earth, the intense heat of the sun's rays poured upon the earth continuously since the sun was formed, would long since have evaporated the last drop of water from the earth, and thus rendered our globe incapable of supporting either plant or animal life. Thus, in addition to separating the waters above it from the waters beneath it, the firmament or heaven confines the atmosphere and waters to the earth, and thus contributes to the preservation of its plant and animal life. Hence, but for the existence of the firmament the earth, like the moon, would be a barren waste, without water, without atmosphere and without plant and animal life.

It is well known that cold air is heavier than hot air. Hence, if it were discovered that the temperature of a greenhouse was not the same throughout, it would be found that the colder, heavier air was below, at the floor; and that the hotter lighter air was above, and immediately under the glass. But these conditions are reversed in the earth's " enormous coating of air." The warm stratas of air found below, at the earth's surface, while the colder stratas of air are found above. As has been shown, the comparatively high temperature found immediately about the earth's surface in the temperate and torrid zones of the globe is not due to the earth's "enormous coating of air." On the contrary, the air derives its temperature from the objects with which it is brought in contact; for example: Place a hot stove in one end of a large hall, the air immediately about the stove will partake of the temparature of the stove; and the surrounding air will be warmed and its temperature raised as far as the heat from the stove is radiated. Then place a 200 pound block of ice in the opposite end of the hall, and the air immediately about the ice will partake of the temperature of the ice; and the surrounding air will be cooled, and its temperature lowered as far as the cold from the ice is radiated. This disposition of the air to partake of the temperature of the objects with which it is brought in contact, explains the singular fact that the comparatively warm stratas of the earth's atmosphere are found below, at and near the earth's surface, while the cold stratas are found above. This, as has been shown is due to the fact that the lower stratas of air derive their comparatively high temperature from the "hot sunbeams" which are concentrated about the earth's surface. This being true it follows that the upper stratas of the atmosphere derive their extremely low temperature from some object at its limits which is intensely cold; and the Bible teaches us that this is the firmament which envelops the earth and its atmosphere. Hence, the higher we ascend into the upper regions of the atmosphere, the nearer we approach the firmament, and the colder it gets. The presence of this intensely cold firmament, intervening between the earth and the sun explains the otherwise unexplainable fact cited by Prof. Ball, that, instead of it getting hotter as we approach the sun, it actually gets colder. On ascending from the earth in our approach to the far-distant sun with its intense heat, we first approach the comparative near firmament with its intense cold. Hence, the nearer we approach the sun the colder it gets.

The disposition of the atmosphere to partake of the temperature of any object with which it comes in contact, taken in connection with the presence of this intensely cold firmament at the outer limits of our atmosphere, and the concentration of the "hot sunbeams" at the earth's surface, explains the apparent reversal in this case, of the rule that the colder air is found below, and the hotter air above.

If the firmament was not intensely cold, and if it was not incapable of being heated — if it had no special temperature of its own, but, like the atmosphere, it would partake of the temperature of any object with which it came in contact — the hot sunbeams poured upon it in their passage to the earth throughout the ages since the sun was formed, would have heated it to a high temperature; this heat from the firmament would have been radiated into the upper regions of the atmosphere, with nothing to modify it; this excessive heat radiated from the hot firmament above, and combined with the heat radiated from the hot sunbeams concentrated at the earth's surface, would have raised the temperature of the atmosphere, and the surface of the earth, and its waters, to such a height as to render it impossible for either plant or animal life to exist on this globe. But, as has been shown, the firmament has a peculiarly low temperature of its own; it is perhaps the coldest object in the universe. The Mount Whitney observations estimate the temperature of space, which is the heaven, at 450° below zero, and it is incapable of being heated. Its intense cold lowers to below the freezing point, the immense volume of the earth's atmosphere down to within about two miles of the earth's surface, where its cold is modified by the heat which is radiated from the hot sunbeams concentrated at the surface of the earth. The presence of this immense volume of cold air above, contributes largely to render wholesome the air we breathe; a greater or less amount of the cold air from above is continually being borne down into the warm stratas of air below, which it displaces; this cold air is in its turn warmed by the hot sunbeams, while the warm air which it displaces is forced out into the upper regions of frost where it is cooled and purified, and in the course of time will return to the earth, cool and pure. This process by which the lower stratas of the earth's atmosphere are purified, and its proper temperature maintained throughout the different seasons, contributes largely to the health and comfort of both man and the animals.

Though we are opposed to the theory that the earth was formerly a molten mass, it seems reasonable to suppose, and there is much to indicate, that in the movement of the enormous masses of matter which were concentrated in the earth, and its atmosphere, and the firmament, there was an immense amount of heat generated; and that the entire volume of the earth's atmosphere reached a higher temperature at that early period than it has since attained, under the influence of the sun's heat. This being true, it follows that in the early history of our globe, the firmament performed a most important work in cooling and purifying the atmosphere, and thus hastened the preparation of the earth for the introduction of plant and animal life. This cooling process began, of course, at the outer limits of the atmosphere, at a distance of perhaps several hundred miles from the earth's surface, and was necessarily very gradual. Let us bear in mind that we are now discussing a period in the world's history prior to the formation of the sun, moon, and stars; and that in the movement of these great masses of matter which were concentrated in the celestial bodies, an immense amount of heat was generated, and that doubtless a greater or less amount of this heat was radiated to the earth, thus counteracting to some extent the influence which the firmament was exerting upon the atmosphere to lower its temperature.

The cooling of this immense mass of heated, imprisoned air would necessarily be a very slow process, and even under the most favorable conditions would require ages for its accomplishment; the cooling of the entire mass was never completed; it is evident that it was not God's intention that it should be, as shown by the fact that while this cooling process was going on, vegetation was introduced upon the earth. Had nothing interposed to counteract the influence of the firmament, the temperature of the entire volume of the earth's atmosphere would have been lowered below the freezing point, as the great bulk of it is to-day, and the surface of the earth and its waters would have been covered with a sheet of ice; and the vegetation of the earth would have been utterly destroyed. This we know never occurred; on the contrary, as we shall hereafter show, the high temperature and general atmospheric conditions so essential to the growth of plants, prevailed over the entire globe. We shall show that during this period, known as the *Carboniferous Age*, which existed long prior to the formation of the sun, the earth produced and maintained a considerable amount of vegetation.

We shall also show that it was not until the latter part of the Carboniferous Age in what is known as the "Permian Period" of that age, that the sun, moon, and stars were formed, and the *seasons* established; and the beneficent influences which God designed that the celestial bodies should exert upon the earth and its phenomena began to be expressed. After these events the chilling influence of the firmament upon the lower stratas of the atmosphere was counteracted by the concentration of the hot sunbeams upon the earth's surface, and the perpetuation of the plant and animal life of our globe was assured. Thus, it is shown that, in addition to its original office of the separator between the celestial and the terrestrial waters, the firmament or heaven discharges other important offices in God's plan of creation, from which man is largely the beneficiary.

For many centuries the modern world has been deceived and misled by the speculations of atheists and infidels who have vainly attempted to devise a theory that will cover all the phenomena of the universe and explain its existence as the result of "natural causes" working automatically and without design to accomplish their formation; nothing is so absurd to these theorists as the admission that the universe is but the expression of Divine intelligence; nothing to them is so repulsive as the belief in a personal God—the Creator of the heaven and the earth. Hence, we should not be surprised that the firmament occupies no place in their theories.

since its origin is alone traceable to the highest intelligence and the most far-reaching design. Strange as it may seem, it is nevertheless a deplorable fact that the great bulk of those who profess belief in a personal God, most readily accept without question these antiscriptural theories which deny the existence of God. Under the demoralizing influences of the unblushing atheism and infidelity which characterize the age in which we live, the firmament has so long been ignored that its very existence and the beneficent purposes for which it was designed is lost sight of. But this was not the case in the earlier ages; the ancients recognized the reality of the firmament and appreciated its grandeur, its beauty, and its utility; and those of the inspired authors, Moses, David, and Daniel, make special mention of it in their writings. This superb, transparent structure which allows heat and light to penetrate it while declining to extend this privilege to air and water, is an ever active factor in the universe which must be considered; and we feel assured that when this is done our present astronomical views will be very materially modified, to say the least of it.

While the sciences are powerless to aid us in determining the *time* and the *manner* in which the firmament was formed, they furnish, as has been shown, the most positive proof of its *reality;* and nothing is more clearly taught by the sciences than that the earth, and the sun, moon, and stars, are not situated in empty space. The sciences not only acquaint us with the fact that the firmament has a temperature that is extremely low, but, as we shall hereafter show, they enable us to determine the *material* of which the firmament or heaven is composed.

Several of the most prominent of the inspired authors in referring to the Creation, speak of God's having "stretched out the heavens;" and they refer to God as he who "stretchest out the heavens;" for example, Isaiah says: "Thus saith God the Lord, He that created the heavens, and stretched them out." (*Is.* xl, 5). "Thus saith the Lord, the Holy one of Israel * * * I have made the earth, and created man upon it: I, even my hands have stretched out the heavens, and all their hosts have I commanded." (*Is.* xlv, 11, 12). Jeremiah says of God: "He hath made the earth by His power, He hath established the world by His wisdom, and hath stretched out the heavens by his discretion." (*Jer.* x, 12; see also *Jer.* li, 15). Isaiah says of God: "It is He that sitteth upon the circle of the earth, and the inhabitants thereof are as grasshoppers; that stretcheth out the heavens as a curtain, and spreadeth them out as a tent to dwell in." (*Is.* xl, 22). David says: "Bless the Lord, O my soul. * * Who coverest thyself with light as with a garment: Who stretchest out the heavens like a curtain." (*Ps.* civ, 1, 2). The references of the inspired authors to the heavens in the Creation, as something that was stretched out like a "curtain," conveys much the same idea of the heavens as that of John, in his description of the destruction of the universe, in which he says: "And the heaven departed as a scroll when it is rolled together." (*Rev.* vi, 14).

These utterances of the inspired authors show

that, when God had completed the firmament or heaven, which He made in the midst of the waters to separate the celestial waters from the terrestrial waters, He "stretched out" or extended the firmament or heaven to the utmost limits of the material universe. This teaching is sustained by that of the Mosaic Record in describing the work of the fourth creative day, as shown by the following: "And God said, Let there be lights in the firmament of heaven to divide the day from the night." * * * "And let them be for lights in the firmament of heaven to give light upon the earth. * * * And God made two great lights; the greater light to rule the day, and the lesser light to rule the night; He made the stars also. And God set them in the firmament of heaven to give light upon the earth." (*Gen.* i, 14, 15, 16, 17).

Further evidence that God "stretched out," or extended the original firmament to the limits of the universe, is found in the references made to the "open firmament of heaven." In describing the work of the fifth creative day, a part of the animals formed on that day are described as "fowl that may fly above the earth in the open firmament of heaven." (*Gen.* i, 20). Hence, they are described throughout the Bible as "the fowls of heaven." It is plain that "the open firmament of heaven" in which "the fowl may fly," is that immense space intervening between the firmament or heaven and the earth, and in which the atmosphere is situated. This term, "the open firmament of heaven," is a comparative term, and indicates that inasmuch as there is an "open firmament or heaven" beneath, or within the original firmament, that above, or beyond it, there is no "open firmament of heaven"—no empty space—but a closed firmament or heaven, in which the sun, moon, and stars are placed. Hence, they are described as "lights in the firmament of heaven." (*Gen.* i, 14, 15, etc.). And also "the hosts of heaven." (*Deut.* iv, 19; *Deut.* xvii, 3, etc.).

We are thus plainly taught that the heavens and the luminaries — the sun, moon, and stars,— are different formations; that they were made at different periods of time, and were designed for different purposes; and the sciences teach us that they are not even composed of the same materials. The heavens are formations as distinct from the luminaries, as the luminaries are from the earth. Hence, we but confuse ourselves when we confuse the sun, moon, and stars with the heavens in which God placed them.

Let us now compare the teachings of the Bible with those of the sciences as to the situation of the heavens, and that of the luminaries, and the relations which the luminaries and the heavens sustain to each other, and to the earth. After reviewing several theories those distinguished English writers, Mr. H. W. Bristow and Mr. Robert Brown, in their revised edition of Figuier's *World Before the Deluge*, says: "The school of philosophy considered to be the most advanced in modern science, has yet another view of cosmogony, of which we venture to give a brief outline. Space is infinite, says the exponent of this system,* for wherever in imagination

* "Professor Tyndall, in *Fortnightly Review*."

we erect a boundary, we are compelled to think of
space as existing beyond it. The starry heavens
proclaim that it is not entirely void; but the question remains, are the vast regions which surround
the stars, and across which light is propagated, absolutely empty? No! Modern science, while it rejects
the notion of the luminiferous particles of the old
philosophy, has cogent proofs of the existence of a
luminiferous ether with definite mechanical properties. It is infinitely more attenuated, but more
solid than gas. It resembles jelly rather than air,
and if not co-extensive with space, it extends as far
as the most distant star the telescope reveals to us;
it is the vehicle of their light in fact; it takes up
their molecular tremors and conveys them with inconceivable rapidity to our organs of vision. The
splendor of the firmament at night is due to this
vibration. If this ether has a boundary, masses of
ponderable matter may exist beyond it, but they
could emit no light. Dark suns may burn there,
metals may be heated to fusion in invisible furnaces,
planets may be molten amid intense darkness; for
the loss of heat being simply the abstraction of
molecular motion by the ether, where this medium
is absent no cooling could take place.

"This, however does not concern us; as far as
our knowledge of space extends, we are to conceive
of it as the holder of this luminiferous ether, through
which the fixed stars are interspersed at enormous
distances apart." (*The World Before the Deluge*, pp.
24, 25).

We have now before us the teachings of the

Bible and those of the most advanced school of modern science expressed in their own language; we are thus enabled to determine whether there is that sharp conflict between the teachings of scripture and those of the sciences of which we hear so much. And it should be unnecessary for us to state that in presenting the results of Professor Tyndall's investigations, we are not employing the aid of one who was in the least partial to the Bible; on the contrary, as is well known, Professor Tyndall was one of the ablest, as well as one of the most open, pronounced opponents of the Bible.

As has been shown, the Bible teaches that the luminaries are not situated in empty space. As shown by the utterances of Professor Tyndall, modern science teaches that the luminaries are not situated in empty space.

The Bible teaches that God made the luminaries and placed them in the firmament of heaven, a formation which He had prepared for their reception.

Modern science teaches that a "luminiferous ether," "infinitely more attenuated, but more solid than gas," a substance which "resembles jelly, rather than air," surrounds the remotest "star the telescope reveals to us."

The Bible teaches that God made the luminaries and placed "them in the firmament of heaven to give light upon the earth." Thus we are plainly taught that it is not to the luminaries alone, but to this combination of the *luminaries*, and the *firmament of heaven* in which God placed them, that the earth is indebted for its light. This being true, it follows that if either the luminaries or the firmament of heaven, was absent, the earth would be enveloped in darkness. The plan of Creation requires the combination of the luminaries, and the firmament of heaven, in which God placed them, to give light upon the earth.

Modern science teaches that while the luminaries produce the light, this ether, through its vibrations, is the vehicle by which their light is transmitted, "with inconceivable rapidity to our organs of vision." Thus we are taught that it is not to the luminaries alone, but to this combination of the luminaries, and the ether which surrounds them, that the earth is indebted for its light. This being true, it follows that if either the luminaries or the ether which surrounds them was absent, the earth would be enveloped in darkness. Modern science requires the combination of the luminaries and the ether which surrounds them to give light upon the earth.

Thus, instead of a conflict between the scriptures and the sciences upon these great subjects, we find that they are in absolute harmony; the sciences not only prove the reality of the "firmament of heaven," but they acquaint us with the fact that it is composed of ether; and inasmuch as this jelly-like substance extends throughout space and surrounds every star, it necessarily surrounds the earth which is in the midst of the stars. The masses of this ether which mark the boundaries of our atmosphere, permit the rays of heat and light to penetrate it without affecting its extremely low temperature; but being impervious to air and water, it holds the earth's water and its atmosphere to the earth; it evidently discharges the same office for every other planet in the universe; it is this great firmament of ether which surrounds every star, that holds the waters of Mars to Mars; and the clouds and vapors of Jupiter to Jupiter, and so on.

Had Professor Tyndall and his followers obeyed the Saviour's command, "Search the scriptures," they might have discovered the perfect harmony which really exists between the scriptures and the sciences; and their unfair criticisms and their unjust assaults upon the Bible would not have been made. No theory which proposes to attribute the existence of the phenomena of the universe to "natural causes," can explain the origin of this great firmament of ether; in its silent grandeur it presents the most crushing proofs of the falsity of all such theories. The Bible alone explains the origin of this wonderful formation. Hence, apparently infinite in its length and breadth, and in its height and depth; unsurpassed in all inanimate nature, in point of utility; and peerless in its grandeur and its beauty: "The heavens declare the glory of God, and the firmament showeth His handiwork."

CHAPTER IV.

Nebular Theory.

There are only two schools of learning which propose to explain the existence of the heavens and the earth with all their phenomena. These are (1) the Bible school of Divine Creation; (2) the Atheistic school of Evolution, or Natural Development. This is admitted by Professor Haeckel, the great German naturalist, upon whom the mantle of authority in the evolution world descended at the death of Darwin. In discussing the origin of plant and animal life, Professor Haeckel says:

"As is now very generally acknowledged, both by the adherents of and the opponents to the theory of descent, the choice in the matter of the origin of the human race lies between two radically different assumptions: We must either accustom ourselves to the idea that the various species of animals and plants, man included, originated independently of each other, by the supernatural process of a Divine 'creation,' which as such is entirely removed from the sphere of scientific observation; or, we are compelled to accept the theory of descent in its entirety, and trace the human race, equally with the various plant and animal species, from an entirely simple primeval parent form. Between these two assump-

94

tions there is no third course." (*The Evolution of Man*, Vol. II., pp. 36, 37).

The School of Creation as presented by the Bible, teaches that the heaven and the earth, with all their phenomena, is the product of Divine creation. Hence, they are artificial — the product of Divine art — and the laws which govern them are God's laws. In direct opposition to this scriptural school, the School of Atheism teaches that the heaven and the earth, with all their phenomena, is the result of *natural causes*, working automatically, and of course without design, to accomplish their formation; and that the laws which govern them are *natural laws*.

As shown in the first chapter of this volume, the School of Creation is by far the most ancient of these ancient schools of learning; and its great truths were taught by the Creator to our first parents in the Garden of Eden, and were transmitted by Adam to his descendants in the "book of precepts" which God delivered to him. In the following pages we shall combat the theory of development at every point; we shall show that in addition to its being antiscriptural, it is irrational and unscientific; we shall show that so far from having progressed, man has not even held his own. As a matter of fact we of modern times are just emerging from the "Dark Ages," into which God in His wrath and disgust plunged the whole world of mankind after the crucifixion of the Saviour, and in which all knowledge of the arts and sciences was practically lost, and in which ignorance and superstition ruled supreme. Our egotism leads us into the error of supposing that we are the most intellectual, learned, and accomplished people that ever lived upon the earth; and we ignore the evidence which explorers among ancient ruins are continually discovering of the high intellectuality, learning, and culture of the ancients; we disregard the facts established by this mass of evidence that nation after nation in the past, and upon every continent of the earth, has ascended to the loftiest positions of knowledge and refinement, and then descended by some demoralizing course which led to individual and national degeneracy, and finally consigned their descendants to barbarism and savagery; laid their superb civilizations in ruins; and the greater part, if not all, of their knowledge acquired through ages of investigation was lost to the world. We also disregard the fact that our great achievements in the realms of art and science have all been accomplished in the last few centuries; for example: The great law of gravitation, a knowledge of which is so essential to the astronomer, was not understood by the moderns until explained and given to the world by Newton in A. D. 1687. The modern world was in ignorance of the existence of the planet Uranus until Herschel discovered it in 1781. The great planet Neptune was discovered simultaneously in 1846 by the mathematicians, Le Verrier of France and Adams of England. The satellites of the planets, and many of the laws governing the celestial bodies, are recent discoveries by modern astronomers, though doubtless known to the ancients. The ancients were aware that the earth is a globe; but this knowledge was lost to the world, and at the time of Bruno, A. D. 1600, the Catholic church, which claimed about all the learning and authority in Europe at that time, taught that the earth was a plane. The ancients possessed and lost the telescope, one of the most essential instruments in studying the heavens; the modern telescope was first made in Holland in A. D. 1608; it was improved upon by Galileo in 1610, and successive improvements have brought it to its present state of perfection. The same is true of all, or nearly all, our modern inventions and discoveries; they are merely reproductions. A knowledge of these things was as essential to the ancients as to the moderns; and the same lofty grade of intellect which produced them in modern times produced them in ancient times. All the facts indicate that the ancients acquired and lost a knowledge of astronomy as well as of other subjects, that we, who are just emerging from the "Dark Ages," have not yet attained to.

In discussing the antiquity of the science of astronomy, Professor Ball says:

"The history of astronomy is, in one respect, only like many other histories. The earliest part of it is completely and hopelessly lost. The stars had been studied, and some great astronomical discoveries had been made, untold ages before those to which our earliest historical records extend. For example, the observation of the apparent movement of the sun, and the discrimination between the planets and the fixed stars, are both to be classed among the discoveries of pre-historic ages. Nor is it to be said that these achievements related to mat-

ters of an obvious character. * * The patient observations of the early astronomers enabled the sun's track through the heavens to be ascertained, and it was found that in its circuit amid the stars and constellations our luminary invariably followed the same path. This is called the *ecliptic*, and the constellations through which it passes form a belt around the heavens known as the *zodiac*. It was anciently divided into twelve equal portions or 'signs,' so that the stages on the sun's great journey could be conveniently indicated. The duration of the year, or the period required by the sun to run its course through the heavens, seems to have been first ascertained by astronomers whose names are unknown. The skill of the early Oriental geometers was further evidenced by their determination of the position of the ecliptic with regard to the equator, and by their success in the measurement of the angle between these two important circles on the heavens. * * *
But we are far from having exhausted the list of great discoveries which have come down from an unknown antiquity. Correct explanations had been given of the striking phenomenon of a lunar eclipse, in which the brilliant surface is plunged temporarily into darkness, and also of the still more imposing spectacle of a solar eclipse, in which the sun himself undergoes a partial or even a total obscuration. Then, too, the acuteness of the early astronomers had detected the five wandering stars or planets; they had traced the movements of Mercury, and Venus, Mars, Jupiter, and Saturn. They had observed with awe the various configurations of these

planets. * * * At length a certain order was perceived to govern the apparently capricious movements of the planets. It was found that they obeyed certain laws." (*Ibid*, pp. 2, 5, 6).

In discussing the ancient Egyptians, Mr. Goodrich says: "The signs of the zodiac were certainly in use among the Egyptians 1722 years before Christ. One of the learned men of our day, who for fifty years labored to decipher the hieroglyphics of the ancients, found upon a mummy-case in the British Museum a delineation of the signs of the zodiac, and the position of the planets; the date to which they pointed was the autumnal equinox of the year 1722 B. C. Professor Mitchell, to whom the fact was communicated, employed his assistants to ascertain the exact position of the heavenly bodies belonging to our solar system on the equinox of that year. This was done, and a diagram furnished by parties ignorant of his object, which showed that on the 7th of October, 1722 B. C., the moon and planets occupied the exact point in the heavens marked upon the coffin in the British Museum." (*Columbus*, p. 22).

Mr. Donnelly says: "The knowledge of the ancients as to astronomy was great and accurate. Callisthenes, who accompanied Alexander the Great to Babylon, sent to Aristotle a series of Chaldean astronomical observations which he found preserved there, recorded on tablets of baked clay, and extending back as far as 2234 B. C. Humbolt says: 'The Chaldeans knew the mean motions of the moon with an exactness which induced the Greek astronomers to use their calculations for the foundation of a

lunar theory.' The Chaldeans knew the true nature
of comets, and could foretell their reappearance. 'A
lens of considerable power was found in the ruins of
Babylon; it was an inch and a half in diameter and
nine-tenths of an inch thick.' (*Layard's Nineveh
and Babylon*, pp. 16, 17). Nero used optical glasses
when he watched the fights of the gladiators; they
are supposed to have come from Egypt and the east.
Plutarch speaks of optical instruments used by
Archimedes 'to manifest to the eye the largeness of
the sun.' 'There are actual astronomical calculations in existence, with calendars formed upon them,
which eminent astronomers of England and France
admit to be genuine and true, and which carry back
the antiquity of the science of astronomy, together
with the constellations, to within a few years of the
Deluge, even on the longer chronology of the Septuagint.' (*The Miracle in Stone*, p. 142). Josephus
attributes the invention of the constellations to the
family of the antediluvian Seth, the son of Adam,
while Origin affirms that it was asserted in the Book
of Enoch that in the time of that Patriarch the constellations were already divided and named. (*Atlantis*, pp. 453, 454).

Thus it is shown that so far from astronomy
being a modern, it is one of the most ancient
of the sciences; it was not only familiar to
the ancients of postdiluvian times, but the antediluvians were familiar with it. Not only were
the constellations divided and named in the time of
Enoch, the seventh from Adam, but the "*invention
of the constellations*" is accredited to the family of

Seth, the third son of Adam.   These incidents furnish additional proof that God revealed to Adam a knowledge of the great events of Creation, just as He afterwards revealed them to Moses; they also go far to prove that just as God inspired Moses to write a narrative of the Creation for the benefit of the moderns, so did He inspire Adam to write a narrative of the Creation for the benefit of the ancients. The knowledge of the heavens, the waters above the heavens, and the celestial bodies which David displayed, was derived from the narrative of Creation which God inspired Moses to write; while the knowledge of astronomy which the immediate descendants of Adam displayed was derived from the account of the Creation which God inspired Adam to write. That intimate knowledge of the phenomena of the heavens, which enabled Seth to divide and name the constellations, could only have been acquired at that early period from Adam's inspired book; and the distinction which Seth derived from his acceptance of it, has survived the ravages of time, and has handed his name down to us from a remote antiquity as the earliest, and perhaps the most accomplished astronomer the world has ever known. The modern world should have profited by Seth's example, and should have accepted the word of God as David did; but instead of this, we find professed Christians either ignoring the Mosaic Record, or engaged in vain attempts to twist its utterances into some semblance of harmony with the speculations of infidels and atheists.

Prominent among the antiscriptural theories of

modern time, is that invented by the French infidel,
La Place, and commonly known as the "Nebular
Hypothesis." This theory professes to explain the
origin of the earth and the celestial bodies. The
Nebular Theory combined with the Theory of Descent, which attributes the origin of plant and animal life to spontaneous generation, form what is
termed the theory of *Evolution* or the theory of *De-
velopment*, which thrusts |God aside, denies the
existence of an intelligent Creator, repudiates the
Bible, and accredits the phenomena of the universe
to *natural causes*. The Nebular Theory is sustained
by the great majority of scientists. Strange as it may
seem this antiscriptural theory is advocated, with
but few exceptions, by those who profess to believe
the Bible.

In discussing this theory, which he warmly advocates, Professor Guyot says:

"In the genesis of our solar system, as explained
by the genius of La Place and submitted by Stephen
Alexander to exhaustive calculations, the result of
which amounts almost to a demonstration of its
truth, we see how a family of planets has been detached from a vast central body which holds them
in bondage by the power of its mass.

"This last history, which immediately concerns
the earth as one of the daughters of our sun, is so
important in helping us to understand the phases of
development undergone by our globe, that it may
be well to give a short outline of the foundation
upon which it rests.

"1. It is found that the distances of the orbits

of the planets from the sun follow a nearly regular law, which is, that, starting from the orbit of Mercury, and counting the place of the asteroids as one planet, each succeeding orbit is about double the distance of the preceding one.

"2. On the whole, the planets nearer the sun are smaller than the more distant ones.

"3. Their density is increasing with their nearness to the sun.

"4. All the planets and their satellites revolve around the sun in the same direction and nearly in the same plane as the equator of the sun itself.

"5. The velocity of their revolution is diminishing with their distance from the sun.

"6. The rapidity of their rotation on their axis, on the contrary is increasing.

"All these coincidences point to a common law which seems to indicate a community of origin. * * * He assumed as his starting-point, the sun as a nebulous star with a powerful nucleus, revolving on its axis, and when hot, gaseous atmosphere extended beyond the limit of the orbit of Neptune. Plunged in the cold abysses of heaven, in which it loses incessantly, by radiation, a part of its heat, it cools and contracts; its centrifugal force increasing rapidly at the same time. Under its action, the cool and heavier particles rush toward the equatorial parts, where, owing to the continual contraction of the main body, they are soon left behind in the shape of a ring similar to those which we observe around Saturn.

"According to the laws of motion, the ring continues to move with the same velocity as the main body from which it was detached. But as the ring itself shrinks in cooling, its inner surface, receding from the sun, begins to move less rapidly, while the outside, approaching nearer the sun, moves with greater rapidity. The equilibrium being thus disturbed, the ring tends to break up, and the outside, gaining upon the inside, the whole is rolled up into a globular mass with a rotary motion in the same direction as that of the ring itself. The result is a planet revolving around the sun and in the plane of its equator. By further contraction of the sun, the same process is repeated and new planets are formed. They decrease in size because the detached rings grow less at every step. They increase in density, because the later planets are detached when the density of the sun is increased.

"The larger planets have a more rapid rotation because they have been contracting during a longer period of time." (*Creation*, pp. 67, 68, 69, 70; see also Ennis, *The Origin of the Stars*; Dawson, *The Origin of the World*, etc).

Dr. Patterson, in discussing the Nebular Theory, says: "*The theory is contradicted by the densities of the planets.* At the time La Place constructed his theory, the densities of the planets were either unknown or erroneously valued. He constructed his theory to suit these errors. Astronomers are now agreed as to the error of Newton, and La Place, and Kepler, in supposing that the densest bodies were those nearest the sun. Kepler declares 'the sun to be the densest of all cosmical bodies; because it moves all others which belong to his system.'

Newton argues: 'The bodies of Venus and Mercury are more ripened and condensed, on account of the greater heat of the sun. The more remote planets, by want of heat, are deficient in these metallic substances and mighty minerals with which the earth abounds. Bodies are denser in proportion to their nearness to the sun.'

"La Place calculated his system accordingly, and made his outside planets, which were first cast off, light in proportion to their distance from the sun, while those nearest, which had condensed most, were made heavy accordingly. For instance, he calculated the density of Mercury, to make it square with his theory, at 2.585; which indeed was a little less than what was then generally supposed; while it is in reality now found to be only one-half of that, or 1.234—a very little heavier than the earth. The sun, which ought to be the densest body of the system by the theory, is actually much lighter than the earth, and stands fifth in the order of densities. There is no correspondence whatever between the distances and the densities of the planets. The actual order of the solar system as to density, is given by Humbolt as follows: Saturn, 0.140 of the earth's density; Uranus, 0.178; Neptune, 0.232; Jupiter, 0.243; Sun, 0.252; Venus, 0.940; Mars, 0.958; Earth, 1; Mercury, 1.234.* Thus it appears that the sun is but little denser than Neptune, the outer planet of the system—exactly the reverse of La Place's nebular hypothesis.

"This objection, of the inconsistence of densi-

* Cosmos, xv. p. 446.

ties, comes with even greater force from the comets
of our system. They are by far the most numerous
family we have. Kepler says that there are more
comets in the heavens than fishes in the ocean. At
any rate, astronomers calculate their numbers within
our solar system at two or three millions. Now
these, according to the theory, should not be within
the solar system at all, nor within millions of miles
of it, but away in the outer margins of space among
the nebulæ, since they are lighter than vanity.
Every comet which shows its light head among
solid worlds mocks at the Nebular Hypothesis.

" *The other arrangements of the solar system were
found to be equally at variance with the demands of the
theory.* The orbits of the comets, being inclined at
all angles to the sun's equator, are often out of the
plane of his rotation, and fly right in the face of the
theory. The moons of Uranus revolve in a direction
contrary to all the other bodies, and so contrary to
the theory. The palpable difference between the
luminosity of the sun and of the other bodies, is in
itself a sufficient refutation of the theory which
would make them all out of the same matter and
by the same process, and moreover refutes the
notion of their common origin by any mere mechanical law, as Newton shows: 'The same power, whether
natural or supernatural, which placed the sun in the
center of the six primary planets, placed Saturn in
the center of the orb of his five secondary planets,
and the earth in the center of the moon's orbit; and,
therefore, had this cause been a blind one, *without
contrivance or design*, the sun would have been a

body of the same kind with Saturn, Jupiter, and the earth; that is, *without light and heat.* Why there is one body in our system qualified to give light and heat to all the rest, I know no reason but because the author of the system thought it convenient." (*Errors of Evolution,* pp. 34, 35, 36).

Sir Robert S. Ball, in discussing the Nebular Theory, says: "Such is, in fact, the doctrine of the origin of system which has been advanced in that celebrated speculation known as the nebular theory. Nor can it ever be more than a speculation; it can not be established by observation, nor can it be proved by calculation. It is merely a conjecture, more or less plausible, but perhaps in some degree necessarily true, if our present laws of heat, as we understand them, admit of the extreme application here required, and if also the present order of things has reigned for sufficient time without the intervention of any influence at present unknown to us." (*The Story of the Heavens,* p. 500).

Thus, this distinguished scientist frankly asserts that the Nebular Theory is simply a *speculation:* that *it can never be more than a speculation;* that *it cannot be established by observation, nor can it be proved by calculation;* that *it is merely a conjecture more or less plausible.* Yet we find professed Christians advocating this *speculation,*—this mere *conjecture* of an infidel—when to do so requires them to repudiate the word of God; nothing is more clearly taught in the Bible than that the *earth* was the first of the great bodies formed; while La Place "assumed," that the *sun* was the first of the great bodies formed; and that the earth was formerly a gaseous ring thrown off from the sun. Hence, Professor Guyot, in advocating this theory refers to the earth as "one of the daughters of our sun."

In discussing the Nebular Theory, and the motions of the planets, the distinguished astronomer Richard A. Procter says:

"Now, the French astronomer La Place showed how all these motions would have resulted if the solar system had once been a great mass of intensely hot vapor turning round and round as upon an axis. This whirling mass of vapor would contract as it parted with its heat, and, as it contracted, would whirl more swiftly. This increase of its rotating movement would cause the outer parts to be separated, and a ring would thus be thrown off. This ring would eventually break up and form a minor vapor mass, circling around the remainder of the contracting mass. Moreover, La Place showed that the mass thrown off would rotate in the the same direction in which it revolved. Now, we have only to conceive this process repeated several times as the vapor mass continued to contract to understand the formation of the primary planets. We have only to suppose further that the larger vapor masses thrown off, as supposed, themselves contracted in the same way, and thus formed subordinate systems, to understand the existence of satellite systems like those circling around Saturn, Jupiter, Uranus and Neptune. A ring such as the ring of Asteroids or the Saturnian rings would, under exceptional circumstances, be formed instead of a planet or satellite.

And thus the main features of the solar system are accounted for.

"But this ingenious theory does not account for some peculiarities which are scarcely less remarkable than those upon which it is based. In particular it does not account for the strange disposition of the masses of the solar system. Why should the inner family consist of minor bodies, in the main unattended, while the outer consists of giant orbs with extensive families of satellites? Why should the innermost members of the outer family of planets be the largest, while just within there lies the family of asteroids, not only individually minute, but collectively less (as Leverrier has proved) than Mars, or even Mercury? Why should the two middle planets of the inner family be the largest members of that family? La Place's theory gives no account of these peculiarities; nor perhaps could it be insisted that these peculiarities should be explained; yet, if any other theory should give an account of these features, explaining also the features which we have seen accounted for, then such theory would have a decided advantage over La Place's. It is to be noticed also that La Place's great nebulous contracting mass is a very unsatisfactory conception to begin with. No such mass *could* rotate as a whole. And lastly, La Place's theory does not in any way correspond with processes still taking place within the solar system. It gives no account of the immense number of meteor flights and comets still existing within the solar domain." (*The Expanse of Heaven*, pp. 181, 182, 183).

It is one of the peculiarities of the atheist, that his cosmogonies are based upon mere *assumption.* Allow the atheists to "assume" that this or that was the case, and then permit him to support his assumption with a string of "ifs," of greater or less length, and it is possible that he will evolve a theory which, when viewed merely upon its surface, may seem more or less plausible; but a critical investigation of it reveals the fact that it is founded upon mere supposition, and that from beginning to end it is simply an imaginary affair. It is another peculiarity of the atheist that he embelishes his theory with a bewildering array of scientific terms, and then attempts to palm the whole off on us as *science.* But as a matter of fact the only scientific thing about his theory are the scientific terms which he employs in describing it, and the greater or less number of known facts which he attempts to prove it in harmony with. But his *theory* as such, from the mere assumption upon which it is based, to the erroneous conclusions to which he argues, is the purest fiction. So it is with La Place's theory. "He assumed as his starting-point, the sun a nebulous star with a powerful nucleus revolving on its axis, etc." (*Guyot*). Hence, to accept La Place's theory, we must first accord his assumption upon which it is based, all the value which we accord to a demonstrated fact; and, as has been shown, we must reject the teachings of the Bible, that the earth was the first of the great bodies formed; but this is not all: to accept the theory of La Place as to the manner in which the sun, moon and stars, and the earth were

formed, not only requires us to reject the Bible with
reference to the heavens and the purposes for which
they were designed, but also requires us to reject
the teachings of the sciences as to the existence of
the ether of which the heavens are composed, and
the purposes which it subserves.

We feel assured that the following conclusions
are unavoidable: (1) Suppose we accept La Place's
assumption that the sun was a nebulous star with a
powerful nucleus revolving on its axis; a moment's
reflection must convince us that this immense gaseous mass could rotate only in obedience to certain
laws governing the movement of matter; and the
presence of these laws must be accepted as the most
positive evidence of the existence of an intelligent
law-maker; intelligence of the highest order is as
essential in the enactment of laws governing the
movement of matter as it is in the enactment of
laws governing the actions of an individual or a nation. Hence, these laws under the influence of
which La Place assumed that this immense gaseous
mass rotated, would not do away with the necessity
for an intelligent law-maker—a Creator; on the contrary, the presence of these laws would but prove
the existence of such a being. Neither is there anything in the scriptures, nor in the sciences, to indicate (as many professed Christians who advocate
the theory of development would have us believe),
that God enacted certain laws to govern the movement of matter, and then left the formation of the
heavens and the earth and their phenomena to the
execution of these laws through some process of de-

velopment; on the contrary, the Mosaic Record says
God made the heavens; God made the sun, moon,
and stars; God made the plants and the animals;
and God created man; and in summing up the results of the creative week the inspired writer gives
the finishing blow to the theory that the Plan of
Creation was perfected and the universe completed
by the execution of certain laws governing the
movement of matter, as shown by the following:
"Thus the heavens and the earth were finished, and
all the host of them." There was nothing left to
development; all things were *finished;* when God
"rested" on the seventh day "from all His works
which He had made," the universe was perfect in
all its details.

(2) If we would further admit that it is possible for the earth and the planets to have been
formed by gaseous rings thrown off from the sun,
as La Place assumed, we would still be at a loss to
account for the existence of the ether of which the
heavens are composed; this ether which occupies all
the intervening space between the sun and the
planets could not have been thrown off in the form
of gas by the sun; it is plain that if this ether which
more resembles "jelly than air," and which surrounds the sun, and the earth, and every star, was
in existence prior to the formation of the sun, its
presence would have effectually restrained the sun
from throwing off into space the gaseous rings of
which La Place assumed the earth and the celestial
bodies were formed; if, on the other hand, the ether
made its appearance after the earth and the celestial

bodies were formed, from what source did it emanate, and by what process was it formed? Neither La Place nor any one of his many followers would render themselves so ridiculous as to assert that the nebulas theory can explain the origin of this ether; on the contrary, the very presence of this ether, which is revealed by the scriptures and the sciences, furnishes the most positive proof of the falsity of his theory.

To accept the nebular theory we must believe as La place evidently did, that the sun, moon and stars are situated in empty space, instead of being surrounded by an ether which is the vehicle of their light. The existence of this ether was established by the English astronomer, Thomas Young, who was born in A. D. 1773, and died in 1829; consequently the existence of this ether was established in the days of La Place; yet this ether occupies no place in his theory; and the most charitable view to take of the matter is, that La Place was not aware of its existence, for had he known of it he would have seen at a glance that his theory could not explain its origin; and consequently his anti-scriptural and unscientific theory would not have been thrown upon the world to deceive and damn its millions, as it has done.

As has been shown, this immense mass of ether of which the heavens are composed is the vehicle by which the light of the lumunaries is conveyed to our globe; and inasmuch as the nebular theory presupposes that the sun, moon and stars are situated in empty space, and makes no provision for this ether, it follows that if the universe had been constructed according to the theory of La Place, there would have been no medium by which the light of the luminaries could have been conveyed to our globe, and without this medium the earth would have been enveloped in darkness, and consequently would have been incapable of producing and maintaining either plant or animal life. Evidently it is well that God—a practical Creator, rather than La Place—an infidel speculator—was the designer of the universe.

This almost limitless mass of ether of which the heavens are composed, and which surrounds the earth, the sun, and "even the remotest star the telescope reveals to us," is the most extensive formation in all the material universe; the earth, and the celestial bodies are mere atoms compared to it; yet the theory of La Place, so far from explaining its origin, utterly ignores its existence; in addition to this we have shown by the testimony of that eminent scientist, Mr. Procter, (1) that no such mass of "hot, gaseous atmosphere" as La Place assumed as his "starting point" *could* rotate as a whole. This being true, the nebular theory falls still-born from the imagination of its author; for, if this immense gaseous mass could not, and did not rotate on its axis, the results which La Place claimed accrued from this process could not have been accomplished. (2) "That it does not account for the strange disposition of the masses of the solar system," as noted by Mr. Proctor. (3) That "it gives no account of the immense number of meteor flights and

comets still existing in the solar domain." When we
add to these discrepancies the fact that it is incompetent to explain the origin of the ether of which the
heavens are composed, and which is the vehicle by
which light is transmitted to all parts of the universe, it becomes plain that if we accord the nebular
theory all that its most ardent advocate claims for
it, it could account for only a mere fractional part of
the phenomena of the universe. And we feel assured
that the time is not far distant when the intelligence
of the world will repudiate this miserable theory
which is in such direct conflict with the teachings
of the scriptures and the sciences.

The confident tone assumed by the modern
advocates of the nebular theory, is in striking contrast to the "distrust" with which its author
regarded it as shown by his utterances quoted by
Mr. Ennis La Place's "System du Monde" as given
in the translation of J. Pond, F.R.S. (London, 1829).
In giving his theory of the planetary system to the
world La Place says: "Whatever may have been the
origin of this arrangement of the planetary system,
which I offer with that distrust which every thing
ought to inspire that is not the result of observation
or calculation, it is certain that its elements are so
arranged that it must possess the greatest stability,
if foreign observations (influences?) do not disturb
it." (See *The Origin of the Stars*, p. 381).

In view of its open conflict with well-established
facts, it is plain that the nebular hypothesis richly
merits the *distrust* with which its author regarded it:
it is also plain that its utter worthlessness is revealed

by the following law laid down by Huxley, who says: "Every hypothesis is *bound to explain,* or at any rate *not to be inconsistent with, the whole of the facts it professes to account for;* and if there is a *single one of these facts* which can be shown to be inconsistent with (I do not mean to be inexplicable by, but contrary to) the hypothesis, *such hypothesis falls to the ground—it is worth nothing.* One fact with which it is *positively inconsistent* is worth as much, and is as powerful in negativing the hypothesis *as five hundred."* (*Lecture on the Origin of Species,* p. 140).

CHAPTER V.

The Dry Land and the Plants.

"All flesh is grass." (*Is.* xl, 5; *1 Ps.* i, 24).

"And God said, Let the waters under the heaven be gathered together unto one place, and let the dry land appear: and it was so.

"And God called the dry land earth; and the gathering together of the waters called He seas: and God saw that it was good.

"And God said, Let the earth bring forth grass, and herb yielding seed, and the fruit tree yieldeth fruit after his kind, whose seed is in itself upon the earth: and it was so.

"And the earth brought forth grass, and herb bearing seed after his kind, and the tree yielding fruit, whose seed was in itself, after his kind: and God saw that it was good.

"And the evening and the morning were the third day." (*Gen.* i, 11, 12, 13).

As shown in the preceding chapter, the inspired writer of the narrative of Creation is silent as to the *time* when the earth was formed; its formation may have began, and perhaps did begin, with the movement of matter on the first creative day; and it may have been completed on that day; or, it may not have been completed until after the formation of the firmament or heaven which envelops it was

117

411

completed on the second creative day. Be this as
it may, the language of our text leaves no room for
doubt that on the opening of the third creative day,
the earth was already formed. Hence, the first command given on that day was, "Let the waters under
the heaven be gathered together unto one place,
and let the dry land appear: and it was so."

We are thus taught (1), that though the earth
was already formed at the beginning of the third
creative day, it was enveloped in water. This places
the Mosaic Record in harmony with the sciences
which teach that in the early history of our globe
"the ocean was universal"—the whole earth was
enveloped in water. (See *The World Before the Deluge*, p. 95, Fiquier. Also *Creation*, p. 79, Guyot.
The Origin of the World, p. 174, Dawson. *Moses and
Geology*, p. 93, Kinns). (2) That the waters enveloping the earth, perhaps a greater or less
amount of which was in the form of vapor,
which extended from the earth's surface to the
firmament, was condensed into water, and this water
"gathered" into the indentations on the earth's
surface which God prepared for their reception, and
which he called "seas." (3) That God's commands,
"Let the waters under the heaven be gathered together unto one place," and "Let the dry land appear," were executed, as shown by the fact that the
inspired writer says, "And it was so." (4) That the
inspired writer of the *Narrative of Creation* thus emphatically commits the Bible to the teaching that the
earth was the first of the great bodies formed.

Inasmuch as the inspired author is silent as to

when the formation of the earth began, or when it was completed, we have no data upon which to base a decision upon this subject, for the sciences can throw no light upon these questions.   There is a strong disposition on the part of men to theorize upon this subject, and to speculate as to how, and when, the earth was formed; but with no data, either scriptural or scientific, to guide them to correct conclusions, their speculations must inevitably culminate in so many *guesses;* and the mere fact that in most cases the *guesser* is a man of scientific attainments does not raise his *guess* to the dignity of a science, since *science* is something *known*. Hence, all attempts to explain the *time* and the *manner* in which the earth was formed is not only the height of folly, but is actually criminal, because misleading.   The necessity for caution in this matter is shown by the statement of Sir Charles Lyell, the great English geologist, who says: "In the year 1806 the French Institute enumerated no less than eighty geological theories which were hostile to the scriptures; but not one of these theories is held to-day."   Is it not creditable to the Bible that these theories which were hostile to it, were abandoned because of their falsity?

For a time the controversy waxed hot between the advocates of the igneous theory, and those of the aqueous theory of the origin of the earth; the former insisting that the earth was formed through the agency of fire, and the latter maintaining that the earth was formed through the agency of water. But as the theory of La Place, which assumes the

413

earth to have formerly been a molten mass, was
generally accepted, the igneous theory gained the
ascendancy over its rival. This theory teaches that
the earth was formerly a molten mass, which, in
the process of cooling gradually formed a crust
around its molten interior, and that this crust is
now many miles thick. The majority of these theorists estimates the thickness of the " earth's crust,"
to be from twenty-five to thirty-five miles; but Dr.
Hopkins, an equally "high authority," estimates
"the probable thickness of the earth's solid crust at a
minimum of 800 miles." (*The World Before the Deluge*, p. 88). The great discrepency between the estimates of these " savants" reveals the fact that they
are utterly unreliable; estimates, to be of any value,
must be based upon facts; but the estimates of these
gentlemen are based upon mere conjecture. This is
further shown by the fact that, the deepest excavations made in the earth, have not exceeded two
miles. Hence, no man knows what exists in the
earth at a depth of 800 miles, or even twenty-five
miles.

We have shown (1) that, for some good reason
known only to Himself, God declined to acquaint
Moses as to the *time* and manner in which the
earth was formed. (2) That the sciences can throw
no light upon these questions. (3) That man is ignorant, and must forever remain in hopeless ignor-
rance of even the materials and the forces which
were employed in the construction of the earth.
This being true, it follows that the modern theorists
who, with no data to aid them in reaching correct

conclusions, attempt to explain the origin of the earth, might have profited by the crushing rebuke which God administered to Job out of the whirlwind: "Who is this that darkeneth counsel with words without knowledge? Gird up thy loins like a man; for I will demand of thee, and answer thou me. Where wast thou when I laid the foundations of the earth? declare, if thou hast understanding. Who hath laid the measures thereof, if thou knowest? or who hath stretched a line upon it? Whereupon are the foundations thereof fastened? or who laid the cornerstone thereof; when the morning stars sang together, and all the sons of God shouted for joy?"

As has been shown, we are absolutely ignorant of and have no means of ascertaining what the conditions are, or what exists in the interior of the earth at a depth of 4,000 miles, or 1,000 miles, or 100 miles, or even 10 miles from its surface. Hence, when the scientist proposes to enlighten us upon these subjects, he at once abandons the domain of science where he is guided by facts, and enters the boundless realm of speculation where his imagination is his only guide. While this is true, the science of geology is invaluable because of the assistance it renders us in ascertaining the order in which the plants and animals made their appearance on the earth. We are thus enabled to compare the teachings of the geological record with those of the Mosaic Record upon this subject. Thus, the declaration of Job holds good: "Speak to the earth and it shall teach thee."

Geology is the science of the earth. When

viewed in the light of this science, the various stratas of the earth may properly be regarded as so many pages in the geological history of our globe. Those stratas which were in process of formation when the first plants and animals made their appearance on the earth, contain more or less of their remains. The remains of the first plants and animals are found in the lowest stratas of the earth; while those of more recent origin are found in the upper stratas. Thus the geological record is formed; and when these stratas are undisturbed the remains of plants and animals which they contain furnish us a record which throws an immense amount of light upon the history of plant and animal life on our globe.

Recognizing the Mosaic Record as God's Word, and the facts presented by the geological record as God's works, we feel assured that the teachings of these great records will harmonize to a nicety when each is carefully investigated and properly understood. Hence, we feel no hesitancy in comparing the *Narration of Creation* with the geological history of plant and animal life on the earth as revealed by scientific research. And we have now reached a point in our investigations where the results of geological research enables us to compare the two records.

We should note the fact that the inspired writer commits the Bible to the teaching that plant life preceded animal life on the earth. We quote the following high authorities on the distinctive characteristics of plants and animals. Professor Dana says: " Plants find nutriment in carbolic acid, appropriate the carbon and excrete oxygen, a gas essential to animal life; animals use oxygen in respiration, and excrete carbonic acid, a gas essential to vegetable life.

"Plants take inorganic material as food, and turn it into organic; animals take this organic material thus prepared (plants), or other organic materials made from it (animals), finding no nutriment in inorganic matter. The vegetable kingdom is a provision for the storing away or magazining of force for the animal kingdom." (*Manual of Geology*, p. 115).

Dr. Kinns says: "The exact period when plants first appeared cannot be told, for their delicate structure is such that their earliest forms may have been entirely destroyed. We may be certain, however, that they preceded animals, for as they can derive their nourishment and add to their tissues from inorganic matter, which animals cannot do, it would be necessary for them to have existed in some form first for animals to feed upon." (*Moses and Geology*, p. 145).

Professor Guyot says: "The most important function of the plant in the economy of nature is to turn inorganic into organic matter, and thus prepare food for the animal. Nothing else in nature does this work. The animal cannot do it, and starves in the midst of an abundance of the materials needed for the building up of its body. The plant stores up force which it is not called upon to use; the animal takes it ready-made as food, and expends it in activity. The plant, therefore, is the indispensable basis

of all animal life; for though animals partially feed
upon each other, ultimately the organic matter they
need must come from the plant." (*Creation*, pp. 88,
89).

Having shown that vegetation, which is essential to the existence of the animal, necessarily preceded animal life on the earth, it is now in order for
us to investigate that part of our text which describes
the introduction of plant life.

"And God said, Let the earth bring forth grass,
the herb bearing seed, and the fruit tree yielding
fruit after his kind: and it was so."

It will be observed that the inspired writer
divides the plants into three classes: grass, herbs
bearing seed, and fruit trees yielding fruit, all after
their kind.

Dr. Kinns in discussing this text says: " For the
present, I will show that a better translation of the
verses relating to the advent of vegetable life will
prove the marvelous correctness of Moses' statements.   I would just say that in endeavoring to give
a more suitable rendering of this and other passages,
I have consulted high authorities, and have been
aided by some of our most eminent scholars, whom
I have mentioned in my preface.   These gentlemen
confirm Dr. Kitto's explanation of this verse, that
the word *deshe*, translated 'grass,' is applicable to
every kind of verdure in the state of sprouting.

"Secondly, that *esebh*, rendered 'herb,' denotes
a higher order of plants propagated by seeds, for as
Kitto says, the words 'herb yielding seed' are very

emphatic in the original; they are, litterly, *herb seed-ing seed*, exactly imitated in the Septuagint version.

"Thirdly ('*ēts p'rî*) fruit trees may refer to certain trees of the Devonian and Carboniferous periods, some of which approached to true fruit trees. Here, then, we get much light upon the matter; for such translations enable us to see that the Geological and Biblical statements are not at variance." (*Moses and Geology*, p. 144).

In discussing our text, Professor Dawson says: "*Deshe*, translated 'grass' in our version, is derived from a verb signifying to spring up or bud forth; the same verb, indeed, used in this verse to denote 'bringing forth' literally causing to spring up. Its radical meaning is therefore, vegetation in the act of sprouting or springing forth. * * * 'With respect to the use of the word in this place, I may remark: (1) It is not correctly translated by the word 'grass'; for grass bears seed, and is, consequently, a member of the second class of plants mentioned. Even if we set aside all ideas of inspiration, it is obviously impossible that any one living among a pastoral or agricultural people could have been ignorant of this fact. (2) It can scarcely be a general term, including all plants when in a young or tender state. The idea of their springing up is included in the verb, and this was but a very temporary condition. Besides, this word does not appear to be employed for the young state of shrubs or trees. (3) We thus appear to be shut up to the conclusion that *deshe* here means those plants, mostly small and herbaceous, which bear no proper seeds;

in other words, the cryptogamia—as fungi, mosses, lichens, ferns, etc.   The remaining words are translated with sufficient accuracy in our version.   They denote seed-bearing or phœnogamous herbs and trees.   *   *   *   'The arrangement of the plants in three great classes of cryptogams, seed-bearing herbs, and fruit bearing trees differs in one important point, —viz.: the separation of herbaceous plants from trees —from modern botanical classification.   It is, however, sufficiently natural for the purposes of a general description like this, and perhaps gives more precise ideas of the meaning intended than any other arrangement equally concise and popular. It is also probable that the object of the writer was not so much a natural history classification as an account of the *order* of creation, and that he wishes to affirm that the introduction of these three classes of plants on the earth corresponded with the order here stated.   This view renders it unnecesary to vindicate the accuracy of the arrangement on botanical grounds, since the historical order was evidently better suited to the purpose in view, and in so far as the earlier appearance of crytogamous plants is concerned, it is in strict accordance with geological fact."   (*The Origin of the World*, pp. 186, 187, 188).

Thus it is shown (1) that the inspired writer divides the plants into three classes: "*Sproutage*" (Cryptogamia—as fungi, mosses, lichens, ferns, etc., which are seedless, and reproduce from *spores*.) *Herb bearing seed.*   (Herb is "a plant, the atom of which is not woody; a plant producing shoots only of annual duration from the surface of the earth."

Herbaceous plant is one "the stem of which perishes annually; one producing an annual stem from a perennial root.") And *Fruit Trees.* (2) That the teachings of the Mosaic Record with reference to the *order* in which these three classes of plants made their appearance upon the earth corresponds with the *Geological Record* upon this subject. The vegetation which was introduced upon the earth on the *third* cosmogonic day was confined to *wild* plants, which subsist without cultivation; in a subsequent chapter we shall show that *domestic* plants, which require cultivation, made their appearance on the earth simultaneously with *man* on the *sixth* day.

The vegetation of the earth attained its greatest luxuriance in what is known as the "Carboniferous Age;" and this age is divided into three periods: The Subcarboniferous, the Carboniferous, and the Permian. (*Dana*).

The following description of the flora of the Carboniferous Age is taken from Figuire's *World Before the Deluge:*

"In the history of our globe the Carboniferous period succeeds to the Divonian. It is in the formation of this latter epoch that we find the fossil fuel which has done so much to enrich and civilize the world in our own age. * * * 'The monuments of this era of profuse vegetation reveal themselves in the precious coal-measures of England and Scotland. These give us some idea of the rich verdure which covered the surface of the earth, newly risen from the bosom of its parent waves. It was the paradise of terrestrial vegetation. The grand *Sig-*

gillaria, the *Calamites*, and other fern-like plants,
were especially typical of this age, and formed the
woods, which were left to grow undisturbed; for as
yet no living Mammals seem to have appeared;
everything indicates a uniformly warm, humid temperature, the only climate in which the gigantic ferns
of the coal-measures could have attained their magnitude.   *   *   *   'Conifers have been found of
this period with concentric rings, but these rings
are more slightly marked than in existing trees of
the same family, from which it is reasonable to assume that the seasonal changes were less marked
than they are with us.   *   *   *   'The fundamental
character of the period we are about to study is the
immense development of a vegetation which flourished in remote ages of the world. Buried under
an enormous thickness of rocks, it has been preserved to our days, after being modified in its onward nature and external aspect. Having lost a
portion of its elementary constituents, it has become
transformed into a species of carbon, impregnated
with those bituminous substances which are the ordinary products of the slow decomposition of vegetable matter.

"Thus coal, which supplies our manufacturers
and our furnaces, which is the fundamental agent of
our productive and economic industry — the coal
which warms our houses and furnishes the gas
which lights our streets and dwellings — is the substance of the plants which formed the forests, the
vegetation, and the marshes of the ancient world at

a period too distant for human chronology to calculate with anything like precision. * * *

"Let us pause for a moment, and consider the general characters which belonged to our planet during the carboniferous period. Heat—though not necessarily excessive heat—and extreme humidity were then the attributes of its atmosphere. The modern allies of the species which formed its vegetation are now only found under the burning latitudes of the tropics; and the enormous dimensions in which we find them in the fossil state prove, on the other hand, that the atmosphere was saturated with moisture. Dr. Livingston tells us that continual rains, added to intense heat, are the climatic characteristics of Equatorial Africa, where the vigorous and tufted vegetation flourishes which is so delightful to the eye.

"It is a remarkable circumstance that conditions equable and warm climate, combined with humidity, do not seem to have been limited to any part of the globe, but the temperature of the whole globe seems to have been nearly the same in very different latitudes. From the equatorial regions up to Melville Island, in the Arctic Ocean, where in our days eternal frost prevails—from Spitzbergin to the center of China, the carboniferous flora is identically the same. When Novaia Similia and New South Wales had a flora much alike, when the same species, now extinct, are met with of equal development at the equator as at the pole, we cannot but admit that at this epoch the temperature of the globe was nearly alike everywhere. What we call *climate* was

unknown in these geological times. There seems to
have been then only one climate over the whole
globe. It was at a subsequent period, that is in
Tertiary times, that the cold began to make itself
felt at the terrestrial poles.   *   *   *

"The ferns, which in our days and in our climate, are most commonly only small perennial
plants, in the carboniferous age sometimes presented themselves under lofty and even magnificent
forms.

"Every one knows those marsh plants with
hollow, channelled, and articulated cylindrical stems;
whose joints are furnished with a membranous, den-
ticulated sheath, and which bear the vulgar name of
'mare's tails,' their fructification forming a sort of
catkin composed of many rings of scales, carrying
on their lower surface sacs full of spores or seeds.
These humble Equiseta were represented during the
coal-period by herbaceous trees from twenty to
thirty feet high and four to six inches in diameter.
Their trunks, channelled longitudinally, and divided
transversely by lines of articulation, have been preserved to us: they bear the name of *Calamites*.
They seem to have grown by means of an under-
ground stem, while new buds issued from the
ground at intervals.   *   *   *

"The *Lycopods* of our age are humble plants,
scarcely a yard in height, and most commonly
creepers; but the Lycopodiaceæ of the ancient
world were trees of eighty or ninety feet in height.
It was the *Lepidodendrons* which filled the forest.
Their leaves were sometimes twenty inches long,

and their trunks a yard in diameter. Such are the
dimensions of some specimens of *Lepidodindron cari-*
natum which have been found. Another Lycopod
of this period, the *Lomatophloios crassicaule*, attained
dimensions still more colossal. The *Sigillarias* sometimes exceeded 100 feet in height. Herbaceous
Ferns were also exceedingly abundant, and grew beneath the shade of these gigantic trees. It was the
combination of these lofty trees with such shrubs
(if we may so call them), which formed the forests
of the Carboniferous period. * * *

"This flora, then, consists of great trees, and
also of many smaller plants, forming a close, thick
turf, or sod, when partially buried in marshes of almost unlimited extent. There have been described
as characterising the period, 1,700 species of
plants belonging to families which we have already
seen making their first appearance in the Devonian
period, but which now attain a prodigious development. * * * Such is a general view of the features
most characteristic of the coal-period, and of the primary epoch in general. It differs altogether and
absolutely, from that of the present day; the climatic conditions of these remote ages of the globe,
however, enables us to comprehend the characteristics which distinguish its vegetation. A damp atmosphere, of an equable rather than intense heat
like that of the tropics, a soft light veiled by permanent fogs, were favorable to the growth of this
peculiar vegetation, of which we search in vain for
anything strictly analogous in our own days. The
nearest approach to the climate and vegetation pro-

per to the geological period which now occupies our attention, would probably be found in certain islands, or on the littoral of the Pacific Ocean—the island of Chiloe, for example, where it rains 300 days in the year, and where the light of the sun is shut out by perpetual fogs; where arborescent ferns form forests, beneath whose shade grow herbaceous ferns, which rise three feet and upwards above a marshy soil, which give shelter also to a mass of cryptogamic plants greatly resembling, in its main features, the flora of the coal-measures."

In closing his discussion of the three classes of plants described in our text, Dr. Kinns says: "Here I must clear up another difficulty. It will be noticed that though I give other meanings to the words translated 'grass' and 'herb,' I still adhere to the word 'fruit trees' (*'ēts p'rî*) ; but instead of there being an error in point of time, I can show that both in the Devonian and Carboniferous periods there existed numerous trees of the Coniferous order, the seed-vessels of which might be properly styled fruit. * * * 'Some of the seed-vessels were quite surrounded with fleshy coatings, which might, as in the Ginkgo of Japan, have constituted edible fruits. * * * 'The interior integument is very thick and cellular, and was, no doubt, once fleshy. The second coat was thinner, but hard, and marked by three ridges. This coating, being all that commonly remains in a fossil state, has suggested the name of Trigonocarpon. Within this were the third and fourth coats, both of which are very delicate membranes, and may possibly have been two plates belonging to one membrane. Lyell says its geological importance is great; for so abundant is it in the Coal Measures that in certain localities the fruit of some species may be procured by the bushel. 'On the whole,' Sir Joseph Hooker says, 'these fruits are referable to a highly-developed type, exhibiting extensive modifications of elementary organs for the purpose of their adaptation to special functions; and these modifications are as great, and the adaptaion as special, as any to be found amongst analagous fruits in the existing vegetable world."' (*Ibid*, pp. 156, 157, 158, 159).

Thus, the geological record sustains the Mosaic Record in its teaching that these three great classes of plants, "Sproutage," "Herb-bearing seed," and "Fruit-trees," made their appearance in the order stated.

CHAPTER VI.

LUMINARIES.

"And God said, let there be lights in the firmament of heaven to divide the day from the night; and let them be for signs, and for seasons, and for days, and for years.

"And let them be for lights in the firmament of the heaven to give light upon the earth: and it was so.

"And God made two great lights; the greater light to rule the day, and the lesser light to rule the night: he made the stars also.

"And God set them in the firmament of heaven to give light upon the earth.

"And to rule over the day and over the night, and to divide the light from the darkness: and God saw that it was good.

And the evening and the morning were the fourth day." (*Gen.* i, 14, 15, 16, 17, 18, 19).

We should note that in addition to producing light, the celestial bodies were designed for other purposes—"to divide the light from the darkness," and for "signs, and for seasons, and for days and years;" that the "greater light"—the *sun*—should "rule the day," and the lesser light—the *moon*—should "rule the night." And that they discharge

134

428

the duties for which they were designed is attested
by the inspired writer, who says, "And it was so."

Here we have the most positive proof that one
of the purposes for which the sun and moon were
formed was for "days," and that prior to the fourth
creative day there could be no such thing as a
"solar day," or day of twenty-four hours, beginning
with the rising, and ending with the setting of the
sun; and that the six creative days, three of which
passed before the sun existed were not solar days,
since there was no sun to mark their beginning and
ending. Hence, the Bible is silent as to length of
the creative days, as well as that of the *seventh* day,
in which God rested from his works; while the results of all scientific research prove that they were
immense periods of time; and this is further shown
by the fact that the *seventh* day upon which God
rested from His works, has continued for thousands
of years with no evidence at present that it is near-
ing its close.

The separation of "the light from the darkness,"
thus producing day and night, and the division of
time into months and years, are processes too well
understood to require discussion here; while it is
equally well known that the signs of the Zodiac are
derived from the celestial bodies:

"There stay until the twelve celestial signs
Have brought about their annual recoming."
—*Shakespeare*.

The atheists and infidels who, as a class, are advocates of the Nebular Hypothesis, delight to ridicule the teaching of the Bible that plant life was in-

troduced on the earth prior to the formation of the sun, moon and stars; and many professed believers in the Bible combat this teaching of the Mosaic Record, which is so directly opposed to their theory.

We should note the fact that the introduction of plant life was the last event of the third creative day; and immediately following this event the formation of the sun, moon and stars began on the fourth creative day. As has been shown, the three classes of plants — *Sproutage*, *Herb-bearing Seed*, and *Fruit Trees*, made their appearance on the earth in the order stated; but there is nothing in the Mosaic Record to indicate that these three classes of plants all made their appearance on the third creative day. Hence, the mere introduction of plant life on the third creative day would meet all the requirements of the Mosaic Record. On the other hand, the geological record shows that fruit trees made their appearance in the Devonian Age, long after the celestial bodies were formed. We have no means of ascertaining the precise period when vegetation made its appearance on the earth, but the geological record indicates that it occurred in what is termed *Archæan Time*. In discussing this period, Mr. Dana says:

"No distinct remains of plants have been observed. The occurrence of graphite in the rocks. and its making 20 per cent. of some layers, is strong evidence that plants of some kind, if not also animals, were abundant. For graphite is carbon, one of the constituents of wood and animal matters; and mineral coal, whose vegetable origin is beyond question, has been observed, in the carboniferous rocks

of Rhode Island, changed to graphite; and even coal
plants, as ferns, occur at St. Johns, New Brunswick,
in the state of graphite. Further, the amount of
graphite in the Laurentian rocks is enormous. Dawson observes (taking his facts from Logan) that it is
scarcely an exaggeration to maintain that the quantity of carbon in the Laurentian is equal to that in
similar areas of the Carboniferous system. * * *
In Europe, graphite occurs in the Archæan rocks of
Bavaria; anthracite has been observed in the iron-
bearing rocks of this age at Arendal, Norway; and
carbonacious (partly anthracite) and bituminous substances are distributed through layers of Archæan
gneiss and mica schist at Nullaburg, in Wermland,
Sweden, constituting 5 to 10 per cent., facts pointing clearly to the existence of life before this era. * *

"The plants must have been the lowest of Cryptogams or *flowerless* species, and mainly at least, *marine Algæ* or *Sea-Weeds;* for the Primordial beds
next succeeding contain remains of nothing higher.
This argument from the Primordial excludes all
mosses and the ordinary terrestrial plants; but not
necessarily lichens, since these grow in dry places,
and could not have contributed to marine deposits
if they had existed. It is hence possible that, besides sea-weeds in the water, there were *lichens* over
the bare rocks. The easily destructible *fungi* may
also have lived in damp places." (*Manual of Geology,* pp. 157, 158).

According to the theory of La Place, the earth
was formerly a molten mass which, in the process of
cooling formed a crust around its molten interior;

as the globe continued to cool, its crust thickened
until the temperature of the waters and the surface
of the earth were sufficiently reduced as to make it
possible for vegetation to exist, when plant life made
its appearance as the result of *spontaneous generation;*
during this period the earth, but recently elevated
above the waves of the "primeval ocean," was enveloped in dense clouds and vapors which excluded
the greater part of the sun's light and heat until the
clouds and vapors were dissipated in the latter part
of the Carboniferous Age; but during the continuance of the clouds and vapors there was sufficient
light for vegetation, while the excluded heat of the
sun was compensated for by the internal heat of the
earth, which stimulated the growth of the profuse
vegetation of that early period, and produced that
uniformity of temperature of the earth's surface
which existed from pole to pole.

If we accept the Nebular Hypothesis which
teaches that the sun is older than the earth, and that
it is in fact the parent of the earth, we must reject
the Bible which teaches that the earth is older than
the sun, and that vegetation was introduced upon
its surface before the celestial bodies existed; we
must also accept the theory that the earth was
formerly a molten mass; that the heat which stimulated the growth of vegetation down to the Permian
period, and produced an even temperature throughout the earth's surface at that remote period was derived from the molten interior of the earth; while
the light in which the vegetation of Archaean time
flourished was *obscured sunlight.* But as has been

shown, the Nebular Hypothesis is a mere speculation at best; and its falsity is demonstrated by its conflict with the scriptures, and with well established scientific facts; and also its failure to explain more than a fractional part of the phenomena of the universe.

On the other hand, if we reject the Nebular Hypothesis with all its absurdities, and adhere to the Bible, we must explain the source from which the heat and light necessary for vegetation was derived prior to the existence of the sun, moon and stars; and happily, as might have been expected, modern science comes to the support of the Bible by furnishing a solution of this problem. In discussing this question we should bear in mind (1) That, "*Heat and light are but different intensities of the vibratory motions of matter.*" (2) That in the movement of these great masses of matter which were concentrated in the earth and its enveloping firmament, an immense amount of heat was generated, which raised the temperature of the earth's surface, its waters, and its atmosphere to a point far too high to make it possible for plant life to have then existed on the globe. (3) That when the firmament which surrounds the earth was completed on the second creative day, it confined the heat of the earth's surface and its waters, and its atmosphere, to the earth, just as it confines the earth's waters and its atmosphere to the earth to-day. This immense amount of heat had no means of escape save by abstraction from its contact with the intensely cold firmament above; this cooling process was necessarily very slow, and doubtless extended through that long period of time described in the Mosaic Record as the *third day*. Thus, by the abstraction of its excessive heat the earth was prepared for the introduction of plant life. (4) That the first event of the third creative day was the separation of the "dry land" from the waters that enveloped it; this was necessarily a slow process, and doubtless required ages for its accomplishment. (5) That during the period when the earth was enveloped in water, and for a long time after, the dry land was separated from the waters, the atmosphere being at a high temperature, was saturated with water, for the disposition of air is to take up vapor from water with which it is brought in contact in proportion to its temperature. (6) That the introduction of plant life on the earth was the last event of the third creative day; and immediately preceded the opening of the fourth creative day. (7) That on the fourth creative day, the formation of the sun, moon and stars began. (8) That in the movement of these immense masses of matter of which the sun, moon and stars were formed, there was an enormous amount of heat generated; and that a great amount of this heat was radiated to every part of the earth's surface, and stimulated the growth of the vegetation of the earth until the formation of the celestial bodies was completed, when the heat from this formative process ended, and was compensated for by the heat derived from the sun. In addition to stimulating the growth of vegetation, the heat which resulted from the movement of matter in the formation of the celestial bodies, doubtless retarded the cooling of the earth's atmosphere, and contributed largely to prolonging that evenness of temperature at the earth's surface which characterized those early periods. (9) That in the movement of these great masses of matter which were concentrated in the celestial bodies in the process of their formation, there was a considerable amount of light—*cosmic* light—generated; and that an amount of this light, sufficient for the needs of vegetation, penetrated the vapors which then enveloped the earth, just as the rays of light from the sun afterwards did. Thus, with the aid of modern science, which teaches that heat and light are but different intensities of the vibratory motions of matter, we find that in the movement of these enormous masses of matter which were concentrated in the celestial bodies on the fourth creative day, we have the true source from which the heat and light necessary for vegetation, was derived at that remote period when plant life was introduced on our globe.

To suppose that in the movement of those enormous masses of matter which were concentrated in the sun, moon and stars, neither heat nor light was generated, would compel us to reject the teaching of modern science that *heat and light are but different intensities of the vibratory motions of matter.* The Bible plainly teaches that each of the six creative days were distinct periods of time; and in the very nature of things, the line of demarcation between them was sharply drawn. Hence, the ending of one of the creative days was instantly followed by its succeeding day; and thus the last event of the one day was immediately followed by the first event of the succeeding day; for example: the introduction of plant life—the last event of the third creative day, was immediately followed by the movement of matter in the process of its formation into the sun, moon and stars, on the fourth day, and in the movement of these immense masses of matter all the heat and light necessary for vegetation was produced, when the vapors which enveloped the earth were dissipated in the latter part of the Carboniferous Age, the "two great lights" at once entered upon the duties for which they were designed—"for signs, and for seasons, and for days and years." This event is marked in the *Geological Record* by the appearance of *concentric*, or season rings on the forest growths of the Permian period; these season rings mark the advent of the *seasons*.

The following definition of the term *seasons* is sufficiently accurate for our purpose, since it shows that the *seasons* produce the variations in climate, and consequently exert the most direct influence upon vegetation. Hence, prior to the advent of the *seasons*, the *climate* of the globe was identical from pole to pole—in fact, properly speaking, there was no such thing as climate; the temperature was the same on every portion of the earth's surface, as shown by the fact that vegetation at the equator was identical with that at the poles:

"Season. * * *

"I. Lit. and Astron.: The alternations in the relative lengths of day and night, heat and cold, etc., which take place each year. * * * The essential astronomical fact on which the recurrence of the successive seasons depends is that the axis of the earth always points in the same direction, whatever portion of the orbit the earth may at the time be traversing. The inclination of the equator to the ecliptic is 23° 27′. On June 21st, when the sun is at the highest point of the ecliptic, the north pole necessarily inclines toward the sun, and is as much irradiated as it ever can be by his beams, whilst the south pole, on the contrary, is as little. It is therefore midsummer in the northern, and midwinter in the southern hemisphere. Six months later, December 21st, the southern pole points towards the sun. It is, therefore, now midwinter in the northern, and midsummer in the southern hemisphere. At the intermediate periods (March 21st. and September 21st.) the axis of the earth is at right angles to the direction of the sun; hence, in both hemispheres it is the equinox—the vernal at the former date in the northern, and at the latter in the southern hemisphere." *(Universal Dictionary,* p. 4, 170).

After discussing the profuse vegetation of the Carboniferous Age, Dr. Kinns says of the Permian period: "In the Permian system the profuse vegetation of the Carboniferous no longer existed; but the fossil remains of plants show a great increase of ligneous or woody tissue, which could only have been produced by the presence of unclouded sunlight. Most of the trees I described in the last chapter were of a soft and pulpy nature, with no season-rings, for huge trunks several feet in diame-

ter were found in the coal compressed and flattened
where they lie in a horizontal or inclining position;
season-rings, however, are found in the flora of the
Trias and Secondary strata." (*Ibid*, p. 188).

Sir Robert S. Ball in discussing the sun, says:
"In commencing our examination of the orbs which
surround us, we naturally begin with our peerless
sun. His splendid brilliance gives him the pre-
eminence over all other celestial bodies. The dimensions of our luminary are commensurate with
his importance.

"Astronomers have succeeded in the difficult
task of ascertaining the exact figures, but they are
so gigantic that the results are hard to realize. The
diameter of the orb of day, or the length of the axis,
passing through the center from one side to the
other, is 865,000 miles. Yet this bare statement of
the dimensions of the great globe fails to convey an
adequate idea of its vastness. If a railway were laid
round the sun, and if we were to start in an express
train moving sixty miles an hour, we should have to
travel for five years without intermission night or
day before we had accomplished the journey.

"When the sun is compared with the earth the
bulk of our luminary is still more striking. Suppose
his globe were cut up into one million parts, each of
these parts would appreciably exceed the bulk of the
earth. Were the sun placed in one pan of a mighty
weighing balance, and were 300,000 bodies as heavy
as our earth placed in the other, the luminary would
turn the scale. * * *

"The actual distance of the sun from the earth

is about 92,700,000 miles; but by merely reciting the figures we do not receive a vivid impression of the real magnitude. * * * It would be necessary to count as quickly as possible for three days and three nights before one million was completed; yet this would have to be repeated nearly ninety-three times before we had counted all the miles between the earth and the sun." (*The Story of the Heavens*, pp. 26, 27, 28).

Mr. Richard A. Proctor says:

"In long past ages there were nations that worshiped the sun. He was their God; he seemed to them as a being of might, 'rejoicing as a giant to run his course,' and capable not only of influencing the fortunes of men and nations, but of hearkening and responding to their prayers. A vain thought truly, for the creature was worshiped and the Creator forgotten. Yet of all the forms of religion in which created things were worshiped sun-worship was the least contemptible. Indeed, if there is any object which men can properly take as an emblem of the power and goodness of Almighty God, it is the sun.

"The sun is an emblem of the Almighty in being the source whence all that lives upon the earth derives support. Our very existence depends on the beneficient supply of light and heat poured out continually upon the earth by the great central orb of the planetary scheme. Let the sun forget to shine for a single day, and it would be with us even as though God had forgotten our existence, or had remembered us only to punish; myriads of creatures now living on the earth would perish, uncounted millions would suffer fearfully. But let the sun's rays cease to be poured out for four or five days, and every living creature on the earth would be destroyed. Or, on on the other hand, even a worse (or at least more sudden and terrible) fate would befall us if an angel of wrath 'poured out his vial upon the sun, and power were given unto it to scorch men with fire.'

"Yet again the sun is an emblem of the Almighty in the manner in which he bestows benefits upon us and is forgotten. Day after day we enjoy the sun's light and heat; clouds may conceal him from our view, much as troubles may cause us to forget God; and the heat he pours out may seem sometimes insufficient or excessive, even as in our ignorance we are dissatisfied with the blessings bestowed by the Almighty. Yet these very clouds are among the good works we owe to the sun—they bring the rain which 'drops fatness upon the earth;' and without the changes of the season there would be neither the time of harvest nor the time of vintage. The cold of winter and the heat of summer, at which we often repine as excessive, are as necessary for our wants as the cool breeze and the genial warmth of spring or autumn.

"We commonly forget, also, that the sun, besides sustaining us by his light-giving and heat-supplying powers, keeps us always near to him by that mighty force of attraction which his vast bulk enables him to exert. When we look at the sun as he rises (even as 'the glory of God coming from the way of the east'), how seldom is the thought present in our minds that in that ruddy orb there exists the most tremenduous power, swaying not only this vast globe on which we live, but orbs yet vaster than she is, and traveling on far wider courses; that the light and heat which seem to be gathering forces as he rises, are in reality poured forth with fullness, even while as yet, owing to our position, we receive but little of them—nay, that during the dark hours of the night they have been poured forth abundantly upon the earth, and that so rich is the sun in power and beneficence, through the might of his Creator and ours, that our earth is nourished and supported by the two thousand millionth part of the heat and light which he pours forth!   *   *   *

"If we would rightly measure the sun's activity as a dispenser of God's gifts of light and heat, we must consider what our earth receives.   *   *   * It has been calculated that the heat received by the earth during twenty-four hours would be sufficient to raise an ocean 250 yards deep, covering the whole surface of the earth from the temperature of freezing water to that of boiling water. And this, be it remembered, is less than 2,000 millionth part of the heat which the sun pours out into space during the same interval of time. Ceaselessly the wonderful stream of heat-waves is poured out on all sides. So energetic is it that the heat emitted in a single second would suffice to boil 195 millions of cubic miles of ice-cold water. Or, to take another illustration, which recent experience as to the value of our coal supplies will bring home to many of us with peculiar force— in order to produce by the burning of coals the supply of heat which we receive from the sun, there

would have to be consumed on every square yard of
the sun's surface no less than six tons of coal per
hour; while, if a globe as large as our earth had to
maintain such a supply of heat, it would be necessary that on every square yard of its surface more
than three tons of coal should be consumed in every
second of time." (*The Expanse of Heaven*, pp. 11, 12,
13, 16, 17).

In discussing the moon, Sir Robert S. Ball
says:

"If the moon were suddenly struck out of existence, we should be immediately apprised of the
fact by a wail from every sea-port in the kingdom.
From London and from Liverpool we should hear
the same story—the rise and fall of the tide had almost ceased. The ships in dock could not get out;
the ships outside could not get in; and the maritime
commerce of the world would be thrown into dire
confusion.

"The moon is the principal agent in causing the
daily ebb and flow of the tide, and this is the most important work which our satellite has to do. The fleets
of fishing boats around the coasts time their daily
movements by the tide, and are largely indebted to
the moon for bringing them in and of the harbor.
Experienced sailors assure us that the tides are of
the utmost service to navigation.   *   *   *

"The brilliancy of the moon arises solely from
the light of the sun which falls on the not self-lumi-
nous substance of the moon. Out of the vast flood
of light which the sun pours forth with such prodi-
gality into space the dark body of the moon inter-

cepts a little, and of that little it reflects a small fraction to illuminate the earth. The moon sheds so much light, and seems so bright, that it is often difficult at night to remember that the moon has no light, except what falls on it from the sun. Nevertheless, the actual surface of the brightest full moon is perhaps not much brighter than the streets of London on a clear sunshiny day. * * *

"The brilliancy and apparent vast proportions of the moon arise from the fact that it is only 240, 000 miles away, which is a distance almost immeasurably small when compared with the distances between the earth and the stars. * * * When we measure the actual diameters of the two globes, we find that of the earth to be 7,918 miles, and of the moon, 2,160 miles, so that the diameter of the earth is nearly four times greater than the diameter of the moon. If the earth were cut into fifty pieces, all equally large, then one of these pieces rolled into a globe would equal the size of the moon. The superficial extent of the moon is equal to about one-thirteenth part of the surface of the earth. The hemisphere our neighbor turns towards us exhibits an area equal to about one twenty-seventh part of the area of the earth. This, to speak approximately, is about double the actual extent of the continent of Europe. The average materials of the earth are, however, much heavier than those contained in the moon. It would take more than eighty globes, each as ponderous as the moon, to weigh down the earth." (*The Story of the Heavens*, pp. 49, 50, 51, 52).

In discussing the moon, Mr. Proctor says:

" Although the sun must undoubtedly have been the first celestial object whose movements or aspect attracted the attention of men, yet it can scarcely be questioned that the science of astronomy had its real origin in the study of the moon. Her comparatively rapid motion in her circuit around the earth afforded in very early ages a convenient measure of time. The *month* was, of course, in the first place, a lunar time-measure. The *week*, the earliest division of time (except the day alone) of which we have any record, had also its origin in the lunar motions." (*The Moon*, p. 1).

In further discussing the moon, Mr. Proctor says:

"I have spoken of the reverence with which men in long past ages contemplated the sun. * * * And many nations worshipped him as a god. But with this worship there was commonly associated a subordinate worship of the moon; and among some nations the moon was esteemed the greater deity.

"Our month, although not according with the lunar month, nevertheless had its origin in the study of the lunar motions, as indeed the name of this interval of time sufficiently indicates. I need hardly remind the reader, again, of the part which the moon takes in fixing the dates of the Jewish movable festivals, while our own movable festivals in like manner depend on the moon's motions, the Paschal full moon determining Easter Day, and the other movable feasts following accordingly.

"The benefits rendered by the moon as a light-giver at night need hardly be insisted upon. Whe-well has well remarked, in his Bridgewater Treatise, that 'a person of ordinary feelings, who on a fine moonlight night' (moonlit is the more correct expression) 'sees our satellite pouring her mild radiance on field and town, path and moor, will probably not only be disposed to 'bless the useful light,' but also to believe that it was 'ordained' for that purpose. The great mathematician La Place adopted an opposite view. Setting himself boldly, one may say defiantly, against the wholesome belief that there is method and design in the works of the Creator, he sneers at the belief of 'those partisans of final causes who have imagined that the moon was given to the earth to afford light during the night.' This 'cannot be so,' he remarked, 'for we are often deprived at the same time of the light of the sun and the moon,' and he proceeds to show how the moon might so have been placed as to be always 'full,' in other words, opposite the sun. * * *

"La Place's device, however, involves the necessity of a moon of different size and distance. He shows how a moon about four times as far off as our moon really is, would revolve around the earth in the same time the sun apparently does, and would present always a full aspect—if originally placed opposite the moon. It is a slight objection to this imagined state of things that, for La Place's moon to appear as large as ours, it should have a diameter about four times as great, and be in fact as large as our earth, while the motions assigned to it require that it should not be more massive than the present moon. Thus it would have to be made of material exceedingly light, about sixty times lighter than the present substance of the moon. This would be about seventeen times lighter than water, and more than four times lighter than cork. We know of no such substance, and therefore it seems idle to discuss further La Place's daring notion. But this also may be remarked: that although such a moon as he described might for a very long period continue always exactly opposite the sun, yet in the course of time this moon would gradually fall away from that position; for the motions both of the earth and of this imagined moon could not possibly remain absolutely uniform. Thus at length a time would come when this moon, instead of being always 'full,' would be always 'new,' that is, always on the same side as the sun, and so give no light at all, even if she did not eclipse the sun.

"On the whole, we may be content to accept the moon as we find her, and to 'bless her useful light,' without being particular to inquire whether another moon might not have given us more light, or under more convenient conditions.   *   *   *

"It is clear that the action of the moon in raising a great tidal wave is of important service to the inhabitants of the earth. It is probable, indeed, that the tides are absolutely necessary to preserve the ocean waters in a healthy condition by continual movement. But the tidal wave discharges special services exceedingly important to mankind. The building and launching of ships would be rendered a task of much greater difficulty if it were not for the alternate rise and fall of the sea. No one, again, who is familiar with life at the seaside, and particularly in cities placed near the mouths of great tidal rivers, can fail to recognize abundant evidence of the importance of the variations of the sea's level in many nautical and commercial processes.

"But perhaps the greatest benefit conferred by the moon on mankind is one which few are aware of. It may truly be said that each year hundreds of lives that would otherwise be endangered are rendered safe by her means. It is known then when our seamen pass far beyond the sight of land, their safety depends on their observations of the celestial bodies. By such observations they are enabled to learn where they are, or, in technical words, their latitude and longitude—that is, their distance north or south of the equator, and their distance east or west of some fixed station, such as Greenwich. Now, their latitude is easily determined by observations of the sun or stars, whose altitude when due south depends solely on the latitude. But it is different with the longitude, for when we travel due east or west we do not find the apparent paths of the sun and stars changing at all. The only change which takes place is in the time at which the celestial bodies rise and set. It is, of course, noon when the sun is due south, wherever the observer may be (at least in our northern hemisphere). But it is not Greenwich noon, unless the observer is due north or south of Greenwich. If he is east of Greenwich it is past Greenwich noon when it is noon for the observer's station, and if he is west of Greenwich it is before Greenwich noon when the sun is due south. If he has a clock showing Greenwich time he can thus learn how far east or west he may be. Now, the moon, properly observed, serves for the seaman the part of a clock which can never go wrong. The stars serve as the marks on the great dial plate of the heavens, by which the position of the moon — the moving hand — can be determined with the utmost nicety. Calculations are then applied to show precisely where the moon would be seen among the stars if the observer were at the center of the earth instead of at his actual station. And then a reference to the Nautical Almanac shows precisely what is the Greenwich time. Thence the observer learns how far east or west he is of Greenwich. And often, after many cloudy nights have passed, the observation of the moon has shown the sailor that owing to currents and misjudged rate of sailing he has been far out in his reckoning; and he has been saved by the moon from a great danger. So that we may find a new meaning in the words of the inspired Psalmist: 'They that go down to the sea in ships, that do business in great waters; these see the works of the Lord, and His wonders in the deep.'" (*The Expanse of Heaven*, pp. 20, 23, 24. 25, 27, 28, 29).

These are a few of the many important offices

which the celestial bodies perform for the earth, its plant and animal life, and for man; but their mention should be sufficient to enable us to realize how foolish, to say nothing of how ungrateful, it is for us to make common cause with atheists and infidels in their attempts to deprive God of the credit due Him for His works, by assigning their origin and operations to mere *chance.*

CHAPTER VII.

THE FORMATION OF THE ANIMALS
AND
THE CREATION OF MIND.

"And God said, Let the waters bring forth abundantly the moving creature that has life, and fowl that may fly above the earth in the open firmament of heaven.

"And God created great whales, and every living creature that moveth, which the waters brought fourth abundantly, after their kind, and every winged fowl after his kind, and God saw that it was good.

"And God blessed them, saying, Be fruitful, and multiply, and fill the waters in the seas, and let fowl multiply in the earth.

"And the evening and the morning were the fifth day." (*Gen.* i, 20, 21, 22, 23).

In the preceding chapter it was shown (1) that plant life preceded animal life on the globe. (2) That the three classes of forest plants—Sproutage, Herb-bearing seed, and Fruit trees, made their appearance on the earth in the order stated in the Mosaic Record, but that these three classes of plants did not *all* make their appearance on the third creative day, but only the *first*, and *lowest* class of these plants; and that the *last*, and *highest* class of

156

plants—fruit bearing trees—did not make their appearance until the Permian period, which occurred during the sixth creative day, as shown by the remains of land animals found among the vegetable remains of that period. Hence, the greatest event of the third creative day was the introduction on the earth of *life—plant life*—in its simplest form. While the Mosaic Record is silent upon the subject, the Geological Record clearly shows that during the fourth creative day, in which the celestial bodies were formed, the plant life of the globe was confined to the simplest forms—the lowest class—of vegetation—*sproutage;* and a moment's reflection should convince us that it would require an immense period of time for the decomposed remains of such delicate plants as sea-weeds, ferns, lichens, etc., to form a strata of soil of any considerable thickness. The slowness with which these delicate plants form a strata of earth of any great thickness explains the fact that the remains of the earliest animals are found associated with the remains of early plant life. Hence, the mere fact that we find remains of animals associated in some of the oldest stratas of the earth, is no evidence that plant life and animal life made their appearance on the earth simultaneously; in fact the earliest stratas show only the remains of plant life, while the Mosaic Record teaches that a long period of time—the fourth creative day —intervened between the introduction of plant and animal life.

The *Geological Record* sustains the Mosaic Record in its teachings that animal life as presented in the fish, followed the introduction of plant life. Professor Dana, in discussing the life of the Lower Silurian, says:

"The Primordial rocks have afforded evidence *only* of *marine* life.

"1. Plants. Algæ, or seaweeds, of the kind called *Fuciods*, are the only forms observed. The slabs of sandstone are sometimes covered throughout with veriform casts of what appear to be stems of this leathery kind of seaweed. Some of the fossils formerly regarded as indications of plants, are now believed to be worm-tracks or borings. But others show by their branching forms that they are true Fuciods.

"2. Animals. The species observed are all invertibrates; they pertain to the four sub-kingdoms. Protozoans, Radiates, Mollusks, and Articulates." (*Manual of Geology*, p. 169).

It will be observed that our text describes two distinct kinds of animals which were introduced upon the globe on the fourth creative day; the one to inhabit the waters, the other to "fly above the earth in the open firmament of heaven."

In the English version of our text, the Hebrew word *tannin*, which signifies great stretched-out sea monsters, is translated *whales*. Professor Dawson says:

"It is interesting to know that the philologists trace a connection between *tannin* and the Greek *teino*, Latin *tendo*, and similar words, signifying to stretch or extend, in the Sanscrit, Gothic, and other languages, leading to the inference that the Hebrew word primarily denotes a lengthened or extended creature, which corresponds well with its application to the crocodile. Taking all the above facts in connection, we are quite safe in concluding that the creatures referred to by the word under consideration are literally reptilian animals; and from the special mention made of them, we may infer that, in their day, they were the lords of creation." (*The Origin of the World*, pp. 214, 215).

Those huge monsters of the Triassic period, the Ichthyosaurus, and the Plesiosaurus, and others of their kind were doubtless the creatures referred to by the inspired writer. Fossil remains of the Ichthyosaurus show it to have attained a length of thirty feet; the fossil remains of the largest Plesiosaurus known is in the museum of the Royal Society of Dublin, and measures twenty-three feet. Mr. Kinns says: "Professor Owen says that he is justified in recording sixteen different species of the Plesiosaurus; and it is to him, in his 'Report on British Reptiles,' I owe the information that the Ichthyosaurus and Plesiosaurus were most probably cold-blooded animals and breathed atmospheric air." (*Moses and Geology*, p. 287).

Before entering upon a discussion of the fowl, we desire to correct an error into which the atheists have led us by classing the Ichthyosaurus, Plesiosaurus, and other amphibians with the Pterodactyl and other winged creatures under the general term, *reptiles;* thus placing representatives of two different *kinds of flesh*—that of the fish and fowl in one class. This is not only unscientific, but is antiscriptural in

Fig. 1. IDEAL BATTLE BETWEEN THE ITCHYOSAURUS AND PLESIOSAURUS.
—From Figuire. The World Before the Deluge.

that, it conflicts with the Mosaic Record, which
teaches that the fish, of which the amphibians are a
part, were made to inhabit the waters; while the
fowl, of which the Pterodactyl and other winged
creatures of the kind are a part, were made to "fly
above the earth in the open firmament of heaven;"
this classification of the atheist is also in direct conflict with Paul's teaching that, "All flesh is not the
same flesh: but there is one kind of flesh of men,
another flesh of beasts, another of fishes, and another of birds." (*I Cor.* xv, 39). Thus, the inspired Apostle teaches that there are *four* different
kinds of flesh on the globe, and that the flesh of the
fowl is as distinct from that of the water animals as
if they inhabited different planets. This being true,
it is a plain infringement upon God's Plan of Creation to place representatives of these two *kinds of*
flesh in one class as *reptiles.*

We also desire to call attention to another error
into which the atheists have led us by placing certain small animals—"creeping things"—belonging to
the flesh of the fish, and that of the fowl, and that of
the beast, in one class under the general term, *in-*
sects. This classification is (1) *unscientific,* because
it is false and misleading. (2) It is *antiscriptural,*
because it is in conflict with the Mosaic Record
which teaches that these creatures were designed for
different *spheres,* a part of them having been made to
inhabit the waters, another part to fly in the air,
while the remainder were made to occupy the dry
land; it is also in conflict with Paul's teaching as to
the four kinds of flesh, since it places representa-

tives of three different *kinds of flesh* in one class. (3) It restricts the term *fowl* to the birds or feathered tribe, thus destroying the harmony which exists between the Mosaic Record and the Geological Record, and brings them in conflict. The Mosaic Record teaches that the *fowl* preceded the land animals on the globe, while the Geological Record shows that the land animals preceded the *feathered* tribe on the globe. The first land animals and the first members of the feathered tribe made their appearance in what is termed *Mesozoic Time*. Mesozoic Time is divided into three periods. "Beginning with the earliest they are: 1. The Triassic Period; 2. The Jurassic Period; 3. The Critaceous or Chalk Period." (*Dana*). The first land animals—representatives of the *flesh of beasts*—were *marsupials*, and made their appearance on the earth in the *Triassic* Period; while the first members of the *feathered* tribe appeared in the Jurassic Period. In describing the life of the Jurassic Period as shown by its fossil remains, Mr. Dana says: "Birds occur fossil at Solenhofen, both their bones and impressions of their feathers." (*Manual of Geology*, p. 446). Thus, it is plain that, if we restrict the Biblical term *fowl*, to the *feathered* tribe, we at once bring the Mosaic Record in conflict with the Geological Record. But the Biblical term *fowl* has a wider significance and should not be restricted to the *feathered* tribe, as shown by the law given Israel, in which is named certain animals belonging to the three *kinds of flesh* which they might eat, and those which they should not eat. After naming certain

animals belonging to the *flesh of beasts*, and those of
the fishes which it was lawful for the Israelites to
eat, and others which it was unlawful for them to
eat, the inspired writer names certain animals belonging to the *flesh* of the fowl which it was lawful
to eat, and others which it was unlawful to eat;
among these we find the *beetle*, the *grasshopper*, the
bat, etc.   (See *Levit.* ii, 19, 22).

Thus we find that the beetle, the grasshopper,
and the locust which, in common parlance are
termed *insects*, are really *fowl;* while the *bat*, which
scientists now class with amphibians as a *reptile*, is
also a fowl. Thus, the Mosaic law throws a flood of
light upon the Mosaic Record as to what animals are
embraced under the term *fowl*, and indicates that all
winged creatures which "fly above the earth" are
fowl. This includes the neuroptera, coleoptera, or-
thoptera, etc., which scientists class as *insects*. The
neuropters and other small winged animals made
their appearance in Paleozoic time, as did the bat
family; the earliest representatives of the bat family
were "huge reptilian bats, veritable flying dragons
with a spread of wings from ten to twenty feet."
(*Allen*).

Thus we are enabled (1) to appreciate the value
of Paul's teaching that, "There is one kind of flesh
of men, another flesh of beasts, another of fishes,
and another of birds;" and to realize that at the
close of the sixth creative day, every creature on
the globe belonged to one or the other of these four
kinds of flesh.   (2) That with the aid of the Mosaic
law we are enabled to determine that the small

FIG. 2. IDEAL LANDSCAPE OF THE LIASSIC PERIOD.

—From Figuire, The World Before the Deluge.

winged animals which are commonly termed *insects*, as well as the large winged animals which are termed *flying reptiles*, are included in the biblical term *fowl*. (3) That the Geological Record sustains the Mosaic Record in its teaching that animal life made its first appearance on the globe in the fish; and that the introduction of the fowl followed that of the fish, thus preceding the land animals.

During those immense periods of time described in the Mosaic Record as the *first*, *second*, *third*, and *fourth* days, the efforts of the Creator were confined to the handling of matter, in the production of light, the formation of the heavens and the earth, the introduction of plant life, and the formation of the celestial bodies. But the *fifth day*, unlike its predecessors, is distinguish by the introduction on that day, of a *new element*—a *creation*—which appeared for the first time in the material universe simultaneously and in combination with matter as presented in the physical organism of the fish. The advent of this creation is described as follows: " And God created great whales, and every living creature which the waters brought forth abundantly after their kind." *(Gen.* i, 21).

Theologians, and such scientists as accept the Bible, have agreed that this new element—this *creation*—was *animal life*; this view of animal life finds no support in either the scriptures or the sciences. *Life—physical* life—is not a *creation*—neither *plant life* nor *animal life*, and the Mosaic Record does not describe it as such. But aside from the teachings of the scriptures and the sciences, it is easy to see that there is not that difference between *plant life* and *animal life*, as would justify us in deciding that plant life was simply a *combination* of the elements inherent in matter, and that animal life was a *creation* distinct from matter. Both plant life and animal life have their *germs*, " containing the same elements in the same proportions." (*Dana*). Each has its circulating fluid; its formative period; its youth; its maturity; its decline, and its final dissolution.

Prof. Dana says: "The vegetable and animal kingdoms are the opposite, but mutually dependent sides or parts of one system of life. (*Manual of Geology,* p. 115). This being true, it follows that, if life was a new element in the material universe, it would have been described as a *creation*, when plant life, which is simply "one side or part," of the "system" first appeared on the earth; and since plant life, the first "side or part" of the life system to appear on the earth, is not described by the inspired writer as a *creation*, it would be absurd to suppose that animal life, the other "side or part" of the "system," which afterwards appeared was a *creation*. In other words, if the elements of *life* was a *creation* distinct from *matter*, the inspired writer would have described them as such when they first appeared in the plant. That the elements of life are not *creations* distinct from *matter*, but are merely elements *inherent* in matter, is shown by the more detailed description of the origin of plants, given in the fourth and fifth verses of the second chapter of Genesis, as follows:

"These are the generations of the heavens and the earth, when they were created, in the day that the Lord God made the earth and the heavens; and every plant of the field before it was in the earth, and every herb of the field before it grew."

Thus, we are plainly taught that the elements of plant life, which are identical with those of animal life, are merely parts of the original *creation*—*matter;* and that they were created in matter "in the beginning;" and consequently existed in matter prior to its formation into the earth. Thus, by creating in the molecules of matter the elements of life, "the Lord God" made "every plant of the field before it was in the earth, and every herb of the field before it grew." Hence, the combination of these original elements into plants and animals, and the first appearance of these on the earth were not *creations*, and are not so described by the inspired writer.

Further evidence that the elements of life—both plant and animal life—were not *creations*, but mere formations out of the original creation—*matter*—is shown by the identity of language used by the Lord in commanding the earth and the waters to bring forth plants and animals, as follows:

"And God said, Let the earth bring forth *sproutage, the herb yielding seed, and the fruit tree yielding fruit*, after his kind, whose seed is in itself upon the earth; and it was so.

"And God said, Let the waters bring forth abundantly the moving creature that hath life; * * * and it was so. And God said, Let the earth bring forth the living creature after his kind; * * * and it was so." (*Gen.* i, 11, 20, 24).

What "was so"? Simply that, in obedience to Divine command the earth and the waters combined the elements of life and brought forth plants and animals.

Inasmuch as the "system of life" is not a *creation*, we must seek elsewhere for the new element— the *creation*—which made its appearance on the fifth creative day in combination with matter as presented in the physical organism of the fish. To accomplish this, we must first ascertain what character pre-eminently distinguished not only the highest, but the lowest order of animal from the plant. In discussing this question, Prof. Dana says: "Plants have no consciousness of self, or of other existences; animals are conscious of an outer world, and even the lowest show it by avoiding obstacles. (*Ibid*, p. 116).

The *physical* organism of the fish is merely a combination of the elements of matter; but *consciousness* is a something distinct from matter, as shown by the fact that it does not exist in light, nor in the heavens, nor in the luminaries; it was a new element which God introduced into the material universe on the fifth creative day. Hence, the inspired writer describes it as a creation. But what is consciousness? Mr. Webster defines it as, "The knowledge of sensations, or what passes in one's own mind." (*Unabridged Dictionary*). Consciousness is, "The power, faculty, or mental state of being aware of one's own existence, condition at the moment, thoughts, feelings, and actions." (*Universal Dictionary*).

Inasmuch as consciousness is always associated with mind, and is never found in separation from it, we are forced to recognize it as one of the many attributes of mind; and inasmuch as the animal's possession of mind is the character which pre-eminently distinguishes the animal from all that preceded it in the universe, we must decide that this new element—this *creation*—which God introduced into the material universe on the fifth creative day, in combination with *matter* as presented in the physical organisms of the first animals, was *mind* in its simplest form. Hence all animals possess mind in greater or less degree.

Thus, while observation may acquaint us with many of the attributes of mind and its possibilities, the Bible alone gives us a knowledge of the *origin* of mind; that it is one of the three *creations* of which the universe is composed. This invaluable knowledge must have been one of man's earliest possessions, and was doubtless revealed by God to Adam, who transmitted it in his "book of precepts" to his descendants. But when Adam's "book" and its teachings were disregarded and lost, this knowledge was also lost; and for ages man remained in ignorance upon this subject, until it was restored to him by the inspired writer of Genesis. It was doubtless retained by those who adhered to the Bible, until the dispersion of the Israelites from Judea, and the descent of the whole world of mankind into the atheism, ignorance, and superstition of the Dark Ages, which followed the crucifixion of the Saviour, when it was again lost, or rather forgotten, for it remained a matter of scriptural record; but for centuries its existence was overlooked, until, in the year 1898, we called attention to it in our first publicacation.* During the many centuries in which the teachings of the Bible that there are three creations—Matter, Mind, and Soul—were forgotten by men, the mind creation and the soul creation were confused, and the terms *mind* and *soul* were employed indiscriminately to describe the mind; at the same time there were many who rejected the atheistic theory of man's descent from the ape, and insisted upon the scriptural teaching that there is no kinship between man and the animals; that man possesses immortality, while the animal is merely mortal; that man is an heir to eternity, while the animal is simply a creature of time. These people desired to distinguish between man and the animal, but they had been misled into believing that *mind* and *soul* were identical; and that the "mind or soul" was the immortal part of man. Their acceptance of this error naturally led them into the further error of supposing that mind was peculiar to man; that he alone possessed the faculty of *reason;* and that the animals possess mere *instinct.* But, as a matter of fact, *instinct* is merely one of the attributes of the mind, and is common to man and the animals.

This antiscriptural theory that Mind and Soul are *identical;* that the mind is the immortal part of man, leading as it inevitably does, to the conclusion that mind is peculiar to man, and that the animal

* "The Negro not the son of Ham, or, Man not a species divisible into Races."

possesses mere *instinct*, has proved most pernicious, since it did much toward destroying the distinctions which God made between man and the animals, and led us to accept into the Adamic family as a "man and a brother" a creature whom God made an ape; this assault upon God's plan of creation led to amalgamation with this animal; and amalgamation—that crime of crimes—has not only depopulated nations, but continents of their Adamic stock, and has damned millions upon millions of souls.

The fallacy of this theory that mind is peculiar to man, and that animals possess mere instinct, has long since been exposed; the most competent observers are now agreed that mind is common to man and the animals. Hence, both man and the animals possess the faculty of *reason*, the difference between them in this respect being merely one of degree.

In discussing this subject, Mr. Darwin says:

"Of all the faculties of the human mind, it will, I presume, be admitted that *Reason* stands at the summit. Only a few persons now dispute that animals possess some power of reasoning. Animals may constantly be seen to pause, deliberate and resolve. It is a significant fact, that the more the habits of any particular animal are studied by a naturalist, the more he attributes to reason and the less to unlearned instincts. * * * No doubt it is often difficult to distinguish between the power of reason and that of instinct. For instance, Dr. Hays, in his work on 'The Open Polar Sea,' repeatedly remarks that his dogs, instead of continuing to draw sledges in a compact body, diverged and separated

when they came to thin ice, so that their weight
might be more evenly distributed. This was often the
first warning which the travelers received that the
ice was becoming thin and dangerous. Now, did
the dog act thus from the experience of each indi-
dual, or from the example of the older and wiser
dogs, or from an inherited habit, that is from instinct? * * *   We can only judge by the circumstances under which actions are performed,
whether they are due to instincts, or to reason, or to
the mere association of ideas; this latter principle,
however, is intimately connected with reason. A
curious case is given by Professor Mobius, of a pike,
separated by a plate of glass from an adjoining aqua-
rium stocked with fish, and who often dashed himself with such violence against the glass in trying to
catch the other fishes, that he was sometimes completely stunned. The pike went on thus for three
month, but at last learned caution, and ceased to do
so.   The plate of glass was then removed, but the
pike would not attack these particular fishes, though
he would devour others which were afterwards introduced; so strongly was the idea of a violent shock
associated in his feeble mind with the attempt on
his former neighbors. If a savage, who had never
seen a large plate-glass window, were to dash himself even once against it he would for a long time
afterwards associate a shock with a window frame;
but very differently from the pike; he would probably reflect on the nature of the impediment, and be
cautious under analogous circumstances. Now, with
monkeys, as we shall presently see, a painful or dis-

agreeable impression, from an action once performed, is sometimes sufficient to prevent the animal from repeating it.   If we attribute this difference between the monkey and the pike solely to the
association of ideas being so much stronger and
more persistent in one than the other, though the
pike often received much the more serious injury,
can we maintain in the case of man that a similar
difference implies the possession of a fundamently
different mind?

"Houzeau relates* that, while crossing a wide
and arid plain in Texas, his two dogs suffered greatly
from thirst, and that between thirty and forty times
they rushed down the hollows to search for water.
These hollows were not valleys, and there were no
trees in them, or any other difference in vegetation;
and, as they were absolutely dry, there could have
been no smell of damp earth.   The dogs behaved as
if they knew that a dip in the ground offered them
the best chance of finding water, and Houzeau has
often witnessed the same behavior in other animals.

"I have seen, as I dare say have others, that when
a small object is thrown on the ground beyond the
reach of one of the elephants in the zoological gardens, he blows through his trunk on the ground
beyond the object so that the current reflected on
all sides may drive the object within his reach.
Again, a well-known ethnologist, Mr. Westropp, informs me that he observed in Vienna a bear deliberately making with his paw a current in some water,
which was close to the bars of his cage, so as to

* *Faculités Mentales*, 1872. tom. ii. p. 265."

draw a piece of floating bread within his reach.
These actions of the elephant and bear can hardly
be attributed to instinct, as they would be of little
use to an animal in a state of nature. Now, what is
the difference between such actions, when performed
by an uncultivated man, and by one of the higher
animals?

"The savage and the dog have often found
water at a low level, and the coincidence under such
circumstances has become associated in their minds.
A cultivated man would perhaps make some general
proposition on the subject; but from all we know of
savages, it is extremely doubtful whether they would
do so, and a dog certainly would not. But a savage,
as well as a dog, would search in the same way,
though frequently disappointed, and in both it seems
to be equally an act of reason, whether or not any
general proposition on the subject is consciously
placed before the mind. The same would apply to
the elephant, and the bear making currents in the
water. The savage certainly would neither know
nor care by what law the desired movements were
affected; yet his act would be guided by a rude process of reasoning, as surely as would be a philoso-
pher in his longest chain of deductions. There
would no doubt be this difference between him and
one of the higher animals; that he would take notice of much slighter circumstances and conditions,
and would observe any connection between them
after much less experience, and this would be of
paramount importance. I kept a daily record of the
actions of one of my infants, and when it was about

eleven months old, and before he could speak a single word, I was continually struck with the greater quickness with which all sorts of objects and sounds were associated together in his mind, compared with that of the most intelligent dogs I ever knew. But the higher animals differ in exactly the same way in this power of association from those low in the scale, such as the pike, as well as in that of drawing inferences and of observation.

"The promptings of reason, after very short experience, are well shown by the following actions of American monkeys, which stand low in their order. Rengger, a most careful observer, states that when he first gave eggs to his monkeys in Paraguay they smashed them and thus lost much of their contents; afterward they gently hit one end against some hard body, and picked off the bits of shell with their fingers. After cutting themselves only *once* with any sharp tool, they would not touch it again, or they would handle it with the greatest caution. Lumps of sugar were often given them wrapped up in paper; and Rengger sometimes put a live wasp in the paper, so that in hastily unfolding it they got stung; after this had *once* happened they always first held the packet to their ears to detect any movement within. * * * Mr. Belt, in his most interesting work (*The Naturalist in Nicaragua*, 1874, p. 119), likewise describes various actions of a tamed Cebus, which, I think, clearly show that this animal possessed some reasoning power.

"The following cases relate to dogs: Mr. Colquhoun winged two wild ducks, which fell on the

farther side of a stream; his retriever tried to bring
over both at once, but could not succeed; she then,
though never before known to ruffle a feather, deliberately killed one, brought over the other, and returned for the dead bird. Col. Hutchinson relates
that two partridges were shot at once, one being
killed, the other wounded; the latter ran away and
was caught by the retriever, who on her return
came across the dead bird; 'she stopped, evidently
greatly puzzled, and after one or two trials, finding
she could not take it up without permitting the escape of the winged bird, she considered a moment,
then deliberately murdered it by giving it a severe
crunch, and afterward brought away both together.
This was the only known instance of her ever having
willfully injured any game.' (*Dog Breaking*, 1850,
p. 46). Here we have reason, though not quite perfect, for the retriever might have brought the
wounded bird first and then returned for the dead
one, as in the case of the two wild ducks. I give the
above cases as resting on the evidence of two independent witnesses, and because in both cases the re-
trievers, after deliberation, broke through a habit
which is inherited by them (that of not killing the
game retrieved), and because they show how strong
their reasoning faculty must have been to overcome
a fixed habit.

"I will conclude by quoting a remark by the illustrious Humboldt: 'The muleteers in South
America say, I will not give you the mule whose
step is easiest, but *la mas racional*—the one that reasons best;' and, as he adds, 'this popular expression,

dictated by long experience, combats the system of animated machines better perhaps than all the arguments of speculative philosophy.' Nevertheless some writers even yet deny that the higher animals possess a trace of reason; and they endeavor to explain away by what appears to be mere verbage, all such facts as those above given.

"It has, I think, now been shown that man and the higher animals, especially the primates, have some instincts in common. All have the same senses, intuitions and sensations—similar passions, affections, and emotions; even the more complex ones, such as jealousy, suspicion, emulation, gratitude, and magnanimity; they practice deceit and are revengeful; they are sometimes susceptible to ridicule, and even have a sense of humor; they feel wonder and curiosity; they possess the same faculties of imitation, attention, deliberation, choice, memory, imagination, the association of ideas and reason, though in very different degrees. The individuals of the same species graduate in intellect from absolute imbecility to high excellence. They are also liable to insanity, though far less often than in the case of man. * * *

"It has often been said that no animal uses any tool; but the chimpanzee in a state of nature cracks a native fruit, somewhat like a walnut, with a stone. Rengger easily taught an American monkey thus to break open hard palm nuts; and afterwards of its own accord it used stones to open other kinds of nuts, as well as boxes. It thus also removed the soft rind of fruit that had a disagreeable flavor.

Another monkey was taught to open the lid of a
large box with a stick, and afterwards it used the
stick as a lever to move heavy bodies; and I have
myself seen a young orang put a stick into a cre-
vice, slip his hand to the other end, and use it in a
proper manner as a lever. The tamed elephants in
India are well known to break off branches of trees
and use them to drive away the flies; and this same
act has been observed in an elephant in a state of
nature. I have seen a young orang, when she
thought she was going to be whipped, cover and
protect herself with a blanket of straw. In these
several cases stones and sticks were employed as
implements; but they are likewise used as weapons.
Brehm ('Thierleben,' B. i, s. 79, 82) states, on the
authority of the well-known traveler Schimper,
that in Abyssinia, when the baboons belonging to
one species (*C. gelada*) descend in troops from the
mountains to plunder the fields, they sometimes en-
counter troops of another species (*C. hamadryas*),
and then a fight ensues. The geladas roll down great
stones, which the Hamadryas try to avoid, and then
both species, making a great uproar, rush furiously
against each other. Brehm, when accompanying
the Duke of Coburg-Gotha, aided in an attack with
fire-arms on a troop of baboons in the pass of Mensa
in Abyssinia. The baboons in return rolled so many
stones down the mountain, some as large as a man's
head, that the attackers had to beat a hasty retreat,
and the pass was actually closed for a time against
the caravan. It deserves notice that these baboons
thus acted in concert. Mr. Wallace ('The Malay

Archipelago,' Vol. i, 1869, p. 87), on three occasions
saw female orangs, accompanied by their young,
breaking off branches and the great spiney fruit of
the Durian tree, with every appearance of rage;
causing such a shower of missles as effectually kept
us from approaching too near the tree. As I have
repeatedly seen, a chimpanzee will throw any object
at hand at a person who offends him.   *   *   *

"In the Zoological Gardens, a monkey, which
had weak teeth, used to break open nuts with a stone;
and I was assured by the keepers that after using
the stone he hid it in the straw, and would not let
any other monkey touch it. Here, then, we have
the idea of property; but this idea is common to
every dog with a bone, and to most or all birds with
their nests." (*The Descent of Man*, pp. 84, 85, 86,
87, etc).

After referring to the resemblances between
the anatomy of man and the superior order of apes,
Prof. Quatrefags says: "Passions, sentiments and
characters establish between ourselves and animals
equally close relations. The animal loves and hates;
we recognize in it irritability and jealousy; unweary-
ing patience, and immutable confidence. In our
domestic species, these differences are more apparent, or perhaps we only notice them more closely.
Who has not known dogs which have been playful
or snappish, affectionate or savage, cowardly or
courageous, friendly with everybody, or exclusive
in their affections.

"Again, man has true instincts, were it only
that of sociability. Faculties, however, of this order,

which are so fully developed in certain animals, in man are evidently very much reduced in comparison with the intelligence.

"The relative development of the latter certainly establishes an enormous difference between man and animal. It is not, however, the *intensity* of a phenomenon which gives value to it from our point of view, but simply its *nature*. The question is whether human intelligence and animal intelligence can be considered as of the same order.

"As a rule, philosophers, psychologists, and theologians have replied in the negative, and naturalists in the affirmative. This opposition can be easily understood. The former make the human mind, considered as an indivisible whole, their principal study, and attribute to it all our faculties. Unable to deny the similarity, external at least, between certain animal and human acts, and yet being anxious to clearly distinguish man from the brute, they have given to the acts different interpretations as they have been performed by one or the other. Naturalists have regarded the phenomena more closely without thinking of anything else, and when they have seen the animals behave in the same manner as they themselves would have done under the given circumstances, they have concluded that the motives must be fundamentally the same. I must ask permission to remain a naturalist, and to recall some facts, and regard them from this point of view.

"The theologians themselves allow that the animal possesses sensation, formation, and association of

images, imagination, and passion. (R. P. de Bonniot).
They allow that the animal feels the relation of fitness
or of unfitness between sensible objects and his own
senses; that it experiences sensible attractions and
repulsions, and acts perfectly in consequence, and
that *in this sense the animal reasons and judges.*
(l'Adde A. Lecompte).   Therefore, they add, we
cannot doubt but that the animal possesses a principle
superior to that of mere matter, and we may even give
it the name of mind. (R. P. Bonniot).   But in spite
of all, theologians and philosophers maintain that the
animal cannot be intelligent, because it has neither
innate sense, consciousness, nor reason.

"Let us leave for a moment the last term, with
which the idea of phenomena which we shall presently discuss, is connected in the mind of our opponents.   Is it true that animals are wanting in
innate sense, and are not conscious of their actions?
Upon what facts of observation does this opinion
rest? We each one of us feel that we possess this
sense, that we enjoy this faculty.   By means of
speech we can convey to another the results of our
personal experience.   But this source of information is wanting when we come to deal with animals.
Neither in them nor in ourselves are innate sense
and consciousness revealed to the outer world by
any special characteristic movement.   It is, therefore, only by interpreting these movements, and by
judging from ourselves, that we can form an idea of
the motives from which the animal acts.

"Proceeding in this manner, it seems to me impossible to refuse to allow animals a certain amount

of consciousness of their actions. Doubtless they do not form such an exact estimate of them, as even an illiterate man can do. But we may be very certain that when a cat is trying to catch sparrows on the level ground, and creeps along the hollows, availing herself of every tuft of grass, however small, she knows what she is about, just as well as the hunter who glides in a crouching attitude from one bush to another. We may be equally sure that kittens and puppies, when they fight, growl and bite without hurting each other, know very well that they are playing, and not in earnest.

"I must beg permission to relate the remembrance of my struggles with a mastiff of pure breed, and which had attained full size, remaining, however, very *young* in *character*. We were very good friends, and often played together. As soon as ever I assumed an attitude of defense before him, he would leap upon me with every appearance of fury, seizing in his mouth the arm which I had used as a shield. He might have marked my arm deeply at the first onset, but he never pressed it in a manner that could inflict the slightest pain. I often seized him by his lower jaw with my hand, but he never used his teeth so as to bite me. And yet the next moment the same teeth would indent a piece of wood I tried to tear away from them.

"This animal evidently knew what it was doing when it feigned the passion precisely *opposite* to that which it really felt; when, even in the excitement of play, it retained sufficient mastery over its movements to avoid hurting me. In reality it *played a part in a comedy,* and we cannot act without being conscious of it." (*The Human Species,* pp. 18, 19, 20, 21).

Mr. Darwin relates the following incident to which Sir Andrew Smith, a zoologist "of scrupulous accuracy," was an eye witness: "At the Cape of Good Hope an officer had often plagued a certain baboon, and the animal, seeing him approaching one Sunday for parade, poured water into a hole and hastily made some thick mud, which he skillfully dashed over the officer as he passed by, to the amusement of many bystanders. For long afterward the baboon rejoiced and triumphed whenever he saw his victim." (*Ibid,* p. 78).

Had this officer "plagued" some ten year-old boy, who retaliated upon him as the baboon did, would we have attributed the boy's actions to *instinct?* When man and the animal perform the same actions under the same circumstances, how unreasonable it is in us to decide that the former was actuated by *reason,* while the latter was guided by mere *instinct.*

In discussing the acts of the gibbon ape, Prof. Huxley says: "Duvancel affirms that he has seen the females carry their young to the water side and there wash their faces. They are gentle and affectionate in captivity — full of tricks and pettishness, like spoiled children, and yet not devoid of a certain conscience, as an anecdote told by Mr. Bennett (*Wanderings in New South Wales,* p. 156), will show. It would appear that his gibbon had a peculiar inclination for disarranging things in the cabin.

Among these articles a piece of soap would especially attract his notice, and for the removal of this he had been once or twice scolded. 'One morning,' says Mr. Bennett, 'I was writing, the ape being present in the cabin, when casting my eyes towards him, I saw the little fellow taking the soap. I watched him without his perceiving that I did so; and he occasionally would cast a furtive glance towards the place where I sat. I pretended to write; he, seeing me busily occupied, took the soap, and moved away with it in his paw. When he had walked half the length of the cabin, I spoke quietly, without frightening him. The instant he found I saw him he walked back again, and deposited the soap nearly in the same place from whence he had taken it. There was certainly more than instinct in that action; he evidently betrayed a consciousness of having done wrong both by his first and last action — and what is reason if that is not an exercise of it?" (*Man's Place in Nature*, pp. 43, 44, 45).

The facts above cited fully sustain our contention that *reason*, one of the loftiest faculties of the mind, is possessed by the animals in greater or less degree; that mind is a creation distinct from matter; that mind made its appearance in combination with matter in the physical organization of the fish on the "fifth day" of the cosmogonic week. The advocates of the modern theory, that reason is peculiar to man, also insist that conscience, that ever alert monitor that rebukes us for our misdeeds, is also peculiar to man; but conscience, like reason, is simply one of the attributes of mind, and the animals possess it in a greater or less degree, as shown by the following incident, quoted in *Anthropology for the People*. The author says: "A late report of something like the conscience of the human being in an animal is the following, for which the New York *Commercial Advertiser*, June, 1889 is responsible:

"Spring brings the turnpike musicians and monkeys in great numbers. While one pair of these were giving a concert on Main Street in Carbondale, Pa., to a crowd of youngters and two inebriate countrymen, one of the men gave the monkey a cent, for which it doffed its cap jauntily. Then the countryman teased the little animal until at last it buried its teeth in the man's finger to the bone. When the blood gushed from the wound the monkey looked regretfully at the finger, then into the man's face, and handed back his money. No amount of persuasion would induce the penitent animal to again accept the coin, though it was repeatedly offered, and though he accepted money from others all around him."

Commenting on the actions of this little monkey in returning his victim's money, the author of *Anthropology for the People*, says: "We venture the assertion that a more satisfactory proof of the existence of conscience cannot be found among African savages." In this opinion we heartily concur. The conscience-smitten little animal not only manifested regret for the injury he had inflicted on his persecutor, but did all in his power to make compensation.

CHAPTER VIII.

Cattle, Creeping Things, and Beasts— the Ape a Biped.

"And God said, Let the earth bring forth the living creature after his kind, cattle, and creeping things and beast of the earth after his kind, and it was so.

"And God made the beast of the earth after his kind, and cattle after their kind, and every creeping thing that creepeth upon the earth after his kind: and God saw that it was good." (*Gen.* i, 24, 25).

It will be observed that God treats the land animals, with many of which man is to be closely associated in his daily life, very differently from the manner in which He treats the "fowls of the air" or the "fish of the sea," in that He divides them into three classes: *cattle, creeping things,* and *beasts.* This classification is observed throughout the scriptures. It will also be observed that God commanded the earth to "bring forth" the land animals in the order stated: (1) cattle, (2) creeping things, (3) beasts.

Modern theologians, both Jew and Gentile, who have noticed this peculiar classification, and have attempted to explain it, consider that the broad distinction which God makes between the *cattle* and the *beasts,* is due to the difference in the *food* upon which these animals subsist; that the *cattle* are *herbivorous* animals, and the *beasts* are *carnivorous* animals.

186

Prof. Guyot says: "In the tertiary the herbivorous animals, domesticated by man, are named cattle; while the others, including the carnivorous, are called wild beasts, and the smaller ones, the creeping things." (*Creation*, p. 119).

Chancellor Dawson says: "1. The first tribe of animals noticed here is named *b'hemah*, "cattle" in our version, and in the Septuagint "quadrupeds," in one of the verses, and "cattle" in the other. Both of these senses are of common occurrence in the scriptures, cattle or domesticated animals being usually designated by this word; while in other passages, as in I Kings iv, 33, where Solomon is said to have written a treatise on "*beasts*, fowls, creeping things and fishes," it appears to include all the mammalia. Notwithstanding this wide range of meaning, however, there are passages, and these of the greatest authority in reference to our present subject, in which it strictly means the herbivorous mammals, and which show that when it was necessary to distinguish these from the predaceous or carnivorous tribes, this term was specially employed. In Leviticus xi, 22-27, we have a specification of all the Behemoth that might and might not be used for food. It includes all the true ruminants, with the coney, the hare, and the hog, animals of the rodent and pachydermatous orders. The carnivorous quadrupeds are designated by a different generic term. In this chapter of Leviticus, therefore, which contains the only approach to a system in natural history to be found in the Bible, *b'hemah* is strictly a synonym for *herbivora*, including especially ungulatis and rodents. That this is its proper meaning here is confirmed by the considerations that in this place it can denote but a part of the land quadrupeds, and that the idea of cattle or domesticated animals would be an anachronism. At the same time there need be no objection to the view that the special capacity of ruminants and other herbivora for domestication is connected with the use of the the word in this place.

"2. The word *remes*, 'creeping things' in our version, as we have already shown, is a very general term, refering to the power of motion possessed by animals, especially on the surface of the ground. It here in all probability refers to the additional types of terrestrial reptiles, and other creatures lower than the mammals introduced in this period.

"The compound term (*hay'th-eretz*) which I have ventured to render 'carnivora,' is literally animal of the land; but though thus general in its meaning, it is here evidently intended to denote a particular tribe of animals inhabiting the land, and not included in the scope of the two words already noticed. In other parts of scripture this term is used in the sense of a 'wild beast.' In a few places, like the other terms already noticed, it is used of all kinds of animals, but that above stated is its general meaning; and perfectly accords with the requirements of the passage.

"The creation of the sixth day therefore includes—first, the herbivorous mammalia; second, a variety of terrestrial reptilia, and the other lower forms not included in the work of the previous day;

third, the carnivorous mammalia." (*The Origin of the World*, pp. 231, 232).

We agree with Chancellor Dawson upon certain points in his argument, and disagree with him upon other points, as follows:

1. We agree with him that the land animals are divided into three classes, translated in the English version of the Bible, "cattle," "creeping things," and "beasts."

2. That *remes*, translated "creeping things" in our version, describes a variety of animal forms which made their appearance on the earth, intermediate between the cattle and the beasts.

3. We agree with him that the term "beast of the earth," in our version, is not in this case "general in its meaning;" that is, it is not a general term intended to include all the land animals.

4. We disagree with him in his opinion that the term "beast of the earth" in our version, is "intended to denote a particular tribe of animals inhabiting the land." On the contrary, we hold, and shall hereafter show, that the term "beast of the earth," denotes a *particular member* of a tribe of animals after whose *kind*—the *beast kind*—it was made; and that this class of animals—the *beast* kind are as distinct from the "cattle," as they are from the "creeping things." We shall also show that these three classes of animals — "cattle," "creeping things," and "beasts," made their appearance on the earth in the order stated.

5. We disagree with him in his opinion that the "cattle" are herbivorous animals, and that the

"beasts" are carnivorous animals, for the following reasons: (1) Because there are numerous animals— some among our domesticated animals—which are both *herbivorous* and *carnivorous,* that is, *omnivorous;* consequently they cannot be classed with either the *herbivores* or the *carinvores,* and all attempts to do so would beget endless disorder and confusion, which is the opposite of that perfect order and harmony which characterizes all of God's works. (2) Because it brings the Mosaic Record with its teaching that the "cattle" were the first land animals to appear, in direct conflict with the Geological Record and its teaching, that the first land animals to appear on the earth were *insect eating* marsupials (*Dromatherium sylvestre*) —*carnivores.* (3) The error in which Mr. Dawson and his fellow theologians, both Jew and Gentile, have fallen on this subject is clearly shown by the presence of these animals which are both *herbivorous* and *carnivorous,* that is, *omnivorous,* and consequently cannot be fairly classed as *herbivores* or *carnivores.*

    6. We insist that the distinction which God makes between the "cattle" and the "beasts" is not based upon the nature of the food upon which these animals subsist; but the distinction between "cattle" and "beasts" is based solely on the differences in their *physical structures* that the "cattle" are *quadrupeds,* and the "beasts" are *bipeds.* We feel assured that every unprejudiced mind will agree with us that there is a *broader,* more permanent distinction between the *quadruped* animal and the *biped* animal than could possibly exist between the *herbiv-*

orous animal and the *carnivorous* animal; and the preference which should be given our view upon this subject over those of the modern theologians is greatly enhanced by the presence of that numerous class of animals, which are both *herbivorous* and *carnivorous;* and which cannot be fairly classed with either the herbivores, or the carnivores.   Hence, the presence of these *omnivorous* animals practically destroys the accepted distinction between "cattle" and "beasts"—that the former are *herbivorous*, and the latter are *carnivorous* animals—and necessitates the creation of a *third* class for the *omnivorous*. This we have no authority to do. The Mosaic Record divides the higher animals into *two* classes, "cattle" and "beasts;" and every one of these animals belongs in one or the other of these two classes.

Our contention that the distinction which the inspired writer makes between the "cattle" and the "beasts" is due to the fact that the former are *quadrupeds*, and the latter *bipeds*, has the following advantage: (1) It recognizes the broad, impassible gulf which God created between the quadruped and the biped. (2) Since there is no animal which is at once a quadruped and a biped, it enables us to place all the higher animals in two classes, without reference to whether they are *herbivorous, carnivorous,* or *omnivorous*.   (3) It harmonizes the teachings of the Mosaic Record with those of the Geological Record as to the order in which the three classes of land animals made their appearance on the earth. (1) "Cattle" (*quadrupeds*). (2) "Creeping things," a

variety of animal form. (3) "Beasts" (bipeds—
apes).

The quadrupeds and the bipeds present the
strongest contrast to each other in their general
physical and mental organisms; but more especially
in their extremities or limbs and in the terminations of their limbs, and in their *posture*.

The quadrupeds ("cattle") are that class of
animals whose fore extremities or limbs are *legs*,
which terminate in hoofs, or paws, as the case may
be; their posture when standing or walking is on
"all fours."

The bipeds ("beasts") are that class of animals,
each of whose fore or upper extremities is an *arm*,
which terminates in a *hand;* and each of whose
hinder or lower extremities is a *leg* which terminates in a *foot;* they also have the erect posture, or
the ability to assume it at will.

Prof. Huxley, in discussing the habits of the
so-called "anthropoid or man-like ape," says:

"There is good testimony that various species
of gibbon readily take to the erect posture. Mr.
George Bennett (*Wanderings in New South Wales*,
Vol. II, chap. viii), a very excellent observer, in
describing the habits of a male *Hylobates syndac-
tylus* which remained for some time in his possession, says: 'He invariably walks in the erect
posture when on a level surface. * * * 'He
walks rather quick in the erect posture, but with a
waddling gait, and is soon run down if, whilst pursued, he has no opportunity of escaping by climbing. * * * 'When he walks in the erect posture,

he turns the leg and foot outwards, which occasions
him to have a waddling gait and to seem bow-
legged.'

"Dr. Burroughs states of another gibbon, the
Horlack or Hooluk:

" 'They walk erect; and when placed on the
floor, or in an open field, balance themselves very
prettily by raising their hands over their head and
slightly bending the arm at the wrist and at the
elbow, and then run tolerably fast, rocking from
side to side.' "   (*Man's Place in Nature*, pp. 39, 40).

The evident fact that the "cattle" are *quadrupeds;* and that the "beasts" or apes are bipeds must
have been known to the ancients in the ages which
immediately followed the Deluge; but when the
great bulk of mankind renounced monotheism, in
their descent to atheism, amalgamation, and polytheism, this fact, together with other invaluable
knowledge, was lost. But in the course of time,
God in His mercy took pity on their ignorance, and
restored this long lost truth to the world through
Moses; it was doubtless retained by the Jews and
many Gentiles, until after the crucifixion, the dispersion of the Jews, and the decent of both Jew and
Gentile, under the curses of God, into that frightful
period in the world's history, known as the "Dark
Ages," in which ignorance, superstition, and crime
reigned supreme, when it was again lost. It is evident that during the "Dark Ages," the term "cattle"
(*b'hemah*), was restricted to a few of our domestic
animals, and so remains; but it is significant that
these are all *quadrupeds.* When the knowledge

that the apes are bipeds was lost, these creatures
finally came to be regarded as *quadrumana*, or four-
handed animals. This error prevailed until a few
decades ago, when its falsity was revealed by comparative anatomy; it was then discovered that there
is no *quadrumana* or "four-handed" animal, and
that all apes, from the lowest to the highest, are *bipeds*, or two-legged animals. The distinguished honor
of this great discovery belongs to that most accomplished naturalist, the late Prof. Thos. H. Huxley,
who published it to the world in the year 1860.
Though it must be admitted that Prof. Huxley lived
and died in utter ignorance of the important bearing his discovery has on the biblical subject now
under discussion; and even the advocates of the
Bible failed to recognize its value and importance,
until the author of this work called attention to it
in his lectures* which appeared in the year 1899.
But the discovery that the ape is a biped, is so far-
reaching in its consequences; so direct is its assault
upon universally accepted theories; so irresistible
is its tendencies to demolish long cherished religions
and other beliefs, that it is denied that cordial welcome which should always be extended to the truth.

In his great work on comparative anatomy, in
which he demonstrates that the fore or upper extremities of every ape are arms terminating in hands,
and that their hinder, or lower extremities, are legs
terminating in feet, Mr. Huxley says:

"Man has been defined as the only animal pos-

* "The Negro not the son of Ham, or Man not a species divisible
into Races."

sessed of two hands terminating his fore limbs, and two feet ending his hind limbs, while it has been said that all the apes possess four hands. * * * 'That the * * * proposition should have gained general acceptance is not surprising—indeed, at first sight, appearances are much in its favor. * * * Before we can discuss the * * * point with advantage we must consider with some attention, and compare together the structure of the human hand and that of the human foot, so that we may have distinct and clear ideas of what constitutes a hand and what a foot.

"The éxternal form of the human hand is familiar enough to every one. It consists of a stout wrist, followed by a broad palm, formed of flesh, and tendons, and skin, binding together four bones, and dividing into four long and flexible digits, or fingers, each of which bears on the back of its last joint a broad and flattened nail. The longest cleft between any two digits is rather less than half as long as the hand. From the outer side of the base of the palm a stout digit goes off, having only two joints instead of three; so short, that it only reaches to a little beyond the middle of the first joint of the finger next it; and further remarkable by its great mobility, in consequence of which it can be directed outwards, almost at a right angle to the rest. This digit is called the 'pollex,' or thumb; and, like the others, it bears a flat nail upon the back of its terminal joint. In consequence of the proportions and mobility of the thumb, it is what is termed 'opposable;' in other

words, its extremity can, with the greatest ease, be
brought into contact with the extremities of any of
the fingers; a property upon which the possibility
of our carrying into effect the conceptions of the
mind so largely depends.

"The external form of the foot differs widely
from that of the hand; and yet, when closely compared, the two present some singular resemblances.
Thus the ankle corresponds in a manner with the
wrist; the sole with the palm; the toes with the fingers; the great toe with the thumb. But the toes,
or digits of the foot, are far shorter in proportion
than the digits of the hand, and are less movable, the
want of mobility being most striking in the great toe
—which, again, is very much larger in proportion to
the other toes than the thumb to the fingers. In
considering this point, however, it must not be forgotten that the civilized great toe, confined and
cramped from childhood upwards, is seen to a great
disadvantage, and that in uncivilized and bare-footed
people it retains a great amount of mobility, and
even some sort of opposability. The Chinese boat-
men are said to be able to pull an oar; the artisans
of Bengal to weave; and the Carajas to steal fish
hooks by its help; though, after all, it must be recollected that the structure of its joints and the arrangement of its bones necessarily render its prehensile
action far less perfect than that of the thumb.

"But to gain a precise conception of the resemblances and differences of the hand and foot, and the
distinctive characters of each, we must look below

the skin, and compare the bony framework and its motor apparatus in each.

"The skeleton of the hand exhibits, in the region which we term the wrist, and which is technically called the *carpus*—two rows of closely-fitted polygonal bones, four in each row, which are tolerably equal in size. The bones of the first row with the bones of the fore-arm, form the wrist or joint, and are arranged side by side, no one greatly exceeding or overlaping the rest.

"The four bones of the second row of the carpus bear the four long bones which support the palm of the hand. The fifth bone of the same character is articulated in a much more free and movable manner than the others, with its carpal bone, and forms the base of the thumb. These are called *metacarpal* bones, and they carry the *phalanges*, or bones of the digits, of which there are two in the thumb and three in each of the fingers.

"The skeleton of the foot is very like that of the hand in some respects. Thus there are three phalanges in each of the lesser toes, and only two in the great toe, which answers to the thumb. There is a long bone termed *metatarsel*, answering to the metacarpel, for each digit; and the *tarsus*, which corresponds with the *carpus*, presents four short polygonal bones in a row, which correspond very clearly with the four carpal bones of the second row of the hand. In other respects the foot differs very widely from the hand. Thus the great toe is the longest digit but one; and its metatarsel is far less movably articulated with the tarsus, than the metacarpel of the thumb with the carpus. But a far more important distinction lies in the fact that, instead of four more tarsal bones there are only three; and that these three are not arranged side by side, or in one row. One of them, the *os calcis* or heel bone (*ca*), lies externally, and sends back the large projecting heel; another, the *astragalus* (*as*), rests on this by one face, and by another, forms, with the bones of the leg, the ankle joint; while a third face, directed forwards, is separated from the three inner tarsel bones of the row next the metatarsus by a bone called the *scaphoid* (*sc*).

"Thus there is a fundamental difference in the structure of the foot and the hand, observable when the carpus and the tarsus are contrasted; and there are differences of degree noticeable when the proportions and the mobility of the metacarpals and metatarsals, with their respective digits, are compared together.

"The same two classes of differences become obvious when the muscles of the hand are compared with those of the foot.

"Three principal sets of muscles, called 'flexors,' bind the fingers and thumb, as in clinching the fist, and three sets—the extensors—extend them, as in straightening the fingers. These muscles are all 'long muscles;' that is to say, the fleshy part of each, lying in and being fixed to the bones of the arm, is, at the other end, continued into tendons, or rounded cords, which pass into the hand, and are ultimately fixed to the bones which are to be moved. Thus, when the fingers are bent, the fleshy parts of the flexors of the fingers, placed in the arm, contract, in virtue of their peculiar endowment as muscles; and pulling the tendinous cords, connected with their ends, cause them to pull down the bones of the fingers towards the palm.

"Not only are the principal flexors of the fingers and of the thumb long muscles, but they remain quite distinct from one another throughout their whole length.

"In the foot, there are also three principal flexor muscles of the digits or toes, and three principal extensors; but one extensor and one flexor are short muscles; that is to say, their fleshy parts are not situated in the leg (which corresponds with the arm), but in the back and in the sole of the foot— regions which correspond with the back and the palm of the hand.

"Again, the tendons of the long flexor of the toes, and of the long flexor of the great toe, when they reach the sole of the foot, do not remain distinct from one another, as the flexors in the palm of the hand do, but they become united and commingled in a very curious manner, while their united tendons receive an accessory muscle connected with the heel bone.

"But perhaps the most absolutely distinctive character about the muscles of the foot is the existence of what is termed the *peronæus longus*, a long muscle fixed to the outer bone of the leg, and sending its tendon to the outer ankle, behind and below which it passes, and then crosses the foot obliquely to be attached to the base of the great toe. No muscle in the hand exactly corresponds with this, which is eminently a foot muscle.

"To resume, the foot of man is distinguished from his hand by the following absolute anatomical differences:

"1. By the arrangement of the tarsal bones.

"2. By having a short flexor and a short extensor muscle of the digits.

"3. By possessing the muscle termed *peronæus longus*.

"And if we desire to ascertain whether the terminal division of a limb, in other Primates, is to be called a foot or hand, it is by the presence or absence of these characters we must be guided, and not by the mere proportions and greater or lesser mobility of the great toe, which may vary indefinitely without any fundamental alteration in the structure of the foot.

"Keeping these considerations in mind, let us now turn to the limbs of the gorilla. The terminal division of the fore limb presents no difficulty—bone for bone and muscle for muscle are found to be arranged essentially as in man, or with such minor differences as are found as varieties in man. The gorilla's hand is clumsier, heavier, and has a thumb somewhat shorter in proportion than that of man; but no one has ever doubted its being a true hand.

"At first sight, the termination of the hind limb of the gorilla looks very hand like, and as it is still more so in many of the lower apes, it is not wonderful that the appellation 'Quadrumana,' or four-handed creatures, adopted from the older anatomists by Blumenbach, and unfortunately rendered current by Curvier, should have gained such wide acceptance as a name for the Simian group.   But the most cursory anatomical investigation at once proves that the resemblance of the so-called 'hind hand' to a true hand is only skin deep, and that in all essential respects the hind limb of the gorilla is as truly terminated by a foot as that of man.   The tarsal bones, in all important circumstances of number, disposition, and form, resemble those of man.   The metatarsals and digits on the other hand, are proportionately longer and more slender, while the great toe is not only proportionally shorter and weaker, but its metatarsal bone is united by a more movable joint with the tarsus.   At the same time, the foot is set more obliquely upon the leg than in man.

"As to the muscles, there is a short flexor, a short extensor, and a *peronæus longus*, while the tendons of the long flexors of the great toe and of the other toes are united together and with an accessory fleshy bundle.

"The hind limb of the gorilla, therefore, ends in a true foot, with a very movable great toe.   It is a prehensile foot, indeed, but in no sense a hand; it is a foot which differs from that of man not in any fundamental character, but in mere proportions, in the degree of mobility, and in the secondary arrangement of its parts.

"It must not be supposed, however, because I speak of these differences as not fundamental, that I wish to underrate their value.   They are important enough in their way, the structure of the foot being in strict correlation with that of the rest of the organism in each case. Nor can it be doubted that the greater division of physiological labor in man, so that the function of support is thrown wholly on the leg and foot, is an advance in the organization of very great moment to him; but, after all, regarded anatomically, the resemblances between the foot of man and the foot of the gorilla are far more striking and important than the differences.

"I have dwelt upon this point at length, because it is one regarding which much delusion prevails; but I might have passed it over without detriment to my argument, which only requires me to show that, be the differences between the hand and foot of man and those of the gorilla what they may—the differences between those of the gorilla and those of the lower apes are much greater.

"It is not necessary to descend lower in the scale than the orang for conclusive evidence on this head.

"The thumb of the orang differs more from that of the gorilla than the thumb of the gorilla differs from that of man, not only by its shortness, but by the absence of any special long flexor muscle. The carpus of the orang, like that of most lower apes, contains nine bones, while in the gorilla, as in man and the chimpanzee, there are only eight.

"The orang's foot is still more aberrant; its very long toes and short tarsus, short great toe, short and raised heel, great obliquity of articulation in the leg, and absence of a long flexor tendon to the great toe, separating it far more widely from the foot of the gorilla than the latter is separated from that of man.

"But, in some of the lower apes, the hand and foot diverge still more from those of the gorilla than they do in the orang. The thumb ceases to be opposable in the American monkeys—is reduced to a mere rudiment covered by the skin in the spider monkeys—and is directed forwards and armed with a curved claw like the other digits, in the marmosets —so that, in all these cases, there can be no doubt but that the hand is more different from that of the gorilla than the gorilla's hand is from man's.

"And as to the foot, the great toe of the marmoset is still more insignificant in proportion than that of the orang—while in the lemurs it is very large, and as completely thumb-like and opposable as in the gorilla—but in these animals the second toe is often irregularly modified, and in some species the two principal bones of the tarsus, the *astragalus* and the *os calcis*, are so immensely elongated as to render the foot, so far, totally unlike that of any other mammal.

"So with regard to the muscles. The short flexor of the toes of the gorilla differs from that of man by the circumstance that one slip of the muscle is attached, not to the heel bone, but to the tendons of the long flexors. The lower apes depart from the gorilla by an exaggeration of the same character, two, three, or more slips becoming fixed to the long flexor tendons—or by a multiplication of the slips. Again, the gorilla differs slightly from man in the mode

of interlacing of the long flexor tendons; and the
the lower apes differ from the gorilla in exhibiting
yet other, sometimes very complex, arrangements of
the same parts, and occasionally in the absence of
the accessory fleshy bundle.

"Throughout all these modifications it must be
recollected that the foot loses not one of its essential
characters. Every monkey and lemur exhibits the
characteristic arrangement of tarsal bones, possesses
a short flexor and short extensor muscle, and a *peron-
œus longus*. Varied as the proportions and appearance of the organ may be, the terminal division of
the hind limb remains, in plan and principle of construction, a foot, and never, in those respects, can be
confounded with the hand." (*Man's Place in Nature*,
pp. 102, 112 inc).

This mass of evidence from the highest authority on the subject establishes the fact there is a vast
difference between the physical structure of the
"beasts" and the "cattle." And clearly indicates
that these differences are the proper basis upon
which to place the distinction which God made between them.

It is evident that in God's plan of creation, the
apes occupy a position intermediate between that of
the quadrupeds and man. But, though the lines of
distinction are broad and clearly drawn between the
quadrupeds and the lemur—the lowest ape—they
are small and insignificant, compared to the great
gulf which intervenes between the highest ape and
man. With each ascending step in the ape series,

their contrast to the quadrupeds, and their resemblance to man becomes more marked.

Mr. Huxley says, (*Ibid*, p. 101).

"Whatever part of the animal fabric—whatever series of muscles, whatever viscera might be selected for comparison, the result would be the same—the lower apes and the gorilla differ more than the gorilla and the man."

The distinctions between the "cattle" and the "beasts" as shown in their extremities and in the termination of these, may be summed up as follows:

The four extremites in the "cattle" are all legs, hence they are quadrupeds. And their four extremities all terminate in hoofs or paws, as the case may be.

The fore or upper extremities of the beasts, like those of man, are arms, each of which terminates in a hand.

The hind or lower extremities of the beasts are legs, hence, like man, they are bipeds. Between the "cattle" or "quadrupeds," with their four legs terminating in hoofs or paws, as the case may be, and the "beasts" or "bipeds" with each of their arms terminating in a hand, and each of their legs terminating in a foot, there is a gulf which is far greater than that between the anthropoid and the negro, or any of the so-called "lower races of men."

It is universally admitted that the *biped* is a higher grade of creation than the *quadruped*. If man was the only biped, and had the ape family never existed, it would never have occurred to a naturalist, however sceptical he might be, that man

had descended from the quadruped, and through
these from the lowest form of animal life. The gulf
between them would have been too wide for man to
have closed with a leap. Hence, man would have
been recognized, as the Bible teaches, a *Creation* as
separate and distinct from the fish and fowl and
beast as he is from the plant or the planet. But the
apes, like man and the quadrupeds, have an exist-
tence. And though man, in his criminal folly, has
seized upon them as the weapon with which to assail
the Word of God, they will yet prove the inestimable blessing to man which God, in His wisdom and
love, designed they should be. The vast width and
importance of the great gulf which separates between
quadrupeds and bipeds has always been recognized
and appreciated.

When man was recognized as the only biped,
and the anatomy of the apes was not clearly understood, these creatures were seized upon by the sceptical scientists, and urged forward as the transitional
forms through which man descended from the
quadrupeds, and through these, from the lowest
form of animal life, thus spanning this otherwise impassable gulf. But the critical investigations of Mr.
Huxley reveal the startling truth that the location
of this gulf has been wholly misunderstood. This
great naturalist proves by comparative anatomy that
the gulf which separates between the quadrupeds
and the bipeds is situated, not between the quadrupeds and man, but between the quadrupeds and
apes.

Heretofore we have been led to suppose that the

quadrupeds on the one side, and man on the other side, constituted the shores of the great gulf which intervenes between quadrupeds and bipeds, while the ape series, as a bridge, spans this gulf and thus forms a natural connection between its opposite and distant shores. But comparative anatomy demonstrates that no such connection exists; and that the quadrupeds on the one side, and the apes on the other, and not man and the quadrupeds, constitutes the opposite shores of this gulf.

At a glance we might be led to suppose that this discovery would lessen the width, and correspondingly lessen the value of this dividing gulf. But careful investigation must convince us that no such result can ensue.

Formerly it was supposed that apes were four-handed animals. Hence, the term "quadru-mana" was applied to them. Since they were supposed to have four hands, they were supposed, of course, to have four arms; for it would be as absurd to suppose that a leg could terminate in a hand, as to suppose that an arm could terminate in a foot. But Mr. Huxley has demonstrated by comparative anatomy that the ape, like man, is a biped. Hence, he occupies the same side of the great gulf which separates between quadrupeds and bipeds that man occupies. We thus discover that the absurd theory that the apes span this gulf, and form the connecting link—the link of kinship—between man and the quadrupeds, and through these, with the lowest order of animal life has its origin and existence solely in the fertile imagination of the evolutionists, and is not founded upon facts.

If, upon going on a journey, we were led to suppose that a stream was bridged at a certain point, until upon reaching it we find that the stream had never been bridged, this circumstance would not lessen the width of the stream. So it is in this case. The world has been led to believe that man is the only biped, and that the apes spanned the great gulf which separates between the quadrupeds and man, thus forming the link of kinship between them. But now when we find that no such connection exists, this circumstance does not lessen the width, nor reduce the value of the gulf itself in the least. It remains the same wide impassable gulf.

Now, that comparative anatomy establishes the fact that man is not the only biped, and that the great gulf between the quadrupeds and bipeds lies, not between the quadrupeds and man, but between the quadrupeds and apes, no naturalist will assert that this gulf is spanned by any intermediate class of creatures whose fore legs, terminating in hoofs or paws, gradually develop through the series, into arms terminating in hands, and the terminations of whose hind legs in hoofs or paws gradually develop into feet. And unless the evolutionists can demonstrate the existence of such an intermediate class of creatures connecting the "cattle" or quadrupeds with the "beasts" or apes, through a gradually developing and unbroken series, "The Theory of Descent," with its "missing links," its inconsistencies, and its demoralizing, degrading infidelity must be abandoned.

The non-existence of such a series forming a connecting link—the link of kinship—between the "cattle" or quadrupeds, and the "beasts" or apes, at once establishes the truth of the scriptural teachings of Divine Creation, and demonstrates the falsity of "The Theory of Descent."

Mr. Huxley, to whom the world is indebted for this evidence that the ape is a biped, which is so essential to a proper understanding of the scriptures, was an open, pronounced foe to Christianity, and was one of the ablest, most persistent assailants of the Bible the world has ever known. Utterly ignorant of the true teachings of the Bible, he lived and died unconscious that his most brilliant achievement in the realm of science—his proof that the ape is a biped—developed the most positive, absolute proof of the inspiration of the scriptures. This fact, taken in connection with his open, aggressive hostility to God's word reminds us that David said, in addressing God: "Surely the wrath of man shall praise Thee."

Having shown by comparative anatomy that the higher land animals are naturally divided into two distinct classes—*quadrupeds* and *bipeds*—we feel assured that the broad distinction which the inspired writer makes between "cattle" and "beast" is based upon the fact that the "cattle" are *quadrupeds,* and that the "beasts" are *bipeds—apes.* We shall now submit our interpretation of the terms "cattle" and "beasts" to the decisive test of the science of geology; if our interpretation of the Mosaic Record is correct the Geological Record, in harmony with the Mosaic Record, will show that these two classes of animals made their appearance on the earth in the order stated: First, "cattle" (*quadrupeds*); second, "beasts" (*bipeds—apes*); with the "creeping things" (a variety of animal forms) intervening between them.

But, before entering upon this subject, we desire to correct another error into which the scientists have led us by placing the whale family, the higher land animals and man, in one class, as *Mammals*. Thus disregarding Paul's teaching that the fish, land animals, and man, each represent different *kinds of flesh*. Nothing is gained by placing these creatures in one class, even though they are all mammals, as shown by the following definition of the term:

"Mammals (from Lat. *mama'lis*, pertaining to or having breasts; deriv. of *mam'ma*, breast, pap, teat): the highest class of the vertebrate branch of the animal kingdom, and therefore the most specialized or highest group of living creatures. The class includes all vertebrates with warm blood, a heart of four chambers, the lower jaw composed of two branches articulated with the skull, and the body partly or wholly covered with hair. It thus includes man, all the higher quadrupeds, and the various whale and porpoise-like animals which possess hair only in the embyonic state and often then only on the upper lip. The habit of bringing forth the young alive is not exclusively a character of the mammals, being shared by various reptiles and fishes. On the other hand the lowest of the mammals, the menotremes lay eggs similar to those of snakes, and the mannos or milk glands of the female are scarcely differentiated." (*Universal Encyclopedia*).

Thus, we find that the term mammal—which includes man who brings forth his young alive, and the menotremes, which lay eggs—is a very latitudinous term, to say the least of it. The fact that we have permitted scientists with atheistical tendencies to place man and certain animals in one class, is largely responsible for our ignorance of the broad distinction which God made between man and the animals, and the confusion which has resulted from our unpardonable ignorance upon this most important subject.

In our chapter on the introduction of the fish and the fowl, we have shown that the earliest of these animals to make their appearance on the globe, were the lowest orders. Hence, we should not be surprised that representatives of the "cattle" or quadrupeds, the first of the land animals to make their appearance on the globe, should be of the lowest orders.

In discussing these, Mr. Dana divides them into two classes, as follows:

"Mammals—The highest group of vertebrates are of two grand divisions:

"1. The *ordinary or True Viviparous Mammals*, such as the monkey, lion, elephant, ox, bat, mouse, whale, etc.

Period.

Period				Species
	Permian			Permian
	Carboniferous.		14c	Upper Coal Measures
			14b	Lower Coal Measures
			14a	Millstone Grit.
	Subcarboniferous.		13b	Upper.
			13a	Lower.
	Catskill.		12	Catskill
	Chemung.		11b	Chemung.
			11a	Portage.
	Hamilton.		10c	Genesee.
			10b	Hamilton.
			10a	Marcellus.
	Corniferous.		9c	Corniferous.
			9b	Schoharie.
			9a	Canda-Galli.
	Oriskany.		8	Oriskany.
	Lower Helderberg.		7	Lower Helderberg.
	Salina.		6	Salina.
	Niagara.		5c	Niagara.
			5b	Clinton.
			5a	Medina.
	Trenton.		4c	Cincinnati.
			4b	Utica.
			4a	Trenton.
	Canadian.		3c	Chazy.
			3b	Quebec.
			3a	Calciferous.
	Primordial or Cambrian.		2b	Potsdam.
			2a	Acadian.
	Archæan.		1	Archæan.

FIG. 3.

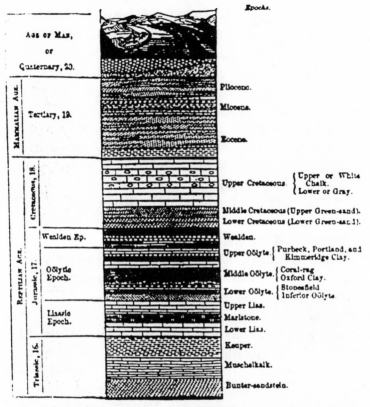

FIG. 3 (Continued). GEOLOGICAL RECORD.

—*From Dana, Manual of Geology*

"2. The *Semi-oviparous mammals*, which are, with
one exception, Marsupials.   Birth takes place before
the ordinary degree of maturity in the embryo is attained, and they thus approximate to oviparous vertebrates.   The immature young in these marsupials
are passed into a pouch (*marsupium*), situated over
the venter of the mother, in which they are nourished from her teats, until the degree of maturity

required for independent existence is attained. They are the lowest, and geologically the earliest, of mammals." (*Manual of Geology*, p. 416).

Let us bear in mind that, while all the so-called mammals are not "cattle" or quadrupeds, all the "cattle" or quadrupeds are included in what is termed *mammals*.

In discussing the animal forms of one of the early geological ages — the Triassic period of Mesozoic Time — Mr. Dana says:

"The only mammal thus far discovered in the American rocks was made known by Professor Emmons. The specimens are two jaw-bones found in North Carolina. According to Professor Owen, they belonged to an insectivorous (insect-eating) marsupial near the modern genus *myomecobius* of Australia. The species has been named, by its discoverer, *dromatherium sylvestre*. Mammals of similar kinds probably spread over the continent, and may have been of many species." (*Ibid.* pp. 415, 416). In discussing the animal life of the Triassic period in Europe, Mr. Dana figures a tooth of a marsupial — *Microlestes anticus Plien.*, which he says "was closely related to that of North Carolina." (*Ibid*, p. 427). Throughout Mesozoic Time, few, if any, of these so-called mammals higher than the marsupial existed. But following this period, in what is termed "The Tertiary, or Mammallian Age," all the higher land animals, such as the camel, horse, elephant, etc., appeared. Following the marsupials came a variety of animal forms, bugs, worms, snakes, and other small animals, which are properly described in scripture as the "creeping things." (See *Manual of Geology*). Following these in what is termed the Eucine period of the Tertiary came the apes. In discussing the life of the Eocene, Mr. Dana says: "Besides the species akin to the Ungulates, there were also * * * Monkeys related to the Lemurs. (*Ibid*, p. 504). Thus the Lemurs, the lowest form of the apes, were the first apes or "beasts" to make their appearance on the earth. The higher forms of apes came at a later period.

Thus, the Geological Record sustains the teachings of the Mosaic Record as to the order in which the three classes of land animals made their appearance on the globe: 1st. Quadrupeds (cattle). 2nd. A variety of animal forms (creeping things.) 3rd. Apes—bipeds (beasts).

CHAPTER IX.

THE BEAST OF THE FIELD.

The "beast of the earth" and the "beast of the field."

"And God made the beast of the earth after his kind, and cattle after their kind, and every creeping thing that creepeth upon the earth after his kind: and God saw that it was good." (*Gen.* i, 25).

What is the beast of the earth, and after what "kind" is he? In this connection we may also ask, what is the "beast of the field," and after what "kind" is he? It is plain that the "beast of the earth" and the "beast of the field" were made "after" the "beast," or ape "kind;" that these terms describe an ape.

In the previous chapter we have seen that Mr. Dawson renders the "compound term *hay'th-eretz*" "carnivora," and says "it is here intended to denote a particular tribe of animals inhabiting the land." We have taken issue with him on this subject, and have shown that the Hebrew term translated "beast of the earth" in our version of the Bible, denotes the highest race of the ape species, and has no reference to the carnivora.

The fact that the "beast of the earth" is not a general term intended to include all the land animals, is shown by the Mosaic Record; in our text

216

this creature is shown to have been made "after" the "kind" of that class of animals termed "beast" in contradistinction to the "cattle" and the "creeping things." Further evidence that the term "beast of the earth" is not a general term intended to include all the land animals, is shown by the narrative of the Deluge: "And God blessed Noah and his sons, and said unto them: Be fruitful, and multiply, and replenish the earth. And the fear of you and the dread of you shall be upon every beast of the earth, and upon every fowl of the air, upon all that moveth upon the earth, and upon all the fishes of the sea; into your hand are they delivered." (*Gen.* iv, 1, 2).

God thus placed into the hands of Noah and his sons (1) the "beast of the earth;" (2) the "fowl of the air;" (3) "all that moveth upon the earth;" (4) the "fishes of the sea." It is significant that in this text God treats the land animals very differently from the manner in which He treats the "fowl of the air" and the "fishes," in that He divides them into two parts; the one part is represented by the "beast of the earth;" the other part by "all that moveth upon the earth," which, of course, embraces the rest of the land animals; and as if to emphasize the distinction which He makes between them, God separates the "beast of the earth" from the rest of the land animals by placing the fowl of the air between them. This cannot be accidental; God never does anything by accident; what God does, He does with the most positive, absolute design; and in this case He evidently designed to impress upon our minds the fact that the term "beast of the earth" is not a general term intended to include all the land animals, nor even the carnivora, but that it describes a particular race of the beast or ape species.

The following language of David to Goliath throws a flood of light on the "beast of the earth:" "This day will the Lord deliver thee into mine hand; and I will smite thee, and take thine head from thee; and I will give the carcases of the host of the Philistines this day unto the fowls of the air, and to the wild beasts of the earth." (*I Sam.* xvii, 46).

This reveals the startling fact that the "beast of the earth" is a *man-eater,* and not one of the recognized apes of to-day is a *man-eater;* many of the apes, and especially the so-called anthropoids, may attack a man, and even kill him, but they will not eat his flesh. But David realized that there existed in his day a great man-eating ape. The disposition of this ape to feed upon the flesh of man, reveals the fact that the "beast of the earth" and the "beast of the field" are *identical,* as shown by the language of Goliath to David: "And the Philistine said unto David: come to me, and I will give thy flesh to the fowls of the air and to the beasts of the field." (*I Sam.* xvii, 44). Thus Goliath testifies to the existence of a great man-eating ape, known in his day as the "beast of the field." All the circumstances indicate that this creature is identical with the "wild beasts of the earth," referred to by David in his controversy with Goliath as above quoted. In Psalm L, verse 11, David refers to the "wild beasts of the field." One would naturally suppose that the term

"beast of the field" would be applied solely to domesticated animals of draught and burthen which
men employ in cultivating their fields; but such is
not the case; anciently, as above shown, the term
"beast of the field" was applied to a certain race of
the ape species, without reference to whether they
were in a "wild," or in a domesticated state.

In all ages of his history, man has shown a
strong disposition to cultivate the most criminal relations with this beast; their indulgence in these
shameless crimes not only led God to destroy nation after nation from the face of the earth, but has
even led Him to obliterate continents; it frequently
occurs that God in His wrath and disgust, decrees
that peoples who abandon themselves to these degrading crimes, shall die violent deaths; and that
their flesh shall furnish food for this man-eating ape.
In these just, but terrible judgments, we find additional proof that the "beast of the earth," and the
"beast of the field" are identical; and that this great
ape is a man-eater. In support of our position we
quote from the scriptural record as follows:

The following is God's threat against the Israelites should they violate His laws; and we should
bear in mind that one of His laws to Israel was,
Thou shalt not lie with any beast.

"And thy carcasses shall be for meat unto the
fowls of the air, and unto the beasts of the earth, and
no man shall fray them away." (*Deut.* xxviii, 26).

Israel violated God's law and the following
judgment was issued against them:

"And the carcasses of this people shall be meat

for the fowls of heaven, and for the beasts of the earth; and none shall fray them away." (*Jer.* vii, 33; see also *Jer.* xvi, 4, *Jer.* xix, 7, *Jer.* xxxiv, 20).

Israel was led into the indulgence of these crimes by her priesthood, as shown by God's judgment against them, as follows:

"Son of man prophesy against the shepherds of Israel, prophesy, and say unto them, Thus saith the Lord God unto the shepherds: Woe be to the shepherds of Israel that do feed themselves! Should not the shepherds feed the flocks? Ye eat the fat, and ye clothe you with the wool, ye kill them that are fed: but ye feed not the flock. * * * And they were scattered, because there is no shepherd: and they became meat for the beasts of the field, when they were scattered. * * * Therefore, ye shepherds, hear the word of the Lord; As I live, saith the Lord God, surely because my flock became a prey, and my flock became meat to every beast of the field, because there was no shepherd, neither did my shepherds search for my flock, but my shepherds fed themselves, and fed not my flock; Therefore, O, ye shepherds, hear the word of the Lord; Thus saith the Lord God; Behold, I am against the shepherds; and I will require my flock at their hand, and cause them to cease from feeding the flock; neither shall the shepherds feed themselves any more; for I will deliver my flock from their mouth, that they may not be meat for them." (*Ezek.* xxxiv, 2, 3, 4, 5, etc.).

In God's threat against Israel in case they violated His laws, He said their flesh should be meat for the "beasts of the earth;" when they allowed the clergy ("shepherds") to lead them into violating the laws of God, He gave their flesh as meat to the "beasts of the field." This furnishes the most positive proof that the "beast of the earth" and the "beast of the field" are identical; and that these two terms were applied to a man-eating ape.

The following is one of God's judgments against the Egyptians:

"Son of man, set thy face against Pharaoh King of Egypt, and prophesy against him, and against all Egypt: Speak and say, Thus saith the Lord God; Behold, I am against thee, Pharaoh King of Egypt. * * * Thou shalt fall upon the open fields; thou shalt not be brought together, nor gathered: I have given thee for meat to the beasts of the field and to the fowls of heaven." (*Ezek.* xxix, 2, 3, 5).

The following is God's judgment against Gog:

"Thou shalt fall upon the mountains of Israel, thou, and all thy bands, and the people that is with thee: I will give thee unto ravenous birds of every sort, and to the beasts of the field to be devoured." (*Ezek.* xxxix, 4).

This mass of scriptural evidence from the inspired writers clearly establishes the existence of a great man-eating ape, known to the ancients as the "beast of the earth" or the "beast of the field." The loss of all knowledge of the existence of such an animal explains our failure to properly understand and appreciate the Bible; and our ignorance upon this subject is largely due to the absurd interpretation of the biblical terms "cattle" and "beast" made by modern theolgians, both Jew and Gentile.

In discussing the above texts, we should bear in mind that we are not discussing tribes of savages in some wild jungle overrun with carnivorous quadrupeds such as the lion, tiger, leopard and the like. The Israelites, Egyptians, etc., were among the cultivated and enlightened people of ancient times; and their countries where the distressing scenes above narrated were enacted were densely populated, and in the highest state of cultivation: no large carnivorous quadrupeds roamed at large through these countries in those days. A moment's reflection should convince us that it would require thousands of carnivorous animals, whether quadrupeds or bipeds, to devour the flesh of the immense number of people who were slain in the wars with which God afflicted these nations for their crimes.

The "beast of the field" is not a carnivorous quadruped, as the modern theologian would have us believe; on the contrary, like man, the "beast of the field" is *omnivorous*, as shown by the following law which God gave Israel: "And six years thou shalt sow thy land, and shalt gather in the fruits thereof: But the seventh year thou shalt let it lie still; that the poor of thy people may eat; and what they leave the beasts of the field may eat. In like manner thou shalt deal with thy vineyard, and with thy oliveyard." (*Ex.* xxiii, 10, 11).

What use would the products of the fields, or the grapes and the olives be to carnivorous quadrupeds such as the lion, tiger, wolf etc.? These carnivores would starve to death in the midst of the greatest abundance of such food. And it would be absurd to suppose that God would command the Israelites to turn their domestic quadrupeds of draught and burthen loose in their vineyards and orchards to browse, trample down, and destroy them every seven years; besides these animals will not eat grapes and olives.

These "beasts of the field" were servants of the Israelites; they owned tens of thousands of them. It was their criminal relations with these apes which led to the destruction of the Israelites as a nation, and their dispersion among the nations of the earth. We shall hereafter prove that the "beasts of the field" were servants to the Egyptians, Babylonians, and all nations of antiquity, as well as to many nations of modern times. The Bible makes special mention of the beast of the field as a *servant*.

As shown in the Mosaic Record, this man-eating ape made its appearance as the "beast of the earth;" this creature stands at the head of the ape family, just as the lion stands at the head of the cat family. The physical and mental organisms of the ape are in nearer approach to those of man than are those of the "cattle" or quadrupeds. This fact, taken in connection with their possession of the erect posture, or the ability to assume it at will, prove them to be the highest grade of animal. This being true it follows that the "beast of the earth," standing at the head of this remarkable family of animals, would possess a finer physical and mental organism than any of the so-called anthropoids, and would in this respect be in nearer approach to man than any other ape. Hence, the "beast of the earth" is the only anthropoid or man-like ape. It was evidently his possession of much finer physical and mental organisms than any other animal, and which pre-eminently fits him for the position of servant, that prompted Adam to name him the "beast of the field." "And Adam gave names to all cattle, and to the fowl of the air, and to every beast of the field." (*Gen.* ii, 20). This is the first mention made of this animal under the name of "beast of the field" but after this he is frequently referred to under this name, and under the name of "beast of the earth," and often, merely as the "beast." The quadrupeds are often mentioned as "cattle" "herds," or "flocks;" and individual species of quadrupeds are often referred to as the horse, ox, swine, etc. But the apes are never referred to as cattle, herds or flocks. By observing this rule we will be greatly aided in our investigations of the Bible. But, we should remember that the cattle, and even the creeping things, like the apes, are all *beast*, in the sense that they belong to the *flesh of beasts*. The term "beast," is frequently employed by the inspired writers; sometimes it is intended to include all the land animals; occasionally it refers to a quadruped; but generally it is used to describe the ape. However, by observing the connection in which it is used, we will find no difficulty in determining the matter.

For many centuries the world has been enveloped in a night of *atheism;* the atheists' views concerning man and his relations to the animals are expressed in the theory of evolution, which degrades man to the level of the brute by attempting to establish between man and the animals a "blood relationship." Under these demoralizing conditions man's true relations to the animals as defined by the inspired writers have been forgotten. The boundary —the line of separation—which God established between man and the animals has also been obliterated; the gibbon, orang, chimpanze, and gorilla, erroneously termed "anthopoid," or "man-like" apes, though unfit for domestic purposes, are recognized as the highest grade of animal, and are now supposed to mark the line of separation between man and the apes. All knowledge of the "beast of the field," whose possession of more perfect physical and mental organisms pre-eminently distinguishes him from the lower apes, and correspondingly approximates him to man, is *lost*, save as we find his existence, and the physical and mental character which distinguish him, a matter of scriptural record.

Under the influence of atheism, and the consequent loss of all knowledge of the teachings of the Bible upon these important subjects, the world has been led to believe that the following characteristics are peculiar to man: (1) Mind (the animals being accredited with mere *instinct*).   (2) Articulate speech.   (3) A well-formed hand and foot.   (4) The erect posture.   (5) The ability to fashion implements for a definite purpose. The Duke of Argyll, quoted by Sir John Lubbuck (*Origin of Civilization*), while admitting that monkeys use stones to break nuts, says: "Between these rudiments of intellectual perception and the next step (that of adapting and fashioning an implement for a particular purpose), there is a gulf in which lies the whole immeasurable distance between man and the brutes. (6) It is also universally taught that woman (the Adamic female), is the only creature with which man (the Adamic male), may associate himself carnally and produce offspring that will be indefinitely fertile; and that man, (the Adamic male), is the only creature with which woman (the Adamic female), may associate herself carnally and produce offspring that will be indefinitely fertile.

It is easy to show that these characteristics are all combined in the beast of the field. When the minds of men are freed from the grasp of atheism, and the great intellects of the world are turned upon the Bible, (as they will be), it will be discovered that man possesses just two characteristics that are peculiar to him: (1) His flesh is a different *kind of flesh* from that of the fish, and fowl, and beast. (2) Man possesses an immortal soul, itself a part of the substance of God.

The importance of the beast of the field in God's plan of creation is shown by the fact that he shares with man the distinction of having been specifically mentioned in the narrative of creation; the rest of the animals are merely included under the heads of fish, fowl, and beast.

The tempter of Eve was a beast of the field, as shown by the language of the text: "Now, the serpent was more subtle than any beast of the field which the Lord God had made." This animal possessed articular speech, as shown by its conversation with Eve, which is a matter of scriptural record; it also possessed the erect posture, as shown by the curse which God directed against its posture, and which resulted in depriving it of the erect posture and degrading it to that of the lowest of the creeping things. The beast of the field has a hand, as shown by God's command to the Israelites with reference to Mount Sinai: "There shall not a hand touch it * * * whether it be a beast or man." (*Ex.*, xix, 13). We also find that in the book of Jonah reference is made to a beast with a hand: "But let man and beast be covered with sackcloth and cry mightily unto God: yea, let them turn every one from the evil of his way, and from the violence that is in their hands." (*Jon.* iii, 8). It is significant that the Rig Veda of the ancient Aryans, also describes in *two* places a beast with a *hand*. The fact that this beast was commanded, like the men of Nineveh, to "cry mightily unto God," indicates that, like the men of Nineveh, he possessed articular speech. The language of the text also indicates that this beast, when domesticated, and associated with civilized people, is habitually *clothed*. The beast has a *foot:* "No foot of man shall pass through it, nor foot of beast shall pass through it." * * * (*Ezek.* xxix, 11).

The genital organs of this beast are so nearly similar to those of man, and his seminal fluid is in such close affinity to that of man, that sexual union between opposite sexes of man and this beast may result in the production of offspring that will be indefinitely fertile; this is demonstrated in the case of

Cain, whose wife, though not of his *kind of flesh*, bore him offspring that was indefinitely fertile. The Bible abounds with instances of this kind; in fact, the Bible is largely a history of the long, destructive conflict which has raged between God and man, because of man's social, political, and religious equality with this beast, and the amalgamation to which these crimes inevitably lead.

The Bible tea. hes that man was not created and turned loose upon the earth like an animal with nothing to do beyond the gratification of his natural desires; but that he was created for, and assigned to a great task—the development of all the resources of the earth; in the accomplishment of this task he was commanded to exercise control over the animals; to develop all the resources of this globe would require a long period of time, and an incalculable amount of labor, and the initial step in this great task is soil tillage; and when Adam was created he was placed in the Garden of Eden, "to dress it and to keep it." This implies his possession of domestic plants and they require cultivation. Yet it is a significant fact that Adam was not compelled to personally till the ground, and thus eat bread in the sweat of his face until *after* he had violated the laws of God; and then only as a punishment for his crime: "And unto Adam he said, Because thou hast hearkened unto the voice of thy wife, and hast eaten of the tree, of which I commanded thee, saying, Thou shalt not eat of it: cursed is the ground for thy sake; in sorrow shalt thou eat of it all the days of thy life. * * * In the sweat of thy face shalt thou eat

522

bread, until thou return unto the ground. * * *
Therefore the Lord sent him forth from the Garden
of Eden, to till the ground from whence he was
taken." (*Gen.* iii, 17, 19, 23).

Observe the language of the text: *Because* * * *
thou hast eaten of the tree whereof I commanded
thee, saying, Thou shalt not eat of it, * * * In
the sweat of thy face shalt thou eat bread." etc.
Thus clearly stating that this was a sentence which
God imposed upon Adam for his violation of His
law. But this sentence, that he should personally
till the ground, and thus eat bread in the sweat of
his face, was confined to Adam who had offended;
there is nothing in the text to indicate that it descends to his unborn offspring who had not offended;
we shall hereafter prove that it did not so descend.
Inasmuch as this was a sentence imposed upon
Adam for his violation of God's law, it follows that
if he had not violated God's law, he would not have
been compelled to *personally* "till the ground," and
thus eat bread in the sweat of his face; at the same
time it must be admitted that the obligation to dress
and to keep the Garden of Eden, which required soil
tillage, was binding upon Adam from the moment of
his assignment to this task. But how was Adam to
dress and keep the Garden of Eden, which required
soil tillage, and not personally till the ground? If
we adhere to the universally accepted theory that
man is the only creature capable of making and
handling tools, this question brings us face to face
with an issue which involves the validity of the
Bible, since it reveals an apparent contradiction in

the teachings of scripture. The Bible plainly teaches: (1) That God created Adam and placed him in the Garden of Eden to dress it and to keep it, which required him to cultivate it, and this of course necessitates manual labor. (2) That Adam lived for a very considerable time in the Garden of Eden in perfect harmony with his Maker, and obeyed the laws of God, which required him to dress and to keep the Garden, that is to cultivate it; but that he finally violated Divine law; then, as a punishment for his offense, God compelled him to *personally* "till the ground," and thus eat bread in the sweat of his face.

In order to reconcile this apparent descrepancy, we must repudiate the modern theory that man is the only creature who possesses the ability to make and handle tools; we must accept the teachings of the scriptures and the sciences that there is an animal upon which God bestowed physical form and mental capacity sufficient to enable it to discharge the duties of servant; this creature must of course be a *tool-making, tool-handling* animal.

Such an animal must have *hands;* this necessitates his being a biped, for no quadruped could meet these requirements; it would be as absurd to suppose that a leg could terminate in a hand as to suppose that an arm could terminate in a foot. Hence, we must seek this animal among the apes. And not one of the recognized apes of to-day could discharge the multifarious duties of a servant; we must seek for a higher grade of ape than any of these; and inasmuch as the so-called anthropoids can walk erect, it would require but a slight improvement on their organism to produce an ape whose habitual posture would be the erect. Besides, as it was a part of God's plan of creation to provide man with a servant in the person of a tool-making, tool-handling ape, no good reason could be advanced why this creature should be *mute;* a mute servant would be at a great disadvantage, and his value correspondingly lessened. On the other hand, the value of a servant is immeasurably increased by the possession of articulated speech; articulate speech is as essential in the *servant* as in the *master.*

With the aid of a lot of tool-making, tool-handling animals possessing the erect posture and articulate speech, and thus fitted for discharging the duties of servant, it would have been easy for Adam "to dress and to keep" the Garden of Eden, with all the cultivation that this would require, with only such physical labor as is inseparable from mental labor. With the assistance of such creatures it would also have been possible for the descendants of Adam to have developed all the resources of this globe with only such physical labor as is inseparable from mental labor.

In discussing the possible achievements of a tool-making, tool-handling animal, Mr. Darwin says: "One can hardly doubt that a man-like animal who possessed a hand and arm sufficiently perfect to throw a stone with precision, or to form a flint into a rude tool, could with sufficient practice, as far as mechanical skill alone is concerned, make almost anything which a civilized man can make." (*Descent of Man*, p. 56).

God made just such an animal, and designed that he should be a servant to man, and we shall hereafter prove that the evidences of his art which antedate the creation of man, are found upon every continent of the earth, and he exists upon one of the continents of the earth to-day. These animals did all the manual labor in the Garden of Eden that was necessary "to dress it and keep it," while Adam did the mental labor. But when Adam violated Divine law God deprived him of these animals—his servants—and compelled him to *personally* "till the ground," and thus eat bread in the sweat of his face as a punishment for his crime. This animal was designed in the creation to do the manual labor necessary to "subdue" the earth, under man's intelligent control.

The presence of this animal clearly indicates that it was not the design of the Heavenly Father that His earthly son should be the subject of manual labor beyond that which is inseparable from mental labor. The theory of the modern theologian, both Jew and Gentile, that it was the original design of God that man should eat bread in the sweat of his face, finds no support in scripture. On the contrary, it is opposed by the plain teachings of the Bible.

When the fish, and fowl, and beasts, were all made after their kind, God then said: "Let us make man in our image, after our likeness: and let them have dominion over the fish of the sea, and over the fowl of the air, and over the cattle, and over all the earth, and over every creeping thing that creepeth upon the earth." (*Gen.* i, 26). In this proposition to make man, the central idea is "dominion"—*control*. In this text the design of God in creating man is clearly revealed; man's duties were to be *mental* rather than *physical*; he was to be the dominant, controlling power of the earth. The idea of man being the subject of manual toil is wholly disassociated with the expressed design of God in creating man.

When man was created, "male and female," "God blessed them and said unto them, be fruitful and multiply, and replenish the earth, and subdue it; and have dominion over the fish of the sea, and over the fowl of the air, and over every living thing that moveth upon the earth." (*Gen.* i, 28). In this assignment of man to the duties upon the earth for which he was designed, the central idea is "dominion"—*control*. No hint is here conveyed that it was God's intention to consign man to a life of physical toil; on the contrary, the plain language of the text shows that man was made ruler of the earth. Man's exalted position is clearly defined by David when, in speaking of God's creation of man, he said: "Thou madst him to have dominion over the works of Thy hands; Thou hast put all things under his feet: All sheep and oxen, yea, and the beasts of the field; the fowl of the air, and the fish of the sea, and whatsoever passeth through the paths of the sea." (*Ps.* viii, 8).

Further evidence that it is not God's desire that man should lead a life of physical toil, is shown by his generous treatment of the Israelites in giving them the land of Canaan: "And it shall be, when the Lord thy God shall have brought thee into the land which he sware unto thy fathers, to Abraham, to Isaac, and to Jacob, to give the goodly cities, which thou buildest not, and houses filled full of all good things, which thou fillest not, and wells digged, which thou diggest not, vineyards and olive trees, which thou plantest not," etc. (*Deut.* vi, 10, 11).

The highly developed condition of this country is shown by the fact that it supported "seven nations" greater than Israel. This "goodly land" with its great wealth, the accumulation of ages, was divided among the tribes of Israel, and was subdivided among the families composing those tribes. This, with their immense wealth in "jewels of silver, and jewels of gold," of which they had "spoiled the Egyptians," was sufficient to make every Israelitish family rich; and thus place them beyond the necessity of physical toil. Besides, the Canaanites owned immense numbers of beasts of the field, and these with the rest of their possessions were transferred to the Israelites; we have already shown that the Israelites were given special commands with reference to allowing the beasts of the field a part of the products of their fields, vineyards, etc., every seven years; and in this we have the most positive proof that these animals were numbered among their possessions.

God's treatment of the Israelites in giving them the land of Canaan, with all that was necessary for their comfort and happiness, and His treatment of Adam in giving him the Garden of Eden and all that was necessary for his comfort and happiness was identical. God gave the Israelites, who were descendants of Adam, the land of Canaan which they

had not developed; and provided them with immense numbers of beasts of the fields as servants to
serve them; and it would be unreasonable to suppose that God did more for the Israelites in their
depraved, fallen condition, than he did for "Adam
the son of God" in his original state of purity.
Hence, we should not be surprised to find that God
gave Adam the Garden of Eden, the most magnificent estate the world has ever known, and one which
Adam had not developed; and that He had also provided him with numbers of the beasts of the field as
servants to serve him. The cases of Adam in Eden
and the Israelites in Canaan clearly prove that it was
not the original design of God to consign man to a
life of physical toil, but that this distressing condition is a punishment which God visits upon man for
violating Divine law. That God desired that man
should do only such physical labor as is inseparable
from mental labor, is shown by his providing him
with a high-grade ape in the person of the beast of
the field which, as a servant, should serve him.

In the following narrative of the plagues sent
upon the Egyptians to compel them to release the
Israelites, a flood of light is thrown upon the distinctions between "cattle" and "beasts," and the relative value of each. After afflicting the Egyptians
with lice, fleas, etc., God said to Moses, "Go unto
Pharaoh, and tell him, Thus saith the Lord God of
the Hebrews, Let my people go, that they may serve
me. For if thou refuse to let them go, and will hold
them still, behold the hand of the Lord is upon thy
cattle which is in the field, upon the horses, upon

the asses, upon the camels, upon the oxen, and upon the sheep; there shall be a very grievous murrian. And the Lord shall sever between the cattle of Israel and the cattle of Egypt: and there shall nothing die of all that is the children's of Israel. And the Lord appointed a set time, saying, Tomorrow the Lord shall do this thing in the land. And the Lord did that thing on the morrow, and all the cattle of Egypt died: but of the cattle of the children of Israel died not one. And Pharaoh sent, and, behold, there was not one of the cattle of the Israelites dead. And the heart of Pharaoh was hardened, and he did not let the people go. And the Lord said unto Moses and to Aaron, Take to you handfuls of ashes of the furnace, and let Moses sprinkle it toward the heavens in the sight of Pharaoh. And it shall become small dust in all the land of Egypt, and shall be a boil breaking forth with blains upon man, and upon beast, throughout all the land of Egypt. And they took ashes of the furnace, and stood before Pharaoh; and Moses sprinkled it up toward heaven; and it became a boil breaking forth with blains upon man, and upon beast." (*Ex.* ix, 1, 2, 3, etc.).

The broad distinction which God makes between the cattle and the beasts, is shown (1) by the fact that the cattle were afflicted on one day; while the beast were afflicted on the following day. (2) That the cattle were afflicted with a "very grievous murrian," while the beast were afflicted with "boils, breaking forth with blains," just as the Egyptians were. The fact that the beasts were afflicted with the same disease as were the Egyptians, while the

cattle were afflicted at a different time, and with
a different disease, clearly proves that the physical
organism of the beast was altogether different from
that of the cattle, and correspondingly approximated
that of man. The significance of this is further increased when we consider that each succeeding
plague visited upon the Egyptians was more injurious to them than its predecessor. This indicates the
relative value of the cattle and the beasts; and shows
that the beasts were far more valuable than the cattle. This is easily comprehended when we understand that the cattle were quadrupeds, horses, oxen,
camels, sheep, etc.; while the beasts were servants
(bipeds—apes). Prior to the late sectional war in
the United States, the people of the Southern States,
like the Egyptians, owned their own servants, as well
as domestic quadrupeds, such as horses, oxen, sheep,
etc. Their servants were far more valuable than
their quadrupeds; a negro servant was worth from
$1,000.00 to $1,500.00; while a horse was worth, say
$100.00; a cow or ox, $25.00; a sheep, $2.00, and so
on. The relative value of the cattle or quadrupeds
and the beasts or servants, was perhaps much the
same in Egypt at the time of which we are writing.

Further evidence of the broad distinction between the "cattle" and the "beasts" and their relative value, is shown by the fact that the Egyptians
are accredited with owning both cattle (quadrupeds)
and beasts (servants), while the Israelites are accredited with owning cattle (quadrupeds), but no
beasts (servants) see (*Ex.* x, 9, 24, 25; *Ex.* x, 11, 38).
This is explained by the fact that the Egyptians were

the masters of the country and were rich and able to own servants; while the Israelites were themselves in bondage to the Egyptians, and were poor and unable to own servants.

The following are lists of personal property owned by Abraham and Esau, his grandson:

"And he said, I am Abraham's servant. And the Lord hath blessed my master greatly; and he has become great; and He hath given him flocks and herds, and silver, and gold, and men servants, and maid servants, and camels and asses." (*Gen*. xxiv, 34, 35).

"And Esau took his wives, and his sons, and all the persons of his house, and his cattle, and all his beasts, and all his substance, which he had got in the land of Canaan, and went into the country from the face of his brother Jacob. For their riches were more than that they might dwell together; and the land wherein they were strangers could not bear them because of their cattle." (*Gen*. xxxvi, 6, 7).

Abraham and Esau were kinsman; they lived in Canaan, though at different times; they were engaged in the same pursuits; they were each rich; they each owned immense herds of cattle of various kinds; yet we find that Abraham is accredited with owning herds and flocks (cattle), and servants, but no beasts; while Esau is accredited with owning cattle and beasts, but no servants. We can readily understand that Abraham's servants attended to his cattle; but who attended to Esau's cattle? Did his "beasts" do this? If they did not, what did they do, and what use did he have for them? The distinction between

Esau's "cattle" and his "beasts" is as marked as that between Abraham's "herds and flocks" and his "servants." The Babylonians, Israelites, Egyptians, Romans, etc., owned both white and black servants; perhaps Abraham did; he certainly owned white servants, for, in obedience to Divine command, he circumcised them, and it is highly probable that at least a part of his servants were blacks. However, we are not so much interested in Abraham's servants as we are in Esau's *beasts*. From the characteristics possessed by the beast of the field, it is evident that Esau's "beasts" were "beasts of the field," and that they discharged the duty of servants in attending to Esau's "cattle;" and it is highly probable, that a part, at least, of Abraham's servants were "beasts of the field." All the circumstances indicate that, (with the exception of Abraham's *white* servants), the beasts of Esau, and the "servants" of Abraham were "beasts of the field;" and that in ancient times, the terms "beast," "beasts of the field," and servant, were all applied to the "beasts of the field."

The most positive evidence that God designed the "beasts of the field" as servants to man, and that the ancients owned and employed them in the capacity of servants, is shown by the following: "And now have I given all these lands to Nebuchadnezzar, the King of Babylon, my servant; and the beasts of the field have I given him also to serve him." (*Jer.* xxvii, 6). Thus God took from certain nations their servants, the "beasts of the field," and gave them to Nebuchadnezzar "to serve him."

We have frequently approached clergymen of

the Jewish, Catholic, and Protestant faith, with the
inquiry, what are the beasts of the field, so often referred to in the Bible? The substance of their reply
has invariably been that, "the beasts of the field are
our domestic quadrupeds of draught and burthen,
with which we cultivate our fields, and use for other
domestic purposes." The absurdity of this explanation is shown by the fact that our domestic quadrupeds with which we cultivate the fields, and use for
other purposes of draught and burthen, are all
herbivorous animals; they subsist on grass, hay, and
the cereals; not one of them is *carnivorous;* they are
not even *omnivorous;* and certainly our horses, oxen,
camels, etc., would not feed upon the flesh of man;
besides, according to the Bible classification of the
land animals, our horses, oxen, camels, etc., would
be placed under the head of *cattle.* On the other
hand the Biblical "beast of the field," is *omnivorous*;
and even prefers the flesh of man as food. Besides,
under the Biblical classification of the land animals,
the "beast of the field" must be placed under the
head of *beasts*, (bipeds—apes). In addition to this,
the "beast of the field" possesses all the characteristics of a servant, which pre-eminently distinguish
him from the "cattle" or quadrupeds.

One who had never investigated the subject,
would naturally suppose the Jewish rabbi of to-day
is perfectly familiar with the language of his ancestors of thirty or more centuries ago; and that he
could promptly give us the proper definition of any
word in the Hebrew language. But, unfortunately,
this is not the case; the Jew possesses a mere frag-

ment of the language of his ancestors; the definition of many Hebrew terms is lost, and their true meaning is as much a matter of doubt and speculation with the Jew of to-day as with the Gentile. We assert without fear of intelligent contradiction, that, if a copy of the Mosaic Record, written as it originally was, in the ancient Hebrew, could be found to-day, neither Jew nor Gentile could properly read and interpret it. Having lost the meaning of many terms which the ancient Hebrews applied to certain animals, the Jew of to-day, like the Gentile, is unable to identify many animals by their ancient Hebrew names. From the many cases of this kind which we might quote, we present the following:

In discussing the Hebrew term *sheretz*, Mr. Dawson says:

"One peculiar group of *sheretz* is especially distinguished by name—the *tanninim*, or 'great whales' of our version. It would be amusing, had we time, to notice the variety of conjecturers to which this word has given rise, and the perplexities of commentators in reference to it. In our version and the Septuagint it is usually rendered dragon; but in this place the seventy have thought proper to put *ketos* (whale), and our translators have followed them. Subsequent translators and commentators have laid under contribution all sorts of marine monsters, including the sea-serpent, in their endeavors to attach a precise meaning to the word; while others have been content to admit that it may signify any kind or all kinds of large aquatic animals." (*The Origin of the World*, p. 213).

Discussing the term *tan*, Mr. Dawson says:

"Tan occurs in twelve places, and from these we can gather that it inhabits ruined cities, deserts, and places to which ostriches resort, that it suckles its young, is of predaceous and shy habits, utters a wailing cry, and is not of large size, nor formidable to man. The most probable conjectures as to the animal intended is that of Gesenius, who supposes it to be the jackal." (*Ibid*, p. 213, 214).

"Behemoth—This word has long been considered one of the *dubia vexata* of critics and commentators, but modern commentators generally believe the hippopotamus to be denoted by the original word. Behemah and behemoth are general terms for all large mammalia, in which it is constantly used in the Hebrew; and also the specific designation of the hippopotamus; to this animal, and to this alone, it can apply in the book of Job; and in this case only the translators of A. V. being without accurate knowledge, wisely abstained from any attempt to render the original. * * * It has been said that some parts of the description in Job cannot apply to the hippopotamus; the 20th verse, for instance, where it is said: The mountains bring him forth food." (*Smith, Dictionary of the Bible*, Vol. I, p. 383).

The hippopotamus is an amphibian, and it would be absurd to suppose that "The mountains bring him forth food;" water animals do not seek their food on the mountains.

Smith's Dictionary of the Bible, written by Sir William Smith, is a standard authority with both the

Jew and Gentile clergy of the day; yet it can give us no information that will enable us to identify the *behemoth*. The same is true of other animals, among them the "beast of the field;" and if Jewish theologians possessed any knowledge of these matters the Gentiles could obtain it of them; but the Jew has lost this knowledge.

As a matter of fact, in the days of Ezra, "the Hebrew language was already a dead language. The popular dialect was the Aramaic, and the Hebrew of Moses, David, and the prophets had become a sort of classical and sacred language, known only to the oldest and the learned. It was an object of academical acquisition. It was therefore necessary to explain and translate or expound the writings." (Philip Schaff, Art. The Bible, Appleton's *Universal Encyclopædia*, Vol. II).

Aramaic was the language of a Semetic people who lived north of Palestine. "The Aramaic language, a branch of the Semitic, was divided into two forms or dialects—the Syriac, or West Aramaic, and the Chaldee, or East Aramaic. The former was the language commonly spoken by the Jews in Palestine at the Christian era." (C. H. Toy, Art. Aramaïc, *Ibid*, Vol. I).

Mr. Schaff, in discussing the desire of the Jews for a knowledge of the original Hebrew, after their return from the Babylonian captivity, says: "One result of the zeal of the Jews for the original Hebrew was the publication of paraphrases in the Aramaic or popular dialect, which were called Targumim (From a root signifying to 'interpret'). They present the rabbinical and traditional interpretation of the scriptures." (*Ibid*, Vol. II).

"Targum: A name given by the Jews to the Aramæan translations and paraphrases of the Old Testament which became necessary when Hebrew was superseded by Aramæan as the spoken language of Palestine. The word occurs for the first time in Ezra iv, 7; but it is impossible to say when these translations were first made—unofficial ones probably at an ealy date." (*Ibid*, Art. Targum, Vol. XI).

Thus it is shown (1) that the Hebrew was a dead language at least twenty-five centuries ago; (2) that the Aramaic language superseded the Hebrew, and became the popular language of the Jews in Palestine centuries before the birth of Christ. (3) That when the Aramaic superseded the Hebrew as the popular language of Palestine, it was necessary to translate and to paraphrase certain parts of the Old Testament into the Aramaic; (4) that such translations and paraphrases were called *Targum*.

In contemplating the Targum, and the probable motives which led to its production, it becomes plain that, the learned paraphrasers who translated it into the Aramaic, fully realized that it contained the true meaning of certain passages and terms in the old Hebrew scriptures, which it was absolutely necessary for the masses of the people to understand. No other motive could have led those learned Hebrews to paraphrase certain passages and terms of the old Hebrew scriptures, and not the whole. These paraphrases were known to be of vital importance; and it is significant that the Hebrew term translated "beast of the field," in our English version, is found in the Targum. The Targum removes all doubt as to whether the "beast of the field" is a quadruped, or a biped, and contributes much toward identifying this animal. Hence, these ancient paraphrases are of vital importance.

It frequently happens that even fairly well educated people find it difficult to remember the definition of a term such as paraphrase, which is not in every day use; this lapse of memory may occur when there is no dictionary at hand; for the benefit of those who may be thus embarrassed while reading this part of our work, we give the definition of the term paraphrase. "Paraphrase: 1. A free translation or rendering of a passage; a re-statement of a passage, sentence, or work, in which the sense of the original is retained, but expressed in other words and generally more fully, for the purpose of clearer and fuller explanation; a setting forth in ample terms of the signification of a text, passage, or word. * * *

"2. To express, explain, or interpret in fuller and clearer words the significance of a passage, statement or work; to translate or re-state freely and fully but without losing or changing the original meaning." (*Universal Dictionary*, Vol. III).

Thus the Targum was merely an Aramæan translation of the Hebrew in which certain passages, terms, etc., were re-stated, 'but expressed in different words,' 'without losing or changing' the sense of the original Hebrew.

Sir William Smith gives the following definition of the term 'beast':

"Beast. 1. B'hemah, (*jumentum, bestia,* animantia, pecos; 'beast,' 'cattle'), which is the general name for 'domestic cattle' of any kind, is used to denote 'any large quadruped,' as opposed to fowls and creeping things; or, the word may denote a wild beast.

"2. Bĕ'ir (*jumentum,* 'beast,' 'cattle') is used used either collectively of 'all kinds of cattle' like the Latin pecos; or, especially of 'beasts of burden.' This word, which is much rarer than the preceding, though common in the Aramaic, is derived from a root 'to pasture.'

"3. Chayyâh (*fera, animantia, animal*; 'beast, wild beast'). This word, which is the feminine of the adjective 'living,' is used to denote any animal. It is, however, very frequently used specially of 'wild beast,' when the meaning is often more fully expressed by the addition of the word (*hassâdeh*) (wild beast) of the field. * * * Similar is the use of the Chaldee (*chayyâh*).

"1. The rendering of four Hebrew words in the A. V., and of three in the R. V. (*chayyah, fera, animal, animantium;* Arab. hayah) signifies simply 'a living thing' but is generally applied to wild animals. * * * 'In most passages, however, whether with or without the words 'of the field,' it is used for wild animals generally, frequently contrasted with birds.

"2. (*Ziz,* * * *fera, ferus*) occurs twice—viz. Ps. i, 11; Levt. xxx, 13—and is rendered by the A. V. 'wild beast.' The word is from the unused root *zooz,* 'to move oneself,' and is a common noun signifying 'that which moves,' having no reference to any special animal; the word *sâdeh*, 'of the field' being in each instance coupled with it.

"3. (*Tziyyim*, * * *bestia, dæmonia, dracones*). i. e. 'inhabitant of the desert' * * * *tziyyah*, 'a desert' or a 'drought;' and frequently of man (as in Ps. lxx, 14), but in three passages—Is. xiii, 21; xxxiv, 14; Jer. i, 39—applies to some wild animal, and translated in the A. V. and R. V. 'wild beast of the desert.' As in each of the three passages it is coupled with *iyyîm*, also distinguishes some specific creature. But as to the meaning, ancient versions and critics are alike in uncertainty, scarcely any two agreeing. Bachaot (*Hieroz* ii, 206) argues strenuously in favor of the wild cat, referring to the Arabic not very dissimilar name *tzaiwa;* and also suggesting that there is reference to the cry of the wild cat, along with the howling of the jackal. But the meaning is not very cogent. * * * Others have suggested the hyena, but this seems to be indicated by another word—*tzebua* (Jer. xii, 9). The Chaldee has apes (cercopithecus),* the Targum *semiæ*, and others bubo, 'the great owl,' but most have left it general; and Gesenius (*sub voce*) adopts this view, and here we may be content to leave it." (*Dictionary of the Bible*, Vol. I, p. 383).

[*Note. Sir William Smith's selection of Cercopithecus as the "beast of the field" was wholly gratuitous. He might with just the same propriety have selected any other ape from the Lemur to the Gorilla. Cercopithecus is a tailed ape of Africa; it is one which we would never associate in our mind with the *field*; it is unfit for domestic purposes, while as has been shown, the Biblical beast of the field was designed for a *servant*; again, the beast of the field is a *mtu-eater*, but no such charge can be brought against *Cercopithecus.*]

From the above quotations, it must be plain to our readers that we have sustained by proof our contention that the Jew has long since practically lost the language of his ancestors of thirty or more centuries ago; that the modern world possesses a mere fragment of the old Hebrew language which died and was superseded in Palestine by the Aramaic, ages ago. This is clearly shown by the fact that modern theologians, both Jew and Gentile, are utterly unable to indentify many animals by their Hebrew name; prominent among these is that great man-eating animal which figure so prominently as the *beast of the field.*

In the preceding pages we have shown that the beast of the field possesses certain peculiar characteristics which pre-eminently distinguish him from all other animals; and that God in His wisdom, His mercy, His love, has made these characteristics of this beast, a matter of *scriptural record;* we have also shown that these characteristics pre-eminently fit this animal for the position of *servant* which God designed him to occupy; and that the ancients owned and used him as a servant; and that God took from certain nations their "beasts of the field," and gave them to Nebuchadnezzar to *serve him.*

When viewed in the light of the scriptural record of this beast and his characteristics, the guesses of the would-be Hebrew scholars and theologians of modern times as to the identity of this animal, are absolutely ridiculous; some guess that the wild cat was the animal referred to; others that it was the hyena, others, the owl, etc.; while some guess that the

"beast of the field" is a general term. With the latter
view Sir William Smith appears to coincide, and he
says, " here we may be content to leave it."

If these distinguished gentlemen had noted
God's gift of the "beast of the field" to Nebuchadnezzar, they must have seen that God designed to
punish the people from whom He took these animals, and that in bestowing them upon Nebuchadnezzar, God proposed to correspondingly benefit
him. It is evident that it was not the intention of
the great Babylonian monarch to engage in the me-
nagerie business, or to start out on the road with a
traveling circus, or something of that kind. Hence,
he would not desire to be burthened with all the
hyenas, wild cats, owls, and such like to be found in
the various countries which he invaded and conquered. How could these animals possibly "serve
him?" Their whole idea of the "beasts of the field"
is perfectly absurd, and could only have originated
in the grossest ignorance of the plain teaching of the
Bible.

The embarassment under which these gentlemen labored in vain, to identify the "beast of the
field," is due solely to their failure to realize that
the distinction between the "cattle" and the
"beasts" is based upon the fact that the "cattle" are
quadrupeds, and that the "beasts" are *biped-apes*.
Had they known this, they would have seen that
the "beast of the field" is an ape, and that in the
creation, he was made after his "kind," the "beast,"
—ape or biped "kind."

For nearly twenty centuries, the Jews as a people, occupied a peculiar position among the nations of the earth, by their adherence to monotheism and the School of Divine Creation, as taught in the Bible. But their history shows that they would occasionally yield to the demoralizing influences by which they were surrounded, and renounce monotheism, and the doctrine of Divine Creation, and descend to atheism as expressed in the theory of evolution, and would even embrace idolatry. Evolution naturally tends to greatly modify and lessen, if it does not wholly obliterate the distinction between the quadruped and the biped, by declaring the latter to be merely a development of the former. Hence, under the influence of evolution it would be easy for a people to lose sight of the distinction which the Bible makes between the "cattle" or quadrupeds, and the apes or bipeds.

When the Israelites would renounce monotheism and accept the theory of evolution, God would visit upon them the most terrible punishments; the Babylonian captivity was one of these; under the pressure of these punishments, they would finally renounce atheism and idolatory, and return to monotheism, as they did in the days of Ezra, and they would be restored to Divine favor. It is evident that at some period intervening between the days of Ezra and the birth of Christ, they again renounced monotheism and accepted the theory of evolution; and during this period, under the demoralizing influence of evolution, they finally lost all knowledge of the fact that the ape is a biped. Ezra was called "a second Moses and the restorer of the law. He was the first 'scribe' and raised the scribe above the priest. He collected and arranged the ancient writings, and so laid the foundation of the canon." (Schaff.) It was Ezra who compelled the Jews to put away their "strange wives," and the "children" they had begotten by them. As the "restorer of the law" he taught Israel the true distinction between the "cattle" and the "beast," as well as the distinction between man and the animals; with this knowledge regained they were enabled to identify the "beast of the field." Their acceptance of the teachings of Ezra, restored them to Divine favor. Hence, in these respects their condition was much the same as it was in the days of Moses. This enables us to understand that it was after the days of Ezra, and before the birth of Christ, that the Jew lost his knowledge of the fact that the ape is a biped.

In the meantime the Septuagint, or Greek translation of the scriptures, was written; the Septuagint was completed about the year 285 B. C.

Before the birth of the Saviour they again returned to monotheism; they accepted the Septuagint, and adhered to it until after the crucifixion of the Saviour, when they abandoned it and turned to the Hebrew scriptures as they have them to-day. When the Jews returned to monotheism, and accepted the Septuagint, they observed that it made a distinction between the "cattle" and the "beasts;" but like our English version it did not state in just so many words that the "cattle" were *quadrupeds* and that the "beasts" were *bipeds—apes;* and having lost all

knowledge that the ape is a biped, and of the true
distinction between the "cattle" and the "beasts,"
the Jews were misled into believing that the "cattle"
were *herbivorous* quadrupeds, and that the "beasts"
were *carnivorous* quadrupeds; and this false pernicious theory has survived to our day, and is now
universally taught by the Jewish, Protestant and
Catholic clergy. The Saviour and His disciples en-
deavored to eradicate from the minds of men all
false theories as to the animals, and man's relation
to them, and restore the teachings of the Mosaic
Record; but their efforts were only partially successful, especially among the Jews, and the good results
which they anticipated, were short lived.

From that remote period in which the Jew lost
his knowledge of the fact that the ape is a biped, the
world was in ignorance upon this important subject,
with the exception of a century or two after the birth
of Christ, until a few decades ago, Professor Huxley
discovered through his researches in comparative
anatomy that the ape is a biped; but even when this
fact was published, the modern clergy failed to recognize its significance; and Huxley's great discovery,
which is worth more to the world than the discovery
of America, or a thousand planets like Uranus, received no notice at the hands of modern theologians.

When the characteristics of the "beast of the
field," as above shown, are viewed in the light of
Prof. Huxley's discovery, it is easy to see that this
creature is an ape; and from our quotation from
Smith's Dictionary of the Bible, it is plain that in
the old Hebrew scriptures the Hebrew term, trans-

lated "beast of the field" in our English version of the Bible, meant *ape;* and that the ancient Hebrews recognized the "beast of the field" as an ape. All doubt upon this most important subject is removed by the fact that, when in very ancient times the translating and paraphrasing of the old Hebrew scriptures into the Targum occurred, the term "beast of the field" was translated *simiac,* which means *ape;* while in the Chaldee translation of the old Hebrew scriptures, our term "beast of the field" was translated *ape.*

Let us bear in mind that the translating and paraphrasing of the old Hebrew scriptures into the Aramaic was not done by strangers for strangers; nor by the Jews for strangers; but was done by the most competent Jews for the Jews. When this translation was made the Aramaic language had superseded the Hebrew in Palestine, and was the popular language of the masses; but at the same time there were perhaps thousands of old and learned Jews besides the priesthood, who were familiar with the Hebrew language, and being vitally interested in the translating and paraphrasing of the scriptures, they would readily detect any errors in the work, and see to it that they were corrected; the same is true of the Chaldee translation of the scriptures. But such was not the case with the Septuagint or Greek version of the Bible. When the Septuagint was translated, the Hebrew had been a dead language for centuries.

We have now shown (1), by comparative anatomy that the whole ape family are bipeds. (2) That

the distinction between the "cattle," and the "beasts"
is based upon the differences in their physical and
mental organisms; that the "cattle" are *quadrupeds*,
and the "beasts" are *bipeds—apes*. (3) That the
Hebrew term, translated "beast of the field" in the
English version of the Bible, meant ape in the old
Hebrew scriptures, as shown by the fact that in the
most ancient translation of the Hebrew this term is
translated *ape*. In the following chapter we shall
appeal to the science of comparative anatomy to aid
us in identifying this great animal which figures so
prominently throughout the scriptures.

CHAPTER X.

THE "BEAST OF THE FIELD" IDENTIFIED WITH THE AID OF COMPARATIVE ANATOMY.

The white is the highest, and the negro the lowest, of the so-called "five races of men;" and they present the most striking contrast to each other in their physical and mental characters, their modes of life, habits, customs, manners, language, gestures, etc. No cross between the negro and any of the so-called brown, red, and yellow races, will produce the pure white. No cross between the white and any of the so-called brown, red, and yellow races, will produce the genuine negro. This indicates that the white and the negro are the originals whom God made. This being true, it is necessary for us to ascertain the relations which God established between them.

In discussing the characteristics of the white (the so-called "Caucasian race"), Theodore Parker says: "The Caucasian differs from all other races; he is humane, he is civilized, and progresses. He conquers with his head as well as with his hand. It is intellect, after all, that conquers, not the strength of man's arm. The Caucasian has been often the master of the other races—never their slave. He has carried his religion to the other races, but never taken theirs. All the great limited forms of monarchy are Caucasian. Republics are Caucasian. All the great

255

sciences are of Caucasian origin; all inventions are Caucasian; literature and romance come from the same stock; all the great poets are of Caucasian origin. No other race can bring up to memory such celebrated names as the Caucasian race."

Mr. Morris says: "It may be remarked that all the savage tribes of the earth belong to the negro or the Mongolian races. * * * On the other hand, the Caucasian is pre-eminently the man of civilization. No traveler or historian records a savage tribe of Caucasian stock." (*The Aryan Race.*) This indicates that between the white and the negro, there is a deep, wide, impassable gulf, which is not the result of any development on the part of the white, nor of retrogression on the part of the negro; its significance is immeasurably increased by the fact that its existence is traceable through the scriptures, the sciences, profane history, tradition, and monumental evidence to the remotest antiquity.

On one side of this great gulf stands the cultured, progressive white, whose flashing intellect, restless energy, and indomitable courage discovers, conquors, and develops continents. On the opposite, and far distant shore of this great gulf, stands the ignorant, savage negro, whose mental indolence and incapacity accomplish nothing. History records no achievements of his. His thousands of years lived out upon the earth, are as barren of results as those of the gorilla. Throughout his whole existence he figures only as a savage or a servant. No "woolly-haired nation has ever had an important history." (*Haeckel.*)

These incontrovertible facts constitute the greatest problem with which man was ever confronted. This great problem — the "negro problem" — has challenged the attention, and baffled the best efforts of the brightest intellects of the earth. Atheism has grappled with this problem only to be vanquished by it. And in the hands of modern religionists, the mystery which has so long enveloped it, grows deeper and more appalling. Yet it must be admitted that the facts we have cited, and which combine to form this vexed problem, are simply *effects*, which, like all effects, are traceable to a *cause*. In our efforts to discover this *cause*, we feel assured that our only hope of success lies in the scriptures and sciences. Recognizing the Bible as the highest tribunal — the court of last resort — we shall appeal to it in this grave emergency, confident that, with the aid of the sciences, we shall accomplish the desired end.

The Bible teaches that man was created a *single pair*, "in the image of God." And that the animal like the plant was made "after his kind." And we feel assured that after carefully considering this most important subject, even the most skeptical must admit that the white, with his exalted physical and mental characters, and the negro with his degraded physical and mental characters, are not the descendants of one primitive pair. This conclusion has long since been reached by the closest observers and the most profound thinkers of the age.

In discussing this question, Professor Haeckel says: "The excellent paleontologist, Quenstedt, was right in maintaining that, 'if Negroes and Caucassians were snails, zoologists would universally agree that they represented two very distinct species which could never have originated from one pair by gradual divergence." (*History of Creation*).

Thus, when viewed from a scriptural standpoint, it is evident that, if the white is the being created "in the image of God," the negro is merely an animal and was made "after his kind." And a glance at the negro indicates the *kind*; his very appearance suggests the *ape*. Mr. Darwin says, "The resemblance to a negro in miniature of Pethecia satanus, with his jet black skin, his white rolling eyeballs and his hair parted on the top of the head, is almost ludicrous."

Prof. Wyman says: "It cannot be denied, however wide the separation, that the negro and orang do afford the points where man and brute, when the totality of their organization is considered, most nearly approach each other." Prof. Haeckel quotes a great English traveler who lived a considerable time on the west coast of Africa, who says: "I consider the negro as a lower species of man, and cannot make up my mind to look upon him as a man and a brother, for the gorilla would then also have to be admitted into the family."

Prof. Winchel says: "The inferiority of the negro is fundamentally structural. I have enumerated the points in his anatomy in which he diverges from the white race, and have indicated that, in all these particulars, he approximates the organisms below. * * * It follows that what the negro is structurally, at the present time, is the best he has ever been. It follows that he has not descended from Adam." (Pre-adamites). It also follows that if the negro "has not descended from Adam," he does not belong to the *flesh of man*, and

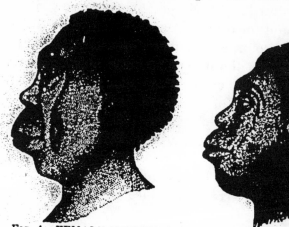

FIG. 4. FEMALE HOTTENTOT.   FIG. 5. FEMALE GORILLA.
—*From Winchell. Preadimites.*

being a land animal, he necessarily belongs to the *flesh of beasts*.

Mr. Morris says: "The negro is normally peaceful and submissive. His lack of enterprise must keep him so. Education with him soon reaches its limit. It is capable of increasing the perceptive, but not of strongly awakening the reflective, faculties. The negro will remain the worker. * * * Of the two great modern divisions of civilized mankind, the workers and the thinkers, the negro belongs by nature to the former class." (*The Aryan Race*, pp. 312, 313).

The observations of the high authorities above quoted are fully sustained by comparative anatomy.

As above shown, the white and the negro are the originals whom God made; when compared with the other so-called "races of men," or with each other, one of the most peculiar physical characteristics of each is presented by their complexions; the one being white and the other black. It is admitted that white is not a color, and that black is not a color; yet it is significant that the white, colorless complexion of the white is in absolute contrast to the black, colorless complexion of the negro.

The theory was formally entertained, and is still adhered to by many, that the dark complexion of the negro, and that of the other so-called "lower races," is the result of climatic influence. But scientific investigation has long since disproven this absurd theory.

In his discussion of this subject, Prof. Winchell says:

" The yellow-tawny Hottentots live side by side with the black Kaffirs. The ancient Indians of California, in the latitude of forty-two degrees, were as black as the negroes of Guinea, while in Mexico were tribes of an olive or reddish complexion, relatively light. So in Africa, the darkest negroes are at 12 or 15 degrees north latitude; while their color becomes lighter the nearer they approach the equator. 'The Yoloffs,' says Goldbury, ' are a proof that the black color does not depend entirely on solar heat, nor on the fact that they are more exposed to a vertical sun, but arises from other causes; for the further we go from the influence of its rays, the more the black color is increased in intensity.' So

we may contrast the dark-skinned Eskimo with the
fair Kelts of temperate Europe.   If it be thought
that extreme cold exerts upon color an influence
similar to that of extreme heat, we may compare the
dark Eskimos with the fair Finns of similar latitudes.   Among the black races of tropical regions
we find, generally, some light-colored tribes interspersed.   These sometimes have light hair and blue
eyes.   This is the case with the Tuareg of the Sahara, the Affghans of India, and the aborigines of
the Orinoco and the Amazons.   The Abyssinians of
the plains are lighter colored than those of the
heights; and upon the low plains of Peru, the Anti-
sians are of fairer complexion than the Aymaras and
Qeuichuas of the high table-lands.   Humboldt says:
'The Indians of the torrid zone, who inhabit the
most elevated of the Cordillera of the Andes, and
those who are engaged in fishing at the 45th degree
of south latitude, in the islands of the Chonos
Archipelago, have the same copper color as those
who, under a scorching climate, cultivate the banana
in the deepest and narrowest valleys of the equinoc-
tial region.'" (*Ibid*, pp. 185, 186).   Thus it is shown
that neither altitude nor latitude produces any
marked change in the complexion.

In explaining the true cause of the differences
in complexion, observable among the so-called
"races of men," Topinard says:

"The color of the skin, hair, and eyes, is the result of a general phenomenon in the organism,
namely, the production and distribution of the coloring matter.   The skin of the Scandinavian is white,

almost without color, or rather rosy and florid, owing
to the transparency of the epidermis allowing the red
coloring matter of the blood to be seen circulating
through the capillaries. * * * The skin of the
negro of Guinea, and especially of Yoloff, the darkest of all, is, on the contrary, jet black, which is
caused by the presence in the minute cellules on
the deep surface of the epidermis of black granules,
known as pigment.   The black layer thus formed by
these cellules, which used to be called *rete mucosum*
of Malpighi, remains adherent sometimes to the
dermis and sometimes to the epidermis on removing
the latter, after previously submitting the skin to
maceration. This pigment is found in all races,
whether black, yellow, or white, but in very different quantity; hence, their various tones of color,
from the lightest to the darkest whites, who readily
become brown on exposure to light, are undoubtedly
provided with it. It is always more abundant in
the scrotum and round the nipple.   It is very visible
on the mucous membrane of negroes, which are frequently surrounded by masses of it, notably on the
vault of the palate, the gums, and the conjunctiva,
which we have also met with in young orangs."
(*Anthropology*, pp. 342, 343).

Quatrefages, in discussing this question, says:
"With all anthropologists, I recognize the high value
of the color of the skin as a character. * * * 'We
know that it does not result from the existence or
disappearance of special layers.   Black or white, the
skin always comprises a white *dermis*, penetrated by
many capillaries, and *epidermis*, more or less trans-

parent and colorless. Between the two is placed the *mucous layer,* of which the pigment alone in reality varies in quantity and in color according to the race. All the colors presented by the human skin have two common elements, the white of the dermis and the red of the blood. Moreover, each has its own proper element, resulting from the colorings of the pigment. The rays reflected from these different tissues combine into a resultant which produces the different tints and traverses the epidermis. The latter plays the part of roughened glass. The more delicate and the finer it is, the more perceptible is the color of the subjacent parts. * * * From the preceding, we can also understand why the white alone can be said to turn pale or to blush. The reason is, that in him the pigment allows the slightest differences in the afflux of the blood to the dermis to be perceived. With the negro, as with us, the blood has its share in the coloring, the tint of which it deepens or modifies. When the blood is wanting, the negro turns grey from the blending of the white of the dermis with the black of the pigment." (*The Human Species,* pp. 356, 357).

It is thus shown by the highest scientific authorities, that the black, colorless complexion of the negro, is not due to climatic influences; but results solely from the black pigment intervening between the *dermis* and the *epidermis.* Like every other part of the organism, this pigment is liable to disease. One of the diseases to which the pigment is subject, is known as *albinism.* The victims of this disease are called *albinos.* Dr. Topenard, in discussing albinism

and albinos, says: "Albinos are individuals in whom
the pigmentary matter is so far deficient that the
skin and hair are colorless, the iris is transparent,
and the choroid coat destitute of the dark pigment
for the absorption of redundant rays of light. In
consequence of this, they are unable to bear sunlight, and see better at night than during the day.
Their eyeballs are affected with a perpetual oscillating
movement, their skin and hair are colorless, or of a
dull white, the eyes reddish, the transparency of the
tissues showing the blood circulating through the
capillaries. They are often indolent, and without
muscular vigor. There are partial albinos, in whom
the above symptoms are observed, but in a less
degree." (*Anthropology*, p. 161).

The white epidermis of the white is relatively
thin, and emits a slight odor which is not offensive.
In strong contrast to this, the negro has a "thick
epidermis, cool, soft and velvety to the touch, mostly
hairless, and emitting a peculiar rancid odor, compared by Pruner Bey to that of the buck goat."
(Prof. Keane quoted in *Anthropology for the People*,
p. 20). Topenard, referring to the repulsive order
of the negro, says: "The characteristic effluvium
from the hold of a slave-ship can never be got rid
of." (*Ibid*).

"There seems to be a difference between the
blood of the white man and that of the negro, too
subtle to be detected by microscopic observation,
but proved by experimental test. The skin of the
white man inserted in the flesh of the negro becomes
black, and the skin of the negro grafted on the white

man turns white. Nothing but the blood could produce this change." (*Anthropology for the People*, p. 21).

The long, fine, silken hair of the white is in absolute contrast to the short, coarse, woolly hair of the negro. Each individual hair of the white is cylindrical. Hence, its section is circular. In contrast to this, each individual hair of the negro "is flattened like a tape." Hence, "its section is oval." (Haeckel, *History of Creation*, Vol. ii., pp. 414, 415). The hair of the white is inserted obliquely into the scalp; in contrast to this, the hair of the negro "is inserted vertically into the scalp." (Winchell).

Prof. Winchell says: "The condition of the hair is found to sustain relations to climate no more exact than the complexion. The Tasmanians, in latitude forty-five degrees, had hair as woolly as that of the negros under the equator. On the contrary, smooth hair is found extensively in tropical latitudes, as among the Australians, the Blacks of the Deccan (India), and the Himyarites of the Yeman, in Arabia. Similar absence of correlation between stature and environment has been ascertained." (*Preadimites*, pp. 186, 187).

Dr. Topenard says: "No explanation can be given as to the varieties of the hair in its fundamental types. For example, the straight and the round, the woolly and the flat hair, as seen under the microscope. In this lies the most serious objection to the theory of the derivation of characters from one another. In the present state of science we have no explanation to give on the subject." (*Anthropology*).

The statements of this distinguished anthropologist deserves our most earnest consideration. He frankly admits that science can give no explanation of why the hair of the white is long, fine, and round, and is inserted obliquely into the scalp; while the hair of the negro is short, coarse, and flat, and is inserted vertically into the scalp. He also admits that in these striking contrasts "lies the most serious objection to the theory of the derivation of characters from one another;" or, in other words, in these opposing characters "lies the most serious objection to the theory" that either the white or the negro developed the one from the other. It is also plain that in these opposing characters presented by the hair of whites and negroes "lies the most serious objection" to the modern church theory that the whites and the negroes are the progny of *one primitive pair*.

"Dr. Brown of Philadelphia, the distinguished microscopist, has thoroughly investigated the hair of 'the human races, and has shown conclusively that the pile of the negro is really wool. He is the best authority on this point, and is, on that account, quoted in the *Encyclopædia Britanica*. The following is a summary of his conclusions: * * 'The hair of the white man has, besides its cortex and intermediate fibres, a central canal, which contains the coloring matter when present. The pile of the negro has no central canal, and the coloring matter is diffused, when present, either throughout the cortex or the intermediate fibres. Hair, according to these observations, is more complex in its structure than wool. In hair, the enveloping scales are comparatively few, with smooth surfaces, rounded at their points, and closely embracing the shaft. In wool, they are numerous, rough, sharp-pointed, and project from the shaft. *Hence, the hair of the white man will not felt; that of the negro will.* In this respect, therefore, it comes nearer to true wool." (*Anthropology for the People*, pp. 104, 105).

Commenting on the wool of the negro, the author of *Anthropology for the People*, says: "It is impossible to conceive any natural cause that could have changed the hair of the white man into the wool of the negro. If the negro has sunk from the Adamic race to what he now is, what caused the central canal in his pile to disappear, and by what natural cause could it be restored? Can the evolutionist explain it on his theory? Can the monogist explain it on his?"

In the white, the pilous system is highly developed; this is in striking contrast to that of the negro, which is notably deficient. Of the negro, Topenard says: "The beard is scant, and developed late. The body is destitute of hair, except on the pubis and armpits." (*Ibid*, p. 488). Winchell says: "As to the pilous system it is deficient in the negro. The hairs of the head are black and crispy, with a transverse section, and are inserted vertically in the scalp. The skin is black, velvety, and comparatively cool." (*Ibid*, p. 174).

The comparatively short, broad skull of the white is in striking contrast to the long, narrow skull of the negro. The length and narrowness of the negro skull is a character of the ape. Prof. Winchell says: "A certain relative width of skull appears to be connected with energy, force and executive ability." This explains the negro's lack of executive ability— God made him so. The significance of this is easily seen when we pause to reflect that the task to which man was assigned in the creation required the highest executive ability. Winchell, quoting from Broca, says: "(1) The face of the negro occupies the greater portion of the total length of the head. (2) His anterior cranium is less developed than his posterior, relatively to that of the white. (3) His occipital foramen is situated more backward in relation to the total projection of the head, but more forward in relation to the cranium only. In other words, the negro has the cerebral cranium less developed than the anterior." (*Preadimites*, pp. 169, 170).

"In the negro skull the sphenoid does not, generally, reach the parietals, the coronal suture joining the margin of the temporals. The skull is very thick and solid, and is often used for butting, as is the custom of rams. It is flattened on the top, and well adapted for carrying burdens." (*Ibid*, p. 171). "The cephalic index—among Noachites (whites), ranges from 75 to 83 degrees; among negroes, from 71 to 76 degrees. (*Ibid*, p. 246).

Dr. Winchell, in discussing cranial capacity, says: "Capacity of cranium is universally recognized as a criterion of psychic power. No fact is better established than the general relation of intellect to weight of brain. Welker has shown that the

brains of twenty-six men of high intellectual rank
surpassed the average weight by fourteen per cent.
Of course quality of brain is an equally important
factor; and hence not a few men with brains even
below the average have distinguished themselves for
scholarship and executive ability. The Noachites
possess a mean capacity of 1,500 cubic centimeters.
Among negroes, 1,360 cubic centimeters." (*Ibid*, p.
246).

"The average weight of the European brain,
males and females, is 1,340 grammes; that of the
negro is 1,178; of the Hottentot, 974, and of the Australian, 907. The significance of these comparisons
appears when we learn that Broca, the most eminent
of French anthropologists, states that, when the European brain falls below 978 grammes (mean of
males and females), the result is idiocy. In this
opinion Thurman coincides. The color of the negro
brain is darker than that of the white, and its density and the texture are inferior. The convolutions
are fewer and more simple, and, as Agassiz and
others long ago pointed out, approximate those of
the quadruma." (*Ibid*, pp. 249, 251).

The theory of evolution has long misled the
world into believing that all bipeds with the erect
posture, articulate speech, a well formed hand and
foot, and the abiltity to make and handle tools, are
men. As a result of this false teaching, we have no
estimates of the average brain weight of the adult
Adamic male nor of the Adamic female. But
there can be no doubt that the average brain weight
of the adult Adamic male may safely be placed at

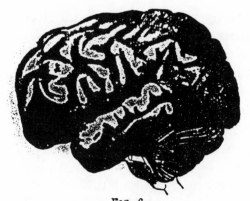

FIG. 6.
PROFILE VIEW OF THE BRAIN OF THE ORANG OUTANG.

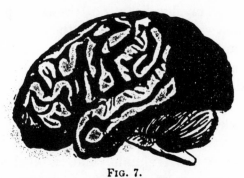

FIG. 7.
PROFILE VIEW OF THE BRAIN OF THE BUSHMAN VENUS.

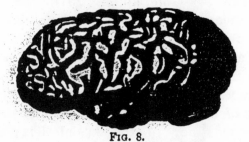

FIG. 8.
PROFILE VIEW OF BRAIN OF GAUSS, THE MATHEMATICIAN.

—From *Winchell, Preadimites.*

not less than 1,500 grammes. This average is far below that of many individual whites, for example:

	Weight of brain.	
	grammes.	ounces
Cavier—63 years old—naturalist, .	1829.96	64.54
Byron—36 years old—poet, . . .	1807.00	63.73
Lejisens Dirichlet—50 years old—		
mathematician, ...	1520.00	53.61

—(*Quatrefages, The Human Species*, p. 411).

The table from which these brain weights were taken contains the brain weights of several distinguished individuals which fall below the average. This indicates that, in determining the relative intelligence of individuals, there are other factors to be considered besides the weight and volume of the brain. While admitting that "there is a certain relation between the development of the intelligence and the weight and volume of the brain," Quatrefages says: "But at the same time we must allow that the material element, that which is appreciable to our senses, is not the only one which we must take into account, for behind it lies hidden *an unknown quantity, an X*, at present undetermined and only recognizable by its effects." (*Ibid*, p. 413). To demonstrate this truth, it is only necessary to compare the achievements of the whites with those of the negro and the mixed-bloods.

The relatively short, narrow jaw of the whites is in striking contrast to the long, broad jaw of the negro. The length and breadth of the negro's jaw is a character of the ape. The jaws of the negro, like those of the other apes, "extend forward at the expense of the symmetry of the face, and backward at the expense of the brain cavity." Quatrefages says: "It is well known that in the negro the entire face, and especially the lower portion, projects forward. In the living subject it is exaggerated by the thickness of. the lips. But it is also apparent in the skull, and constitutes one of its most striking characters." (*Ibid*, pp. 390, 391).

Dr. Winchell says: "The amount of prognathism is another marked criterion of organic rank. One method of expressing this is by means of 'auricular radii,' or distances from the opening of the ear to the roots of the teeth, and to other parts of the head. Among Europeans, the distance to the base of the upper incisors is 99, but among negroes it averages 114. On the contrary, the average distance to the top of the head is, among Europeans, 112, but among negroes, 110. The distance to the upper edge of the occipital bone is, among Europeans, 104, among negroes, 104. These measurements prove that the negro possesses more face, and particularly of jaws and less brain above. Other measurements furnish a similar result, and show also that the development of the posterior brain, in relation to the anterior, is greater in the negro. Prognathism is likewise expressed by means of the 'facial angle,' or general slope of the face from the forehead to the jaws, when compared with a horizontal plane. Among the Noachites, the facial line is nearest perpendicular, giving an angle of 77 degrees to 81 degrees. Among the negroes it averages only 67 degrees." (*Preadimites*, p. 247).

In contrasting the negro skull and face with

those of the white, Topinard says: "The *norma ver-ticalis* is of an elliptical shape. The supra-iniac portion of the occipital is frequently projecting, its lateral portions are flat and vertical, the curved temporal lines describe an arc corresponding with the mass of temporal muscles, which are inserted beneath them; the temporal shelf itself is larger than that of the white. The frontal is articulated frequently with the temporal; the greater wings of the sphenoid are consequently not articulated with the parietal. The cranial sutures are more simple than in the white type, and are obliterated sooner. (*Gratiolet*). The squamo-temporal, and the spheno-parietal frequently form a horizontal straight line. The forehead is narrow at the base, sometimes receding and rather low; sometimes straight and bulging (bombe) at the summit. The frontal bosses are often confluent, or replaced by a single and median protuberance. * * * The orbit moreover are microsemis, that is to say, short from above downwards. * * * The eyeballs are close to the head, and the palpebral apertures are nevertheless small and are on the same horizontal line. * * * The nose is developed in width at the expense of its projection; its base is large and crushed in, owing to the softness of the cartilages, and spreads out into two diverging alæ, with elliptical nostrils more or less exposed. This extremity is also trilobed. The skeleton of the nose platyrrhinian (54.78); the two bones proper are occasionally united as in apes. The inferior border of the aperture is obliterated, or replaced by a sort of platform, the boundary between the nasal fossæ and

the sub-nasal region being undefined in proportion
to the very slight development of the median spine.
* * * The prognathism of the negro extends
within certain limits to the entire face. All the
parts of the superior maxilla contribute to it, and
even the pterygoid processes, which are drawn forward by the development of the jaw; but it is only
really characteristic and considerable in the sub-
nasal region and in the teeth. It frequently exists
also in the lower jaw, that is to say, the chin recedes,
and the teeth project obliquely forwards. The teeth
themselves are wider apart than in the white races,
beautifully white, very firm and sound. Lastly, the
ears are small, round, their border not well curled,
the lobule short and scarcely detached, and the audi-
tory opening wide. The neck is short." (*Anthropology*, pp. 488, 489, 490).

  "The space between the eyes of the negro is
larger and flatter than in the white." (Topenard).
"The eye of the negro affords a peculiarity of structure strikingly different from the white man. It has
been long known, and was described by Dr. Samuel
A. Cartright, of Natchez, Mississippi, nearly fifty
years ago, in simple, non-technical language. He
says: 'If you look into the inner angle of the eye,
next to the nose, and slightly elevate the eyelids,
you will discover nothing in the white man's eye but
a small prominence, or glandular-like substance, and
a very small semi-lunar membrane. The prominence is composed of seven distinct crypts, or sacs,
filled with an unctious fluid, and has seven distinct

openings, or orifices. The semi-lunar membrane is for the purpose of directing the tears into a sac, which lies behind and below the prominence. But if you look into the eye of the negro, in the same manner, you will discover that his eye has an additional expansion of the above-mentioned membrane, or, in other words, an additional contrivance, consisting of a membranous wing expanded underneath a portion of the upper eyelid, and that when the eye is exposed to a bright light, the membranous wing covers a considerable portion of the globe of the eye. You will find the same membranous wing still more fully developed in birds, forming a kind of curtain, or third eyelid, called by naturalists the nictating membrane, evidently to guard their eyes against the dazzling influence of the sun's rays. The master may neglect to provide his slaves with a covering for the head to shield the eyes from the brilliancy of the sun while laboring in the fields, and such neglect would greatly increase the irksomeness of labor under a tropical sun, if God, in His good providence, had not provided them with the above-mentioned contrivance to protect the eyes against the brightness of the solar rays. You have, no doubt, frequently seen slaves throw off their hats as an incumbrance and voluntarily expose themselves bare-headed to the sun, without suffering any inconvenience from the intensity of his light.'" (*Anthropology for the People*, pp. 21, 22).

The prominent nose of the white is in striking contrast to the flat nose of the negro, which has the appearance of having been crushed in. The flat nose of the negro is another characteristic of the ape. "The cartilage at the end of the nose of the white man is divided, or split, as any one can test by placing a finger on the tip of that organ; but in the negro nose this split does not exist, nor does it exist in mulattoes. The prostate gland in the negro is bilobular, or, to put it in popular terms, it may be said to be divided into two parts, like the quadrumanous organization. The absence of the 'nasal spine' in the negro is another singular difference." (*Anthropology for the People*, pp. 20, 21).

The comparatively thin lips of the white are in striking contrast to the thick, fluffy lips of the negro. This thickness of the lips is another character of the ape.

Quatrefages says: "The thousand differences of form and dimensions which exhibit, from the negro of Guinea with his enormous, and, as it were, turned-up lips, to certain Aryan or Semitic whites, can neither be measured nor described. * * * It may, however, be remarked that the thickness of the lips is very marked in all negroes, in consequence of their projection in front of the maxillary bones and the teeth. The mouth of the negro presents another character which seems to me to have been generally neglected, and which has always struck me. It is a kind of clamminess at the outer border of the commissures, and seems to prevent the small movements of the corner of the mouth which play such an important part in the physiognomy. The dissections of Mr.

Harny have explained these facts. They have shown that in the negroes the muscles of this region are both more developed and less distinct than in the whites." (*The Human Species*, p. 367).

The prominent chin of the white is in striking contrast to the retreating chin of the negro. This retreating chin is another character of the ape. Winchell says: "The retreating contour of the chin, as compared with the European, approximates the negro to the chimpanzee and lower mammals." (*Ibid*, p. 251).

The front teeth of the white, set perpendicularly in the jaw, are in striking contrast to the front teeth of the negro, which set slanting in the jaw. The slanting teeth is another character of the ape. Haeckel describes as "Prognathi" those whose jaws, like those of the animal snout, strongly project, and whose front teeth, therefore, slope in front; and men with straight teeth "orthognathi, whose jaws project but little and whose front teeth stand perpendicularly."

Dr. Middleton Michel, Professor in the South Carolina Medical College, quoted in *Anthropology for the People*, says: "The larynx is formed of true and false cartilages. The textural peculiarity of these false cartilages is that they are delicate, pliable, elastic, and never undergo ossification. To this class belong the epiglottis and the cartilages of Santorini and Wrisburg. The so-called cartilages of Wrisburg, cuneiform or cruciform cartilages, as they are also designated, are developed within the aryteno epiglottidian folds, one on each side of the rima glottidis, or chink of the glottis. Of all these intrinsic pieces forming or supporting the wind pipe, none are so inconstant, and, when present, even variable as to size, as the Wrisburg cartilages; scarcely any larger than the Santorini cartilages, they, at best, are concealed within the mucous folds of the aryteno epiglottic larynx, and are very difficult to find. In the white subject I have never met them, and when to the touch and sight they were discernable, it has always been in the negro. I have made a special investigation of this point, and I would caution those who seek to discover these delicate nodules of fibro-cartilage that, when the scalpel would fail to discover them, their presence is often satisfactorily revealed by simply rolling the aryteno epiglottic folds between the thumb and fore-finger. as then the touch at once detects the firmer resistance of an extremely delicate body unfolded within these mucous layers and embedded among the minute granules of sparcely-scattered laryngeal glands."

The relatively long, slender neck of the white, is in striking contrast to the short, thick neck of the negro. The short, thick neck is another character of the ape. Burmeister, quoted by Hartman, says: " The negro's thick neck is the more striking, since it is generally allied with a short throat. In measuing negroes from the crown of the head to the shoulder, I have found the interval to be from nine and a quarter to nine and three quarter inches. In Europeans of normal height this interval is seldom less than ten inches, and is more commonly eleven inches in women, and twelve in men. The shortness of the neck, as well as the relatively small size of the brain pan, and the large size of the face, may be more readily taken as an approximation to the Simian type, since all apes are short-necked. * * * This shortness of the neck of the negro explains his greater carrying power, and his preference for carrying burdens on his head, which is much more fatiguing to the European on account of his longer and weaker neck." (*Anthropoid Apes*, pp. 100, 101).

In the negro, "the *clavicle* is longer in proportion to the *humerus* than in the white. His *radius* is perceptibly longer in proportion to the *humerus*—thus approximating to that of the ape. The *scapular* is shorter and broader." (*Preadimites*, p. 171). "Among negroes, the forearm is longer, in proportion to the arm, than is the case with whites. The same is true of anthropoid apes. (*Ibid*). Topinard says: "The arm is shortest in whites, longest in negroes. Frequently in the latter, the extremity of the middle finger touched the patella; once it was twelve millimeters below its upper border, as in the gorilla." (*Ibid*, p. 335). Quatrefages says: "I have already observed that the upper limb is a little longer in the negro than in the white. The essential cause of this difference is the relative elongation of the fore-arm. M. Broca, after comparing the radius and humerus of the two races, gives 79.43 for the negro, and 73.82 for the European." (*The Human Species*, p. 399).

Prof. Winchell says: "Among negroes the capacity of the lungs is less than among the whites, and the circumference of the chest is less." (*Ibid*, p. 173). Quatrefages says: "The thoracic cage presents some facts sufficiently well proved. In consequence of the form of the sternum, the greater or less curvature of the ribs, it is generally broad and flattened in the white, narrow and prominent in the negro." (*Ibid*, p. 397).

Topinard says: "M. Pruner-Bey speaks of two important characters which remind one of the ape. The three curvatures of the spine are less pronounced in the negro than in the white; his thorax is relatively flat from side to side, and slightly cylindrical. The shoulders, he adds, are less powerful than in the European. The umbilicus is nearer the pubis; the iliac bones in the male are thicker and more vertical, The neck of the femur is less oblique." (*Anthropology*, p. 490).

Topinard says: "Camper and Soemmering observed that the pelvis of the negro in its *ensemble* is narrower than that of the white. * * * In 1826 Vrolik came to the conclusion that the pelvis of the male negro—from its strength and thickness—from the want of transparency in its iliac fossæ—from the higher projection of its superior extremity, and from the spinous processes of the iliac bones being less projecting and less separated from the cotyloid cavities, approximates to that of animals, while the

pelvis of the negress maintains a certain slender-
ness." (*Anthropology*, pp. 305, 306). "Weber found
that in each of the races he had studied, the pelvis
presented a predominant form, which, on that account alone, became characteristic. He regarded
the inlet as being generally oval and of large transverse diameter in the white * * * cuneiform and
of large antero-posterior diameter in negroes. * * *
M. Verneau confirms the assertions of the greater
number of his predecessors, as to the reality of the
characters of race to be found in the pelvis.
Amongst these characters, there are some which
have been pointed out in the negro as *indications of
animalism.* * * * In fact, the verticality of the
ilia, and the increase of the antero-posterior diameter of the pelvis in the negro, have been chiefly
insisted upon as recalling characters which may be
observed in mammilla generally, and particularly in
apes." (*The Human Species*, pp. 397, 398). Winchell says: "The negro pelvis averages but $26\frac{1}{2}$
inches in circumference; that of the white race is 33
inches. In the negro it is more inclined, which is
another quadmanous character." (*Preadamites*, p.
249).

Topinard places the relative length of the femur
to the tibia at 67.22 in the negro, and 69.73 in the
white. (*Ibid*). In contrasting the following characters of the negro with those of the white, Topinard
says: "The femur is less oblique, the tibia more
curved, the calf of the leg high and but little developed, the heel broad and projecting, the foot long,

but slightly arched, flat, and the great toe rather shorter than in the white. Negresses age rapidly, their breasts elongate after the first pregnancy, and become flabby and pendulous." (*Ibid*, p. 490.) The thin calves set high on the leg, the projecting heel, etc., are all characters of the ape. Topinard also points out differences between whites and negroes in their muscular systems, vessels, viscera, and all the internal organs, and says: "No doubt special peculiarities in the internal generative organs will be discovered. The nervous system has been the subject of closer study. Soemmering, and after him Jacquart, demonstrated that the nerves of the negro, particularly those at the base of the brain, are larger than those of the European. It has been ascertained that his cerebral substance is not so white." (*Ibid*, pp. 307, 308, 309).

Quatrefages says: "Relatively to the white, the negro presents a marked predominance of peripheral nervous expansions. The trunks are thicker, and the fibres more numerous, or perhaps merely easier to isolate and to preserve on account of their volume alone. On the other hand, the cerebral centers, or at least the brain, appear to be inferior in development." (*Ibid*, p. 401). There are also some slight variations between the respiration, circulation, animal temperature, secretions, etc., of the white man and the negro. (*Ibid*, 409).

Dr. Mosley, quoted by Winchell, says: "Negroes are void of sensibility to a surprising degree. They are not subject to nervous diseases. They sleep soundly in every disease, nor does any mental disturbance keep them awake. They bear chirurgical operations much better than white people; and what would be the cause of insupportable pain to a white man, a negro would almost disregard." (*Preadamites*, p. 178). Dr. Winchell says: "The mental indolence of negroes is further shown in the comparative records of insanity and idiocy. While among whites, mania occurs in the proportion of 0.76 per thousand, among negroes it is only 0.10 per thousand. While idiocy among the former is 0.73 per thousand, among the latter it is 0.37 per thousand." (*Ibid*, p. 182). "In the negro, the development of the body is generally in advance of the the white. His wisdom teeth are cut sooner; and in estimating the age of his skull, we must reckon it as at least five years in advance of the white." (*Ibid*, p. 175). The exemption of the negro from malarial diseases, and sundry other pathological affections of the white race, is another significant diagnostic." (*Ibid*, p. 180). Quatrefages says: "Of all human races the white is the most sensitive to marsh fevers, and the black the least so. On the other hand, the negro race suffers more than any other from phthisis." (*Ibid*, p. 426).

Dr. J. Hendree, of Aniston, Alabama, in writing to Professor Winchell, says:

"Let me mention one fact especially, drawn from my own experience of forty years. The coarseness of their (the negroes) organization makes them require about double the dose of ordinary medicine used for whites."

Dr. M. L. Barrow, of Drayton, Georgia, writing to Dr. Winchell, says:

"I have practiced among the negroes for over forty years. * * * Your information in respect to the doses of medicine for the colored people, corresponds with my experience—except as regards opiates; and perhaps they will bear large quantities of these, as I have known some to take very large doses with impunity." (*Preadamites*, p. 177).

Desirous of comparing the anatomy of one of the so-called "lower races of men," with that of the white and the apes, Prof. Huxley selected as his specimen, a "Bosjesman Negro," from one of the so-called "black races" which he, Winchell and others, class as negroes. After comparing the physical and mental organisms of the "Bosjesman Negro," with those of the white, on the one side, and with those of the gorilla, chimpanzee, and other apes on the other side, Prof. Huxley states the result of his observations as follows: "The difference between the highest and lowest men is far greater, both relatively and absolutely, than that between the lowest man and the highest ape. The latter, as has been seen, is represented by, say, twelve ounces cerebral substance absolutely; or by 32:20 relatively; but as the largest recorded human brain weighed between 65 and 66 ounces, the former difference is represented by more than 33 ounces absolutely, or by 65:32 relatively. Regarded systematically, the cerebral differences of man and apes are not of more than generic value—his family distinction resting chiefly on his dentition, his pelvis and his lower limbs.

"Thus, whatever system of organs be studied, the comparison of their modifications in the ape series leads to one and the same result—that the structural differences which separate man from the gorilla and the chimpanzee are not so great as those which separate the gorilla from the lower apes." (*Man's Place in Nature*, pp. 122, 123).

Thus, Prof. Huxley found by comparative anatomy that the difference between the physical and mental organism of the white and "Bosjesman Negro" are immeasurable; he also found that the differences between the physical and mental organism of the "Bosjesman Negro" and the gorilla and chimpanzee, are not so great as those which separate the gorilla from the tailed apes; that they *are not of more than generic value.* In view of the fact that comparative anatomy furnished Prof. Huxley the most abundant, absolute proof that the negro is an ape, it would be interesting to learn upon what authority he declared him a "man." He proved him a monkey, and pronounced him a man—proved him a beast and accepted him as a brother.

The above comparisons clearly show that in his physical and mental organisms, the negro differs from the white; and that at every essential point he approximates the organisms below. We have also shown that in their ability to make and handle tools, the lower apes closely approach the negro. Yet none of the lower apes, not even the so-called anthropoids, can discharge the many duties which devolve upon servants. They could never handle and care for domestic animals, work metals, fashion implements, break the ground, plant, cultivate, and harvest crops; and build houses, fences, etc. In addition to this, it is significant that no one of the so-called anthropoids can be said to be "most absolutely like man." The gorilla approaches nearest to man in the structure of the hand and foot, the chimpanzee in important structural details in the skull, the orang in the development of the brain, and the gibbon in that of the thorax." (*The Evolution of Man*, Vol. II, p. 181).

When we pause to reflect that all knowledge of the fact that the negro is an ape, was lost to the world ages ago, it is easy to see that, but for the existence of the lower apes, it would be impossible for us, at this late day, to prove that he is not a man; and this, too, in the face of the fact that, in his physical and mental characters, his habits, mode of life, manners, gestures, language, and his achievements, he is in striking contrast to the white. But with this interesting family of animals, shading up from lemur to the negro, we are able with the assistance of the scriptures and the sciences to determine that the negro is one of the ape family; that he simply stands at the head of the ape family, as the lion stands at the head of the cat family. Hence, the lower apes, though unfit for general domestic purposes, are invaluable, in that they enable us to determine beyond question the negro's true position in the universe—that he is merely an ape.

The negro possesses articulate speech, the erect posture, a well-formed hand and foot, and is withal a tool-making, tool-handling animal. These characteristics pre-eminently fit him for the position of servant, while the low order of his mentality disqualifies him for a higher sphere; as is well known, the negro is an animal with which man may associate himself carnally, and produce offspring, that will be indefinitely fertile, and capable of utilizing the arts of civilization, and of acquiring a knowledge of God and His dealings with man; besides, it should be borne in mind that, though the negro is omnivorous, he manifests a strong preference for the flesh of man as an article of food. These characteristics clearly identify the negro as the creature described in scripture as the *beast of the field.*

CHAPTER XI.

The Creation of Man.

"And God said, Let us make man in our image, after our likeness: and let them have dominion over the fish of the sea, and over the fowl of the air, and over the cattle, and over all the earth, and over every creeping thing that creepeth upon the earth.

"So God created man in his own image, in the image of God created he him; male and female created he them:

"And God blessed them, and God said unto tnem, Be fruitful, and multiply, and replenish the earth, and subdue it: and have dominion over the fish of the sea, and over the fowl of the air, and over every living thing that moveth upon the earth" (*Gen.* i, 26, 27, 28).

The broad distinction which the inspired writer makes between man and the animals, and plants which preceded him is shown as follows:

1. In the proposition to make man: "Let us make man," etc.

2. That neither the earth nor the waters would be allowed to bring forth man; God Himself would create man.

3. That, unlike the animals and plants, man was not made after any kind, but was created "in the image of God"—"after His likeness."

288

582

4. That, unlike the plants and animals, which were made in great numbers and varieties, man was created a single pair.

5. That, unlike his treatment of the animals, the inspired writer tells us that God designed man for a specific work; that man was to have dominion over the earth and the animals.

6. That when created, man was commanded to "subdue" the earth, and "have domain over the fish of the sea, and over the fowl of the air, and over every living thing that moveth upon the earth."

It is plain that to "subdue" the earth means to develop its resources; for, just in proportion as man subdues a piece of wild uncultivated land, he necessarily reduces it into a cultivated state, and developes its resources. Hence, the Biblical term "subdue," in this text, and our term "develop," are synonyomous. To "have dominion" means to dominate—to have control. Hence the term "dominion" in this text, and our term "control" are synonymous. Thus, man was designed to develop all the resources of this globe, and when created he was at once assigned to this great task. He was also designed to "have dominion"—to exercise control over the animals and utilize them in his efforts to accomplish the development of the earth. This was a task of such magnitude as only the mind of Diety could have conceived; and man's successful accomplishments of it required that man be endowed with mind of the highest order—mind at once legislative, executive, and judicial; and man's brilliant achievements when viewed in the light of history, traditions, monumental evidence, and our daily observation, shows that he was thus endowed. All the indications point to the fact that if man had respected the design of God in creating him, and had applied himself to the accomplishment of the great task for which he was designed, and to which he was assigned in the creation, this earth would long since have been in the highest state of cultivation; its resources would all have been discovered, appreciated, and developed. The besetting sin which degraded man from his first and high estate, as the dominant power of the earth, will be fully revealed in the following pages of this work.

It will be observed that in our English version of the Bible, the Mosaic account of the creation is divided into two chapters. As above quoted, the first chapter acquaints us with the leading events of the creation in the order of their occurrence, beginning with the creation of matter, and ending with the creation of man; the design of God in creating man, and the duties to which he and his descendants were assigned in the creation. If the narrative of creation ended with the first chapter of Genesis, we could readily see that no kinship exists between man and the animals; that they were made at different periods; and were designed for different purposes; that man was designed to rule, and the animals to be controlled. But we would be hopelessly ignorant upon the following important subjects: (1) What character in man pre-eminently distinguishes him from the animals, and establishes between God and man the close relationship of father and son; thus making man an immortal being—an heir to eternity—while the animals are mere creatures of time. (2) How man was brought into existence, and what elements entered into his composition. (3) What new element was introduced into the material universe on the sixth creative day in combination with matter and with mind as presented in the physical and mental organisms of Adam, and which elevated man to the lofty dignity of a *creation.* (4) Was man and woman created simultaneously, or did one precede the other, and if so, which one? These and other important questions would have been left to mere speculation. But, happily the narrative of creation extends through the second chapter of Genesis; and in this chapter we are given a more detailed account of the origin and location of the elements of plant and animal life—that they are inherent in matter; the material of which man's physical organism is formed; the manner of his formation; the elements which enter into his composition, and which pre-eminently distinguish man from the animals; establishes between God and man the close relationship of father and son; and thus endows man with immortality; and also enlightens us as to this new element which made its first appearance in the material universe in combination with matter and with mind in Adam; the fact that the male side or part of the Adamic creation preceded the female; that man, unlike the animals, was assigned to a definite place of abode, and to a specific task in the Garden of Eden, etc.

In verse 7 of the second chapter of Genesis the inspired writer says:

"And the Lord God formed man of the dust of the ground, and breathed into his nostrils the breath of life; and man became a living soul."

The information contained in this text is invaluable for the following reasons:

1. The "dust of the ground" of which "God formed man is a part of the original creation—*matter*. This being true, it follows that man's physical organism is composed of matter; and that man's physical life, like that of the plant or the animal, is derived from the elements of life, which are inherent in matter.

2. It enables us to realize that the broad distinction which exists between man and the animals is not due to man's possession of more perfect physical and mental organisms; for, in these respects the difference between them is merely one of *degree*, not of *kind*. Hence, when, in the Creation, man's physical and mental organisms were completed, he, like the animals, was simply a combination of matter and mind. At this period in his history there existed between God and man, as existed between God and the animals, only such relationship as naturally exists between the Creator and His creature—the relationship of the artist to the product of his art. In this condition, man, possessed of physical and mental organisms of the highest order—and life—

physical life—derived from the combination of the elements of life, which were inherent in the matter of which his physical organism was composed, might have lived out a mere animal existence on the earth, without further endowments from the hand of God. If mated with a female whose exalted physical and mental organisms corresponded with his own, he might even have begotten offspring which would have been indefinitely fertile, and to whom he would transmit his elevated physical and mental characters; in this case, however, Adam and his progeny would have been mere animals, distinguished from the fish, and fowl, and beasts only as these are distinguished from each other; and, like their fellow animals, they would have had no knowledge of, nor interest in, an eternity beyond.

But such was not God's will; it was not a part of His plan of creation that man should thus be placed on the base level of the brute; with no laws governing his conduct save those which govern the animals in their relations to each other; with no hope of present or future reward as an incentive to the performance of good acts; and no fear of present or future punishment as a restraint upon the commission of bad acts; it was not God's intention that man should live out a mere animal existence on the earth—a mere creature of time; He had no desire that between Himself and man there should exist only such relationship as naturally exists between the Creator and His creature—the relationship of the artist to the product of his art.

God entertained nobler, grander, more sublime
conception with regard to man, that peerless creature
whom He proposed to honor by the bestowal of His
likeness, and His image, and to whom He would con-
fide dominion over the works of His hands.   He
desired that between Himself and man there should
exist a close relationship of father and son; that
the intercourse between the Heavenly Father and
His earthly son should not be confined to time, but
would continue throughout eternity; this required
that, in addition to his physical life, derived from
matter, man should be endowed with immortal life;
this required that God would incorporate with man's
physical and mental organisms, a part of His own
substance; in the accomplishment of this ennob-
bling, far-reaching design, "God breathed into
man's nostrils the breath of life, and man became
a living soul." Thus the three creations, Matter,
Mind, and Soul, which are necessary to perfect man,
were combined in "Adam, the son of God."

"The breath of life"—immortal life—itself a
part of His own substance, which God breathed into
man's nostrils, was a new element—a *Creation*—
which was thus introduced into the material universe; and when God incorporated it with the physical and mental organisms of Adam, He at once
established between Himself and man the close relationship of father and son, transformed him from a
mere combination of matter and mind, to the lofty
dignity of a Creation. "Thou mad'st him a little

lower than the angels, and hast crowned him with glory and honor."

If further evidence was necessary to show that Adam was the son of God, our Saviour furnishes it by His recognition of the pure-blooded descendants of Adam as His brethren and sisters. (*Matt.* xii, 49; also *Mark* iii, 35). We might also point to the fact that the ancestry of the Saviour is traced to "Adam, the son of God." (*Luke* iii, 38).

Well might David exclaim in contemplating God's creation of man: "I will praise Thee, for I am fearfully and wonderfully made; marvelous are Thy works; and that my soul knoweth right well. My substance was not hid from Thee, when I was made in secret, and curiously wrought in the lowest parts of the earth. Thine eyes did see my substance, yet being imperfect, and in Thy book all my numbers were written, which in continuance were fashioned, when as yet there was none of them." (*Ps.* cxxxix).

Man and woman were not created simultaneously; the male side or part of the Adamic creation was first created, and afterwards the female; but what length of time intervened between these great events, we have no means of ascertaining; but that it was a considerable period, is indicated by the fact that it was in this interval that "Adam gave names to all cattle, and to the fowl of the air, and to every beast of the field." To successfully accomplish this great task would have been creditable to a Linnæus or Cuvier; it was a mental work requiring the ut-

most observation and the finest discrimination.
Hence, Adam's successful accomplishment of it, goes
far to prove the splendor of his intellectuality.

When the great task of naming the animals was
finished, the earth was not graced by the presence
of woman; "for Adam there was not found an
helpmeet for him." So long as only the male side
or part of the Adamic creation was in existence, it
was incomplete, and utterly incapable of obeying the
first command given in the creation, "be fruitful
and multiply." Realizing this, the great Artist of
the universe looked out upon His yet unfinished
creation, and said: "It is not good that man should
be alone; I will make him a helpmeet for him.

"And the Lord God caused a deep sleep to fall
upon Adam and he slept; and He took one of ribs,
and closed up the flesh instead thereof. And the rib,
which the Lord God had taken from man, made he
a woman, and brought her unto the man."

Forgetful that like produces like, and that by
virtue of this principle the native characteristics of
man must have been more or less active in all ages
of his history, we, of modern time are accustomed to
boast our greater enlightenment as compared to that
of the ancients; and in proof of this, we proudly
point to the sacredness of marriage, woman's honorable position in society, and her higher education.
But scraps of very ancient history, bits of monumental evidence, and fragments of old traditions
that have survived the ravages of time, and descended to us, all point to the fact that this is merely

a reformatory movement, which indicates a disposition on our part to return to primitive conditions. Among the Egyptians, that ancient people who filled the valley of the Nile with magnificent cities, adorned with sumptuous palaces, splendid temples, and all the evidences of the highest culture, the position of woman was honorable and marriage was sacred; not even the king was allowed a plurality of wives; woman's mental faculties were highly cultivated, and her rights respected and carefully guarded; the wife could hold property in her own right and manage her financial affairs; and if divorced, her dower was returned to her with a high rate of interest. Among the Toltics, that great people who developed one of the splendid civilizations of America in ancient times, the position of woman was honorable; her mental faculties were highly cultivated, and marriage was sacred. Among the Aryans, who, thousands of years ago, developed the magnificent civilization of ancient India, marriage was sacred, the position of woman was honorable, and the culture bestowed upon her mental faculties is attested by the Vedas, which abound in beautiful hymns and poems, which were composed and written by the ladies and queens of the Aryans.

When we ascend the stream of time in our efforts to discover the fountain source of this exalted characteristic in man—his respectful devotion to woman, it leads us to the Creation. We find that the earliest manifestation of this ennobling characteristic was displayed in the first recorded utterance of Adam, on his reception of that lovely "help-meet" which God made for him: "This is now born of my bones, and flesh of my flesh, she shall be called woman, because she was taken out of man. Therefore shall a man leave his father and his mother, and shall cleave unto his wife; and they shall be of one flesh."

We would search the annals of the world in vain for a sentiment at once more chaste, more chivalrous, and more devotional to our mother's lovely sex; no one of the intrepid knights who weilded a lance in the Age of Chivalry, ever gave utterance to a sentiment more chivalrous, toward the lady of his choice, whose feelings, whose interest, and whose honor he stood pledged to defend with his life. But in view of the fact that man's chivalrous devotion to his mother's sex, is a character peculiar to man; that it is traceable to the Creation, and had its origin in Adam, we should naturally expect to find traces of it in the literature and traditions of those ancient peoples, the remains of whose splendid civilization, even in their ruins, at once excites the wonder, and challenges the admiration of the modern world. Hence, to our minds there was no occasion for the surprise which greeted the announcement made some fifty years ago that, in addition to their religious, scientific, historical, and poetic literature, the ancient Hindoos possessed many beautiful dramas.

One of these fine dramas, "Sakoontala," was composed by Kalidasa, an ancient Hindoo bard, who is styled "the Shakespeare of India." Sakoontala was translated into English by Professor Monier Williams, who says of it: "Indeed the popularity of this play with the natives of India exceeds that of any other dramatic, and probably of any other poetical composition. But it is not in India alone that the Sakoontala is known and admired. Its excellence is now recognized in every literary circle throughout the continent of Europe; and its beauties, if not universally known and appreciated, are at least acknowledged by many learned men in every country of the world. The four-well known lines of Goethe, so often quoted in relation to the Indian drama, may be here repeated:

'Would'st thou the young year's blossoms and the fruits of its decline,
And all by which the soul is charmed, enraptured, feasted, fed?
Would thou the earth and heaven itself in one sole name combine?
I name thee, O Sakoontala! and all at once is said.'

* * * 'Alexander Von Humbolt, in treating of Indian poetry, observes: 'Kalidasa, the celebrated author of the Sakoontala, is a masterly describer of the influence which nature exercises upon the minds of lovers. * * * Tenderness in the expression of feeling, and richness of fancy, have assigned to him his lofty place among the poets of all nations.'" (See introduction to *Sakoontala*, pp. 6, 7, 8).

The lofty, chivalrous sentiments toward woman,

which characterized the utterances of Adam on his reception of Eve, breathes in every line of the following beautiful tribute which Kalidasa pays to woman:

"Man's all-wise maker, wishing to create
A faultless form, whose matchless symmetry
Should far transcend Creation's choicest works,
Did call together by His mighty will,
And garner up in His eternal mind,
A bright assemblage of all lovely things:
And then, as in a picture, fashion them
Into one perfect and ideal form."

(*Sakoontala*, p. 43).

Prior to the advent of man, there was no connecting link—no bond of kinship between God and the material universe; the relationship between them was merely that of the architect to the structure He had devised and builded. All things in the material universe were mortal, there was nothing immortal. But the proposition to make man, as above quoted, announced the end of these conditions; it heralded the advent of a being who would form the link of kinship between the Creator and His creation. In the execution of this Divine proposition man was created as above described. And our acceptance of the Mosaic account of creation, leaves us no alternative than to decide that man is a *creation*, just as matter and mind are *creations*. This being true, it follows that man is no more akin to the animals than he is to the plant or the planet. Paul furnishes further evidence of this in his declaration: "All flesh is not the same flesh; but there is one kind of flesh of men, another flesh of beasts, another of fishes, and another of birds." Thus we are emphatically taught that these four kinds of flesh are as distinct from each other as if the one made its appearance upon and inhabited the earth, the other Saturn, the other Mars, and the other Jupiter. This being true, it follows that we might with just the same propriety consider man a member of the siderial kingdom as to consider him merely a member of the animal kingdom. Hence, to recognize any kinship between man and the animals, we must repudiate the teachings of Moses and St. Paul.

Prior to the advent of woman, the inspired writer says: * * * "For Adam was not found an helpmeet for him." (*Gen.* ii, 20). This was due to the fact that Adam was the sole representative of the *flesh* of man. Then, in order that there should be no doubt as to whether Adam and Eve were of "one kind of flesh," God made the female man out out of the male man. Thus completed and prefected by the presence of woman, the Adamic family could beget offspring, and increase its numbers on the earth, and ultimately discharge the duties for which they were designed, and to which God assigned them in the Creation. Let us bear in mind that man the male, and woman the female, are the mutually dependent sides or parts of the *immortal life system* of the earth. Hence, the presence of each is necessary to the existence and perpetuation of the system.

The combination of the three creations—matter, mind and soul, as they exist in man, are transmitable through pure Adamic channels; that is, by sexual intercourse between man and woman. Hence, when the male and female sides or parts of the Adamic creation were perfected in Adam and Eve, God commanded them to "be fruitful and multiply and replenish the earth." The reasons for this are evident: (1) Immense numbers of men and women were necessary in order to develop the resources of earth, and exercise control over the animals. (2) That, by a life of obedience to God's laws, Adam and Eve, and their descendants, would fit their souls for the realms of the blest, so that when their physical dissolution occurred, they would be gathered to their reward in eternity, and thus increase the population of heaven.

In discussing this question, let us bear in mind that matter is the basis of all formations in the material universe, whether it exists alone as in the plant; or in combination with mind, as in the animal; or in combination with mind and soul, as in man. It should be unnecessary to say that the reproduction of these three creations, as they exist in plants, in animals, and in man, are governed by laws which God enacted in the creation; and which are positive and unerring in their operations and results.

By way of ascertaining the operations and results of these laws, we shall first investigate the reproduction of plants, in which only the matter creation is represented; and, inasmuch as the manner in which they are reproduced is generally understood, we shall take as our illustration the flowering plants, in which the sexes are represented in the male and in the female bloom. It is well known that the reproduction of these plants results from the union of the *pollen*, or fecundating dust of the stamen of the male bloom with the pollen or fecundating dust of the pistil of the female bloom. This indicates that one side or part of the matter creation, with all the elements of life—physical life—exists in the male bloom; and that its corresponding side or part exists in the female bloom; these opposite, but mutually dependent sides or parts, each act as a magnet which attracts its corresponding side or part in the opposite sex; and, when the two are united in the female bloom, the matter creation is perfected and reproduced in the young plant. But if, as frequently occurs, the matter creation as it exists in its imperfect state in the respective germs of the male and female blooms, are not united in the female bloom, these vital elements are wasted, and the reproduction of the matter creation in the young plant is not accomplished.

The same law governs the reproduction of the animal, in which the two creations—matter and mind—exist in the respective germs of the male and the female. One side or part of the matter creation, with all the elements of life—physical life—and one side or part of the mind creation, exists in an imperfect state in the male animal; the corresponding sides or parts of these imperfect creations exist in the female animal. Observation teaches that by uniting the imperfect sides or parts of these creations in the female, results in their being perfected and reproduced in the young animal. This indicates that each of these creations maintains its individuality in their respective germs of the male and the female animal, and that each side or part of these imperfect creations acts as a magnet, which attracts its corresponding side or part in the opposite sex. Hence, when sexual union occurs, each side or part of these two creations—matter and mind—are united and perfected in the female, conception and birth results, and the combination of matter and mind as they existed in the parents is reproduced in the offspring.

But if, as frequently occurs, from various causes, these imperfect matter and mind creations, as they exist in the respective germs of the male and female animal, are not united and perfected in the female, these vital elements are wasted, conception does not result, and the reproduction of these two creations in a young animal is not accomplished. The strength of our argument is demonstrated by the actions of our domestic fowls; it frequently occurs that the female fowl, when not associated with the male fowl, will lay eggs; but such eggs will not "hatch." This is due to the fact that but one side or part—the female side or part of the two creations, matter and mind, as they existed in the germ of the female—was represented in the egg; their corresponding side or part in the male, which was necessary to perfect the two creations in the female, were not present; and as a result the effort of the female to reproduce these two creations in a young animal, independently of the male, was abortive.

The same law which governs the reproduction of the matter creation in the plant, and the reproduction of the matter and the mind creations in the animal, must also govern the reproduction of the three creations—matter, mind, and soul—as they exist in the respective germs of the male and female man. One side or part of the matter creation with all the elements of physical life; and one side or part of the mind creation; and one side or part of the soul creation with its peculiar characteristic—*immortal* life—exists in an imperfect state in the germ of the male man; the corresponding sides or parts of these imperfect creations exist in the germ of the female man. By the union of these imperfect creations in the female man, they are perfected and reproduced in the offspring. This indicates that each of these imperfect creations maintains its individuality in the respective germs of the male and the female man; and that each of these imperfect creations acts as a magnet, which attracts its corresponding side or part in the opposite sex. When sexual union occurs, each side or part of these imperfect creations unites with its corresponding side or part in the female, and is thus perfected; conception results, and the three creations —matter, mind, and soul—are reproduced in the offspring. Thus, it is shown that the reproduction of the immortal soul, in combination with matter and with mind as it exists in man, is as natural and as

simple a process as the reproduction of the animal
or the plant; and that it is governed by the same
laws.

The most positive evidence that Adam was conscious of the fact that he was not a mere combination of matter and mind; that he was not an animal;
that he was not akin to the animals; but that he was
a distinct creation; that he possessed an immortal
soul, itself a part of the substance of God; that his
soul formed the bond of kinship between himself
and God; that when the hour of his physical dissolution arrived his soul would take its flight from
the scenes of earth to an endless existence in eternity; his knowledge of all these facts is shown by
his explanation of why he called the name of his
wife Eve: "Because she is the mother of all living." (*Gen.* iii, 20).

All the facts indicate that this explanation was
made before Eve had conceived by Adam, and consequently before she became a mother. But para-
doxical as it may appear, his explanation is sustained
by the scriptures, which teach us that the animal
possesses mere physical or mortal life; while in
addition to his physical life, man possesses *immortal*
life. This being true, it follows that, from the
moment of its conception, the offspring of the
female animal begins to die, in the sense that each
moment of its existence brings it nearer to the time
of its final dissolution. Hence, in this sense, the
female animals may with propriety be regarded as
the mothers of a'l dying. But this does not apply

to women. Adam was fully aware that in the ovaries of Eve there was one side or part of the three creations,—matter, mind, and soul; that the corresponding sides or parts of these creations existed in himself; and that when these imperfect sides or parts were united and perfected in Eve, she would give birth to an immortal being.

Thus it is shown: (1) That by incorporating "a living soul"—itself a part of the substance of God—with Adam's physical and mental organisms, God established between Himself and Adam the close relationship of father and son. (2) That this relationship is transmitable through pure Adamic channals to the remotest descendants of Adam. Hence, every pure-blooded descendant of Adam and Eve are sons or daughters of God, as the case may be. Further evidence of this is furnished by the Virgin Mary and her conception of the Saviour. Immediately before the occurrence of this great event, one side or part—the female side or part—of the matter, mind, and soul creations reposed in the womb of Mary; ordinarily, these imperfect sides or parts of these three creations would have been perfected by being united through sexual contact with their corresponding male sides or parts. But God willed it otherwise; He desired a "begotten son," who, as His heir and representative, would act as mediator between God and man, and re-establish between them the cordial relations which had so long been interrupted. In the execution of this design, God, not by the sexual act, but simply by the exercise of His creative power, sup-

plied and united the imperfect female sides or parts
of the three creations in the womb of Mary, with
their corresponding male sides or parts; Mary conceived, and in due process of time, Jesus Christ, the
Founder of Christianity and the Redeemer of the
World, was born.

As above shown, the Bible teaches that there are
three Creations—matter, mind, and soul; and that
the soul creation is as distinct from mind, as mind
is distinct from matter. We have also shown that
Adam fully realized this, and that his possession of
a Soul, which is peculiar to man, pre-eminently distinguishes man from the animal. This essential
knowledge which God bestowed upon Adam for the
benefit of the Adamic family in all ages, doubtless
occupied as conspicuous a place in Adam's book as
it does in our Bible. But, when Adam's book was
lost in the ages following the Deluge, the knowledge
of these three elements was handed down by tradition and thus became more or less garbled and confused. However, we find traces of them in the literature of the civilized nations of antiquity of whose
cosmogonies we have any knowledge. But, finally,
God made a second revelation of the existence of
these creations to Moses, who transmitted them to
the Jews in his account of the creation. The Jews,
and doubtless many Gentiles, knew of these three
creations and the distinctions between them until
long after the crucifixion; besides, our Saviour recognized the distinctions between these three creations in His command: "Thou shalt love the Lord

thy God with all thy heart; (physical organ, composed of matter), and with all thy soul (the immortal
organ), and with all thy mind," (the mental organ).

But during the "Dark Ages" the existence of
these three creations and the distinctions between
them, like the distinctions between the "cattle" or
quadrupeds, and the "beasts" or *bipeds* (apes), were
lost. When this sad event occured the mind creation and the soul creation came to be regarded as
identical, and the terms "mind or soul," were
employed to describe the mental organism. At the
same time there were many persons who adhered to
the belief of their ancestors that man is immortal;
and they insisted upon making a distinction between
man and the animals; but with the Bible distinctions upon this subject lost, and with mind and soul
blended and confused, as the " mind or soul," they,
in their ignorance, were led to believe that mind is
peculiar to man; and that the animals possessed
mere instinct. This great error which had its origin
in the "Dark Ages" of ignorance, superstition,
and crime, has survived to our day, and is now
universally entertained by the Jew and the Gentile,
the Catholic and the Protestant alike; and thus practically eliminates the soul creation from modern
theology. The leading authorities of the age make
no distinction between mind and soul. As evidence
of this, we quote Professor Robert Young in his
" Analytical Concordance of the Bible," in which he
proposes to give "every word in alphabetical order,
arranged under its Hebrew or Greek original, with

the literal meaning of each, and its pronunciation."
Professor Young defines the term " Mind " as
follows:

" Mind—

1. Imagination, frame, formation, *yetur*.
2. Heart, *leb*.
4. Soul, *breath*, *nephesh*.
5. Mouth, *peh*.
6. Spirit, *ruach*."

—(*Analytical Concordance*, pp. 661, 662).

Sir William Smith, another leading authority,
makes no distinction between mind and soul. (See
Dictionary of the Bible). The misconception as to
the identity of mind and soul which universally prevails among both Jew and Gentile theologians, is
clearly shown by the utterances of Dr. Robert T.
Young, a prominent educator of Nashville, Tenn.,
who, in his work, " *The Negro, a Reply to 'Ariel*,' "
pp. 28, 29, says:

"The whole world is made up of mind or soul
and matter. The term matter is a name which we
apply to a certain combination or properties, or to
certain substances which are solid, extended and
divisible, and which are known to us only by these
properties. The term mind, in the same manner,
is a name which we apply to a certain combination of functions, or to a certain power which we
feel within us, and is known to us only by these
functions. Matter we know only by our senses.
Mind or soul by our consciousness. (*Dr. Aber-
combie*)."

This blending and confusing of the mind and soul creations has the following disastrous results:

1. It is at once an open, gratuitous insult to God, and the most positive, direct assault upon His plan of creation, since it proposes to throw open the portals of eternity alike to man and the animals.

2. It proposes to eliminate the soul creation from the material universe; and thus destroy the bond of kinship between God and man; deprives man of any special claim to immortality, and dethrones him from his lofty position as a distinct *creation.*

3. It degrades man to the base level of the brute; for, as has been shown, mind is common to man and the animals, the difference between them in this respect being merely one of *degree*, not of *kind.* Hence, if the mind and soul are identical, why should not the "mind or soul" of the animal be as immortal as the "mind and soul" of man? Thus it is plain that man's claim to immortality is absolutely ridiculous when based on nothing more than the superiority of his mind over that of the animal.

The teachings of the modern clergy, both Jew and Gentile, that mind and soul are identical, and the employment of the terms "mind or soul" to describe the mental organ, though in conflict with the scriptures, is in absolute harmony with the teachings of modern materialism, as shown by the utterances of Professor Haeckel, the leading materialist of the age, who says:

"With regard to the human 'soul organ,' the

brain, the application of the fundamental law of biogeny has been firmly established by the careful empiric observations. The same may be said of its functions, the 'activity of the soul.' For the development of a function goes hand in hand with the gradual development of every organ. The morphological differentiation of the various parts of the brain corresponds with its physiological separation or 'division of labor.' Hence, what is commonly termed the 'soul' or 'mind' of man, (consciousness included) is merely the sum total of the activities of a large number of nerve cells, of which the brain is composed. Where the normal arrangement and function of these latter does not exist, it is impossible to conceive of a healthy 'soul.' This idea which is one of the most important principles of our modern exact physiology, is certainly not compatible with the wide-spread belief in the 'personal immortality of man.' However, this dualistic dogma, which is met with among the lower races of men in the greatest variety of forms, is no longer tenable. The wonderful advances made in experimental physiology and psychiatry, as well as in comparative pyschology and ontogeny, have, during the last half-century, removed stone after stone from the mighty sub-structure upon which this dogma stood so apparently unassailable. However, it lost its hold by the grand biological discoveries of the last two decades, above all by the complete uplifting of the veil which had hitherto concealed the mystery of fertilization. We now know for certain, and can demonstrate the fact at any moment under the microscope, that the wonderful process of fertilization is nothing more than the commingling of two different cells, the copulation of their kernals. In this process the kernal of the male sperm-cell transmits the individual peculiarities of the father, the female egg-cell transmits those of the mother; the inheritance from both parents is determined by the commingling of both kernals, and with it likewise begins the existence of the new individual, the child. It is against all reason to suppose that this new individual should have an ' eternal life ' without end, when we can minutely determine the finite beginning of its existence by direct observation." (*History of Creation*, pp. 493, 494, 495).

Thus, as above shown, the modern clergy, both Jew and Gentile, Catholic and Protestant, are in open conflict with the Bible in their efforts to blend and confuse mind and soul, they are in absolute harmony with the teachings of atheism. If further evidence was required to show the broad distinction which exists between mind and soul, we might, among other scriptural writers, quote Peter, who says of the antediluvians: "Which some time were disobedient, when once the long suffering of God waited in the days of Noah, while the ark was a preparing, wherein few, that is, eight souls were saved by water." (*1 Peter*, iii, 20).

There were as many *minds* "saved" in the ark as there were men, women, and animals, but there were only *eight souls* "saved;" these were Noah and his wife, and his three sons and their wives.

All the facts relative to the creation of man justifies us in asserting that Adam, fresh from the hands of his Creator, bearing the "image of God," presented in his physical, mental, and soul organisms, the grandest specimen of manhood the world has ever known; and that Eve, fresh from the hands of her Creator, with the "image of God" stamped upon her fair brow, presented in her physical, mental, and soul organisms, the loveliest specimen of womanhood, that ever graced the earth.

CHAPTER XII.

The Theory of Descent.

Having reviewed the teachings of the scriptural school of Divine Creation, as revealed in the language of the inspired authors, it is only fair to our readers to present the teachings of the atheistic school of Natural Development, as set forth in the language of its leading advocates. As shown in a previous chapter of this work, the general theory of development is, as it were, divided into two parts: the first part treats of the origin of the earth and the celestial bodies; and materialists generally accept the Nebular Theory as the correct solution of this problem. The other part of the theory of development treats of the introduction of plant and animal life; and the origin of plants, animals and man. This part of the theory is known as "The Theory of Descent." The advocates of this theory assume that plant and animal life is the result of "spontaneous generation." Thus, the "Nebular Hypothesis" and "The Theory of Descent," combine to form what is known as "The Theory of Natural Development," or "The Theory of Evolution."

.   In discussing the origin of animal life, Prof. Haeckel says: "The most ancient ancestors of man, as of all other organisms, were living creatures of

315

the simplest kind imaginable; organisms without
organs, like the still living monera.   They consisted
of simple homogeneous, structureless, and formless
little lumps of mucous or albuminous matter (plas-
son), like the still living *protamœba primitava*.   The
form value of these most ancient ancestors of man
was not even equal to that of a cell, but merely that
of a cytod; for, as in the case of all monera, the
little lump of protoplasm did not as yet possess a
cell-kernel.   The first of these monera originated in
the beginning of the Laurentian period by spontaneous generation, or archigony, out of so-called "inorganic combinations;" namely, out of simple combinations of carbon, oxygen, hydrogen, and nitro-
gen."   (*History of Creation*, p. 380).

Mr. Haeckel's theory of the origin of life by
spontaneous generation is in striking contrast to
that of Mr. Darwin, who believed that God created a
few simple "forms," and that these evolved through
higher forms to culminate in man.   Mr. Darwin
says:

"There is a grandeur in this view of life, with
its several powers, *having been originally breathed by
the Creator into a few forms or into one.*   *   *   *   *
The similar framework of bones in the hand of a
man, wing of a bat, fin of a porpoise, and leg of a
horse   *   *   *   and innumerable other such facts,
at once explain themselves on the theory of descent
with slow and successive modifications.   *   *   *
In regard to the members of each great kingdom,
such as vertebrata, articulata, etc., we have distinct

evidence * * * that within each kingdom *all the members are descended from a single progenitor.* * * * All the living forms of life are the lineal descendants of those which lived long before the Cambrian epoch." (*Origin of Species,* pp. 420, 425, 428).

In opposition to this, Mr. Haeckel says: "But a truly *natural and consistent* view of organisms *can assume no supernatural act of creation for even these simplest original forms,* but only a coming into existence by spontaneous generation. From Darwin's view of the nature of species we arrive, therefore, at the natural theory of development. * * * The fundamental idea which must necessarily lie at the bottom of all natural theories of development is that of a gradual development of all (even the most perfect) organisms out of a single or out of a very few quite simple and quite imperfect original beings *which came into existence not by supernatural creation but by spontaneous generation,* or archigony, *out of inorganic matter."* (*Ibid,* Vol. I, pp. 48, 75).

In a more detailed description of the monera, Mr. Heackel says: "Formerly, when the doctrine of spontaneons generation was advocated, it failed at once to obtain adherents on account of the composite structure of the simplest organisms then known. It is only since we have discovered the exceedingly important monera, only since we have become acquainted in them with organisms not in any way built up of distinct organs, but which consist solely of a single chemical combination, and yet grow, nourish and propagate themselves, that this great difficulty has been removed, and the hypotheses of spontaneous generation has gained a degree of probability which entitles it to fill up the gap existing between Kaut's cosmogony and La Mark's Theory of Descent.

"Only such homogeneous organisms as are yet not differentiated, and are similar to inorganic crystals in being homogeneously composed of one single substance, could arise by spontaneous generation, and could become the primæval parent of all other organisms." (*Ibid*, pp. 418, 419).

In contradiction of Mr. Haeckel, Mr. Darwin says: "We cannot fathom the *marvellous complexity* of an *organic being;* but on the hypothesis here advanced *this complexity is much increased.* Each living creature (Mr. Haeckel recognizes the monera, as the living creature) must be looked upon as a *microcosm—a little universe—*formed of a host of *self-propagating organisms,* inconceivably minute, *and as numerous as the stars of heaven.*" (*Animals and Plants,* Vol. II, p. 483).

This shows that the monera is not a "structureless," "homogeneous," "lump of albumen," "composed of one single substance," and "not in any way built up of distinct organs, but which consists solely of a single chemical combination." Mr. Darwin, a most competent judge, says it is nothing of the kind; but that "each living creature must be looked at as a microcosm—a little universe—formed of a host of self-propagating organisms, inconceivably minute, and as *numerous as the stars of heaven.*"

Professor Huxley adds his testimony to that of Mr. Darwin as follows: "No living being (the monera is a 'living being') is throughout of homogeneous substance; the most of them are highly complex, from the union of many dissimilar parts. The statement of this structure constitutes anatomy, and if it is carried down to the minutest microscopic elements of the organism it is called histology." (*Elementary Physiology,* p. 15).

Thus, according to these great naturalists, the monera is not a "formless," "homogeneous," "simple lump of albumen," composed of "a single chemical combination." Mr. Darwin says: "*Each living creature* must be looked at as a *microcosm—a little universe*—formed of a host of *self-propagating organisms,* inconceivably minute, *and as numerous as the stars of heaven.*" Huxley says: "*No living being* is throughout of *homogeneous substance;* the most of them are highly *complex, from the union of many dissimilar parts.*"

Add to the statements of these naturalists Mr. Haeckel's own admission, and not a vestige of his theory of spontaneous generation is left. He says: "Only such *homogenous organisms* as are yet not *differentiated* and are *similar* to the organic crystals, in being *homogeneously* composed of *one single substance,* could arise by spontaneous generation." This being true, it follows that, since "*no living being* is throughout of *homogeneous* substance;*" but that

"*each living creature* is a *microcosm—a little universe*"
in itself—formed of a host of *self-propagating organisms*, Mr. Haeckel's theory of spontaneous generation, based upon the monera, falls still-born from
the imagination of its author.

Mr. Haeckel further says: "When the' monera
moves itself, there are formed on the upper surface
of the little mucous globule, shapeless, finger-like
processes, or very fine radiated threads; these are
the so-called false feet, or pseudopodia. The false
feet are simple, direct continuations of the shapeless albuminous mass, of which the whole body consists. We are unable to perceive different parts in
it, and we can give a direct proof of the absolute
simplicity of the semi-fluid mass of albumen, for,
with the aid of the microscope, we can follow the
moneron as it takes in its nourishment. When
small particles suited for its nourishment—for instance, small particles of decayed organic bodies or
microscopic plants and infusoria—accidently come
in contact with the moneron, they remain hanging
to the sticky semi-fluid globule of mucus, and here
create an irritation, which is followed by a strong
afflux of the mucus substance; and, in consequence,
they become finally completely enclosed by it, or are
drawn into the body of the moneron by displacement of the several albuminous particles, and are
there digested, being absorbed by simple diffusion
(*endosmosis*).

Thus, in describing the habits of the monera,
Mr. Haeckel tells us that it moves from place to

place with the aid of "finger-like processes"—"so-called false feet"—that it takes into its body "small particles of decayed organic bodies," which "are there digested." These things could only be accomplished with the aid of organs which were designed for the purposes which they serve. The "finger-like processes"—the so-called "false feet," the digestive apparatus, etc., are all so many *organs*. Yet, at the outset, Mr. Haeckel describes the monera as "*organisms without organs*."

In describing the propagation of monera, Mr. Haeckel says: "All monera propagate themselves only in a non-sexual manner by monogony. * * * When such a little globule, for example, a protamœba or a protogenes, has attained a certain size by the assimilation of foreign albuminous matter, it falls into two pieces; a pinching-in takes place, contracting the middle of the globule on all sides, and finally leads to the separation of the two halves. Each half thus becomes rounded off, and now appears as an independent individual, which commences anew the simple course of vital phenomena of nutrition and propagation." (*Ibid*, p. 191).

Thus the monera propagates itself by *self-division*. Each half is the same individual duplicated; by this process there can be no such thing as *inheritance;* for inheritance implies *parent* and *offspring*. This being true, there can be no "inherited" variations to transmit to descendants. Hence, the most remote descendants of the first monera would simply be an exact duplicate of the original. There could be no variations. This places the monera "beyond the influence of ' natural selection.'" Mr. Darwin says: "Unless favorable variations be *inherited* by some at least of the offspring, *nothing can be affected by natural selection.*"

"Natural selection acts *only* by the preservation and accumulation of small inherited modifications."

Any variation which is *not inherited* is unimportant for us." (*Origin of Species*, pp. 9, 75, 80).

Thus it is shown that Mr. Darwin's theory of "natural selection, or survival of the fittest," of which Mr. Haeckel is so ardent an advocate, does not apply to the monera; for, where there is no *inherited* qualities—no variations—there can be no "natural selection;" no "survival of the fittest;" and consequently no evolution from this simple creature to higher organisms.

And again, according to Mr. Darwin's theory of "natural selection or survival of the fittest," if the descendants of the most ancient monera had been modified or improved, the improved varieties would have supplanted the parent forms, and the latter would have become extinct.

Mr. Darwin says: "New varieties continually take the place of and *supplant the parent forms.*"

"New and improved varieties will *inevitably supplant and exterminate the older.*"

"*In all cases* the new and unimproved forms of life *tend to supplant the old and unimproved forms.*" (*Origin of Species*, pp. 266, 292, 413).

The very fact that the monera of to-day is the

exact duplicate of the monera of ages ago, is proof positive that no new and improved varieties have been developed in all the ages that have passed; for, had there been, the improved varieties, according to Mr. Darwin's theory, would long since have supplanted and exterminated the parent forms; but such was not the case; the monera is perhaps to-day the most numerous of all living beings, covering almost the entire bottom of the ocean. From remote ages this "simplest of all organisms" has gone on propagating itself by self-division, each half duplicating the original, and utterly incapable of the least variation; as shown by the fact that, not a single specimen of a modified or improved variety, either alive or in a fossil state, has ever been discovered. Thus Mr. Haeckle's theory of spontaneous generation based on the monera, when viewed even in the light of "natural selection or survival of the fittest," falls to the ground on the very threshhold of its existence.

The theory of spontaneous generation is based upon a false assumption; the assumption that the distinction between *inorganic matter*, and *organic life*, is found in the greater or less simplicity of the organisms of the latter. This is a great mistake; there is a vast difference between the simple structure of the monera and the complex structure of the man; but there is no difference between the *life*—physical *life* —which animates and perfects the simple organism of the monera, and the physical *life* which animates and perfects the complex organism of the man.

Life—physical life—is identical, whether it exists in the most simple or the most complex organism. Hence, it is their possession of life—physical life—which alike distinguishes the monera and man from inorganic matter, and not the greater or less simplicity of the organisms of the latter. Their failure to note these facts has led the advocates of spontaneous generation to suppose that between inorganic matter and the simple organism of the monera, there is a gap so small that, in the remote past, under favorable conditions, spontaneous generation might have spanned it. From this false premise they argue that, from the complex organism of man, down through the animal kingdom, there is an ever-increasing simplicity of organism—a gradually shading down, as it were, to reach the monera, which, in the extreme simplicity of its organism, is but little removed from inorganic matter. But, as a matter of fact, there stands between inorganic matter and organic life, a deep, wide, and impassable gulf, which spontaneous generation could never span. On one side of this great gulf stands inorganic matter; on its opposite, and far distant shore, stands organic life, in all the simplicity and complexity of its organisms. Hence, the simple organism of the monera is as far removed from inorganic matter as is the complex organism of man. Then add to this the fact that even the simplest animal organism possesses mind—a creation distinct from inorganic matter, and the great gulf which separates inorganic matter from organic life, is immeasurably increased.

Mr. Haeckel's opinion of the simple organism of the monera is in striking contrast to that of Mr. Darwin, who says: "The most *humble organism* is something *much higher than the inorganic dust* under our feet; and no one with an *unbiased mind* can study *any living creature, however humble,* without being struck with enthusiasm at its *marvelous structure* and *properties.*" (*Descent of Man,* p. 165).

How any rational man can entertain the idea that inorganic matter, which is destitute of intelligence, or any ability to plan and construct, could possibly devise and form the "marvelous structure" of an animal organism, is beyond our comprehension; and then, as if to make the absurdity more absurd, to suppose that inorganic matter, which is never associated with mind, transferred mind to the animal organism it had so miraculously brought into existence!

Mr. Darwin, the great high priest of evolution, admits that evolution is incompetent to explain the origin of either mind or life. He says: "In what manner the mental powers were first developed in the lowest organisms is as hopeless an inquiry as how life itself first originated. These are problems for the distant future, if they are ever to be solved by man." (*Descent of Man,* p. 66).

Mr. Haeckel admits that not a single case of spontaneous generation has ever been observed. He says: "The origin of the first monera by spontaneous generation appears to us as a simple and necessary event in the process of the development of the earth. We admit that this process, as long as it is not directly observed or repeated by experiment, remains a pure hypothesis. But I must again say that this hypothesis is indispensable for the consistent completion of the non-miraculous history of creation, that it has absolutely nothing forced or miraculous about it, and that certainly it can never be disproved." (*History of Creation,* Vol. I, p. 422).

In the face of the facts above set forth, Mr. Haeckel's sweeping claim that the monera is "the most ancient ancestor of man, as of all other organisms," is shown to be absolutely ridiculous. It should be unnecessary to state that this atheistic theory, which denies the existence of a personal Creator, and proposes to establish a "blood relationship" extending throughout the animal kingdom from the monera to man, is opposed to every teaching of the Bible. While we hold with the Bible that the elements of life—*physical life*—are inherent in matter, we insist that spontaneous generation is powerless to combine them in plants and animals. This marvelous result can only be accomplished by a *Thus saith the Lord.*

Thus, according to Mr. Haeckel, the monera marks the first "Ancestral Stage" in man's progenitors; from this humble beginning he tells us that our "animal ancestors," evolved through the fish, and fowl, and beast, to reach what he terms the

"Twenty-third Ancestral Stage," in the so-called anthropoids or man-like apes, the gorilla, chimpanzee, orang, and gibbon.

According to Prof. Haeckel, the "seventeenth stage" of our *animal ancestors* consisted of a family of animals to which he has given the name *Protamnion*. This family of animals are expected to furnish the transitional forms through which the fish developed into *land animals* on the one side, and *fowls* on the other. As might have been expected, zoology knows nothing of such a family of animals; and geological research has never discovered the least vestige of such creatures. They never existed. However, the necessities of his theory demand them, and to meet the demand the evolutionist was forced to draw on his imagination. The necessities of evolution also required that this purely hypothetical family should be amphibians; a branch of which developed wings, and thus became progenitors of all the fowls. "A wing of a bird has a score or more of distinct, ingenious, but co-ordinated parts and devices, each of which is essential to make it useful, the whole showing unmistakably the work of the highest order of intellectual skill and designing capability."—(Hall). The evolutionist expects us to believe that this wonderful mechanical structure was developed by a branch of his wingless amphibians; the development of wings was, of course, accomplished under Mr. Darwin's law of *natural selection, or survival of the fittest;* but the initial step in the production of a wing must be made by the animal independent of *natural selection;* natural selection can not produce an organ of any kind, nor ever cause the least variation. Mr. Darwin says: "Several writers have misapprehended or objected to the term *natural selection.* Some have even imagined that natural selection induces variability, whereas it merely implies only the preservation of *such variations as arise* and are *beneficial* to the being under its conditions of life—unless *favorable variations* be inherited by some at least of the offspring, *nothing can be affected by natural selection.*" (*Origin of Species,* pp. 63, 80).

The next question which suggests itself is: Was it possible for wingless amphibians to suddenly develop wings? According to Mr. Darwin's law of natural selection, which Prof. Haeckel is an ardent advocate of, evolution can not operate by *sudden leaps,* but by *short and slow steps.* "Natural selection *acts only* by taking advantage of *slight successive variations;* she can never take a great and sudden leap, but must advance by *short* and sure, though *slow steps.*" Natural selection is a *slow process,* and the same favorable conditions must long endure in order that any marked effect should thus be produced." (*Origin of Species,* pp. 97, 156).

Thus these *wingless* amphibians never hastily developed *wings,* since this would be a *great and sudden leap.* This leaves us no alternative than to suppose that they developed their wings by a *slow process* extending through many successive generations during a long period of time. But here we are again met by Mr. Darwin, who says: "Natural selection *acts exclusively* by the preservation and accumulation of variations which are *beneficial.*" (*Origin of Species*, p. 413).

Thus it is plain that under Mr. Darwin's law of *natural selection, or survival of the fittest,* no family of *wingless* animals could ever develop a *wing;* a wing in its incipient stages would be of no use to the animal; it would require nourishment to sustain and develop it; it would require strength to transport it; in many cases it would be in the animal's way, and would at all times prove a useless and burdensome appendage; a mere stub of a wing could not under any circumstances meet the requirements of the law of natural selection by being *beneficial* to the animal "under its conditions of life." Hence, under the operations of the law of the *survival of the fittest,* it would be destroyed. Mr. Darwin frequently states that *natural selection* "acts exclusively," "acts only," "acts solely," in preserving variations which are *beneficial.* He repeatedly says: "This preservation of *favorable* individual differences and variations, and the *destruction of those which are injurious,* I have called *natural selection, or survival of the fittest.*" (*Origin of Species*, p. 63).

Thus it is shown that Prof. Haeckel's *wingless* Protamnion could not have suddenly developed *wings,* for natural selection *can never take a great and sudden leap, but must advance by slow steps;* neither could the Protamnion develop wings by a gradual process, extending through many generations, for

the wing, in its incipient stages—a mere stub—
would have been destroyed under the law of the
survival of the fittest, as a harmful and useless appendage. Hence, which ever horn of the dilemma
we lay hold of, the result is the same—the wingless
animal can never develop a wing. Thus, this boast-
ful theory of evolution is shattered by the wing of
a bird.

The general theory of evolution existed thousands of years before Darwin was born; yet, in his
theory of "natural selection, or survival of the
fittest," he gave to evolution all the strength which
it enjoys, but, as above shown, his theory gave evolution its death blow, by making it impossible for
this theory to explain the origin of the fowls. At
the same time, he exposes the utter worthlessness of
his own theory of "natural selection, or survival of
the fittest;" he says: "If it could be demonstrated
that any *complex organ* existed, which could not
possibly have been formed by numerous successive
slight modifications, *my theory would absolutely break
down.*" (*Origin of Species*, p. 146).

The wing of a bird is certainly a "complex
organ," which, as has been shown, *could not possibly
have been formed by numerous successive slight modifications.* Strange as it may seem, Mr. Darwin calls
attention to this fact, and thus demonstrates the
falsity of his theory. Referring to the wings of the
ostrich which are useless for purposes of flight, and
merely aid the animal in running, Mr. Darwin says:
"As organs in this condition would formerly, when

still less developed, have been of even less use than at present, *they cannot formerly have been produced through variations and natural selection,* which acts solely for the preservation of *useful modifications.*" (*Origin of Species,* p. 398).

Thus, by its author's own admission, the theory of natural selection *absolutely breaks down.* Since the school of evolution, with its so-called law of *natural selection, or survival of the fittest,* can not produce a bird's wing, or even the wings of the tiniest animal that flies, we have, according to Mr. Haeckel, no alternative than to accept the teaching of the scriptural school that God made the fowl. In the face of the above facts, the skeptic should lay aside his skepticism, and admit the existence of an intelligent Creator who designed that wonderful organ, the bird's wing, which enables the animal possessing it to overcome the law of gravitation, and soar amid the clouds.

But it is not only the inability to develop wings on wingless animals that the theory of evolution breaks down through the influence of *natural selection, or survival of the fittest;* it breaks down at an infinite number of points. The evolutionist will admit that the earliest animals to appear on the globe were the invertebrates; these could never have developed into the vertebrates; the invertebrates could not have suddenly developed a vertebral column, or even a single vertebra, for this would be a *sudden leap,* and *natural selection advances by slow steps;* neither could the invertebrates develop a vertebral column by a slow process, for the incipient vertebra would not be *beneficial* to the animal; hence, under the operations of the *survival of the fittest*, it would be destroyed as a useless and harmful growth—a mere monstrosity. The same is true of the skulless animals which were the first to make their appearance on the globe; these could not have suddenly developed skulls, for this would have been a *sudden leap* which is utterly opposed to *natural selection*, which advances by *slow steps;* neither could those ancient *skulless* animals have developed *skulls* by a gradual process, for the incipient skull would not be *beneficial* to the animal, and under the operations of the *survival of the fittest* would be destroyed as harmful and useless. The same is true of the *finless* animals which were the earliest forms to appear on the globe; these could not have suddenly developed fins, for *natural selection* only advances by *slow steps*, says Mr. Darwin; neither could the *finless* animal develop fins by a gradual process, for only the perfect fin could be *beneficial* to the animal; hence, the incipient fin, being useless and unfit to survive, would have been destroyed under the operations of the *survival of the fittest*. The same argument applies to the *legless* animals which preceded the animals with legs; take, for example, the great amphibians of the early geological periods; according to the evolutionists these immense animals with their powerful legs descended from animals which had no legs; according to Darwin's theory of *natural selection,* or *survival of the fittest*, the legless ancestors of these gigantic amphibians could never have developed legs, either suddenly or by a gradual process, for the reasons above given. So it would have been with Prof. Haeckel's imaginary *protamnion*, which he would have us believe were the ancestors of our land quadrupeds; had this hypothetical family of amphibians had a real existence, their ancestors would have been animals with no legs; they could not have suddenly developed legs, for this would have been a sudden and long leap; and *natural selection* makes no *sudden leaps*, but *advances by slow steps;* neither could they have developed legs by a gradual process extending through many generations, for the incipient legs would not have been *beneficial* to the animal; on the contrary, it would have been a harmful and useless appendage, which, under the operations of the *survival of the fittest*, would have been destroyed in its incipiency.

As has been shown, the immense amphibians were followed by the comparatively small marsupials; the former inhabited the water, and the latter inhabited the land; in their physical organisms, their habits, the manner of their reproduction, etc., they presented the strongest contrast to each other; the deep, wide gulf which separated them was spanned by no intermediate forms. This should occasion no surprise, for, according to St. Paul, the amphibians belonged to the flesh of "fishes," while the marsupials belonged to the "flesh of beasts."

Prior to the appearance of the whale family there were no mammals; and it is plain that natural development, acting under Darwin's theory of *natural selection or survival of the fittest*, could never have produced a mammal. Only the perfected mammæ, with its intricate system of glands, etc., for the secretion of milk, could be *beneficial* to the animal in enabling it to nourish its young; this could not have been developed suddenly, for *natural selection* only advances by *slow steps;* neither could the mammæ have developed gradually through many generations, for in its incipient stages it would not have been *beneficial* to the animal by assisting it to nourish its young; hence, under the operations of *the survival of the fittest*, it would have been destroyed as useless and harmful.*

Mr. Darwin, like all evolutionists, insists that the most complex organisms have developed from the most simple, through the "transmutation of species," under the operations of "natural selection or survival of the fittest." If this were true, the stratas of the earth would abound with the fossil remains of transitional forms in every stage of development from lower to higher species; but scientific research discovers no fossil remains of such transitional forms; on the contrary, the geological record shows that new species made their appearance sud-

*[NOTE—After investigating the bearing of "natural selection or survival of the fittest" on the general theory of Development, as above set forth, we were surprised to find that another had anticipated us along this line, and had long since reached the same conclusions. The views of this brilliant writer are found in "The Problem of Human Life; Here and Hereafter," published by Hall & Co., of New York. For a more elaborate discussion of the subject our readers are referred to the above work.—THE AUTHOR].

denly. Commenting on the absence of any evidence
in support of the theory of "the transmutation of
species," Prof. Winchell says: "The great stubborn
fact which every form of the theory encounters at
the very outset is that, notwithstanding variations,
we are ignorant of a single instance of the derivation of one good species from another.   The world
has been ransacked for an example, and occasionally
it has seemed for a time as if an instance had been
found of the origination of a genuine species by so-
called natural agencies; but we only give utterance
to the admissions of all the recent advocates of de-
rivative theories when we announce that the long-
sought *experimentum crucis* has not been discovered." (*Doctrine of Evolution*, p. 54).   Mr. Darwin
says: "Scarcely any palæontological discovery is
more striking than the fact that the forms of life
change almost simultaneously throughout the
world." (*Origin of Species*, p. 297).   The above
facts cited by Winchell and Darwin are fatal to the
theory of evolution, and clearly point to *creation* as
the only explanation of the origin of species.

If further proof of the utter absurdity of the
theory of evolution were required, it is furnished by
that remarkable family of animals—the *apes*.   This
is especially unfortunate for the evolutionist, since
he claims a *blood relationship* with these animals,
and for whom he entertains the most affectionate
regard, recognizing them as the *immediate progenitors
of man*.   However, every scientist will admit, and no
intelligent evolutionist will deny that, at a certain

period in the remote past, the *four* extremities of the higher land animals were *legs* terminating in *hoofs* or *paws;* and that suddenly there appeared upon the earth a distinct and higher class of animals—the *apes*—whose hinder or lower extremities were *legs* terminating in *feet,* and whose fore or upper extremities were *arms* terminating in *hands.* Between these two distinct classes, the one *quadrupeds,* and the other *bipeds,* there could be no transitional forms. Surely even the fertile imagination of an evolutionist should revolt at the suggestion that the hoofs or paws which terminated the hinder legs of a certain class of quadrupeds, suddenly differentiated into *feet;* and that their *fore* legs which terminated in hoofs or paws, suddenly differentiated into *arms* terminating in *hands.* The idea that a *quadruped* could ever develop into a *biped* is too absurd for serious consideration. Hence, every ape that ever lived upon the earth, or that will ever live, at once furnishes the most positive proof of the falsity of the theory of evolution, and the truth of *creation.* While we have little hope that any array of facts, however powerful, could influence the materialistic evolutionist, the facts above cited should afford food for reflection to that rapidly-increasing class of theologians who style themselves *theistic evolutionists* (whatever that may mean).

After referring to the close blood relationship between man and the so-called anthropoids, Mr. Haeckel says: "The most general conclusions arrived at from these most careful comparisons is that each one of the four man-like apes stand nearer to man in one or several respects than the rest, but that no one of them can in every respect be called absolutely the most like man. The orang stands nearest to man in regard to the formation of the brain, the chimpanzee in important characteristics in the formation of the skull, the gorilla in the development of the feet and hands, and, lastly, the gibbon in the formation of the thorax." (*Ibid*, p. 377).

Describing what he terms the "Twenty-fourth Ancestral Stage," Mr. Haeckel says: "Although the preceding stage is already so nearly akin to genuine man that we scarcely require to assume an intermediate connecting stage, still we can look upon the speechless primeval man (*alali*) as this intermediate link. This ape-like man, or pithecanthropi, very probably existed toward the end of the tertiary period. They originated out of the man-like apes, or anthropoids, by becoming completely habituated to an upright walk, and by the corresponding stronger differentiation of both pairs of legs. The fore-hand of the anthropoids became the human hand, their hinder hand became a foot for walking. Although these ape-like men must, not merely by the external formation of their bodies, but also by their internal mental development, have been much more akin to real man than the man-like apes could have been, yet they did not possess the real and chief characteristic of man, namely, the articulate human language of words, the corresponding development of a higher conciousness, and the formation of ideas. * * *

"Genuine men *developed* out of the ape-like men of the preceding stage by the gradual development of the animal language of sounds into a connected or articulate language of words. The development of this function, of course, went hand in hand with the development of its organs, namely, the higher differentiation of the larynx and the brain. The transition from speechless ape-like men to genuine talking men probably took place at the beginning of the Quatenary period, namely, the Diluvial period, but possibly even at an earlier date, in the more recent Tertiary." (*Ibid*, p. 398, 399).

Continuing, Mr. Haeckel says: "Those processes of development which led to the origin of the most ape-like men out of the most man-like apes, must be looked for in the two adaptive changes which, above all others, contributed to the making of man, namely, *upright walk* and *articulate speech*. These two physiological functions necessarily originated together with two corresponding morphological transmutations, with which they stand in the closest corelation, namely, the *differentiation of the two pairs of limbs and the differentiation of the larynx*. The important perfecting of these organs and their functions must have necessarily and powerfully reacted upon the differentiation of the brain and the mental activities dependent upon it, and thus paved the way for the endless career in which man has since progressively developed, and in which he has far outstripped his animal ancestors.

"The first and earliest of these three great processes in the development of the human organism probably was the higher differentiation and the perfecting of the extremities which was effected by the habit of an upright walk. By the fore feet more and more exclusively adopting and retaining the function of grasping and handling, and the hinder feet more and more exclusively the function of standing and walking, there was developed that contrast between the hand and foot which is indeed not exclusively characteristic of man, but which is much more strongly developed in him than in any of the apes most like men. This differentiation of the fore and hinder extremities was not merely most advantageous for their own development and perfecting, but it was followed at the same time by a whole series of very important changes in other parts of the body. The whole vertebral column, and more especially the chest, the girdle of the pelvis and shoulders, as also the muscles belonging to them, thereby experienced those changes which distinguish the human body from that of the most man-like apes. There transmutations were probably accomplished long before the origin of articulate speech; and the human race thus existed for long, with an upright walk and the characteristic human form of the body connected with it, before the actual development of human language, which would have completed the second and more important part of human development. We may, therefore, distinguish a special (24th) stage in the series of our human ancestors, namely, speechless man (*Alalus*), or ape-man (*Pithecathropus*), whose body was indeed formed exactly like that of man in all essential characteristics, but did not as yet possess articulate speech.

"The origin of *articulate language*, and the *higher differentiation and perfecting of the larynx* connected with it, must be looked upon as a later, and the most important stage in the process of the development of man. It was, doubtless, this process which above all others helped to create the deep chasm between man and animals, and which also first caused the most important progress in the mental activity and the perfecting of the brain connected with it." (*Ibid*, pp. 405, 406, 407).

Mr. Haeckel admits that geological research, which has discovered some remains of about all that ever existed on the earth, has never found the least trace of such a creature as his "Speechless Man." Yet with that unparalleled audacity which is characteristic of him, he proceeds to describe it as though he had a specimen before him.

He says: "We as yet know of no fossil remains of the hypothetical primeval man (*protanthropus alavis*—Homo primigenius). But considering the extraordinary resemblance between the lowest woolly-haired men and the highest man-like apes, which still exist at the present day, it requires but a slight stretch of the imagination to conceive an intermediate form connecting the two, and to see in it an approximate likeness to the supposed primeval man, or ape-like man. The form of their skull was probably very long, with slanting teeth; their hair

wooley; the color of their skin dark, of a brownish
tint. The hair covering the whole body was probably thicker than in any of the still living human
species; their arms comparatively longer and stronger;
their legs, on the other hand, knock-kneed, shorter
and thinner, with entirely undeveloped calves; their
walk but half erect." (*Ibid*, p. 438).

Continuing, Mr. Haeckel says:

"The difficulties met with in classifying the different races and species of men are quite the same as
those which we discover in classifying animal and
vegetable species. In both cases forms apparently
quite different, are connected with one another by a
chain of intermediate forms of transition. In both
cases the dispute as to what is a kind or a species,
what a race or a variety, can never be determined.
Since Blumenbach's time, as is well known, it has
been thought that mankind may be divided into five
races or varieties, namely: (1) the Ethiopian, or black
race (African negro); (2) the Malayan, or brown
race (Malays, Polynesians and Australians); (3) the
Mongolian, or yellow race (the principal inhabitant
of Asia and the Esquimaux of North America); (4)
the American, or red race (the aborigines of America); and (5) the Caucasian, or white race (Europeans, North Africans and south western Asiatics).
All these five races of men, according to the Jewish
legend of creation, are said to have descended from
"a single pair"—Adam and Eve—and in accordance
with this are said to be varieties of one kind or
species. If, however, we compare them without

prejudice, there can be no doubt that the differences of these five races are as great and even greater than the 'specific differences' by which zoologists and botanists distinguish recognized good animal and vegetable species (bonæ species)." (*Ibid*, p. 412).

The opinion most generally entertained by the leading advocates of evolution is, that this purely hypothetical creature, "Speechless Man," differentiated into the negro with articulate speech; the great majority of the negroes developing no higher, thus presenting a case of "arrested development;" but that in the course of time a branch of the negroes differentiated into Malays; the great majority of the Malays developing no higher; and thus presenting another case of "arrested development;" but that in the course of events a branch of the Malays developed into Indians; the great majority of the Indians developing no higher, and thus presenting another case of "arrested development;" but that in the course of events a branch of the Indians developed into Mongolians; the great majority of the Mongolians developing no higher, and thus presenting another case of "arrested development;" but that at some remote period a branch of the Mongolians differentiated into Caucasians (whites). Mr. Haeckel differs somewhat from the older evolutionists, as shown by the following: "A great many reasons might be advanced in favor of the opinion that the primeval men of the Lissotrichous species (the primary forms of straight-haired men) were derived from the South Asiatic anthropoids, whereas the primeval men of the Ulotrichous species (as the primary forms of the four wooly-haired tribes) were derived from Central African man-like apes." (*Ibid*, Vol. II, p. 439).

The evolutionist takes the fish, and fowl, and beasts, and man, and masses them into what he terms "the zoölogical system;" he then divides "the zoölogical system" into classes, orders, genera, species, races, sub-races, and varieties. Having decided that man is simply an animal, the evolutionist places him in "the zoölogical system" with the rest of the animals; he then decides, (1) that man belongs to the class—mammalia; which embraces all creatures that suckle their young; this includes man, the apes and quadrupeds among the land animals, and the whale family among the fish; (2) that he belongs to the order—bimana; this "order" embraces not only man, but every member of the ape species from the lemur on up to and including the negro; (3) that man belongs to the genus—homo; this not only includes the so-called "Caucasian race" (Homo Mediterraneuse); the so-called "Mongol race" (Homo Mongol); the so-called "Indian race" (Homo Americanus); the so-called "Malay race" (Homo Malayus); the so-called "Negro race" (Homo Niger); but necessarily embraces "Speechless Man" (*Protanthropos atavis-Homo primœgenius*), the first man; (4) that the "Species Man," the so-called "Human Species," is divisible into five races of men; and that these may be divided into sub-races, and varieties.

Thus, according to the theory of natural development or evolution, man is simply a highly developed species of ape—the human species—and this human species is divisible into five or more races of men.

It should be unnecessary for us to state that this cold, uncompromising materialism; this demoralizing atheism, which degrades us to the level of the brute, by declaring the existence of a "blood relationship" between man and the animals, denies to man *immortality*.

In the preceding pages of this work we have presented the teachings of the two great schools of learning, Divine Creation and Natural Development or Evolution; we have presented the leading features of the school of Creation, in the language of the inspired authors; we have also presented the leading features of the school of Evolution, as far as our limited space would permit, in the language of its leading advocates; and we feel assured that even the most skeptical will see that these two schools are opposites; that the most open, direct conflict exists between them; and that no amount of reasoning can possibly reconcile the differences between them. How can we hope to harmonize the Word of God with this theory which denies the existence of God? A moment's reflection should convince us of the hopelessness of such a task. Hence, our acceptance of the teachings of one of these schools, necessarily carries with it our rejection of the other. The teachings of these opposing schools are in conflict at every point;

and it is not only foolish but criminal to attempt to
blend and confuse them by accepting the teachings
of the one on certain points, and rejecting the teachings of the other on those points; when we indulge
in this folly we have as a result a blended, distorted
mixture of the two which bears little or no resemblance to either of the originals; no leading advocate
of evolution would accept this unnatural mixture,
and every believer in the Bible should reject it. For
example: the Bible teaches that man was created "in
the image of God." Evolution teaches that man is
simply a highly developed species of ape, who traces
his descent back through a long line of "animal ancestors" to the lowest form of animal, itself the
result of "spontaneous generation." How can we
ever reconcile these conflicting teachings? The Bible
teaches that "all flesh is not the same flesh: but
there is one kind of flesh of man, another flesh of
beasts, another of fishes, and another of birds."
Hence, there is no kinship between creatures belonging to two different kinds of flesh; that there is no
kinship between man and the animals; but that God
and man are akin. Evolution teaches that there is
a link of kinship extending from the monera on
up through the fish, and fowl, and beast, to form a
"blood relationship" with man; that all flesh *is* the
same flesh, since man and the animals are all akin.
Hence, from the monera to man there is just *one*
flesh in different stages of development. How can
we hope to harmonize the teachings of evolution that
man and the animals are of the same flesh, with the

Bible teaching that there are four different kinds of
flesh with no more kinship between them than if
they each made their appearance upon and inhabited
different planets?

If we accept the teachings of Moses, that God
made the animals, like the plants, after their kind,
the theory of the evolutionist falls still-born from
the imagination that conceived it; if we accept the
teaching of Paul that the fish and fowl and beast, each
represent a different "kind of flesh," the theory that
the fish developed into the fowl on the one hand,
and the land animals on the other, and through
these into the man, receives its *death blow*.   If we
accept the teachings of Moses that God created man
in his own "image;" and if we accept the teachings
of Luke that Adam was the son of God; and if we
accept the teaching of Paul that even the flesh of
man is a different "kind of flesh" from that of the
animals, the theory of the evolutionist that man is a
highly developed species of apes—the human
species—and that this human species is divisible into five races of man, falls to the ground.   If, on the
other hand, the teachings of evolution are true, the
teachings of Moses and Paul are false, and should be
repudiated; and inasmuch as all the inspired writers
of the Bible were in harmony with Moses and Paul,
their teachings must also be false, and consistency
demands that their writings should be repudiated;
this accomplished, the Bible, with all its elevating,
ennobling, soul-inspiring teachings, would be practically obliterated from the earth; and the dream of

the atheist would be realized in the universally accepted belief in the existence of a universe without a God, a creation without a creator, man without religion, and the world without a Sabbath or a Bible. However much professed Christians may differ with us on these questions, no well informed atheist will do so; we have seen that Haeckel emphatically states that the Schools of Creation and Evolution are *opposites.*

The terms "tribes," "nations," and "empires," are political terms, and it is significant that the inspired writers invariably employ these political terms—tribes, nations, and empires—in describing the relations of men. On the other hand, the terms "human species," and "races of men," are an inseparable part of the theory of evolution. Hence, it should occasion us no surprise when we find that, *not one of the inspired writers makes the slightest allusion to such a thing as a human species or a race of men.*

Throughout the Bible we find no mention of such a thing as a "zoölogical system" in which man is thrust with the animals; no such thing as a "class mammalia," in which man is placed with the higher land animals and the whale family; no such thing as an "order bimana," in which man is placed with the apes as a two-handed animal; no such thing as a "genus homo," embracing "speechless man (Homo Primigenius);" the Negro man "(Homo Niger);" the "Malay man (Homo Malayus);" the "Indian man (Homos Americanus);" the "Mongolian man

(Homos Mongol) ; " the " Mediterranean (white) man
(Homo Mediterranese) ; " no such thing as a " species,
man," embracing five or more "races of men." As
might have been expected, these misleading terms
which were born of the purest atheism, are conspicuous in scripture by their *absence*. These facts
should afford professed Christians food for grave reflection.

The terms "species" and "races" are scientific
terms; they belong to natural science, and are used
to describe natural relations; and there is in natural
science the same broad distinction between *species*
and *races*, as exists in mathematics between *units*
and *fractions*. A. De Quatrefages, Professor of Anthropology in the Museum of Natural History, in
Paris, France, a standard authority upon such questions, says: "*Species* is the *unit* and the *races* are
the *fractions* of this unit." The terms *species* and
races are applicable to both plants and animals, since
these were made in great numbers and varieties;
while there are such differences between certain
plants and between certain animals as justifies the
naturalist in deciding that they are different families
or species, there are such resemblances between
certain members of these families or species, as justifies the naturalist in deciding that they are branches
or races of these species. Thus, species is the unit
of which races are the fractions. To illustrate: the
ape is a species of animal, but this *species* is formed
of a number of *races;* the lemur is one race of the
ape species; the gorilla is another race; the negro

is another race of the ape species, and so on throughout the series. Hence, a *species* is composed of a greater or less number of *races;* while a *race* is a fractional part of a *species.*

This enables us to realize that God never intended that man, like the plants and animals, should be a species, or a race. Man was created a single pair, and a single pair is not *species,* since *races* which are essential to the formation of a species is wanting in man; neither was this single pair a *race,* since it was not a fractional part of a *species.* Thus, the theory now universally taught, that man is a species which is composed of five or more races of men, is at once opposed to the scriptures and the sciences.

From the above facts it is plain (1) that the theory now universally taught, that man is a s*pecies* which is divisible into five or more *races of men,* of which the white is the highest and the negro the lowest race, with the browns, reds and yellows as intermediate races in different stages of development, is an inseparable part of the atheistic theory of evolution. (2) That it was atheism that took the negro out of the ape family, where God made him, and thrust him into the family of man; and that only the purest, most unadulterated atheism keeps him there. This being true, it follows that, when atheism is repudiated, and the teachings of scripture are universally accepted, the negro will at once retire from his present unnatural position in the family of man, and resume his proper place among the apes.

The fact that the offspring resulting from unions between whites and negroes are *fertile*, is accepted as proof positive that they are merely different *races* of the same *species;* for, the opinion is generally entertained, that the offspring resulting from unions between different *species* are always *barren*. This theory advanced by the older naturalist, is now exploded. Dr. Topinard says: "Between species the crosses are common and fertile * * * as the progeny of the hare and the rabbit, the dog and the wolf, the jackal and the fox, the camel and the dromedary, the alpaca and the llama or vecuna, the horse and the zebra or wild mule, the bison and the European ox, etc. There is, therefore, no reason to suppose that we have been deceived as to the reality of certain species; and that such were only varieties. * * * It is now certain that the limit of species is not an absolute obstacle to fertility, and consequently that its circumscription has nothing decided about it." (*Anthropology*, p. 368).

Prof. Quatrefages says: "Sexual unions in plants, as in animals, can take place between individuals of the same species and the same race; further between different races of the same species, and finally, between different species. In the two latter cases we have what is called a cross. This crossing, itself, is differently named according to whether it takes place between different races or different species. In the first case it produces a mongrel, in the second a hybrid. When the cross unions are fertile the product of the union of mongrels is called a mongrel, the product of the union of hybrids, a hybrid." (*The Human Species*, p. 63).

In the atheist's division of the so-called "Zoological system," the animals of different genera, are not so nearly related to each other as those of different species; and again, the animals of different orders are not so closely related to each other as those of different genera. Dr. Topenard says: "It is stated that individuals of different Orders have given birth to offspring, as between the bull and the mare, whose progeny or jumarts inhabitated the Atlas mountains and the mountains of Piedmont. It is a better authenticated fact that the phenomenon takes place between different genera. M. de Bouills, in 1873, described the offspring of the cross between the Ibex of the Pyrenees and the domestic goat. The Pehuelhas in the Chilian Alps crossed this latter with the sheep and obtained a very vigorous breed called *chabins* (buck sheep), whose decendants, fertile through an indefinite number of generations, are of considerable commercial value on account of their skins and fleeces, known by the name of 'pellons.'" (*Ibid*, p. 367).

Thus, it is shown that not only a cross between different species, but even a cross between different genera will produce offspring that is indefinitely fertile; and, "it is stated that individuals of different Orders have given birth to offspring" that is fertile. Hence, the mere fact that the offspring of Whites and Negroes are fertile, is no evidence that they are of the same species, or the same genera, or even of the same order. On the other hand, as we shall hereafter show, the Bible teaches that unions between individuals of different *kinds of flesh*—those of man and beast—will be indefinitely. fertile.

The want of space forbids our further discussion of the theory of development. However, in view of the facts above set forth, it should be an affront to our intelligence to ask us to believe that, not only the earth and the celestial bodies; not only plant and animal life, but that even man, with his flashing intellect and his immortal soul, "were once latent in a fiery cloud."

CHAPTER XIII.

The Garden of Eden.

"And God planted a garden eastward in Eden; And there he put the man whom he had formed. And out of the ground made the Lord God to grow every tree that is pleasant to the sight, and good for food; the tree of life also in the midst of the garden, and the tree of knowledge of good and evil. And a river went out of Eden to water the garden; And from thence it was parted, and became four heads. The name of the first is Pison. * * * And the name of the second river is Gihon. * * * And the name of the third river is Hiddekel. * * * And the name of the fourth river is Euphrates. And the Lord God took the man, and put him into the Garden of Eden to dress it and to keep it. And the Lord God commanded the man, saying, Of every tree of the garden thou mayest freely eat. But of the tree of the knowledge of good and evil, thou shalt not eat of it: for in the day thou eatest thereof thou shalt surely die." (*Gen.* ii, 8, 9, 10, 11, 12, etc.).

"——Man He made of angel form erect,
  To hold communion with the heavens above,
  And on his soul impressed His image fair
  His own similitude of holiness,
  Of virtue, truth, and love; with reason high
  To balance right and wrong, and conscience quick
  To choose or to reject; with knowledge great,

353

Prudence and wisdom, vigilance and strength,
To guard all force or guile; and, last of all,
The highest gift of God's abundant grace,
With perfect, free, unbiased will. Thus man
Was made, upright, immortal made, and crowned
The king of all; to eat, to drink, to do
Truly and sovereignly his will entire;
By one command alone restrained, to prove,
As was most just, his fillial love sincere,
His loyalty, obedience due, and faith.
And thus the prohibition ran, expressed,
As God is wont, in terms of plainest truth:
'Of every tree that in the garden grows
Thou mayest freely eat; but of the tree
That hath of good and ill, eat not,
Nor touch; for in the day thou eatest, thou
Shalt die. Go, and this one command obey;
Adam, live and be happy, and with thy Eve,
Fit consort, multiply and fill the earth.'
Thus they, the representatives of men,
Were placed in Eden—choicest spot on earth;
With royal honor and with glory crowned,
Adam, the lord of all, majestic walked,
With God-like countenance sublime, and form
Of lofty towering strength; and by his side
Eve, fair as morning star, with modesty
Arrayed, with virtue, grace, and perfect love:
In holy marriage wed, and eloquent
Of thought and comely words, to worship God
And sing His praise—the Giver of all good.
Glad, in each other glad, and glad in hope."
                                    —*Pollok.*

Man could no more develop a civilization, and depend upon the wild plants of the forest for his supply of vegetable food, than he could, and depend upon the chase for his supply of animal food. Hence, domestic plants and domestic animals are essential to civilization. With domestic plants, man can increase his supply of both vegetable and animal food to meet the demands of an increasing population. Domestic plants are dependent upon cultivation for their existence. Without culture, they either rapidly degenerate, or soon die out and disappear altogether. This is especially true of the *cereals* from which man derives his supply of bread. Domestic plants have not, as the atheist would have us believe, been developed from "wild originals;" *they were God's special gift to man.* Without them man could never develop the resources of the earth. The obligation to do this devolved upon Adam from the moment of his assignment to this task. Hence, he had no time to develop *wild originals* into *domestic* plants. Many of these so-called " wild originals," are merely *degenerate domestic plants,* which have survived some old civilization, in which they were cultivated. This absurd idea that the domestic plants were all developed from "wild originals," is a part of *The Theory of Development,* which denies the existence of a *Creator,* and attributes everything to *natural causes.* According to this theory, man developed from the ape; then, by ages of cultivation, man developed the domestic plants from those which originally were wild. The whole proposition is *atheism, pure and simple.* Yet we see it accepted and advocated by professed Christians.

Dr. Macmillan says of *corn:* "God gave it to Adam, we have every reason to believe, in the same perfect state of preparation for food in which we find it at the present day. It was made expressly for man, and given directly into his hands. 'Behold,' says the Creator, 'I have given you every herb-bearing seed which is upon the face of all the earth' —that is, all the cereal plants, such as corn, wheat, barley, rice, maize, etc., whose peculiar distinction and characteristic it is to produce seed. * * * The word of God plainly tells us this, and nature affords a remarkable corroboration of it. We cannot regard it as an accidental, but, on the contrary, as a striking, providential circumstance, that the corn plants were utterly unknown throughout the geological periods. Not the slightest trace or vestige of them occurs in any strata of the earth, until we come to the most recent formations, contemporaneous with man. They are exclusively and characteristically plants of the human epoch; their remains are found in deposits near the surface, which belong to the existing order of physical conditions. * * * There is another proof that corn was created expressly for man's use in the fact that it has never been found in a wild state. * * * Where are the wild grasses which, according to some authors, cumulative processes of agriculture, carried on through successive ages, have developed into corn, wheat, and barley? Much has been written, and many experiments have been tried to determine the natural origin of these cereals, but every effort has hitherto proved in vain.

Reports have again and again been circulated that corn and wheat have been found growing wild in some parts of Persia and the steppes of Tartary, apparently far from the influence of cultivation; but, when tested by botanical data, these reports have turned out in every instance to be unfounded. Corn has never been known as anything else than a cultivated plant. The oldest records speak of it exclusively as such. * * * History and observation prove that it cannot grow spontaneously. * * * Neglected of men, it speedily disappears and becomes extinct. * * * All this proves that it must have been produced miraculously, or, in other words, given by God to man directly in the same abnormal condition in which it now appears; for nature never could have developed or preserved it. In the mythology of all the ancient nations it was confidently affirmed to have had a supernatural origin. * * * Let me bring forward one more proof of special design, enabling us to recognize the hand of God in this mercy. Corn is universally diffused. It is almost the only species of plant which is capable of growing everywhere, in almost every soil, in almost any situation. In some form or other, adapted to the various modifications of climate and physical conditions which occur in different countries, it is spread over an area of the earth's surface as extensive as the occupancy of the human race. * * * Corn, as the German botanist, Von Meyer, says, precedes all civilization; with it is connected rest, peace, and domestic happiness, of which the wandering savage knows nothing. In order to rear it, nations must take possession of certain lands." (*Bible Teachings in Nature*, Chap. v).

While we appreciate the force of Mr. Macmillan's argument that *cultivation* is essential to the existence of *corn*, we feel assured that he was unfortunate in his selection of a text to support his position. The production of *seed* is not a character *peculiar* to the *cereals* or any *domestic* plant. Seed-bearing plants existed upon the earth long ages previous to the creation of man. Many of the land animals and fowls from which man was designed to derive his supply of *animal* food, subsisted on these *seeds;* and do so still; while many other animals from which man was designed to derive his supply of *animal* food subsisted on *foliage*, and do yet. In this sense we may understand the text: "Behold I have given you every herb-bearing seed, which is upon the face of all the earth, and every tree in which is the fruit of a tree yielding seed; to you it shall be for meat. And to every beast of the earth, and to every fowl of the air, and to everything that creepeth upon the earth wherein there is life, I have given every green herb for meat."

We are thus taught: (1) That God made the wild forest growths and gave them to man. They never developed from lower forms. The pine has always been a pine; the oak has always been an oak; the beech has always been a beech; and so on throughout the list. (2) That it was not, as many suppose, the design of God that man should subsist solely on a *vegetable* diet; but that, in addition to this, he should have a supply of *animal* food. (3) That in the wild forest growths, provision had been made for the subsistence of the land animals and fowls, which preceded man; and over which man was commanded to "have dominion," and from which he was to derive his supply of animal food. Hence, "They shall be to you for meat." Thus, long previous to the creation of man there was provision made for his supply of *animal* food. This view of the text is further sustained by the fact that *after* the creation of man, there was a special provision made for his supply of *vegetable* food, as shown by the following:

"And the Lord God planted a garden eastward in Eden; and there he put the man whom He had formed. And out of the ground made the Lord God to grow every tree that is pleasant to the sight, and good for food."

We are thus clearly taught that, just as the Israelites were given homes in a highly developed country which *they* had not developed, so was Adam given a home in a highly developed section of country which *he* had not developed. The land of Canaan which was given to Israel, was developed by the Canaanites. The Garden of Eden, which was given to Adam, was developed by God Himself. A moment's reflection should convince us that the efforts of the Canaanites in developing the land of Canaan is not to be compared to the effort of God in developing the Garden of Eden; and that no home which man has ever prepared for himself in any land, could compare with that peerless home which the Great Architect of the universe prepared in Eden for His earthly son.

So far as our reading and our observation extends, little or no attention is paid to the biblical description of the Garden of Eden; while many professed Christians regard it as a myth, and the incidents associated with it, as mere *allegories*.

We are not of those who regard Eden as a *myth*. The Garden of Eden had an existence as real as that of Jerusalem or Rome. Neither are we of those who regard the incidents connected with it as *allegories*. These were real occurrences which have led to the most important events in man's history, and are even now leading to others as momentous.

The biblical description of the Garden of Eden, and the incidents associated with it, are an inseparable part of the inspired writings; and as such, are entitled to the same consideration and respect as any other part of the scriptures. The theologians, who assume the authority to decide that the Garden of Eden is a *myth* and that the events associated with it are mere *allegories*, should feel it a duty incumbent upon them to tell us when *myths* and *allegories* end in Genesis, and where a plain statement of facts begin. If Genesis is false, upon what principal would we decide that any other book in the Bible is true? If the books of the New Testament have any basis in fact, their ultimate basis is the book of

Genesis. If Genesis is false, the super-structure—Christianity—is a *fraud*, and religion a *farce*.

By carefully analyzing the biblical description of the Garden of Eden, we are enabled to decide intelligently as to whether or not it was the design of God that man should be the subject of manual toil. Let us bear in mind that we are now discussing a period in the world's history prior to the advent of woman. When Adam was created and placed in the Garden of Eden, "there was not found a help-meet for him." He was the sole representative of his *kind of flesh*. A proper understanding of this most important subject of *flesh* enables us to realize and appreciate the full import of Adam's declaration upon his reception of Eve: "This is now bone of my bones, and flesh of my flesh."

The biblical term "trees" includes all plant-life that was represented in the Garden of Eden; and is not confined to the larger growths which we term "trees." It includes all the domestic fruit and nut-bearing trees, and the vines, cereals, vegetables, etc., which are "good for food." And also every plant "that is pleasant to the sight," which man cultivates for their beauty and fragrance. The domestic *food* and *ornamental* plants are *God's special gift to man*, and made their first appearance upon the earth in the Garden of Eden. The most positive evidence of this is furnished by geological research, which proves that the earliest evidence of the existence of domestic plants is found in the *Neolethic* or *Age of Polished Stone*. It is a *significant fact* that no evidence of the existence of domestic plants is found in the *Palaeo-lithic* or *Age of Rough Stone*. In that age agriculture was unknown, and nearly all the domestic plants are dependent upon culture for their existence. Without cultivation they soon disappear. This is especially true of the *cereals*.

From the biblical description of the Garden of Eden, we are taught as follows:

1. That God planted it. This in itself should be a sufficient guarantee that it was absolutely perfect in all of its details. What an exhibition of parental love was there displayed by the Heavenly Father for His earthly son, in thus providing for his daily wants, and in beautifying and adorning the garden that was designed to be his earthly place of abode! What an exhibition of utility its crops must have presented, in which was represented every plant that was "good for food!" What a spectacle of beauty and fragrance must have been presented by this garden, in which was displayed the matchless taste of the Great Artisan of the heavens and the earth!

2. That every domestic plant that is "pleasant to the sight" was represented there. Not single specimens, but doubtless in greater or less profusion. Think of the territory it would require to accommodate even a few specimens of every domestic plant which man cultivates for their beauty and fragrance. Besides many of the wild plants are beautiful and fragrant; and these doubtless contributed their beauty and fragrance to heighten the charms of the Garden of Eden.

3. That every plant that is "good for food," was represented there. The cereals, vegetables, fruits, nuts, and vines—all the *food* plants. Think of the territory these would require. This was not a mere experiment station, planned and planted by the Creator of the universe, it was *par excellence, the model farm*, in which the *food* plants were not represented merely by a few specimens of each. They were "planted" in such quantities as was necessary to supply the needs of man, and the animals, which were required to *dress* and *keep* the garden. There were fields of maize, wheat, rye, oats, barley, rice—all the cereals; gardens in which every domestic vegetable was grown; orchards, and vineyards of luscious fruits and grapes; parks with trees laden with edible nuts; and meadows and pasture lands for the cattle. Utility, beauty, and fragrance struggled for the mastery in this peerless estate. No accomplishment of man, the *creature*, can compare with this masterpiece of God, the *Creator*. Doubtless it was the design of its Divine artist that this matchless combination of heavenly art and earthly beauty and fragrance should stand throughout the ages as a model from which man might derive valuable suggestions in his efforts to beautify and adorn his home.

4. Further evidence of the magnitude of the Garden of Eden is found in the fact that it required *a river to water it.* "And a river went out of Eden to water the garden." We are thus told in plain language that the Garden of Eden was not depend-

ent upon the *seasons* for its supply of water, but upon the *river that went out of Eden;* just as the valley of the Nile is not dependent upon the *seasons* for its supply of water, but upon the *river Nile.* And a moment's reflection should convince us that just as it requires an extensive system of irrigation to transfer the waters of the Nile to every portion of the Nile valley, for agricultural purposes, so would it require an extensive system of irrigation to transfer the waters of "the river that went out of Eden," to every part of the Garden of Eden for agricultural purposes.

Additional evidence of the great extent of that beautiful garden in which "the Lord God planted" all the *food* and *ornamental* plants, which depend upon cultivation for their existence, is found in the narrative of the *fall*, as follows:

And the serpent "said unto the woman, Yea, hath God said, Ye shall not eat of every tree of the garden. And the woman said unto the serpent, We may eat of the fruit of the trees of the garden: But of the fruit of the tree which is in the midst of the garden, God hath said, Ye shall not eat of it, neither shall ye touch it, lest ye die. And the serpent said unto the woman, Ye shall not surely die: For God doth know that in the day ye eat thereof, then your eyes shall be opened, and ye shall be as Gods, knowing good and evil. And when the woman saw that the tree was good for food, and that it was pleasant to the eyes, and a tree to be desired to make one wise, she took of the fruit thereof, and did eat, and gave also unto her husband with her; and he did eat." (*Gen.* iii, 1, 2, 3, 4, 5, 6). *But when the woman saw that the tree was * * * pleasant to the eyes:* Thus clearly indicating that this *tree*, which was situated in the midst of the Garden of Eden, was so far removed from the immediate place of abode of the Adamic pair in the garden, that the *woman* had never seen it. "But when the woman saw that the tree was good for food, and that it was pleasant to the eyes, and a tree to be desired to make one wise, she took thereof, and did eat, and gave also unto her husband with her; and he did eat."

The magnitude of the Garden of Eden is thus shown by the fact that it accommodated, in greater or less profusion, specimens of all the ornamental plants which man prizes and cultivates for their beauty and fragrance; and was also sufficiently extensive to accommodate in greater or less quantities the domestic plants upon which man relies for his supply of vegetable food. Its great extent is further shown by the fact that it required a river to water it. To "water the garden" with the waters of the river would require a system of irrigation. Thus, the disposition of the Atlanteans, Egyptians, Ancient Americans, etc., to rely upon the *certainty* of *irrigation*, rather than upon the *uncertainty* of the *seasons*, for water for agricultural purposes, is traceable to the Garden of Eden.

Let us bear in mind, that we are now discussing a period in the world's history long prior to the time when God delegated to man the power to perform

miracles; and that Adam is not accredited with performing any miracles. God placed Adam in the
Garden of Eden "to dress it and to keep it." This
simply meant that Adam was to cultivate and harvest
the various crops, plan, construct, and operate a system of irrigation to transport the water of the "river"
to every part of the garden for agricultural purposes; and to "keep" this immense estate in the
highest state of cultivation. It was simply a plain
business transaction, such as we observe in every
day life. A man owns a fine estate, but for some
reason prefers not to take upon himself the manage-
ment of it; in this case, he employs an agent,
and assigns him to this duty; but he does not expect
his agent to perform the manual labor; this is performed by servants which the master provides.
There was nothing supernatural in the discharge of
the duties to which Adam was assigned in the Garden of Eden.

Let us also bear in mind that Adam's assignment to this duty occurred long prior to his *fall;*
and that it was not until after this event, and as a
punishment for his violation of Divine law, that God
sentenced him to personally " till the ground," and
thus compelled him to " eat bread" in the sweat of
his face. Hence, while it is evident that, " to dress,"
" and to keep" the Garden of Eden was a duty which
devolved upon Adam from the moment of his assignment to this task, it would be a reflection upon
the wisdom, and justice, and love, and mercy of
God to decide that Adam would have been com-

pelled to personally "till the ground," and thus "eat bread" "in the sweat" of his "face," even if he had never violated Divine law. Yet it would be absurd to suppose that this lone man could, from year to year, plant, cultivate and harvest the crops of every plant "that is good for food;" cultivate the vineyards of domestic grapes; and the orchards of domestic fruits, propagate and cultivate the myriads of ornamental plants which contributed their beauty and fragrance to embellish this magnificent estate; and also construct and operate a system of irrigation to transport the waters of the "river" to every portion of the garden for agricultural purposes, with only such assistance as the *quadrupeds* could render him.

But when we lay aside our absurd theories, and accept the teachings of scripture and of science, that the negro is an ape, and that man was designed to have, and commanded to exercise "dominion" over him in common with the rest of the animals; and that in common with the domestic animals of draught, burden and food, Adam possessed such numbers of negroes, in the Garden of Eden, as enabled him "to dress it and to keep it," the whole proposition is simplified, and its accomplishment made easy.

The negro, as he existed previous to the creation of man, relied chiefly upon the proceeds of the chase for subsistence; and his descendants pursued *this one vocation* from generation to generation, as does the undomesticated negro of to-day. But it must be borne in mind that Noah and his sons owned the negroes which survived the Deluge. Hence, the undomesticated negro of *modern times* is the descendant of the domesticated negro of *ancient times.*

Man, whom God designed to subdue the earth and have dominion over fish, and fowl, and beast, pursues an almost infinite number of vocations, many of which tend to the development of the resources of the earth. This course has characterized him from the earliest ages of his history. As shown by the Bible, Adam was placed in the Garden of Eden, "to dress it and to keep it." In this we find the most positive proof that domestic plants, which require cultivation, were first introduced upon the earth in the Garden of Eden, in which *God planted* them immediately after the creation of man. This indicates that Adam at once proceeded to engage in agriculture—the basis of all civilization. His immediate offspring also engaged in the pursuits of civilized life. His first son was a farmer and, like all farmers, cultivated domestic plants. The wild forest growths thrive without cultivation. Adam's second son engaged in rearing domestic animals. "Abel was a keeper of sheep, but Cain was a tiller of the ground." Thus, the first and second sons of Adam were each engaged in the essential pursuits of civilized life; and it is a significant fact that Cain, the first child born to the Adamic creation, was *a tiller of the ground.*

We are thus taught that man was not created an ignorant, degraded savage and turned loose in the forest with no special aim in life; and left to subsist as best he could upon the wild fruits and the proceeds of the chase, until, in the course of ages, he would learn to domesticate animals, work metals and acquire such knowledge of plants as would enable him to realize that, by cultivation, he could develop " wild originals " into *domestic plants*.

Man was placed in a *garden*, and he and his descendants were assigned to a specific work.   A garden which the great artist of the universe planted for His earthly son; a garden, "out of the ground " of which "made the Lord God to grow every tree that is pleasant to the sight and good for food;" a garden which contained in abundance not only every plant that is "good for food," but one in which myriads of flowering plants contributed their wealth of beauty and fragrance to make the primitive home of the Adamic family, the most superb estate the world has ever known.   Not only the most valuable of the food plants require cultivation, but many of the flowering plants which man prizes for their beauty and fragrance, and with which he adorns his home, perish if neglected.   It would have been folly on the part of God to bring into existence a class of plants which require *cultivation*, when "there was not a man to till the ground."   Hence, the domestic plants, which require cultivation, were brought into existence *after* the creation of man.

We accept the Bible as God's word; we also accept the truths which scientific research has discovered as God's works.   But we insist that there must be no discrepancy between the teachings of the scriptures and those of the sciences; and we feel assured that if each is properly interpreted they will harmonize.

As has been shown, the Bible teaches that *domestic* plants, and *agriculture* were introduced upon the earth immediately after the creation of *man*. On the other hand, science teaches that *art* preceded domestic plants, and consequently agriculture, on the earth, by perhaps *thousands of years*. If we adopt the universally accepted *theory* that the ability to fashion implements for a *particular purpose* is a character *peculiar* to *man*, how are we to reconcile the teachings of scripture with those of science on these essential points? Geological research demonstrates that the earliest evidences of *art* were found in the Palæolithic Age, or Age of Rough Stone, in which agriculture was unknown. The *chipped flints* of that remote age were merely the rudely fashioned weapons of war and of the chase. Neither in the material out of which they were fashioned, nor in the purposes for which they were designed were they such as man could have used in the cultivation of plants, which was necessarily the initial step in his efforts to *subdue the earth*. What manner of creature was this who fashioned the chipped flints of the earlier Stone Age? To which one of the four *kinds of flesh* did this ancient artisan belong? Certainly not to the *flesh of men*, for domestic plants and agriculture were unknown to him; and we are plainly taught by the Bible that *man, domestic plants* and *agriculture* were introduced upon the earth almost simultaneously; Adam was placed in that beautiful garden which *God planted eastward in Eden,* to *dress it and to keep it.* To *dress* and *keep* a garden requires *soil tillage.*

The only way to reconcile these essential truths is to lay aside our absurd *theories,* and the prejudices which have grown out of them, and accept the teachings of scripture and of science that there is a *tool-making, tool-handling animal.* The existence of such a creature is clearly implied in the Bible, in that (1) While man was designed to *subdue the earth,* that is, to develop its resources, and was assigned to this task when created, it was not until *after* he had violated Divine law that he was compelled to *personally till the ground;* and thus *eat bread in the sweat of his face.* (2) From this the inference is fair that, if Adam and his descendants had never violated God's law, they would not have been sentenced to manual toil; yet the obligation to develop the resources of the earth, was binding upon them from the moment of their assignment to this task. (3) This indicate the necessity for and demonstrates the existence of a tool-making, tool-handling animal, which, in the capacity of servant could perform the *manual* labor necessary to develop the resources of the earth under man's control. (4) Man's appointment in the creation to *dominion over all the earth,* demonstrates his great mental superiority; while his subsequent history and achievements fully confirm it. (5) The ancient artisan who fashioned the chipped flints of the earlier stone period, like the rest of the animals, was introduced upon the earth previous to the creation of man and the introduction of domestic plants and agriculture. (6) Not belonging to the *flesh of men*, he necessarily belonged to one of the other three *kinds of flesh;* and being a *land animal*, he belonged to the *flesh of beasts.* (7) If there were no tool-making, tool-handling animal, *art*, like *domestic plants*, and *agriculture*, would have *followed* the creation of man. In this event the earliest evidences of art found on the globe would have been *metallic implements*, such as man devises for the cultivation of plants, the erection of mechanical structures, etc. But this would imply that man was designed to perform the *manual toil* as well as the *mental labor* necessary to *subdue the earth*, and such was not the case. God in his wisdom and love provided man with a high grade ape in the person of the negro, who is fully competent to discharge all the duties of *servant.* The negro, like man was ushered into the world unprovided with weapons, offensive or defensive; but soon realizing the necessity for these, his mechanical skill, an essential part of the equipment of a *servant*, enabled him to fashion for himself rude weapons of *stone.* So crude were these chipped flints that, for years after their discovery by Europeans, scientists denied that they were *artificial;* the very suggestion was ridiculed and denounced. "A purely geological question was made the subject of religious controversy." "The honor of having dispersed all doubts and inspired conviction" is due to the French *savant*, M. Boucher de Perthes. (*Man Before Metals—Joly*).

Once the chipped flints were recognized as *artificial*, they were universally regarded as the work of man. They were promptly seized upon by the advocates of *the Theory of Development* as the most positive evidence that man developed from the ape into an ignorant, degraded savage, with no ability to domesticate animals; and with no knowledge of domestic plants, agriculture or metals; a mere hunter who subsisted on the wild products of the forest and on the proceeds of the chase, with only such meager intelligence as would enable him to fashion rude weapons of stone. With the *theory* universally taught and accepted, that *man* is the only tool-making, tool-handling animal, and with the chipped flints recognized as *artificial*, the conclusion was irresistible that they were the works of man; and that all subsequent *art and civilization* traced its origin to these humble beginnings. Nothing could be more *anti-scriptural*. Hence, nothing more *absurd*. Man was created to *subdue the earth* and *have dominion* over the animals; *domestic plants* were God's special gift to *man;* and *metallic implements* are essential to the cultivation upon which they depend for existence. Hence, *man never developed through an Age of Stone*. Thus, the chipped flints of the earlier Stone Age, which furnish the most absolute proof of the truth of the Bible, have been seized upon and used as the most positive evidence of its falsity. In the meantime the *modern clergy*, ignorant of God's plan of creation, have either accepted this atheism or ignored the whole subject with all its vital importance. If we accept the chipped flints of the *diluvium* as the works of *man*, it follows that we must also accept *the Theory of Development.* In this event, the *Bible*, with its teachings of *Divine Creation*, must *go.*

A certain amount of plausibility was given *the Theory of Development* from the fact that, in Europe, the "Palæolithic," or "Age of Rough Stone" implements, was immediately followed by what is termed the "Neolithic," or "Age of Polished Stone" implements; and this, in its turn, by an "Age of Bronze." In the Age of Polished Stone, a greater variety of material was employed, such as bone, horn, wood, etc., while their *stone* implements were often finely wrought and sometimes *polished.* But, from the fossil remains of the artisans of the polished flints of the later Stone Age, we find that they were neither *whites* nor *negroes,* but *mixed bloods,* in whom, as a class, a predominance of Adamic blood, carrying with it a corresponding increase of intelligence, enabling them to produce a better class of implements.

A moment's reflection should convince us that, to successfully conduct an estate of such magnitude as the Garden of Eden, an immense number of domestic animals of draught, burden, and food would be required. We are taught that "Abel was a keeper of sheep," and, though he may have devoted most of his attention to sheep raising, it is reasonable to suppose that he also possessed other domestic animals, such as the horse, ox, swine, etc. Cain, like Adam, "was a tiller of the ground;" and his farming operations, conducted with the assistance of a greater or less number of negroes, required domestic animals of draught, burthen, and food; and we have the most positive evidence that Cain possessed domestic animals, and carried them with him to the "land of Nod," for his mixed-blooded descendants were cattle raisers. "Jabal * * * was the father of such as dwell in tents, and of such as have cattle." (*Gen.* iv, 20). It would be unreasonable to suppose that these mixed-bloods possessed domestic animals, which their Adamic ancestor did not have; on the contrary, it would be in keeping with the results of our observation to decide that their white ancestor possessed domestic animals which his mixed-blooded descendants inherited.

It would also be impossible to successfully cultivate an immense estate like the Garden of Eden without metallic implements; inasmuch as Adam's duties in the Garden of Eden began as soon as he was assigned to the task of cultivating it, he had no time to acquire a knowledge of metals in the ordinary way; for this would require years of investigation. Hence, it is evident that, among other things, God must have imparted to Adam a knowledge of metals, and the process of mining, working, and fashioning them into implements; and Cain must have acquired this knowledge from Adam, for he was also a farmer and would need metallic implements. We find that Cain's mixed-blooded descendants possessed a knowledge of metals. Tubal-Cain was "an instructor of every artificer in brass and iron." (*Gen.* iv, 22). The mixed-bloods never acquire a knowledge of metals and the manner of mining, working, and fashioning them into implements through their own exertions; they inherit them from their white ancestors. Tubal-Cain evidently inherited his knowledge and skill from Cain, and inasmuch as God never made any special bestowals on Cain, it is evident that he inherited it from Adam, to whom God gave it. In all ages of his history we find man (the white) in possession of a knowledge of metals, and the manner of mining, working, and fashioning them into implements; on every continent of the earth we find the remains of ancient civilizations which are crumbling into ruin from age alone; in the beauty and finish of their designs these old ruins present evidences of the most accomplished art; the decorations, inscriptions, and every hewn stone in these old cities testify to the fact that their architects were metallurgists; it would be absurd to suppose that the artisans, who built and decorated those ancient structures of hewn stone, accomplished their task without metallic implements. Not only this, but we find that the knowledge of brass, which is a combination of 70 parts copper to 30 of zinc, is traceable through Tubal-Cain and Cain to Adam.

To acquire a knowledge of metals and the manner of mining, working, and fashioning them into implements; or combining different metals to form a desired metallic substance, are accomplishments far beyond the intellectual ability and inventive skill of the negro, or the mixed-bloods; and are such as only the white is capable of.

In discussing this question, De Gobineau says: "The white race has great physical vigor, capacity and endurance. It has an intensity of will and desire which is controlled by intellectuality. Great things are undertaken readily, but not blindly. It manifests a strong utilitarianism, united with a powerful imagination, which elevates, ennobles and idealizes its practical ideas. The negro can only imitate, the Chinese only utilize, the work of the white; but the latter is abundantly capable of producing new works. He has as keen a sense of order as the yellow man, not from a love of repose, however, but from the desire to protect and preserve his acquisitions. He has a love of liberty far more intense than exists in the black and yellow races, and clings to life more earnestly. His high sense of honor is a faculty unknown to the other races, and springs from an exalted sentiment of which they show no indications. His sensations are less intense than in either black or yellow, but his mentality is far more developed and energetic." (*Moral and Intellectual Diversity of Races*).

Here we have the most positive proof that the white is the creature whom God designed and equipped, mentally and physically, to develop the resources of the earth, and have dominion over the animals; and the past history of civilization fully confirms it; the white is to-day, what he has been in all ages of his history—the great building, developing, power of the earth. Hence, when in some pathless jungle, or on some deserted plain, or in some isolated valley, or perhaps on some island of the sea, we discover the remains of some ancient civilization which presents even in its ruins the evidences of fine architectural skill and taste on the part of its builders, we may confidently say: *This is the work of the white.* Mr. Morris says: "It may be remarked that all the savage tribes of the earth belong to the Negro or Mongolian races. No negro civilization has ever appeared. No Mongolian one has ever greatly developed. On the other hand, the Caucasian is preeminently the man of civilization. No traveler or historian records a savage tribe of Caucasian stock." (*The Aryan Race*).

We often hear modern theologians assert that "Adam was a red man." In explanation of this we are told that in the Hebrew, "Adam signifies *red*." This modern idea could only have been conceived in the grossest ignorance, strongly tinged with the most unblushing infidelity. The Hebrew was not the language of Eden. The Bible plainly teaches that the language of Adam was transmitted to his post-diluvian descendants through Noah; and that for a considerable period after the Deluge it was the one universal language of the globe. "The whole earth was of one language and one speech." (*Gen.* ii, 1). But the Bible also teaches that at the Tower of Babel their original language was broken up into a number of languages, of which the Hebrew is one. Hence, the mere fact that in the Hebrew the term "Adam" signifies *red*, is no evidence, whatever, that it had any such significance in the original language of

man.   On the contrary, if, in the original language
of man, the term Adam had any significance as to
complexion, all the facts indicate that it signified
white; for *white* was, unquestionably, the complexion
of Adam.

In the first chapter of this work we have shown
that the most ancient and reliable traditions of men
assert that Adam was the father of arts and letters;
that he wrote a book of precepts which God gave him
in the Garden of Eden.   Hence, Adam was the first
author; and the Bible plainly teaches that he was the
first agriculturist; the first horticulturist; the first
keeper and breeder of domestic animals; the first mechanic; for it required the highest mechanical talent
and the finest engineering skill to construct the irri-
gating system of the Garden of Eden.   Adam's possession of these great intellectual gifts should occasion
us no surprise, when we pause to reflect that every
intellectual faculty displayed by the men of this and
other ages, were inherited from Adam, upon whom
they were Divine bestowals.   With God as his instructor, Adam had opportunities for acquiring
knowledge which none of his descendants have enjoyed.   During his stay in Eden, it was Adam's high
privilege to imbibe wisdom direct from the Fountain
of all Wisdom; and the record of his achievements,
as above set forth, indicates that he profited by it.
Hence, all the facts indicate that, in addition to being
the most intellectual, Adam and Eve, in the Garden
of Eden, were the most learned, cultured, and refined people that ever graced the earth.

In this professedly Christian age we hear much

of the "great intellectual development and progress made by the human race in modern times." In addition to the atheism openly expressed in the term "human race," this statement carries with it the implication that we have developed higher and have progressed further, intellectually, from our "animal ancestors" than the ancients had. But even disregarding this atheism, expressed and implied, and confining the question to man (the white), we find nothing in the scriptures, the sciences, profane history, tradition or the evidence of the old civilization to sustain it. On the contrary, these are all against it. The ancients were familiar with the sciences, especially the science of astronomy; we have shown that tradition asserts that in the days of Enoch, the seventh from Adam, the constellations were already divided and named. On every continent of the earth we find the remains of superb civilizations, which testify to the fact that the ancients were the most accomplished artisans. The architectural remains of the ancients, even in their ruins, and such fragments of their literature as have descended to us, at least equal the best products of modern minds. What have we in architecture which, in point of solidity, purity of design, and in the elegance and beauty of its finish, will equal that of ancient Greece, Egypt, India, the Island of Java, or Central America? What have we in literature that equals the Bible? In addition to all this we are reminded that if the stream of humanity that flowed out from Adam and Eve has risen above its source, *it's the first stream that ever did.*

Further evidence of the culture and refinement of Adam and Eve, and their immediate descendants, is found in the fact that Cain's mixed-blooded descendants possessed the harp and the organ. "Jubal * * * was the father of all such as handle the harp and the organ." (*Gen.* iv, 21). Their possession of the harp and the organ, two instruments that have never been improved upon, leads us to infer that they possessed other musical instruments. Their possession of these fine musical instruments clearly indicates the culture and refinement which existed in the sixth generation of the mixed-blooded descendants of Cain. And no one would suppose that the pure-blooded descendants of Adam, in the time of Seth, were less cultured and accomplished than the mulatto descendants of Cain. This indicates that the culture and refinement of the whites and mixed-bloods of that remote period was much the same as that enjoyed by the most cultivated classes of whites and mulattoes in our day; yet if we were to enter the home of some rich, educated mulatto in our community and found that he possessed the harp or the organ, or other fine musical instruments, and that he and his family handled those instruments with consumate skill, it would never occur to us that they had *invented* them; we would know that the whites invented them; neither would we suppose that they had inherited their fine musical talent from the negro, since he never had it to transmit; we would know that their musical talent *was inherited* from their *white* ancestors.

Where did the mixed-blooded descendants of

Cain obtain their knowledge of the art of music, and the art of fashioning and handling such instruments as the harp and the organ? Was this knowledge the result of *development* in the course of a few generations? The thought is inadmissible; and would be so pronounced by the most ardent advocate of the theory of development. No mixed-blood ever developed the art of music, nor invented such instruments as the harp and organ; though they can be taught to construct and handle almost any instrument.

Inasmuch as the knowledge of the art of music, and the art of fashioning and handling musical instruments, which the mulatto descendants of Cain possessed, was not the result of development, we have no alternative than to decide that they inherited them from their white ancestor, *Cain;* and inasmuch as there were no special Divine bestowals upon Cain, we must decide that he inherited from Adam the fine musical talent, and perhaps the knowledge of musical instruments, which he transmitted to his mulatto offspring. Thus we find that musical talent, in its highest state of perfection, like every other exalted characteristic which man possesses, is traceable to Adam, upon whom God bestowed it. Hence, it requires no stretch of the imagination to suppose that the charms of beauty and fragrance, which characterized the primitive home of our first parents in Eden, was heightened by their innocent songs of joy and praise blending with the soft, sweet strains of instrumental music.

CHAPTER XIV.

THE FALL OF MAN.

"Oh lovely, happy, blessed, immortal pair!
Pleased with the present, full of glorious hope!
But short! the song that sings their bliss!
Henceforth, the history of man grows dark:
Shade after shade of deepening gloom descends,
And innocence laments her robes defiled.
Who farther sings, must change the pleasant lyre
To heavy notes of woe. Why?—dost thou ask,
Surprised? The answer will surprise thee more.
Man sinned; tempted, he ate the guarded tree;
Tempted of whom thou afterward shall hear.
Audacious, unbelieving, proud, ungrateful,
He ate the interdicted fruit and fell."

—Pollok.

"Now the serpent was more subtle than any beast of the field which the Lord God had made. And he said unto the woman, Yea, hath God said, Ye shall not eat of every tree of the garden? And the woman said unto the serpent, We may eat of the fruit of the trees of the garden: But of the fruit of the tree which is in the midst of the garden, God hath said, Ye shall not eat of it, neither shall ye touch it, lest ye die. And the serpent said unto the woman, Ye shall not surely die: For God doth know that in the day ye eat thereof, then your eyes

383

shall be opened, and ye shall be as Gods, knowing
good and evil. And when the woman saw that the
tree was good for food, and that it was pleasant to
the eyes, and a tree to be desired to make one wise,
she took of the fruit thereof, and did eat, and gave
also unto her husband with her; and he did eat.
And the eyes of them both were opened, and they
knew that they were naked; and they sewed fig
leaves together, and made themselves aprons. And
they heard the voice of the Lord God walking in the
garden in the cool of the day: And Adam and his
wife hid themselves from the presence of the Lord
God amongst the trees of the garden. And the Lord
called unto Adam and said, Where art thou? And
he said, I heard thy voice in the garden, and I was
afraid, because I was naked; and I hid myself. And
He said, Who told thee that thou wast naked? Hast
thou eaten of the tree, whereof I commanded thee
thou shouldst not eat? And the man said, The
woman whom thou gavest to be with me, she gave
me of the tree, and I did eat. And the Lord said
unto the woman, What is this that thou hast done?
And the woman said, The serpent beguiled me, and
I did eat.

"And the Lord God said unto the serpent, Because thou hast done this, thou art cursed above all
cattle, and above every beast of the field; upon thy
belly shalt thou go, and dust shalt thou eat all the
days of thy life: And I will put enmity between
thee and the woman, and between thy seed and her
seed; it shall bruise thy head, and thou shalt bruise
his heel.

"Unto the woman He said, I will greatly multiply thy sorrow and thy conception; in sorrow thou shalt bring forth children; and thy desire shall be to thy husband, and he shall rule over thee.

"And unto Adam he said, Because thou hast hearkened unto the voice of thy wife, and hast eaten of the tree whereof I commanded thee, saying, Thou shalt not eat of it: cursed is the ground for thy sake; in sorrow shalt thou eat of it all the days of thy life; thorns also and thistles shall it bring forth to thee: and thou shalt eat the herb of the field; in the sweat of thy face shalt thou eat bread, till thou return unto the ground; for out of it wast thou taken: for dust thou art, and unto dust shalt thou return.

"And Adam called his wife's name Eve; because she was the mother of all living. Unto Adam also and to his wife did the Lord God make coats of skins, and clothed them.

"And the Lord said, Behold, the man is become as one of us, to know good and evil: and now lest he put forth his hand, and take also of the tree of life, and eat, and live forever: therefore the Lord sent him forth from the Garden of Eden, to till the ground from whence he was taken." (*Gen.* iii, 1, 2, 3, etc.).

In commenting on the first verse of Genesis, in his attempt to identify the Tempter of Eve, Dr. Adam Clark, says: "Verse 1. (Now the serpent was more subtle.) We have here one of the most difficult as well as the most important narratives in the whole book of God. The last chapter ended with a short, but striking account of the perfection and felicity of the first human beings, and this opens with an account of their transgression, degradation, and ruin. That man is in a *fallen* state, the history of the world, with that of the life and miseries of every human being, establishes beyond successful contradiction. But *how*, and by what *agency*, was this brought about? Here is a great mystery; and I may appeal to all persons who have read the various comments that have been written on the Mosaic account, whether they have ever yet been satisfied on this part of the subject, though convinced of the fact itself. *Who* was the *serpent?* Of what kind? In what *way* did he seduce the first happy pair? These are questions which *remain yet to be answered*. The whole account is either a *simple narration of facts*, or it is an allegory. If it be a historical relation, its literal meaning should be sought out; if it be an *allegory*, no attempt should be made to explain it, as it would require a distinct revelation to ascertain the sense in which it should be understood, for fanciful illustrations are endless. Believing it to be a *simple relation of facts* capable of satisfactory explanation, I shall take it up on this ground, and by a careful examination of the original text, endeavor to fix the meaning and show the propriety and consistency of the Mosaic account of the fall of man. The chief difficulty in the account is found in the question: Who was the *agent* employed in the seduction of our first parents.

"The word in the text which we, following the Septuagint, translate *serpent*, is * * * *nachash;* and, according to Bextorf and others, has *three* meanings in scripture.

" 1. It signifies to *view* or *observe attentively*, etc.

" 2. It signifies *brass, brazen*, and *fetters of brass*, and in several places, steel. * * *

" 3. It signifies a *serpent*, but of what kind is not determined. * * * In *Eccles.* x, 11, the creature called nachash, of whatever sort, is compared to the babbler. * * *

" We have already seen that * * * *nachash* signifies to *view attentively*, to *acquire knowledge* or *experience* by *attentive observation;* * * * I have learned by experience; and this seems to be the most general meaning in the Bible. The original word is by the Septuagint translated * * * a serpent, not because this was its *fixed*, determinate meaning in the sacred writings, but because it was the best that occurred to the translators, and they do not seem to have given themselves much trouble to understand the meaning of the original, for they have rendered the word as variously as our translators have done, or rather our translators have followed *them*, as they give nearly the same significations found in the Septuagint. * * * From the Septuagint, therefore, we can expect no light, nor indeed from any other of the ancient versions, which are all *subsequent* to the Septuagint, and some of them actually made from it. In all this uncertainty, it is natural for a serious inquirer after truth to look everywhere for information. And in such an inquiry the Arabic may be expected to afford some help, from its great similarity to the Hebrew. A root in this language, very nearly similar to that in the text, seems to throw considerable light on the subject. * * *

chanas or *khanasa* signifies *he departed, drew off, lay hid, seduced, slunk away;* from this root come *akhnas,* * * * *khanasa* and *khanars,* which all signifies an *ape,* or *satyrus,* or any creature of the *simia* or ape genus. It is very remarkable also that from the same root comes *khanas,* the *devil,* which appelative he bears to that meaning of *khanasa,* he *drew off, seduced,* etc., because he *draws* men *off* from righteousness, *seduces* them from their obedience to God, etc., etc. * * * Is it not strange that the *devil* and the *ape* should have the same name, derived from the same root, and that root so very similar to the word in the text? But let us return and consider what is said of the creature in question. *Now the nachash was more subtle arum,* more wise, cunning, or prudent, *than any beast of the field which the Lord God had made.* In this account we find: (1) That whatever *nachash* was, he stood at the *head* of all inferior animals for wisdom and understanding. (2) That he *walked erect,* for this is necessarily implied in his punishment—*on thy belly* (*i. e.,* on all fours), *shalt thou go.* (3) That he was *endowed with the gift of speech,* for a conversation is here related between him and the woman. (4) That he was also endowed with the *gift of reason,* for we find him reasoning and disputing with Eve. (5) That these things were *common to this creature,* the woman no doubt having often seen him walk erect, talk and reason, and therefore she testifies *no kind of surprise* when he accosts her in the language related in the text: and, indeed, from the manner in which this is introduced, it appears to be only a part of a conversation that had passed between them on the occasion: *Yea, hath God said,* etc.

"Had this creature never been known to speak before his addressing the woman at this time and on this subject, it could not have failed to excite her *surprise,* and to have filled her with *caution,* though from the purity and innocence of her nature, she might have been incapable of being affected with *fear.* Now, I apprehend that none of these things can be spoken of a *serpent* of any species. (1) None of these ever *did* or ever *can* walk erect. The tales we have heard of two-footed and four-footed serpents are justly exploded by every judicious naturalist, and are utterly unworthy of credit. The very name *serpent* comes from *serpo,* to creep, and therefore to such, it could be neither *curse* nor *punishment* to go on their bellies, *i. e., to creep on,* as they had done from their creation, and must do while their race endures. (2) They have no *organs* for *speech* or any kind of articulate sound; they can only *hiss.* It is true that an *ass,* by miraculous influence, may speak; but it is not to be supposed that there was any miraculous interference here. *God* did not qualify this creature with speech for the occasion, and it is not intimated that there was any *other agent* that did it; on the contrary, the text intimates that *speech* and *reason* were natural to the *nachash;* and is it not in reference to this the inspired penman says: *The nachash was more subtle or intelligent than all the beasts of the field that the Lord God had made?* Nor can I find that the *serpentine genus* are remarkable for *intelligence.* It is true the *wisdom of the serpent* has passed into a proverb, but I cannot see on what it is founded, except in reference to the passage in question, when the nachash, which we translate *serpent,* following the Septuagint, shows so much intelligence and cunning; and it is very probable, that our Lord alludes to this very place when He exhorts His disciples to be *wise*—prudent or intelligent *as serpents,* and it is worthy of remark that He used the same term employed by the Septuagint in the text in question: *The serpent was more prudent or intelligent* than all the beasts, etc. All these things considered, we are obliged to seek for some other word to designate the *nachash* in the text, than the word *serpent,* which, on every view of the subject, appears to me inefficient and inapplicable. We have seen above that *khanas, akhnas,* and *khanros,* signify a creature of the *ape* or *satyrus* kind. We have seen that the meaning of the root is, *he lay hid, seduced, slunk away,* etc., and that *khanas* means the *devil,* as the inspirer of evil, and seducer from God and truth. *See Gollins* and *Wilmet.* It therefore appears to me that a creature of the *ape* or *orang outang* kind is here intended.

"Should any person who may read this note object against my conclusions, because apparently derived from an Arabic word which is not exactly similar to the Hebrew, though to those who understand both languages the similarity will be striking, yet, as I do not insist on the *identity* of the terms, though important consequences have been derived from less likely etymologies, he is welcome to throw the whole of this out of the account. He may then take up the Hebrew root only, which signifies to *gaze, to view attentively, pry into, inquire narrowly,* etc., and consider the passage that appears to compare the *nachash* to the *babbler,* (*Eccles.* x, 2), and he will soon find, if he have any acquaintance with creatures of this genus, that for *earnest, attentive watching, looking,* etc., and for *chattering* or *babbling,* they have no fellows in the animal world. Indeed, the ability and propensity to chatter is all they have left, according to the above hypothesis, of their original gift of speech, of which I suppose them to have been deprived at the fall as a part of their punishment." (*Clark, Commentary,* Vol. I, pp. 45, 46, etc.).

We have quoted at length from the above named work (1) because its author, Dr. Clark, was a modern clergyman—a minister in the Methodist Church. (2) Because this distinguished commentator utterly repudiated and clearly disproves the modern theory that the tempter of Eve was a snake. (3) Because he proves that the tempter of Eve was an *ape,* which habitually walked erect, *talked* and *reasoned,* as shown by the fact that the woman was not in the least alarmed, or even surprised, when he engaged her in the conversation recorded in the text; on the contrary, she was evidently accustomed to seeing this animal walk erect, talk and reason; consequently she felt no surprise when he addressed a question to her, and manifested no hesitancy in replying to him. The whole transaction shows that their conversations were common occurrences.

Dr. Clark manifested a commendable independence of thought and action when he abandoned the absurd theory of the modern clergy that the tempter of Eve was a snake; he made a creditable advance upon the snake theory when he proved the tempter of Eve an ape; yet it is at once a matter of surprise and regret that after thus advancing so far in the right direction, he should have stopped at one of the so-called anthropoids—the orang—when a step further would have taken him to the negro, the identical ape he was seeking. The negro meets all the requirements of the case, and he is the only animal that does; he possesses the erect posture, articulate speech, and more reasoning capacity than any other animal; and these characteristics place him at the head of the apes, and consequently "at the head of all inferior animals for wisdom and understanding." Besides, the negro is an inveterate talker—"babbler"—and is withal one of the noisest animals in the world.

The negro is the only animal that could have understood the relation between God and man, and the relations between man and the plants and animals in the Garden of Eden; and the knowledge of these relations was one of the characteristics of the tempter of Eve; in addition to understanding these relations which God established, the negro is the only animal with mental capacity sufficient to devise a scheme to deceive man into disregarding these relations, and thus violate the laws of God; and all these things the negro did.

The orang, like the snake, would be incapable of understanding the relations which God established between Himself and man, and those between man and the plants and animals; and being ignorant

of the existence of these relations, it would never occur to either the snake or the orang, to devise a
scheme to deceive man into disturbing these relations, and thus violate the laws of God. Neither
could these animals, or any animal, except the negro, execute such a scheme for the want of articulate speech. Hence, we fail to see that the embarrassment under which Dr. Clark labored on account
of the fact that the Bible accredits the tempter of
Eve with articulate speech, was in the least modified
by his exchange of the *snake* for the *orang*. In his
efforts to relieve himself of this embarrassment, Dr.
Clark advances the theory that all the orangs originally possessed the "gift of speech," but "at the
fall" God "deprived" them of this gift, "as a part of
their punishment." But this theory finds no support in scripture; on the contrary the text is clearly
against it.

The Bible plainly states that *just three individuals*
participated in the fall of man; and names Adam,
Eve, and *nachash* or *serpent*, as the guilty parties.
The acts which each of these individuals committed
are clearly stated, as are the punishments which God
meted out to each of them. There is absolutely nothing in the text to justify Dr. Clark in entertaining the
remotest suspicion that God "deprived" the tempter
of Eve of the "gift of speech;" the individual ape,
nachash or *serpent*, which tempted Eve, was one of
many of its kind; and all of these "walked erect,
talked and reasoned," but they were not parties to
the serpent's offense, and certainly there is nothing
in the text to indicate that these unoffending ani-

mals were punished in any way. As a matter of fact, nachash was one of many negroes in the Garden of Eden; nachash offended God and was terribly punished, by being compelled to go on its belly; but it was not deprived of speech, and its unoffending kindred were not deprived of their erect posture, articulate speech, etc., for the negro of to-day, and of all past ages, has possessed these characteristics. For example: Before the late sectional war in the United States, many men in the Southern States owned negroes; if one of his negroes offended, his master punished him, but the rest of his negroes who had not offended were not punished; it would have been a grave injustice to have punished them; is God less just than man?

Dr. Clark observed that a part of the punishment which God inflicted on the tempter of Eve, was directed at this animal's *posture*, for he says: "that he *walked erect*, for this is necessarily implied in his punishment—on thy belly (*i. e.*, on all fours) shalt thou go." Man and the negro possess the erect posture, and "go" upon their two legs; the apes below the negro may walk erect at will, but they habitually support their bodies with both their arms and legs in walking, and this somewhat resembles the "cattle;" the "cattle" or quadrupeds "go" on all four of their legs; there are many of the small animals among the "creeping things" which have a greater or less number of legs upon which they "go;" but among the "creeping things," there are a number of animals, such as worms, snakes, etc., which have no legs, and these "go" on their bellies;

the latter are the lowest, and in point of posture the most degraded of the creeping things. We have shown that the "beast of the field" and the negro are identical. Hence, God's curse upon the tempter of Eve, "cursed art thou above every beast of the field," deprived this creature of the erect posture. "Cursed art thou above all cattle" prevented this creature from going on all fours. "On thy belly shalt thou go" degraded this creature in point of posture to the lowest of the "creeping things." This curse wrought the most radical change in the posture of this negro, and was a terrible punishment. But this would not have been the case if the tempter of Eve had been a snake. The only way a snake can "go" is on its belly. Hence, God's curse, "on thy belly shalt thou go," would not have wrought any change in its posture, nor occasioned it the least inconvenience or suffering.

The opening verse of the narrative of the fall plainly shows that the tempter of Eve was a beast of the field: "Now the serpent was more subtle than any beast of the field which the Lord God had made." Observe (1) that here there is a comparison drawn. (2) That this comparison is drawn between the tempter of Eve and the other beasts of the field. (3) That the comparison drawn in this text is not between the tempter of Eve and the animals in general, but is confined strictly to the tempter of Eve and the other beasts of the field: "Now the serpent was more subtle than *any beast of the field* which the Lord God had made." It must be admitted that, the fact that the tempter of Eve was a beast of the

field, would not have been more clearly indicated
had the text read: Now the serpent was more subtle
than any other beast of the field which the Lord God
had made.

In a previous chapter we have shown that the
term "beast of the field" is not a general term, but
that it is a term applied to a particular race of the
ape species; and with the aid of comparative anatomy, we have identified the negro as the biblical
"beast of the field." Hence, if our text with its
terms had been translated into English, it would
read: Now nachash, or serpent, was more subtle
than any negro which the Lord God had made. Nachash, translated *serpent*, in our English version of
the Bible, was merely the name given this negro by
Adam, to distinguish it from the other negroes in
the Garden of Eden.   "Adam gave names to all cattle, and to *every beast of the field.*"

It is evident that all the embarrasment under
which the world has so long labored in its efforts to
identify the tempter of Eve, is due to the following
causes: (1) That about eighteen centuries ago all
knowledge of the fact that the ape is a biped was
lost to the world.   (2) That at about the same time
the world lost all knowledge of the fact that the
negro is an ape; that God designed him as a servant to man, and that he was owned and used by the
ancients as a servant; that he is referred to in scripture as the beast of the field; and that his leading
characteristics are a matter of scriptural record; prior
to these events, monotheism and a belief in the inspiration of the scriptures was practically confined

to the Jews; the rest of the world, with perhaps the exception of an individual or a family here and there, were abandoned to atheism and polytheism; and among the Jews atheism and polytheism prevailed to some extent.

When Christianity superseded Judaism the knowledge of the fact that the ape is a biped, and the negro an ape, was restored to the world; and the Saviour and His deciples employed every argument at their command to eradicate from the minds of men the false theories of atheism, and convince them of the truth of the scripture; but their teachings survived only for a season; soon after the death of the last of the apostles the followers of the Saviour split up into a number of warring factions, which gradually lost all true knowledge of the teachings of the Bible; in this condition they fell an easy prey to the atheism of the age; the theory of evolution which teaches that the negro is a "lower race of the human species," was blended with the teachings of scripture, and was universally taught and accepted; under these demoralizing conditions, continued for generations, all knowledge of the fact that the negro is an ape, was lost, and, under the influence of atheism, he came to be universally regarded as a man. Then God, in His wrath and disgust, plunged the whole world of mankind into that distressing period of ignorance, superstition, and crime which is fitly termed the *Dark Ages*. In the meantime, the various Christian sects were consolidated into the Catholic church. The mercenary priesthood of this church were at once ignorant of the teachings of scripture and indifferent

to the welfare of the people; their highest ambition
was to acquire for their sect universal political supremacy and power, as well as universal religious
supremacy and power.   The scriptures were supplanted by the traditions of the church; the laws of
God were set aside by the "Bull" of the Pope; de-
bauchery, crime, and bloodshed characterized the
reign of the priesthood, who claimed to be the representatives of the Prince of Peace; and death, inflicted with the most fiendish tortures, was promptly
meted out to the "heretic" whose nature revolted
at such atrocities, and whose voice was raised in
protest against crimes that were daily committed in
the name of religion.   Under these distressing conditions, the masses sank to the lowest depths of
ignorance and superstition, and so remained for
centuries. The first rays of light and hope, which
penetrated this benighted age, were ushered in by the
reformation.   A very considerable portion of the
pure-blooded whites of Europe, following the leadership of Martin Luther, repudiated Catholicism and
inaugurated a movement which resulted in the establishment of Protestantism; the beneficial results
of this movement were further increased by the invention of the printing press and the consequent
dissemination of learning among the people of all
classes.

When the Protestant clergy and laity began to
investigate the scriptures, they at once found themselves confronted with the fact that the Bible teaches
the existence of a beast which habitually "walks
erect, talks, and reasons;" and that this animal was

the tempter of Eve; but all knowledge of the fact
that the negro is an ape, and that he is the beast
which had figured so prominently in the fall of man,
had long been lost; centuries had passed since atheism had taken the negro out of the ape family, and
thrust him into the family of man, as a "lower race
of the human species;" for centuries the negro had
been received into the Church as a "man and a
brother." During the Dark Ages the negro had been
accepted into the Adamic family without question;
and it never occurred to the early Protestants to
make any inquiry as to his antecedents. The profane literature of the ancients which would doubtless have enlightened them upon the subject, had
all been destroyed; and modern science was unborn.
Failing to find among the recognized animals of the
day, any creature which could possibly meet the
scriptural requirements, the most skeptical of the
early Protestants were led to believe that the Bible
narrative of the fall of man is merely an *allegory;*
and this pernicious belief has survived to our day,
and is now entertained in quarters where we should
least expect to find it.

Others among the early Protestants who were
desirous of adhering to the Bible, conceived the idea
that the tempter of Eve was "an invisible, spiritual
being, and this absurd idea has also survived to our
day; but it is plainly disproven by the language of
the curse which God put upon the tempter of Eve:
" I will put enmity between thee and the woman, and
between thy seed and her seed; it shall bruise thy
head, and thou shalt bruise his heel." This leaves

no room for doubt that the tempter of Eve was a material creature; a creature of flesh and blood—an offspring-bearing animal.

Numerous theories have been advanced as to the identity of the tempter of Eve; but they are all more or less absurd, and so far from being sustained by the scriptures, they are all purely imaginary. The most general opinion among the early Protestants was that the tempter of Eve was a snake; and this opinion is generally held by the Jewish and Gentile clergy and laity of to-day; many of the advocates of the snake theory hold that God endowed the snake with speech in order that he might tempt man to his ruin; it is easy to see that this theory makes God the principal, and the most guilty participant in the fall of man. This theory is at once too absurd and blasphemous for serious consideration. There are others who hold that the snake was merely the agent employed by an invisible arch fiend to tempt man to his ruin; these people hold that the snake was deprived of the gift of speech as a punishment for his offense, and that he was also compelled to "go" on his belly ever after.

As above shown, Dr. Clark came nearer the truth when he repudiated the snake theory and fixed upon the ape as the tempter of Eve; but he fell far short of the truth when he selected the orang; and he was compelled to advance the absurd theory that the whole race of orangs once possessed the erect posture and articulate speech; and that God deprived the whole race of orangs of the erect posture and the "gift of speech," as a punishment for the acts of one of their number. It is surprising that men will persist in palming off on the world a lot of *home-made* scripture when they have already more *genuine* scripture than they can understand. As shown above, the punishment inflicted on the tempter of Eve was confined to the individual animal which offended; and there is not one particle of evidence to indicate that it was deprived of articulate speech. Dr. Clark, in common with all modern theologians who accept the Bible, insists that the animal which tempted Eve was merely the "agent" of an invisible arch fiend, commonly called the *devil;* this theory teaches that there were *four* active participants in the fall of man—Adam, Eve, the serpent and the devil, which controlled the serpent; and this too, in the very face of the plain teaching of the Bible, that there were but *three* parties implicated—Adam, Eve, and the serpent.

The modern theory that the animal which tempted Eve was merely the "agent" or tool of a supreme, invisible arch fiend which desired the ruin of man, is opposed to the evident meaning conveyed by the text: "Now the serpent was more subtle than any beast of the field which the Lord God had made." Thus the inspired writer emphatically states that the tempter of Eve was more "subtle," that is, more "sly in design," more "artful," more "cunning," more "crafty," "than any beast of the field which the Lord God had made;" and was consequently more capable of devising and executing a scheme to deceive man into violating the laws of God. On the other hand, there is not the slightest hint conveyed by the text that the animal which deceived Eve was in the least influenced or controlled by any supernatural agency.

In our forthcoming work on the book of Revelation we shall prove that the modern theory that there is a supreme, invisible arch fiend, called the "devil," or "satan," who stands for all that is wicked and corrupt, as God stands for all that is good and pure, had its origin, and exists solely in the grossest ignorance and superstition. The modern believers in "His Satanic Majesty" will have the opportunity of doing for this much talked-of gentleman, what they have never done—the opportunity of proving his *reality*. In pursuing their investigation along this line these gentlemen might profit by the hint dropped by Dr. Clark, who, in discussing certain terms in the Arabic language which is closely related to the Hebrew, says: "Is it not strange that the *devil* and *ape* should have the same name, derived from the same root, and that root so very similar to the word in the text?" We have a multitude of "devils," but no one of them is *supreme;* and none of them are *invisible.*

All the circumstances indicate that the beast of the field which tempted Eve was a *negress,* who served Eve in the capacity of maid servant; that Eve became too confidential and familiar with this negress and was imposed upon by her. The language of the text clearly indicates that this negress was aware of the fact that Adam and Eve were prohibited from eating the fruit of a certain tree in the garden, and subsequent events confirm it; yet in

FIG. 9. EVE AND HER TEMPTER.

pretended ignorance, she approaches her mistress
with the question: "Yea, hath God said, Ye shall
not eat of every tree in the garden?" It is evident
that this was the initial step in the execution of a
cunningly devised scheme to deceive the woman
into violating the laws of God. At this critical juncture Eve made that fatal mistake which involved the
world in sin, and the disastrous train of evils that
have grown out of it; instead of sending this pre-
sumptuous negress away with a reprimand, the unsuspecting woman in the simplicity of her nature replied: "We may eat of the fruit of the trees of the
garden, but of the fruit of the tree which is in the
midst of the garden God hath said, Ye shall not eat
of it neither shall ye touch it, lest ye die." Note the
adroitness with which this negress approached Eve
upon this subject! And, emboldened by her success in gaining the confidence of her mistress, she
flatly contradicted the Word of God by saying, "Ye
shall not surely die. For God doth know that in
the day thou eatest thereof, then your eyes shall be
opened, and ye shall be as gods, knowing good and
evil." Thus, by one bold, skillful move this impu-
dent negress instilled into the woman's mind distrust
of God; engendered in her heart discontent with her
position; and aroused in her nature the unholy ambition that she and her husband "be as gods."
The iniquitous designs of the negress were successful. Eve, accompanied by Adam, and doubtless by
the negress proceeded to the forbidden tree, "and
took of the fruit thereof, and did eat, and gave also
unto her husband with her, and he did eat."

Thus, it is clearly shown that the scriptural narrative of the fall of man, accredits no characteristic to the tempter of Eve that is not found in the genuine negro. This, taken in connection with the fact that the Bible teaches that Adam, Eve, and the serpent were the only parties implicated, leaves modern theologians no basis for their theory that there was a *fourth* party implicated; and that this fourth party was an invisible arch fiend, called the "devil" or "satan."

We are taught by the modern theologians that Adam and Eve committed their first sin by eating the forbidden fruit; but to accept this theory we must disregard the narrative of creation, which teaches that the design of God in creating man, was that he should have dominion over the animals; and that when man was created he was assigned to this task. Inasmuch as the tempter of Eve was an animal, it follows that it was the duty of Adam and Eve to control it in common with the rest of the animals. But instead of controlling this negress, Eve accepted the negress as her counselor, and allowed the negress to control her, and induced Adam to do likewise; and she counseled them to their ruin. Thus, it is plain that when Adam and Eve accepted this creature as their counselor, they not only violated the laws given man in the creation to "have dominion" over the animals, but they outraged the very design of God in creating man. Their acting upon the advice of the negress by eating the forbidden fruit, was their second offense; when they accepted the negress as their counselor, they necessarily descended to social equality with her. This reveals the startling fact that it was man's social equality with the negro that brought sin into the world. This being true, it follows that man's social equality with the negro will keep sin into the world, and will bring upon man the just condemnation of God. Besides, man's social equality with the negro tends to political and religious equality; and these three, or any one of them, inevitably leads to amalgamation—itself the most infamous and destructive crime known to the law of God.

CHAPTER XV.

THE HISTORY OF CAIN.

"And Adam knew Eve his wife; and she conceived and bear Cain, and said, I have gotten a man from the Lord. And she again bear his brother Abel, and Abel was a keeper of sheep, but Cain was a tiller of the ground. And in process of time it came to pass, that Cain brought of the fruit of the ground an offering unto the Lord. And Abel, he also brought of the firstlings of his flock and of the fat thereof. And the Lord had respect unto Abel and to his offering; but unto Cain and to his offering he had not respect. And Cain was very wroth, and his countenance fell."

We are thus taught that these brothers were engaged in different persuits; the one "was a keeper of sheep;" the other "was a tiller of the ground." Hence, they were not rivals in business; and had each of them lived in obedience to the laws of God, their offerings would have been alike acceptable to God. But such was not the case. Abel was a good man, and loved God and had faith in Him; (see *Heb.* xi, 4), this led him to respect and obey the laws of God. Hence, God had respect for Abel as a man; and this led Him to respect Abel's offering. But Cain was a bad man; he cherished no love for God, and no respect for His laws; and this led him to

407

violate the laws of God. Hence, God had no respect
for Cain as a man; and this led Him to reject Cain's
offering. The nature of their respective offerings
had nothing to do with God's acceptance of the one
and His rejection of the other. The whole question
hinged upon the position which each of these brothers held in the esteem of God. God had respect for
Abel; but for Cain He had no respect.

"And the Lord said unto Cain, Why art thou
wroth, and why is thy countenance fallen? If thou
doest well, shalt thou not be accepted? And if thou
doest not well, sin lieth at the door; and unto thee
shall be his desire, and thou shalt rule over him."
(*Gen.* iv, 6, 7).

This clearly shows that Cain was not only a violator of the laws of God, but that he had an accomplice in his crime. There was something which had
desire for Cain, and no inanimate object can entertain desire. To have desire, requires both life and
intelligence; and inasmuch as individuals of the
same sex have no desire for each other, we would
naturally decide that this creature which had desire
for Cain, was a female; the mere fact that the inspired writer refers to it in the masculine is no evidence that it was not a female. In describing the
animals, the inspired writers frequently refer to both
sexes in the masculine. For example: "God made
every winged fowl after his kind." "Let the earth
bring forth the living creature after his kind," etc.
(*Gen.* i, 22, 24). Now we know that both sexes were
included in these commands; and again, the *sun*,
which is without sex, is referred to in the masculine:

"His going forth is from the end of the heaven, and his circuit from the end of it." (*Ps.* xix, 6).

The evident fact that Cain's associate in the crime which cost him the respect of God, was a female which had desire for him, indicates that the *sin* which lay at his "door," was the result of his desire for her; and that she was his paramour. "Unto thee shall be his desire, and thou shalt rule over him," was a sentence which God imposed upon Cain and his paramour. Further evidence of this is found in the striking similarity of God's language in imposing this sentence to that which He used in imposing His sentence upon Eve. To the woman who sinned, God said: "Thy desire shall be to thy husband, and he shall rule over thee." (*Gen.* iii, 16). To the man Cain, who had sinned, God said: "Unto thee shall be his desire, and thou shalt rule over him." Thus it is plain that the sentence which God imposed upon Eve was identical with that which He imposed upon Cain's associate in crime. This identity of sentence furnishes the most positive proof that Cain's accomplice was a female. In each case God decreed that the female should have desire for a particular male, and that this particular male should "rule over" the female which had desire for him.

When we compare the sentence which God imposed upon Eve, and to which Adam was made a party, with the sentence which He imposed upon Cain's paramour, and to which Cain was made a party, we find that in each case the result to the parties interested was *identical*. The relation of husband and wife which existed between Adam and Eve in the days of their innocence, was sanctioned by the law given man in the Creation, "be fruitful and multiply;" but under the changed condition wrought by their fall, God saw fit, by special decree to bind and confine them in their sexual relations to each other, changing their former relations only so far as to place the offending woman in subjection to her husband whom she had misled. The sentence which God imposed upon Cain and his paramour, being identical with that imposed upon Adam and Eve, necessarily had the same result. It bound them together in the relation of husband and wife, and confined them in their sexual relations to each other; and at the same time placed Cain's wife in subjection to him.

The inspired apostle Jude, not only furnishes the most positive evidence that Cain's associate in crime was a female, but that she was not of the Adamic *flesh*. Jude at once arraigns the men of his day on the charge of amalgamation—"giving themselves over to fornication, and going after strange flesh;" and urges the followers of Christ to "keep" themselves "in the love of God."

Jude says: "Beloved, when I gave all deligence to write unto you of the common salvation, it was needful for me to write unto you and exhort you that ye should earnestly contend for the faith which was once delivered to the saints. For there are certain men, crept in unawares, who were before of old ordained to this condemnation; ungodly men, turning the grace of our God into lasciviousness, and denying the only Lord God and our Lord Jesus Christ. I will therefore put you in remembrance, though ye once knew this, how that the Lord, having saved the people out of the land of Egypt, afterward destroyed them that believed not. And the angels, which kept not their first estate, but left their own habitation, he hath reserved in everlasting chains under darkness unto the judgment of the great day. Even as Sodom and Gomorrah, and the cities about them, in like manner, giving themselves over to fornication and going after strange flesh, are set forth for an example, suffering the vengeance of eternal fire. Likewise these filthy dreamers defile the flesh, despise dominion, and speak evil of dignitaries. Woe unto them for they have gone in the way of Cain." (*Jude* i, 3, 4, etc.).

We are thus taught: (1) that the crime of fornication, with which the Jews and other ancient people are charged by the inspired writers, and which led to the destruction of "Sodom and Gomorrah and the cities about them," is traceable to Cain, who was the first to lead off in this wicked course. Hence, Jude describes it as "the way of Cain." (2) That *fornication*, according to scripture, is "going after strange flesh."

The Bible describes two offences which result from illicit intercourse between the sexes; the one is "adultery," the other is "fornication." We, of modern times, are taught that *adultery* is the "unfaithfulness of any married person to the marriage bed." (*Webster's Dictionary*). And that *fornication* is "the incontinence or lewdness of unmarried persons, male or female." (*Ibid*). But this definition of *fornication* was not held by the founder of Christianity. On the contrary, our Saviour said: "Whosoever shall put away his wife, except it be for fornication, and shall marry another, committeth adultery; and whoso marrieth her, which is put away, committeth adultery." (*Mat.* xix, 9). Thus, the Saviour not only draws a broad distinction between fornication and adultery, but He teaches that a married person may commit *fornication;* and if a man and wife are divorced and either, or both of them, marry another, they commit *adultery*, but not fornication. Our Saviour also shows fornication to be a more heinous offense than adultery, by making it the only ground for divorce. It is also taught that nations may become involved in fornication. (See *Ezek.* xvi, 26, 29).

That God's sentence upon Cain and his partner in sin established between them the relation of husband and wife, is shown by the fact that *after* their sentence, Cain is accredited with a wife, while *prior* to this event he is merely credited with a paramour of "strange flesh," with whom he committed *fornication*, as shown by the following: "And Cain went out from the presence of the Lord, and dwelt in the land of Nod, on the east of Eden. And Cain knew his wife, and she conceived and bear Enoch." (*Gen.* iv, 16, 17).

There is absolutely nothing in the scriptural record that justifies us in supposing that Cain obtained his wife in the land of Nod; on the contrary, the record clearly shows that she was his paramour when he and his brother Abel brought their offerings to the Lord; and that it was his criminal relations with her that cost Cain the respect of God and led to the rejection of his offering. And as a punishment upon Cain for his criminal relations with her, God by special decree established between them the relation of husband and wife. Upon their arrival in the land of Nod, "Cain knew his wife," in the sense that she conceived and bare Enoch; just as, after being driven from the Garden of Eden, "Adam knew Eve, his wife," in the sense that she conceived and bare Cain.

Upon Cain's history, as upon many other parts of Bible history, Paul's declaration that, "there is one kind of flesh of men, another flesh of beasts, another of fishes, and another of birds, proves invaluable, since it enables us to solve many of the so-called *mysteries* of the Bible. Jude tells us that Cain committed *fornication* by "going after strange flesh." When we turn upon Jude's statement, the light of Paul's declaration as to the four different *kinds of flesh*, it becomes plain that Cain's paramour was not of Cain's "kind of flesh"— she was not of the "flesh of men"—she was not a *woman;* but was a creature of "strange flesh;" and being a land animal, she belonged to the *flesh of beasts*. Hence, Cain's wife was a beast; yet his wife of strange flesh bare Cain offspring that was indefinitely fertile. His son Enoch had numerous descendants—children, grand-children, great grandchildren, etc.

In a previous chapter we have shown that Cain's

mixed-blooded progeny compare favorably, in point of intelligence and culture, with the most intelligent and cultured of the mixed-bloods of our day. They were great cattle raisers; they mined, and worked metals and fashioned them into implements; they were skillful mechanics and accomplished musicians; they evidently cultivated domestic plants, especially the food plants, and they possessed a knowledge of God and His dealings with Cain, as shown by the utterances of one of them who had slain a man: "Hear my voice; ye wives of Lamach, hearken to my speech; for I have slain a man to my wounding, and a young man to my hurt. If Cain shall be avenged seven fold, truly Lamach seventy and seven fold." (*Gen.* iv, 23, 24).

In view of the characteristics of the beast of the field, as we find them recorded in scripture, it is plain that Cain's wife was a beast of the field—a *negress;* and it is highly probable that she was the immediate offspring of the negress who tempted Eve; and that God's curse upon the tempter—"I will put enmity between thee and the woman, and between thy seed and her seed; it shall bruise thy head and thou shalt bruise his heel"—was fulfilled in the disasters which befell Cain as the result of his criminal relations with her.

Thus, the testimony of the inspired writers, Moses, Jude and St. Paul, sweeps away the veil of mystery which for so many centuries has enveloped the marital relations of Cain, and throws a flood of light upon the most important events in his history.

When we appeal to science to identify this creature of "strange flesh" with which Cain committed *fornication*, and which bore him offspring as above described, she promptly invades the so-called "human species," and points to the negro as the highest race of ape, and the only creature of the lower kinds of flesh with which man may associate himself carnally and produce offspring which will at once be indefinitely fertile, and capable of acquiring a knowledge of God and the arts of civilization. Throughout his whole history, man has manifested a strong disposition to abandon himself to this loathesome, destructive crime, and this is rendered even more conspicuous by the fact that Cain, the first child born to the Adamic Creation, *fell*, the *victim of amalgamation.*

Inasmuch, as all knowledge of the fact that the negro is an ape was lost centuries ago, the modern theologian was led to decide that Cain took his sister to wife; but had this been true, she would not have been of "strange flesh;" Cain and his wife would have been of *one flesh*—the "flesh of men;" besides, *sin* would not have lain at Cain's "door" as the result of his act. He would simply have obeyed the law given man in the Creation, "be fruitful and multiply." The only way in which the immediate sons of Adam could have preserved and increased the Adamic flesh was by taking their sisters to wife. Seth and his younger brothers did this, and they were never censured for it. On the contrary, Seth, the third son of Adam, was highly honored by taking his sister to wife, since it placed him in the line of descent from Adam to Jesus Christ. Hence, he occupies an exalted position in the genealogical tables of the Bible, as one of the ancestors of the Messiah.

Further evidence that Cain's wife was not of the "flesh of men"—that she was not a woman—is found in the fact that Seth was the third child born to Adam, and took the place of Abel whom Cain slew, as shown by the record: "And Adam knew his wife again ; and she bore a son, and called his name Seth: For God, saith she, hath appointed me another seed instead of Abel, whom Cain slew." (*Gen.* iv, 25). And there were no daughters born to Adam until after the birth of Seth, as shown by the record: "And the days of Adam after he begat Seth were eight hundred years, and he begat sons and daughters." (*Gen.* v, 4). The profane history of this early period has long since been lost. But the history of Adam's immediate descendants is of such vital importance to the men of subsequent ages, that God inspired Moses to write it; and if there had been any daughters born to Adam and Eve prior to the birth of Seth, Moses would have made some mention of them; the inspired writer mentions the sons born to Adam before the birth of Seth, as well as those born after that event; and if there had been daughters born to Adam *before* the birth of Seth, why should he decline to mention them as well as those born *after* that event ? If we accept the Bible account of the immediate offspring of Adam as an inspired narrative, we have no alternative than to regard it as full and authentic.

Hence, we must stand by the record, and decide that there was no daughter born to Adam until after the birth of Seth. Thus the history of Cain's marital relations fully sustains the teachings of Jude that Cain's paramour was not of his *kind of flesh*—she was not of the "flesh of men"—hence, she was not a woman—but was a creature of *strange flesh* with which he committed fornication; for nothing is more clearly taught in the Bible than that Cain had a wife before Seth was born.

Cain being the eldest son of Adam, it is plain that, in the ordinary course of events the first female child born to the Adamic family would, upon reaching maturity, be given in marriage to Cain; but Cain's loathsome crime in cultivating sexual relations with a beast had rendered him unfit for the companionship of a pure woman. Besides, God's sentence upon Cain and his paramour bound Cain to this beast in the relation of husband all his life, and forever restrained him from holding sexual relations with woman. And as a result, the beautiful Adamic woman who, in all her virgin loveliness, would have been the wife of Cain, would now become the wife of his brother, Abel. In his jealousy and rage upon realizing this, we might find an explanation of why, "Cain rose up against Abel his brother and slew him."

When viewed from the atheist's standpoint, that man is a species composed of a greater or less number of races, the history of Cain and his descendants presents little to interest, and is of no practical value; on the contrary, it is altogether unsatisfactory and misleading. But when viewed in the light of the scriptures and the sciences, it at once becomes a subject of the most absorbing interest and importance. God's utter abhorrence of amalgamation is shown in the disasters which He visited upon Cain; while God's wondrous love for man is displayed in His formation and preservation of the genealogical table of Cain's descendants, in which it is made a matter of scriptural record that there is a beast with which man may associate himself carnally and produce offspring that will be at once indefinitely fertile, and capable of acquiring a knowledge of God and the arts of civilization.

Inasmuch as Cain's wife was a negress, her offspring were necessarily mixed-bloods. This explains why Cain and his descendants were thrust out of the line of descent from Adam to Jesus Christ; and the line of descent as shown in the genealogical tables is made to pass through Seth, the third son of Adam, and through his descendants of pure Adamic stock. Cain and his wife disappear from the records, and all trace of them is lost after the birth of Enoch, and the building of the city which Cain named after his son, Enoch.

Thus it is shown: (1) That the rejection of Cain's offering was solely due to the fact that God had no respect for Cain as a man, because he was a violator of the law of God. (2) That Cain had an accomplice in his crime. (3) That his accomplice was a female of " stange flesh " with whom he committed " fornication." (4) That his paramour was a " beast of the field "—an ape. (5) That, as a punishment for his loathsome crime, God bound him to this beast in the relation of husband, and forever debased him from holding marital relations with woman. (6) That his wife bore him offspring that was indefinitely fertile, and capable of acquiring a knowledge of God and the arts of civilization. (7) That the genealogical table of Cain's descendants serves no other purpose, and was merely designed as a scriptural record of the fact that there is a beast with which man may associate himself carnally and produce offspring that will be indefinitely fertile, and capable of acquiring a knowledge of God and the arts of civilization. What other good purpose does this genealogical table of Cain's descendants perform? Why does the inspired writer give us a list of the principal characters among Cain's offspring by his wife of "strange flesh," with their occupations, etc., for five generations, and then stop, when he gives us a list of pure-blooded whites extending from Adam to Jesus Christ? This genealogical table of Cain's descendants serves a purpose; it is simply a scriptual record of the fact that there is a beast with which man may associate himself carnally and produce offspring possessing the characteristics of mixed-bloods. (8) That no lower grade of ape *than the negro meets* the scriptural requirements.

Cain's wife being a negress—an ape—she, like every other animal, was simply a combination of *two creations*—matter and mind; and was consequently a mere creature of *time*. On the other hand, Cain, being a man, was a combination of *three creations*— matter, mind, and soul; and was consequently an *im-*

mortal being. This unnatural condition of affairs suggests the inquiry, was it possible for Cain to transmit the soul creation to his mulatto son Enoch and his progeny, and thus establish between God and these mixed-bloods, the relation of father and son? To answer this question, we must investigate the laws which govern the reproduction of the *creations*, as they exist in man and the animals.

The negro, like every other animal, being merely a combination of two creations—matter and mind— it follows that one side or part of the matter creation, and one side or part of the mind creation, exists in an imperfect state in the male negro; the corresponding sides or parts of these imperfect creations exists in the female negro. In the sexual act each side or part of these creations maintains its individuality, and acts as a magnet which attracts its corresponding side or part in the opposite sex; and when united and perfected in the female, conception and birth ensues, and the two creations— matter and mind—are reproduced in the young negro.

Thus, *two* creations—matter and mind—combine to perfect the negro. But it requires the combination of the *three* creations—matter, mind, and soul— to perfect man. Hence, while but two creations— matter and mind—exist in an imperfect state in the germs of the male and the female negro, as mutually dependent sides or parts of the life system of the animal, the three creations—matter, mind, and soul exist in an imperfect state in the germs of the male and female man, as mutually dependent sides or parts of the life system of man; and so great is the attraction between the matter and mind creations as they exist in the imperfect state in the germs of man and the negro, that sexual intercourse between the two may unite and perfect these two creations. But the imperfect side or part of the soul creation as it exists in the germ of the man, finds no corresponding side or part in the negro; as a result the soul creation having no attraction, remains passive. Hence, if conception ensues from the union of the germs and the consequent perfecting of the matter and mind creations of man and the negro, this *passive* creation forms no part of the offspring of this unnatural union. Thus, neither the male nor the female side or part of man can transmit the three creations—matter, mind, and soul—to their offspring by the negro, in whom the matter and the mind creations alone exist. In other words, the male and the female can only transmit to their offspring such of these creations as are common to both parents.

Thus, it is plain that only the sides or parts of matter and the mind creations, as they existed in the respective germs of Cain and his negro wife, were united and perfected in their offspring; while the side or part of the soul creation, as it existed in an imperfect state in Cain, found no corresponding side or part in his negro wife, remained passive in the sexual act, and consequently formed no part of the offspring of this unnatural union. Hence, Cain's mulatto son was wholly animal—a mere combination of matter and mind—and being utterly destitute of a soul, there existed no kinship between God and

Cain's son, Enoch.   Hence, when a man becomes so
degraded as to associate himself carnally with the
negro, his act brings into operation the law which
governs the reproduction of the creations, which
makes it impossible for man to transmit to his offspring by the beast the slightest kinship with God.

This law becomes active and operates with the
same result when man associates himself carnally
with the mixed-bloods without reference to what
their proportions of white and black blood may be.
The immediate offspring of man and the negro—
the half breed—like the negro, is merely a combination of matter and mind; consequently, in associ-
ating himself carnally with the mixed-bloods, man
would continually oppose three creations—matter,
mind, and soul—as they exist in their imperfect
state in his germ, to only two creations—matter
and mind—as they exist in their imperfect state in
the germ of the mixed-bloods.   Hence, it could only
be possible to unite and perfect the matter and the
mind creations as they exist in their imperfect state
in the respective germs of man and the mixed-bloods,
and thus reproduce them in the offspring.   But the
side or part of the soul creation, as it exists in its imperfect state in the germ of the man, finding no corresponding side or part in the mixed-bloods with
which it might be united and perfected, is not affected
in the sexual act, and remains passive; hence, it forms
no part in the offspring.   This unvarying law would
hold good through millions of generations.   Man
cannot transmit to his offspring by the negro, the

least vestige of the soul creation. Hence, *no mixed-blood has a soul.*

In addition to this, a moment's reflection should convince us that, inasmuch as God declined in the creation, to establish any kinship between Himself and the animals, it follows that he would not make it possible for man to do so by an act, which, of itself, is a violation of that Divine law: *"Thou shall not lie with any beast."*

The social equality with the negro to which Adam and Eve descended in the Garden of Eden, culminated in Cain's abandoning himself to amalgamation with the negro; in the absence of a female of his *kind of flesh*, he selected a paramour of *strange flesh*—a negress. In this age of atheism, in which the negro is universally recognized as "a lower race of the human species," and man's marriage with him universally sanctioned by the church, and almost universally sanctioned by the state, it is difficult for us to comprehend the depth of depravity to which Cain descended by cohabiting with a negress; neither is it easy for us to understand the crushing degradation to which God subjected Cain by binding him in marriage to the base-born object of his lust. Like the antediluvians, and the people of Sodom and Gomorrah, and like the Egyptians, Babylonians, and Israelites, etc., we, of modern times, have "gone into the way of Cain;" but when we accept the teachings of the scriptures and the sciences, that the negro is an ape, we should be able to look upward from the depths of depravity to which we have descended, at least so far as to realize that, in binding Cain in marriage to a beast, God inflicted upon him the most degrading punishment. The Bible abounds with instances in which individuals and nations cultivated marriage relations with the negro and with the mixed-bloods, but in every case these marriage relations were the voluntary acts of these individuals and nations. But Cain's case is the only one on record where God, by special decree, bound a man in marriage to the beast with which he had committed fornication. Hence, the degrading punishment which God visited upon Cain—the first amalgamationist—is unparalleled in His dealings with men.

It was evidently God's intention to make an example of Cain, by inflicting upon him a punishment so degrading as to restrain others from "going after strange flesh." But the infamy which God heaped upon Cain failed to restrain others from going "in the way of Cain," as shown by Jude's reference to "the angels which kept not their first estate, but left their own habitation, * * * giving themselves over to fornication, and going after strange flesh. * * * These filthy dreamers defile the flesh, despise dominion, and speak evil of dignitaries. * * * Woe unto them, for they have gone in the way of Cain." (*Jude*).

The "angels" above referred to, were not *celestial*, but *material* beings. They were the early descendants of Adam who "left their own habitation"—the Adamic flesh, as presented in woman—"going after strange flesh"—the flesh of beasts, as presented in the negro. Those "filthy dreamers" "despised dominion" over the negro in common with the rest of the animals, and preferred social equality with him and the amalgamation to which it inevitably leads.

Additional proof of the prevalence of amalgamation among the antediluvians is shown by the following: "And it came to pass, when men began to multiply upon the face of the earth, and daughters were born unto them, that the sons of God saw the daughters of men that they were fair: and they took them wives of all which they chose. And the Lord said, my spirit shall not always strive with man, for that he also is flesh: Yet his days shall be an hundred and twenty years. There were giants in those days; and also after that, when the sons of God went in unto the daughters of men, and they bear children to them, the same became mighty men which were of old, men of renown." (*Gen.* vi, 1, 2, 3, 4).

We observe that these texts plainly show: (1) That there is a broad distinction made between the "sons of God," and the "daughters of men." (2) That their inter-marriages were criminal. (3) That God had striven with man to induce him to refrain from such marriages. (4) That God was growing weary of striving with man—"My spirit shall not always strive with man, for that he also is flesh;" thus clearly stating that, like man, these creatures, with which man was contracting these unlawful marriages, were creatures of *flesh*. (5) That God gave man 120 years in which to abandon his wicked course, and return to his duties and to a life of obedience. (6) That, in some cases, the offspring resulting from the unions between the " sons of God" and "the daughters of men," were of such extraordinary size as to be termed "giants;" and it is significant that the mixed-bloods of postdiluvian times were physical *giants;* such, for example, was Goliath, the Philistine whom David slew; such also were the Anakims. (*Deut.* ii, 10, 11). The skeletons of ancient Indians have been found which were of such extraordinary size as to lead to their being termed "giants." And we occasionally find "giants" among the mixed-bloods of to-day; on the other hand, we find among the mixed-bloods, tribes composed of individuals so diminutive as to be termed "pigmies" or "dwarfs." But whether *giants* or *pigmies,* these monstrosities are always *mixed-bloods;* the tribes of pigmies to be found to-day are neither white nor black, but some shade of brown, red, or yellow; and the fossil remains of either pigmies or giants will show the evidence of *crossing.* The pure whites vary in size; but these variations never extend from *pigmies* to *giants.* In no case do they develop into physical giants; neither do the pure whites produce pigmies or dwarfs; except in isolated individual cases, and then only as the result of accident or disease. The same is true of the pure-blooded negroes; they produce no giants and no pigmies.

In commenting on the "sons of God," and the "daughters of men," and their unlawful unions and progeny of giants, Lenormant pronounces it "the *crux intrepretum* of the first part of Genesis." Various efforts have been made to solve the question as to who were the "sons of God" and who were the "daughters of men." Hence, this question has been the subject of endless speculation and controversy. Many of the early Catholic writers even went so far as to suppose that the "sons of God" were celestial beings, who became infatuated with the beauty of the women of the earth—the "daughters of men"—and formed marriage alliances with them which led to the production of an unnatural progeny in the form of *giants*. (*Beginning of History*, pp. 299, 300).

Let us bear in mind that these early Catholic writers lived and wrote at a time when all knowledge of the fact that the white is the only man, and that the negro is an ape, were lost; that they lived at a time when atheism had misled the world into accepting the degrading theory that man is a species of which the white is the highest and the negro is the lowest race, with the browns, reds, and yellows as intermediate races in different stages of development. Under the demoralizing influence of this destructive theory, they recognized the negro as "a man and a brother;" and also recognized his mixed-blooded progeny—the so-called brown, red, and yellow races —as "men and brethren." Blinded by this false teaching of atheism, they could see nothing criminal in the marriage of whites with these so-called "lower races of men." Hence, when they observed the broad distinction made between the "sons of God" and the "daughters of men," the criminality of their marriages, and the unnatural offspring resulting therefrom, together with the terrible punishment which God visited upon them because of these crimes, the early "fathers of the church" conceived the absurd idea that the "sons of God" were angels who fell from their high estate through their guilty loves for the women of the earth—the "daughters of men."

But when we lay aside our atheism and accept the teachings of the scriptures and the sciences that the white is the *only man*, and that the negro is an *ape*, and view this whole subject in the light of Cain's history, as above set forth, it becomes plain that the "sons of God" were the pure-blooded male descendants of "Adam, the son of God;" and that the "daughters of men" were mixed-blooded females; they were the offspring of amalgamation between the Adamic *males* and the negro *females*. Thus it will be seen that the inspired writer describes them to a nicety; their fathers were *men;* hence, they were the "daughters of men;" but their mothers were not *women*, they were *negresses*—"beasts of the field"—*apes.*

Continuing his narrative of the criminal marriage of the "sons of God" with the "daughters of men," the disposition which God made of them and their unnatural progeny, the inspired writer says: "And God saw that the wickedness of man was great in the earth, and that every imagination of the thoughts of his heart was only evil continually. And it repented the Lord that He had made man on the earth, and it grieved Him at his heart. And the Lord said, I will destroy man, whom I have created, from the face of the earth; both man and beast, and the creeping things, and the fowls of the air; for it repenteth Me that I have made them." (*Gen.* vi, 5, 6, 7).

Thus God's abhorrence of amalgamation is shown by the fact that, after striving for ages to induce man to abandon his wicked course, He was disposed, in His wrath and disgust, to destroy from the earth both man and the animals. But just at this critical period—the most critical in man's history—"Noah found grace in the eyes of the Lord." (*Gen.* vi, 8).

"These are the generations of Noah: Noah was a just man and perfect in his generations, and Noah walked with God." (*Gen.* vi, 9). There are three characteristics here recorded of Noah, and they are evidently given as so many reasons why Noah found grace in the eyes of the Lord: (1) "Noah was a just man." (2) He was "perfect in his generations." (3) "Noah walked with God;" that is, he was obedient to the laws of God. There was nothing uncommon in Noah's possession of the first and third of these characteristics; many men preceded Noah, and many came after him who possessed these characteristics; on the other hand, the *second* characteristic, that he was "perfect in his generations," is shared by every pure-blooded descendant of Adam; but the *record* of it, unlike the characteristic itself, is *peculiar* to Noah. No such record is found of the great antediluvian patriarch, Enoch (the seventh from Adam), who, like Elijah, was translated; nor of Abraham; nor of Moses; nor of David; nor even of Jesus Christ. Is it not peculiar that in all Bible history, there is just this one individual of whom it is recorded, that he was "perfect in his generations?" The fact that Noah was "perfect in his generations" was not the result of any act of his; and all credit for its existence in him is wholly due to his ancestors who transmitted to him from Adam, in uncorrupted line of descent the pure Adamic stock. The fact that he was "perfect in his generations" was one of the reasons why "Noah found grace in the eyes of the Lord," when viewed in the light of all its attendant circumstances, necessarily carries with it the implication that there were others in Noah's time, who were *not perfect in their generations*. Now, if Noah was "perfect in his generations," because his ancestors transmitted to him in uncorrupted line of descent from Adam, the pure Adamic flesh, and there were others in Noah's time who were not perfect in their generations, by assosociation, with whom did their ancestors transmit to them a corrupted line of descent from Adam?

Illicit intercourse between the Adamic males and females indicates a corrupt condition of their morals; but the offspring of such illegal unions will be as perfect in their generations—as pure in their genealogy—as if the relations of their parents had been legitimate. As long as man's sexual relations are confined to the Adamic *flesh*, their genealogy is perfect and their line of descent pure. This being true, it follows that the genealogy of the antediluvians—their line of descent from Adam—could only have been corrupted by their sexual relations with some other "kind of flesh," which resulted in the production of a fertile progeny. This enables us to realize the *deep significance* of this record concerning Noah's genealogy. The antediluvians had *gone in the way of Cain;* amalgamation had become general and widespread among them.   Hence, when God decided to preserve Noah and his family from whom the Adamic stock of postdiluvian times are descended, He made it a matter of scriptural record that there was no taint of negro blood in Noah's veins; he was a pure-blooded descendant of Adam—he was *"perfect in his generations."*   Noah's wife was also a pure-blooded descendant of Adam, for, had there been any taint of negro blood in her veins, he could not have lain with her and "walked with God."   Noah and his wife being pure-blooded descendants of Adam, their sons—Ham, Shem, and Japheth—were necessarily the same; and their wives were of pure Adamic stock, or they would not have been preserved, but would have been destroyed with the rest of the mixed-bloods.

Amalgamation is the sole charge recorded against the antedilivians, as shown by the following: "The earth also was corrupt before God, and the earth was filled with violence.   And God looked upon the earth and behold it was corrupt; for all flesh had corrupted His way on the earth.   And God said to Noah: The end of all flesh is come before me; for the earth is filled with violence through them; and, behold, I will destroy them with the earth."   (*Gen.* vi, 11, 12, 13).

Inasmuch as "all flesh" on the earth had been "corrupted," it is pertinent to inquire as to how many kinds of flesh there are on the earth.   To ascertain this, we should first turn upon this question the light of Paul's declaration: "That there is one

kind of flesh of men, another flesh of beasts, another
of fishes, and another of birds," thus making *four*
different *kinds of flesh;* then turn upon this question
the light of the Mosaic record, which teaches that
the fish were made to inhabit the waters; that the
fowl were made to "fly above the earth in the open
firmament of heaven;" while man and beast were to
occupy the dry land.   This enables us to see that
there are only two kinds of flesh which belong
strictly to the earth; and that these are the "flesh of
men," and the "flesh of beasts."

As has been shown, no form of lust to which
man can abandon himself within the Adamic family
can corrupt the "flesh of men."   However unlawful
the intercourse between men and women may be,
the offspring will be of pure Adamic *flesh.*   The same
is true of the animals.   No hybridization which may
occur between the different species or races of beasts,
can corrupt the flesh of beasts; the hybrids, or mongrels, resulting from such unions are the pure flesh
of beasts.   To corrupt the flesh, there must be sexual intercourse between *two different kinds of flesh,*
and the corrupted flesh will express itself in the *off-*
spring.   For example: the flesh of man is a different "kind of flesh" from that of beasts; while the
negro, being simply a race of the ape species, belongs to the flesh of beasts.   Hence, when a man associates himself carnally with a negress, the *flesh* of
that man is not corrupted by his intercourse with
that beast; neither is the flesh of the negress corrupted by her intercourse with the man; the flesh of
each is as pure after their sexual contact as it was be-

fore. But should their intercourse result in conception and birth, the corrupted flesh will express itself in the offspring—the mulatto—which is not the pure flesh of man, as was its Adamic parent; neither is it the pure flesh of beast, as was its Negro parent; it is what the inspired writer describes it as being, *corrupted flesh*, resulting from amalgamation between two different kinds of flesh.

Having decreed the destruction of the inhabitants of the earth by a flood, God commanded Noah to build an ark in which he and his family, together with a male and female of the fowls and land animals should be preserved. "Thus did Noah; according to all that God commanded him, so did he." (See *Gen.* vi, 14, 17, 18, 19, 22). Thus it is shown that man's criminal relations with the negro led God in His wrath and disgust to "bring upon the earth," the deluge, the most terrible cataclysm the world has ever known. In a previous chapter we have shown that the waters which God employed to deluge the earth, were *celestial* waters. Thus, through the agency of a deluge, which was necessarily universal, God destroyed from the earth, the corrupted flesh and those who were instrumental in corrupting it, and restored the flesh of the earth to its original purity.

CHAPTER XVI.

Amalgamation and Its Results.

Through the agency of the deluge, which was universal, God destroyed from the earth the corrupted flesh resulting from amalgamation between man and the negro; and also destroyed the degraded amalgamationists whose loathsome crimes had corrupted, in God's eye, the earth itself. "And Noah only remained alive, and they that were with him in the ark." Thus the flesh of the earth was restored to its original purity. The negro entered the ark as an ape and was preserved with the rest of the animals.

As shown in a previous chapter, Adam and Eve, our first parents, were the most intellectual, cultivated, and refined people that ever graced the earth; their home in Eden was the most superb estate the world has ever known; they not only possessed a knowledge of the great events of the Creation, but, with God as their tutor, were instructed in all the arts of civilization, including a a knowledge of letters. This great mass of invaluable knowledge Adam transmitted to his descendants, who added to it such knowledge as they acquired from time to time. With all these advantages in their favor, we risk nothing in asserting that, in the long period intervening between the crea-

434

tion of man and the deluge, the descendants of Adam, with that lofty intelligence, ambition and energy, which characterizes the white, developed upon a considerable portion of the earth a splendid civilization, which was at least the peer of any of postdiluvian times. But, unfortunately, they descended to amalgamation with their negroes—they went "in the way of Cain;" and so hateful was this crime in the eyes of God that He not only destroyed them and their civilization, but even the land which they occupied. "And the Lord said, I will destroy them with the earth." (*Gen.* vi, 13). This, of course means that He would destroy "them" and the portion of the earth upon which they dwelt.

In the midst of this great antediluvian civilization, Noah and his family were born and reared. This illustrious family brought with them from their antediluvian home, and transmitted to their descendants, a thorough knowledge of the arts and sciences which had been accumulating in the Adamic family for ages. This explains the accomplished skill displayed by the most ancient postdiluvian artisans, whose architectural remains are invariably the most superb. Mr. Taylor says: "To see gold jewelry of the highest order, the student should examine that of the ancients, such as the Egyptians, Greek, and Etruscan in the British Museum, and that of Mediæval Europe. The art seems now to have passed its prime, and become a manufacture, of which the best products are imitations from the antique." (*Anthropology*, pp. 243, 244).

At the close of the deluge "God blessed Noah

and his sons and said unto them: Be fruitful, and multiply, and replenish the earth. And the fear of you, and the dread of you shall be upon every beast of the earth, and upon every fowl of the air, upon all that moveth upon the earth, and upon all the fishes of the sea; into your hands are they delivered." (*Gen.* ix, 1, 2). God thus gave Noah and his sons the domain over the earth and the animals that He gave Adam in the Creation. And the Lord said in His heart, I will not again curse the ground for man's sake; for the imagination of man's heart is evil from his youth; neither will I smite everything living as I have done. While the earth remaineth, seed time and harvest, and cold and heat, and summer and winter, and day and night shall not cease. (*Gen.* viii; 21, 22).

Having shown the true origin of the negro, as taught by the scriptures and the sciences; and inasmuch as we have investigated the atheist explanation of his origin as expressed in the theory of development, it seems only fair to examine the modern church theory of the origin of the negro. This theory would have us believe that the negro is the son of Ham, Noah's youngest son; and that his physical and mental inferiority to his "white brother" is the result of a curse which Noah put upon Ham for his offensive conduct toward him. This absurd theory had its birth in the Dark Ages; and has descended to us from that frightful period of ignorance, superstition and crime, and because the church advocates it we are expected to accept it as "both sound and sacred." But since the Hamitic origin of the negro is opposed to all the results of scientific research, and to all observation and experience, we should not be surprised to find that it is in conflict with the scriptures, upon which it is claimed to be based.

The Bible teaches that after the deluge, "Noah began to be an husbandman and planted a vineyard. And he drank of the wine and was drunken; and he was uncovered in his tent. And Ham, the father of Canaan, saw the nakedness of his father, and told his brethren without. And Shem and Japheth took a garment and laid it upon their shoulders and went backward, and covered the nakedness of their father; and their faces were backward and they saw not their father's nakedness. And Noah awoke from his wine and knew what his younger son had done unto him. And he said, cursed be Canaan; a servant of servants shall he be unto his brethren. And he said, blessed be the Lord God of Shem; and Canaan shall be his servant. God shall enlarge Japheth, and he shall dwell in the tents of Shem; and Canaan shall be his servant." (*Gen.* ix, 20, etc.).

This is evidently a simple narrative of a son's disrespectful conduct toward his inebriated father, and the injustice displayed by the father in his manner of resenting it: no sane mind could have any respect for Noah's drunken desire to punish Canaan, an unoffending child, for an act which his father committed, and to which Canaan was not a party; and it is highly probable that when Noah recovered from the effects of the wine he was heartily ashamed of it, for when sober he "was a just man." Yet strange to say, the curse which Noah, in his drunken spite desired to inflict upon Ham's unoffending little boy, is advanced in this professedly enlightened age as an explanation of the origin of the negro; and stranger still is the fact that millions of intelligent people accept it.   But let us investigate this su'ject further and see what we are compelled to believe in order to accept this absurd explanation.

1. We must disregard the plain teaching of the Bible that Noah performed no miracles, and believe that he performed the most wonderful miracle the world has ever known; for, if he transformed a white-skinned, silken-haired boy, who was born in the "image of God," into a black-skinned, woolly-haired negro with all the physical and mental characters of the ape, this miraculous act stands unsurpassed in all history.   We are aware that many, who recognize the absurdity of the whole proposition, attempt to minimize the result by insisting that this transformation was not accomplished suddenly; but that under the operations of Noah's curse, Canaan and his descendants, in the course of time, were transformed into negroes.   But this only exaggerates the absurdity of the whole proposition, since it accredits Noah with bringing into existence a law which would accomplish this result; and only God Himself could enact such a law.   Besides, God has not only cursed individuals, but nations, and even continents, and in no instance did His curse change their physical and mental characters.   Hence, we accredit to Noah a power which God Himself never exercised.   And there is nothing in scripture to in-

dicate that Noah possessed any authority or power to thus afflict Canaan or anyone else. In addition to this, the narrative plainly shows that God was not a party to the disgraceful incidents recorded in our text, but that the whole affair was confined to Noah and his family.

2. To accept this theory, we must believe that a wise, just, merciful, and loving God would consent that Noah, in his drunken rage, should visit this terrific curse upon Canaan, an unoffending child; and that, in addition to this, He would lend his aid to the perpetuation of this curse on the descendants of Canaan throughout all time.

3. We must believe that Noah's curse deprived Canaan of the exalted physical and mental characters which, as has been shown, distinguish the white from the negro, and gave him the degraded physical and mental characters which approximate the negro to the lower organisms.

But the absurdity of this theory does not end here. It will be observed that the narrative plainly teaches that Canaan was the only individual upon whom Noah manifested any desire to visit this dire calamity; there was no white female cursed and transformed into a negress to mate with Canaan, and thus enable him to beget a progeny of negroes. Hence, in the absence of a negress, he had no alternative than to take a wife from among the whites; for he certainly had a wife, by whom he became the father of the Canaanites. Our personal observation of the results of amalgamation between whites and negroes, enables us to see at a glance that the off-

spring resulting from the union of a male negro and
a white female would not be negroes, but half-breeds
—mulattoes.   These, upon reaching maturity, would
not have intermarried among themselves, but would
have taken husbands and wives from among the
whites.   The offspring resulting from these inter-
marriages between whites and mulattoes would not
have been negroes; but three-quarters white.   Thus,
through the intermarriage of these mixed-bloods with
whites, each succeeding generation of the descendants of Canaan would have grown whiter, and their
hair straighter, until finally it would be difficult, if
not impossible, to distinguish them from pure whites.
Under these conditions, it is plain that Canaan could
never beget a pure-blooded negro, and that when he
had lived out his days and died, he would have been
the *last*, as the advocates of this theory would have
us believe he was the *first* negro, and the origin of
the negro of subsequent ages would remain unexplained.   Thus, when we view this narrative in the
light of our personal observations, it at once becomes
plain that, to ask us to accept the absurd theory of
the Hamitic origin of the negro, is simply an appeal
to our credulity.   The negro is not the son of Ham;
he is not a descendant of Adam.   On the contrary,
as shown by the scriptures and the sciences, the genuine negro is an ape, and, like all the apes, he made
his appearance on the earth long prior to the creation
of man.

When the incidents related in this narration are
viewed in a rational way, it becomes plain that when
Noah awoke from his wine he was highly offended

at the indignities which Ham had put upon him; and that he desired to retaliate; and realizing that it would be more hurtful to Ham's feelings to say something offensive to Canaan, than if he said the same thing to Ham himself, Noah said: "Cursed be Canaan, a servant of servants shall he be unto his brethren." By way of further showing his resentment toward Ham, and his appreciation of the conduct of Shem and Japheth, Noah said, "God shall enlarge Japheth, and he shall dwell in the tents of Shem; and Canaan shall be his servant." That Noah's curse upon Canaan was merely the spiteful utterances of an old man just coming out of his cups, that God never sanctioned it, and that it had no effect upon Canaan and his descendants, is clearly proved by the fact that it was not fulfilled. On the contrary, the very reverse is true; for example: While the Israelites, who were the descendants of Shem, were servants to the Egyptians, who were the descendants of Ham, the Canaanites, the descendants of Canaan, whom Noah cursed, were the possessors of one of the richest countries on the globe, a country which God pronounced "a goodly land,"— "a land flowing with milk and honey."

Further proof that Noah's drunken utterances had no effect upon the relations of Canaan and his descendants to Shem and Japheth and their descendants, is shown by the language of Moses in explaining why God dispossessed the Canaanites of their country and gave it to Israel. It was not in fulfillment of Noah's curse upon Canaan, nor because of the "righteousness of the Israelites," but "for the wickedness of those nations." (*Deut.* ix, 4). And when the land of Canaan was given to the Israelites, they were not ordered to enslave them, but to "utterly destroy them, and leave nothing alive that breatheth." (*Deut.* xx, 16, 17). This absurd theory of the Hamitic origin of the negro offers the only explanation of the origin of the negro, which lays any claim to a scriptural basis. But, as a matter of fact this theory is as anti-scriptural, as it is unscientific and irrational; for this reason it has been repudiated by many of the leading theologians of our day. However, the majority of the laity adhere to it as one of the most cherished traditions of the church.

After the deluge, Noah and his family, with their negroes, and other domestic animals, domestic plants, metallic implements, etc., settled upon one of the continents and developed a great civilization. In the course of time they increased in number, and sent out colonies to other continents; these colonists carried with them their negroes, and other domestic animals, domestic plants, and all the appliances of civilized life, and developed those great civilizations, the remains of which are found on every continent of the earth. "And the sons of Noah that went forth of the ark were Shem, Ham, and Japheth. * * * These are the three sons of Noah, and by them was the whole earth overspread." (*Gen.* ix, 18, 19). "And the whole earth was of one language and one speech." (*Gen.* xi, 1).

All the facts indicate that for a long period after the deluge, the descendants of Noah respected the

design of God in creating man, lived in obedience to
Divine law, and maintained that dominion over the
negro in common with the rest of the animals, which
God designed them to have, and commanded them
to exercise.   This period is referred to in the ancient
book of the Quiches, the "Popul Vuh," as one in
which the *whites* and the *blacks* lived together "in
great peace," "and all seem to have spoken one language." (*Bancroft's Native Races*, Vol. V, p. 548).
This goes far to sustain the teachings of scripture
that, in the remote past, there was one universal
language; then the black servant spoke the language
of his white master.   It is significant that the *Popul
Vuh* mentions only the whites and blacks, which indicates that, at that remote period, they represented
the population of the earth; no mention is made of
any brown, red, or yellow inhabitants, and these
would certainly have been mentioned, had they then
existed.   The statement of the *Popul Vuh* also indicates that some ancient white was the author of this
old American book.

Further evidence of the presence of whites and
blacks in America in the remote past is furnished by
Mr. Donnelly who says, Quetzalcoatl, the leader of
the Nahua family, who was deified, is described as *a
white man*, with strong formation of body, broad forehead, large eyes, and *flowing beard*. (*Atlantis*, p.
165).

"On the monuments of Central America there
are representations of bearded men. How could the
beardless American Indian have imagined a bearded
race?" (*Ibid*). Prof. Wilson describes the hair of

the ancient Peruvians, as found upon their mummies, as "a lightish brown and of a fineness of texture which equals that of the Anglo-Saxon race." (*Ibid*). Hayward says that in the early part of the century, three mummies were found in a cave on the south side of the Cumberland river (Tennessee), who were buried in baskets as the Peruvians generally buried; their skin was white and their hair auburn and of a fine texture. (*Natural and Aboriginal History of Tennessee*). Mr. Donnelly says: "Very ancient ruins, showing remains of large and remarkable edifices, were found near Huamanga, and described by Ciecade Leon. The native traditions said this city was built by bearded white men who came there long before the Incas and established a settlement." (*Ibid*).

"Desare Charney has published in the *North American Review* for December, 1880, photographs of a number of idols exhumed at San Juan de Teotihuacan, which show striking negroid faces." (*Ibid*). Dr. Le Plongeon says: "Besides the sculptures of long-bearded men seen by the explorer at Chichen Itza, there were tall figures of people with small heads, thick lips and curly, short hair or wool, regarded as negroes. * * * We always see them as standard or parasol bearers, but never engaged in actual warfare." (*Maya Archæology*). Thus it is shown that in the remote past the relations between the whites and negroes in America was that of master and servant. We also find the white and the negro figured on the monuments of ancient Egypt, the latter "with halters about their necks," indicating that they were in servitude. (*Preadimites*, p. 206).

Some conception of the ancient civilization of America may be acquired from the fact that such high authorities as Charnay, Stevens, and Dupaix pronounce the architectural remains of Central America to equal in solidity, beauty, and finish the best specimens of Egypt, Rome, or Greece. "The Peruvians made large use of aqueducts, which they built with notable skill, using hewn stone and cement, and making them very substantial. One extended four hundred and fifty miles across sierras and over rivers. * * * The public roads of the Peruvians were most remarkable; they were built of masonry. One of these roads ran along the mountains through the whole length of the empire, from Quito to Chili; another, starting from this at Cuzco, went down to the coast, and extended northward to the equator. These roads were from twenty to twenty-five feet wide, were macadamized with pulverized stone mixed with lime and bituminous cement, and were walled in by strong walls more than a fathom in thickness. In many places these roads were cut for leagues through the rock; great ravines were filled up with solid masonry; rivers were crossed by suspension bridges, used here ages before their introduction into Europe." (*Ibid*).

Of Gran-Chimu, Mr. Donnelly says: "Its remains exist to-day, the wonder of the southern continent, covering not less than twenty square miles. Tombs, temples, and palaces arise on every hand, ruined but still traceable. Immense pyramidal

structures, some of them half a mile in circuit; vast
areas shut in by massive walls, each containing its
water tank, its shops, municipal edifices, and the
dwellings of its inhabitants, and each a branch of a
larger organization; prisons, furnaces for smelting
metals, and almost every concomitant of civilization
existed in the ancient Chimu capitol. One of the
pyramids, called the 'Temple of the Sun,' is 812 feet
long by 470 wide and 150 high. These vast structures have been in ruins for centuries." (*Ibid*).
The splendid civilization of the ancient Americans
extended from New York to Chili; and from the
Atlantic to the Pacific; it was of the same high order
as those of Java, India, Egypt, Rome, Greece, etc.

The magnitude of those superb old civilizations,
extending over the various continents, indicates that
their development was the work of ages; and that
the nations which developed them must have numbered their whites and negroes by the hundreds of
millions. What became of them? What became of
those hundreds of millions of whites? They have
long since disappeared from three of the five continents; a mere remnant of their white descendants
are left, and these are practically confined to Europe
and America. What became of those hundreds of
millions of negroes? They have disappeared from
four of the five continents. Their pure-blooded descendants are now confined to a few tribes in Africa.
Where did all these so-called brown, red, and yellow
"races of men" come from which we find in possession of the remains of these great civilizations, and
which in the sum of their characters are not distin-

guishable from the known offspring of whites and
negroes in our midst? These miserable, worthless .
creatures never developed the civilization they possess, and as a rule they have no idea who did. In
many cases the remains of superb civilizations are
found in sections which are now inhabited by wild,
hunting tribes of savages.

The atheist, with his theory of development can
throw no light on these grand old civilizations; their
very existence goes far to prove the falsity of his
theory. Ages ago these superb old civilizations were
the centres of wealth, culture, and refinement; their
crumbling ruins, now often found in pathless jungles,
or in barren wastes—the abodes of barbarians and
savages—tells a tale of retrogression that is frightful to contemplate.

When we appeal to the scriptures for information as to the architects of these ancient civilizations,
we are taught that Noah and his family were the
finest specimens of antediluvian culture and refinement; that they built the ark, and preserved the
animals and the domestic plants from the deluge; that
they transmitted to their descendants their knowledge and refinement; and that by them "was the
whole earth overspread." That they were whites is
shown by the fact that all the great civilized nations
of antiquity were their descendants, and were whites.
When we appeal to the sciences for light on this subject, we are taught that, "No negro civilization has
ever appeared; no Mongolian one has greatly developed." "The white is pre-eminently, the man of
civilization." When we appeal to profane history we

are taught that the white has been in all ages of his history what he is to-day—the great, building, developing power of the earth. When we appeal to tradition, we find that in many cases the savages now in possession of these old civilizations have traditions that their ancestors were *white*. When we appeal to the monuments, we find the bearded white figured on monuments as old as the edifices and other evidences of these by-gone civilizations, and the whole crumbling into decay from age and neglect. And, as has been shown, the negro also, is sometimes figured on these ancient monuments; and we have also shown that, in those remote ages the white and the negro held the same relation to each other that they have in all subsequent ages—the white was the master— the *thinker;* the negro was the servant—the *worker.* If we desired further evidence of the existence of the whites and the negroes on the various continents, in the remote past, it is found in the fact that the so-called brown, red, and yellow races, now in possession of the remains of these old civilizations, are, in the sum of their characters, identical with the known offspring of whites and negroes in our midst.

No naturalist will deny that Blumenbach's division of the so-called "human species" into "five races of men," was based strictly upon geographical lines, and not upon what the atheist would term *racial distinctions.* In Europe the complexions range from pure white to dark brown. In Africa they range from shades so light as to be almost white, to brown, red, yellow, and pure black. In Asia they range from light yellow to brown and black. In

Oceanica the complexions are light yellow, copper-colored, and dark brown.

In America, prior to its discovery by Columbus, the complexions ranged from nearly white in the Mandans, Tuscaroras, Zunians, etc., to brown, red, yellow, and black. Among the Mandans were found blue, gray, and hazel eyes, while many had hair that was white from infancy to old age. (*Catlin*). Among the so-called Malay, Indian, and Mongolian races are to be found individuals and tribes whose resemblance to each other is so strong as to make it impossible to distinguish them. And we might add representatives from Southern Europe and from certain African tribes. In support of our position we quote from Fontaine, who says: "If a congregation of twelve representatives from Malacca, China, Japan, Mongolia, Sandwich Islands, Chili, Peru, Brazil, Chickasaws, Comanches, etc., were dressed alike, or undressed and unshaven, the most skillful anatomist could not, from their appearance, separate them." (*How the World was Peopled*, pp. 147, 244). Fontaine might well have added representatives of our mulattoes to his list, as shown by the following:

"BELLE WEDS A NEGRO.

"White Girl Bought a Country Home Where She Lives with Her Dusky Groom.

"SPECIAL TO THE POST-DISPATCH.

"PHILADELPHIA, May 4.—Miss Emma Bethel, whose father was a physician of note, and who was a leader in exclusive society in West Philadelphia, has been married to Howard Lee, colored, formerly

employed as butler by John C. Uhle, a relative of
the young woman.   While residing with the Uhles
several months ago Miss Bethel met Lee, who acted
as her coachman when she drove out to dispense
charity.   Mr. Uhle heard rumors that the coachman
was in love with Miss Bethel, and discharged him.
Not long afterwards Miss Bethel, who had independent means, announced that she intended to
purchase a summer residence in Hammonton, N. J.
After Miss Bethel took possession of the house, Lee
also appeared.   Shortly Miss Bethel and he called
upon the Rev. Mr. Albrum and were married.   Mrs.
Lee is pretty and is 30 years old.   While living here
she was a liberal contributor to the Episcopal
Church, which she attended, and was active in the
work of the parish.   Lee is tall and quite dusky.   *
*   *   A dispatch from Hammonton, N. J., says that
Mr. and Mrs. Lee live on the outskirts of the town.
The man has passed as an Indian, Mrs. Lee said
to-day."   (*St. Louis Post-Dispatch*, May 4, 1901).

Thus, we find that we are producing Indians
here in the United States, by amalgamation between
whites and negroes.   But this is merely the fullfil-
ment of the predictions of the most competent observers.   Referring to the writings of Mr. Reclus,
and l'Abbe Brasseur de Bonbourg, Quatrefages says:
"Both these authors seem to admit that at the end
of a given time, whatever be their origin, all the descendants of whites or of negroes who have emigrated
to America will become red-skins."   (*The Human
Species*, p. 255).   What is the "red-skins?"   Simply
a *savage*.   Thus, under the demoralizing, degrading

influences of our social, political, and religious systems, we are descending to *savagery*—to ruin in time and to hades in eternity.   Further evidence of this is found in the following:

"SPECIAL TO THE POST-DISPATCH:

"CHICAGO, July 17—'The American people in their physical character are turning more and more like Indians every day. The only thing that prevents the people of the United States from becoming exactly similar to the nomadic tribes of Indians in facial characteristics is the intermarriage between residents of this country and emigrants from foreign lands.' This is the statement made by Prof. Frederick Starr to his class in anthropology at the University of Chicago to-day. 'If the immigration laws should once be strictly enforced, a few years would see us all Indians. Once make the cry general that America is being used as the dumping ground of European nations, and so stir up public spirit as to exclude foreign elements, and it would only take a few years for the Indian to haunt his old time pastures again.'"   (*St. Louis Post-Dispatch*, July 17, 1901).

Though perhaps not intended as such, it is nevertheless plain that no more severe arraignment of our social, political, and religious systems; no greater exposure of the emptiness of our accustomed boast, that "we are an enlightened, progressive people;" no more positive proof that we are in reality a *dying nation*—that we are descending to savagery— than is found in the fact stated by Prof. Starr, that "the American people in their physical characters are becoming more and more like Indians every day;" that *the only thing* that prevents us from becoming Indians is our intermarriage with emigrants from *foreign lands* and that if the foreign element was excluded, "it would only take a few years for the Indian to haunt his old time pastures again." In other words, but for the influence of white stock from Europe, we would soon become Indians, and consequently *savages*. This humiliating admission, coming from a distinguished American anthropologist, should arouse us to a sense of our danger.

Prof. Starr offers no explanation of why the American people are turning to Indians, neither does he suggest a remedy; he merely intimates that we are kept white by the inflow of Europeans; but he fails to show that we draw our white stock only from northern and central Europe, while unfortunately the great bulk of emigrants come from the dark, mixed-blooded nations of southern Europe. It is easy to see that our population of supposed whites is steadily growing darker, and that our population of supposed negroes is steadily growing correspondingly lighter. This is due solely to amalgamation, which tends to mix all the white blood with all the black blood. When this disastrous result is consummated, the population of this country will settle down to about the level of the Indian; in sections where the white blood largely predominates, we will duplicate the Mandans, Tuscaroras, Zunians, etc. In sections where the negro blood largely predominates, we will duplicate the black tribes of California, the Kaws of Kansas, the Carribs, etc. Under the curses of God, our civilization will be laid in ruins, and our descendants of a few centuries hence will be naked savages in the woods—the *Indian will haunt his old time pastures again.*

The fact that, by a few centuries of amalgamation between whites and negroes, we have produced Indians, and that, as a result of this loathsome crime, our whole population is becoming "more and more like Indians every day," is the most positive proof that the original Indian is simply the result of amalgamation between the whites and negroes who settled upon this continent after the deluge. It is an affront to our intelligence to ask us to believe that, in the remote past, the same class of creatures were produced by development from the ape that we now produce by amalgamation between whites and negroes. "Besides Indians, we are producing Malays by the tens of thousands; the absolute similarity between the characters of many of our mulattoes and the Filipinos has led the American soldiers in the Philippines to pronounce the Filipinos *negroes.* Aguinaldo can be duplicated a thousand times over among our mulattoes. In addition to this, a close observer can see good specimens of Chinese, Japanese, Koreans, etc., among our mulattoes. Yet the atheists have deceived the whole world into believing that these so-called Malays, Indians, and Mongolians are lower races of men which have descended from the ape in remote ages, and which, in their various stages of barbarism and savagery, present so many cases of *arrested development.* Surely, there are not two ways of producing these creatures, one by amalgamation between whites and negroes, the other by development from the ape.

As shown in a previous chapter, the pure white and the pure black—man and the negro—are the originals whom God made; this is proved by the fact that neither can be produced by any cross, and neither can *survive a cross*. The progeny resulting from any cross to which either man or the negro is subjected are neither man nor negro, but *mixed-bloods*. On the other hand, we have demonstrated here in the United States that the physical and mental characters of the so-called brown, red, and yellow races can be produced by centuries of amalgamation between whites and negroes.

Amalgamation is one of the most stealthy crimes, often requiring centuries for the accomplishment of its work of absorbing and destroying both the whites and the negroes in a nation. When this crime begins, the relation of master and servant usually exists between the whites and negroes, and it is at first confined to the white males and the black females. Upon reaching maturity a greater or less number of their mixed-blooded progeny, both males and females, will mate with negroes; besides more or less of the white males will have paramours among both negroes and mixed-bloods. The negro thus becomes the prey not only of the white males, but the mixed-bloods of both male and female. Under these conditions, it is simply a question of time when the negroes will be absorbed and destroyed, and their descendants become mixed-bloods. We have demonstrated this in the United States. The systematic importation of negroes from Africa to this country began in A. D. 1619; though a few negroes were imported here by the Spaniards as early as the 16th century. Amalgamation at once began, and to-day there is not a *pure blooded neqro* in America; the last one has disappeared from this continent, and their descendants are all mixed-bloods; however black their skin, or however woolly their hair may be, they will present in some character the evidence of crossing. Since amalgamation with the whites and mixed-bloods has destroyed the pure negro in our midst, it is easy to see that amalgamation between the whites and mixed-bloods will destroy the pure whites. When this dire calamity is accomplished, this continent will again be populated with mixed-bloods— Indians. The fact that amalgamation will destroy both the pure white and the pure negro is easily demonstrated. Let a pure white take a pure negress to wife and raise a family; when the white father and negro mother dies, the pure white and the pure negro in that family are gone; their progeny are mixed-bloods; it is plain that this would hold good with a nation or a continent as the result of amalgamation between whites and negroes; though in the case of a nation it might require centuries. Let us bear in mind that neither the white nor the negro can absorb the mixed-bloods; on the contrary, the mixed-bloods absorb both the white and the negro when either are brought in sexual contact with them; their offspring are mixed-bloods, without reference to whether they are mated with whites, negroes or

mixed-bloods. For this reason, they are a dangerous, destructive element, and one which God detests.

Woman, the female side or part of man, is the
vital point of the Adamic Creation; and so long as
the marriages of the Adamic females of a nation are
confined to Adamic males, the Adamic stock of that
nation cannot be absorbed by amalgamation. While
amalgamation between the Adamic males, negresses
and mixed-blooded females is being carried on, the
Adamic females, declining to descend to the low level
of the negro and mixed-bloods, are confining their
marriage relations to the Adamic males, and are producing pure Adamic offspring to much the same extent
as if no amalgamation was going on. But unfortunately, the mixed-blooded progeny of the Adamic males
and negresses and mixed-blooded females, by mating
continuously with Adamic males, grow whiter and
whiter, and their hair longer and straighter with each
succeeding generation, until finally it would be difficult for the ordinary observer to distinguish them
from pure whites. They may then remove to some
distant section of country and pass themselves off as
pure whites, and inter-marry with Adamic females.
The offspring of these unhallowed unions will marry
pure whites, and perhaps never know that they are
of negro extraction; but the Adamic stock will be
absorbed and destroyed as far as they inter-marry
with them. In the meantime, God may visit His
curse upon them in the form of famine, pestilence,
war, etc., to force them to abandon their evil way;
should they persist in it, He may destroy them and
lay their civilizations in ruins; or, He may abandon

them to the natural results of their crime; in this event the negroes will first be absorbed by association with the white males and the mixed-bloods; the whites will then be absorbed through their associations with the mixed-bloods. When this occurs, that nation's relation to God, its relations to the earth and the animals has completely changed. Its former population of whites and negroes were parts of God's Creation, while their mixed-blooded progeny have resulted from the violation of His law. This change, which required centuries for its accomplishment, was so gradual as to pass unnoticed at the time; and the cause of it was never investigated and ascertained. When the whites are all destroyed, their country, with its national name, wealth, religion, their knowledge of the arts and sciences, is inherited by their mixed-blooded descendants; when the white blood largely predominates in them, they may, under favorable circumstances, retain more or less of their inherited civilization for an indefinite period, but they add nothing to it; and when they lose an art, or any part of their inherited knowledge, they never regain it; such was the case with the Mexicans, Peruvians, Chinese, Japanese, Hindoos, Greeks, Turks, Egyptians, etc. But in most cases they are driven from their civilization in the forest, and, with no capacity to develop a civilization, they descend to savagry; this is shown in the case of the Navajoes. They were an agricultural community when the Spaniards entered Mexico. When attacked by the Spaniards they abandoned their homes and fled to the mountains; they made no effort to develop a civilization, but became a wild, blood-thirsty band of savages, and have so remained. (*Baldwin, Ancient America,* p. 68). This explains the origin of the wild hunting tribes of browns, reds, and yellows which are found upon the various continents.

Under the influence of the law of heredity, any physical or mental character is transmittable. "Intellectual qualities are transmitted, as well as physical characters." (*Topinard*). When amalgamation between the Adamic males and the negresses and mixed-blooded females in a nation is carried on until the mixed-blooded males are able to impose themselves on the Adamic females as whites and inter-marry with them the Adamic Creation is successfully assailed at its vital point—the *female;* and only the intervention of the Almighty could prevent its Adamic stock in that nation from being ultimately destroyed. The false teaching of atheism that the negro is a lower "race of man" is now beginning to degrade woman to the level of the negro; here and there in this country Adamic females are marrying those whom they recognize as negroes; but to the honor of the sex it may be said that the women who thus lower themselves are either moral degenerates or religious fanatics.

The fact that the negro possesses the moral faculty to some extent is regarded by many as evidence that he is a man—that he has a soul. But before hastily deciding that this is so, we should remember that there are three distinct creations— matter, mind, and soul; and that every thing in the material universe is a part of one or the other of these

three creations. This being true, we should first ascertain which of these creations the moral faculty
is a part of. Since it does not exist in the plant it is
evidently not a part of the matter creation. Hence,
it is either a part of the mind creation, or the soul
creation. If it is a part of the soul creation it is peculiar to man. If it is a part of the mind creation
the animals share it with man. It is the moral faculty which enables man to distinguish between right
and wrong; that it is right to obey, and wrong to
disobey God. But for the presence of this faculty
in man, he could not justly be held responsible for
his acts. The same is true of the animals; it is the
moral faculty in them that enables them to understand that it is right to obey, and wrong to disobey
their master. Then, if by accident, or disease, the
mind of either man or the animal is impaired, the
moral faculty is correspondingly impaired; if, as in
the case of an insane man, woman, or animal, the
mind is affected to such an extent as to temporarily
or permanently destroy the reasoning faculty, the
moral faculty is temporarily or permanently destroyed, as the case may be; the very moment that
either man or the animal ceases to be a rational
being, he ceases to be a moral being. Then, if his
mind is restored, his moral faculty is at once restored; and again, the moral, like any attribute of
the mind, may be cultivated and developed, or it
may be neglected and dwarfed; this is easily seen by
comparing the cultivated with the uncultivated man,
or the domesticated with the undomesticated animal. Thus, it is shown that the moral faculty is a

part of the mind creation, which is common to man and the animals. Hence, the mere fact that the negro possesses the moral faculty in any degree is no evidence that he is a man, or that he has a soul. The same is true of the mixed-bloods. The moral faculty being a part of the intellectual, it is transmittible. Hence, the mixed-blood might in some cases inherit the high moral characters of the white, together with other intellectual qualities. Quatrefages, in discussing the results of crossing, says: "In the formation of a new being, the action of heredity is divided into as many *cases* as there are *charters* to transmit. Both father and mother tend to reproduce themselves in their offspring; there is, consequently a struggle between both natures. But the battle, if we may use the expression, results in a number of single combats in which each parent may be in turn victor or vanquished. * * We know how far this victory can go, and how the two natures can, so to speak, divide the product between them. Lislet Geoffroy, entirely a negro physically, though entirely a white in character, intelligence, and aptitudes, is a striking example of it." (*The Human Species*, p. 268). This explains why a mixed-blood sometimes possesses fine intellectual qualities occasionally allied with rather elevated moral qualities; these were inherited from some Adamic ancestor; but as a rule, the intellectual and moral characters of the mixed-bloods approximate those of their negro ancestors, and are of a very low order.

The following estimates of brain weights, collected by Sanford B. Hunt, of the Federal army during the late civil war in the United States, show that the blood of the white tends to elevate, and that the blood of the negro tends to lower the mentality of individuals, tribes and nations:

	Weight of Brain. Grammes.
"24 whites, ...	1424
25 three parts white, ...	1390
47 half white, or mulattoes, . .	1334
51 one-quarter white, ...	1319
95 an eighth white, ...	1308
22 a sixteenth white, ...	1280
141 pure negroes, ...	1331 "

—(*Topinard, Anthropology*, p. 312).

Commenting on these estimates, Topinard says: "This would lead us to believe that the mixed-breeds assimilate the bad more readily than the good." (*Ibid*).

These estimates are quoted by Winchell, Quatrefages, and other scientists. Though fair to the negro, and the grades of mixed-bloods referred to, it is plain that they place the white at a disadvantage, since they are evidently confined to the common white soldiers; the higher grades of officers, and the most intellectual among the citizens of the United States were not represented; if they had been, the average brain weight of the whites would have been raised to the average of Noachites—1500 grammes. However, Hunt's estimates show that man (the white) is a distinct creation, and that whites and negroes are not different races of one species of animal. Breeders who attempt to produce new varieties by crossing, experience great difficulty because of the disposition of the offspring to revert to one or the other of its parent stocks. But as shown by Hunt's tables, if the offspring of man and the negro were mated with pure negroes for ages, they would never revert to the negro; but while approximating a lower grade of ape would retain the characters of mixed-bloods. The same result must necessarily ensue if the offspring of whites and negroes were mated continuously with whites for ages; they could never revert to the pure white; the ape can never be bred out, nor the soul creation bred in, the offspring of man and the negro; though they might take on more and more the physical and mental characters of the white, they must remain mixed-bloods. The fact that the mixed-bloods cannot revert to either of their parent stocks proves that whites and negroes are not of the same *kind of flesh.*

If the white and the negro were different races of one species of animal, their immediate offspring would take a position in point of brain weight, midway between the two, with a brain weight of 1,377½ grammes; but, as Hunt shows, the half white has an average brain weight of 1,334 grammes; this is only three grammes in excess of that of the negro, and 90 grammes less than that of the white soldier. Hunt also shows that if the half white is mated with the pure negro, the brain weight of their offspring—the one-quarter white, is lowered to 1,319 grammes; this is 12 grammes less than that of the pure negro; and if the one-quarter white is mated with the pure negro, the brain weight of their offspring—the one-eighth white, is reduced to 1,308 grammes; and if the one-eighth white is mated with the pure negro, the brain weight of their offspring—the one-sixteenth white, falls to 1,280 grammes. This is 23 grammes below that of the pure negro. This indicates that, with this rapid fall of brain weight with each succeeding generation, and the process continued, the brain weight of their offspring would ultimately fall to the level of that of the gorilla, which is 600 grammes, according to Huxley.

Thus is shown that the mixed-bloods, in whom the negro blood largely predominates over that of the white, is more degraded and ape-like in their physical and mental organisms, and consequently more depraved in their modes of life, customs, etc., than the pure negro. This explains the following facts stated by Winchell: "The measurements already given show the Australian to possess an organism quite inferior to that of the negro. In intelligence he is said to be so low as to be unable to count five. Of the Aetas of the Philippines, De la Geronniere says they gave him the impression of being a great tribe of monkeys; their voices recalled the short cry of these animals, and their movements strengthened the analogy. * * * Some of the American tribes remain at the lowest point of degradation. This is the case with the Fuegians, and the Botecudos of Brazil have often been cited. Of the latter, Lallemand says: 'I am sadly convinced that they are monkeys with two hands.'" (*Ibid*, pp. 267, 268).

The above facts, when viewed in the light of

Hunt's estimates, show the effects of amalgamation upon cerebral development, and clearly shows how these so-called brown, red, and yellow races originated. When the white is mated with the negro, the brain weight of their offspring is neither that of the white nor that of the negro; the same is true of their physical characters, they are neither white nor black, but some shade of brown, red, or yellow. The half white, when viewed from the atheist standpoint, and compared with their white and black ancestors, presents all the physical characters of a new "race of men," with a brain weight of 1,334 grammes. Say there were 3,000 of these half whites, and that 1,000 of them found mates among themselves; their offspring would be half white with a brain weight of 1,334 grammes. Let another thousand of the half whites mate with pure whites, their progeny would be three-quarters white, with a brain weight of 1,390 grammes. We would thus produce another so-called "race of men." Let the remaining 1,000 half whites mate with pure negroes; their offspring would be one-quarter white, with a brain weight of 1,319 grammes. We would then have another so-called "race of men," making in all three new so-called "races of men," as widely different in their physical as in their mental qualities. If each of these three classes of creatures were placed upon an island in the ocean, and thus separated from each other and isolated from the rest of the world, and the marriage relations of each confined to their own class, they would ultimately settle down to some fixed type. It is easy to see that the number of these so-called "races of men" could be increased to any desired extent by mating these three classes of mixed-bloods with pure whites, with pure negroes, and with mixed-bloods of different grades; the progeny of each cross would present a new "race of men" in the eyes of the atheist.

Hunt's estimates show there is a differrence of 93 grammes, between the brain weight of the white soldier and the negro; while there is a difference of 110 grammes, between the brain weight of the three-quarter white and the one-sixteenth white. Thus, the difference in brain weight between the extremes of mixed-bloods is greater than that between the whites and the negroes. Hence, at this stage, we might confine ourselves to the mixed-bloods in our efforts to produce new "races of men" by crossing, and still have a wider range than we had with the whites and negroes with which we began. However, we might largely increase this range by mating the progeny of three-quarter whites with whites, and by mating the progeny of the one-sixteenth white with negroes. In the offspring of the former, the increase of brain weight would correspond with the increase of white blood; in the offspring of the latter the decrease of brain weight would correspond with the increase of negro blood. These differences in their mental qualities, would be accompanied with corresponding differences in their physical qualities. The rapid reduction in brain weight which each infusion of negro blood, as shown by Hunt's estimates, demonstrates that, if the progeny of the one-sixteenth white were mated continually with pure negroes for centuries, they would ultimately fall as low in point of brain weight as the diminutive Hindoos, who are quoted by Huxley at 27 ounces.

Thus it is shown: (1) That all of the so-called brown, red, and yellow "races" to be found on the different continents can be produced by amalgamation between whites and negroes; and this is the only process by which they can be produced. This explanation of their origin is sustained by the scriptures and the sciences; arrayed against i is the undemonstrated and undemonstrable theory of the atheist that these degraded creatures developed from the ape. (2) That these so-called brown, red, and yellow "races," which apparently span the gulf between the whites and the negro, and which shade up from almost pure black to almost pure white, thus giving the Theory of Descent the little plausibility it enjoys, are really the result of amalgamation between whites and negroes. (3) That if all these mixed-bloods were destroyed, and only the white and the negro remained, no advocate of the Bible, however partial he might be to the negro, would consent to believe that the white and the negro are the progeny of one primitive pair; neither would the most avowed opponent of the Bible consent to believe that there could possibly be such a thing as a "human species" composed of only two "races of men," the one *white* and the other *black*, and in absolute contrast to each other in their physical and mental organisms and in their modes of life, aspirations, customs, habits, manners, gestures, etc.

We have now shown: (1) That after the deluge

Noah and his family, with their negroes and other domestic animals, domestic plants, metallic implements and all the appliances of civilized life, settled upon one of the continents and developed a great civilization which finally spread to other continents. "By them was the whole earth overspread." They were one people and spoke one language. "Behold the people is one and they have all one language." (*Gen.* xi, 6). *The whole earth was of one language and one speech.* (2) That Noah and his family were white. (3) That their white descendants have disappeared from three of the five continents, leaving a mere remnant in parts of Europe and America. (4) That their negroes have disappeared from four of the five continents, the remnant of them being confined to a few tribes in Africa. (5) That the greater part of their once splendid civilizations are now in ruins. (6) That now the great bulk of their descendants on the various continents are brown, red, and yellow barbarians and savages, which, in the sum of their characters, are *identical* with the known offspring of whites and negroes in our midst.

These facts indicate that, after living obediently to the laws of God for a long period after the deluge, the descendants of Noah forgot God, and their obligations to Him, and violated His law by descending to amalgamation with their negroes; then the smiles of heaven in which they had prospered were withdrawn, and the curses of God were visited upon them in the form of war, famines, pestilence, etc., to compel them to abandon their wicked, destructive course. But they persisted in it with the results above shown. In order to appreciate the value of these great truths, we must disabuse our minds of the false teachings of atheism with reference to man's development; we must accept the teachings of the Bible that man was created *man;* that he was created "a little lower than the angels;" that he has not *developed,* but *retrograded.*

CHAPTER XVII.

AMALGAMATION THE PARENT OF ATHEISM AND IDOLATRY.—THE MISSION OF JESUS CHRIST.

The course of the modern amalgamationist, and the origin and spread of amalgamation in modern times, throws a flood of light on the ancient amalgamationist, and the spread of amalgamation in ancient times. When amalgamation began in this country, the man who was so degraded as to take a negress to wife was looked upon with scorn and contempt, and was ostracised from the society of decent people; and this is the case in some sections to-day. Many of the States of this government enacted laws against amalgamation. But at the same time transient amours were tolerated; this resulted in the utter destruction of our genuine negroes, and the production of an immense mixed-blooded population that will yet absorb the whites if they are allowed to remain here.

When viewed in the light of these modern events, it is plain that the first amalgamationists were severely denounced and punished by their neighbors who were aware that amalgamation was the most infamous crime known to the law of God, and that its indulgence had led to the destruction of the antediluvians. Under these circumstances it would seem only natural that those ancient amalga-

469

mationists, who were determined to pursue their sinful course, should desire that some semblance of respectability be given their acts; the only way possible to do this was by devising some iniquitous scheme by which the negro and the mixed-bloods would be received into the family of man; for at that remote period, and for long afterwards, the negro was known to be a beast—*the beast of the field.* Doubtless the God-fearing people of that age did their utmost to stamp out amalgamation; but despite their efforts it spread until in many sections of the earth the pure whites and pure negroes were destroyed and their country populated with mixed-bloods; general demoralization, and the increase of every form of crime, kept pace with the rapid growth of amalgamation; this demoralizing condition of affairs gave the amalgamationist his opportunity; and he availed himself of it by renouncing God, and repudiating the doctrine of Creation, and devised the theory of development. Taking advantage of the existence of the various tribes and nations of mixed-bloods, he combined them with the whites and negroes as different "races" of the "species—man." By this means the negro and the mixed-bloods were thrust into the family of man, where they have since remained, in contempt of God's plan of Creation, and in wanton violation of His law. Thus *amalgamation became the parent of atheism,* with its theory of *development.* This theory gradually broadened out, and finally crystalized into the general theory of development, which attributes the whole phenomena of the universe to *natural causes.*

The literature of these ancient peoples, like their civilizations, has long since crumbled into dust. Hence, it is impossible for us at this late day to ascertain the exact date upon which this crime was committed. However, we have reliable data which proves that it occurred between the Deluge and the birth of Abraham. The theory of development doubtless existed together with idolatry among the antediluvians; if so, the evolutionist, the idolator, with the amalgamationist and mixed bloods, were destroyed by the Deluge. The fragment of Plato's history of Atlantis contains the first mention of the "races of men" to be found in profane history. Plato lived 300 years B. C.; he was the descendant of Solon, the great law-giver of Athens. Solon spent ten years in Egypt, where he first heard of Atlantis and the records concerning it to be found in the sacred registers of Egypt. He was granted permission to examine them, and obtained the data from which to write a history of Atlantis. But Solon died before completing his work. His data seems to have fallen into the hands of Plato, who began to write a history of Atlantis; but after writing a description of the continent, its population, products, wealth, religion, culture, power, etc., Plato died, leaving a mere fragment of history, which, if finished, would have been an invaluable contribution to the literature of the world. The sacred registers of Egypt were so much more ancient than the historical records of the Greeks, that an Egyptian priest said to Solon: "You have no antiquity of history, and no history of antiquity." These terms of the atheist

could only have originated in the atheistic school of
development; they are always employed by the advocates of the theory of man's descent from the ape.
However, their presence in the sacred registers of
ancient Egypt indicates that the theory of development was universally taught in that remote period,
in perhaps as systematized and elaborated a form as
it is in our day; and it is possible that it had existed
among the ancients from a period so remote that it
is doubtful whether the Egyptians of Solon's day
were aware of the time or place of its origin.

The continued existence of this degrading, destructive theory was insured by man's criminal lust,
to which it owed its origin; it was universally taught
in the ages preceding the birth of Christ, and forms
the basis of the theory of development, as shown by
the statement of Prof. Haeckel, who says: "We will
here mention only that as early as the seventh century before Christ, the representatives of the Ionian
philosophy of nature, Thales, Anaximenes, and Anaximander, of Miletus, and more especially Anaximander, established important principles of our modern monism. Their teaching pointed to a uniform
law of nature as the basis of the various phenomena,
a unity of all nature and a continual change of forms.
Anaximander considered that the animalcules in
water came into existence through the influence of
the warmth of the sun, and assumed that man had
developed out of fish-like ancestors. At a later date
also we find in the natural philosophy of Heraclitus,
and Empidocles, as well as in the writings of Dem-
ocritus and Aristotle, many allusions to conceptions

which we regard as the fundamental supports of our modern theory of development. Empedocles points out that things which appear to have been made for a definite purpose may have arisen out of no purpose whatever. Aristotle assumes spontaneous generation as the natural manner in which the lower organisms came into existence." (*History of Creation*, Vol. I, pp. 78, 79).

Thus, we find that in remote ages it was taught that man is merely a species of animal which is composed of races of men who trace their descent through the lower organisms to "fish-like ancestors," themselves the result of *spontaneous generation*. Thus, the theory of these ancient atheists, like that of the modern atheists, taught that from man's "fish-like ancestors" on up to, and including man, there is just *one flesh* in different stages of development. Hence, according to this theory, all flesh is *akin*. This theory proposed to degrade man to the level of the brute, by establishing a blood relationship between man and the animals. It was this theory that practically swept monotheism from the earth prior to the birth of Abraham. It was to counteract the degrading influences of this theory that God raised up the nation of Israel; and when the Israelites became the victims of this theory, as they often did, God sent prophet after prophet to induce them to renounce this pernicious theory which degrades man to the level of the negro and the mixed-bloods. But, disregarding every influence that was brought to bear, they adhered to this theory and the demoralizing influences which it exerts, until every circle of society was permeated and corrupted by it. Then God sent His son, Jesus Christ, but, like many of the prophets who preceded Him on this mission, He lost His life in the vain effort to eradicate from the minds of men this demoralizing theory, and counteract its degrading influences. In Paul's day the theory of development threatened to sweep the church from the narrative of creation upon which the Saviour established it, and land it a wreck on the quicksands of atheism and negroism where we find it to-day. It was in his fierce struggle with this theory and its false teachings that Paul exclaimed: "All flesh is not the same flesh; but there is one kind of flesh of man, another flesh of beasts, another of fishes, and another of birds." But despite every effort to eradicate it, this destructive theory has survived to our day, and is now universally taught and accepted by professed Christians; and as a result, the negro and the mixed-bloods are now recognized as lower races of men who must be developed and christianized. This is a plain violation of the law of God. The negro, being an ape, was not involved in the fall of man. Hence, he is not included in the plan which God devised for man's redemption. The mixed-bloods were not in existence at the time of Adam's *transgression;* they are simply the ultimate result of his violation of God's law in descending to social equality with the negro in Eden.

Prior to the creation of man, the negro had no more idea of God or of Divine worship than a gorilla. But the link of kinship which God established between Himself and man, forms a bond of love and sympathy between them which makes it possible for man to recognize the existence of, respect, and worship, an all-wise, all-powerful, but invisible God.   But no kinship, and no bond of love and sympathy exists between God and the mixed-bloods.   Hence, though these creatures inherit from their white ancestors a belief in God and a pure form of religious worship, they can not long retain it when left to themselves; when relieved of the influence of the white, they soon lose all confidence in an invisible God; they want a God that they can see; and in the absence of such an one they make for themselves Gods of stone, wood, or metal, or deify some animate or some inanimate object as the case may be.   Hayti illustrates the truth of this.   The "black republic" of Hayti was formally acknowledged by England in 1825.   That rich, productive island was turned over to the negroes and mixed-bloods: they were provided with organized political and religious systems, with schools, churches, and all the appliances of civilization; yet in spite of the efforts of both Catholics and Protestants, they have descended to fetish worship.   They not only sacrificed their own offspring to snakes, but they eat the sacrifice; their disgusting ceremonies end in a drunken debauch which is characterized by the most indiscriminate intercourse between the sexes. (Sir Spencer St. John, *Hayti or The Black Republic*).   This enables us to realize that the offspring of whites and negroes ultimately descend to idolatry; though there are many tribes of mixed-bloods who have lost all knowledge of a God, and have no form of religious worship. Thus, strange as it may seem, amalgamation is not only the parent of atheism, which denies the existence of God, but is also the parent of idolatry with its worship of many gods.

This reveals the startling truth that the idolatry for which God punished Israel and her neighboring nations, had its origin in amalgamation. When the whites of a nation are absorbed by amalgamation, their mixed-blooded descendants ultimately descend to idolary; this idolatry spreads to the mixed-bloods of neighboring nations, and may even spread among the whites of those nations, as shown in the case of Solomon. Solomon took wives of the mixed-blooded females of the Egyptians, Ammonites, Moabites, Edomites, Zidonians, and Hittites. These were nations with which God forbade Israel to inter-marry; and Solomon's mixed-blooded wives led him into idolatry. (See *I Kings*, xi). Ahab did the same. (See *I Kings*, xvi). When idolatry first enters a nation it appeals to the depraved nature of the mixed-bloods. The men have no confidence in the idol; but the obscene rites, and the indiscriminate intercourse between the sexes which usually characterizes the worship of idols, appeals to their lusts, and in order to gratify these unrestrained they renounce God, abandon His worship, and embrace idolatry. Their descendants are raised in the midst of amalgamation and idolatry; and in the course of time they lose all knowledge of the true God, and become heathen. Hence, the heathen are not negroes; neither are they mixed-bloods. The heathen are pure-blooded descendants of Adam, who have lost their knowledge of God through their ancestors' descent to amalgamation and idolatry; and it was to these that God sent the prophets, the Saviour, and His disciples to reclaim.

When, after the deluge, amalgamation began among the descendants of Noah, it continued to spread, destroying the whites and negroes in nation after nation, and populating them with mixed-bloods until, in the course of time, the earth was in much the same condition that it was prior to the deluge; as amalgamation increased, the mixed-bloods increased at the expense of the pure whites and the pure negroes; and atheism and idolatry, the twin crimes which owe their birth to amalgamation, increased at the expense of monotheism. This struggle for supremacy between monotheism on the one side and atheism and idolatry on the other, finally culminated in war. In our next book of this series we shall show that in these great religious wars, which lasted for centuries, and in which every continent was involved, the earth was drenched in blood. In this long, unequal struggle monotheism was practically swept from the globe, and the sacred writings, which had been handed down from Adam through Noah and his family, were all destroyed. When this sad event occurred God's plan of Creation as revealed to Adam survived only in tradition, and these traditions in their oral transit through the centuries became so corrupted with errors and superstitions as to be practically worthless; these old corrupted traditions linger now in the cosmogonies of the Chinese, Hindoos, Babylonians, Egyptians, etc.

The God-believing, God-loving people, widely scattered among the remnant of pure whites, became more and more powerless to withstand the overwhelming tide of atheism, negroism and idolatry that had practically swept monotheism from the globe; and the destruction of both man and the negro, and the consequent destruction of God's plan of creation, was as seriously threatened as before the deluge. In this grave emergency God conceived the design of raising up for Himself a great nation— a *chosen people*—a people whom He desired should be *peculiar*, in that they would never descend to amalgamation, atheism, and idolatry. In the execution of this design God selected Abraham, of Uz, in Chaldea, and said unto him: "Get thee out of thy country, and from thy kindred, and from thy father's house, unto a land that I will show thee. And I will make thee a great nation, and I will bless thee, and make thy name great; and thou shalt be a blessing. And I will bless them that bless thee, and curse them that curse thee; and in thee shall all the families of the earth be blessed." (*Gen.* xii. 1, 2, 3).

God directed Abraham to the land of Canaan, and said unto him, "Lift up now thine eyes * * For all the land which thou seest, to thee will I give it and thy seed forever." (*Gen.* xiii, 14, 15).

The Canaanites had descended to amalgamation with their negroes; though there were more or less of pure whites among them, and some of these survived to a late period in Israelitish history. This is shown in the case of Uriah, the Hittite, whom David had killed that he might possess himself of Uriah's wife. However, the mixed-bloods had become so white that it was impossible to distinguish them from whites in many cases. Hence, it was dangerous to inter-marry with them, as shown by the fact that, when Abraham's son Isaac reached maturity he was forbidden to take a wife from among the daughters of Canaan; but that he should take a wife from among Abraham's kindred. (See *Gen.* xxiv, 3, 4). This was done, and Isaac took to wife Rebekah, who bore him two sons, Esau and Jacob. Esau intermarried with the Canaanites; and Rebekah, fearing that Jacob might do likewise, said to Isaac, "I am weary of my life because of the daughters of Heth: if Jacob take a wife of the daughters of Heth, such as these which are of the daughters of the land, what good shall my life do me?" (*Gen.* xxvii, 46). This Godfearing, devoted mother realized that if Jacob took a wife from among the mixed-blooded females of Heth and begat a progeny of mixed-bloods, her life would be lived in vain. And Isaac, startled at the thought, "called Jacob and blessed him * * 'and said unto him, Thou shalt not take a wife from among the daughters of Canaan. Arise, go to Padan-aram to the house of Bethuel, thy mother's father; and take thee a wife from thence of the daughters of Laban, thy mother's brother. And God Almighty bless thee * * and multiply thee, that thou mayest be a multitude of people; and give thee the blessing of Abraham * * * and to thy seed with thee, that thou mayest inherit the land wherein thou art a

stranger, which God gave unto Abraham.'" (*Gen.*
xxviii, 1, 2, 3, 4). Jacob took to wife Leah and Ra-
chel the daughters of Laban. Jacob and his family,
consisting of seventy souls, moved into the land of
Egypt, where they were well treated for a time, but
their descendants were finally enslaved and held in
bondage for about 400 years; but God kept His promise to Abraham, and released them from bondage,
and directed them to the land of Canaan. He gave
them an organized system of political government,
and an organized system of religion; and in order to
counteract the teachings of atheism as set forth in the
theory of evolution, God inspired Moses to write the
Narrative of Creation, and the early history of the
Adamic family as set forth in the Pentateuch.

God forbade the Israelites to inter-marry with the
Canaanites, saying: "Neither shall thou make marriages with them; thy daughter thou shalt not give
unto his son, nor his daughter shalt thou take unto
thy son." (*Deut.* vii, 3). "But of the cities of these
people which the Lord thy God doth give thee for
an inheritance, thou shalt save alive nothing that
breatheth: But thou shalt utterly destroy them."
(*Deut.* xx, 16, 17). At the same time they were permitted to inter-marry with nations "afar off." (*Deut.*
xx). After enumerating and forbidding every form
of lust which it was possible for the Adamic family
to indulge among themselves, God enacted the most
stringent law against their amalgamation with the
negro, and affixed the death penalty to the violation
of the law, as follows: "Neither shalt thou lie with
any beast to defile thyself therewith; neither shall

any woman stand before a beast to lie down thereto; it is confusion." (*Levt.* xviii, 23). And if a man lie with a beast, he shall surely be put to death: and ye shall slay the beast. And if a woman approach unto any beast, and lie down thereto, thou shalt kill the woman and the beast; they shall surely be put to death; their blood shall be upon them." (*Levt.* xx, 15, 16). Continuing, God said: "Defile not ye yourselves in any of these things; for in all these the nations are defiled which I cast out before you; and the land is defiled; therefore I do visit the iniquity thereof upon it; and the land itself vomiteth out its inhabitants. Ye shall therefore keep my statutes and my judgments, and not commit any of these abominations * * * that the land spue not you out also when ye defile it, as it spued out the nations that were before you." (*Levt.* xviii, 24, 25, 26, 28). God thus specifically charges the Canaanites with lying with beasts. In this we have the most positive proof that there is a beast with which a man may lie, just as he would with a woman, or, to which a woman might "lie down thereto," just as she would to a man.

Corrupt and defile are synonymous terms, and investigation of this subject will show that amalgamation with the negro is the only crime that will (1) corrupt the flesh; (2) that will corrupt the earth itself in God's eye; (3) that will bring upon its perpetrators the penalty of death, under the law of God. Previous to the deluge, God looked upon the earth and said: "It was corrupt; for all flesh had corrupted His way on the earth." This, as has been shown, could only have resulted from amalgamation. Previous to the entry of the Israelites into Canaan, God said of Canaan: "The land is defiled." He charges the Canaanites with lying with beast, and this corrupted the flesh of Canaan as it corrupted the flesh of the antediluvians; and in each case God destroyed the corrupted flesh, and the amalgamationists who corrupted it. He destroyed the antediluvians by the deluge, and the Canaanites by a war of extermination.

The immediate offspring of man and the negro the mulatto—is the result of man's violation of that Divine law, *thou shalt not lie with any beast;* and under the penalty which God attached to the violation of this law, the mulatto was doomed to instant death in the moment of conception. This being true, it follows that neither the mulatto nor his ultimate offspring can ever acquire the right to live; that they have no rights, social, political, or religious; this is shown by God's destruction of the antediluvians, and His command to Israel to destroy the Canaanites without regard to age or sex, and "leave nothing alive that breatheth," and take their possessions. The immediate offspring of man and the negro is merely the result of man's violation of Divine law, and, as such, is not a part of God's creation. Hence, its ultimate offspring could never become so; it was corrupted flesh to begin with, and can never become pure by reverting to either man or the negro. Neither can there be any peace between God and man as long as these monstrosities are allowed to defile the earth with their presence.

God made Jerusalem the religious center of the world; the pure-blooded descendants of Adam, whatever their nationality, were entitled to membership in the Jewish church by complying with its laws. God desired that Israel would disseminate the plan of Creation, as set forth in the Mosaic Record, among the pure-blooded descendants of Adam, and counteract the degrading influences of idolatry and the theories of atheism; that all should know that man had not descended from "fish-like ancestors," themselves the result of "spontaneous generation;" but that man was created "the son of God," and that he is not a highly developed species of ape which is composed of five or more races of men in different stages of development; but that he is a separate creation, wholly distinct from the animals.

But the Israelites seemed to have no appreciation of the great mission which they were brought into existence to accomplish; they thought only of the gratification of their own desires; instead of responding to the just requirements of God by reclaiming their fellowmen from the errors and crimes into which they had fallen, they abandoned themselves to the indulgence of the follies and crimes they were commanded to eradicate. Once settled in their new homes they disregarded the laws of God, and as Josephus says, "were full of the evil doings that were common among the Canaanites." They not only descended to amalgamation with their negroes, and inter-married with the mixed-blooded nations they were commanded to destroy, but they even renounced God and embraced idolatry. The history of the Israelites from Sinai to the crucifixion is largely a narrative of their descent to idolatry and fornication; no charge made against them is more common than that of fornication. They went *in the way of Cain.* A notable instance of this is presented in the case of King Solomon, who not only took wives of the mixed-blooded princesses of nations with which Israel was forbidden to inter-marry, but he had negro concubines, as shown by the utterances of one of them as follows:

"Let him kiss me with the kisses of his mouth; for thy love is better than wine. Because of the savior of thy good ointments thy name is as ointment poured forth, therefore do the virgins love thee. Draw me; we will run after thee: the king hath brought me unto his chambers: we will be glad and rejoice in thee, we will remember thy love more than wine. * * * I am black, but comely, O ye daughters of Jerusalem, as the tents of Kedar, as the curtains of Solomon. Look not upon me because I am black, because the sun hath looked upon me: * * * While the king sitteth at his table, my spikenard sendeth forth the smell thereof. A bundle of myrrh is my well beloved unto me; he shall lie all night between my breasts. * * * Behold, thou art fair, my beloved, yea pleasant: also our bed is green." (*Cant.* i, 2, 3, etc.). The disgusting spectacle of Solomon's black concubine exulting over the "daughters of Jerusalem" because of the favor shown her by the king, has been often repeated in our day; in our own country many a black concubine, who had received the attentions of some demoralized father, husband, son or brother, has thus exulted over his injured mother, wife, daughter, or sister.

In this age of atheism and infidelity the inhabitants of the earth, without regard to their physical and mental characters, or the laws of God, are all included under the term "people." But no such pernicious course was pursued by the inspired authors; they divided them into *three classes:* (1) "People." (2) "No people," or "those which are not a people." (3) "The mingled people."

The "people" are evidently the pure-blooded descendants of Adam; this is proved by the fact that the Israelites, whom God so often befriended, are referred to as "people." "Those which are not a people," or "no people," were certainly animals— "beasts of the field"—negroes. God warned the Israelites through Moses that if they cultivated criminal relations with them that He would use these creatures as a weapon against them. He said, "I will move them to jealousy with those which are not a people." In addition to this He says, "I will provoke them to anger with a foolish nation." (*Deut.* xxxii, 21). Many centuries after this event, when the Israelites had abandoned themselves to the most criminal relations with these creatures "which are not a people," and had been led off into idolatry, and were suffering the vengeance of God for their crimes, Paul charged them with not being ignorant upon this subject, and reminded them of the warning God had given them through Moses; Paul said to them: "Did not Israel know? First, Moses saith,

I will provoke you to jealousy by them that are no
people, and by a foolish nation I will anger you."
(*Rom.* x, 19). These creatures "which are not a
people" were not of the flesh of men—they were
beasts—apes; and if the theologian thinks they were
not negroes, he should inform us as to what animal
the inspired writers referred to.

The "mingled people" were evidently *mixed-
bloods;* mixing and mingling are synonymous terms;
these "mingled people" were the result of mingling
man's blood with the blood of beasts—beasts of the
field—they were the offspring of whites and negroes;
they presented the physical and mental characters
of man blended and confused with those of the negro; they were neither man nor negro, but were the
result of man's violation of God's law against *confusion.* (See *Levt.* xviii, 23). They were a "mingled
people."

Further evidence of the fact that the "mingled
people" were mixed-bloods, is found in the fact that,
like the antediluvians, Canaanites, etc., they were
destroyed by Divine edict: "The Word of the Lord
came again unto me, saying, Son of man, prophesy
and say,   *   *   *   the day is near, even the day of
the Lord is near,   *   *   *   and the sword shall
come upon Egypt, and great pain shall be in Ethiopia,   *   *   *   Ethiopia, and Libya, and Lydia, and
all the mingled people, and Chub, and the men of
the land that is in the league, shall fall by the
sword." (*Ezek.* xxx, 1, 2, 3, 4, 5; see also *Jer.* xxv).
Thus we find that the Ethiopians of the times of

Jeremiah and Ezekiel were a "mingled people"—mixed-bloods.

The fact that the Ethiopians of to-day, in Africa, are blacks, has led many to suppose that the ancient Ethiopians of the time of Moses were blacks—negroes. This is a sad mistake. However, this error has been seized upon by modern amalgamationists as proof of God's approval of amalgamation between whites and negroes; in support of their pernicious theory, its advocates point to the fact that Moses married an Ethiopian woman, and insist that she was black; the fact that Miriam, the sister of Moses, was punished with leprosy for complaining against Moses for marrying an Ethiopian woman, is seized upon as further evidence of God's approval of amalgamation. But this is all wrong; nothing could be more absurd, and nothing more blasphemous, than to suppose that God would select a degraded amalgamationist, with a black wife, to lead the Israelites to Canaan. It will be remembered that the Israelites were forbidden to inter-marry promiscuously with other nations, for amalgamation was common in that remote period, as it is to-day; realizing this, Miriam feared that the Ethiopian wife of Moses might be a mixed-blood, and she expressed her displeasure at his marriage. But this was a reflection on God, who approved of the marriage of Moses to the Ethiopian woman, and Miriam was severely punished. The very fact that God approved of the marriage of Moses to this Ethiopian woman, is the most positive proof that she was of pure Adamic stock—that she was *white.*

In addition to this, modern research has demonstrated beyond all doubt that the original Ethiopians were not Africans, but Asiatics. The seat of the Ethiopian Empire was situated "in the province of Omar, in southern Asia." (*Preadamites*, p. 17. Observe the long list of high and recent authorities cited by Prof. Winchell in support of this). The Ethiopians developed on the Arabian peninsula, in Asia, one of the finest civilizations of ancient times. This is further evidence that they were not blacks, but whites, for scientific research has shown that "no negro civilization has ever appeared;" but that the white is the great building, developing power of the earth. The Ethiopians were one of the most enlightened, enterprising, and powerful nations of their day. They developed a commerce which extended over a considerable portion of Asia and Africa, and perhaps Europe. The history of such a people must have been an important one; in this, we find further proof that they were not negroes: the most careful research shows that "no woolly-haired nation ever had an important history." The whites have always been the commercial power of the globe.

Mr. Bancroft says: "The Semites early peopled the Arabian peninsula and established a state in Ethiopia, as some believe, before Egypt had attained its full development. The Ethiopians established a commerce on the Red Sea with the eastern coasts of Africa and with India, and contributed greatly to the resources of ancient Egypt." (*Footprints of Time*, p. 33). Thus, according to this learned historian, and other high authorities, the Ethiopians were not the sons of Ham, but were the descendants of Shem. It should prove a trifle embarrassing to the advocates of the theory that the original Ethiopians were negroes, when they are called upon to explain how the Ethiopians, who were one branch of the family of Shem, were *black*, while the Israelites, another branch of the family of Shem, were *white*.

It is probable that more or less amalgamation existed among the Ethiopians of Moses' day; they were originally of pure white stock, and that more or less of this stock remained at that period is shown by the fact that the marriage of Moses with an Ethiopian woman received the sanction of God. Additional proof that they were originally pure whites who were finally absorbed by amalgamation with their negroes, is shown by the fact that nearly nine hundred years after the time of Moses we find them described as a "mingled people" and included in the list of that class of nations who were destroyed by Divine edict. We should bear in mind that at one period of its history the inhabitants of a nation may consist of pure whites and pure negroes; the whites may descend to amalgamation, and in the course of centuries both the pure whites and the pure negroes will be absorbed, and their descendants will all be mixed-bloods. This was the case with the Ethiopians. This destructive crime destroyed the great nations of antiquity, and populated the greater part of every continent of the earth with mixed-bloods.

All the facts indicate that the Ethiopians sent

out a colony from their empire in Asia which settled
on the upper Nile. These colonists with their negroes developed a fine civilization, but finally descended to amalgamation, and both whites and negroes were absorbed, and their civilization was laid
in ruins. Their mixed-blooded descendants are now
found in Nubia, Sennaar, Kardofan, and Abyssinia.
"The population of this vaguely defined region is a
mixture of Arabian and Libyan races with the genuine Ethiopians. The latter had well-formed limbs,
and a facial outline resembling the Caucasian in all
but its inclination to prominent lips and a somewhat
sloping forehead. Their language was Semitic." C.
K. Adams, *Universal Encyclopedia*, Art., Ethiopia).

Thus, we find in these modern Ethiopians of
Africa the "facial outline resembling the Caucasian,"
blended with the "prominent lips" and "sloping
forehead," which is a character of the negro. We
might add that his complexion is another character
of the negro. In this blending of the characters of
whites and negroes, in the modern Ethiopians, we
find the most positive proof of their being mixed-
bloods. In the face of these evidences of crossing,
there is not an anthropologist on the earth who
would accept the theory that the Ethiopian of to-day
is a genuine negro. The very fact that the modern
Ethiopians of Africa are mixed-bloods, shows that
they trace their descent to whites and negroes.

The original Ethiopians who developed the
splendid civilization of the Arabian peninsula, descended to amalgamation with their negroes and
their descendants became *colored;* and however much

they might desire it, they could never revert to the complexion of their white ancestors. It was doubtless his knowledge of this that led Jeremiah to contemptuously ask: "Can the Ethiopian change his skin, or the leopard his spots?" This passage has been seized upon as proof that the Ethiopians of that period were black; but there is nothing in the text to warrant such construction. They might have been of any other complexion; besides it is plain that it would be as impossible for the whites, or the reds, or the yellows, to change their complexion, as it would be for the blacks to change theirs. Amalgagamation alone can change the complexion ("skin") of a tribe or a nation. In discussing these questions, we should bear in mind that the disposition of the ancients to migrate from one country to another was much the same as it is with the moderns. Ebedmelech, the Ethiopian, who befriended Jeremiah, presents a case in point. (*Jer.* xxxviii). Ebedmelech was evidently a white whose ancestors, more or less remote, migrated from Ethiopia to Judea, and thus escaped amalgamation and the destruction which befel their kinsman in Ethiopia. The advocates of the theory that the original Ethiopians, like their mixed-blooded descendants were blacks, would have us believe that the Queen of Sheba, who visited Solomon, was a negress; but this is a mere assumption, and is not supported by the least shadow of proof. For aught we know, she was a pure-blooded white.

In discussing Meroe, Mr. Charles R. Gillett says it was "the name given by Cambyses to the Ethiopian city Saba, in honor of his sister, who died there. It was situated on the Nile between the fifth and sixth cataracts, in upper Nubia. * * * After the decay of Napata, * * * it became the Ethiopian capital. * * * The Greek tradition that Meroe furnished the original Egyptian civilization is wrong, being based, probably, on limited observation and temporary relations. * * * The pyramids of the region were of late construction, dating from 600 to 100 B. C., and are simply formal imitations of those of Egypt." (*Universal Encyclopedia*, Art. Meroe).

The above statement fully confirms our contention that the original Ethiopians were not Africans, but Asiatics; that they were not blacks, but whites; and that at some period intervening between the time of Moses and the time of Ezekiel, they sent a colony of whites with their negroes into Africa. This colony settled on the Nile, in what is now Nubia, and developed a splendid civilization, the remains of which are in existence to-day. This colony of white Ethiopians survived the destruction of the mother country, which occurred in the days of Ezekiel, more than 500 B. C. We find these white Ethiopians in Africa developing their country, building monuments, etc., down to a period 100 B. C. Doubtless a considerable number of them survived until long after the birth of Christ. It is highly probable that more or less of them embraced Christianity; the Ethiopian eunuch whom Phillip baptised presents a notable example of this. However, they finally went "in the way of Cain," and were destroyed; their civilization was laid in ruins, and their mixed-blooded descendants exist to-day in Africa in various stages of barbarism and savagery.

After the original Ethiopians were destroyed in Asia, the world lost all knowledge of their former existence, and the African Ethiopians came to be regarded as the only Ethiopians. But it is plain that if we accept this theory the Bible with its teaching that the Ethiopians were destroyed 500 years before Christ is disproved; for we find them (in Africa) building monuments, etc., 100 B. C. But when we understand that there was a great Ethiopian empire in Asia from which the African Ethiopians were a colony, and that it was the parent country that was destroyed, the whole subject becomes plain.

Further evidence that the Israelites violated the laws of God by descending to amalgamation with the negro and mixed-bloods, is shown by the following: "For mine eyes are upon all their ways. * * * And first I will recompense their iniquity and their sins double; because they have defiled mine inheritance with the carcasses of their detestable and abominable things." (*Jer.* xvi, 17, 18). Israel was God's "inheritance." (See *I Kings*, viii, 51; *Isaiah*, xix, 25, etc.). Thus, by their amalgamation they had filled Israel—the nation of Israel— with the "carcasses" of "things"—mixed-bloods— that were "detestable and abominable" in the eyes of God; and by so doing they *defiled the land* as the Canaanites did.

Prior to the time of Jeremiah, the Israelites had persisted in amalgamation for so long a period that their mixed-blooded progeny were not distinguish-able from pure whites; and the whole nation had become so demoralized and degraded that even the women of Israel were marrying mixed-bloods; and as a result it was unsafe for a man to take a wife from among them, and God forbid Jeremiah to do so, saying: "Thou shalt not take thee a wife, neither shalt thou have sons and daughters in this place. For thus saith the Lord concerning the sons and concerning the daughters that are born in this place, and concerning their mothers that bare them, and concerning their fathers that begat them in this land: They shall die grievious deaths; they shall not be lamented, neither shall they be buried; but they shall be as dung upon the face of the earth; and they shall be consumed by the sword, and by fam-ine; and their carcasses shall be meat for the fowl of heaven, and for the beasts of the earth." (*Jer.* xvi, 2, 3). Thus it is a matter of scriptural record that, in the eyes of God, the mixed-bloods are only fit *for dung on the face of the earth.*

Despite every effort made to reclaim them, the Israelites persisted in their amalgamation, atheism, and idolatry, and thus defiled the land until, as God had threatened, it spued them out also, as it spued out the nations that were before them. In the meantime God sent prophet after prophet to induce them to abandon their wicked course; but they mal-treated and often killed them; and as a last resort He sent His son Jesus Christ, and they maltreated and killed Him also. That the mission of the Saviour was identical with that of the prophets who preceded

Him is shown by His parable: "There was a certain householder, which planted a vineyard, and hedged it round about, and digged a winepress in it, and built a tower, and let it out to husbandmen, and went into a far country: And when the time of the fruit drew near, he sent his servants to the husbandmen, that they might receive the fruit of it. And the husbandmen took his servants, and beat one, and killed another, and stoned another. Again he sent other servants more than the first: And they did unto them likewise. But last of all he sent unto them his son, saying, They will reverence my son. But when the husbandmen saw the son, they said among themselves, This is the heir; come, let us kill him, and let us seize on his inheritance. And they cast him out of the vineyard, and slew him." (*Mat.* xxi, 33, 34, etc.).

In this parable it is plain that God is represented by the "householder;" the earth by the "vineyard;" souls by the "fruit;" the prophets by the "servants;" and Jesus Christ by "the son and heir." We are thus taught (1) That the earth is God's "vineyard." (2) That the fruit He desires of it are souls. (3) That man is the husbandman to whom He let it out, and whom He desired to produce souls which, by a life of obedience to God, would be fitted for the realms of the blest in eternity, and thus increase the population of heaven. But amalgamation produces no souls. Hence, the apostle Jude compares the mixed-bloods to *clouds without water,* and *trees without fruit,* that is *bodies without souls.* Referring to the mixed-bloods as participants in Divine worship, Jude says: "These are spots in your feasts of charity, when they feast with you, feeding themselves without fear." Jude also displays an intimate knowledge of the disposition of the mixed-bloods to boast their white blood regardless of whether they are born in or out of wedlock, when he compares them to "raging waves of the sea, foaming out their own shame." (See *Jude*, verses 12, 13). (4) The Saviour's parable teaches that each succeeding prophet came on the same mission as did the first one; and that the "son and heir," Jesus Christ, came on the same mission as the prophets who preceded Him; and a moment's reflection should convince us that if the first "servant" or prophet had succeeded in his mission, the second one would not have been sent; and if any subsequent one had succeeded, the "son and heir" would not have been sent. Hence, the coming of the Saviour to reclaim man was a *last resort;* but He failed in His mission, as did the prophets who preceded Him; and atheism is as universally taught to-day, and amalgamation as universally indulged, as they were prior to the birth of Christ.

In His efforts to redeem the whole Adamic family, both Jew and Gentile, the Saviour issued His great decree: "Go ye into all the world, and preach the gospel to every creature." (*Mark*, xvi, 15). No decree was ever more misunderstood than this, and none more abused. In the very nature of things, the execution of this decree was confined to the pure-blooded descendants of Adam, who *alone* are involved in Adam's transgression; if proof of this is required, the Saviour furnishes it in the following decree: "Give not that which is holy unto the dogs, neither cast ye your pearls before swine, lest they trample them under their feet and turn again and rend you." (*Mat.* vii, 6). This prohibitory statute proves the existence of an animal upon which we, in our ignorance of God's plan of creation, might be misled into attempting to christianize under the impression that he is a man; and this is shown to be true when we turn upon this decree the light of Paul's teaching that, "there is one kind of flesh of men, another flesh of beasts," etc. We find that the swine, the dog, and the negro, all belong to the *flesh of beasts*. The scriptures are pronounced "holy." (*Rom.* i, 2). While the kingdom of heaven is likened to "goodly pearls." (*Mat.* xiii, 45, 46). Thus we are justified in deciding, that "that which is holy," and which God forbids man to give unto the dogs, is the Bible; and that the "pearls" which God forbids man to cast before swine, is the kingdom of heaven. Thus is becomes plain that this statute was intended to confine the Bible and Divine worship to man, and that it excludes the negro in common with the rest of the animals. This being true, it follows that it is as criminal to confer the Bible on the negro, as to confer it on the dog; and that it is as criminal to attempt to christianize the negro, as the swine. Man can make no distinction between one animal and another in these respects. This prohibitory statute embraces the mixed-bloods.

Further evidence that the negro and the mixed-bloods are not included in the Plan of Salvation, is found in the statement of Paul, who says that in his day, the gospel "was preached to every creature under heaven." (*Col.* i, 23). That is, it reached "every creature" for whom it was designed. Yet neither the Saviour nor His disciples preached the gospel to the negroes and mixed-bloods throughout Africa; nor to the Hindoos, Chinese, Japanese, etc., of Asia; nor to the Malays, Australians, etc., of Oceanica; nor to the Indians of North and South America; nor to the Basques, Laplanders and Fins of Europe. Thus, under the direction of the Saviour and His disciples, the gospel was confined to a fractional part of the inhabitants of the earth; and this fractional part was in exact proportion to its population of pure whites; while there were not only tribe after tribe, and nation after nation, but even *continents* to which the gospel was not sent at all. In the face of these significant facts it is pertinent to inquire where the modern church obtained its authority to send the gospel promiscuously throughout the globe. The extension of the gospel to the negroes and mixed-bloods is a plain violation of Divine law, and is due solely to the influence of atheism with its teaching that man is a highly developed species of ape of which the white is the highest, and the negro the lowest race, with the reds, browns, and yellows, as intermediate races in different stages of development. We should profit by the sad experience of every nation of antiquity, whose ruined civilizations testify that man's social, political, and religious equality with the negro and the mixed-bloods inevitably leads to amalgamation, the most loathsome, destructive crime to which man can descend. The fact that as the result of amalgamation our population of supposed whites is growing darker; and that our population of supposed negroes is growing lighter, should warn us that already we have strayed too far in forbidden paths; we should call a halt, ere amalgamation adds our beloved country to the long list of nations whose wrecks are thickly strewn along the shores of time. Our very existence as a people at once demands that we repudiate the false teachings which have brought us to the verge of ruin, and promptly return to first principles. The demoralizing conditions which confront us on every side should enable us to realize that what the world wants is primitive Christianity; it wants a religious system based squarely on the narrative of the Divine Creation, and not on the atheistic theory of evolution; it wants a religious system that will bring our social, political, and religious systems into harmony with the laws of God; it wants a religious system that will recognize and respect the broad distinction which God made in the Creation between man and the animals; and any religious system which declines to meet these requirements is simply a delusion and a snare.

THE END.

LIST OF AUTHORITIES CITED.

501

Inasmuch as this work is based on the Bible, the inspired authorities quoted are too numerous to index.

THE ADAMIC LIBRARY.

As the result of amalgamation, three continents of our earth with their civilizations were destroyed by Divine Edict and replaced by immense oceans. While for this crime nation after nation, under the curse of God, has disappeared from the remaining continents, leaving little or nothing to indicate their former existence, the Scriptures, the Sciences, Profane History, Tradition, the evidence furnished by ancient ruins and monuments place in our hands an amount of data sufficient to enable us to write an approximately correct history of our globe from the Creation to the Twentieth Century of the Christian Era. This invaluable fund of information will be given to the world for the first time in the Adamic Library. This Library will be composed of a series of books, each treating of *different subjects* and *complete in itself.*

The second book of this series will be a work on Spiritualism, in which the reality and evils of spiritualism will be fully exposed. By ALMINA THOMAS.

The third book of this series will be a work on the Book of Revelation, in which John's figurative language will be reduced to plain English, and his revelations shown to be in harmony with Profane History, Tradition, and Modern Science. By CHARLES CARROLL.

The fourth, fifth, sixth, seventh and eighth books of this series will each be devoted to a history of one of the five continents from the Deluge to the Twentieth Century of the Christian Era. By CHARLES CARROLL.

Other books of this series will be announced later.

These books will contain about 500 pages each, and will be bound in English Silk Cloth, price $2.00; Buckram, price $2.50; Half Morocco, price $3.00.

ADAMIC PUBLISHING CO.
ST. LOUIS, MO.

SOURCES

THE BIBLICAL AND "SCIENTIFIC" DEFENSE
OF SLAVERY

A Minister [D.G. Phillips]. *Nachash: What Is It? or An Answer to the Question, "Who and What Is the Negro?" Drawn From Revelation.* Augusta: James L. Gow, 1868. (Courtesy of Trinity College Library, Hartford, CT)

Sister Sallie [Reverend Thompson?]. *The Color Line. Devoted to the Restoration of Good Government, Putting an End to Negro Authority and Misrule, and Establishing a White Man's Government in the White Man's Country, by Organizing the White People of the South.* [Memphis: n.p., 1875?]. (Courtesy of Boston Public Library)

Lester, A. Hoyle. *The Pre-Adamite, or Who Tempted Eve? Scripture and Science in Unison as Respects the Antiquity of Man.* Philadelphia: J.B. Lippincott & Co., 1875. (Courtesy of Harvard University Library)

Carroll, Charles. *The Tempter of Eve; or, The Criminality of Man's Social, Political, and Religious Equality with the Negro, and the Amalgamation to Which These Crimes Inevitably Lead. Discussed in the Light of the Scriptures, the Sciences, Profane History, Tradition, and the Testimony of the Monuments.* St. Louis: Adamic Publishing Company, 1902. (Courtesy of Lexington Theological Seminary Library)

CONTENTS OF SERIES

Other Books by John David Smith

Window on the War: Frances Dallam Peter's Lexington Civil War Diary, with William Cooper, Jr. (1976)

Black Slavery in the Americas: An Interdisciplinary Bibliography, 1865–1980 (2 vols., 1982)

An Old Creed for the New South: Proslavery Ideology and Historiography, 1865–1918 (1985; reprint edition, 1991)

Dictionary of Afro-American Slavery, with Randall M. Miller (1988)

Ulrich Bonnell Phillips: A Southern Historian and His Critics, with John C. Inscoe (1990)